W9-AFC-541

Governments and Politics of the Contemporary Middle East

THE DORSEY SERIES IN POLITICAL SCIENCE

EDITOR   Norton E. Long   *University of Illinois*

AKE   *A Theory of Political Integration*

BROWN & WAHLKE (eds.)   *The American Political System: Notes and Readings*

DRAGNICH   *Major European Governments*   3d ed.

EDELMANN   *Latin American Government and Politics: The Dynamics of a Revolutionary Society*   rev. ed.

FROHOCK   *The Nature of Political Inquiry*

GRIPP   *Patterns of Soviet Politics*   rev. ed.

ISAAK   *Scope and Methods of Political Science: An Introduction to the Methodology of Political Inquiry*

ISMAEL   *Governments and Politics of the Contemporary Middle East*

JACOB & ATHERTON   *The Dynamics of International Organization: The Making of World Order*

JACOBINI   *International Law: A Text*   rev. ed.

LUTTBEG   (ed.)   *Public Opinion and Public Policy: Models of Political Linkage*

MACRIDIS & BROWN   *The De Gaulle Republic*

MACRIDIS & BROWN (eds.)   *Comparative Politics: Notes and Readings*   3d ed.

MANGONE   *The Elements of International Law*   rev. ed.

MEEHAN   *Contemporary Political Thought: A Critical Study*

MEEHAN   *Explanation in Social Science: A System Paradigm*

MEEHAN   *The Theory and Method of Political Analysis*

MEEHAN   *Value Judgment and Social Science: Structures and Processes*

MINAR   *Ideas and Politics: The American Experience*

MURPHY   *Political Theory: A Conceptual Analysis*

NAGEL   *The Legal Process from a Behavioral Perspective*

ROBINSON   *Congress and Foreign Policy-Making: A Study in Legislative Influence and Initiative*   rev. ed.

ROELOFS   *The Language of Modern Politics: An Introduction to the Study of Government*

SARGENT   *Contemporary Political Ideologies: A Comparative Analysis*

SIGLER   *Courts and Public Policy: Cases and Essays*

SIGLER   *An Introduction to the Legal System*

SPIRO   *World Politics: The Global System*

WASBY   *The Impact of the United States Supreme Court: Some Perspectives*

WESSON   *Soviet Foreign Policy in Perspective*

Governments and Politics of the Contemporary Middle East

TAREQ Y. ISMAEL

Associate Professor of Political Science
The University of Calgary, Alberta, Canada

WITH CONTRIBUTIONS FROM

A. M. Abu-Hakima, Kamel S. Abu Jaber, Harry Howard,
Kenneth E. Koehn, Abdul H. Raoof, Bernard Reich,
William Sands, Michael W. Suleiman, Walter Weiker,
Manfred W. Wenner, and Marvin Zonis

1970

THE
DORSEY PRESS   HOMEWOOD, ILLINOIS
IRWIN-DORSEY LIMITED, GEORGETOWN, ONTARIO

© THE DORSEY PRESS, 1970

First Printing, May, 1970

Library of Congress Catalog Card No. 78-112831

Printed in the United States of America

Preface

Although books on every aspect and every country of the Middle East abound, there is no current volume geared specifically to the novice in Middle Eastern studies that attempts the comprehensive task of bringing together the pertinent background material, the pervasive fundamental changes that have been occurring in the area since World War II, and the specific political situation in each individual country. Hopefully, this book successfully realizes such a combination with the aim of providing the student who has little background in Middle Eastern studies with a cognizance of the basic factors shaping the area.

In order to give this book a depth and perception that no single author could achieve in such a diverse area, the chapters on the individual countries were written by scholars who possess particular expertise in the areas they treated. Also, the examination of current political trends (Chapter 5) and the concluding chapter on the international relations of the Middle East were prepared by noted scholars. Thus, the book brings together a variety of approaches, a fund of knowledge, and a broad base of scientific objectivity.

The book is divided into four parts. Part I is designed to provide a general overview of the Middle East's physical and social geography and history up to World War II. Part II is an examination of the forces that have shaped contemporary Middle Eastern politics: Islam, nationalism, modernization, and current political trends. Part III is a study of the comparative politics of the Middle East with emphasis on the political institutions and processes, and the domestic and foreign policies, of each country. And, finally, Part IV describes the historic development and present circumstances of the Middle East's international relations.

I wish to thank all of those people who have made this book possible. My special thanks go to those contributing scholars who have added so much to this endeavor. I also wish to express my appreciation to Professor Muhsin Mahdi of Harvard University for his helpful comments on the section of the book that discusses Islam, to Professor Bernard Reich of George Washington University for reviewing the section on Zionism, and to Professor Walter Weiker of Rutgers:

v

The State University for reviewing the section on Turkish nationalism. All the contributing authors and myself wish to express our appreciation to Professor Manfred Halpern of Princeton University who, after reading the entire manuscript, offered thoughtful criticisms that were invaluable to our efforts. Of course, each author assumes sole responsibility for the opinions and conclusions expressed in his respective chapters. I am also indebted to Professor Frances Huston of Eastern Washington State College for her expert editorial comments; to Mrs. Vera Espe for typing the manuscript; to the Cartographic laboratory, under the supervision of Professor Charles Booth, of Eastern Washington State College, for preparing the maps; to my graduate assistants Mr. Glenn Knight and Mr. Frank Sauser; and last, but certainly not least, to my wife, who spent many hours aiding me in the preparation of this manuscript.

April, 1970   Tareq Y. Ismael
Calgary, Alberta

Contents

PART III
COMPARATIVE GOVERNMENTS

The Northern Belt

The Fertile Crescent

PART IV
INTERNATIONAL RELATIONS OF THE MIDDLE EAST

part I

THE MIDDLE EAST IN PERSPECTIVE

chapter 1

Introduction

WHAT IS THE MIDDLE EAST?

The Middle East, roughly located between southwestern Asia and the eastern Mediterranean, does not constitute a distinct geographic region. Although it is chiefly distinguished from Europe by religion, from the Far East by culture, and from central Asia by geography, and is generally considered to center in the Fertile Crescent, its periphery is not clearly demarcated by any of these factors. For this reason the term *Middle East*, along with the term *Near East* has never applied to a specific region or set of countries. Its meaning has been determined by political rather than geographic factors and therefore has changed in correspondence to the growth of Western interest and involvement in the area.

Of the two designations, the Near East is actually the older, originating around the 15th century with the early European explorations to find new routes to the East. The lands farthest from Europe came to be called the Far East, while those between Europe and the Far East were called the Near East. Later, the term was used to designate the lands ruled by the Ottoman Empire after 1453. Even the French term *Levant*, which translates as "the rising of the sun," means the East. Also, European archaeologists use the term Near East to distinguish the ancient civilizations of Mesopotamia, Egypt, and Persia from those of the Far Eastern civilizations of China and Japan. Clearly, both terms are European in origin and have little meaning at all from an Asian or African geographic point of view.

The term Middle East came into popular usage during World War II with the establishment of the British Middle East Command and the Allied Middle East Supply Center. Both organizations served the North African and Asian countries west of India. Since then, the appellation Middle East has become increasingly popular while that of Near East has become somewhat obsolete. Thus, the terms are sometimes used interchangeably, or the Near East may only refer to the Balkans or to the Balkans and Egypt plus those lands near to and east of the Mediterranean, including southwestern Asia. Similarly, the Middle East has been variously defined: The broadest view considers it as the area from Morocco on the Atlantic coast to Pakistan in Asia and from Turkey to Sudan; the narrowest definition concedes only the Arab countries on the eastern Mediterranean, plus Turkey, Israel, and Iran; many other delimitations span the gap between these two.

The problems inherent in such a confusion of nomenclature become apparent when we examine the U.S. government's use of the terms Near East and Middle East. For example, Secretary of State John Foster Dulles, in his statements on the Eisenhower Doctrine to House and Senate Committees in 1957, defined the Middle East as the area extending from Libya in the west to Pakistan in the east, and from Turkey in the north to the Arabian peninsula in the south and including Ethiopia and Sudan. He also indicated that the terms Middle East and Near East are interchangeable. A year later, on August 13, 1958, President Eisenhower, in his address to the emergency special session of the United Nations General Assembly dealing with the Lebanese and Jordanian crises, used the term Near East but did not mention the Middle East. The State Department, in answering reporters' queries on this, indicated that the terms Near East and Middle East are reciprocal, but that they included only the countries of Egypt, Syria, Israel, Jordan, Lebanon, Iraq, Saudi Arabia, and the Persian Gulf sheikdoms. Thus, the Secretary of State and the State Department each defined the Middle East quite differently. Such was the extent of confusion that in 1959 a geographer of the State Department concluded that the Middle East cannot be defined. [1] Britain, which has had a long history of involvement in the area, has had no less a problem with these amorphous terms and in 1947 that government commented, "Where precision would be required we should not use these terms."[2]

Because of the confusion about the proper use of the term Middle East, the first task is to clearly define the area in question. The view most commonly held in the literature, and the one adhered to in this book, is that the Middle East is that area centered on the Fertile Crescent and including the states of Turkey, Iran, Iraq, Syria, Lebanon, Israel, Jordan, Egypt, and the states and sheikdoms of the Arabian peninsula (see map below). This division, like any other, is rather arbitrary, but it takes into account the major characteristics shared by the included states and not shared by the excluded states.

With two exceptions—Lebanon and Israel—the states of the area are predominately Muslim. In Lebanon, there is no conclusive evidence as to the presence of either a Christian or a Muslim majority. In Israel, Judaism is the

---

[1] G. Etzel Pearcy, "The Middle East—an Indefinable Region," *Department of State Bulletin* (March 23, 1959), 407-416; reprinted as Department of State Publication No. 6806, Near East and Middle Eastern Series 39.

[2] Roderic H. Davison, "Where Is the Middle East," 13-29, ed. Richard H. Nolte, *The Modern Middle East* (New York, 1963), p. 29.

FIGURE 1-1

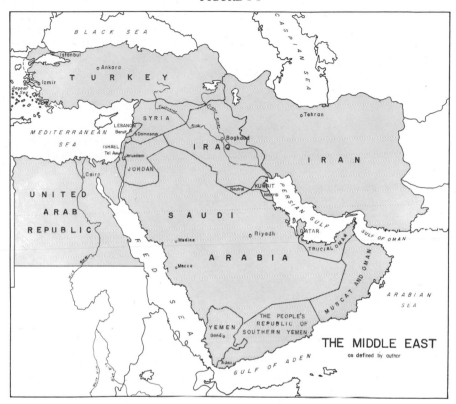

THE MIDDLE EAST
as defined by author

principal religion. The other states, although they have Christian and Jewish minorities, are overwhelmingly Muslim. This common faith is not necessarily a unifying factor, however, because of the existance of many sects within the Islamic faith and because there are other predominantly Muslim states outside this area. With three exceptions—Israel, Turkey, and Iran—these states are preeminently Arab, and even Israel has had a large number of Arabs within her borders, especially since June 1967. Turkey is one of the other exceptions, but as the former center of the Ottoman Empire, her influence in the Middle East and the traits she has in common with the cultures of the Arab states cannot be ignored. Iran is not an Arab state, but she is certainly Muslim and is geographically integral to the concept of a Middle East.

With the exception of Egypt, all of these states are located in Asia. Sudan, Morocco, and Algeria, despite their majorities which are Arab in culture and Muslim in religion, were excluded because of their geographic position as African states. But obvious involvement in the politics of the area, as well as her importance in the Osmanli era, tie Egypt to the Middle East rather than to the North African region.

The physiographical factor, although secondary, has had considerable influence upon the history and the development of the region. The entire territory is typically arid, from the low desert of Egypt's Qattara Depression to the highest desert of Iran; therefore, its development is primarily dependent upon the availability of a constant supply of sufficient water. Although industrialization may alleviate the area's dependence upon water supplies, at present the agricultural economy of the states in the region makes this a problem of prime importance. Even the recent process of modernization has not relieved the situation, since the population has grown more rapidly than the water supply.

Except in the north, where the border is mountainous, and on the western and southern borders of Egypt, which are artificial, the natural boundaries of the area under study are marine. If we exclude Egypt, which is included as an adjunct to the region for social and political reasons, the remainder of the area may be seen as a fairly contiguous land mass, for most Middle Eastern national boundaries are artificial. The Black Sea on the north, the Mediterranean on the west, the Persian Gulf (the Arab Gulf), the Gulf of Aden, and the Indian Ocean on the south and east delimit the entire territory.

THE IMPORTANCE OF THE MIDDLE EAST IN WORLD AFFAIRS

The historic role of the Middle East in world affairs has derived from its location as the cultural and economic intermediary between Europe, Asia, and Africa. Such Far Eastern commodities as silk, sugar, citrus fruit, paper, gunpowder, and the compass were introduced to Europe through the agency of the Middle East. The Middle East preserved, expanded, and passed on to the West the philosophic and scientific ideas of the Greeks and Hindus; and it was there that the religions of Judaism, Christianity, and Islam were born. The area has been contended over by every conqueror moving from one to another of its three neighboring continents and has been successively incorporated into the Persian, Greek, Roman, Arab, Mongol, Tartar, and Turkish empires. It has been the key to the Orient; the bridge connecting Africa, Asia, and Europe; and a chief trade center for millennia.

The importance of the position of the Middle East as a corridor of East-West communication, somewhat diminished by the 15th century discovery of a sea route to India, has been revived in modern times by the Suez Canal and the advent of air travel. Today, the area is a node of air and sea traffic. The value of its waterways—the Turkish Straits, the Suez Canal, the Red Sea, the Bab-al-Mandeb, the Straits of Armuz, and the Persian Gulf—for communication, travel, and trade is illustrated by the disconcertion of world powers at the 1956 and 1967-70 stoppage of the Suez Canal. Ships flying the flags of more than fifty different nations pass through this waterway annually. And a major portion of Europe's lifeblood—Middle Eastern oil— is shipped via the Canal.

The position of the Middle East on the air routes is as vital to communications and trade today as its age-old caravan routes were formerly.

The international airports at Istanbul, Beirut, Cairo, Khartoum, and Dhahran serve almost every international airline. Amply illustrating the area's importance as a communication link between East and West is the fact that there are more B.O.A.C. scheduled departures for the Middle East than for any other non-European area.

It is the production of oil, however, that overshadows all of the Middle East's other functions. The oil of the Middle East provides power for much of Europe and Asia. Some 75 percent of Western European power needs and 90 percent of the needs of Japan are supplied by the area's oil fields. This great wealth in a strategic material has made the Middle East an arena for contention between the great powers. During World War II, Germany and the Allies each sought to secure Middle Eastern oil while denying it to the enemy. With the end of the war, some arrangement was necessary for the sharing of access to this resource among the victors. It is true that the U.S.S.R. is a net exporter of oil and is not interested in Middle Eastern oil per se. However, because Middle Eastern oil is the key to the economy of Western Europe and a basic resource in global defense its continued unimpeded availability is of vital economic and strategic importance. According to the distinguished scholar John S. Badeau, "the first and foremost [interest of America] is that the Middle East, or any vital part of it, shall not be occupied or controlled by a foreign power hostile to the United States and the free world. Such a power could either deny oil and passage to the West, or use access to them as diplomatic blackmail to force changes in Western policy."[3]

The Middle East is also important to world affairs in the politics of the Third World, *i.e.*, the neutral or nonaligned countries of Africa and Asia, emerging or developing, that are looking for solutions to their many problems. The Middle East, particularly Egypt, has taken the lead in encouraging solidarity among the neutralist states and has taken something of a leading position in the Third World.

Thus, with the many problems arising from its attempts at rapid modernization, with the conflict between Israel and the Arab states and the conflict among the Arab states themselves, with the importance of Middle Eastern oil, with the influence of the Middle East in the Third World, and with the strategic position of the Middle East in world politics, it is apparent that the Middle East is a key area in the future of international relations.

PHYSICAL GEOGRAPHY

Physiography

The Middle East is an area of contrasting geographical features that range from swampy regions where coal beds are formed to steep cliffs and jagged peaks. Most of Arabia is a slanted coastal block that climbs gradually from sea

---

[3] John S. Badeau, *The American Approach to the Arab World* (New York, 1968), p. 22.

level in the northeast to 12,000 feet in the southwest until it reaches Yemen, where a sharp drop occurs and the land rushes down into the troughs and rifts that comprise the Red Sea and the Gulf of Aden. The southern plateaus, other than the break at Yemen, continue into North Africa without much change or disturbance in the landscape, creating a region of seemingly endless, relatively flat, sank-covered surfaces as in much of the Libyan Sahara, Egyptian, and Arabian deserts. Central Turkey and central Iran are also elevated plateaus that sometimes reach a height of 8,000 feet. But it is the various systems of rugged mountains with their formidable topography, deep valleys, and sheer drops to narrow coastal lowlands that vividly command the Middle Eastern scene. The Caucasus Mountains, which divide the Black and Caspian seas, tower to 19,000 feet; the Zagros Mountains, a wide system of ranges, thrust to the southeast across the face of Iran; and in Turkey the Toros Daglari (the Taurus Mountains) overshadow the Anatolian Plateau, and the Elburz group command the southern shores of the Caspian coast.

In the region where Syria, Israel, Jordan, Lebanon, and Iraq lie, there is a zone where the ancient, unfolded plateaus and the marked crustal convulsions which dominate the major portion of the Middle East converge into relatively serene and pleasing landforms where man is neither engulfed by vast monotonous expanses nor overwhelmed by the magnitude of ominous mountains and lofty peaks. In this area, hospitable to man, civilization first blossomed forth, and this same geological territory now contributes a significant amount of petroleum to the thirsty work horses of the mechanized world.

Two other important physical features of the Middle East are the rivers and waterways which have played eventful political, economic, and social roles in their respective regions. The Nile River is made up of several streams which flow from central Africa and Ethiopa and merge together to amble over a relatively flat territory in the Sudan and roar through a cataract zone north of Khartoum. Then, below Aswan, and during the rest of its journey through the U.A.R., the river follows a long, fertile valley until it reaches Cairo, where it separates into two branches and enters the delta. The Nile follows a seasonal variation in the volume of water it transports. Every summer the river rises and during the month of August it reaches a high point that is about 18 feet above the annual low in April and May. In the process it deposits in Egypt over 100 million tons of silt, a sedimentary material rich in minerals and other substances vital to plant life. Since the building of the Aswan High Dam, of course, the amount of silt moving down the river has been considerably lessened.

The Tigris-Euphrates river system is the other important river system in the Middle East. These two rivers begin in the mountains of eastern Turkey and are enlarged as they wind through tortuous channels until they reach the plains of Syria and Iraq. Thousands of years ago rich sediment carried by the Tigris and Euphrates rivers created, between Baghdad and what is now the present shoreline of the Persian Gulf, a broad, fertile valley out of the basin that once held waters of the Persian Gulf. Today, the rivers join approximately 230 miles south of Baghdad to form the Shatt-al-Arab and from the travel 70 miles further to the coast of the Persian Gulf. Both the Tigris and the Euphrates are lowest during the fall and highest during the months between December and June; the Tigris generally reaches its flood stage of 18 feet in April, but the Euphrates usually does not overflow until May.

The waterway from the Black Sea to the Aegean, which separates Europe from Asia and which is commonly referred to as the Straits, has been significant in the affairs of men throughout all history. At the southwestern outlet of the Black Sea lies the Bosporus, a narrow passage that never reaches a width greater than two miles and that extends for 16 miles between Asiatic and European Turkey. However, the Bosporus is a deep channel ideally suited for the docking and unloading of heavily laden, deep draft vessels. On the shores of the inlet where the Bosporus enters the Sea of Marmara stands Istanbul, one of the legendary cities of the Middle East. Istanbul, known variously throughout history as Byzantium and Constantinople, has been one of the most important cities in the history of civilization.

The Sea of Marmara, which is 60 miles wide, marks the second stage of the passage to the Mediterranean from the Black Sea and extends for some 125 miles to the southwest, where it joins the Dardanelles, an ancient strait that accounts for the final 25 miles to the Aegean. The Dardanelles is two and a half to four and a half miles wide and is referred to in Greek mythology as the Hellespont, the sea where Helle fell from the ram with the golden fleece and drowned.

Climate

There has been little documentation of climatic change during the last five thousand years in the Middle East, although Cladium Ptolemy wrote of frequent afternoon showers in the now desert city of Alexandria in 150 A.D. Generally speaking, the Middle East experiences a Mediterranean climate. Along the coasts of the Black, Caspian, and Mediterranean seas winter precipitation, caused by the westward flow of maritime air, is the rule, and many areas experience as much as 30 inches yearly. In the summer this flow of air is largely inhibited by the appearance of higher pressures in the western Mediterranean, and sunny days with blue skies prevail. The territories which receive the most rain during the winter months are those regions whose coastlines face west and are backed by rapidly rising highlands, such as are found in Lebanon, Israel, and western Asia Minor. Where these geographic features are missing, rainfall in any season becomes scarce, and it is always scarce in the interior. Egypt and the plateaus of Arabia, Iran, and Turkey have vast expanses of desert. In addition, the rains in these areas are not only seasonal but extremely erratic. Damascus has an annual rainfall of about ten inches, but it has received as much as four inches in one morning. In the mountains of eastern Turkey and Iran greater precipitation occurs, but winter is still by far the wettest season with additional months of snow contributing significantly to the yearly average. There are two climatic exceptions to the rhythm of moist winters followed by summer droughts: the monsoon region of southern and southwestern Arabia, which acquires most of its precipitation during the months of July, August, and September; and the Black Sea coast of Turkey, which gets its rain throughout the year.

The temperatures of the various regions in the Middle East, as in all other places, depend greatly on altitude and latitude. In the mountainous areas of Arabia winters can be quite harsh and cold. This can also be said of Asia Minor and a major portion of Iran because of their accessibility to the cold air pockets formed over the Eurasian land mass. To the south, however, the seas exert a tempering influence. During the daylight hours of summer, temperatures often exceed 100° F. in Egypt, Arabia, Iran, and the interior of Turkey, but nights are generally cool everywhere except in some lower valleys and along the coasts of the Persian Gulf, the Red Sea, and the Mediterranean, where the humidity is extremely high.

ETHNIC GEOGRAPHY

Just as there is little accord among scholars as to the exact boundaries of the Middle East, there is also little agreement among anthropologists concerning the defintion of the term *race*. Most modern writers feel that if true biological divisions ever did exist among men, they were obscured and diffused long before the advent of recorded history as early men wandered extensively over the broad reaches of their natural environment and intermixed freely with the peoples of other regions. Since the intermingling of races is especially characteristic of the Middle East, an attempt to group these peoples racially would be virtually impossible, and they will therefore be grouped according to the languages they speak and the religions they practice.

Language

The three major linguistic categories in the Middle East are the Semitic, Turkish, and Iranian. The Semitic group is by far the largest and includes modern Arabic and Hebrew. Of these two, Arabic is the prevailing tongue. In fact, it is an important unifying factor in the Arab Middle East. Wherever Arabic is spoken there exists among the people a common social and cultural heritage based on the history and myths that are an integral part of the culture. Arabic predominates throughout the Middle East except in Turkey, Israel, and Iran; and its major subdivisions are the Egyptian, Syrian, Iraqi, and Arabian Peninsular dialects. However, the extensive variations in grammar, vocabulary, and pronunciation that occur within these general subdivisions are prominent enough to identify a speaker's origin.

Approximately two thousand years ago Arabic was just one of a dozen Semitic tongues and was found primarily in central Arabia. Historical knowledge of the Semitic languages begins with the written records left by the Akkadians, a people who occupied an ancient country north of Babylonia and preceded the Babylonians and Assyrians in the Middle Eastern area. The origin of present day Arabic and Hebrew script has been traced to the Phoenician civilization. The emergence of modern Arabic dates from the fourth to sixth centuries A.D. Following the advent of Islam during the seventh and eighth centuries, Arab conquests spread the language throughout the area so that it currently occupies a position of cultural dominance.

As has been previously noted, Arabic often displays marked regional differences. Wherever Persian, Turkish, English, French, or other foreign words and phrases have worked themselves into the language, they have exerted a substantial influence. However, written Arabic is essentially the same throughout the Middle East and has changed very little during the last thousand years. The Koran, written in the seventh century, has from its firt appearance served the Arab nations and the Muslim world as a model of literary excellence.

A relatively recent development in Arabic has been the emergence of a new idiom made up of a blend of the classical and colloquial elements already existing in the language. This new idiom has been influenced most by the Egyptian and Syrian dialects and has become the stylistic standard for newspapers, radio broadcasts, motion pictures, and other media of mass communication in the Arab speaking regions of the Middle East.

The other Semitic language found in the area is a revived and simplified Hebrew so similar to Arabic in grammar, vocabulary, sentence structure, and script that knowledge of the one facilitates study of the other, for many of the words in both languages have the same cognates. Modern Hebrew, however, which is found predominantly in Israel, has been greatly colored by the speech of the numerous European immigrants who have swelled the population of this new country.

The second largest linguistic category in the Middle East is Turkish, a member of the Turkic family of languages. Turkish is found not only in Turkey proper but in Iran, Afghanistan, the central Asian and Caucasian areas of the Soviet Union, and scattered throughout the Arab nations as well. The Turks are originally descended from a number of tribes which migrated from central Asia during the eleventh and twelfth centuries and are related to the Huns—a fierce Asiatic people who, led by Attila, invaded the Middle East and eastern and central Europe in the fourth and fifth centuries A.D.

Today, Turkish (an agglutinative language), has proved to be a flexible one well-suited to handle the complexities of modern existence and the demands of a rapidly expanding body of administrative and scientific knowledge. Both nouns and verbs in the language are equipped with a convenient system of prefixes and suffixes so that the meaning of a single root can be augmented and modified in a dozen expressive ways.

During various periods of history Turkish has been transcribed in Syriac, Tibetan, Armenian, Greek, and Hebrew characters. In western Asia Turkish has been almost exclusively written in Arabic script, a medium fundamentally unsuited for the task. However, in 1928 it was decreed that within the borders of the Turkish Republic the official alphabet would be composed of Latin letters and, in a burst of national pride, it was also decided at this time to purge the language of its Arabic and Persian vocabulary in favor of a true Turkish idiom. In a sense this latter effort has failed because it has been accompanied by a wholesale adoption of French and English words. In addition, the attempt to purify the language has created new difficulties: Significant differences now exist between the current Turkish of the Republic and the Turkish of those communities outside of the Republic which still adhere to the composite medieval diction and the Arabic form of writing; and a widening gulf now exists between the old Turkish literature and the new.

Iranian is the third largest linguistic category in the Middle East. It belongs to the Indo-European family of languages, a family whose parent tongue disappeared from the human scene sometime before 2000 B.C. It is believed that the almost mythical Indo-European population inhabited the mainland of Europe and the western part of Asia, but because the Indo-Europeans existed as a coherent community before the invention of writing and thus left no recorded evidence behind them, the location of their original home can only be approximated. Today, the Persian-speaking Iranians number over twenty million and occupy an area centered in the great plateau of Iran that covers 629,180 square miles of land. However, Iranian languages, due to early migrational periods, can also be found in territories as remote as southern Russia and central China.

A tongue that is linguistically related to Iranian is Kurdish, known also as Kurdistani or Kirmanji. Kurdish is the language of a people who are found throughout northern Syria and Iraq, eastern Turkey, northeastern Iran, and Russia. The Kurds represent a minority group in the regions they inhabit and observe obedience and loyalty only to their own tribal organizations, a custom which has brought them into open conflict with various national governments. Originally nomadic herdsmen, the Kurds are fiercely independent, traditionally proud, warlike and predatory, and they follow a way of life that has changed very little since the Middle Ages. Dealing with them on an administrative level has proved next to impossible, and whenever central authorities have attempted to assert their influence overt warfare has often resulted.

Religion

Religion has played an important role in the affairs of the Middle East for centuries and has not only provided a basis for national and ethnic unity, but also a source of diversity. Islam, Judaism, and Christianity—which originated in the Middle East—are the dominant religions (as shown in the map below), and a significant number of those who worship in these faiths are more likely to identify with their religion than with their political state

Islam, at least numerically, is the most influential religion in the Middle East. Those in the area faithful to Islam number approximately 85 to 90 million. Early in its history, Islam divided into two major sects, the Shi'i and the Sunni. The Shi'i sect, found predominantly in Iraq and Iran, is divided into a number of subsects, *i.e.* Imami, Ismaili, and Zaidi. In addition, there are a number of

FIGURE 1-2

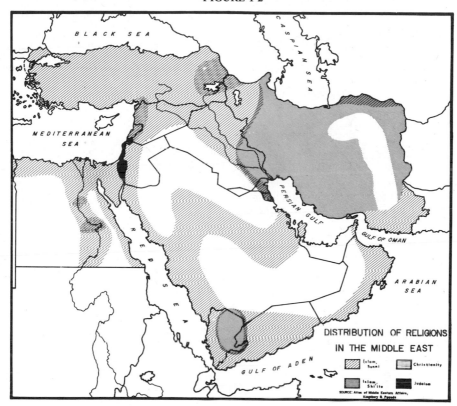

DISTRIBUTION OF RELIGIONS
IN THE MIDDLE EAST

Islam, Sunni   Christianity

Islam, Shi'ite   Judaism

SOURCE: Atlas of Middle Eastern Affairs,
Kingsbury & Pounds

Islamic heterodox and offshoot sects which include Druze, Yazidi, Ibadi (modern Kharijite), Alawi (Nusayri), Ali-Ilahi or Ahl al-Haqq, and Bahai.

It is the Sunni division of Islam, however, which predominates. This sect represents 90 percent of all Muslims and is the principal faith of Egypt, Syria, Jordan, the Arabian peninsula, and Turkey. The Sunni branch of Islam is divided into four "schools of law": the Hanifite, the Malikite, the Shafite, and the Hanbalite. Each of these schools has its distinct interpretation of scripture and tradition.

The Coptic church in Egypt, with approximately 2,000,000 members, and the Greek Orthodox church in Syria and Lebanon, with about 400,000 members, are the largest Christian organizations found in the Middle East. In addition, there are small groups of Nestorians and Armenian and Syrian Orthodox scattered throughout the area. Originally, the Coptic church evolved in Alexandria, the Greek Orthodox in Constantinople, and the Syrian or Jacobite in Antioch. The Roman Catholic church, which is currently represented in the Middle East by various uniate churches, such as the Greek Catholic, Coptic Catholic, and Syrian Catholic, first arose in Rome.

The Jewish faith is the third most significant religion in the Middle East and, aside from traces of the lost Samaritan and Daraite sects, generally follows the traditional canons set forth by a native orthodox Rabbinate Judaism. Jewish communities can be found in most Middle Eastern states, such as Iraq, Syria, Lebanon, and Eqypt, but since 1948 the largest concentrations have, of course, been found in Israel.

ECONOMIC GEOGRAPHY

Agriculture

Harsh climatic conditions have long been a source of concern to agricultural specialists in the Middle East. Farming has been generally restricted to those regions that lie outside the vast stretches of desert and steppe, and thus it has been confined to relatively small areas. It is estimated that only 7 to 10 percent of the total area is suitable for cultivation.

The seasonal concentration of rainfall seriously limits the amount of ground that can be productively utilized. Except in the mountains, most precipitation occurs during only one or two months; the rest of the year remains virtually arid. Moreover, except for the Euphrates, Tigris, Nile, and Karun rivers, Middle Eastern rivers are small, and the lakes have a high saline content. (The map below details the major irrigated areas of the Middle East.) Therefore, in many areas dry farming is necessary and a system of two or three year rotation of the land is often unavoidable. Another difficulty is that in territories, such as Iraq, the rivers flood every spring when additional water is least needed.

In view of these Middle Eastern environmental factors, agriculture must still be carried on in a primitive fashion until modern systems of irrigation, flood control, and farming can be developed to offset long summer droughts and the unequal distribution of water. At present, chemical fertilizers and scientific methods of grazing and harvesting are almost unknown. In addition, up-to-date farm equipment is scarce. During 1954, for example, 60.5 percent of the world's total tractor supply was being used in the United States, while less than 1 percent was utilized in the Middle East (excluding Israel). Instead, handmade, manually employed cultivating tools are most often used to prepare the soil. However, following recent land redistribution in Iran, Syria, and the United Arab Republic, modern farming techniques are being introduced.

In the Middle East farming is carried on largely for local consumption except for the raising of cotton, which is Egypt's chief export, and for dates and olives. Also, a fourth of Israel's agricultural produce is exported. Though the region boasts an extensive grain belt, it is still unable to produce the amount of food required to sustain its population. Generally speaking, Turkey, Iraq, and Syria harvest a surplus of wheat and even manage to export some barley and rice. However, Iran, Israel, and Egypt are commonly forced to import grain.

The principal plants that have been developed from the flora native to the area—besides wheat and barley—are broad beans, rye, leeks, onions, lentils,

FIGURE 1-3

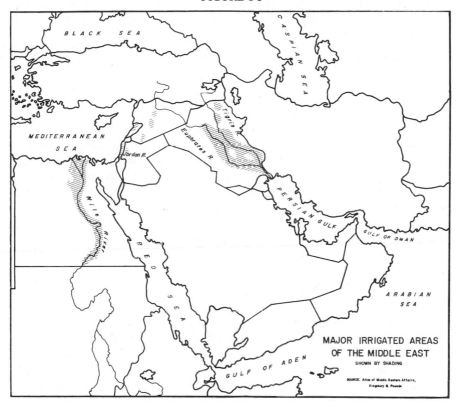

MAJOR IRRIGATED AREAS
OF THE MIDDLE EAST
SHOWN BY SHADING

SOURCE: Atlas of Middle Eastern Affairs,
Kingsbury & Pounds

grapes, figs, garlic, apricots, peaches, apples, plums, pears, pomegranates, melons, dates, olives, walnuts, and almonds. Wheat and barley are by far the most important grains cultivated in the Middle East and are largely produced in the north, where climatic conditions are favorable to their growth. Barley is particularly favored in Iraq, Iran, and Syria because of its greater resistance to insects and environmental extremes. Rye is a crop that does well in the foothills and the colder regions of Iran and Turkey. As one moves south towards southern Arabia, corn and drought-resistant cereals, such as millets and sorghums, become the principal plants grown. In those areas of the desert where water is available and in other regions where irrigation is possible, such as in Lower Egypt, Iran, and southern Iraq, rice (which requires a great deal of heat and moisture) is popular because of its high yield per unit of land.

In addition to the basic grains, the Middle East also boasts a wide selection of fruits and nuts. Hazelnuts and figs are grown in Turkey; apples are found in the highlands of Lebanon; apricots, melons, and pistachios are raised in Iran; and, wherever hilly regions and moderate, dry weather occur together (as they do in the foothills of Asia Minor, Lebanon, and Israel) grapes are cultivated and harvested in large quantities. Oranges are the principal citrus fruit produced in the Middle East and represent a significant portion of Israel's export profits. They are also grown in parts of Iran, the Levant, and southern Turkey.

Even more important than the vine to the diet of a great number of Middle Easterners are the date and olive crops. The olive represents a significant source of fat and is used in the preparation of a variety of tasty, nourishing dishes. Requiring considerable winter precipitation and long, dry summers, the olive tree is raised primarily in the valleys of southwest Turkey and, on a more limited basis, in Iran and along the coasts of Syria, Lebanon, and Israel. On the other hand, the date requires endless heat and often fails to mature properly if temperatures drop below 64° F. Thus the date palm thrives around the oases of the Arabian peninsula. However, the most abundant date harvests are obtained where either irrigation or rivers ensure a surplus of water. For this reason the district of Basra, in southern Iraq, exports 80 percent of the world's supply of dates.

One of the more profitable commercial plants being grown in the Middle East today is Egypt's long-fibered cotton, which is cultivated on 20 percent of her agricultural land and accounts for four fifths of her total exports. Turkey and Iran, as well as other nations of the Fertile Crescent region, also raise cotton but their annual yields are relatively modest in comparison to Egypt's bountiful harvests. Flax, hemp, and silk are produced in Syria, Iraq, Jordan, and Israel—but in quantities too small to be utilized as market crops.

Some of the secondary crops being produced in the Middle East are coffee, cultivated on the mountain slopes of Yemen; tea, raised along Turkey's Black Sea coast and the Caspian shore of Iran; and both sugar beets and sugar cane, harvested primarily in Turkey. Turkey also grows tobacco near its Aegean Sea coast, and small quantities of the plant are found in Iran, northern Iraq, and along the Levantine coast.

No survey of the Middle Eastern agricultural scene would be complete without at least a brief look at those animals upon which the pastoral and rural dwellers depend for food and income. Sheep and goats, numbering in the tens of millions, are found throughout the region, and it is believed by conservation specialists that their destructive grazing habits have contributed significantly to the disappearance of large areas of native vegetation. Nomadic tribes, who depend upon their livestock for survival, possess approximately 80 percent of these animals; the remaining 20 percent represent the herds and flocks of the settled farmers.

The cattle of the Middle East, in comparison with cattle in other parts of the world, are generally not significant. They are small in size and their milk yield is so low that most of them are used primarily as draft animals. It is not unusual to see donkeys and cows yoked together and pulling plows in the fields of the Middle East. However, in regions, such as the Nile Delta and the marsh lands of southern Iraq, the water buffalo is the principal beast of burden.

The horse is gradually becoming a thing of the past in the Middle East, as in other regions of the world. The camel is still utilized by the nomadic tribes in their long journeys across the deserts and arid steppes, but in the rural areas the economical donkey has become the most common means of transportation.

Resources

Oil is by far the most important mineral resource the Middle East possesses. No one knows for sure how great the oil reserves are, but it is apparent that they have not yet been fully explored. For instance, in 1964 it was estimated that 68 percent of the world's total proven oil reserve lay in the Middle East, yet only 34 percent of this reserve was actually mined and processed. However, Middle Eastern oil is not equally distributed throughout the area. Some oil is found in Turkey, Egypt, Syria, and Israel, but the truly large fields are located in Kuwait, Iraq, Iran, and along the Persian Gulf in Saudi Arabia and the sheikdoms. Kuwait accounts for about 20 percent of the world reserve, while Saudi Arabia accounts for 19 percent, Iran for 12 percent, and Iraq for 8 percent.

A variety of mineral resources are found in the Middle East, but other than oil, only the red iron oxide and turquoise of Iran and the potash of Jordan are produced and exported in any quantity. There exist in Turkey and Iran large deposits of coal and lignite, but these beds have only been exploited during recent years. In addition to widespread but individually small pockets of gold, silver, copper, and iron ores, the Middle East also possesses considerable amounts of chromium and manganese and small amounts of antimony, molybdenum, mercury, and cobalt.

Other Middle Eastern resources are extensive basalt, granite, marble, porphyry, sandstone, and limestone quarries, and the natural clays which have been used by many cultures for the production of fine ceramics.

Industry

Industry, relatively speaking, is almost nonexistent in the Middle East. Outside of the oil industry, the indifference of private investors and the shortage of trained administrators, skilled workers, and power have greatly limited the Middle East's ability to manufacture goods that can compete in price and quality on the world market. Only in the U.A.R., Israel, and Lebanon do textiles and other manufactured items represent a significant proportion of total exports. Nevertheless, there has been a recent surge of industrialization brought about by such measures as state capitalism in Turkey and Iran, socialism in the U.A.R. and Syria, tariff protection for private industry in Lebanon and Iraq, the investment of oil income in Iraq and Iran, and financial and technical assistance from abroad.

The growth of industry has resulted in the rise of a new working class. This group, though still small, has formed organized unions and influenced legislators to enact laws favorable to labor and has thereby created a working environment that may one day encourage further industrial expansion. A well-trained, satisfied body of workers is essential to industry, and benefits, such as workmen's compensation and high wages, are sure to attract and retain the type of individuals necessary to operate a modern manufacturing system at peak efficiency. However, it is estimated that the number of people currently engaged in Middle Eastern industry is very small in comparison with the total agricultural population. A survey in Egypt, with a relatively large proportion of industrial workers, indicates that less than 6 percent of the nation's manpower resources are employed in an industrial capacity. Even in those countries where the production of oil is the dominant factor of economic existence, usually no more than 1 percent of the labor force is actively concerned with oil-connected enterprises.

While the industrial sector is small, nevertheless it is rapidly growing in some states. For example, in 1954 industry contributed 19.7 percent to the domestic product of Israel, 13.3 percent to the domestic product of Turkey, 12.1 percent to the domestic product of Lebanon, and 10.6 percent to the domestic product of Egypt. Although complete figures are not available, it is believed that by 1964 the contributions of industry to the domestic products of Israel, Turkey, and Egypt had risen to 27 percent, 17 percent and 22 percent respectively. The industrial sector in the U.A.R. has realized the highest development rate of income in the world. The following charts illustrate the dramatic growth experienced by its major industries from 1952 to 1965.

FIGURE 1-4
Industrial Output Value
(1952, 1960, 1965)

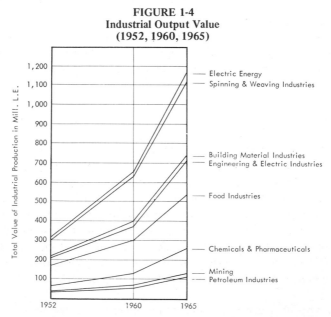

Graph adapted from U.A.R., *Statistical Handbook,* 1952-1965 (Cairo: Central Agency for Public Mobilisation and Statistics, April 1966), p. 75.

FIGURE 1-5
U.A.R. Index Numbers of Industrial Production
(1951/1952, 1964/1965)

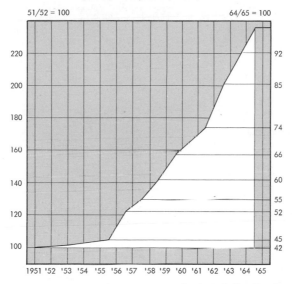

Graph adapted from U.A.R., *Statistical Handbook,
1952-1965* (Cairo: Central Agency for Public Mobilisation
and Statistics, April 1966), p. 59.

The increase of oil production and export, however, overshadows industrialization. In 1964 oil accounted for about 93 percent of Iran's total exports and for about 90 to 95 percent of Iraq's. In fact, in 1966 the Middle East became the world's largest producer with a total estimate of 471 million tons while the United States dropped to second place with 462 million. In comparison, the world's third largest oil producing region, the Sino-Soviet area, had an estimated output of slightly over 290 million tons. The graph below clearly illustrates the Middle East's dominance in oil production. Thus, it is not surprising that oil tankers traveling to and from the ports of the Middle Eastern oil states accounted for more than two-thirds of the merchant tonnage handled by the Suez Canal prior to its closure in June 1967.

The table below details the Middle East's total oil production in 1967 of 504,585,000 metric tons listed by country.

	1,000 Metric Tons		*1,000 Metric Tons*
Saudi Arabia	129,594	Qatar	15,479
Iran	129,345	U.A.R	7,000[a]
Kuwait	115,203	Bahrain	3,405
Iraq	60,085	Turkey	2,400[a]
Neutral Zone	21,600	Oman	2,000
Abu Dhabi	18,339	Israel	135[a]

[a]Estimated

FIGURE 1-6

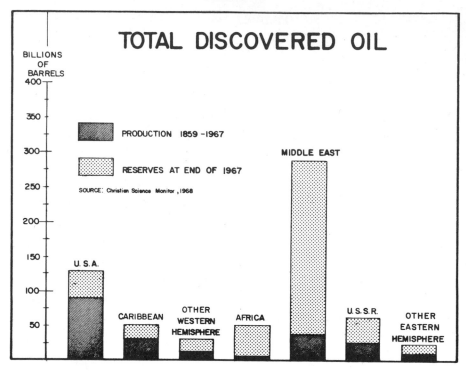

SOCIAL GEOGRAPHY

Middle Eastern society is in the process of a socio-economic and political revolution and is currently experiencing important and sweeping changes in its basic structure. Yet traditional social patterns, such as kinship-based social groupings and the rule of Sharia Law (Islamic law), are generally more resistant in rural than in urban areas. Therefore the process of change is uneven and must be considered separately for the urban dweller, the villager, and the nomad.

City Life

Although rural life accounts for the major share of population, city life represents a disproportionate share of influence in the Middle East. The urban developments are the centers of the economic, social, political, and religious activities carried on in the area. In fact, the economic dominance of the cities has contributed significantly to the poverty of the rural regions. In many cases absentee landlords and merchants who control and manipulate the profits of rural produce have been able to accumulate most of the surplus agricultural wealth in the cities. In addition, the city is the focus of all political power.

One of the major problems of the Middle East has been the rapid growth of urban centers. Since the 1940's, the number of people moving from the rural areas of the Middle East to the cities has drastically increased. Among the reasons for this migration are industrial employment, higher wages, and improved medical facilities found in the cities. Frequently, the youth of the Middle East have been unwilling to remain in the villages and have sought, instead, the opportunities and social stature of urban life. The chart below records a dramatic rise in the population of several cities and suggests how extensive migration from the country has been. Of course, a higher birth rate and a longer life expectancy have also contributed to urban growth.

Urban Population
(approximate figures)

Cities	1940s	1960s
Alexandria	1,000,000	2,000,000
Baghdad	350,000	2,000,000
Beirut	200,000	750,000
Cairo	1,400,000	4,000,000
Damascus	200,000	600,000
Teheran	500,000	2,000,000

Rural Life

Except in Israel, where it is estimated that 84 percent of the population lives in cities, the predominance of rural life is one of the primary features of Middle Eastern society. Approximately seven-tenths of the population live in the countryside and are principally engaged in agricultural pursuits. Like the nomad, the average Middle Eastern peasant, or *fallah*, exists as his ancestors existed centuries before him. He lives in a village near to or surrounded by the fields he works during the day. The tools that he uses—the sickle, the threshing board, and the wooden plow—are the same tools that have been used to cultivate the land for over 2,000 years. Until recently, the land that he farms was the property of a relatively few powerful landlords, such as tribal sheikhs and absentee owners. Prior to the fifties, approximately 70 percent of the *fallahin* were either tenants or share croppers. In recent years land reform programs in the U.A.R., Iraq, Syria, Yemen, and Iran have greatly reduced the number and size of large landholdings, with the result that the *fallahin* in these areas increasingly own the land they till. In conjunction with the land reform programs, the governments are encouraging the introduction of modern farming techniques and equipment and are attempting to replace the cash crop system with a food crop system.

The rural Middle East is plagued by problems endemic to most developing areas—high birth and mortality rates, malaria and typhoid perpetuated by inadequate sanitation, and malnutrition. Until recently, it was estimated that out of every 1,000 births approximately 200 children died, and of those who survived at least 80 percent contracted trachoma and various intestinal disorders before they matured. Widespread illiteracy inhibits improvements in these tragic conditions of village life. Only 10 to 15 percent of the total rural population

Middle East Population Data

	World	Iran	Iraq	Israel	Jordan	Kuwait	Lebanon	Saudi Arabia	Southern Yemen	Syria	Turkey	UAR	Yemen
Population:													
Mid-'69 estimate (millions)	3551	27.9	8.9	2.8	2.3	0.6	2.6	7.2	1.3	6.0	34.4	32.5	5.0
Birth rate (per 1,000)	34	50	48	25	47	52	–	–	37	–	46	43	–
Death rate (per 1,000)	15	20	–	6.6	16	6	–	–	8	–	18	15	–
Percent rate current growth	1.9	3.1	2.5	2.9	4.1	7.6	2.5	1.8	2.2	2.9	2.5	2.9	–
Number of years to double	37	23	28	24	17	9	28	39	32	24	28	24	–
Infant mortality (under 1 yr. per 1,000)	–	–	–	25	–	37	–	–	80	–	161	120	–
Percent under age 15	37	46	45	33	46	38	–	–	–	46	44	43	–
1980 projection (in millions)	4368	38	13.8	–	3.3	–	3.6	9.4	1.6	9.2	48.5	46.7	6.9
GNP per capita (in $ U.S.)	589	250	270	1160	220	3410	480	240	–	180	280	160	90

Source: adapted from *1969 World Population Data Sheet*, Population Reference Bureau, Information Service, Washington, D.C.

know how to read or write. Here too, however, the governments are making slow but meaningful progress in overcoming these conditions. In many nations systems of compulsory education have been instituted that insure at least a minimal education to the peasant and offer to the superior student an opportunity for advanced education. Comprehensive sanitation projects have been undertaken to eradicate sources of disease. Iraq, for example, has attempted to eliminate the widespread marsh areas that were notorious for parasitic infestations—hookworm, bilharzia, and ankylostomiasis. Technical and educational public health programs are also making progress in improving sanitation and combating malnutrition.

Nomads

Like the urban dweller, the nomad too is passing through a transitional period and is currently in the process of changing from a migratory to a sedentary member of Middle Eastern society. National governments have recently found it necessary to restrict or control the freedom of movement the tribes have enjoyed for centuries, and modern weapon systems have rendered the more warlike wanderers vulnerable even in their traditional strongholds, the desert and mountains. Moreover, as the area under cultivation has increased, the grazing lands which the tribes depend upon to support their livestock have rapidly dwindled. Consequently, many nomads have already sought employment in the oil and mining industries and others have joined various military and public organizations. Thus, it seems that Middle Eastern nomadism will eventually disappear. For example, in 1938 there were over 600,000 tribesmen in Iraq, but today they number less than 150,000. It is estimated, however, that there are still approximately 1,500,000 nomads in central Arabia; 1,000,000 in Iran and Turkey; and about 250,000 in Syria.

Nomadic existence is centered in the raising of sheep and goats and in the production of milk, butter, cheese, and wool. In fact, the various tribes depend heavily on their flocks and herds to sustain life, although the mobile and heavily armed tribesmen have traditionally supplemented their income with random but effective assaults on the outskirts of urban areas. For many tribes raiding and pillage has long been an economic necessity—often the only alternative to starvation during years of drought when the grass has failed to replenish itself sufficiently to feed their animals.

The most important organization in the nomad's life is the tribe, which basically consists of a number of families who have been brought together through marriage and who follow a leader called a *sheikh* by the Arabs and a *khan* in Iran. The office of a sheikh or khan is decided partly by heredity and partly by merit, and it commands the intense loyalty of all members of the tribe. Although most tribes are found within the borders of the several Middle Eastern states, they seldom recognize any government but their own, a practice that has often outraged central authorities. The tribe is usually large enough to survive in a hostile environment, but it is limited in size by the resources of the district it inhabits. Occasionally an exceptional leader has been able to combine the tribes into larger federations. These federations, however, have lasted for relatively short periods and were generally marked by intertribal feuds and jealousy. On the whole, the nomad's way of life and his social ideals, which include personal bravery and tribal prestige, do not permit the formation of extensive political unions.

There are two forms of nomadism in the Middle East. The "horizontal" nomads occupy the desert and follow the rain. During autumn and winter, seasonal precipitation extends the grazing area available for their sheep and goats and the tribes are able to remain relatively stationary for long periods of time. However, during the summer months, they must seek out distant water supplies for their flock and herds or perish. On the other hand, the "vertical" nomads follow the vegetation that blossoms at increasingly higher altitudes during the summer in the mountainous regions of Iraq, Turkey, and Iran, and then winter each year on the plains.

In order to remain highly mobile, nomads have only a few personal possessions. Their tents, customarily black, are woven of either goat or camel hair and are easily folded and moved; furniture is kept to a minimum, and usually consists of only a few daily utensils and a floor rug or mats.

SELECTED BIBLIOGRAPHY

Roderic H. Davison's excellent article, "Where Is the Middle East," in *The Modern Middle East*, ed. Richard H. Nolte (New York, 1963), is a definitive treatment of the problems of consistently locating the Middle East in time and space. For detailed geographic surveys treating the area by individual countries and geographic regions, see George B. Cressey, *Land and Life in Southwest Asia* (Philadelphia, 1960), and W. B. Fisher, *The Middle East, A Physical, Social, and Regional Geography*, 3d ed. (London, 1956). In addition, *Atlas of the Arab World and the Middle East* (New York, 1960) provides information on the physical characteristics, resources, population, and climate. An excellent and regularly updated reference volume is *The Middle East and North Africa*, published by Europa Publications Limited, London.

Stephen H. Longrigg's book, *The Middle East: A Social Geography* (Chicago, 1963), is a comprehensive social, political, and economic survey of the area. Another excellent and concise reference is the Royal Institute of International Affairs' book, *The Middle East, a Political and Economic Survey* (London, 1950, 3d ed., 1968).

The New Metropolis in the Arab World, ed. Morroe Berger (New Delhi, 1963) is a series of articles which examines the problems of urban growth in the Arab world. For an excellent anthropological study of the Middle East, see Carleton S. Coon, *Caravan: The Story of the Middle East* (New York, 1951).

The following series of periodicals and reference works provide a constant source of timely and scholarly articles on every facet of study pertaining to the

Middle East: *International Journal of Middle Eastern Studies*, published by the Middle East Studies Association of North America (New York, N.Y.); *The Middle East Journal*, published by the Middle East Institute, Washington, D.C.; *The Moslem World*, published by the Hartford Seminary Foundation, Hartford, Conn.; *American Universities Field Staff Reports* (Northeast Africa and Southwest Asia Series, American Universities Field Staff, Inc., New York); *The Journal of Developing Areas*, Western Illinois University, Macomb, Ill.; and for an excellent detailed chronology of current events in the Arab world see *Chronology of Arab Politics* by the Political Studies and Public Administration Department of the American University of Beirut, published quarterly since 1963. They also annually publish *Arab Political Documents*, a translation of documents from domestic and inter-Arab politics.

chapter 2

Evolution of the Contemporary Middle East

Although historians disagree over the exact location of the birthplace of Western civilization, they do agree that it originated in the Middle East, either in the Nile Valley or in Mesopotamia along the Tigris-Euphrates River. From the earliest period, the area was the crossroads of migrating peoples. Successive invasions into the area, occurring approximately between 5000 B.C. and the time of Christ, made it a melting pot of races and cultures. The first of the invaders, an Asiatic type of the Mediterranean race called the Sumerians, established a number of city-states between the Tigris and the Euphrates rivers. The prosperity of these city-states attracted from the surrounding areas Semitic peoples who first founded the state of Akkad along the middle Euphrates about the beginning of the third millenium B.C. For a thousand years Sumerian and Akkadian states competed with each other. The threat of outside invasion by the non-Semitic Elamites resulted, however, in the unification of all Mesopotamia by Hammurabi of Babylon about 1700 B.C. During this same period, the Hamites established in the Nile Valley a monarchial state which they were able to hold relatively undisturbed until about 500 B.C. when the Persians established their empire. Semite tribes from Arabia, meanwhile, continued to fill the area between Sumeria and the Nile, establishing states in the area known as the Fertile Crescent.

From 1700 to 100 B.C. the Indo-European invasions brought successive waves of conquerors, each of whom extended the empire of his predecessors. Thus, the Persians, by 500 B.C., were able to establish an empire bordered by the Indus River, the Black Sea, and the western border of Egypt. The Persian Empire, a monarchial state, was effectively controlled by the appointment of satraps to the governorship of its territorial subdivisions and by the use of spies

FIGURE 2-1

ANCIENT   MIDDLE
EAST   CIVILIZATIONS

AFTER   ARAMCO   HANDBOOK,   1960

who watched the satraps and reported directly to the emperor. The Persians also built a highway, the Royal Road, from Sardis on the Aegean to their capital at Susa. This road, excellently policed, both facilitated East-West trade and ensured communication within the empire.

One of the major problems facing the Persian Empire was the expansionist tendencies of the Greeks. The ultimate failure to control the Greeks was to have a dramatic impact upon the development of the Middle East. The conquests of Alexander the Great ushered in a new age not only for the Greeks but also for the groups who resided in the birthplace of civilization. It had been Alexander's wish to blend the cultures of Greece and Persia; and before his early death in 323 B.C. he was partially successful in Hellenizing the Middle East through his encouragement of intermarriage between his soldiers and the women of conquered peoples and his founding of a number of cities styled after those of

Greece. After Alexander's death, the empire broke up into a series of kingdoms ruled by his generals. The Hellenizing effects of his conquest, however, were more permanent. For the next two centuries the Middle East continued to be a wealthy area high in intellectual and artistic achievement but low in political stability.

About the first century B.C. the Romans, then the most powerful people in the Mediterranean area, began to extend their influence into the Middle East through arbitration with the warring states there. Eventually the Romans established political control over the area except for the eastern part of Persia, where first the Parthian Empire and then the Sassanids maintained predominance. The area remained under imperial regulation until the time of Constantine, when it fell under the authority of Constantinople.

Roman control of the Middle East, however, was never complete. The first centuries of occupation saw a number of large-scale uprisings, and the Parthians and Sassanids remained a constant threat to the security of first the Romans and later the Byzantines.

It might be expected that the spread of Christianity throughout the Roman Empire would have brought unity, but in fact it did not. From Constantinople to North Africa each area developed its own heresy, and the only link between them was that they were all split from Rome and the West.

Into this mass of political and religious strife came the Arab invasions from the Arabian peninsula. The Arabs had formed economic ties between the city-dwellers and their own nomadic bands. Thus, as the cities allied with the Arab tribes began to seek power on the basis of their position on the East-West trade routes, western influence fell away.

ISLAM AND THE ISLAMIC EMPIRE

By the seventh century, Mecca, midway on the trade route between Yemen and Syria, was the principal center of the Arabian peninsula. It had become a wealthy and independent city which had achieved its position of eminence through trade and financial speculation in the Red Sea and eastern Mediterranean territories. The city maintained relations with the tribes in the surrounding area, but carefully kept itself neutral in the conflicts between the Sassanid and Byzantine empires. The city government consisted of a council of clan leaders but each clan was independent of the council and responsible for itself. Religion in Mecca was diverse, ranging from magic and pantheism to a clan-centered code of honor. The city was, however, developing a concept of monotheism.

In this environment the Prophet Muhammad, a Meccan native, began preaching a religion of individual surrender to a monotheistic God. At first his movement drew a number of converts from the middle class; however, the wealthy feared that monotheism would lessen the number of pilgrimages to the Kaaba, a pantheistic shrine, and would destroy the pilgrim trade. As a result, economic sanctions were taken against the new religionists, the Muslims, and conversions ceased. In 622, therefore, Muhammad moved with his followers to Madinah where by acting as arbitrator for the city's clans and by reshaping his religion he was able to establish himself as overlord. Eight years of warfare with Mecca followed, but finally that city was brought to terms and Muhammad returned as its master. During those eight years of warfare, Islam spread throughout the Arabian peninsula and the social precepts of Islam were developed.

From the death of Muhammad in 632 until the establishment of the Umayyad Dynasty at Damascus in 661, the Muslim leaders were chosen by the chief men of Mecca and Madinah. Each of the four leaders chosen during this period—Abu Bakr, 'Umar, 'Uthman, and 'Ali—was named in his turn Khalifah (Caliph or successor) and functioned as both religious and political head of the Muslim world. And during their years in power, these four men succeeded in completely entrenching Islam on the Arabian peninsula and wresting from the Byzantine and Sassanid Empires the lands of Syria, Palestine, Egypt, Iraq and Iran.

During the reign of the first four Caliphs, a single family called the Umayyads had been gathering power through administrative ability. After the assassination of Ali in 661, this family established a dynasty which was to last for nearly a century. The Umayyads made four marks on the Islamic world: They moved the capital to Damascus; they added North Africa, Spain, and part of Asia to the empire; they reorganized the imperial administration; and they changed the elective caliphate to a hereditary system. The Umayyads at first partitioned the empire into five viceroyalties ruled by their appointees. Then, because of the lack of trained Arab personnel, they left the administration of each of these areas in the hands of those who had administered them before the conquest.

During the last half of the Umayyad reign, however, the Middle East was torn by civil wars. Charges of corruption against the Damascene rulers aided the Abbasids, descendants of Muhammad, in their claim to the caliphate. In 750 Abu al-Abbas overthrew the Umayyads and founded the Abbasid dynasty. The Umayyads, however, retained control of Spain.

Following their rise to power, the Abbasids moved the capital to Baghdad and from there ruled, through their *wazirs* (viziers), steadily dwindling dominions. In 788 an independent state was established in Morocco; in 800 the governor of Africa declared his independence; in the middle of the ninth century Egypt began her own dynasties. Finally, in the 10th century the Fatimids of Egypt succeeded in establishing a western Muslim world that stretched from Syria to the Straits of Gibraltar. And in the East all the Muslim provinces in and near India fell away from Baghdad. In the 11th century the Seljuk Turks, fierce invaders from the East, seized the last of the Abbasid Empire.

Concurrent with the Abbasid political decline, however, was the development of a rich culture. Notable contributions were made to philosophy and poetry, and the distinct Abbasid architecture evolved: a style which features tall minarets and complex geometrical designs which has had influence throughout the world. The works of the Greek scholars were translated, studied, and supplemented, and work of original and lasting value was done in medicine, astronomy, and geography.

By the 11th century both the Seljuk and Fatimid empires began to disintegrate and break up into numerous petty states. Thus, unable to present any organized resistance, these states watched helplessly as the European crusader drove a wedge of control into Syria and Palestine during the 12th century. The crusaders' fortunes in the Middle East were directly related to Muslim unity. Thus, when Salah-al-Din Alayyubi (Saladin) was able to regroup the torn Muslim world—starting with Egypt, then proceeding to Syria, northern Iraq, Hijaz, Nubia, and North Africa—he was able to extend his influence from the Nile to the Tigris. Upon his death, however, the crusaders gained back their lost territory and were able to hold it until the Mamluks gained firm control of Egypt. But even as the Mamluks were driving the Europeans from the Middle East, they were required to meet a new threat. The Mongol hordes of Genghiz Khan and his successors invaded from the East in a wave of destruction and conquest. They conquered as far as Damascus until in 1260 they were defeated and thrown out of Syria.

The Mamluk rulers of Egypt, the Turkish warrior slaves of Egypt's former rulers, established feudalism as the new social order. But the conquests of the Mongolian Turks, led by Timur Leng (Tamerlane), in the last part of the 14th century ended Mamluk control east of Egypt, resulted in a subdued and diminished Ottoman state, and left Iran dismembered and weak.

OTTOMAN EMPIRE

When Constantine moved the Roman capital to Constantinople, he created a buffer state between Europe and the Middle East. Originally the Byzantine Empire controlled the entire Middle East; but over its thousand year life span the empire was reduced to a single city-state straddling the Bosporus. Nonetheless, because of its strategic position, the impregnable city of Constantinople was able to maintain itself until the Turks captured the city in 1453.

From the time of the Seljuk invasions, the Turks had come to dominate the Middle East, largely at the expense of the Byzantines. By the last half of the 12th century, the Sultanate of Rum and the holdings of Salah-al-Din included the greater part of Islam. The Mongol invasions, however, destroyed both these states. Then, about 1300, Osman, a Turkish chieftain, began to consolidate by conquest and alliance a number of small towns in Asia Minor. Although Osman died in 1326, the Ottoman Turks continued to expand their sphere of influence in the Middle East. In 1354 an earthquake destroyed the walls and fortifications of Gallipoli and thus enabled the Ottomans to cross the Dardanelles and gain a foothold in Europe. From there, aided by the chaos created by the Black Death, they were able to extend their dominion into the Balkans. At the same time, they pressed south and east, establishing their control over the greater part of Asia Minor. Ottoman expansion in the east, however, was met by Tamerlane. Tamerlane defeated Bayezid I in 1402 at the Battle of Ankara and then conquered to the west as far as the Mediterranean. Rather than holding Ottoman territory directly, in exchange for an oath of allegiance, Tamerlane divided the Ottoman conquests of Europe and the early holdings of Osman and Orhan I (Osman's son) in Asia among Bayezid's sons. Upon Tamerlane's death in 1405 the Ottoman amirs asserted their independence of the Timurids, but the Ottoman state remained fragmented among Bayezid's four sons.

It was one of the sons of Bayezid, Mehmed I, who reunited the Ottoman state and set it again on the path of conquest. His grandson Mehmed II pushed into Hungary and southern Russia, completed the conquest of Turkey, and in 1453 captured Constantinople (from then on known as Istanbul), thus laying the foundation of the Ottoman Empire. Salim I added Syria, Palestine, Egypt, and Algeria. Suleiman the Magnificent conquered all Hungary, Mesopotamia, and Tripoli. And finally, in the last part of the 17th century, Tunisia, the west coast of Arabia, and small holdings around the Black Sea and the Persian Gulf were brought into the empire, completing its period of expansion.

The Ottoman Empire was ruled from the sultan's court in Istanbul. The sultan was theoretically the absolute ruler of the state and head of the Muslim religion, but considerable power was exercised by the sultan's household. Also, the degree of local autonomy increased with the degree of remoteness from the administrative center at Istanbul. Because the Turks were a minority in their empire, administrators were drawn from any source, including nations outside the empire's borders. Officials, therefore, could be chosen on the basis of ability rather than on the basis of racial or religious prejudice. Indeed, the corps of Janissaries, the famed bodyguard of the sultans, was composed entirely of Islamized Christians. Bribery was common in the appointment of officals; but a palace school was maintained for the education of those who would occupy the higher positions of government, and thus it was ensured that the sultan and his immediate circle of deputies would be men capable of ruling.

The Ottoman Empire exercised considerable influence in European affairs, partly because of its encroachments on European territory and partly because of its control of the East-West trade routes. Particularly strong were the Ottoman ties with the Italian city-states, which represented at that time the western terminus of the trade routes. But these ties were eventually weakened when at the end of the 15th century the Portuguese discovered a new East-West passage around southern Africa.

The 16th century also saw the development of Istanbul as a cultural center. The city was largely rebuilt, and it is still famous for its Ottoman mosques. A

Turkish literature was developed during this period as both poets and historians were retained by the court. Also, Ottoman naval development in the Mediterranean led to advances in geography and map-making.

During the 17th century, however, the Ottoman decline was rapid. A combination of weak sultans, civil wars, and European expansion drove the Ottomans first from Europe and, in the following centuries, from North Africa. At the start of the First World War, the Ottoman Empire was reduced to Turkey, Mesopotamia, Palestine, and the fringes of Arabia.

EUROPEAN INVOLVEMENT

In 1498 Vasco da Gama, a Portuguese navigator, reached India by sailing around Africa. In the years immediately following, other Portuguese retraced da Gamma's route, establishing trading stations in the Persian Gulf and diverting much of the Eastern trade from the earlier routes through the Middle East. For a time the Portuguese enjoyed a monopoly over the Cape route. The transport costs were as much as one-third less than those of the overland route via the Middle East. And to further inhibit overland transport, the Portuguese attempted to blockade shipping on the Red Sea and Persian Gulf. Thus, Libson quickly replaced Venice as the European clearinghouse for Indian goods. When military efforts by the Middle Eastern and European powers failed to destroy the Portuguese trade, first Venice and then France and England signed trade agreements with the Turks to secure more favorable transport terms for their goods across Ottoman territory.

While France and England contended for the Middle East trade, England and Holland supplanted the Portuguese in the East Indies. But Holland, drained by her wars with the English and the French, was unable to compete with England; and the Dutch withdrawal from the East left the British East India Company with a monopoly on the southern trade route.

In the 18th century European expansion became more overt. As governmental authority broke down in the Far and Middle East, France and England sought to secure their trade through physical supervision of the sources and routes of that trade. England seized political power in large parts of the Far East and attempted to do the same in the Middle East. France countered in 1798 with Napoleon's expedition to Egypt. The defeat of the French fleet at Aboukir Bay, however, checked the French and three years later they withdrew their army.

Napoleon's fall left England the dominant power in the Middle East, but the Egyptians had been impressed by the display of efficiency of the French expeditionary force to their country, and Muhammad Ali and his son Ibrahim Pasha laid designs to build a modern, pan-Arab state. Under the leadership of these two men, the Egyptians rapidly expanded into Sudan, Ethiopia, Palestine, Syria, and Arabia. British ties with the Ottomans, however, checked further expansion.

Refused aid by Britain in modernizing their state, Muhammad Ali and

Ibrahim Pasha turned to France. The French responded with trained administrators, military missions, aid in opening schools, and the training of young Egyptians in French colleges. Half of Egypt's trade, however, remained with England, and France's setback in the Franco-Prussian War left the English dominant once more throughout the Middle East.

Besides the modernization of Egypt, the French made yet another great contribution to Middle Eastern affairs. Using a brief period of influence in the Ottoman Empire during the Crimean War, the French pressed for permission to build the Suez Canal. Granted permission by the Ottomans and supported by Russia and Austria, France was able to open the canal in 1869, thus linking the Middle East to the modern West.

The incompetence and extravagance of Muhammad Ali's successors in Egypt resulted in the building up of an enormous national debt to the European powers. In 1879, therefore, France and England established dual political control of Egypt in an effort to secure their investments. When the Egyptians grew restive under this control, Britain in 1882 occupied the country and held all political power there until World War I.

Although British rule was helpful in reducing the Egyptian debt, the country itself was not improved much materially. Further, the use of English officials at all levels of control kept the Egyptians from developing the ability of self-rule.

In the 19th century the Ottoman Empire was the major area of European conflict. The Roman Catholics of France engaged with the Orthodox Christians of Russia in controversies over who should control the Christian holy places in the Middle East; and Russian expansionists desired to secure their entrance to the Mediterranean through the Bosporus and to restore a Christian empire at Istanbul. Austria, fearing that Russia would outflank her from the south, desired to check Russian expansion into Ottoman territory. England, too, was apprehensive about Russian expansion into the Mediterranean. In addition, both England and France were interested in Ottoman territory that lay astride the trade routes to their extensive commercial interests in the Orient. A series of small wars waged between these nations concerned with Turkish territory kept any one of them from dominating the area.

In 1872 a serious threat to Anglo-French interests in Turkey appeared when the Ottomans brought in a German to supervise the building of the Balkan railway system. During the next 30 years, the Germans increased their influence in Turkey through extension of the railroad and through trade agreements with the Ottomans.

20TH CENTURY MIDDLE EAST TO WORLD WAR I

European intervention in the Middle East during the 19th century fostered Arab nationalism. European armies, technicians, and administrators clearly demonstrated the abilities of, and the benefits accruing to, a modernized nation. Christian missionaries aided in establishing Arab schools, thus laying an educational foundation for modernization, and potential Muslim leaders were given the opportunity to observe and learn European methods in the academies of France and Germany. Finally, Muhammad Ali's and Ibrahim Pasha's efforts toward Arab unification encouraged Muslims to consider the possibilities of establishing, and the advantages of operating, a modern Arab state.

The English occupation of Egypt spurred nationalism in that state. The occupation denied educated Egyptians the opportunity for advancement through the use of their abilities. British personnel were brought in to fill administrative positions, thus denying these posts to educated Egyptians. Inspired by the gains of the Young Turks, Egyptian nationalists engaged in violent agitation for self-government.

Concerned for the security of the Suez Canal and their Egyptian investments, the British could not at that time accede to Egyptian demands for immediate self-government. In 1911, therefore, they reasserted their control of Egyptian affairs with the appointment of Lord Kitchener as administrator of Egypt. Kitchener initiated programs of legislative reforms designed to break down the power of Egyptian agriculturists. Although nationalist resistance was strong, an open break was averted by the start of World War I.

The oppression and absolutism of the Ottoman Sultan and the winds of change from Europe led to the growth of Turkish nationalism. In 1889 students at the Istanbul Military Medical College, led by the Albanian student Ibrahim Temo, organized the Committee of Progress and Union, a secret society modeled after the Italian Carbonari societies. The movement quickly branched into the Military Academy, the Naval Academy, the Artillery and Engineering School, the Veterinary School, and the Civil College. With the blessing and support of the major ethnic and religious groups in the Ottoman Empire, the CPU led the revolution of 1908. The Young Turk Revolution, which brought in its wake a declaration of the equality of all races in the Ottoman Empire, had stirred Arab nationalism, especially in Syria and Iraq. By 1909, however, conflict within the CPU divided its members along national lines and resulted in the growth of extremism on both sides. Centralization of government and Turkification of all elements within the empire became the covert objectives of the Young Turks. In the Arab world rapidly growing secret socieites, which at first hoped to gain autonomy within the Ottoman Empire, now advocated complete independence.

German influence had grown with Turkish nationalism. Germany's *Drang nach Osten* (drive to the East) led to German aid in Turkish modernization, development of the Berlin to Baghdad railway, and the eventual emergence of Turkey as Germany's partner.

The first months of World War I saw an uneasy truce in the Middle East, but in October 1914, the British began instigating Arab revolts in Arabia. In the celebrated correspondence between Sharif Husayn of Mecca and Sir Henry McMahon, British High Commissioner for Egypt and the Sudan, McMahon promised the creation of an independent Arab state at the conclusion of the war. This state was to encompass the area demarcated on the north by a line drawn eastward from Alexandretta to the Iranian frontier and thence southward to the

Persian Gulf and to include the entire Arabian peninsula with the exception of Aden. At the same time, however, the Allies were negotiating the division of both Turkish and Arab lands amongst themselves. The Constantinople Agreement of March 1915 gave Russia the right to annex certain areas in Asia Minor and Thrace while guaranteeing the French and British interests in Turkey and Iran. The Treaty of London, signed in April of 1915, gave Italy territorial claims in North Africa and Asia Minor. Finally the secret Sykes-Picot Agreement was concluded in May 1916 defining the exact territories to be taken over by Russia, France and Britain and recognizing the spheres of influence of France and Britain in the Arab territories. In conflict with both the McMahon promises and the Sykes-Picot Agreement, the famous Balfour Declaration was issued on November 2, 1917, promising Palestine to the Zionists as a homeland for the Jews.

Precipitated by the Young Turks' declaration of martial law in Syria and by the execution and deportation of Arab nationalists, the Arab revolt began on June 5, 1916. This revolt, while hardly successful in mobilizing mass Arab support, was immensely helpful to the British in that it diverted Turkish reinforcements from facing the British advance through Palestine, ended German propaganda in Arabia, and forestalled the possibility of a German submarine base on the Red Sea.

BETWEEN TWO WORLD WARS

The Arab revolt of World War I had been purchased at the price of Allied promises of an independent Arab state. At the end of the war, however, each of the victorious western European powers hoped to seize a chunk of Middle Eastern territory. After two years of nearly fruitless negotiations, the treaty of Sèvres with the Ottomans was signed on August 10, 1920. Under this treaty Turkey renounced all claim to Arabia, Egypt, Mesopotamia, and Syria. Britain was given a protectorate over Egypt, a mandate over Palestine, and tutelage over nominally independent Mesopotamia. Syria was placed under a French mandate; and the rulers of Arabia were granted independence.

The end of the war saw the Allies in possession of Turkey. The occupation of that state was left in the hands of the Greeks until such time as the Allies might decide her future. But the Turks, led by Mustafa Kemal, took matters into their own hands. In 1920 the Turks raised the banner of revolt; and at the end of two years of warfare, they had forced the withdrawal of the occupation forces. The Turks established a new government, deposed the Ottoman Sultan, and voided the legislation of his government. In 1922 they met the Allies at the Lausanne Conference to determine Turkey's future. The Lausanne Conference sheared the last remnants of the Ottoman Empire from Turkey, but it left the Turkish Republic an independent state.

In 1923 Mustafa Kemal was elected president of the Republic. Until his death in 1938, he directed the Turks in a six point plan of modernization: Turkey was officially declared a republic; the state was secularized, particularly through the closing of the religious courts and the abolishment of Islam as a state religion; the state was popularized through universal suffrage, equal taxation, universal education, and the establishment of a phonetic alphabet for the increase of literacy; nationalism was encouraged through the glorification of Turkish history and the adoption of family names; foreign trade and agriculture were encouraged, and industrial enterprises were undertaken by the state; and finally, reform was established not as a goal but rather as a continuing process in Turkish life.

The Turks also found it necessary to resolve two problems concerning foreign interests: demarcation of the Iraqi-Turkish frontier in Mosul province, and foreign use of the Dardanelles and the Bosporus. The first issue was resolved by awarding Mosul province to Iraq; in return, Turkey received £500,000 from Iraq and a guarantee of 10 percent of all oil royalties paid to Iraq by the concessionaire for the next 25 years. An international agreement allowing Turkey to fortify the Straits settled the second issue.

In the Fertile Crescent the French established a governorship in Lebanon. In 1936 they agreed to make Lebanon an independent state, but later refused to sign the treaties accomplishing this. In Syria, also under French mandate, independence again was first promised and later denied, and dissension arose between the French and the Syrians over Syria's loss of Lebanon, Latakia, and the Jebel Druze.

The British occupation of Iraq had met with fierce resistance that led to British attempts to form a stable government in that country. In 1921 a king was elected, and the country achieved a state of semi-independence from England. Full independence, however, was not achieved until Iraq was admitted as a member to the League of Nationas in 1932. Oil was the great issue in Iraqi politics, both international and domestic. The Iraqis turned this problem into a source of strength by basing their economy on oil concessions.

Palestine, occupied by the British, was torn by conflict between the Arabs and the Jews. Each group wanted an independent Palestine for itself. Arabs made up approximately 85 percent of the population; but heavy Jewish immigration and effective Zionist representation greatly built up Jewish strength. With the immigration of skilled Jews and with massive financial aid from the world's Jewry, Jewish settlements in Palestine flourished. British rule was a hopeless attempt to aid the Jews while protecting the rights of the Arabs.

Egypt continued after World War I as a British protectorate under martial law. Strong nationalist resistance, however, forced promises of eventual independence. The instability of Egyptian government, Britain's preoccupation with other matters, and British concern for the Suez made this a difficult step. But the Anglo-Egyptian Treaty of 1936 began the process of making Egypt an independent state.

Elsewhere, Great Britain maintained its influence on the southern coast of the Persian Gulf, and Ibn Saud consolidated the Arabian peninsula under his rule and in 1927 proclaimed himself King of Hijaz and Nejd.

Iran, an independent state at the start of World War I, successfully resisted British attempts to incorporate her into the British Empire and Russian attempts to secure Iranian territory after the war. Then, in 1920 Reza Khan overthrew the Iranian government and attempted to establish a republic modeled after Mustafa Kemal's Turkey. Religious opposition, however, prevented this transformation, and in 1925 Reza Khan became shah.

Reza Khan's strength was sufficient to accomplish several reforms: The power of religion and of religious institutions was reduced; 15,000 miles of roads and the Trans-Iranian railway were built; efforts were made toward the improvement of irrigation and other agricultural methods; and a number of industries were started by the state. Also, the oil concessions to Britain were modified to bring greater Iranian control to and more profit from this important commodity.

In international affairs Iran sought close ties with Germany to protect her from British and Russian encroachments. The advent of World War II, however, ended German influence and forced Iran to cooperate with Britain and Russia.

At its beginning, World War II was seen by most Middle Eastern peoples as a European affair which had little effect on them. Only Turkey saw herself in the path of aggression; but since German and Russian dominance were equally repugnant to her, she maintained a careful neutrality. Iran attempted to tie herself to Germany, but England and Russia occupied the country, deposed Reza Shah, and forced Iranian cooperation. The collapse of France weakened French control in Lebanon and Syria and attempts made after France's liberation to reassert that control were met by British intervention. Iraqi nationalists endeavored to capitalize on Britain's weakness in the early part of the war to stage a revolt, but they were unsuccessful. In Palestine, the Arabs were unconcerned with the war, but Nazi atrocities against the European Jews led to the creation of a Zionist Brigade and to frantic Jewish immigration. This massive and illegal immigration in turn led to increased hostilities between Arabs and Jews, and Palestine erupted with terrorism. Egypt was used as a staging area for the British army, and Egyptian troops fought in the desert and in defense of Eqypt.

At the end of World War II Britain remained the paramount power in the Middle East, maintaining effective control over Egypt, Palestine, Transjordan, Iraq, southern Arabia, and the Persian Gulf. But Britain emerged from the war a weakened state unable to withstand nationalist pressures fomenting in the states under her suzerainty. The story of Britain's withdrawal from the Middle East and the forces acting within and upon each country in the area are taken up in Part II.

SELECTED BIBLIOGRAPHY

Excellent histories on the Middle East abound, and those that are mentioned here are intended only to give the student a starting point. In a single excellent volume Sydney Nettleton Fisher, *The Middle East: A History*, 2nd ed. (New

York, 1968), has concisely, yet comprehensively, treated the entire span of Middle Eastern history. Philip K. Hitti's book, *History of the Arabs*, 8th ed. (London, 1963), is the classic study of the emergence and decline of the Arab empire. And Bernard Lewis' brief account, *The Arabs in History,* 3rd. ed. (London, 1956), places the Islamic empire in its proper historical perspective. William Yale, in *The Near East: A Modern History* (Ann Arbor, 1958), treats the area's history up to the Second World War and contains some stimulating analyses. Carl Brockelmann's study, *History of the Islamic Peoples* (New York, 1947), is a highly detailed historic survey and an indispensable reference work. The most recent book in the field is Yahya Armajani's well-written volume *The Middle East: Past and Present* (New York, 1969). Parts II and III of L. S. Stavriano's book, *The Balkans Since 1453* (New York, 1958), have an excellent account of the rise and fall of the Ottoman Empire. And Harry N. Howard's book, *The Partition of Turkey: A Diplomatic History, 1913-1923*, 2nd ed. (Norman, Oklahoma, 1963), is the best account of the fragmentation of the Ottoman Empire. For an account of Arab-Allied relations and the rise of King Faisal following World War I see Zeine N. Zeine, *The Struggle for Arab Independence* (Beirut, 1960). Finally, George Lenczowski, *The Middle East in World Affairs,* 3rd ed. (Ithaca, 1964) provides an expert account of the area since World War I.

part II

THE CONTEXT OF
MIDDLE EAST POLITICS

chapter 3

The Heritage of Islam

Islam is not itself a political system. Rather, it is a religion and a way of life that relates to both the individual and the community. All human action and interaction within the Muslim community is, theoretically, regulated by Islam. There is no distinction between the secular and the religious. And because some human activity is political in nature, politics in the Middle East is affected by Islam.

Attempts have been made to find within Islam a coherent political theory. The difficulty involved here, however, is that no such unified theory exists. Although Muslim politics is derived from the religious and social teachings of Islam and although Islamic concepts of God, Man, and the world have placed certain limitations upon, and have guided in certain directions, the development of Muslim politics, it is expediency, tempered by Islamic law, that has completed the process of political development.

The political unit in the Muslim world today is the nation-state; but the corresponding conceptual unit in Islamic law is the Islamic community. This community is the brotherhood of all Muslims and transcends national boundaries. In the past it has sometimes been a single political unit, though it is today primarily a religious and cultural unit. It is bound by a common belief in one God, the Prophet Muhammad's revelation, and a variety of other common cultural patterns. Its functions have been similar to that of Christianity in Europe: It has provided at times a binding force which has allowed the Middle East to present a unified front to outside interference. It has also been an underlying force in the Islamic empires and in the more recent attempts to form a pan-Arab state.

The community concept, however, is incompatible with the reality of the nation-state. The Middle East does not often act as a single political unit. Early Arab conquests led to the inclusion of diverse racial, linguistic, and cultural groups within the expanding territorial sphere of the Islamic brotherhood. The

41

building of the Arab and Turkish empires led to the assimilation of some of these non-Muslim elements. And finally, European expansion in the 19th century forced a potent injection of Western ideas and practices into the bloodstream of Islam. The results have been a diversification within the Islamic world, leading to the creation of several nation-states exhibiting certain marked differences.

Another shaping element in Islamic politics is the Muslim concept of equality. There is no priesthood in Islam serving as an intermediary between man and God. And because Islam covers all aspects of Muslim life, equality before God becomes, theoretically, equality in all situations. Of course, racial and class distinctions have been made in Middle Eastern states. Observable individual differences are a part of human life. Nonetheless, the theoretical equality of all Muslims is maintained, leading to an awareness that all have some sort of political rights. Non-Muslims, however, have traditionally been considered inferior to Muslims. The relative decline of the communal system and its replacement in recent times by the nation-state have resulted in making differences in religious belief no longer as crucial in defining the rights and duties of the citizen in the nation-state.

Muhammad and the Middle East

In the seventh century the Middle East was an area ravaged by the constant warfare between the decaying Byzantine and Persian empires. The Arabian peninsula was a disunited area where individual cities flourished on the East-West trade routes. But in the vast areas between these cities there were only bands of desert nomads who survived by trading meat, milk, and livestock for the manufactured products of the cities. Then, in 622 in the city of Medina the Prophet Muhammad began to concentrate around his person the ideology to spark a major religion and the power to build a leading empire.

Muhammad, a Meccan aristocrat and trader, first began to teach a doctrine of monotheism when he was about 40 years of age. In the beginning he was quite unsuccessful in his native Mecca. Although a few persons embraced his doctrine, the majority of the wealthy abjured it for fear that it would end the lucrative pilgrimages to Mecca's many shrines. Persecuted in Mecca, Muhammad and his few adherents fled to Medina where they were made more welcome. Muhammad soon became the leader in that city, and Islam began to grow as alliances were made with the surrounding communities and tribes.

At that point, Muhammad felt secure enough to look once more toward Mecca. He initiated raids on the Meccan caravans and, as a result, provoked a punitive expedition against him and his followers. That expedition was defeated; and that defeat and the two battles which followed it brought Mecca under Muhammad's power. The city was treated mercifully and was made the center of the new religion. Shortly after his victorious return to Mecca, Muhammad died.

Muhammad's contribution to the Middle East cannot be overemphasized. Islam has undoubtedly been the greatest single factor in the development of that area. And because of Muhammad's unique position as the Seal of the Prophets, almost all that is Islam can be ultimately traced back to him. The analogies, the traditions, and the Koran all derive from the words and actions of Muhammad. The concepts of centralized authority and of rule by God are both drawn from his own practices in ruling Medina. The first *jihad*, or holy war, was Muhammad's first attack on a Meccan caravan. The religious tolerance and the use of existing administrators in conquered territories, both of which were standard practices in the later empires, were techniques which Muhammad himself used to gain power. So it can be seen that the methods used by Muhammad and the rules laid down by him have served as guidelines throughout the development of the Middle East.

Ironically, Muhammad was not only the originator of the techniques which unified much of the Middle East, but he was also, in a sense, the cause of the great political and religious dispute that disrupted the unity of the Muslim world. Muhammad neglected to deal with the problem of succession, and it was controversy over this problem that caused the Muslim brotherhood to splinter into the various sects that still exist today.

The Islamic State

The Islamic state is a political institution initiated by Muhammad for the purpose of organizing the *umma* (community of believers), preserving the faith, and maintaining and enforcing the word of God. Like any other insititution it consists of a series of interlocking systems. These systems might be reduced to ten: the value system, the normative system, the ideological system, the division of labor and specialization, the status-role system, the regulative system, the socialization system, the power-authority system, the enforcing system, and the maintenance system. The Islamic state, then, may be examined within the context of these systems.

Value System. The Islamic value system is based largely on the heritage of the Arab bedouin. The rigorous environment of the desert Arab bred in him a love of freedom, a sense of equality, and a resolute self-reliance. Among the qualities enshrined in his code of honor, the basis of tribal law, are tenacity, patience, courage, loyalty, hospitality, and protection of the weak. These virtues became the prototype of the Islamic value system not only because the Islamic state was built upon a foundation of pre-Islamic Arabic society, but also because of the predominant position given to the Arabic language by the Koran. Arabic philology became the basis of the religious sciences. In the first four centuries of Islam, Muslim literature was almost entirely written in Arabic. Hence, the literary and social heritage of the ancient Arabs permeated Muslim literature. Their virtues were idealized and their proverbs popularized.

The principal political institution of the bedouin, the tribe, did not become a permanent part of the Islamic system. The ethnocentricity of the tribal structure is inconsistent with the Muslim concept of the state as the community of all believers wherein all loyalties, tribal or otherwise, are superseded by the Muslim brotherhood. It was the absorption of large numbers of non-Arab, multiracial elements without the tribal allegiances of the Arabs which helped the state develop politically beyond its tribal structure.

Normative System. Ideally all Muslims are equal; all their interpersonal relations are ordered by the Koran and formulated in the Islamic law. But the rapid spread of Islam in its first centuries of life precluded putting these ideals into practice. The attempt to organize the expanding empire and to assimilate the new elements within it led to compromises. New normative systems had to be incorporated into the state in order for the Muslims to deal not only with non-Islamic peoples but also with the non-Arab Muslims within the state. In many cases this was accomplished through the nearly total retention of the preexisting norms in a conquered area. The conquered peoples practiced most of their own behavior patterns and conformed to Islam only in its most obvious aspects.

Even in the political and social centers of the state, the Arabic tribal norms were insufficient to meet the expanding needs of empire. The gross inadequacy of tribal norms of conduct for the ordering of a large and heterogeneous state necessitated the creation of new norms of behavior.

Ideological System. Although the Koran contains no systematic presentation of doctrine, there does emerge from the book a consistent ideology. Muslim theologians generally make a distinction between three basic components of this body of belief: religious belief, religious duty, and right conduct.

The essential religious beliefs of Islam are: (1) Belief in the Unity of Allah. "There is no God but Allah, and Muhammad is His Messenger." This creedal formula of Islam is the central doctrine of the Koran. There is one God before Whose judgment all men are equal; and Muhammad was the Seal of the Prophets through whom God revealed His design for society. (2) Belief in the Angels of Allah. The angels are the messengers of Allah and, like men, they are his creatures and servants. Correspondingly, there are devils, or *jinn*, who contrive to lead men astray. (3) Belief in the Prophets of Allah. The Koran teaches that God sent messengers to all peoples throughout history to preach the unity of God and to warn men of the Last Judgment. Muslims are enjoined to believe in all of them although only 28 are mentioned in the Koran, including 18 from the Old Testament and 3 from the New Testament. (4) Belief in the Koran. The Koran, the "Very Word of God," is the last of a series of revelations given to various prophets. It is the Eternal Truth in its final perfect form. (5) Belief in the Last Judgment. There will be a last judgment when each man's deeds will be weighed in the balance. Evildoers and nonbelievers will be assigned to Hell, and righteous believers are assured eternal bliss in Paradise. (6) Belief in the Divine Decrees of Allah. Everything that occurs is predestined by Allah, even man's salvation, damnation, belief, and unbelief. Allah's will is everything, and man's only course is to throw himself upon Allah's divine mercy.

The "Five Pillars" of Islam comprise the religious duties of the faithful Muslim. They include: (1) profession of the creed, "There is no God but Allah, and Muhammad is His Messenger;" (2) prayer five times daily; (3) fasting during the month of *Ramadan*, the ninth month of the Islamic calendar; (4) almsgiving, explicitly enjoined by the Koran as the outward sign of piety and means of salvation; and (5) pilgrimage to Mecca, required of every Muslim who has the economic means to afford it.

The "code of right conduct," as it is embodied in the Koran, directs every aspect of human life whether social, political, economic, or religious from birth until death. It distinguishes what is right from what is wrong by specifically delineating conduct that is required, conduct that is permitted, and conduct that is forbidden. This advanced moral code has succeeded in bringing unity and a sense of brotherhood to what are otherwise heterogeneous peoples.

Division of Labor and Specialization. In the bedouin tribes administrative specialization was at a minimum. Tribal councils handled the few occurring problems. But the spread of Islam brought with it a host of new and complex problems. Should a trade agreement be signed with a state; and, if so, what should be its terms? How was a city to be taken or an army destroyed? How were revenues to be assessed, collected, and apportioned? To handle these and similar problems of administration, specialists were needed. While the empire was expanding, it was customary to retain the preexisting administrations in conquered territories. This practice, however, did not meet the demand for a central administration for the empire. For this purpose the Ottoman Turks created a bureaucracy and trained specialists to staff it. The Ottomans also maintained a palace school in order to ensure that sultans and their advisors would be adequately trained for directing the administration of the empire.

Because Islam conceived of no intermediaries between man and God, the only religious specialization was in the field of legal interpretation and in the office of the caliph, the "successor of the Prophet."

Status-Role System. In Islam it is held that all men are equal before God. Ideally, then, men do not rank each other; but in fact they must. The growth of the Islamic state was so rapid that there was little opportunity to assimilate the conquered peoples into the Islamic culture. Consequently, the state contained a sizeable proportion of free non-Muslims. These people were not a part of the Muslim brotherhood, but they were a part of the Islamic state. As a result their status was low in a society which existed for the benefit of Muslims, and their primary political role was to pay taxes for the support of the state.

Slaves were another distinct group. Because the role of a slave was that of a permanent employee, the slave's status (and the material marks of that status) was relative to the status of his master.

Expertise provided yet another means for distinguishing between men. Men of many skills were needed for the maintenance of the empire, and such men were rewarded with honors and wealth. But the most distinct status-role differentiation occured when the Seljuk Turks invaded the Middle East and established a feudal aristocracy under the Ottoman dynasty. Race then became a determinant of status and role, and as might be expected the Turks, whose role was governing, occupied the top level of society.

Regulative System. Islamic law *(sharia)* derives solely from the word of God as revealed to Muhammad. God is the sole legislator and, therefore, the umma cannot legislate its own law. But rather than constituting a code of law in the modern sense, the sharia is actually an all-encompassing code of ethics that regulates the Muslim's religious, political, social, domestic, and private life. It deals with such problems as criminal law, marriage, inheritance, property, and most other questions of jurisprudence.

The Koran, the embodiment of Muhammad's revelation, is the basic law of the state and its constitution. But since the death of Muhammad, Islam has expanded, moving geographically into wider territories and temporally into newer times, constantly meeting new political realities. The Koran alone could not deal with all situations arising out of the new demands. Consequently, new sources of revelation-derived law were necessary even though new revelations after the death of the Prophet were impossible.

The first answer to the problem was an attempt to increase the original amount of revelation. "Traditions of the Prophet," *(sunna)* consisting of non-Koranic statements traceable back to Muhammad, were compiled by Muslim jurists and theologians in the first centuries after Muhammad's death. The traditions were verified by examining their word-of-mouth line of passage. But the difficulties in checking all the links of an oral transmission over many generations exhausted this source after several centuries.

Two other methods of determining the law were found, however, and their discovery helped to resolve the dilemma. Analogies *(qiyas)* were drawn from the Koran and from the traditions to meet the new situations, and legal decisions based on the principles of the Koran and the Sunna could be made if there was a consensus of the community *(ijma)*. These two principles brought an element of interpretation into Islam and gave it sufficient flexibility to meet a variety of political problems.

Socialization System. The process of cultural transmission in Islam has generally proceeded on two levels. On one level Muslim thought has been recorded in law, literature, and scientific writings. These writings have been preserved, studied, and expanded by a literate minority clustered mainly around a few centers of learning. On the other level, oral transmission has been the major means of socialization. Most Muslims, whether they are born into Islam or are converts to it, learn their culture not only by the usual method of observing the practices of those around them, but also by listening to scholars who devote their lives to researching, studying and memorizing their law and their history.

Power-Authority System. Muhammad, the Prophet of Islam, was also the head of the state. After his death a series of "successors of the Prophet" were elected by leading Muslims to serve as head of both the religion and the state. Thus was initiated the central Islamic institution of the caliphate which endured until 1924. The last of the elected caliphs was supplanted by the Umayyad family who established a dynastic caliphate, only to lose it to the Abbasid family. The Abbasids ruled Islam until the establishment of the Ottoman Empire. Under these dynasties the caliph was the religious and political head of

Islam, employing viceroys to administer the territorial subdivisions of the state. But it was also during this period that imperial subdivisions broke away from the empire.

The Seljuk Turks reunited the empire under a new absolutist institution, the sultanate. The caliphate was retained, although it was shorn of its power, as a means of legitimizing the new institution. By the beginning of the 15th century, however, the two had become one. The sultanate, with its bureaucratic central administration, remained an absolutist government at the head of a feudal aristocracy until the beginning of the 20th century.

Enforcing System. The enforcing system in Islam depends on obedience to the ruler. It is assumed that disobedience to the ruler results in anarchy; and it is further assumed that anarchy is always the poorest choice. But the ruler is also expected to abide by the law. For this reason the Islamic state has had religious courts to interpret the law during most of its history. However, the power of the courts has always been limited, and the enforcing power has generally been in the hands of the ruler and his subordinates.

A central concept to both the enforcing system and the power-authority system is the Islamic view of man as a naturally unruly creature. He is incapable, unless directed, of leading an orderly social life. It is a practical necessity, then, that there be within the state some force capable of restraining men from following their impulses. And because this force is a necessity, it is generally assumed that the order imposed by a bad leader is preferable to the anarchy that would accompany his disposition. Some Islamic scholars disagree with the last point, but, in the main, Muslims have been oriented toward the acceptance of authority. However, there is a basis for resistance to the ruler in Islam. He should conform to the code of ethics laid down in the Koran; if he does not, the umma has the right to overthrow him. For the purpose of government is to ensure man's eternal destiny and his temporal well-being.

Maintenance System. An institutional maintenance system, which is made up largely from the other nine systems, can be divided into two categories: physical-economic maintenance and cultural maintenance.

The Islamic state was born amid battles for a portion of the East-West trade routes; and battles and trade routes provided its physical and economic maintenance. In its first centuries the state expanded rapidly by conquest until, under the Ottomans, it controlled almost all of the East-West trade. Since then the Middle East has attempted, with an increasing lack of success, to provide for its security through trade concessions. In recent years, however, the Middle Eastern states have been more successful in maintaining their political and economic security through oil concessions.

Cultural maintenance in Islam is provided by the belief that Islam is the community of all Muslims, by the belief in one revelation of all law, and by the belief in the legitimacy of all central authority. These beliefs limit the possibilities for the development of heretical sects and limit the political power of those sects that do develop.

Islam Today

The extreme bureaucratization of the Ottoman Empire sapped the strength of medieval Islam, ended all Islamic political expansion, and initiated a period of economic, political, and cultural stagnation. At the same time, Western Europe was experiencing technological growth, political expansion, and the advent of liberalism, and when Ottoman power was withdrawn from vast areas of the Middle East the European powers flowed into those areas. These European penetrations not only resulted in an influx of Western ideas and attitudes, but also provided a measure of the decline in the vitality of Middle Eastern culture.

The political decline of the Muslim world gave birth to a strong reaction throughout the Middle East. Reform movements of many kinds were started, ranging from attempts to impose a strict adherence to the letter of Koranic law to attempts to change the basic doctrines of Islam itself. A particularly powerful reform movement occurred in Turkey during the 19th century. It did not, however, have the necessary force to overthrow the Ottoman inertia. It was the Turkish nationalist movement at the beginning of the present century which overthrew the Ottomans and made possible the process of modernization in Turkey. Since that time the forces of nationalism and modernization have swept through the rest of the Middle East, bringing the same benefits and problems they brought to Turkey.

The major problem of modernization in the Middle East was that of reconciling modernization processes with the social values of Islam. The greatest conflict occurred with the adoption of Western penal codes and family law. This conflict was resolved in Turkey by divesting the sharia, the religious courts, of their secular authority. The result of this move was the first real separation of church and state in Islam. It opened the door to government control and led the government to assume the prerogative of changing the social structure whenever its needs and desires should run counter to the tenets of Islam.

Other attempts to reconcile Islamic law with Western codes have focused on removing certain matters from the jurisdiction of the religious courts and on the reinterpretation of Islamic law. The first method, without the separation of church and state, is merely a stopgap measure; the second method may lead to permanent legal changes within the Islamic world.

The advance of knowledge, occasioned by the growth of science, is also having an impact on Islam. The investigations of science are supported by the Koranic value of the pursuit of knowledge, but the task of reconciling Islamic doctrine to the often conflicting findings of science presents a dilemma for which no adequate solution has as yet been found.

Finally, there are those Muslims who are still trying to reject all Western influences. These puritan elements are seeking to return to the beliefs and way of life of the original Islamic community and thus recapture Islam's former greatness.

Thus, Islam continues to be a major factor in the development of the Middle East, shaping new trends even as it changes with them.

SELECTED BIBLIOGRAPHY

H. A. R. Gibb's concise book, *Mohammedanism: An Historical Survey,* 2nd ed. (New York, 1962), is an excellent introduction to the study of Islam. For a more comprehensive survey, the *Encyclopaedia of Islam*, four volumes, 2nd ed. (Leiden, 1954), provides scholarly articles on all aspects of Islam. G. E. Von Grunebaum's collection of essays, *Islam: Essays in the Nature and Growth of a Cultural Tradition* (London, 1955), considers Islamic culture, its unity, and its interaction with other cultures. Majid Khadduri's unexcelled study, *War and Peace in the Law of Islam* (Baltimore, 1953), examines the nature of the Islamic state and law and explores classical Muslim attitudes toward international relations. For a history of the Islamic empire see John Bagot Glubb, *The Empire of the Arabs* (New Jersey, 1965). Wilfred Cantwell Smith's book, *Islam in Modern History* (Princeton, 1957), is an excellent account of Islam's influence on the contemporary Middle East. Of course, any study of Islam is incomplete without the *Koran*, and A. Yusuf Ali's annotated translation, *The Holy Qur'an: Text, Translation and Commentary* (Washington, D.C., 1946), is highly recommended. For a study of the Prophet Muhammad see Tor Andrae, *Mohammed, The Man and His Faith,* paperback ed. (New York, 1960). Reuben Levy, *The Social Structure of Islam* (Cambridge, 1957), examines social institutions and structures within Islam. The March 1969 issue of *Current History*, Vol. 56, No. 331, provides an excellent collection of articles on the contemporary Islamic world.

chapter 4

The Legacy of Nationalism

Nationalism as a political ideology is a fairly recent phenomenon in the Middle East and at the turn of this century was still only nascent. Since that time, however, the development of the concept of nationalism has been rapid and has proven to be both a constructive and a destructive force in the Middle East. For example, reform and modernization have often been the first goals of the several Middle Eastern nationalisms, and these efforts to reform and to modernize have contributed to the civil and social advancement of the peoples of the area. However, ethnocentrism, irredentism, and national sovereignty have also been integral parts of the nationalist programs; and these aspects of nationalism have resulted in conflict and upheaval, as, for example, in the cases of Turkish versus Arab nationalism within the Ottoman Empire; Zionism versus Arab nationalism; and Turkish, Arab, and Iranian nationalism versus European imperialism.

In this chapter, the genesis of the four major Middle Eastern nationalisms—Arab, Turkish, Iranian, and Zionist—will be traced, and the regional and international implications that the growth of those nationalisms has had will be reviewed.

ARAB NATIONALISM

Arab nationalism has been described as the "principal movement through which the Arab peoples are seeking to reconstruct the foundations of their life, after centuries of suspended animation."[1] It has spread throughout the Arab world with the same rapidity and has generated the same invigorating force as

---

[1] Hazem Zaki Nuseibeh, *The Ideas of Arab Nationalism* (Ithaca, N.Y., c. 1956), p. 207.

did Islam centuries before it. And its significance, not only to the Middle East but to the world as well, is no less than that of Islam at its apogee. The response of nationalism to the challenge of modernization is a decisive factor in determining the future of the Arab people. The direction and orientation of the development of those peoples—indeed, their very fate—will to a large extent be determined by the course of this volatile force. And because the Arabs are the most pervasive and numerous of the Middle Eastern peoples, their destiny cannot but profoundly affect one of the most strategic areas on earth, the Middle East.

Modern Arab nationalism has roots deep in the past. Its inspirations are the achievements and culture of early Islam. Before the advent of Islam the focus of Arab patriotism and loyalty had been either the family or the tribe. Arabs did not feel themselves to be, either socially or politically, part of any other larger unit. Islam, however, drastically changed the political and social focus of the Arab. For as the armies of Islam began those seemingly inexorable marches that were to create the great Islamic empire, an empire that was eventually to stretch from India to Spain, Arabs began to consider themselves more and more as part of the larger Islamic community.

Of course, the Islamic community had an essentially supranational orientation, and the rich Islamic culture that developed during the Middle Ages was a synthesis of many cultures. But because Islam requires that the Muslim read the Koran and pray in the language of the Prophet Muhammad, Arabic became the common language of the Muslim civilization. As a result, the culture of that civilization came to be regarded as Arabic. Thus, all of those who shared in common the Arabic language and the culture of the Muslim civilization came to regard themselves with pride as Arabs, a feeling not too remote from the modern sense of national consciousness.

However, by the 13th century the Islamic empire lay in ruins, and its 14th century successor to power, the Ottoman Turks, devised an administrative technique that tended to nullify nationalist sentiment and to emphasize sectarian differences. The Ottoman millet system organized the subjects of the Ottoman Empire on the basis of religious affiliation rather than on a cultural or linguistic basis. Thus, people who under the Islamic empire would have proudly considered themselves Arabs identified themselves instead, under the Ottomans, as Christians, Jews, or Muslims.

It must not be assumed, however, that all traces of Arab civilization disappeared during the four centuries of Ottoman rule. Indeed, since the Ottoman Turks had adopted Islam and had made sharia law an important part of their government, Arab culture and language not only continued to exist but also played an important role in the Turkish civilization. Thus, when Napoleon invaded Egypt in 1798, elements of the earlier Arab culture were still very much present in the Middle East.

Even though the inspiration of modern Arab nationalism was the culture of early Islam, the actual birth of that nationalism is usually traced to Napoleon's invasion of Egypt. That event in itself did not result in a general Arab awakening, but it marked the beginning of a steady influx of the Western concepts, processes, and techniques that did finally spark the Arab renaissance and awakened many Arabs to the manifold disadvantages of Turkish rule. For an increasing amount of Western intervention and imperialism accompanied the influx of Western modes; and these European encroachments on what was essentially Arab territory, and the resulting exploitation of Arab resources, raised Arab ire against the Turks who seemed unable to protect them from European depredations.

The activities of two Albanians, Muhammad Ali and his son Ibrahim, helped to kindle the fires of a yet nascent Arab renaissance. Muhammad Ali ascended to power in Egypt shortly after French withdrawal early in the 19th century and made Egypt virtually independent of Istanbul. Unquestionably one of the greatest rulers of his time, Ali introduced important reforms in education, agriculture, industry, commerce, sanitation, and social custom. It was, however, the reforms he made in education that were of particular significance to the revitalization of the Arabs. Primary and secondary schools, preparatory schools, a medical college, and a polytechnic school staffed predominantly by Egyptians were established. Also, Egyptian youth were sent to Europe for a Western education, and many schools were opened in Egypt for the training of civil servants.

Complementing his reforms in education, Muhammad Ali established a government printing press at Cairo in 1822 and thus made Cairo the intellectual center of the Arab world. By 1850 the government press had printed over 300 books in Arabic, Turkish, and Persian. It also printed, in both Arabic and French, newspapers that not only disseminated Western ideas but also gave the Arabs a vehicle through which they could regenerate their own literature.

At the same time that Muhammad Ali was introducing his reforms in Egypt, his son Ibrahim was encouraging modernization in Syria. Having succeeded to the governorship of Syria in 1833 as a result of his successful military campaign there against Turkish forces, Ibrahim embarked upon a program of reform similar to that of his father's in Egypt. Sydney Nettleton Fisher writes of Ibrahim's eight-year rule in Syria that "taxes were regularized, justice was more sure for people of all religions, commerce was encouraged, privileges for foreigners were less abused, education was stimulated, law and order were prevalent."[2]

Ibrahim's administration of Syria came to an end in 1840, however, when the British forced Muhammad Ali to withdraw his son from Syria. Nevertheless, Syria remained the cradle of nascent Arab nationalism. For as a result of Ibrahim's edicts, Syria had been opened to American Protestants and French Catholics who were allowed to establish missionary schools. By 1860 the American missionaries had established 33 schools in Lebanon, Syria, and

---

[2] Sydney Nettleton Fisher, *The Middle East: A History* (New York, 1966), p. 282.

Palestine; and in 1866 the influential Syrian Protestant College in Beirut (now the American University) opened its doors. The French missionaries also founded many schools in the area, including the University of St. Joseph at Beirut in 1875. Because these schools taught in Arabic, they helped to revive the Arabic language as a medium of expression and communication for Arab writers and intellectuals and thus fostered the intellectual awakening that was to culminate in the Arab nationalist movement.

The tremendous demand for education that resulted from the establishment of schools in Egypt and Syria was not confined to those two countries alone, however, but spread in unprecedented proportions throughout the Arab world. This demand was partially met by a great increase in the volume of printed material. Publishing houses and newspapers were established in many of the major cities, and the great volume of material printed became both a means for and a measure of the spread of nationalism throughout the Arab provinces of the Turkish empire.

Educational societies to facilitate inquiry into Arab history, art, and literature were also organized during this period. The Society of Arts and Sciences was created in 1847 with the help of American missionaries, and the Jesuits organized the Oriental Society in 1850. Generally, however, Muslim Arabs refused to join these two groups because of their foreign Christian missionary affiliations. But in 1857 the Syrian Scientific Society was established on a nonsectarian basis, and under its auspices Christians and Muslims joined together to foster and develop their common Arabic heritage. From this society came Arab nationalism's first rallying cry: Ibrahim Yaziji's "Ode to Patriotism," a poem appealing to the Arabs to unite and to revolt against Turkish oppression.

The first organized response to Ibrahim Yaziji's appeal for Arab unity and for revolt against the Ottoman Turks came in the form of secret societies which sprang up in Beirut (the center of the movement), Damascus, Tripoli, and other cities. The primary activity engaged in by these societies was the posting of placards which urged the Arabs to insurgence. Such urging proved to be premature, however, since there was not yet a sufficiently widespread sense of Arab national consciousness among the people to rally them to armed revolt; and, as a result, the secret societies proved short-lived. Nevertheless, these secret societies did serve an important purpose, for the placards they posted not only contained statements urging the Arabs to rebellion but also contained specific demands that served as a model for the Arab political programs that were to be later formulated. Included in these demands were: the independence of Syria in union with Lebanon, the recognition of Arabic as a national language, an end to censorship and the removal of other restrictions on the freedom of expression, and the use of locally recruited units on local military service only.[3]

Although the growing sense of Arab national consciousness received its chief impetus from the Arab resurgence in Syria, it was also stimulated by the

---

[3]George Antonius, *The Arab Awakening: The Story of the Arab National Movement* (New York, c. 1939), p.84.

pan-Islamic revival which was occurring in Egypt during this same period. Jemal al Din al-Afgani, the founder of the pan-Islamic movement, had advocated that one of the Islamic states be strengthened to the point that it could unify the Muslim world and thus free it from foreign domination. Al-Afgani, however, did not care which Islamic state united the world of Islam, and it remained for Abdul Rahman al-Kawakebi to draw the distinction between Arab and non-Arab Muslims and to advocate that the Muslim would be united under a Quaraish-born Arab caliph established in Mecca. Kawakebi's proposals captured the imagination of the Arab world and contributed in no small way to the gradual change from Christian to Muslim leadership in the Arab national movement.

After the British occupation of Egypt in 1882, however, Egyptian leaders became preoccupied with the removal of the British; and, thus, it was in Beirut and Damascus that the search for Arab emancipation continued. At the time of the Young Turk revolt in 1908 Arab leaders hoped that the Ottoman program of the Society of Union and Progress would bring about decentralization of the empire and give the Arabs an equal voice in the conduct of the empire. Thus, for a time, the Arabs sought emancipation through cooperation with the Young Turks. As a measure of their sincerity the Young Turks pressured Sultan Hamid into appointing Sharif Husayn as Governor of the Hijaz, Keeper of the Holy Places and Prince of Mecca. When this appointment was made in 1908 the Ottoman Arab Fraternity was created as an Arab society for the defense of the Ottoman Constitution and the promotion of Arab welfare. The society was barely created when in 1909 it and other non-Turkish political groups were forced to go underground by the Young Turks' program of centralization and Turkification.

Numerous Arab societies, some clandestine and some public, developed for the dissemination of Arab national ideas. Notable among them were the Literary Club of Istanbul, the Ottoman Decentralization party in Cairo, al-Kahtaniya, and al-Fatat, of which the two former were public, and the latter two subterranean. The Literary Club, founded in 1909 and recognized by the CUP because of its ostensible cultural rather than political objectives, played a significant role in that it "provided centres in which Arabs from all parts of the empire felt at home and talked freely in an atmosphere in which minds relaxed and the traffic of ideas could move."[4] Its membership reached thousands and branches were established in Syria and Iraq.

The second public group, the Ottoman Decentralization party, was founded in Cairo in 1912 for the purpose of winning equality and autonomy for the Arab provinces within the framework of the Ottoman Empire. Branches were established throughout Syria and close contact was maintained with other Arab nationalist associations. This organization provided the Arabs with the first extensive political machinery that could coordinate their activities and maintain concerted and continuous pressure to achieve a specific political program.

---

[4]Ibid., p. 109.

Al-Kahtaniya, a secret society organized in 1909, also had a well-defined program. It advocated the creation of a Turko-Arab empire on the Austro-Hungarian model. But it was short-lived and its chief contribution to the Arab nationalist movement lay in its attempt to enlist Arab officers serving in the Turkish army into the nationalist movement.

Of these major organizations al-Fatat, a clandestine society organized by Muslim Arab students in Paris in 1911, was the only one to fully reject the idea of collaboration with the Turks and integration into a decentralized empire. It worked for creation of a sovereign Arab state and within a short time became the most effective and widespread force. When in 1913 an interfaith Committee of Reform won public acclaim and enthusiasm for its open circulation of a plan for Arab autonomy, with the consequence that it was disbanded and many of its members arrested, al-Fatat took the initiative to convene the first Congress of Arabs at Paris. Representatives from most of the Arab nationalist organizations participated. The Paris Platform which they promulgated was a moderate program calling for reform within the empire to bring the Arabs and other non-Turkish nationalities a greater amount of local autonomy. As a sop to the Arabs, the Turks ostensibly accepted this program, but it remained unenforced.

Partly out of this hoax was born another party, al-Ahd, organized by Aziz Ali al-Misri, an Egyptian major on the Ottoman general staff who had been a founder of al-Kahtaniya. Al-Ahd advocated essentially the same program as al-Kahtaniya, and in 1914 the Turks arrested al-Misri on a trumped-up charge of treason in the Italian campaigns in Libya and sentenced him to death. Although he was subsequently pardoned due to intervention by the British, al-Misri's arrest and trial not only outraged the Arab leaders but aroused the masses. With this act of tyranny the Turks destroyed any hope for Arab-Turkish cooperation. The Arab national movement now fully crystallized into a drive for an independent Arab state.

Although the various nationalist groups now had unanimity of purpose, the natural Arab proclivity for individualism made it difficult to achieve unanimity of action against the Ottoman government. However, the advent of World War I helped to coalesce the many factions into a united front behind the leadership of Sharif Husayn who favored cooperation with the British and the Allies in return for an independent Arab state. But even though the various factions were united under the leadership of Husayn, many of them still feared that cooperation with the Allies would result in European domination. It was believed that a Turkish defeat would assuredly result in the dismemberment of Arab lands by the French and the British unless some guarantee for the creation of an independent Arab state was agreed upon by one or more of the Allied powers. Therefore, in 1915 the Arab revolutionists drafted the Damascus Protocol embodying their demands for an independent Arab state that would encompass all of the lands of western Asia that were culturally and linguistically Arabic. In return, the Arabs would revolt against the Ottoman Empire. This Protocol was transmitted to Husayn and provided the basis for the ill-fated correspondence between Husayn and Sir Henry McMahon, the British High Commissioner of Egypt. McMahon accepted the conditions of the Damascus Protocol on behalf of the British government, and on June 5, 1916 the Arab revolt was launched.

Thus, when the Paris Peace Conference convened in 1919 Prince Faisal attended as the representative of a people who had made a significant contribution to the Allied war effort. Armed with Allied promises of Arab independence—the Husayn-McMahon correspondence, Britain's Declaration to the Seven (a reaffirmation of Britain's pledge made to seven Arab leaders in Cairo in June 1918), President Wilson's Fourteen Points, and the Anglo-French Declaration of November 1918 (again reaffirming Allied promises)—Faisal prepared to demand the fulfillment of those promises. But Britain had made other treaties and agreements conflicting with Arab aspirations, most notable of which were the Balfour Declaration and the Sykes-Picot Agreement, and did not intend to fulfill its pledge to the Arabs. In an attempt to forestall British and French designs to dismember the Middle East for their own advantages, President Wilson sent the King-Crane Commission to Syria and Iraq to determine the wishes of the people regarding their future rule. Two recommendations, both directly relevant to these agreements, were strongly urged in its report to the conference. One of them stressed that the unity of Syria (which up to that time included Palestine and Lebanon) be maintained, because "the territory concerned is too limited, the population too small, and the economic, geographical, racial, and language unity too manifest, to make the setting up of independent states within its boundaries desirable, if such division can possibly be avoided. The country is very largely Arab in language, culture, traditions, and customs."[5] The second recommendation concerned the establishment of a Jewish national home. The commission reported that the "anti-Zionist feeling in Palestine and Syria is intense and *not lightly to be flouted*."[6] It recommended that the Zionist program be greatly reduced because it could be carried out only by force of arms.

Meanwhile, in realization of French and British intentions to disregard Arab aspirations and with hopes set upon the King-Crane Commission, Arab nationalist leaders in Syria organized elections and convoked the first Arab Parliament on July 2, 1919. This parliament is known as the General Syrian Congress, and the resolutions it passed may be briefly summarized:

(a) Recognition of the independence of Syria, including Palestine, as a sovereign state with the Amir Faisal as king; recognition of the independence of Iraq.

(b) Repudiation of the Sykes-Picot Agreement and the Balfour Declaration and of any plan for the partition of Syria or the creation of a Jewish Commonwealth in Palestine.

---

[5] Ibid., Appendix H, p. 445.
[6] Ibid., Appendix H, p. 449.

(c) Rejection of the political tutelage implied in the proposed mandatory systems; but acceptance of foreign assistance for a limited period provided it did not conflict with national independence and unity, preference being given to American or—failing America—to British assistance.

(d) Rejection of French assistance in any form.[7]

In March 1920 the congress declared the independence of Syria and Iraq and demanded the evacuation of foreign troops. However, in April the Allied Supreme Council met at San Remo; disregarded the congress' decisions, Allied promises, and the King-Crane report; and divided the Arab provinces into several mandates. The mandates as established were Syria and Lebanon under France; and Palestine, Transjordan, and Iraq under Britain. Also, the Balfour Declaration, so abhorrent to the Arabs, was reaffirmed.

The effect of the mandate system on the Arab nationalist movement was most dramatic. Under the Turks the Arabs had at least enjoyed a uniform political status (except for parts of the coastal fringe of the peninsula). Now they were fragmented into a multiplicity of states, each one subjected to the political institutions of its particular mandatory power. Thus, Iraq and Transjordan, under Britain, were monarchial with parliamentary government, and Lebanon and Syria, under France, were republican. Palestine remained without any definite political character. The Arabian peninsula alone remained independent but was itself carved into five relatively weak states which were later unified under Ibn Saud. In all cases these separate states were controlled by French or British commissioners.

As a result of the mandate system, the nationalist movement split and each group became preoccupied with the struggle for power and control within its own locality. Hence, a separate history began for each country. But all Arabs shared the bitter disillusionment with the results of a war that had played so piteously with their dreams of independence and had reduced them from the status of dissatisfied citizens under Ottoman hegemony to hapless subjects under colonial suzerainty.

Although this sense of disillusionment was a common bond that united all Arabs in sympathy, it was not sufficiently strong to regenerate the Arab nationalist movement, and it was not until the eve of World War II that the nationalist movement again fused into a program of united action. The occasion for this united action was the Palestine-Arab revolt of 1936. Committees for the defense of Palestine were organized throughout the Arab world, and in 1938 the various groups merged to form the World Interparliamentary Congress of Arab and Muslim Countries for the Defense of Palestine.

During World War II, unrest continued throughout the Arab lands, resulting in the abortive coups of Rashid Ali al-Gilani in Iraq and General Aziz Ali al-Misri in Egypt. In recognition of this fomenting nationalist dissatisfaction, Anthony

---

[7]Ibid., pp. 293-294.

Eden, the British Foreign Minister, declared in May 1941 that Great Britain realized that "many Arab thinkers desire for the Arab peoples a greater degree of unity than they now enjoy . . . His Majesty's Government for their part will give full support to any scheme that commands general approval."[8] In response to Eden's declaration, Nuri al-Said, Iraqi Prime Minister, circulated his own plan for the creation of a Greater Syria which was to include Syria, Lebanon, Palestine, and Transjordan, and for the formation of an Arab League to include any Arab states that might join. The concept of a Greater Syria was opposed, but the idea of an Arab League gathered support and by 1945 the Arab League pact was formalized with Iraq, Syria, Lebanon, Transjordan, Saudi Arabia, and Egypt as its members. Yemen, Libya, Sudan, Tunisia, Morocco, Algeria, and Kuwait have subsequently joined.

The purpose of the Arab League was to promote cooperation among the member states in communications, health, economics, nationality, extradition, and cultural and social matters. It guaranteed each member's sovereignty and could force no member to take any action. Although the League initially aroused enthusiasm, its failure to effectively organize the Arab states to oppose the Zionists during the Palestine war discredited the organization among Arab nationalists.

The loss by the Arabs of their position in Palestine had larger ramifications than just the condemnation of the Arab League, however. For the Zionist victory led many youthful nationalists to condemn Arab society as a whole and to attempt, within a decade of the Palestine war, nationalist revolutions in Syria, Jordan, Iraq, Lebanon, and Egypt.

TURKISH NATIONALISM

In the 18th century Ottoman control in the Middle East began to fail. Since Turkish administration had been highly centralized in Istanbul with only a network of feudal overlords and governors to control the provinces of the empire, two problems arose. First, the governors, who were semiautonomous because the regions they controlled were generally far removed from the administrative center, repeatedly made attempts to form their provinces into sovereign states. Second, the provinces remained non-Turkish in population and culture and eventually developed a local nationalism of their own.

The central administration itself also began to fail. The sultans had long had the prerogative of appointing favorites to ministerial posts and of accepting gifts for favors. So long as the sultan was the only one operating in this manner, little harm resulted, but when the entire bureaucracy began following this practice, the government became paralyzed by nepotism and bribery.

European military penetration in the Middle East and later penetration by missionaries and businessmen brought with it Western culture. Artifacts of

---

[8]George Kirk, *The Middle East in the War* (London, 1952), p. 334.

Western culture, such as dress and manners, were adopted by many of the educated in the urban centers, but of far more importance was the influx of Western thought which sparked a Turkish intellectual revolution. One of the fruits of this intellectual renaissance was a new literature that transformed the collectivist ideas of European liberals into nationalist programs.

During this period of European expansion into the Middle East, Turkish leaders had ample opportunity to observe and compare the more efficient Western administrative machinery with their own. This comparison made it clear to some of those leaders that administrative reform was both possible and necessary.

Two schools of reform grew up within the empire, both influenced by the Europeans. One school, the idealists, felt that the adoption of Western governmental procedures (along with the philosophy underlying those proce- dures) would lead to the economic and industrial development necessary to bring Turkey to equality with the Western nations. The other school, the realists, felt that technological development was necessary first. Such development, they felt, would force governmental change. The Ottoman administration actually followed both programs, attempting from the top of the administrative pyramid to bring about the use of modern Western tools and techniques at the lower governmental levels.

The first task of the government in its effort to reform was to break the stranglehold of the conservative elements in the army. For this purpose a special artillery unit loyal only to the sultan was devised. This special unit surrounded the barracks of the famed Janissary Corps, the stronghold of conservatism, and annihilated that force. Immediately after it destroyed the Janissary Corps, the artillery unit traveled throughout the country and purged the rest of the army in a similar manner. Once the conservative elements were eliminated, a new army that supported the government in its reform attempts was created.

Backed by its modern army, the government was able to issue two decrees limiting its own powers. First, it gave non-Muslims equal protection under the law; and, second, it reorganized corrupt governmental agencies. Although neither decree was ever fully implemented and although the pressure for reform waxed and waned periodically, these measures considerably increased governmental efficiency. Hand in hand with these reforms, government support was provided for fledgling newspapers and publishing houses, and the number of schools was increased for the purpose of raising literacy.

Finally, in 1876 Midhat Pasha, then grand vizier and last of the great reformers, succeeded in introducing a constitution establishing a two-chamber parliament. However, the sultan, Abdul Hamid II, used the Russo-Turkish war of 1877-78 as a pretext to regain absolute control of the state through the emergency powers clause of the constitution. Thus, the parliament was rendered powerless. Following this, Midhat Pasha and the rest of the reformers were dismissed and then murdered.

Throughout the reform period, concepts of nationalism were being developed. During the first half of the century, the terms for fatherland and nation began to acquire specific reference in terms of the Ottoman state and to take on patriotic overtones. Thus, in 1860 Sinasi, an Ottoman journalist, was able to write an article that discussed the interests of the fatherland and spoke of an Ottoman nation within that fatherland.

Namik Kemal, a gifted contemporary of Sinasi, also wrote of an Ottoman nation within the empire; however, he wished that nation to be Islamic as well as Ottoman. Namik Kemal firmly believed that Muslim values and traditions would be reconciled with his own concepts of nationalism, parliamentary democracy, and individual freedom. He was, in fact, so anxious to preserve the best of Islamic tradition that he suggested the tie of Islamic brotherhood be made the means of implementing modernization not just in Turkey but throughout Asia and Africa.

Abdul Hamid II's return to despotism, which ended the reform movement, was followed by the establishment in Seneva of secret societies which became centers of nationalism. Many of these societies espoused pan-Turanianism, a belief that the Ottoman Turks were part of a larger Turanian race that occupied large portions of Russia, central Asia, and China. The pan-Turanianists fostered racism by concentrating on the ancient history of Turkey and the supposedly original Turkish language. Pan-Turanianism, however, was countered by Ottomanism, a concept which stressed the equality of all subjects of the empire regardless of their race, nationality, or religion.

The secret societies were also divided between those who favored the continuation of centralism and those advocating a movement toward decentralization.

In 1907 at the Ottoman Liberal Congress in Paris, all of these groups were united under the newly reformed Committee of Union and Progress. The committee, consisting mostly of army officers, government officials, and professional men, was dominated by the ideas of Ottomanism and centralization. The committee's program was to oppose the government of Abdul Hamid in every possible way, and in the 1908 revolution the committee forced a return to parliamentary government and sponsored a resurgence of the programs of modernaization and reform.

The next noticeable factor in the growth of Turkish nationalism was the outstanding success of Turkish arms during and immediately after the first world war. The Turkish success in repelling the Allies at Gallipoli and in driving the Greek army of occupation from the country brought feelings of nationalism, already strong in the intellectual centers, to the peasant communities. The common people began to feel pride in regarding themselves as Turks.

But the complete formulation of Turkish nationalism as it was to be practiced under the government of Ataturk came from the pen of the sociologist Ziya Gokalp. From the collectivist philosophy of the French sociologist Emile Durkheim, Gokalp drew the idea of the collective society as an ideal type. But he rejected an international society in favor of a Turkish one, for he held that a state which consisted of two or more cultures would necessarily disintegrate when the separate cultures were reasserted. For the same reason he made a distinction between Western culture and Western civilization; and he rejected the former while accepting the latter.

Gokalp's program, called Turkism, consisted basically of two elements. The first of these was a conscious return to a pure Turkish culture. The Turkish language was to be used, particularly in prayers, and a return was to be made to the presumedly superior morality of the ancient Turks in the areas of national patriotism and family relations.

The second element of Turkism was Gokalp's plan for the collectivization of Turkey. First he said that the power of the religious courts would have to be broken in order to deliver Turkey from theocracy and clericalism. Then he wrote that an "economic patriotism" must be fostered, emulating the prosperity of the ancient Turks but using the productive forces of industrialism and capitalism, with occupational unions and guilds operating as corporate persons. It was assumed that government aid would be necessary to the development of industry.

Thus, as the Ottoman Empire was about to die, many intellectual and political foundations for modern Turkish nationalism were in existence, on which Kemal Ataturk was soon to build a new Turkey.

IRANIAN NATIONALISM

The state of Iran has been strategically important for centuries. Iran sits squarely on the old East-West trade routes, and because of this a great deal of wealth has passed through the area, contributing to the greatness of the former state of Persia. In modern times, Iran has been coveted by both Russia and England. Control of Iran would have provided Russia with Persian Gulf ports for trade and naval activity, and it would have provided England with a link between the Near and Far Eastern segments of the British Empire. Thus the 19th and 20th centuries have been a period of competition between these two powers for influence in Iran. Fear of provoking a major war, however, kept each of the two nations from attempting a physical occupation. Instead, each sought to bind Iran through the purchase of trade concessions.

During the 19th century, Iran was particularly vulnerable to foreign inroads. The rerouting of East-West trade through the Suez Canal deprived Iran of one of its major means of revenue. And the extravagances of a series of shahs completed the job of reducing most of the country to poverty. As a result, Iran was in a state of anarchy. The Shah's control was largely limited to his capital city, and tribesmen and bands of robbers roamed the country, looting as they went. In an effort to fill this power vacuum, the Russians organized the Persian Cossack Brigade. The brigade served both to keep order in the capital and to protect Russian interests in Iran.

In 1890 a group of British merchants succeeded in obtaining a concession for

Iran's tobacco; but this measure aroused a sense of deep outrage in the public—they felt that the handling of Iranian tobacco by infidels defiled it—and public opinion forced the Shah to cancel the concession. At this time, three groups began to emerge as political forces: the clerics, the merchants, and the intellectuals. In 1906 these groups accomplished a nearly bloodless revolution and forced the Shah to institute a constitutional government under parliamentary control. Success, however, drove the three groups from politics: The clerics feared the secularization that would accompany modernization; the merchants received their economic demands and thus were satisfied; and the intellectuals withdrew from the business of politics to the less demanding pleasures of debate.

In 1907 the Anglo-Russian Agreement divided Iran into two spheres of influence. This agreement was bitterly resented by the small group of nationalists, and the country was plunged into civil war as Britain and Russia backed reactionary elements which were united with the Shah in an attempt to remove the constitutional limits on his power. The nationalist forces prevailed, however, and the Shah was exiled in 1909.

For the next two years the Iranian parliament strove to deal with the problems of ensuring civil order and collecting taxes. Failing in their efforts, they hired Morgan Shuster, a New York banker, to provide technical assistance. Shuster organized a gendarmerie to control the tribesmen and bandits, collected taxes, and began to put Iran's financial affairs in order. But when he ignored the division of Iran as outlined in the Anglo-Russian Agreement of 1907, the Russians demanded his dismissal. This broke the spirit of the nationalist movement. Civil order disappeared, and British troops entered the southwestern province of Fars under the pretext of protecting British citizens there.

At the outbreak of World War I, Iran declared her neutrality. The Russian occupation of Azerbaijan and the British occupation of the south, however, made Iran virtually an ally. What there was of a pro-German nationalist element in Iran proved to be very ineffective. This became apparent when the Russian collapse left those areas not occupied by the British in a state of complete anarchy. This state of anarchy, however, was not attributed to any failure on the part of the nationalists, but was attributed instead to the British; and, consequently, when the British proposed in the 1919 Anglo-Persian Treaty to train the Iranian army, build railroads, negotiate a loan, and reorganize government services, they were charged with "colonial generosity" and opposed by a spreading nationalism. The Iranian government that resulted from this nationalism, however, remained unable to cope with the problems of internal disorder and external interference.

In 1921 Sayyed Ziya al-Din Tabatabai, a journalist and nationalist, took over the government by coup and made himself prime minister. In order to accomplish the coup, Tabatabai had found it necessary to ally himself with Reza Khan, an officer of the Persian Cossack Brigade, and continued opposition from the court, the landowners, and the nationalists (who believed the coup had been engineered by the British) left Tabatabai entirely dependent on Reza Khan's cossacks. This dependence enabled Reza Khan to strengthen his own position to the point that he was finally able to exile Tabatabai and to declare himself prime minister.

Reza Khan used his position as prime minister to consolidate Iran's military and police forces, and then used those forces to secure Iran's frontiers and to quell the restive tribes within Iran. In 1924 he tried to establish a republic. This move was defeated by clerical opposition arising from fears of secularization. In 1925 in order to meet that opposition, Reza Khan became Reza Shah Pahlevi. As shah he attempted reforms modeled somewhat after those of Ataturk in Turkey. Rapid westernization was attempted through improvements in communications, education, industry, and transportation. Little attention, however, was paid to the agricultural base of the economy. Unity and stability were achieved, but the state was only partially modernized and the political development of the population was entirely ignored.

Just before World War II, Reza Shah began building ties with Nazi Germany: German technicians were brought in to organize administration, agriculture, and industry; German teachers were secured for Iranian schools; many Iranian students were sent to German schools; and, finally, commercial ties were developed between the two countries. By 1939 over 40 percent of Iranian trade was with Germany.

Reza Shah had hoped that by building strong ties with Germany he could use the might of Germany to offset British and Russian influence in Iran. The result was quite the opposite. Russia, fearing for her southern border, and England, fearing for her eastern empire, occupied Iran. They did agree, however, to withdraw their troops within six months of the signing of an armistice. During the occupation, the Allies forced Reza Shah to abdicate in favor of his son, while they themselves took over the administration of the state.

The end of the war did not bring the withdrawal of all the occupation troops. American and British forces were withdrawn within the agreed time, but Russian troops stayed to support a Soviet engineered revolt in Azerbaijan. Ahmad Qavam, then premier in Iran, obtained the withdrawal of Russian forces by agreeing to form a Soviet-Iranian oil company and to recognize an independent government in Azerbaijan. Then, through a series of maneuvers Qavam succeeded in reoccupying Azerbaijan with Iranian troops and in having his agreement with the Russians voided by the Iranian parliament. The Iranian government was once more in control of the country.

The next problem to be tackled by the government was that of capitalizing on its oil resources. The nationalists felt that their royalties from the Anglo-Iranian Oil Company were insufficient and, although the British made a proposal for a change in payment, an oil committee headed by Dr. Mohammad Mossadeq refused to act on the proposal. Mossadeq instead demanded nationalization of Iran's oil.

Mossadeq was a politician who had made himself a nationalist leader by his stand on the oil question, and, as a result, he became prime minister. His first official act was to evict the Anglo-Iranian Oil Company form Iran, but the consequences of his first act were not at all what he had expected. From 1951 to 1954 Iran was not able to produce oil and, although the world adjusted without much difficulty to the loss of Iranian oil, Iran itself could not adjust so easily to the loss of its substantial oil revenue. Mossadeq's popularity diminished as oil workers went jobless, as the government became financially strained from the loss of royalties, and as Iran's international credit disappeared. Although those segments of Iranian society which were directly affected by the loss of revenue were willing to withstand the strain, other segments, mainly the military, remained discontented and frustrated. Finally, the Shah dismissed Mossadeq and forcibly removed him from his position of control. A new government under General Zahedi imprisoned Mossadeq and settled the oil dispute by a contract with a consortium in the Netherlands. Since that time the Shah has become virtually a dictator.

ZIONISM

Modern Zionism is a socio-political and nationalistic movement whose aim is the ingathering of the Jews as a nation in Palestine. It derives its inspiration from its interpretation of the Judaic religion. Zionist dogma views the Convenant established by God and Abraham, Isaac, and Jacob as assigning the land of Palestine to the Hebrews "for an everlasting possession." It also bases its claim on the fact that the Jews once inhabited that area. Intermittently, from the time of the Diaspora, there was a yearning on the part of some Orthodox Jews to return to the Promised Land. Certain symbolic elements in Judaism dealt with their past glories as a nation, and religious festivals commemorate events in their history as a state. Also, Jewish liturgy is permeated with prayers for a return. In the late 19th century, belief in the return to Zion was transformed from a spiritual to a political Zionism and was translated into a cardinal principle of Jewish nationalism.

Zionism developed as a viable political movement in the late 19th century as a result of anti-Semitism in Europe, particularly among the East European and Russian Jews who suffered manifold disabilities and frequent persecutions. One of the influential works shaping political Zionism at this time was Leo Pinsker's pamphlet, *Auto-Emancipation*, published in 1882. In this book Pinsker argued that legal emancipation was useless because it did not carry with it social emancipation. For this, he declared, the Jews must establish their own nation. In the same year, Pinsker helped establish the organization *Hovevei Zion* (Lovers of Zion) which founded the first Zionist colonies in Palestine supported by funds from abroad. Other settlements followed, peopled mostly by East European and Russian Jews. But this movement was in reality a religious-philanthropic undertaking. It was Theodor Herzl who transformed Zionism into an organized political movement.

Herzl, a Hungarian Jew acting as a correspondent for a Viennese newspaper, was deeply aroused by the anti-Semitism he witnessed while covering the

Dreyfus trial in Paris. As a result, he published in 1895 *Der Judenstaat (The Jewish State)*. In this book he stated that the Jewish problem could not be solved merely by immigration, for Jewish minorities would eventually be persecuted wherever they existed. Herzl considered that a "Society of Jews" might acquire a national territory in either Argentina or Palestine and organize the Jews for immigration to their new home.

In 1897 Herzl called the first World Zionist Congress in Basel, Switzerland, attended by over two hundred delegates. This congress established the World Zionist Organization, the "Society of Jews" foreseen by Herzl in *Der Judenstaat*. It also formulated the "Basel Program" which stated that "the aim of Zionism is to create for the Jewish people a home in Palestine secured by public law."

Herzl, as leader of the World Zionist Organization, attempted through diplomatic channels to get one of the major powers to sponsor a Jewish home in Palestine. In Germany and Turkey he met with little success. The English, however, were more sympathetic. In 1903 they offered what is now Uganda as a site for a Jewish home. Zionist oppostion to this offer was so strong that Herzl, who favored acceptance, supported Uganda only as a temporary home. Nonetheless, the Seventh Congress of the World Zionist Organization after sharp debate rejected the offer completely. From that time on the Zionist organization became unalterably committed to establishing the national home for the Jews only in Palestine.

During this period of attempted diplomacy by the World Zionist Organization, other Zionist groups were established to facilitate Jewish immigration to Palestine. The Jewish Colonial Trust was established in 1901 and the Jewish National Fund was set up at about the same time; both organizations purchased land in Palestine for the settlement of European Jews.

Zionism was not without opposition from within. Several groups from among the Jews themselves opposed the new movement for various reasons. The ultra-Orthodox Jews, which comprised only a very small segment of total world Jewry, believed that the return to Zion could occur only through divine intervention and opposed the political aspects of the movement. The strongest opposition came from the Reform Jews, who considered that Judaism denoted a religion and not a race. Their views primarily represented the assimilationist tendencies of the Jews in Western Europe, England, and America who feared that Jewish nationalism would legally and morally compromise their positions as citizens of their respective states. Thus, a split developed among the Jewish people over the problem of nationhood which exists to the present.

At the outbreak of World War I, the Ottoman government clamped down on Palestine and declared the Zionist movement a subversive element. During the war Jewish leaders gave financial support to the Allied governments, in an effort to gain Allied sympathy for the Zionist movement. Of greater importance toward that end, however, were the contributions of Dr. Chaim Weizmann, a chemistry lecturer at Manchester University and a Zionist leader. During the war, he gained influence in England by developing a cheaper way to produce acetone, an ingredient of the explosive cordite used in artillery shells. Dr. Weizmann used his influence to bend British leaders to support the Zionist cause. At the same time, U.S. Supreme Court Justice Louis Brandeis and Rabbi Stephen Wise, American Jewish leaders, convinced President Wilson that he should support the now favorable British position on Zionism. The result of these persuasive techniques was the Balfour Declaration of 1917, which stated:

> His Majesty's Government views with favour the establishment in Palestine of a national home for the Jewish people and will use their best endeavours to facilitate the achievement of this object, it being clearly understood that nothing shall be done which may prejudice the civil and religious rights of existing non-Jewish communities in Palestine or the rights and political status enjoyed by Jews in any other country.

In 1917 Palestine was freed from Ottoman control. But the Allied powers had made several conflicting agreements over the disposition of that land: the Sykes-Picot Agreement dividing the Middle East into spheres of influence for the Allied powers; the Balfour Declaration, discussed above; and the Husayn-McMahon correspondence promising the Arabs an independent state in the Arab lands of the Middle East. Out of these antithetic promises arose the bitter struggle between Jewish and Arab nationalisms. The Arabs, no less than the Zionists, had a religious and historical attachment to Palestine. In Muslim belief, Jerusalem is a sacred city. Perhaps even greater in importance to the Arab is the fact that Palestine had been continuously occupied by a primarily Arab population since 640. Furthermore, at the close of the war, Palestine's population was comprised of 620,000 Arabs, of whom 550,000 were Muslims, 70,000 Christians, and 50,000 Jews (the majority of which were cultural Arabs). The Arabs feared that unlimited Jewish immigration would displace the Arab population and eventually make Palestine wholly Jewish. The Zionists, on the other hand, considered that the Balfour Declaration promised them a Jewish state in Palestine.

The fate of Palestine thus remained undecided until 1922 when the League of Nations made it a British mandate. The British were given "full powers of legislation and of administration, save as they were limited by the terms of this Mandate." The mandate also instructed the British to work with "an appropriate Jewish agency," on matters affecting the establishment of a Jewish national home. The Zionist Organization became that agency, and the Jews set up a quasi-state within the mandate area. (The activities and organization of the Jewish quasi-state are discussed in greater detail in Chapter 12.)

The advent of World War II sharply curtailed the Zionist activities aimed at Palestinian independence. Hitler's persecution of the European Jews caused both the Zionist Organization and the non-Zionist Jews of Palestine to expend most of their energy in support of the Allied war effort. Over a hundred thousand Palestinian Jews volunteered their services to the Allies, while those who stayed at home threw the agricultural and industrial resources they possessed into the war effort.

The Zionists also put considerable effort into the illegal immigration of European Jewish refugees from Hitler's persecutions. This led to increased friction among the Jews, the Arabs, and the British. The Arabs, inflamed by the swelling Jewish immigration and the fear that Palestine would become a Jewish state rather than an Arab nation, demonstrated and rioted against the Jewish population and British occupation. To quell the unrest the British attempted to limit immigration, and their naval patrols intercepted many refugee ships and sent the occupants to British colonies. In retaliation for the British action, the Stern gang, a small band of Jewish terrorists, maintained a private war with the British.

The revelation at the war's end of the attempted extermination of European Jewry caused world opinion to swing to the support of the Zionists. Inspired by the same horror, the Jews themselves bent all their efforts to the immediate illegal immigration of the European Jews. British attempts to limit the immigration led to open clashes between them and the Jews and to the arrest of many Jews.

Palestine was becoming an unbearable administrative and financial burden to the British. President Truman's promise during the election campaign of 1948 of his support for the immediate immigration of 100,000 Jews into Palestine led Great Britain to declare that Jewish disarmament must precede any large-scale immigration. The Zionists' military organizations, the *Haganah*, the *Irgun*, and the Stern gang, answered the British demand with a military campaign.

Anxious to be rid of its burden, Britain placed the Palestinian problem before the United Nations. A United Nations investigation committee sent to Palestine to study the situation recommended that Arab-Jewish cooperation was unlikely. Consequently, in 1947 the U.N. voted to partition Palestine into an Arab state, a Jewish state, and an international zone around Jerusalem. The already brewing civil war between Arabs and Jews broke out in full scale immediately following the partition proclamation. And in the midst of this strife, on May 14, 1948, David Ben Gurion, head of the Jewish Agency, announced the establishment of the State of Israel. Thus, the "Society of Jews" that Theodor Herzl, the founder of political Zionism, had postulated in 1895, was achieved within 53 years. But this society was created at the expense of Palestinian society. As a result, more than 1,000,000 Palestinians became homeless, hapless refugees. And the Middle East moved into an era of tension, instability, and war.

SELECTED BIBLIOGRAPHY

Hans Kohn's book, *Nationalism and Imperialism in the Hither East* (London, 1932), provides an excellent analysis of the effects of nationalism on the Middle East.

The classic study of Arab nationalism is George Antonius' book, *The Arab Awakening: The Story of the Arab National Movement,* 4th ed. (Beirut, 1961).

Hazem Z. Nuseibeh's work, *The Ideas of Arab Nationalism* (Ithaca, 1956), is the best philosophic study of Arab nationalism.

Zeine N. Zeine's book, *The Emergence of Arab Nationalism: With a Background Study of Arab-Turkish Relations in the Near East* (Beirut, 1966), emphasizes Arab nationalism in the Ottoman period.

For an examination of liberal thought on Arab nationalism, the following two books are most useful:

Albert Hourani, *Arabic Thought in the Liberal Age: 1798-1939* (London, 1962); and Malcolm H. Kerr, *Islamic Reform: The Political and Legal Theories of Muhammed 'Abduh and Rashid Rida* (Los Angeles, 1966).

The following books provide an excellent background for the study of Zionism, its ideology and history: Israel Cohen, *The Zionist Movement* (London, 1945); Ben Halpern, *The Idea of the Jewish State* (Cambridge, 1961); and Theodor Herzl, *The Jewish State: An Attempt at a Modern Solution of the Jewish Question* (London, 1934).

For a survey of Iranian nationalism see the excellent books, Richard W. Cottam, *Nationalism in Iran* (Pittsburgh, 1964), and Leonard Binder, *Iran: Political Development in a Changing Society* (Los Angeles, 1962).

On Turkish nationalism, the following accounts of Ziya Gokalp's ideas are very useful: Ziya Gokalp, *Turkish Nationalism and Western Civilization,* trans. and ed. by Niyazi Berkes (New York, 1959); Uriel Heyd, *Foundations of Turkish Nationalism: The Life and Teachings of Ziya Gokalp* (London, 1950).

For the best account of the young Turk movement see Ernest E. Ramsaur, Jr., *The Young Turks* (Princeton, 1957).

chapter 5

Political Trends in the Middle East: Nationalism, Communism and Socialism*

The enormity of the subject under discussion, the political and ideological movements in the Middle East, cannot be overemphasized. Indeed, it would be nearly impossible to cover the topic in detail even in a book, and thus what follows is only an introduction to give an idea of the general outlines and major landmarks. Each country in the Middle East has developed its own prejudices, preferences, and peculiarities; and a generalization that will fit all situations is sometimes difficult to substantiate. The sections in this chapter attempt as much generalization as is humanly possible. Because the Arab part of the Middle East is the largest and most numerous in terms of population, more emphasis has been placed upon it than on Turkey and Iran. No attempt was made to cover the ideological movements in Israel; since Israel's political trends are not indigenous to the area, its particular case will be considered within the context of the chapter on Israel.

NATIONALISM

There is no doubt that Arab nationalism—with emphasis on both terms, *Arab* and *nationalism*—is a recent phenomenon in the modern history of the Middle East. As a phenomenon brought about due to Western inroads into the area it also afflicted other peoples with its fever; in both Turkey and Iran, as well as in other parts of the world, nationalism has become a very strong political force. While serious consideration of Turkish and Iranian nationalism is included here,

*Kamel S. Abu Jaber, associate professor of government, Smith College.

69

the major emphasis in this section is on the development, elements, aims, and aspirations of the Arab nationalist movement whose torturous and violent path has overshadowed many other aspects of 20th century Middle Eastern society and politics.

Turkey's national development and Turkish nationalism were to take a different path from Arab or Iranian nationalisms where the anti-Western sentiment predominates. Following World War I, Mustafa Kemal rendered the Treaty of Sèvres (by which the Allies reduced Turkey to almost a dependency) a dead letter. In a series of brilliant military and political rounds with the Greeks, the British, and the Italians, Ataturk was able to free Turkey from their influence. Turkey emerged a homogeneous nation with its pride intact. Thus, from the beginning its nationalism was not a bitter defeated one, and therefore was more positive than either Arab or Iranian nationalisms. The Kemalist reforms, some of which were very progressive and revolutionary, put Turkey on the proper road toward progress and modernization. Her proximity to the Soviet Union and the various types of pressures to which she was subjected by her northern neighbor caused her to assume a less hostile posture toward the West and to concentrate on domestic reform. Furthermore, Ataturk's nationalism was based not on an adventurist or expansionist foreign policy. If anything, Ataturk's ambition was to retract Turkey's frontier to include only a homogeneous, purely Turkish nation. Even the Kurds are called "mountain" Turks. With the exception of the District of Alexandretta (a Syrian territory ceded to Turkey by France in 1939 as the price of keeping her neutrality in World War I) there exist few other serious territorial disputes. The leaders since that time have consistently emphasized Turkish nationalism and domestic reforms.

Iran's national development took a different route from that of Turkey. Whereas Turkey was abolishing all remnants of a traditional past—secularization, shedding titles, emancipation of women, etc.—Reza Shah, on the other hand, even saw the necessity of giving himself the title of King of Kings to acquire further legitimacy. While Turkey could easily secularize, this was impossible in Iran where Shi Islam was part of Iranian cultural, religious, and national heritage. Not only was the King of Kings unable to shed traditionalism, his bases of power and support have remained the most traditional *ulema* and the absentee landlords. Until well into the 1950s, the feudal order remained almost intact: a few landlords, rich families, and foreign oil companies at the top and the masses of Iranian people at the bottom. A huge gulf separated them. Doctor Mossadeq's "revolution" in the early fifties must be seen as an attempt not only to rid Iran of obnoxious exploitation but as a national act to alleviate the terrible condition of the masses.

The present Shah, while maintaining the slogan "God, Shah and Fatherland" as a guiding principle for his "white revolution from the throne," has been attempting to introduce a more "positive nationalism." A nationalism with a social content: to alleviate the lot of the average Iranian, raise the standard of living and literacy, and lessen the bitter xenophobic elements of nationalism.

The land reforms instituted by the Shah must be viewed as a gigantic step with which he hopes to change and also widen his base of support from the traditional ulema and landlords to the mass of Iranian peasantry and lower middle classes. The revolution from the " peacock" throne is still in progress, and its success depends largely upon the astuteness and adroitness of the Shah in overcoming the entrenched opposition that has developed and will manifest itself in various forms in the future.

In his interesting book *The Arab Awakening,* George Antonius outlines in detail and with great understanding the rise and development of the Arab nationalist movement.[1] The major concern of the pre-World War I Arab nationalists was to preserve the unity of the Arab people, to import or adapt certain Western institutions deemed good, to instill in themselves awareness as Arabs, and to cause a resurgence of nationalistic sentiment; following the conclusion of that fateful war their major concern was diverted to the achievement of independence and to the restoration of lost unity. There is no doubt that the greatest impetus for this nationalist resurgence came only as a result of the impact of the West and the ensuing contact between the Occident and the Orient. The former, sure of itself, domineering and aggressive; the latter, on the defensive, unsure of itself yet fascinated with this new element. The East awoke to find its self-assumed superiority shattered; the new reality was certainly disagreeable. These Eastern societies discovered" . . . their resources, their civilizations, even their very souls were menaced by a West that was rich and powerful beyond belief . . . "[2] Strength was one element that could have been tolerated by the peoples of the Middle East. What could not be tolerated was the contempt with which the West treated the "natives." As Albert Hourani put it, " . . . the contempt was no less wounding when it was concealed beneath a romantic admiration for the primitive or the exotic . . . it gave rise to a desire to equal the West . . . "[3] Such a desire could not help but be frustrated due, among other reasons, to the impatience of the Arab nationalists and the speed with which they attempted such a resurgence. The West, for its part, continued to regard the area as a sphere of influence whose inhabitants and their desires were of minor importance. Arab hopes and desires clashed with the rock of Western interests and machinations in the region. The contest was unequal, for the Arabs—newly emergent from 400 years of retardative Ottoman rule—were no match for the wits and resources of the West. The result was a "defeated" Arab nationalism.

First Stage: Islamic Reformism, 1880s-1918

The Arab nationalist movement has undergone various stages of development. While the major concern of this essay is to discuss that movement since

---

[1] London, 1938.

[2] Bernard Lewis, "Democracy in the Middle East—Its State and Prospects," *Middle Eastern Affairs,* Vol. VI, No. 4 (April 1955), p. 103.

[3] *Syria and Lebanon* (London, 1946), p. 100.

World War II, a brief look at its earlier development will give further and better understanding. The early nationalists, as Professor Ibrahim Abu Lughod points out, were fond of certain Western institutions and practices: " . . . constitutionalism, especially with reference to limitations on the absolute power of the executive branch; freedom both for the individual and association; and justice." These were considered the underlying causes of Europe's political and social "strength and ascendancy."[4] These early nationalists, really reformers, viewed the West as a model to be imitated. In their writings they hoped for the possibility of a reform—Islamic revival coupled with the introduction of Western liberal ideas.[5] The major thrust of their effort was to reform and adapt the Islamic community to the new challenges.

Second Stage: Nationalist Liberalism, 1918-1948

A new vintage of nationalists emerged after World War I. These were primarily concerned with independence. In their writings and exhortations a new twinge of mild anti-Western resentment emerges. Their major emphasis was on expanding the demand for the importation of Western institutions of liberal democracy and parliamentary government. They were not concerned with the place or fate of religion in their writings. In fact, they tended to dodge the issue and refused to tackle it. Nusseibeh says they either glossed over the issue or were embarrassed by it.[6] In deference to the modern and progressive ideas of the day, the slogan "Religion is for God and the Fatherland for everyone" was advanced. Thus, unlike the Western society where the issue was settled in favor of total secularization, the place of religion in Arab society is still ambiguous. The prime demand of the new post-World War I nationalists was political. They asked for independence from the West and for unity. Internally they advanced few ideas for social or economic reform.

Third Stage: Nationalist Socialism, 1948-1967

The conclusion of World War II signaled the beginning of a new era not only for the peoples of the Middle East but for the colonized people everywhere. The political independence, so long demanded by the liberal nationalists of the time, was finally achieved. They instituted liberal democratic ideas and institutions. However, these institutions were soon rejected in favor of more efficient but authoritarian regimes. Despite their theoretical emphasis on liberality and the free exchange of ideas, these nationalists when in power took

[4]*Arab Rediscovery of Europe* (Princeton, 1963), p. 157.

[5]Full discussion of these nationalists can be found in S. G. Haim, ed., *Arab Nationalism, an Anthology* (Berkeley, 1963); A. Hourani, *Arabic Thought in a Liberal Age* (London, 1962); H. Z. Nusseibeh, *The Ideas of Arab Nationalism* (Ithaca, 1959); and in J. S. Badwau, "The Arab World in Quest of a Future," in J. H. Thompson, and R. D. Reischauer, eds., *Modernizing of the Arab World* (Princeton, 1966).

[6]*The Ideas of Arab Nationalism*, p. 67.

an opposite path. At that time their societies were so fragmented and weak they felt the need to combine all national efforts behind one movement or leader. Now that the evil colonialists had been ousted, the masses and nationalist leaders alike believed a new era was finally at hand; an era of peace, progress, and prosperity. Events in the Middle East soon proved these aspirations to be groundless and bogus. In the Arab world there was terrific disillusionment with the West and its liberal ideas. This disillusionment culminated in the Western creation of the state of Israel in 1948. Added to the humiliation of defeat by the Israeli forces in 1948 was the continued presence of "pockets" of colonial presence and influence in parts of the region. Bitterness acidulated and the disillusionment matured (fermented) into estrangement. Arab masses and nationalist leaders alike began to seek other ideas, ideologies, and inspirations. In the words of Morroe Berger, "Arab liberalism never more than a tender shoot . . . finally withered just after World War II in the white heat of the West's insistence upon maintaining its special position in the Near East and the creation of the state of Israel . . . "[7]

Western insistence on maintaining the status quo, *i.e.*, a divided Arab world, its espousal of the cause of Zionism, its continued sustenance of the state of Israel, and its desire to retain its hegemony over the area, have further alienated Arab nationalists. Western defense schemes (the Middle East Defense Command, the Baghdad Pact, and the Eisenhower Doctrine) were seen as proof of Western desire to maintain its privileges and tie the Arabs to the Western camp. The economic, political, and military aid by the West to Israel was viewed as further proof of Western hostility toward Arab nationalism. The Tripartite Agreement of 1950 (in which the United States, France, and Britain undertook unilaterally to guarantee the territorial integrity and sovereignty of states in the region), the arms supplies, and the French-British-Israeli attack on Egypt in 1956 were further proof of such hostility to the Arabs. The 1967 "war" and the stand taken by the West, America in particular, were further evidence.

Thus the new era, the post-World War II era, saw the introduction of new elements in the nationalist ideology of the Arabs. Xenophobia, often extreme, became a major characteristic of the nationalists of this period. The *West* as a term became interchangeable with such words as *imperialism* and *colonialism*. Robert Waelder stated that the " . . . anti-colonial passions in Asia and Africa have become more inflamed at the very time that more than nine-tenths of the Western colonial empires have become emancipated."[8] Many nationalists came to believe that while colonialism appeared to have retreated politically, it in fact did not. While the Asians, Africans, and Latin Americans were "given" the paraphernalia of political independence, they had little of its spirit. Economically, culturally, even militarily, these nations were still tied to and dependent upon the old colonial powers, now called *allies*. Under the pretext of helping the developing nations to "contain" communism with technical, military, or

---

[7] *The Arab World Today* (New York, 1962), p. 328.
[8] In Morton Kaplan, ed., *The Revolution in World Politics* (New York, 1962), p. 9.

economic aid, Western influence and presence took new forms. Thus, the anti-Western sentiment of Arab nationalism can be explained in historical and contemporary terms. Historically, one can point to the religious-cultural rivalry between Christianity and Islam which often took the form of military confrontations. Also the Western cultural-educational impact that helped awaken Arab nationalism was soon superseded by Western economic and military interests and actual colonization. At the very time that Arab nationalism was awakened after World War I, Western colonialism became a reality in most of the region.[9] The Arab feeling of Western "treachery" and "deceit," and "breach of promises" after both World Wars did not help matters much. In deed as in practice the West disregarded, the nationalists felt, the legitimate desires of the Arab people. The West preached self-determination while it acted, often violently, other-determination.

The rise of two super-powers, the cold war, and the vigorous and dynamic Soviet policy in the Middle East also added dimension to Arab ideology. New avenues, hitherto inaccessible, were made available. Shy at first, the flirtations with the Soviet Union soon became serious, eventually culminating in a "friendly" intercourse. Arab fixation with the righteousness of their cause; their feeling of bitterness against Western treachery; Western insistence on maintaining the status quo; Western espousal of Israel; as well as a new, versatile, and dynamic Soviet foreign policy caused a new reorientation of Arab nationalist sentiment. The United States-Western preoccupation with containing communism caused the rise of *pactomania*. As the West pushed harder for allies, the Arab suspicion grew stronger. Pacts and alliances were viewed as keeping the area tied to Western strings and, worse, guaranteeing the existence of Israel. "How could an ally of Britain or the United States be permitted to fight Israel?" the nationalists asked. Refusing the logic of "the friend of my enemy is my enemy too," the Arabs introduced the principles of *positive neutralism*.

While in the eyes of John Foster Dulles neutrality was tantamount to immorality, the nationalists viewed it as a positive step in the right direction. For President Nasser, neutralism meant political independence. He once stated, "We decided our policy; we said our policy is from Cairo, from Egypt, not London, Washington, or Moscow . . ."[10] It meant that Egypt could draw upon the aid, resources, and ideas of any side. This was further expanded by Michel Aflaq, the founder and philosopher of the Arab Baath Socialist Party, to include "ideological" neutrality, the Arabs being unwilling to accept the capitalist or the communist solution to the achievement of human freedom.[11] Clovis Maqsud relates the phenomenon of neutralism among the developing peoples to their

[9]The exceptions, of course, are Algeria 1830, Aden 1839, Egypt 1882, and Libya 1911. See Dankwart Rustow, in G. A. Almond and J. S. Coleman, *The Politics of the Developing Nations* (Princeton, 1960), p. 381.

[10]*Thawratunah al-Ijtima'iyyah (Our Social Revolution)*, (Cairo, n.d.), p. 72.

[11]M. Aflaq, *et. al., Dirasat Fi al-Qawiniyyah (Studies in Nationalism)*, (Beirut, 1960), p. 32. See also S. al-Bitar, *al-Siyyasah al-Arabiyyah Bain al-Mabda wa al-Tatbiq (Arab Policy between Principle and Practice)*, (Beirut, 1960), p. 33.

desire to achieve a just and peaceful society, neutralism being considered a positive reaction to all power blocs and thereby conducive to the "realization of a true socialist regime . . ."[12] Thus it would seem to have been espoused for political as well as social reasons. Politically, ideologically and socially it stems from the Arab desire for noninvolvement and nonalignment and the resultant freedom to partake of aid from East and West alike.

Contemporary Arab nationalists, dissatisfied with political democracy alone, have been advocating economic democracy and socialism as well. The socialist principles and ideas are viewed as giving Arab nationalism a social content internally. For the Arab nationalists of this period view their battle on two fronts: externally, to liberate themselves from the last vestiges of Western-colonial influence and to liberate Palestine; and internally, to struggle for a better standard of living for the common man. "In the West," says Michel Aflaq, "injustice touches only some classes [of the society while all . . .] the East represents nothing but an oppressed people . . ."[13] internally oppressed by local capitalists, landowner and reactionary forces, externally by the forces of colonialism and neo-colonialism. Viewed in this light, Leonard Binder's statement that Baath ideology is more than an ideological explanation why imperialism must be fought is indeed a harsh judgment.[14] While externally this party's attitude toward the West is negative, internally, and in theory at least, it has been attempting to expand the economic and political opportunities of the average man.

While this new element was called socialism, what was really meant was economic democracy. Many of the traditional Western notions of socialism, like ideas of international brotherhood of all workers, cosmopolitanism, class struggle, and secularism, were not only discarded but hotly denied and rejected; yet it was so christened for want of better terminology. These new nationalists, having sprung from the middle and lower classes, were at close range and in touch with them and to them they felt a *noblesse oblige* that went beyond mere political democracy. This new breed even disparaged "false parliaments" and "meaningless elections." For leaders like President Nasser, democracy " . . . fundamentally means the establishment of social justice and equality for the oppressed classes . . . that . . . government should not be the monopoly of feudalism and exploiting capital, but should be for the welfare of the whole nation . . . It is not created simply by issuing a constitution and setting up a parliament; there is no freedom and no democracy without equality . . . " of opportunity.[15] These nationalists were demanding social and economic equality,

---

[12] *Ma'na al-Hiyad al-Ijabi (The Meaning of Positive Neutrality)*, (Beirut, 1960), p. 114. For a comprehensive study of Arab neutralism see F. A. Sayegh, ed., *The Dynamics of Neutralism in the Arab World*, (San Francisco, 1964).

[13] *Ma'rakat al-Masir al-Wahid (Battle of the Same Destiny)*, (Beirut, 1959), p. 29.

[14] "Radical Reform Nationalism in Syria," *The Muslim World*, Vol. XLIX, No. 3 (July 1959), p. 226.

[15] See Malcolm Kerr, "The Emergence of Socialist Ideology in Egypt," *The Middle East Journal*, Vol. 16, No. 2 (Spring 1962), p. 143.

not political freedom. President Nasser says real freedom is " . . . not in false parliaments which represent a minority ruling the majority . . . "[16] while Kamal E. Rif'at, a socialist author, wonders "where is liberty and democracy when capital reigns? Is there any liberty for the working classes if these classes are under the sway of unemployment and hunger? Is there any freedom of elections when the results of these elections are influenced by those who can buy public opinion . . . ?"[17] Rif'at concludes that the freedom and democracy expounded by the 19th-century philosophers cannot be an adequate basis "for our society."[18] This has been the mood of the nationalists in the era of the fifties and the sixties.

Modern Arab nationalists always characterize their nationalism as peaceful, humanitarian, constructive, nonracist, and nonexclusivist. Speaking at Port Said in 1959 President Nasser said, "We shall work in the future . . . to prove to the whole world that Arab nationalism is a constructive movement . . . "[19] Sati al-Husari, called by many the father of modern Arab nationalist thought, speaks of Arab nationalism as a "peaceful" movement, "nonexpansionist," and "nonexclusivist,"[20] while Michel Aflaq states categorically that an Arab socialist must also be a nationalist, "his nationalism is a guarantee of his humanity."[21] In fact, socialism is ancillary to nationalism, the latter being of more importance. Socialism, true socialism, cannot be achieved without unity; unity, the foremost dream and demand of Arab nationalism with, in the words of Aflaq, "socialism its body . . . unity its soul."[22] It is apparent then that Arab nationalists foresee a role beyond mere improvement of the lot of the common man and beyond political independence and neutralism. They foresee for the Arabs a "mission," a mission that will bring benefits to all of humanity. Unable to accept the idea of only partaking of modern civilization, they feel they also must contribute. This missionary zeal, perhaps a result of the present stagnation and disarray, accounts for part of the difficulty in understanding Arab nationalism.

If unity is the norm, and the present condition is not, it becomes obvious why Arab nationalists continuously emphasize its achievement. In a succinct article entitled "How Strange We Are," Al-Husari expresses the dilemma and difficulty facing Arab unity:

> We revolted against the British and the French, against those who colonized our countries and tried to enslave us. We repeated these "red" revolutions many times and continued "white" revolutions over many generations. We suffered many types of torture, losses, and sacrificed many lives. But, when we were finally liberated, we began to consider the

---

[16]*Thawratunah* . . . p. 14.

[17]"al-Demoqratiyyah f: al-Mujtama al-Kshtiraki," (Democracy in the Socialist Society), *al-Majallah*, No. 68 (September 1962), p. 3.

[18]*Ibid.*, p. 4.

[19]Quoted in Berger, *op. cit.*, p. 370.

[20]*Hawl al-Qawmiyyah al-Arabiyyah (Concerning Arab Nationalism)* (Beirut, 1961), p. 89.

[21]*M'rakat* . . . , p. 29.

[22]*Ibid.*, p. 33.

frontiers they imposed upon us and dismembered our land as sacred. We forgot these frontiers were those of "solitary confinement" and the "house arrest" they imposed!"[23]

Unity is the norm that must be restored. The localism that has flourished since the end of World War I must be eradicated and replaced with unity of the whole Arab world so it can prosper, so it can be strong, so it can stand equal among the other nations of the world. It is ironic that this emotion to unite, this powerful psychological stimulant that underlies Arab nationalism, has also been the most frustrated. While Arab nationalists are aware that historically the Arab world has united for only brief periods, *i.e.*, the political norm being disunity, they are aware that the emotion among the people has always harked back to those brief moments as the norm. They point out that despite many separatist movements in Islam despite the Mongol, Seljuk, Mamluk, Crusader, Ottoman, and finally Western incursions, the feeling of the unity of the Arabic *ummal* (community) is still strong and still alive.

But it is not only emotion and a feeling of historical and cultural association that impels Arabs towards unity. There exists a genuine desire, a recognition on the part of various Arab peoples that they are really one people.[24] That emotion is buttressed by a common language; a language poetic, unique, and rich. The language of the Prophet and the language of the Koran. Many Arabs feel that the return to unity will somehow bring about a reassertion of the noble traits in the Arab character that will once again enable it to achieve self-pride and dignity. In this sense pan-Arabism is a protest against the superimposed artificial frontiers laid down by imperial powers, a protest against the present inferiority and a powerful motivating factor towards progress. Indeed this sentiment has been an integral principal of all ideologies and Arab revolutionary movements. There is also the unity of religion among the vast majority of the Arabs. The Islamic community has always emphasized the unity of the people and the unity of religion and state. That the Arabs feel part and parcel of one geographic area is another element that strengthens the argument for unity. In addition, some modern Arab writers have begun to speak of a "community of interest" among the Arabic peoples. Nusseibeh declares that the "concept of national interest should undoubtedly be regarded as a factor in Arab nationalism, even though some theorists have been reluctant to include it because of its elusive, indefinable, and changeable nature . . . "[25] Nusseibeh also lists other factors which he calls "controversial factors;" among these is the place of religion, race, and the idea of a "special mission." On none of these last three factors has there been complete or partial agreement and the debate still continues.[26]

---

[23] *Op. cit.*, p. 336.

[24] See M. al-Razzaz, *Ma'a lim al-Hayat al-Arabiyaah al-Jadideh (Contours of Modern Arab Life)*, (Beirut, 1960), pp. 265-6. Also I. Jum'a, *al Qawmiyyah al-Arabiyyah (Arab Nationalism)*, (Cairo, 1960), p. 25.

[25] *Op. Cit.*, p. 86.

[26] For details of the arguments, *Ibid.*, pp. 88-97, *passim*.

Long on emotion, the Arab nationalist movement suffers from a dearth of programs, theoretical as well as actual, intended to effectuate unity. There exists no agreement as to what form this unity should take. Should the future united Arab government be a monarchy (constitutional or otherwise), a republic, a dictatorship, or should it be a "peoples republic?" Should it be a confederation, federation, or unitary, or perhaps it should be "corporative?" The historical as well as the present diversity and particularisms of Arab life have made agreement on a single form impossible. Herein lies one difficulty. Then should there be regional unities to precede the grand unity of all the Arabs? Regional unity as "The Fertile Crescent" scheme, "The Nile Valley," "The Arabian Peninsula," and North African unity of "The Maghrib?" Compounding all these diverse elements and ideas is the diverse impact the many European powers have had on various parts of the Arab world. French, Spanish, and Italian in some countries, British in others, with touches of American influence added to traditional Arab-Ottoman-Mamluk-Kurdish ideas, mores, and forms!

The divergent forms of governments, dynasties, republics, and sheikdoms, with their varying levels of socio-economic and political developments, the rise of localisms, provincialisms, and provincial nationalisms, are no less of an impediment. Added to that, of course, is the struggle between the traditional and modernist, between the progressive and the reactionary regimes which culminated in the struggle over the idea of the Islamic Alliance advanced by Saudi Arabia. Culturally there are also vast differences. There is perhaps as much difference between the resident of Damascus or Cairo and that of Mukalla as between an Italian and a Spaniard. The different levels of education and literacy are also factors.

Fourth Stage: Nationalist Radicalism, Contours, 1967 —

Despite all these difficulties, impediments, lack of manifest theory or an actual program, the emotion to unite remains the strongest force behind the Arab nationalist movement. It overrides all other sentiments, programs, or commitments, whether political, religious, or social. Since the defeat by Israel in 1967, where even on that most crucial issue the diverse Arab governments could not coordinate their efforts, the union sentiment has increased. Since 1967 many Arab intellectuals believe their very way of life, the personality of the Arab culture, and the Arab himself to be at stake. Unity had been demanded before 1967 to add to Arab strength. The year 1967 proved there was no Arab strength in disunity, that not only is Palestine at stake, but their very existence as a people. As a result, Arab nationalism received a strong dose of demand for union. The defeat of 1967 also added a brief, almost religious and fanatic, that only force—sheer naked force—will bring about the realization of Arab hopes. The Arab intellectuals and masses alike are still stunned by the speed and magnitude of the defeat. One thing they are sure of, however. They were defeated this time. Governments and people alike. Why? They ask—why? There will come one day when they will discover the answer. The "progressive" "socialist" military regimes that have come to power have too failed like their "not-so-progressive" and "reactionary" adversaries. Basically, these intellectuals reason that the answer lies in disunity.

Conclusion

The nationalists who came after World War II were "positivists." They were committed to action both internally and externally. Their belief in social justice, socialism, and economic democracy stemmed from a genuine concern for the masses of people. The masses that had hitherto escaped the attention of the traditional Middle Eastern leaders. These leaders also believed that political and economic democracy could not be separated; that political democracy was meaningless and that such equality was groundless unless buttressed by social justice. In order to achieve such a better society the leaders, in theory and fact alike, were more concerned about the creation of this harmonious and socially integrated society than about the means with which it was to be achieved. They were not concerned with apologies about the lack of democratic institutions and methods. What they demanded was action, and to achieve the quickest action they infiltrated the army in order to assume the leadership of government. They believed that a positive role for government was absolutely necessary to achieve the "general good" and the common will, and their formidable task was how to ameliorate a culture and a society so it could survive as equal among other nations of the 20th century.

Whatever the countless obstacles it faced and the drawbacks it will face, Arab nationalism believes in a positive role for man in society. That in itself is a terrific change from the previous belief in predestiny and fatalism. It believes in partaking of all types of human knowledge and experience. Its pseudo-Marxist outlook is tempered by humanistic elements. The unity it seeks is both for reasons of strength, to liberate Palestine and maintain independence, and also for preparing the Arabs to contribute to humanity. It is a mystical vision of a civilized people interacting with other civilized peoples. To achieve this goal, socialism both as an ideology and as a program of action is necessary. In the words of Dr. Munif al-Razzaz, Arab nationalism does not believe in agression against others, nor in racism, both characteristics of colonialism. It believes in "independence . . . positive neutrality . . . peaceful co-existence . . . unity. This unity is horizontal, meaning it shall tie the various dismembered parts in one struggling political and economic unit, and perpendicular, meaning it shall fight sectarianism, racism, tribalism, nepotism, and looks to uniting the Arabs . . . the construction of a free dignified existence . . . (institute) liberty. Externally to institute free association with other nations without damaging Arab sovereignty. Internally to bring about (true) liberty . . . socialism . . . the only way to develop our underdeveloped economy . . . "[27] This perhaps catches the feeling and spirit of the modern Arab nationalist movement.

COMMUNISM: A STUDY IN FAILURE

The study of politics and the development of political trends in the Middle East cannot but include a serious consideration of the introduction, development, and influence of the Communist movement. The introduction of this foreign element into the politics of the area has permanently altered the chemistry of the local politics. As a leftist, revolutionary, and progressive ideology it has had a strong appeal among some elements of the intelligentsia. Steeped as it is in pseudo-scientific Marxist jargon that clatters of certainty, it had its initial appeal, on the ideological level, to those in search of certainty in an age of disorder, uncertainty, and chaos. As an ideology promising a better life here and now, its appeal, not surprisingly, was strongest among the disgruntled, the malcontent, the deprived. Initially, these elements, for historical as well as socio-political and economic reasons, were the intelligentsia and the minorities. It is a fact that the minorities constituted the backbone of the Communist parties of the Arab world in the 1920s and 1930s and that their influence in these local parties is still strong. As late as 1947 the Kurds constituted between 35-40 percent of the Iraqi Communist party.[28] The Jews were also very active in the Iraqi party. In 1946-47, 25 percent of its members were Jews, and Sasson Shlomo Dalal became its secretary general until 1949.[29] In addition, the Iraqi party had many Assyrians among its ranks.

In Syria the first secretary of the party was an Armenian, Artin Maduyan, to be replaced in 1934 by Khalid Bakdash, a Kurd.[30] Bakdash remains till this day the secretary of the Syrian party while the influence of the Armenians has continued to remain strong. In Lebanon the Armenian influence in the party remains very strong. The Lebanese Communist party was organized in 1924 at the behest of Joseph Berger, a Polish Jew, and a leader of the Palestine Communist party. Berger served as a liason officer with the Palestine Communist party. He was succeeded by Eliahu Teper, a Lithuanian Jew, who in turn was succeeded by Nikhman Litvinsky, a Russian Jew.[31] Christian Orthodox too have been very active in the Communist movement in the Middle East. Both Fuad Nasir in Jordan and Nikola Shawi in Lebanon are Orthodox.[32] In Egypt the party was founded by Joseph Rosenthal in 1920 and, until World

[27] In Aflaq, et. al., Dirasat F. al-Qawmiyyah, pp. 61-63, passim.
[28] Walter Z. Laqueur, Communism and Nationalism in the Middle East (New York, 1956), p. 225.
[29] Ibid., pp. 234 and 192.
[30] Ibid., p. 141.
[31] N. W. Suleiman, Political Parties in Lebanon (Ithaca, 1967), pp. 60-61.
[32] Christian Orthodox also founded the Arab Baath Socialist party, Michel Aflaq; the Syrian Social Nationalist party (Antun Sa'adeh): and the Arab Nationalist Movement (Dr. George Habash). Their "protest" seems to encompass the entire spectrum of political activity.

War II, 80-90 percent of the membership was composed of foreigners. Jews, Greeks, and Italians were the active elements well into the 1940's when the Communist party of Egypt began to Arabize.[33] In all these parties, however, the bulk of the membership was not the proletariat or peasants but the intelligentsia: high school and college students, lawyers, physicians, teachers, engineers, and generally the educated. While the influence, and in some cases the predominance, of the minorities have subsided over the years, the general intellectual and social make-up of these parties continues to be the intelligentsia of the middle classes and is not of working class origins.

The growth of communist parties and influence in the Middle East have been conditioned by the peculiar geographic as well as historical and socio-economic conditions of the area. In addition, the international Communist movement has had a marked influence on the development of local Communist parties. As elsewhere, the local parties have had to suffer the changes and shifts in Soviet policies over the years. Often the suddenness of the shift has spelled near disaster for the local parties, and it is to their credit that they have survived at all. Among the major conditioning factors of the growth of Communist influence in the Middle East has been the nature of the Marxist ideology itself with its theoretical emphasis on internationalism, class struggle, its view of religion, nationalism, and socialism.

On practically every bend in their torturous road to national independence and unity, Arab nationalists have felt and continue to feel that communism is their enemy and has worked against them. Communist emphasis on internationalism, the brotherhood of the working class everywhere, is not only disparaged but worse, is thought of as anathema to Arab nationalism. Aflaq, the founder of the Baath party, spoke for all nationalists when he pondered, "How can an Israeli and an Arab worker be brothers?" Arab nationalists have also come to feel that the Communist parties were anti-Arab nationalism and anti-Arab unity, the most cherished goal of the nationalists in the 20th century. Some nationalist writers like al-Hakam Darwazeh claim the Communists cooperated with the colonial powers while the Arabs were struggling against them in Syria and Lebanon, and that the Communists betrayed the Algerian revolution.[34] Worse, the various Communist parties in the Arab world acquired the spirit of provincialism endemic to each country and consistently refused to recognize the concept of one Arab nation. Instead, they spoke of particular characteristics of various Arab "nationalities," Egyptian, Syrian, Iraqi, . . . etc.[35] On the Palestine question and the creation of Israel, the local Communist parties have been greatly handicapped. Following closely the Soviet foreign policy lines, the local Communist parties continued until 1947 to resist the idea of creating a Zionist state in

---

[33] Laqueur, *Communism . . .*, pp. 31, 34, and 42.

[34] *al-Shuyu iyyah al-Mahaliyyah (Local Communism)*, 3rd ed. (Beirut, 1963), pp. 460, 507.

[35] See Naji Allush, "The Arab National Struggle and The Arab Communists," *Dirasat Arabiyyah*, Vol. 3, No. 1 (November 1966), p. 28.

Palestine. When the Soviet Union agreed to the Partition Plan, the local parties followed suit and defended the idea of partition. From 1948 till 1955 when the Soviet line and policy regarding the Arabs took another turn, the Communists called for peace between the Arab states and Israel. During this period they defended the "legitimacy" of the Zionist state and claimed that continued tension between the Arabs and Israel benefited only the colonial powers. From 1955 onward the Communists began denouncing Israel as a beachhead of Western imperialism and colonial influence in the region. The Communists, however, never called for the destruction of Israel as a state, again following the Soviet line, which, while denouncing Israel, maintained various types of relations with her.[36] This attitude still pervades the Arab Communist parties.

Sa'dun Hamadi, a Baath party intellectual and one time Agrarian Reform Minister in Iraq, claims communism has come about as a reaction to the deteriorating socio-economic conditions of the working classes in Europe.[37] Should one ponder this statement a little deeper, the reasons for the Communists' difficulties in the Middle East will become clearer. The most obvious remark is that the absolute majority of the peoples of the Middle East are still engaged in agriculture. As such, the Communist response to their problems, while ameliorated later, remained far from satisfactory. Should one think that the appeal of Marxist ideology is strongest among labor, a theoretical precept of this ideology, it becomes apparent why it has encountered difficulty in a basically peasant society. No doubt this lack of "industrial mentality" and its concomitant values of discipline, promptness, and routine have been a handicap.[38] Furthermore, while the Communist parties of the Middle East spoke as if representing the proletariat, they were in fact neither led by nor composed of the working classes. The working classes began to emerge only in the late 1950s and 1960s and have not yet attained the necessary class consciousness nor the numerical strength to be more effective.

Intellectually as well as socially these Communist parties have been composed of the new elite of the emerging middle classes. Their middle class origin is an element of strength as well as a basic reason for their weaknesses. It is an element of weakness in the sense that an average worker—difficult as it may be to find such a one in the Middle East in the first place—will find it impossible to identify or empathize with the past and present leadership of the Communist parties. These are socially, intellectually, and, more importantly, economically so superior to labor that the latter can find no common grounds with the former. The gulf between the leadership and the masses is far too wide and the local parties have not yet attempted to bridge it. In no country in the Middle East did the Communist party seriously attempt to branch out and enlist support among the masses of peasants, while its attempts, vigorous in the

---

[36] See Darwazeh, *op. cit.*, pp. 257-262, *passim*.

[37] *Nahnu Wa al-Shuyu iyyah Fi al-Azamah al-Hadirah (We and the Communists in the Present Crisis)*, (Beirut, 1963), p. 9.

[38] See Manfred Halpern, *The Politics of Social Change in the Middle East and North Africa* (Princeton, 1963), p. 164.

beginning, to organize and dominate labor unions have not succeeded. Walter Z. Laqueur indicates that the Communist movement in the Middle East did not place its emphasis on the "revolutionary mass struggle . . . In party propaganda the feudal regime was attacked . . . If the Communists appealed to *class* interests at all, it was the class interest of the intelligentsia and not of the proletariat . . . "[39] The Communist tactic no doubt was to attract the important elements first and then perhaps turn to a serious appeal to the "toiling classes." It is also possible that the Communists decided it was futile to attempt reaching the masses with, as Manfred Halpern put it, "the Middle East . . . unready to receive modern ideas, including communism . . . "[40] In Iraq the party has almost remained exclusively a students' party, while in Jordan the party made no attempt to seriously reach, enlist, or infiltrate the refugees.[41]

The Communist movement, it seems, never seriously attempted to enlist mass support. Its greatest periods of strength have always coincided with a surge of anti-Western feeling, as in Iran in 1953 when its membership reached between 40,000 and 80,000 members, Syria in the mid 1950s, or in Iraq after the 1958 coup d'etat that brought Abd al-Karim Kassim to power. Thus the degree of its attraction has depended more heavily on the negative xenophobic sentiments of the particular moment than on a sustained, well-organized, mass supported movement. In part this explains the continued weakness of the Communist movement in Turkey where anti-Russian feeling and Soviet threat has been more immediate. Is it possible that the Communist movement in the Middle East is trying yet another road to communism—that of a party of well-disciplined intellectuals, instead of workers, who can take over in time of political crisis and breakdown as in Russia of 1917, or a mass peasant war of liberation as Mao Tse-tung has led in China? The emphasis of the Communist parties of the Middle East on drawing their leadership and support from the middle classes has yet another detrimental factor: By so doing they put themselves in competition with other middle class Middle Eastern parties, instead of recruiting the peasant-working classes. Thus, the competition with the Baath and the Syrian Social Nationalist party has been very keen. Internally the Communist movement of the Middle East has remained a middle class movement struggling against a feudal or semi-feudal order. Even where the feudal order has been broken, and a progressive regime, led by the national bourgeoisie replaced it, the Communist movement still did not succeed. This phenomenon is partly explained by the reluctance of the "new" leadership to relinquish power as well as to a host of other factors. The Soviet Union has always faced a dilemma with regard to cooperation with the national bourgeoisie, for as can be readily seen from their name, they are primarily nationalistic. In the 1920s the Soviet Union was sympathetic with the policies of Mustafa Kemal of Turkey and Shah Reza Pahlevi of Iran. The 1930s saw a switch in this policy and the Comintern banned cooperation with the bourgeois elements and even Ghandi was denounced as a

[39] *Communism* . . . , p. 126.
[40] *Op. cit.*, p. 159.
[41] See Laqueur, *Communism* . . . , pp. 126-7.

British "agent."[42] Not until the death of Stalin was cooperation with the bourgeoisie possible again. The Twentieth Party Congress of the Soviet Union gave the new line its formal benediction. A quick review at the various shifts will reveal the Soviet response was to events in Europe: the rise of Nazi and Fascist danger, the war, the cold war, the nuclear balance-of-terror, and the new theme of peaceful coexistence.

No doubt the greatest handicap facing the Communist movement has been its subservience to the Soviet Union's line of policy. As the line of Soviet policy was drawn to fit its stature as a world power, *i.e.* globally and in response to problems stemming from and peculiar to the nature of the Soviet Union, it was bound to encounter difficulties locally. From the slogan "no cooperation with the national bourgeoisie," popular front cooperation in the 1930s, the various Soviet stands on the Palestine problem, to a hot and cold attitude towards one particular regime or another, the local parties faithfully followed. Constantly following the "foreign" line of Soviet policy the local parties never developed a distinct personality, nor did they offer solutions to problems peculiar to the area. Their main function, the nationalists asserted, was to be a vehicle of Soviet foreign policy. Thus, the nationalists learned to suspect them, use them, but never trust them. The Soviet Union underestimated the strength of the nationalist sentiments and when this line of "no cooperation" policy changed in 1955 the basic lines of the struggle had already been drawn and the nationalists were fully aware of the Communist designs and methods. While the nationalists applauded Rashid Ali's revolt in Iraq in 1941, the Communists scorned it as Fascist; the Communist line on the creation of Israel and Communist condemnation of the Algerian Revolution in 1954 are given as examples of anti-Arab nationalist desires. In 1958 Khalid Bakdash left Syria following the formation of the United Arab Republic, and in Iraq the Communist party advocated "federation" rather than unity.[43] Equally bad was the claim that the local Communist parties had lost their revolutionary spirit and acquired a reformist attitude. The Syrian-Lebanese Communist party, following the Twentieth Party Congress of 1956, advanced "the parliamentary road to achieve the basic reforms."[44]

The weakness of communist ideological appeal in the Middle East attests, in part at least, to the strength of nationalist sentiment and the desire to contribute something indigenous. Furthermore, in both Turkey and Iran, there is genuine fear of the neighbor to the north. Turks and Iranians fear the "bear's" embrace more than they value their anti-Western sentiment. Among the progressive Arab peoples neutrality, positive neutrality, has become a cardinal element of the nationalist movement. In fact, Arab nationalists are also aware of the

---

[42] W. S. Laqueur, "The National Bourgeoisie," *International Affairs*, Vol. 35, No. 3 (July 1959), pp. 324-331, *passim*.

[43] Naji Allush, "The Communist Movement in the Arab Fatherland," *Dirasat Arabiyyah*, Vol. II, No. 3 (January 1966), p. 77.

[44] From "Nahwa Afaq Jadidah" (Towards New Horizons), publication of the Syrian and Lebanese Communist party, (May 1965), and quoted in *ibid.*, p. 77.

Soviet-Communist threat. Ahmad I. Khalaf-Allah, an Egyptian intellectual writing in 1961, identified Soviet imperialism as equally dangerous to Arab nationalism as that of Western imperialism. He saw only one avenue left open to the developing nations to escape the Soviet or Western imperialisms: "cooperative, human, democratic socialism."[45] Arab intellectuals of the post World War II era were intent on choosing their own ideology and perhaps making their own mistakes. Nationally they sought the adoption of socialist ideology for it allowed them maximum maneuverability between East and West. Capitalism entails domestic injustice and exploitation, while communism with its emphasis on class struggle fights disease with disease.[46] Aflaq, who saw the entire East exploited by a predatory colonial West, could not think in terms of class struggle. To him, as to many Arab nationalists and intellectuals, the entire East with all its classes, not just one or more classes within the society, has been oppressed and needs to be liberated. Thus the concept of a battle on "two fronts" developed; internally against the various ills of Arab society (and these the Communists have failed to come to grips with) and externally by fighting for Arab independence and unity. Communist doctrine, tailored for different places, problems and circumstances and designed for the service of the Soviet Union, could not offer attractive solutions to the majority of Middle Eastern peoples. Ahmad Kamal Abul Majd was speaking for a majority of the intellectuals when he asked for an indigenous ideology, a pragmatic ideology, flexible to reflect the needs of Middle Eastern society and not an ideology that would fight " . . . injustice with injustice."[47]

Perhaps the greatest detriment to the Communist party's growth in the Middle East is the fact that it was grafted onto an entirely different milieu. For, like Western liberal institutions, introduced from above either by a colonial power or an over-eager reform-minded group or monarch, it never had mass grassroots support and has never been able to develop it. Also, like Western liberal ideas that came about as a response to peculiar Western historical developments, communist ideology found few ears. Few ears willing, either by personal choice, personal disposition, or for a feeling of national-minority frustration and deprivation, to repeat the jargon and accept it uncritically. Marxism, daughter of an heiress to the humanist tradition in Western political thought, continues to encounter difficulties even in its own habitat. With all its contradictions, its pseudo-scientific solutions, and its jargon-laden literature it was grafted in the Middle East from above. Copied and imitated by certain frustrated intellectuals "above," it remained "above" and failed to enlist and sustain a popular mass movement. In fact, its greatest appeal has been in

---

[45]al-Falsafah al-Ishtirakiyyah Wa al-Demoqratiyyah al-Ta 'awuniyyah (Socialist Philosophy and Democratic Cooperation), (Cairo, 1961), pp. 19-20.

[46]Michel Aflaq, M'rakat al-Masir al-Wahid (Battle of the Same End), (Beirut, 1959), p. 15.

[47]"al-Mithaq al-Watani; Ahdafuhu, Madmunuhu," (The Nationalist Charter; Aims and Content), al-Majallah al-Masriyyah Li al-Ulum al-Siyasiyyah, No. 12 (March 1962), pp. 90-91.

moments of national crisis; invariably this has meant an anti-Western trend in one country or another.

But the existence of the Communist movement in the Middle East cannot be explained simply in negative arguments. The theory of class struggle has been replaced with the theory of struggle against Western imperialism, and certain rigid dogmas have been twisted and bent out of shape to fit the local situation. Marxist hostility to religion has been tactically postponed. Manfred Halpern is of the opinion that such a postponement is deliberate till the Communists take control of the state. To conduct a frontal attack on religion now would mean the Communists would deprive themselves of mass support while they still need it.[48] Many observers of the scene view the greatest attraction to communism as a result of certain similarities between the communist dogma and the religion of Islam. Both, it is said, are "absolute and universal . . . puritan . . . filled with missionary zeal and spiritual fervor, and demand submission of the individual to the community and complete devotion." The analogy goes on to point to a similarity in their dislike for schismatics, differentiation between just and unjust wars; both have their saints, heretics, and deviationists.[49] Bernard Lewis emphasizes the authoritarianism inherent in both systems and adds, "A community brought up on such doctrines will not be shocked by Communist disregard of political liberty or human rights . . . "[50] Of the traditional *ulema* whose Sunni tradition of submission to authority did not prevent them, frequently, from leading revolt against an unjust ruler, Bernard Lewis has them sum up the communist creed as "There is no God and Karl Marx is his Prophet."[51] In part, at least, this is a superficial analysis. True, on the surface, the similarities are extensive, but then what can be said of Islamic dogma can be said of other religious dogmas—Catholic, Christian Orthodox, Episcopalian, or Judaic. All monotheistic religions defer to *one* God and his messenger, or messengers. Furthermore, unlike communist dogma, bound up in materialism and an economic straight jacket, Islam's view is both spiritual and social at the same time. Indeed, it is difficult to completely separate the two. Furthermore, Muslims value religion as part of their historical heritage; *i.e.*, in addition to religious affiliations, a heritage which they cherish, love, and idealize. Moreover, Marxism considers religion an opium and, in principle, rejects and disparages the past.

It is possible that the three greatest elements behind the existence of communism in the Middle East are: the anti-Western sentiment, the instability of the regimes, and the rise of the Soviet Union as a model to be emulated and as a source of aid as well. The anti-colonial-Western sentiment came at about the

---

[48]*Op. cit.*, p. 157.

[49]In *ibid.*, p. 157. See also Bernard Lewis, "Communism and Islam," in W. Z. Laqueur, ed., *The Middle East in Transition*, (New York, 1958), pp. 311-324.

[50]Lewis, *op. cit.*, p. 319.

[51]*Ibid:* p. 321. See the excellent study on the *ulema* by Afaf L. el Sayed, "The Ulema in Egypt during the Early Nineteenth Century," in *Political and Social Change in Modern Egypt*, ed. by P. M. Holt, (London, 1968), pp. 264-280.

same time as colonial retreat. Today's anti-Western sentiment is motivated by the past memories of bitter and treacherous experiences. It is also motivated by the fear that while the West has retreated physically, *i.e.*, Western powers no longer insist on military bases and troops in the country, their colonialism has taken a new shape. Neo-colonialism, it is argued, is couched in aid agreements with strings, in mutual defense agreements like the Middle East Defense Organization of the early 1950s, the Baghdad Pact, and the Eisenhower Doctrine. For the Arabs, the creation of Israel by the Western powers is viewed as a very real evidence of Western insistence on maintaining their hegemony in the region. On the other hand, with the exception of the Turks and Iranians, the peoples of the Middle East have had little experience with the Soviet Union. Warnings of "Soviet imperialist" designs ring hollow; the real danger has always come from the West. A short-sighted view, but one that is real.

The Soviet Union in propaganda directed to the underdeveloped world emphasizes its achievements over a short period of time. No one can deny this impressive achievement, and the Middle Easterners, eager for "instant modernization," are dazzled by the terrific advancement. In their eagerness they may forget the price paid by the Russian peasant and worker to achieve that progress. Should a particular model be adopted at all, it will not necessarily be an exact replica of the Soviet model, but only a variation. Middle Easterners, from Muhammad Ali of Egypt to Kemal Ataturk to Gamal Abdul Nasser, have always been careful to select only certain aspects to be copied—never the total system. While the Soviet model may serve as an inspiration, the Middle Eastern peoples and their intellectuals do not seem ready yet to denounce their heritage, their way of life, and their religion and espouse Communism alone. The Middle East intelligentsia, still puzzled by the speedy decay of certain aspects of their life and emotionally frustrated by the terrific onslaught of "Westernization," may espouse a variation of one authoritarian regime or another. Emotionally as well as psychologically they have rejected and will continue to reject total submission to an alien system. The Soviet Union's entrance into the Middle East following World War II was just as unceremonious and unwelcome as that of any outside power attempting to dominate another. Their "republic" in north Iran speedily collapsed once they withdrew, and their pressure on Turkey (and Greece) caused the American giant to retaliate with the Truman Doctrine. Once the Soviet Union entered the thorny field of Arab politics after 1955 it encountered the same difficulties and frustrations that any other power would have.

Even in the Arab world proper where governmental instability was supposed to enhance Soviet penetration, this has not happened. While military juntas may flirt with the "bear" all have shunned his embrace. They seem to value their independence more than they have been given credit for. Soviet aid, both military and economic, has certainly been a factor in Middle Eastern politics. Syria, the United Arab Republic, and lately even Iran and Turkey have partaken of this source of "unattached" aid. The people receiving aid no doubt have welcomed it and will continue to do so as long as the Soviet Union accepts the fact of their desire to be independent. Middle Eastern regimes, Arab regimes in particular, have always made a distinction between local Communist parties which they have continuously and vigorously suppressed, and their relations with the Soviet Union. The Soviet Union realizes, as does everyone else, that governmental suppression of the local Communist parties has been a terrific handicap to their growth. When Khrushchev attempted to interfere on behalf of the local Communists, Nasser's reply was quick, sharp, and definitely negative. The Middle Eastern attachment to their independence has indeed been a great barrier to Communist expansion.

There is no doubt that since World War II, Middle Eastern peoples have been asking for a more positive role from their governments internally while at the same time extricating themselves from Western ties externally. For most Western observers this seemed a leftward motion and is invariably explained in terms of Soviet influence, expansion, or the appeal of communist dogma. Such rationale is particularly appropriate, it is reasoned, in the case of the Arabs. It seems to escape most Western analysts that it is not the Soviet Union's appeal, nor the literal communist dogma that is attractive, but the negative fact that the Communist movement is in opposition to the West, and that it can be used as a lever against Western hegemony. Thus, communism is attractive to some only as an alternative, a political and social alternative to the frustrations from within, as well as a lever to the external threat. Arab nationalism and Arab socialism have mitigated the growth of the Communist parties in the Arab world. Both offer an alternative that seems more attractive than this foreign dogma. Both emphasize their indigenous nature and that they are a response to local needs, rather than a cold blueprint imported from abroad. In Turkey and Iran local nationalism, social reform, and economic progress were strengthened by real fear from their northern neighbor. In all these countries the dominant desire has been how to achieve progress and modernization. The response, not surprisingly, has been the birth of a local ideology. These local ideologies are a hybrid of various Western systems of thought, including Marxism, and the native culture, religion and heritage. Their hybrid nature makes them more appealing, for along with the scientific, modern, and technical arguments are also advanced arguments about "our" great cultural heritage and "our" glorious past. This combination of the scientific and the romantic, the scientist and the poet, has been thus far too difficult to be overcome by the Communists.

Considering the fact that the Communist movement has been operating in the Middle East since the 1920s, its record has been far from impressive. Communist following is still very small and exceedingly divided into various factions. Factionalism within has been an endemic disease of the Communist parties which they have not been able to overcome. As a result, their numbers have either remained static or in some cases have diminished. While numbers are never a satisfactory barometer of Communist strength, they do offer an idea of its support. The accompanying table indicates their numerical strength.

Middle East Countries and Their
Communist Party Membership*

Country	Number of Members	Percent of Working-Age Population
Iran	1,500	.015
Iraq	15,000	.474
Israel	2,000	.156
Jordan	500	N.A.
Labanŏn	3,000	N.A.
Libya	Nil	.000
Morocco	1,250	.017
Saudi Arabia	Negligible	N.A.
Sudan	2,500	.382
Syria	4,000	.190
Turkey	1,000	.007
U.A.R.	1,000	N.A.
Yemen	Negligible	N.A.

*Source: U. S. Department of State, Bureau of Intelligence and Research, *World Strength of the Communist Party Organizations* (January 1965). The entire table can be found in R. W. Benjamin & J. H. Kautsky, "Communism and Economic Development," *The American Political Science Review,* Vol. LXII, No. 1 (March 1968), p. 122.

As the above table indicates, neither in absolute numbers nor in percentages where these are available are the Communist parties strong. Communist strength has been largely restricted to a small element in the cities and has not yet seriously attempted to reach the countryside. Its adherents, a few dedicated souls, remain to live on the fringe of political events and away from the mainstream of public sentiments. If Communist appeal is at all a serious matter it is not because of the actual strength it presently displays but in its potential, its long term potential to attract more adherents in societies in the process of economic, political, and social development. In the Middle East, one cannot simply explain it in terms of economic development or psychological and emotional factors alone; one has to probe deeper into all modes of human experience and existence.

SOCIALISM

The Middle Eastern Socialist movement of the 1950s and the 1960s is a protest movement against the terrible conditions of the common man, the stagnant economics, and the backward social, economic, and political order that prevail. In Turkey and Iran in the second and third decades of this century a conscious attempt was made by Mustafa Kemal Ataturk and Reza Shah to change the existing order by fiat from above, a palace revolution that only incidentally involved the masses though it was to benefit them indirectly. The revolution from above was slower in reaching the Arab world, but here too, when it finally arrived it shook the social order at its roots. The Middle East entered the 20th century fettered with a stagnant traditionalism that stifled innovation and progress. Ataturk's view was to shed Islam and to secularize the state in the hope that reason and traditional Western liberal thought would enable the new Turkey to catch up to the parade of progress. Kemalist ideology adopted reform rather than revolution as a vehicle for achieving modernity. It was a mass party dictatorship, dominated by the urban intelligentsia and the bourgeoisie, that only partly came to grips with the terrific problems facing Turkey. With 80 percent of the population living in rural areas, the urban ideology was doomed to failure before it began. The Kemalist faith in liberal parliamentary institutions having been given a terrific shock in 1960 and the abortive coup of 1962, it is still too early to predict whether the return to parliamentarian-reform gradualism will succeed. By the mid-1950s the intelligentsia's faith in democracy had been shattered although the intelligentsia still hopes to salvage the spirit of Ataturk's reforms.[52] State control and an emphasis on the state's political rather than economic responsibility was the legacy of Ataturk to his heirs, some of whom, especially Ismet Inonu and Recep Peker, followed it carefully.[53] The Democratic party which came to power in the 1950s was no more successful in instituting the necessary economic reforms than the Republican, its predecessor. The hanging of Prime Minister Menderes in 1961 by a "clearly unconstitutional, military tribunal"[54] emphasized the weakness and perhaps death of liberal institutions.

There is no doubt that the greatest danger to Ataturk's reforms has been due to the obviously large gap between the rulers-intelligentsia and the masses. No serious attempt has been made to bridge this gap, and it is not unlikely that should this gulf remain, a return to military dictatorship will result. The support to the Justice and the New Turkey parties, formed as they were from the ashes of the Democratic party, underlines the inherent danger to the democratic evolutionary reformist republic.

While Turkish nationalism always emphasized its ideological content, its Iranian counterpart never made such claims or pretensions. Iran's introduction to modernity in the 20th century came not as a result of a reformist ideology or leader, but haltingly and hesitantly according to the whim and decree of the Shah. Turkey's "revolution from above" had Kemalist ideology as a frame of reference; Iran's had only *Pahlevism*, a sometimes benevolent dictatorship with no frame of reference and no ideology.[55] Its *raison d'être* many argue is how to maintain and retain power. Haltingly reforms were introduced here and there,

---

[52]See Kemal H. Karpat, "Recent Political Developments in Turkey," in B. Rivlin & Szyliowicz, ed., *The Contemporary Middle East* (New York, 1965), pp. 485 and 487. See also Frederick W. Frey, *The Turkish Political Elite* (Boston, 1965). Chapter 7 (below) on Turkey by Professor Walter Weiker advances a contrary view and a different interpretation.

[53]Kemal Karpat, *Turkey's Politics* (Princeton, 1959), pp. 72-73.

[54]Richard D. Robinson, *The First Turkish Republic* (Cambridge, 1963), p. 268.

[55]See the excellent article by R. H. Pfaff, "Disengagement from Traditionalism in Turkey and Iran," in Rivlin & Szyliowics, *op. cit.,* pp. 417-428, *passim.*

never on a sustained full-fledged attack, and when the opposition proved too strong no reform was made. Well into the 1960s the religious *mullahs* and the landlords remain to wield considerable power. Unlike Turkey, no secularizing reforms could be instituted, *Shiism* being, as it were, part and parcel of the Iranian national character; thus the retarding influences of a superstitious folk-Islam remain.

Reza Shah's greatest ambition was to imitate Mustafa Kemal in Turkey and to rid Iran of foreign influence. He concentrated on strengthening the army, and his internal reforms were geared for a double role of progress internally and emancipation from foreign influence externally.[56] The internal economic policies were haphazard with little planning or principle behind them. Muhammad Reza Pahlevi's reform policies have been more vigorous and better planned than those of his father. The present Shah's commitment to reform became apparent in 1942 with the distribution of his own lands among the peasants.[57] From the beginning the new Shah was hoping to break the feudal order where about 700 landlords each owned about 10 villages, with some owning about 100 villages. A few landlords owned as many as 300 villages! No doubt the Shah then, as well as now, was attempting to gain the allegiance of the mass of peasantry and reform-minded intelligentsia to offset the rising opposition of the urban areas. The Shah's attempt remains just that, for it is still too early to predict whether it has been or will be a success. Unlike Turkey, where the reform-minded leadership relies on the urban areas, in Iran the traditional support for the Emperor has always been the religious *mullahs* and the absentee landlords. Today, the Shah is attempting to change his base of power to a coalition between a benevolent government and the peasantry. The Shah's "White Revolution," introduced from the throne in 1961, was an expansion of his reform programs, and in November of the same year he dissolved the parliament controlled by the landed aristocracy, asserting that it hindered the passage of reform legislation. The Shah's plans to stabilize a faltering economy, expand it, expand economic opportunity, and institute social justice are still pursued. The Shah has manipulated the *Majlis* (parliament), rigged the elections, and depended greatly on the *Savak*, the secret police. The revolution from the throne, with no ideological basis, is still in progress. Progress and modernization are being effected but without an ideological framework. The Fourth Development Plan, instituted in March 1967, aims at alleviating the low literacy rate of the Iranian people.[58]

In the Arab countries the generation that assumed leadership after World War I was imbued with Western liberal ideas. Parliamentary government based upon a semi-laissez faire economic order. Soon the parliaments were corrupted, the liberal institutions were twisted out of shape to maintain the status quo; a reality

---

[56]See George Lenczowski, *The Middle East in World Affairs,* 3rd ed. (Ithaca, 1962), p. 180.

[57]Donald N. Wilbur, *Contemporary Iran* (New York, 1963), p. 181.

[58]For example, see the article by D. R. Francis, "Iran's Own Steel Plant Runs Full Blast," *The Christian Science Monitor* (October 15, 1968).

of a small land-owning aristocracy, allied with a few rich merchants and a vast number of impoverished, landless, and illiterate masses. Parliaments became facades and vehicles for the upper classes to maintain their power, instead of being vehicles for change and progress. Soon too, the establishment began cooperating with the colonial powers, and liberal thought to the contrary, repression became the mode of government. Slowly but surely, however, a new class was beginning to emerge, the middle class. This class, unable to identify with the establishment with its close ties to the colonial power, began advocating liberal ideas of a different vintage. Hesitantly in the beginning, the idea of social justice, of socialism, began to spread until in the 1950s and after it became the manifest ideology and program of action of a number of Arab governments. The bell tolled the demise of Western liberal style governments with the creation of the State of Israel in 1948. From then on, Arab nationalist ideology has continued its leftward movement.

Post-1948 Arab leaders, nationalists that they are, advocate a total reevaluation of Arab economic and socio-political order. The defeat of 1948 shook their faith in liberal institutions; that of 1967 seems to have damaged whatever survived the first defeat. The military weakness displayed by the Arab armies and governments is no doubt a reflection of a sick society—a society that must be somehow revamped, resurrected. The advocacy of socialist ideology, insistant and consistant after 1948, must be viewed with Arab weakness on the battlefield for a background. President Nasser, the Baath party, the Arab Nationalist Movement, and other parties and groups emphasize that Arab weakness in the 20th century is due to social and economic backwardness internally. The whole social order, the collective, must be infused with new blood, new life. The adoption of socialist ideology called *revolution* by some Arab leaders ushered in a new era, a new faith that the lot of the common man can be bettered here and now; that the improvement of his lot increased national strength, added impetus to the argument. Traditional Western liberal thought taught that man's lot could be bettered with a minimum of government interference, the enlightened man can solve individually his own problem. It can be improved, Arab socialists say, but it is government, and not the person, the collective and not the individual, that must become the agency of change.

The belief in the positive role of government to induce changes is the common denominator that all Arab socialists agree upon. Nasserite, Baathist, Algerian, or Iraqi socialists, as well as a number of other small tributaries along the Arab socialist stream, all adhere to the idea of a vigorous governmental role in the social, economic, and political spheres. Transportation, education, health services, and many other social services in practically all Arab countries have become public. In the progressive socialist countries almost all foreign firms and all large domestic companies have been nationalized, land reform and progressive taxation instituted. The government fosters the growth of cooperative societies in all social and economic fields, labor unions, and other such institutions. In fact, it is difficult to think of a single field of economic activity that the government does not promote or control either partially or totally in some Arab countries.

This description, no doubt, is a far cry from the situation of a decade or two ago, and the reason for this must be sought not in terms of economics alone. To reiterate, the greatest motivation behind the adoption of socialist ideology has not been solely concern for the masses, but the weakness—the terrible weakness—displayed by the Arab world vis-a-vis an advancing and strong West. That is why Arab socialists deny the existence of class struggle. It is not one class against another, but the whole society with all its classes that must be liberated from itself and from an imperialist West.[59] In essence, class struggle is translated into anti-Westernism. In its more immediate manifestations, it is translated into an emphasis on neutralism. A neutrality that is tilted to the left and East.[60] Socialism is neither capitalist nor communist and it does not seem to matter that both ideologies have undergone tremendous change and no longer exist in their classical, theoretical forms. Part of the reason for the rejection of both is nationalistic. In the words of Aflaq, "The Arabs are not like any other nation of secondary" importance. They cannot simply imitate, they must create.[61] Over and over again it is pointed out that socialism then is not adopted for its intrinsic merits or out of genuine concern for the masses but only as a vehicle to regain the lost national greatness and glory. Socialism is not only the social content of the dominant ideology, nationalism, it is of secondary importance to it. This fact stems from the Arabs' self-image as carriers of a mission, in Baath parlance an "eternal mission" to participate in human progress and to contribute towards it. In 1959 Nasser spoke of proving to the "whole world" that the Arab national socialist revival is a constructive force to contribute to all mankind.[62] This belief in a mission stems from the Arabs' feeling of a link between the struggle against local corruption; economic, political, and social stagnation; and their struggle against the remnants of colonial influences.[63]

The theoretical formualtions of Arab socialism are not as complex as one first imagines. Their complexity stems from the fact that there are Socialists in power in some countries, like Syria, Iraq, the United Arab Republic, and Algeria, while other Socialist groups are still in opposition. The difficulty is compounded with the profusion of writings on the topic by various self-styled socialist writers who do not seem to belong to any ostensible socialist school or system. The difficulty in discerning the various Socialist groups is further complicated by the seemingly pragmatic approach Arab Socialists seem to prefer. As one time U.A.R. Minister

[59]See Michel Aflaq, *Ma'rakat al-Masir al-Wahid (Battle of the Same End),* (Beirut, 1959), pp. 29-30, *passim.*

[60]See, for example, Salah al-Din al-Bitar, *al-Siyasah al-Arabiyyah Bain al-Mabda' Wa al-Tatbiq (Arab Policy between Principle and Practice)* (Beirut, 1950).

[61]*Fi Sabail al-Ba'th*, p. 193.

[62]See direct quote in Morroe Berger, *The Arab World Today* (New York, 1962), p. 370.

[63]See Gamal A. Nasser, *The Philosophy of the Revolution* (Buffalo, 1959), p. 36, and G. A. Nasser, *Thawratunah al-Ijtima'iyyah (Our Socialist Revolution),* (Cairo, [n.d.]), pp. 8-10, *passim.*

of State and writer, Muhammad Hatim, put it, "One of the great characteristics of our intellectual and spiritual experience has been [the fact that] we did not get involved in theories searching for our life, but . . . in life searching for theories . . . "[64] Michel Aflaq thinks a socialist theory is not necessary; in fact, he attacks abstract theorizing stating, "Society is a living organic being . . . "[65] that defies abstract analysis and would not submit to cold blueprints. Exposed to new problems, searching for plausible solutions, and lacking influential intellectuals and organizations, in the beginning Arab socialism had to rely on the pragmatic approach. In Egypt where socialism was first applied, and later on in Algeria, practice preceded theory. Only in Iraq and Syria, with the accession of the Baath party since 1963, was theory to precede application.[66] Yet even here the exigencies of the moment compelled a disregard for theory. Theory had to conform to the human and environmental circumstances. Thus the remark that Arab socialism may have come about due to necessity rather than reasoned conviction would seem true.

Writing in 1958 Gebran Majdalany listed two main currents of Arab Socialist thought.[67] The first and most important, according to him, is that of the Arab Baath Socialist party, founded in 1943.[68] This party holds the entire Arab world to be a unity of culture and aspirations and its greatest concern is how to reunify this dismembered unity. Its program of action can best be understood from its slogan "Unity, Liberty and Socialism." The order of the words in this slogan is not haphazard, for unity—a nationalist goal—takes precedence over liberty which might be sacrificed should the need arise, and over socialism which is adopted merely as a social content. The Baath party has deliberately maintained a certain amount of vagueness and imprecision in its polemics. This imprecision, this vagueness in its ideological writing, gives the party greater room for maneuverability and tactics. While it advocates liberty for the individual it subjects him to various restrictions and sacrifices him for the group. As a vanguard party, rather as a party that considers itself the vanguard of the toiling masses, it does not permit opposition to exist. Aflaq does not foresee any clash between the individual and the group. Should such a clash exist, it is due to the individual's confusion of priorities, and Aflaq is merciless in his treatment of such dissidents. "Our mercilessness has for its object to bring them back to their true selves which they ignore, to their hidden will which they have not yet

---

[64]"Ahadfunah al-Ishtirakiyyah 'Ala du' al-Mu'tamar al-Watani Li al-Quwa al-Sha'biy-yah," (Our Socialist Aims in Light of the National Conference of Popular Forces), *al-Majallah al-Masriyyah Li Al-'Ulam al-Siyasiyyah,* No. 12 (March 1962), p. 16.

[65]*Fi Sabil . . . ,* pp. 9-11, *passim.*

[66]The Baath was in power from February to November 1963, when it was overthrown by Muhammad A. Aref. The Baath has been in power again in Iraq since July 1968.

[67]In Walter Z. Laqueur, ed., *The Middle East in Transition* (New York, 1958), p. 337.

[68]For a complete study of the program, ideology, and activity of this party, see my book, *The Arab Ba'th Socialist Party: History, Ideology and Organization,* (Syracuse, 1966).

clearly discerned and which is with us even though their swords are raised against us . . . "[69] In the tradition of Rousseau, he wants to force them to be free.

But then Aflaq is a romantic and his humanistic socialism is more in the tradition of a romantic Latin than a pragmatic Anglo-Saxon or scientific German. The Baath wishes to effect a rebirth of the best qualities of the individual, a resurrection of his true "self." Once such a true rebirth of the individual occurs, clash between him and the group will be immediately eliminated.

The second major current of Arab socialism listed by Majdalany is represented by certain parties and groups which base their action upon the present possibilities. Some, like the Progressive Socialist party of Lebanon, advocate socialism more as a vehicle for the ambitions of its leaders rather than a serious conviction.[70] Of his consideration of this party's leader Kamal Jumblatt, M. Suleiman says in one place he is "an idealist" and later he calls him a man who "has not hesitated to align himself with the political right or left when it suited him," which seems to be a contradiction. The fact is that this party, led by one of the most feudal and sectarian leaders in Lebanon, is no more socialist than any other traditional "personal following" party. Socialism is only a slogan to ward off accusations and to attract some attention from the liberals. The National Socialist party of Jordan, also led by a feudal leader, Suleiman al-Nabulsi, is similar to the Progressive Socialist party of Lebanon. Here too the party and its slogans are only a vehicle for ambitious leaders.

A third major current of Arab socialism not listed by Majdalany is that followed by Egypt and Algeria where the state, faced with terrific economic and social problems, has had to assume a major role in these fields. Unlike Syria and Iraq where the Baath had a developed socialist ideology, here socialism came ex post facto and as a response, a pragmatic response, to the problems of the society. The war of liberation against France left the Algerian economy with terrific problems. As late as November 1967, some observers wrote of the formidable underemployment and unemployment. "Half the labor force is jobless and of the 1.5 million Algerians officially considered to be 'employed', one-third works only 50 to 100 days a year. Perhaps most serious, there are virtually no jobs for an ever growing pool of trained manpower, and university graduates are frequently forced to take to menial work."[71] While the above quote overexaggerates the problems Algeria still faces, it does give an idea of the problems yet to be faced. The 1963 Constitution which professed Islam as the national religion also committed Algeria to a socialist program.[72] Domestically, land reform was instituted as well as the nationalization of all foreign trade and

---

[69] Aflaq, *Fi Sabil*, p. 103.

[70] A contradictory view to mine will be found in M. Suleiman, *Political Parties in Lebanon* (Ithaca, 1968), pp. 213-232.

[71] *Newsweek* (November 13, 1967), p. 52.

[72] See Richard M. Brace, *Morocco, Algeria & Tunisia* (Englewood Cliffs, 1964), p. 160.

certain domestic enterprises. With little experience, no ideological frame of reference, and a terrific commitment to raising the standard of living, Ben Bella proceeded on a program of nationalization that included individual movie theaters and hairdressers' shops! The great problems—initial lack of well-trained people to manage the nationalized industries, failure to fully implement the agrarian reform, and the failure of self-management in industry to raise production—added more problems. Furthermore, Ben Bella vacillated between several alternatives: to become an African, pan-Arab, or anticolonial leader. Domestically, he hesitated between Islamic and scientific socialisms.

Ben Bella's commitment to fight colonialism and his avowed aim to help struggling peoples in their fight against colonialism added more problems. In 1965 just before the meeting of African leaders in Algiers, he was toppled and replaced with Colonel Houari Boumedienne, an austere blue-eyed, red-headed bachelor, who had been stressing domestic development before international engagements. Boumedienne's first concerns were how to insure governmental stability, how to decentralize authority, and finally how to provide cogent economic development programs.[73] Boumedienne has stressed what he calls *Algerian* socialism "which will spring from the people, its past, its history, and its civilization . . . "[74] Boumedienne has effected a partial retreat from the near-total nationalization program of Ben Bella and has returned small business to private ownership. He has tried to decentralize state-owned farms, and has nationalized all foreign mines and oil companies. In 1968 one observer stated that Boumedienne's brand of "state capitalism" appears to have established the basis for an industrial economy.[75] Boumedienne's ideological orientation seems to the right of that of his predecessor, and he has been attempting to concentrate on solving his country's domestic problems. He is primarily a nationalist, a pragmatic nationalist who sees little use for extravagant theorizing, and has encouraged, sought, and received closer economic cooperation with France.[76]

In the United Arab Republic, too, socialist practice preceded theory. In fact, and as stated earlier, some Egyptian socialists disparaged theorizing as a waste of time and effort. Society responds to real needs at any given historical moment, and not to a predetermined theoretical program. Of the movement in general, Hans Tutsch says, "Socialism in this part of the world is merely a label covering all sorts of government intervention. There is hardly any serious study of socialist doctrine . . . "[77] The abundance of Arabic writing on socialism today has refuted this observation as too hasty and superficial. Since World War II, Arab nationalists have been preoccupied with socialist ideology as a content to national ideology. Like Baath Socialists, Egyptian Socialists too have rejected

---

[73] *The New York Times,* Sec. 4 (January 16, 1966).

[74] Arslan Humbaraci, *Algeria, A Revolution that Failed* (London, 1966), p. 248.

[75] *The New York Times* (January 26, 1968).

[76] Humbaraci, *op. cit.,* p. 244. See also P. Braestrup & D. Ottoway, "In Algeria, It's Not Yah, Yah, Boumedienne, but Wait and See," *The New York Times Magazine* (February 13, 1966).

[77] In Laqueur, ed., *The Middle . . . ,* p. 23.

both capitalism and communism and emphasize socialism; their socialism is a median between the two.[78] Since 1952, President Nasser's consuming energy has been directed toward how to achieve social justice and how to institute it. Until 1961, he attempted cooperation with domestic capitalists in order to achieve some progress. These mistrusted his motives, and social and economic progress was not as extensive as Nasser had hoped. The 1961 nationalization decrees were not simply an attempt by the state to raise capital. They went far beyond that, for Nasser realized that only through the application of a socialistic program can the backward domestic conditions be alleviated.[79] From then on Nasser has been committed to a radical social program and has succeeded in widening his base of support to include the underprivileged masses of Egypt.

The National Charter (al-Mithaq al-Watani) of 1962, as well as Nasser's reorganization speech of March 31, 1968, emphasize a new base of support for the Egyptian socialist revolution. It is to include five categories: the intelligentsia, national capital, soldiers, workers, and peasants. Nasser's emphasis on these classes does not mean, Egyptian Socialists hasten to defend, that his socialism is for the benefit of some classes over others. Nasser's socialism is to bridge the gap between classes and narrow it until a classless society emerges.[80] He is attempting to achieve a society where social mobility is a reality and where the rigid class structure that Egypt once knew will be completely obliterated. The 1964 Constitution attempts to put these lofty ideas into practice.[81] The difficulties are numerous and many of these ideals are yet to be realized.

A discussion of the particular elements of any or all of the brands of Arab socialism mentioned above would go beyond the scope of this paper. It is evident though that all Arab Socialists have come to reject political democracy as the sole legitimate justification for their societies. What they are demanding now is a certain measure of political democracy and equal opportunity for all the citizens. The rejection of traditional Western liberal thought was soon replaced by the emphasis on the hegemony of one powerful party. There is a need to combine all the national effort to solve "our" societal problems. Multiple parties are too divisive and a luxury that cannot be afforded at this time. In practice, however, the state becomes the principal vehicle for achieving or instituting the desired reforms. The hopeless weaknesses of Arab society vis-a-vis the rest of the world, and especially the Western world and Israel, has forced the majority of Arabs to become preoccupied with national political problems. As further evidence of the weaknesses of the Arab world unfolds with each encounter with

---

[78]See Abdul Qadir Hatim, *Hawl al-Nazariyyah al-Ishtira Kiyyah (Concerning Socialist Theory)*, (Cairo, 1959), p. 32. A much later article expresses the same view. See R. al-Mahjub, "al-Tajribah al-Ishtirakiyyah F; al-Jumhuriyyah al-Arabiyyah al-Muttahidah," (Socialist Experiment in the United Arab Republic), *Dirasat Arabiyyah*, Vol. II, No. 10 (August 1966), p. 26.

[79]See Malcolm H. Kerr, "The Emergency of Socialist Ideology in Egypt," *The Middle East Journal*, Vol. 16, No. 2 (Spring 1962), p. 131.

[80]See al-Mahjub, *op. cit.*, p. 37.

[81]See George Massannat, "Nasser's Search for New Order," *The Muslim World*, LVI, No. 2 (1966), pp. 87-95, *passim*.

Israel, Arab politics further radicalizes. Since the defeat of June 1967, younger and more frustrated Socialists, ideologies of a different and more doctrinaire ilk, have emerged. They all argue that the "older" Socialists, the Baathists, the Nasserites . . . etc. are too bourgeois, too conservative, and too timid. They argue that they have utterly failed to heal the domestic ills of Arab society and have not been able to prevent Israel from further expansion. Like the pre-1948 Arab leaders, these too have failed and must be replaced. These younger revolutionaries argue for a truly popular and highly action-committed, not word-committed, regime. "Socialist" republics, this younger set argues, should be transformed into "peoples" republics. The defeat of 1967 and the stagnation—economic, political, and social—of Arab society that followed has given impetus to a more radical approach.

The Socialist or reformist movement in the Middle East came as a response to the challenges of the modern age. Societies that had for centuries languished in the belief of their supposed superiority awoke to the reality of a bitter weakness. Shocked by the bitter reality, they did not hesitate to shed many aspects of their traditional life and to accept alien thought. Having come on the heels of the failure of Western liberal thought, socialism was bound to be radical. Moreover, unlike the Western experience, in the Middle East socialism came after, not before, the spread of communism. Thus, as a reaction to this communist ideology, further elements of radicalization were introduced. Nebulous a concept as it may be, socialism provides the reformers with the power to act and with the ideological justification for their action.

SELECTED BIBLIOGRAPHY

Despite certain limitations George Antonius's Book *The Arab Awakening* (London, 1938) remains a most valuable source on the early Arab nationalist era. For background and an incisive treatment into earlier Arab thought, Ibrahim Abu Lughod, *The Arab Rediscovery of Europe* is necessary. H. Z. Nusseibeh, *The Ideas of Arab Nationalism* (Ithaca: Cornell, 1956) and S. G. Haim, *Arab Nationalism: an Anthology* (Berkeley: California, 1962) are very useful. The Arabic literature on the topic is extensive and readily available. Historical studies and studies dealing with particular aspects of Middle East politics in Western languages have increased greatly in the last decade. Of particular significance is Manfred Halpern's *The Politics of Social Change in the Middle East and North Africa,* (Princeton N.J.: Princeton U., 1963). Bernard Lewis, *The Emergence of Modern Turkey* (New York: Oxford, 1961) and Kemal Karpat, *Turkey's Politics* (Princeton N.J.: Princeton U., 1959), are very important. Leonard Binder, *Iran: Political Development in a Changing Society* (Berkeley: U. of California, 1962) and Donald N. Wilbur, *Contemporary Iran* (New York: 1963) are good studies. Studies on communism, socialism and political parties are few and far-between. Again L. Binder's *The Ideological Revolution in the Middle East* (New York: Wiley, 1964), and Hisham Sharabi, *Nationalism and Revolution in the Arab*

World (Princeton N.J.: Nostrand, 1966) are a good beginning. Mr. Suleiman, *Political Parties in Lebanon* (Ithaca N.Y.: Cornell, 1967) deals with the range of ideas existing in Lebanon. I. M. Husaini, *The Muslim Brethren* (Beirut: Khayat's, 1956), Kamel S. Abu Jaber, *The Arab Ba'th Socialist Party, History, Ideology and Organization* (Syracuse N.Y.: Syracuse U., 1966) and Labib Z. Yamak, *The Syrian Social Nationalist Party* (Cambridge: Harvard, 1967) are in-depth studies of political movements in the Middle East that are absolutely necessary for the study of ideology in the area. Walter Z. Laquer's studies, *Communism and Nationalism in the Middle East* (New York: Praeger, 1956), and *The Middle East in Transition* (New York: Praeger, 1958) are indispensable.

Of particular interest for the study of modernization in the Middle East are a number of anthologies. William R. Polk and Richard L. Chambers, ed., *Beginnings of Modernization in the Middle East; the Nineteenth Century* (Chicago: The University of Chicago Press, 1968); Sydney Nettleton Fisher, ed., *Social Forces in the Near East* (Ithaca: Cornell University Press, 1955); Walter Z. Laquer's, ed., *The Middle East in Transition* (New York: Praeger, 1958); and Richard H. Nolte, *The Modern Middle East* (New York: Atherton, 1961) are all excellent works. Of more recent vintage are Jack H. Thompson and Robert D. Reischauer, *Modernizing the Arab World* (Princeton, 1966). The problem of economic development is thoroughly explored by Taghi T. Kermani, *Economic Development in Action: Theories, Problems, and Procedures as Applied in the Middle East* (New York: c. 1967).

chapter 6

The Challenge of Modernization

Even the casual observer is readily aware that the Middle East is in a state of political, economic, and social flux. The common upheavals of government, the proliferating problems of massive oil wealth versus mass poverty, the constant tensions of urban stress, and, indeed, the ubiquitous manifestations of nationalisms are all symptoms of a transitional process occurring in the Middle East. But transition from what to what? And if these are but symptoms, then what are the causes? Who are affected and how? And finally, what will be the outcome?

These are the questions we shall investigate in this chapter. They are not all answerable; and none are answered simply. For the process of social change occurring in the Middle East and in many other developing areas throughout the world is so complex, so diversified, and so imperfectly understood that even social scientists are unsure of its nature, its causes, or its effects. Yet, imperfect as our present knowledge is, this chapter should introduce the student to this underlying phenomena essential to an understanding of the Middle East.*

MODERNIZATION DELIMITED

Our first task is to define or at least delimit the process of transition under discussion. Social change, typically defined as an alteration in the beliefs, values, cognitions, and institutions of peoples, is certainly not a new phenomena to the Middle East. Through several millenia the Middle East has experienced successive civilizations, successive foreign invasions, and successive religions (or modifications of existing religious beliefs). Each of these shifts, along with many other internal and external forces, has entailed an adaptive process including

---

*Because modernization in Israel is a special case, Israel has been excluded from this discussion.

100

alteration of the beliefs, values, cognitions, and institutions of the area's diverse peoples.

Modernity

The present process of social change, however, differs markedly from past experiences. That is, the changes occurring are specifically a reaction to the demands made upon social systems by the unprecedented progress in material culture, especially since World War II. It is now possible to mass-produce almost any product, to harness nuclear power, to travel to the moon. It is possible to eliminate poverty, to educate universally, to eradicate completely. It is all of the possibilities of science, technology, and industry combined that have altered our sociology and have brought upon us the modern age.

The modern age, or modernity, does offer man incomparable choices—moral, social, and personal—never before available or comprehensible. David E. Apter, a pioneer in the study of modernization, regards this acceptance of choice as the earmark of modernity: "To be modern means to see life as alternatives, preferences, and choices."[1] And where this limitless range of choice is available to man individually and collectively, a society's attitudes, values and institutions, a people's way of life, must be able to sustain constant and often rapid modification, invention, and innovation—the effects of self-conscious choice.

Of course, modernity manifests itself differently in each society, depending upon historical, environmental, cultural, and other mediating influences. Generally speaking, however, those societies that social scientists assess as modern—the United States, the USSR, Britain, Germany, France, Japan—maintain some similarities in varying degrees that seem to be functionally critical for modernity. These include secularization of beliefs, a sense of mastery over nature, universalistic norms of conduct, and impersonal systems of evaluation. In addition, there are some common structural characteristics which include rationalization of work, functional specifity, and structural differentiation and interdependence.

Traditionalism

Modernity is indeed a way of life. And the concepts, techniques, and institutions necessary for modernity have developed in the Western world over a period of centuries. According to Daniel Lerner "Western men need only reflect on the titanic struggles whereby . . . medieval lifeways were supplanted by modernity. Hindsight now summarizes these struggles as The Age of Exploration, The Renaissance, The Reformation, The Counter-Reformation, The Industrial Revolution."[2] But for the peoples of the Middle East, as for the bulk

---

[1] David E. Apter, *The Politics of Modernization* (Chicago, Ill., 1965), p. 10.

[2] Daniel Lerner, *The Passing of Traditional Society: Modernizing The Middle East* (Glencoe, Ill., 1958), p.43.

of mankind, modernity is a recent challenge. These nonmodern societies—the traditional societies—have developed through the course of centuries different concepts, techniques, and institutions in response to demands different from those made on the West. And whereas modernity requires continuous modification, invention, and innovation for political, economic, and social stability, the traditional society to ensure stability has required a static organization.

This static tendency is the essential characteristic of traditionalism in comparison to modernity. The traditional societies contain no mechanisms for continuous change and therefore find difficulty in meeting the dynamic strains of modernity. And in spite of the apparent vigor of traditional Islamic society—the pervasive way of life in the Middle East for some 1300 years—it has been on the whole static. Manfred Halpern, an eminent scholar of Middle Eastern studies, has said that traditional Islam "bound orthodox and heretic, scholastic and mystic, ruler and people in a single connected system of roles, values, orientations, and action. The combinations possible within that system were varied and unstable, but the system itself left play for all these uncertainties within rigidly defined patterns. It was a system in constant motion, like a prayer wheel, yet always anchored in the same place."[3]

Of course, change—often rapid—has occurred in traditional Islamic society. David E. Apter explains, however, that in traditional societies, "innovation—that is, extrasystemic action—has to be mediated within the social system and linked with antecedent values." Modernity, on the other hand, "presupposes a much more remote relationship between antecedent values and new goals."[4]

Like modernity, traditionalism manifests itself differently in each society, but certain attributes (contrasting sharply with the characteristic functional and structural elements of modern societies) appear to be common to most static societies including, of course, that of traditional Islam. These may be summarized as a lack of structural differentiation, a tendency toward functional diffuseness, particularistic norms, and determinations of status by ascriptive considerations. The contrast generally becomes apparent in analysis of the functioning of the family or clan unit typical of traditional societies. Since no great variety of separate structures for the performance of various tasks exists, a given person may perform a number of functions in the society; leadership and usually membership in the clan or family are hereditary or dependent upon other ascriptive considerations (membership in a particular kinship, age, or sex group). Rules and norms of conduct will typically differ with the roles within the society—as between members and nonmembers of the family unit. A cogent example of this ascriptive accordance of status on a particularistic basis is the *millet* system utilized by the Ottoman Empire. While most modern societies fail

---

[3]Manfred Halpern, *The Politics of Social Change in the Middle East and North Africa* (Princeton, 1963), p. 22.

[4]Apter, *op. cit.*, p. 83.

to differentiate between members of religious communities in their legal codes, under the millet system each religious community was subject to its own code of religious law administered by its own courts.

These functional and structural differences arise from the different patterns of life within the two types of societies. Whereas in the traditional society modernity's lifeways are organized around secularization, commercialization, industrialization, urbanization, education, and mass participation explain the authors of *The Emerging Nations*, "more than 75 percent of the population [live] ... in the countryside and less than 10 percent [are] literate. The round of life is tied to the rhythm of the harvests and to the narrow local scene; to a traditional system of land tenure and the assumption that life for the children and grandchildren is likely to be much as it is and has been in living memory. Social life is built around a close family; traditional political and social relations, long sanctioned by custom, tend to be passively accepted. The government is likely to seem a remote and distant entity associated with extraction of taxes and arbitrary recruitment of sons for military service; and the concept of the nation may often hardly exist."[5]

Modernization

How the traditional societies of the Middle East are adapting to modernity—the process of modernization—is the aspect of social change with which we are concerned. It is not necessarily a change for the better; modernization is not synonymous with progress; modernity is not Utopia; and modern societies are not without deep-rooted and far-reaching problems. Rather, modernity is a new type of challenge to traditional society: a challenge not before available or attainable to individual and collective responsibility in a comprehensible and manipulatable world. But although modernity is now a *fait accompli* in many states, it may not be successfully attained in the Middle East. For modernity is a way of life, and the process of modernization involves a total transformation of traditional society—"a change in what men believe, how men act, and how men relate to each other."[6]

Thus, while the material benefits of modernity are desired by all mankind and have created a "revolution of rising expectations" throughout the world, the attempt to modernize is accompanied by tension and resistance at every level of traditional Islamic society. Patterns of life, long sanctioned by religion and custom, are not easily altered. And even when the traditional structure no longer works to a society's satisfaction "secular enlightenment does not easily replace sacred revelation."[7]

---

[5] Max F. Millikan and Donald L.M. Blackmer, *The Emerging Nations* (Boston, 1961), p. 22.

[6] Halpern, *op. cit.*, p. 3.

[7] Lerner, *op. cit.*, p. 43.

But that traditional Islamic society could not meet the "revolution of rising expectations" set into motion by modern alternatives—to agricultural poverty; to social, economic, and political immobility; to cultural stagnation; to economic inertia; to political irresponsibility; to foreign intervention—is precisely why modernization has ensued in the Middle East. According to Robert E. Ward and Dankwart A. Rustow, "A society as a whole cannot engage in modernization without accepting it, on balance, as beneficial."[8] The process, in other words, is not spontaneous or inevitable. The attempt to fuse traditional structures into a modern framework is a conscious effort that occurred first in limited sectors of traditional Islamic society, such as the military and the bureaucracy. Once the modernization process was set into motion, however, the traditional Islamic structure, already weakened by internal and external tensions, proved unable to adapt effectively. The result has been a dislocation of traditional Middle Eastern society. And because the spread of modernization has been uneven and incomplete, the process has "served to undermine old institutions more effectively than it has yet initiated the effective development of new ones."[9]

The Middle East is indeed in a state of flux. In places, new and old exist together and in tension; in other areas, the old is gone but has not been replaced. There are traditional and modern attitudes, traditional and modern institutions, and traditional and modernizing states juxtaposed and to some extent counteractive in the contemporary Middle East.

MANIFESTATIONS OF MODERNIZATION

At the beginning of this chapter we raised the question who is affected by modernization and how. This question serves here to remind us that, although we will be examining the manifestations of modernization primarily through institutions, we are still talking about people—what they believe, how they act, and how they relate to each other. A *sine qua non* of social change is individual adjustment and "the paramount requirement for the modernization of any society is that the people themselves must change."[10] The drama of modernization, then, works itself out through millions of individual lives and "induces different dilemmas of personal choice."[11] A nomad in Saudi Arabia must choose between his precarious life of freedom and a stable life of circumscription; a fellah in Egypt must choose between rural poverty and urban insecurity; a college graduate in Turkey must choose between religious piety and secular fermentation. Indeed, for most individuals in the Middle East the tension between tradition and innovation imposes itself, in some form, upon the pattern

---

[8] Robert E. Ward and Dankwart A. Rustow, *Political Modernization in Japan and Turkey* (Princeton, 1964), p. 7.

[9] Halpern, *op. cit.*, p. 37.

[10] Millikan and Blackmer, *op. cit.*, p. 23.

[11] Lerner, *op. cit.*, p. 44.

of life, while traditional Islamic society seeks an accommodation with modernity.

certain common values and procedures and meeting certain basic needs of society, are merely the parameters of such change. They reveal measurable and quantifiable evidence of collective human behavior and reflect the tension and upheaval suffered by individuals in a changing cultural milieu. By examining the manifestations of modernization, then, through social, economic, and political institutions—the three general areas of relatively differentiated behavior—we are in effect (if indirectly) answering our question of "who are affected and how."

Social Institutions

Sociologists consider the basic social institutions of any society to be the family, religion, education, economics, and politics. Merely for convenient reference, we have called the nonpolitical and noneconomic institutions social institutions. In discussing the manifestations of modernization within social institutions we will consider only the family, religion, and education. Of course, this by no means encompasses all of the nonpolitical and noneconomic institution of traditional Islamic society. The role and status of women, social stratification, and law (to mention only several) are some of the changing institutions not taken into account primarily because of considerations of space and complexity. By examining some of the characteristics of change in these three most basic social institutions, however, we will see the extent to which the traditional pattern of Middle Eastern life is undergoing modification.

It should be remembered, too, that the classification of institutions as social, political, or economic is often quite difficult, for the institutions of traditional Islamic society are highly integrated. The family, for example, is generally the basic economic unit of rural agricultural areas; the political institutions have revolved, and in some instances still do, around the extended family, that is, the tribe; and religious mores and traditional legal codes support the structure of family organization. Similarly, education, which typically has been a religious function, is now a political function in most Middle Eastern states. The roles, beliefs, and values emanating from one institution, in other words, interact with the relationships within and among other institutions to form an integrated whole out of the many structures that channel behavior within society. And one of the primary results of modernization in the Middle East has been to disturb this balance of reciprocal relationships and in so doing to disrupt the social structure.

The Family. As the primary instrument in the formation of the individual personality, the family is a key institution in any society and is a universal attribute of all known social systems. There is, however, considerable variety in the form taken by the family. The typical traditional Islamic family, with certain exceptions, is patrilineal consanguine, patrilocal, monogamous (although polygyny was permitted), and paternal. That is, descent is reckoned in the male line and based upon all persons in the line of descent rather than upon a single conjugal unit; the sons bring their wives to their father's house; each son generally has one wife (for reasons of economy); and the father or eldest male is usually the chief authority of the family. This extended family evolved into clans and tribes and has been the chief unit of organization in Islamic society.

During the process of modernization, the family, along with other institutions, has been modified. These modifications are primarily based upon shifts in the function of the family caused by a changing configuration of social, economic, and political institutions. The changing functions of the family are largely an effect of the changing bases of Middle Eastern economies and politics. Urbanization and industrialization tend to displace family enterprises and small capitalists and to replace them with larger units of production. Even in agriculture, the formation of collective farms and, on the other hand, the dismantling of large estates have diminished the importance of the family in the economy. As industry begins to hire and classify workers on a skill basis, and as the personal aspect diminishes in agriculture, clan and family organization becomes less important as units of production. As consumption units, moreover, the nuclear family[12] is coming to overshadow the extended family. This is largely because urbanization and increasing mobility have tended to separate members from the larger group.

In much the same way, increasing mobility and industrial organization have modified the welfare functions of the family. Government agencies now take much of the responsibility for the care of the sick, aged, crippled, or very young—a responsibility once taken by the family. This freedom from responsibility has further increased the mobility of younger family members and strengthened the nuclear family at the expense of the extended family. Education and religious instruction are now also less functions of the family than of outside agencies, and this diminishes the family's ability to socialize its children in traditional ways. The fact that younger members often have a more modern education tends to divide the family and to bring the authority of the father into question.

The tendency in the Middle East seems to be toward a more equalitarian,[13] more democratic[14] family, although the change is not consistently rapid. This may mean that modern values will become increasingly acceptable to successive generations, just as national loyalties may be stronger for those who have not been raised in the extended family.

Religion. The definitive characteristic of religious institutions is that they give form and structure to man's relation with the supernatural; they provide a

---

[12] A nuclear family is one based upon the conjugal unit—mother, father and children—rather than all members of a descent line.

[13] In this sense, a family in which the mother and father have approximately equal authority, as opposed to either a paternal or maternal family.

[14] A democratic family may be defined as one in which the children have a substantial, if not equal, role in decision-making.

pattern for religious belief and behavior. In traditional Islam, the core religious values included a belief in the omnicompetence of God, which places all events under supernatural influence. Thus, all institutions bear some relation to religion, and the religious institution performed many functions in the society. In medieval Islam such basic social institutions as education, war, government, law, and the economy were based upon or influenced by religious doctrine. There was, in other words, no clear distinction between religious and secular matters.

During the process of modernization, the chief change in the religious institution has been an attenuation of function. That is, functions have been transferred to other institutions—education, government, and the like—and new functions have not been given to the religious institution. This secularizing trend has been opposed by some parts of the Islamic community; the Muslim Brotherhood, for example, has sought the formation of a theocratic state in the Arab East. Nonetheless, the trend toward secularization has not thus far reversed itself. In Egypt the Islamic leaders have sought to find a new role in a secular state through aiding in the propagation of the government's secular ideas. Even in Saudi Arabia, where the Wahabite sect has been powerful in maintaining the traditional values of Islam, the impact of the modern world, especially since the mid-1950s, has led to a reduction in the importance of religion as a social institution. Similarly, this loss of function may be clearly seen in Turkey, Iran, and Jordan, although religious attachments are still important in the political systems of Lebanon and Iraq.

A loss of the underlying social coherence is the main consequence of this attentuation of the religious function. When so many functions were performed by Islam there was some consistency among those functions. Because Islam was the unifying force, the ultimate *raison d'être* of society, it diffused a common set of values throughout the social structure. The attentuation of Islam's role and the redistribution of its functions among a number of other institutions have eroded this unifying factor. And as yet Middle Eastern society has been unable to replace it. Thus, even though the functions once performed by the religious institution are still being performed and in many instances are being performed at a higher level, the fact that they are now dispersed and, perhaps more importantly, lacking an integrating principle increases the tendency for instability in the Middle East.

Education. Traditional education in the Middle East was primarily informal and even casual. It consisted of the processes of socialization and occurred mainly within the family. Religious schools were almost exclusively devoted to Islamic studies. Formal technical education, only open to a few, was devoted to imparting the specialized knowledge and skills required by such institutions as the military and the bureaucracy. Within this limited educational framework, knowledge and expansion of Islam's rich cultural heritage gradually receded and died. And as Islamic society became physically immobile (that is, territorial expansion ceased) and Ottoman society grew static, the values and social norms inculcated by education became increasingly rigid, as did the social structure itself.

The history of Western intervention into the Middle East and the subsequent growth of nationalisms is to a great extent a story of the expansion of formal education in the area. Chapter 4 relates some of this story. Here we need only point out that under the impact of Western intervention and the early growth of nationalisms formal education became primarily concerned with a rediscovery of classical heritage and a search for cultural identity. And since World War II, formal secularized education under government control has greatly expanded, with the ultimate goal in most states being universal education at the primary and secondary levels.

Yet, although modernization in the Middle East has resulted in an expansion of formal education, both qualitatively and quantitatively, this institution too is in the flux of transition between traditionalism and modernity. First of all, educational expansion is outspacing economic and political modernization. On the simplest plane, there are more people with a higher level of expectations (inculcated by education) than the present political processes can cope with or the economies absorb. This situation is most overt at the level of higher education. For example, in Egypt, only 931 of the 7135 college graduates for the class of 1948-1952 found government employment, the chief source of jobs for the educated in Egypt.[15] Yet, in spite of this inability to absorb the educated into the economy, Egypt continues to maintain a ratio of college students to general population higher than that of some industrialized countries. In fact, Professor Manfred Halpern, writing in 1963, found the ratio of college students to general population in Egypt to be nearly twice that of Britain.[16] This same situation is found again and again in the Middle East. Of 10,000 college graduates in Iraq between 1950-55, for instance, only 1,250 found employment.[17]

Another problem of education in the Middle East, and to some extent an explanation of the above situation, is the discontinuities between the educational content and the needs of a modernizing society. The norms, knowledge, and skills inculcated by education are not altogether relevant to the norms, knowledge, and skills required by a developing country. Again, most overt in higher education, the accompanying table indicates why the educated remain unemployable in the Middle East. Relatively few students are enrolled in the sciences, even though it is the skills of the engineer, the agronomist, and the physicist that the developing society needs.

Thus, while the major characteristic of religious institutions is a loss of functions, the problem of education is an expansion of function. As secular

---

[15]Lerner, pp. 237-38.

[16]Halpern, p. 65.

[17]Halpern, pp. 64-65.

	Sciences*		All Higher Education*			
	1953-54	1963-64	1953-54	1963-64	Change	% of Change
Egypt	17,722	63,014	58,960	142,313	83,353	141.37
Iraq	1,403	4,987	4,931	19,000	14,069	285.32
Jordan	–	84	–	400	400	–
Lebanon	1,850	3,060	5,000	9,000	4,000	80.00
Syria	1,305	5,100	3,000	20,000	17,000	566.67
Saudi Arabia . .	–	400	–	2,000	2,000	–
Totals.	21,366	76,645	71,891	192,713	120,822	168.06

*These figures do not include any students studying abroad, but they do include foreign students studying at these institutions.

Adapted from Fahim Qubain, *Education and Science in the Arab World* (Baltimore, Maryland: Johns Hopkins Press, 1966), p. 505.

values replace religious ethics, the ethical or moral training of the young is being transferred to the school, where such values as nationalism and socialism are taught. It becomes the responsibility of the schools to provide not only these attitudes and values, but also the skills necessary for a developing society. And because the requirements of a developing society change so rapidly it is also a problem of the educational institution to remain relevant to those needs. This key institution is in a very unstable position at present and communicates this instability to the remainder of society.

Economic Development

Because the very survival of a society is dependent upon the production, distribution, and consumption of man's material needs, economic institutions are often the focal point, the cynosure, of patterns of human organization. Thus, many of the functional and structural attributes of modernity are associated with economic factors. In the Western world, where the modern way of life first evolved, modernization in fact occurred as a result of economic change: in conjunction with spiritual, intellectual, social, and political change. In the Middle East, however, economic development is a goal of modernization rather than a cause of it. For it is only through economic development that a modernizing society can achieve its new aspirations for individual and collective "alternatives, preferences, and choices." And the peoples of the Middle East have realized these aspirations before achieving the economic means to attain them.

What is economic development? Is it merely the adoption of technology to methods of production and distribution—an exchange of the tractor for the hand plow, the application of mass production in industry, the substitution of the railroad for the oxen-drawn cart? According to the noted economist Everett E. Hagen, "This is wrong. Economic development is not a matter of substituting the new for the old, whereupon the change is completed."[18] Rather, economic development is a continuing process of increasing productivity.[19]

A modern economy (one which has realized a self-sustaining rate of growth through continuously increasing productivity) differs from a traditional economy in any number of ways, but the key factor is the continuing progress of innovation and organizational change which characterizes the modern economy. The economic problems of innovation and organizational change in an industrialized society are obviously complex. In the traditional economy, however, the problems of innovation—of substituting a tractor for a hand plow—are as much social, psychological, political, and cultural as they are economic. Commercialization, bureaucratization, industrialization, urbanization, and mass education—all concomitants of economic development—have far-reaching effects upon a people's way of life. Economic development not only entails changes in patterns of production, distribution, and consumption; it requires sometimes radical changes in the very culture of a society. It follows from this that some of the key obstacles to economic development are those social attitudes and institutions which obstruct or discourage innovation. And in the Middle East innovation and organizational change are hampered at every level by the resiliency of traditional values, motivations, and aspirations.

Economic development, then, cannot proceed in a vacuum. It must be accompanied by proper supportive changes throughout the entire fabric of society. This is why the road to economic development may be slow, the attempts often frustrating, and ultimate success not assured. These difficulties being kept in mind, let us proceed to a brief survey of economic development in the Middle East by examining the three sectors of the economy: primary, secondary, and tertiary.

Primary Sector. The states of the Middle East are primarily agricultural, and agriculture involves between one half and four fifths of the total populations in these states. Only in Israel, Lebanon, and the oil states of the Arabian peninsula is agriculture surpassed as a source of national income.[20] Agricultural workers receive lower incomes than other workers because of a lower value productivity. The causes contributing to this lower value productivity are scarcity of water, inadequate technological knowledge, and traditional forms of social organization. Also, agricultural production available for sale is limited by high grower-consumption and weaknesses in transportation and marketing.

Attempts to increase agricultural production have been made primarily through land reforms, of which there are three types: (1) transfer of ownership from absentee landlords to peasants on peasant-worked small holdings; (2) consolidation of fragmented holdings; and (3) division of large holdings into small plots. Most land reform in the Middle East has been of the third type. Professor Kermani lists five major objectives of the land reforms: (1) to reduce

---

[18]Everett E. Hagen, *The Economics of Development* (Homewood, Ill., 1968), p. 5.

[19]*Ibid.*

[20]Stephen H. Longrigg, *The Middle East: A Social Geography* (Chicago, 1963), p. 233.

the landholdings and power of large landowners; (2) to increase the security, incentive, and production of the tenants; (3) to steer landowners' income toward industrial investment; (4) to release the underemployed from the farm; and (5) to equalize income distribution and to help create a new middle class.[21] Land reforms are likely to be ineffective, however, if other steps to improve agricultural productivity are not taken.

Secondary Sector. Industrial development is often presented as a panacea for the economic problems of the Middle East, and some industrialization is indeed a necessity if modernization is to be accomplished. But there must also be a proportionate growth in agriculture, for the purchasing power of the population must keep pace with manufacturing production. Until the agricultural sector has further developed, national purchasing power cannot support massive industrialization.

Other factors necessary to industrialization in the Middle East, besides improvement in agricultural production, are the development of broad markets and a base of internal exchange. And it is necessary to provide for the establishment of a system which will not only allow for the development of proper interrelationships between industry and agriculture but which will also allow for the development of proper interrelationships between the various components of the growing industrial complex. It is evident, for example, that the growth of supporting industries may make feasible the establishment of industrial concerns which require complex supply inputs and many components, as is necessary in automobile production, and which may become a major part of economic development and employment.

Tertiary Sector. Development of the tertiary sector of the economy is also necessary, for without adequate communication, transportation, finance, marketing facilities, and the like, the creation of a self-sustaining rate of growth in the economy cannot be achieved. This becomes especially true as the industrial interrelationships envisioned above develop.

A key problem in the development of the economic system of any underdeveloped country is capital formation. The creation of sufficient human and physical capital to form a balanced economy is a necessary condition of development. It is, of course, also necessary to create the ability to utilize this capital in a suitable manner. There is, however, considerable difficulty in releasing either human or physical capital from the agricultural sector due to structural and institutional situations made rigid by social norms and attitudes.

Unless there is an unlimited supply of capital, development in one sector may have to be sacrificed to obtain growth in another, and attempts to advance in all areas may be mutually frustrating. At the same time, the attempted creation of industrial plants in a society which provides no market for their goods is tantamount to waste, and at best merely creates enclaves for the export market which have no substantial effect upon the domestic economy or its

[21] Taghi H. Kermani, *Economic Development in Action: Theories, Problems, and Procedures as Applied in the Middle East* (Cleveland and New York, 1967), pp. 147-148.

development. In large part, however, development will stem from the growth of new attitudes and techniques among the people and this growth can be encouraged only through education.

While certain Middle Eastern countries (Iraq, Iran, Kuwait, Saudi Arabia, and the Persian Gulf sheikdoms) have great financial capital from oil, most of the nations in the region have very limited capital, since they must depend upon agriculture for most of their national product. (Israel is an exception because it has received much capital from abroad.) Where capital is limited, resources must be husbanded, and some care must be taken to ensure that development projects are planned for the most efficient utilization of those resources which are available. It is at this point that government action—either direct control or indirect regulation through tax incentives and judicious application of tariffs, loans, and the like—may be useful in protecting resources and directing development in the most productive areas.

Indeed, government intervention in Middle Eastern economies has been extensive, both in the revolutionary governments and in the traditional sheikdoms, although in the latter national economies are sometimes treated as the household budget of the ruling family. This intervention has been used both to create a balanced economy and to diminish foreign influence and encourage domestic production. However, too often the emphasis has been upon industrial growth, and agriculture has been neglected. Then, too, in some of the oil-rich states, domestic circumstances have provided few good opportunities for investment, and much capital has been invested abroad or squandered. Nonetheless, nationalization of industry and finance, along with redistribution of land, has been a means of providing for economic equality consistent with the goals of social justice and democracy avowed by most of the nations of the Middle East.

Political Modernization

Government is potentially the one structure that can attempt to coordinate and direct the vast social and economic changes which are at the same time transforming Middle Eastern society and creating debilitating imbalances within it. But most Middle Eastern governments seem to lack, in varying degrees and combinations, at least the minimum requirements of/for legitimacy, political consensus, and/or authority essential for such a formidable undertaking. That is not to say that where governments possess these attributes modernization proceeds rationally and purposefully. Even when long-range modernization programs can be undertaken, there are tremendous problems in their implementation. Technical expertise, administrative capability, capital availability, and so on are only some of the instrumental requirements of such programs. In the U.A.R., for example, where President Nasser's government has maintained through the past 18 years legitimacy, political consensus, and authority, some of the major impediments to modernization programs are the rapid rate of population growth, limited resource base, lack of capital, and the pressures of extensive commitments in foreign affairs.

Our point here is simply that most Middle Eastern governments are too unstable, too unpopular, and/or too dependent for their power upon vested interests to even attempt the constructive coordination and direction of social change. They lack the legitimacy, political consensus, and/or authority required to exercise power effectively enough to undertake the setting up of priorities, the long-range planning, and the social and economic mobilization involved in programs of modernization. Or they are unable to withstand the pressures, frustrations, and antagonisms that such programs are likely to generate. Their energies, instead, are sapped in responding to social change and the tension generated by those forces resisting change and those promoting it.

Islam is one of the forces resistant to modernization. As a sociopolitical system, it is inadequate to meet the demands of the modern world environment; while as an ethical and religious system it is still cherished by millions. The difficulty of separating these elements of Islam, together with their association with past Arabic greatness, has led to movements which reject the changes transforming the Middle East and which seek to restore to that area its past social and cultural systems. These movements represented by a number of groups, such as the Moslem Brotherhood, offer an alternate route to security for those who are made anxious by modernization's continual assaults on their traditional values.[22]

As Islam is a broad cultural force resistant to change, so there are broad popular forces for change. Changes in the environment or man's relation to his environment, as a massive population growth relative to resources, may provide or stimulate such a force. A popular force for change must by definition include a significant segment of society that harbors dissatisfaction with the status quo. In the Middle East, however, such popular forces seldom include the peasant masses, who are typically skeptical about the value of change and have been a strong conservative force. This too may be changing (as evidenced by the vast movement of peasants to the cities, the great interest of Turkish peasants in commercialization and in employment of workers abroad, and the ready response of Egyptian peasants to the comprehensive program of the government's Combined Units). Nevertheless, the peasants have more often obstructed than aided programs promoting change. On the other hand, the urban masses with their greater participatory orientation and higher degree of media susceptibility more readily adopt such programs and can often be moved to mass action by such modern and volatile groups as the students.

The tensions arising from frustrated expectations may result in anomic popular forces, as in Egypt's 'Black Saturday' riots in January 1952. The tensions between institutions with different value systems have been generally

---

[22]Halpern, *op. cit.*, chap. 8.

controlled in Lebanon, but in 1958 the heightened consciousness of their Arab identity on the part of the Muslim community lead to serious civil strife. Iraq provides us with an example of tensions between two modernizing institutions. The government signed a new Anglo-Iraqi Treaty in 1948 to aid their program of economic development. The popular belief in political independence conflicted with the government policy and led to riots serious enough to prevent ratification of the treaty.

In order to meet such challenges to its authority as are posed by the mass action of popular forces or by foreign competition, the state will sometimes attempt to modernize itself. Such attempts may lead to a widespread modernization of societal institutions. However, those who initiate attempts at modernization may be caught up in the forces they themselves have loosed. Such was precisely the case when Britain stimulated Arab nationalism during World War II in order to defeat the Turks and then found that nationalism turned against them. Despite the risks involved, however, there are those leaders who are willing to attempt sweeping social reform. Muhammad Ali was certainly one such leader. He substantially modified Egyptian society, especially the economic order, to carry out his projected reforms in the military.

However, even when the state is willing to carry out reforms and even when its leaders are competent and realize the implications of their actions and know how to proceed in their reforms, social organization and cultural values may rob modernization programs of their effect. For instance, if the values of civil servants are in conflict with impersonal, differentiated, routinized administration no amount of bureaucratic reorganization will be truly effective.

Sometimes, indeed, the exuberant hopes of a new regime are so little suited to the realities of its situation that it becomes discredited and is overthrown. Few Middle Eastern revolutionary governments have maintained even a credible figurehead from the traditional monarchy and most of them have broken decisively with the traditions of their society. A revolutionary regime which thus breaks with traditional symbols faces the problem of establishing legitimacy. It must also establish its own symbols around which to create political consensus. It may well be, for example, that the popularity of military regimes in the Middle East is due to the long tradition of military influence in the area. This tradition allows these regimes to draw on many traditional symbols which they may manipulate to gain popular support.

In the United Arab Republic the state has attempted to bring projected institutional changes into coincidence with cultural values in the society through the use of sophisticated socialization techniques. However, traditional attitudes lead the people to view these efforts selectively, and they respond to that information they consider realistic. It seems that rather than responding to the regime's pronouncements about democracy, for example, the people of the United Arab Republic note the fact that the regime communicates in an authoritarian manner and thus disbelieve they are able to influence the regime. In this case, it is apparent that the tensions among institutions have resulted in the creation of attitudes contrary to those desired by the state. In Turkey and

Iran similar regimes with similar histories have followed policies of encouraging economic development, but the Turks have been more successful than the Iranians. David McClelland has hypothesized that the difference is due to cultural factors; the Turks evidence more *n* achievement than do the Iranians, and so are more receptive to change which is identified with advancement.[23]

Also, interest groups opposed to reform may frustrate the state's modernization schemes. In most Middle Eastern countries the power of the landowners and traditional elites has been sufficient to obstruct efforts at reform to a significant extent. Unless the state can mobilize sufficient support to overcome such obstacles, its effectiveness is likely to be severely impaired, and the state may even be reduced to impotence. The Iranian governments of 1906-1921, for instance, were not only unable to improve the social and political systems, but also unable to maintain effective government in the face of foreign and domestic opposition.

When the state itself is unwilling to effect changes or is incapable of doing so, various groups in society may seek control or replace the traditional forms of government. These groups, often fulfilling the role of counterelites, may displace the old regime either to carry on change impossible under the old order or to maintain the functioning of the state. Ataturk, Reza Khan, Nasser, Kassim, and Salal of Yemen all took power in order to replace ineffective and politically bankrupt regimes; all of them, with the possible exception of Kassim, proved more capable in the exercise of power than their predecessors.

Where the power to rule has been the legitimizing factor for government, the army has been the basis of political power. This tradition of recourse to controllers of military force appears to have a limiting effect on the development of political institutions in the Middle East. Political control is commonly gained or lost by military coups rather than by institutionalized forms for the transfer of power. And where formal political institutions have been created in the Middle East they are often bypassed with military force. Syria and Iraq are classic cases of this sort of military influence in politics.

All this does not mean that Middle Eastern governments and political processes are hopelessly the hapless victims "of social and economic forces that willy-nilly control the destiny of the people."[24] Rather, the present instability which characterizes the area's politics is again a symptom of modernization. The change from a politically irresponsible, ascriptive, particularistic, tribal-based hierarchial political structure to the modern nation-state with its universalistic laws, generalized concepts of justice and citizenship, impersonal systems of evaluation, and mass participation not only entails changes in the governmental structure; it requires the creation of an entirely new political system. That is, not only a new configuration of legislative, administrative, and legal organizations but also new modes of articulating, aggregating, and communicating political

[23] David C. McClelland, *The Achieving Society* (Princeton, 1961).

[24] Lucian W. Pye, *Aspects of Political Development* (Boston, 1966), p. 42. But they may well remain so, for as we stated earlier modernization is not necessarily inevitably successful.

interests and, indeed, new roles, relationships, values, and orientations. The process of political modernization, in other words, occurs within a matrix of social change. And because modernization in the Middle East is disorderly, uneven, and incomplete, the political institutions, more conspicuously than other institutions, reflect the present upheaval of society.

The problem of the political system is to translate all of these divergent forces into a coherent social system. For it is only at the level of political action that countries (*i.e.*, geographic units) can be transformed into modern nation-states. We are, in effect then, identifying political modernization as nation-building. The test of it, according to Lucian W. Pye, would involve "first the establishment of a particular set of public institutions that constitute the necessary infrastructure of a nation-state, and second, the controlled expression in political life of the phenomenon of nationalism."[25] While the nations of the Middle East are far from this ideal, some much farther than others, the trend of political modernization is generally in this direction. As is illustrated in Chapter 4, nationalisms have had a profound effect on Middle Eastern nation-building, actually giving the greatest momentum to modernization. Chapter 5, Political Trends, exemplifies the continuing search for a nation-building formula. And Part III, Comparative Government, discusses the political movements and public institutions arising in each state.

THE FORCES OF MODERNIZATION

Modernization in the Middle East is likely to continue as a disruptive rather than an integrative influence as long as it is an erratic process. But there are already powerful forces in the Middle East that are attempting to translate modernization into national goals, to extend it to the tradition-bound rural masses as well as the influentially dominant cities, to generalize modern values, and to institutionalize modern infrastructures. What are these forces for modernization? The middle class, the military, and communications.

The Middle Class

The new middle class in the Middle East, in contrast with the class of entrepreneurs which arose in Europe several centuries ago, is primarily a salaried class composed of intellectuals, professional men, government workers, and aspirants to middle class status (those who have acquired the skills and share the values of this class, but who are without the jobs.)[26] This class, born from the copulation of modern societies with traditional societies and oriented toward modern rather than traditional roles, was considerably influenced by modern thought from its conception. With the proliferation of modern ideas and Western-style education in the Middle East during the 19th century, modern political and social ideals quickly spread among the intelligentsia (see Chapter 4).

---

[25]*Ibid.*, p. 37. Pye uses the term political development.

[26]Halpern, *op. cit.*, Chapter 4.

The administrations set up throughout the area by England and France following World War I became the seed bed for the salaried new middle class. And among this diverse group, drawn primarily from the lower and hitherto uninfluential echelons of society, Western thought modified by indigenous symbols took root. Impatient of traditional values that denied them on an ascriptive basis the status and power consonant to their skills, intolerant of foreign domination that curtailed their freedom of action, and imbued with a sense of nationalism and social conscience, this class has emerged as the principal advocate of modernization in the Middle East.

In its skills, aspirations, and values, this is a modern class; in its dedication to social change, this is a revolutionary class; in its struggle for influence, this class has burst forth into Middle Eastern politics as the most dynamic force in our century, perhaps in several centuries. Why? According to Halpern, "the tasks it must perform in order to create status, power, and prosperity for itself no less than the nation require the establishment of modern, integrating institutions which can mobilize the spirit and resources of the entire nation. At the same time these institutions, by their very nature, are also peculiarly adapted to control by the new middle class.[27] Kamal Ataturk in Turkey, Gamal Abdul Nasser in Egypt, Brigadier General Abd al-Karim Kassim and the Aref brothers in Iraq, Michel Aflaq, Akram Hourani, Salah al-Din al-Bitar and others of the Baath party in Syria symbolize the passing of political power from the traditional rulers to this new middle class. Indeed, they symbolize the passing of traditional politics.

Power for most of them is not an end in itself, it is a means of solving problems, of changing society. The potentialities for change are obvious in a situation where an army, a bureaucracy, a political party, and a ruling elite—all strongholds of the middle class—hold the same or similar values. Furthermore, the constant pressure for change from the aspiring members of the new middle class is not only a dissident voice but a source of reinforcement for the ruling elites drawn from this same class. There are, however, serious ideological divisions within the new middle class that create new tensions and curtail its effectiveness. Nevertheless, as the new middle class is a modern class, its involvement in politics is directed toward new solutions and solutions in accord with modern values of efficiency, rationalism, and popular participation. The choices they make—social, economic, and political—will have a profound impact on the Middle East.

The Military

The military offers to an aspiring young man an introduction to middle class life. Even the illiterate peasants who often compose the enlisted ranks are brought into contact with the modern world to some extent, while the better educated persons who gain entrance to the officer corps are largely separated

---

[27]*Ibid.*, p. 77.

from traditional attachments. The military men are thus in many ways similar to other members of the new middle class. There are three differences which have in large part determined the important position of the military in Middle Eastern politics.

The fact that a military career and martial life are traditionally objects of respect among the people of the Middle East makes the position of the military unique in the political realm. The military's external aspects provides symbolic connections with the martial tradition of Islam. Unlike civil servants and political party heads, military leaders may utilize this traditional respect to legitimize their rule.[28]

The dedication of the military to the service of the state accords with the nationalist principles of the middle class. While military service thus reinforces nationalist feelings, it may not under all circumstances increase loyalty to the government. For example, in order to quell civil disturbances, or used as an instrument of oppression, the military may revolt and take power in the name of the nation.[29] Furthermore, the attachment of military men to nationalist principles is not only a matter of principles and emotion, but is reinforced by a way of life continually reminding the individual of his duty to the nation.

The access of the military to power renders its position quite different from that of most nonmilitary groups. The ability of an officer to use force against the government as well as in support of it and his ability to withhold the use of this force makes it difficult for contestants for power to ignore the military. Further, as the cases of Egypt in 1952 and Iraq in 1958 illustrate, the military form of organization can provide a means for assembling the information and force necessary to perpetrate a coup. Once the legitimacy of the government is vitiated, the internal legitimacy of the command structure gives the military a base of coercive power.

Thus, by reason of their position of traditional respect, their dedication to nationalism in action, and their access to force, the members of the military establishments in the Middle East differ significantly from the other members of the new middle class, whose values they share, in their ability to place their principles in practice.

On the basis of the above description, one could imagine military regimes or parties which, while a dominant nationalist political force, were not in fact modernizing. However, the tendency for states in the Middle East to adopt Western modes of military organization early in the process of modernization has meant that the military has often been more familiar with modernity than other sectors of society and that the military is to outward appearances the most modern organization in society. In addition, the interests of the military in building national security tends to encourage modernizing attitudes, at least toward industrialization and infrastructural development. Thus, the military is a

---

[28]John Bagot Glubb, "The Role of the Army in the Arab World," in Thompson and Reischauer, *Modernization of the Middle East*.

[29]In John C. Campbell, ed. *The Military in the Middle East*.

powerful political force in the Middle East with a distinct interest in modernizing certain other sectors in society.

Communications

The relation of communication to society is intimate. In fact, human society is characterized by man's ability to understand the meaning behind symbols and thus to communicate through the manipulation of symbols.[30] Societies have been differentiated as modern, transitional, and traditional in terms of their communications systems.[31] In a time of social change, the communication of new values, attitudes, and knowledge to all persons in the society is a key factor in maintaining a coherent social order through the transitional period. Differential rates of communication, *i.e.*, differing socialization experiences, may create or exacerbate divisions in a society. A commonly noted occurrence in the Middle East, as elsewhere, has been the separation of the masses from the elites due to the greater familiarity of the latter with Western society and modern values. The often reported "revolution of rising expectations" is a result of communication channels newly opened to previously isolated peoples, and the gap between the aspirations thus generated and the achievement actually gained presents a major political problem throughout the Middle East.

If modernization is viewed as development (that is, progress toward some goal), this goal is often capable of expression in communication terms. If political development is seen as increasing national unity, for example, it may also be seen as involving "extending central communication networks into and across previously isolated sectors of society."[32] In Egypt, the extension of communication networks for social mobilization is a major area of government enterprise.[33] Such measures as literacy rates, newspaper circulation, miles of roads and railways, and radio ownership are frequently used as indicators of economic development. The existence or absence of free elections or a controlled press are used as a measure of democratic or authoritarian societies.

It is thus apparent that modernization may usefully be viewed as a process of communication change and development. An excellent analysis of the relation between communication development and political development, with emphasis on the role of the mass media in social change, concludes that the mass media in the developing countries have failed to aid in the creation of a balance between mobility and stability, but that they have a great potential for constructive

---

[30]Alfred Kuhn, *The Study of Society: A Unified Approach* [Irwin-Dorsey Series in Behavioral Science in Business], (Homewood, Ill., 1963), Parts II and III.

[31]Lucian W. Pye, "Models of Traditional, Transitional and Modern Communications Systems," in, Lucian W. Pye, ed., *Communications and Political Development* [Studies in Political Development Series] (Princeton, 1963), pp. 24-29.

[32]Richard R. Fagen, *Politics and Communication* [Little, Brown Series in Comparative Politics] (Boston, 1966), p. 128.

[33]Leonard Binder, "Egypt: The Integrative Revolution," in Lucian W. Pye and Sidney Verba, eds., *Political Culture and Political Development* [Studies in Political Development Series] (Princeton, 1965).

participation in the modernizing process. In Mr. Lerner's analysis, the mass media may contribute to the development of the empathy necessary to what he terms the Participant Society.[34] In a more negative vein, it may be noted that where communication facilities are government-controlled (as in the entire Middle East with the exception of Lebanon and to a lesser extent Israel and Turkey) or government-owned (as in Egypt, Iraq, and Syria), communication tends to be one-way. Under these conditions, where authoritative communication channels are directed from top to bottom, communication upward diminishes and governmental isolation from the people may result.

CONCLUSION: THE CHALLENGE OF MODERNIZATION

With the relationships within and among family, tribe, and country; village and town; religion and loyalty; land, wealth, and power; and man and nature all changing—with the great gulfs between rural and urban, rich and poor, traditional and modern, expectations and fulfillment—Middle Eastern society can only be seen as transitional: a way-station from the obsolete past to the unknown future. It is evident that the traditional structure is no longer viable; but as yet no new social system has replaced it. And it is probable that a long period of tension and upheaval must precede the formation of such a system. The outcome is unforeseeable, for never before has man had such a range of choice. The challenge of modernization for the Middle East, however, is not so much to choose wisely as to evolve a coherent social system where choice is a way of life.

SELECTED BIBLIOGRAPHY

Most of the works which have been useful in the preparation of this chapter have been cited in the text. Of special interest to the student of modernization are the excellent volumes in the Princeton studies in Political Development:

Lucian W. Pye, *Communications and Political Development* (1963)

Joseph LaPalombara, *Bureaucracy and Political Development* (1963)

Lucian W. Pye and Sydney Verba, *Political Culture and Political Development* (1965)

Dankwart Rustow and Robert E. Ward, *Political Modernization in Japan and Turkey* (1964)

James S. Coleman, *Education and Political Development* (1965)

Joseph LaPalombara and Myron Weiner, *Political Parties and Political Development* (1966)

These provide a comprehensive view of the field from several viewpoints. A more theoretical approach may be found in Gabrial A. Almond and G. Bingham

---

[34]Daniel Lerner, "Toward a Communication Theory of Modernization: A Set of Considerations," in Lucian W. Pye, ed., *Communications and Political Development*, pp. 327-350.

Powell, *Comparative Politics: A Developmental Approach* (Boston, 1966). Dankwart Rustow looks to the relationship between nationalism and modernization in *A World of Nations: Problems in Political Modernization* (Washington, D.C., 1968). The communications approach is reviewed in Richard R. Fagen, *Politics and Communication* (Boston, 1966). David Apter develops a tentative taxonomy from a structuralist approach in *The Politics of Modernization* (Chicago, 1965).

With special relevance to the Middle East, some helpful works have been Dankwart Rustow's chapter in Gabriel A. Almond and James S. Coleman, eds., *The Politics of the Developing Areas* (Princeton, 1960), H. B. Sharabi, *Nationalism and Revolution in the Arab World* (Princeton, 1966), and Morroe Berger's *The Arab World Today* (Garden City, N.Y., 1958). Manfred Halpern's excellent volume, *The Politics of Social Change in the Middle East and North Africa* (Princeton, 1963) is especially informative as a guide to methodology. On the role of the military, see Sydney Nettleton Fisher, ed., *The Military in the Middle East* (Columbus, Ohio, 1963). David Lerner in *The Passing of Traditional Society, Modernizing the Middle East* (New York, 1958) studies the impact of Westernization on the Arab countries, Turkey, and Iran.

Of particular interest for the study of modernization in the Middle East are a number of anthologies. Syndey Nettleton Fisher, ed., *Social Forces in the Near East* (Ithaca: Cornell University Press, 1955); Walter Z. Laqueur, ed., *The Middle East in Transition* (New York: Praeger, 1958); and Richard H. Nolte, *The Modern Middle East* (New York: Atherton, 1961), are all excellent works. Of more recent vintage are Jack H. Thompson and Robert D. Reischauer, *Modernizing the Arab World* (Princeton, 1966). The problem of economic development is thoroughly explored by Taghi T. Kermani, *Economic Development in Action: Theories, Problems, and Procedures as Applied in the Middle East* (New York, c. 1967).

part III

Comparative
Governments

THE NORTHERN BELT

chapter 7

Turkey*

Introduction

Turkey is one of the few countries of the Middle East with a solidly rooted multiparty, open political system. It has reached this point after undertaking some drastic social and political transformations and deliberately coming to grips with some of the major problems involved in modernization. One such transformation was readjusting herself from being a major empire and the dominant power in the area, to being a small state in the modern world. This adjustment affected mostly the upper echelons of Turkish society, and has on the whole been successfully handled. There was also the transformation from a traditional to a modern society and from autocracy to democracy which has affected the Turkish people from top to bottom. This far more fundamental change has proven much more difficult and disrupting, and although it too has been generally well carried through and it appears that multiparty politics is likely to continue in Turkey, many problems remain. Chief among these is the question of whether the pressures for economic development and continuing social change can be successfully accommodated with the pressures for stability and for continuing democracy.

The Context of the Political System

The political system and problems of contemporary Turkey are deeply rooted in Turkish history. As has been discussed earlier in this volume, the Ottoman Empire dominated the Middle East and brought the Turks power and prestige for over five centuries before it succumbed to the onslaughts of nationalism and imperialsim in the 19th and early 20th centuries. The Ottoman period left

---

*Walter Weiker, associate professor of political science, Rutgers: The State University.

Turkey some important political assets. These included a large and relatively well-trained civil bureaucracy and considerable experience in self-government; two things which some other states in the Middle East have been notably lacking. The Ottoman period also left at least the rudiments of such things as an educational system, and a railroad and telegraph network. Perhaps the most important asset was the experience of unsuccessful attempts at reform and an appreciation of some institutional and ideological arrangements which were tried or advocated and which did *not* produce satisfactory solutions to the nation's problems.

The political history of the Ottoman Empire, particularly after the beginning of the 19th century, is one of constant tensions between forces of reform and resistance to reform, tensions often expressed also in terms of centralization versus decentralization in politics and administration. At its height the empire rested on several foundations, all depending on able sultans at the top of the pyramid. One was military success, which served not only for subjugation but also provided the promise of booty and land to attract the loyalty of local notables from whom levies of troops were demanded and who could thus identify their interests with those of the empire. A second pillar, most successful under Suleiman the Magnificent (1520-1566), was a comprehensive and extremely efficiently run administrative system. Personnel for the civil bureaucracy were especially trained in a palace school which practiced extremely rigorous selection and discipline and emphasized loyalty to the Ottoman dynasty as one of its foundations. Third, Suleiman administered the empire with a high degree of equity and justice.

When the line of strong sultans gave way to a succession of weak ones in the 17th and 18th centuries the power of local notables grew stronger to the point where both the military might and the revenues of the government declined, simultaneously weakening the state's ability to handle the rising pressure from abroad. Many central institutions declined. A notable example was the Janissaries. This group had been founded in the 14th century as an elite military force, given special training, status, and rewards. Under strong sultans the Janissaries played their assigned role, but under weak ones the corps began to assert its own power and see to its own welfare prior to the interests of the state. By the 18th century the Janissaries had gotten the right to engage in commercial and other outside pursuits, and to marry and have their sons given preference in joining the corps. They also became a center of reaction until it was abolished by Mahmud II in 1826 as part of his efforts at revitalizing the empire.

By the beginning of the 19th century the Ottomans were beset on all sides. In the Balkans separatist nationalism was soon to detach one province after another from Istanbul's control. Western imperialism was beginning to show strong interests in the Middle East and would soon make great encroachments. And many areas in the Arab world and North Africa, though not directly affected by these two motivations, were not very effectively secured under Ottoman jurisdiction. About this time, however, the dynastic line turned for the better and a series of able, reform-minded sultans ascended the Ottoman throne. The first of these, Ahmed III (1789-1807), lost his life to reactionary forces, but his successor Mahmud II (1808-1839) fared better and began to try to revitalize the empire by reorganizing the army on modern lines, strengthening the administrative apparatus, and particularly by attempting to create feelings of loyalty to the empire on the part of all its constituent groups. The middle 19th century is known as the *Tanzimat* (reorganization) period. It began with the Rescript of the Rose Chamber in 1839 *(Hatt-i Serif of Gülhane)* which proclaimed the equality of all Ottoman subjects before the law and the promise that laws would be enforced justly and honestly. These two reforms were to be the foundation on which loyalty to the empire would be based, on which a new sense of Ottoman nationality would rest.

A variety of implementing schemes followed during the next half century. One was the verbal granting of equality to non-Muslims by such steps as abolishing special taxes on these groups and admitting them to eligibility for service in the army. Equality remained always a fiction, however, for neither the Ottomans nor the non-Muslims really wanted it. The former were far too deeply imbedded in their tradition to be able to accept such equality (even the most strongly reform-minded officials never could bring themselves to completely give up the idea that Islam was an essential pillar of the state). The minorities in turn were either relatively satisfied with their status (most preferred, for example, to continue paying the special tax rather than doing military service) or were determined to gain full independence rather than only improved status within a state not fulfilling their own nationalist ambitions.

Administrative reforms also fared poorly. Attempts to establish provincial and local legislative and consultative councils resulted more often than not in enhancing the powers of local notables without any increased attention to problems, such as public welfare or economic development, or gave administrators excuses for doing little or nothing on the grounds that the councils "disapproved." Attempts to improve the quality of the civil bureaucracy encountered recruitment and promotion by ascription rather than achievement which had come to permeate most Ottoman institutions. It also ran afoul of the determination by even the more reformist sultans to keep control of the government by such measures as retaining the right to transfer provincial governors and other officials at will. This power was used capriciously, thereby predisposing those officials to enrich themselves as quickly as possible before being sent elsewhere and having to start anew, thus discouraging any long-term planning and development efforts that such officials might intend. Midhat Pasha, the best known and probably the most able administrator of this era, was able to achieve impressive successes in provincial administration only by unusually favorable combinations of circumstances and shrewd political maneuvering.

The most dramatic reform scheme of the Tanzimat era was the Ottoman constitution . The brainchild of Midhat Pasha, it was promulgated in 1876 by the recently ascended Sultan Abdul Hamid II after considerable pressure was exerted by forces of reform led by Midhat and a group of intellectuals, writers, and journalists known as the Young Ottomans. The attempt to turn the absolute monarchy into a constitutional one was doomed from the outset, however. For one thing, few of the reformers understood the reasons why parliamentary government worked in the West. Many, including Midhat, in fact, saw the constitution as a panacea for all the empire's ills. For another, many compromises had to be made with conservative elements, and few of the Ottomans themselves were really prepared to create a true democracy (even if the social and economic conditions would have made that possible). In order to restrain the irresponsibility of the Sultan, Midhat "handed down" the constitution and retained a great many powers in his own hands. The Ottoman parliament sat for but ten months in 1877-8 before the shrewd Abdul Hamid was able to exile Midhat and the other reformers and suspend the constitution. The Tanzimat era was over.

The reign of Abdul Hamid lasted until 1908. Although he was extremely conservative and suspicious of all attempts at change, the influx of Western influences could not be stopped. European military and economic power continued to increase and to arouse the resentment of the Ottomans. Railroads and telegraph lines (later to be important in the rise of Ataturk) began to appear. European educational institutions, established in the 19th century partly by missionaries and partly by invitation of the Ottoman government as a part of its "defensive modernization" efforts, brought Western ideas into direct contact with much of the Turkish elite. Two groups were chiefly affected by these influences. One was the intellectuals, who by the last third of the 19th century had become steeped in the thought of the French Revoltuion and other European liberal currents. These "Young Ottomans," included many writers and journalists like Namik Kemal and Ibrahim Sinasi who began to circulate numerous pieces of nationalist and patriotic literature. During the Abdul Hamid period, most were in exile much of the time and made cities like Paris and Cairo centers of Turkish reform agitation. The second group very intimately affected by Western contacts was the military. Military schools had been among the first institutions to be given Western advisors and curricula, and Turkish officers were not only exposed to Western military techniques but also to Western languages and thought. Many were sent to Europe for further training. The intellectuals and the officers were, not surprisingly, at the head of the revolutionary movements of 1908 and 1919.

The Young Turks

The year 1908 found the Ottoman Empire in extremely bad straits. The government was hopelessly in debt and had had to submit to the dictates of European financiers. Egypt was all but independent; indeed Muhammad Ali had almost defeated the Ottomans in the 1830s, succumbing only to Western power, ranged on the Ottoman side. On the north, Russia had won a long string of victories. Internal restlessness was also growing. Then in July 1908 a group of officers led by Colonel Enver led a mutiny which became a revolution when the Sultan was forced to accept the demand for reinstatement of the constitution and reconvene the Ottoman parliament. Abdul Hamid promised his cooperation and was allowed to retain his throne, but after he was implicated in an attempted counterrevolution in March 1909 he was deposed in favor of his brother Mehmet V.

A variety of groups vied for power in the new circumstances. They ran the entire gamut from absolute monarchists to classical liberals, and for a while the political, intellectual, and journalistic scene in Istanbul was extremely lively. The Young Turks, who came to include a large number of officers, politicians, writers, and others, took steps to improve education, public health, found industries, improve the armed forces, and other such efforts. But open competitive politics was short-lived. Foreign pressures soon brought great strains (most of the Balkans proclaimed and/or won their independence between 1908 and 1912, for example). Domestically Enver and his fellow officers grew impatient and intolerant of the need to deal with bickering politicians. The record showed nothing but further decline both internationally and in terms of domestic strength and unity. Thus, in 1913 the Committee of Union and Progress, the officer's political organization, took power and ruled until Turkey's defeat in World War I.

Ideologically most leaders of the Young Turk period were intent on retaining as much of the empire as possible. Three bases were advocated by one group or another as the underpinning for this. Pan-Ottomanism, the unity of all subject nationalities, fared no better than it had during the Tanzimat. Pan-Islam was used by fundamentalists in various ways including a call for holy war against the West in World War I, but it too aroused little response. Pan-Turkism was largely led by Turkish emigres from Russia who sought the unity of the large number of Turkish-speaking peoples there with the Turks of the empire, but this ideal proved completely beyond the Ottoman's abilities to bring about.

Thus the stage was set. World War I brought Turkey final defeat and the Western Allies began revealing plans to dismember what was left of the empire. The Balkan provinces gained complete independence; the Arab states were put under mandates or other arrangements described elsewhere in this book. The most significant incursion, however, was the intention to divide Thrace and Anatolia themselves into spheres for the French, British, Italians, and Greeks. Istanbul was occupied by the Allies in 1919, and the Ottoman government was forced to sign the Treaty of Sèvres which incorporated all the Allied plans.

The lessons of the Ottoman Empire were clear, although few yet appreciated them. The state could be held together only on the basis of true nationalism, and all the ideologies which had recently been tried were irrelevant. It had also to be supplemented by truly reformist administration dedicated to the welfare of the people, and by true national sovereignty. Economic, military, and political strength built on modern foundations were necessary to combat Western imperialism and reassert Turkey's rightful place in the world.

The Nationalist Movement

On May 19, 1919 a general named Mustafa Kemal, later to acquire the name Ataturk (Father of the Turks), landed at the Black Sea port of Samsum to take over the job of inspector of the few army units which remained in Anatolia. Turkey's most successful military hero, he had led the victory over the British navy at Gallipoli and managed to save most of the Turkish forces on the Palestine front in the face of the British assault on that area.

Kemal was an extraordinary man. The son of a minor government official, he had shown ability and determination from an early age when he virtually fought his way to admission to a military school. During his early career, his experience included such things as accompanying Sultan Vahideddin to Germany, service as military attaché in Bulgaria, and dabbling in Istanbul politics. He thus was able to see the problems of the empire at firsthand, and was acquainted with virtually all of those who led the Ottoman government and/or who would be at the forefront of the nationalist movement. More than most Turkish officers he was able to escape being caught up in the Ottoman mentality, perhaps because of his lower middle class origin. Among his most important characteristics were a clear direction and set of goals, an iron-bound determination to achieve them, a prodigious energy (he often worked or held balls and debates on affairs of state through the night), and an extremely keen sense of strategy and tactics. He incorporated in himself the ideals of military hero, virile and fearless man, and leader who exuded confidence. His charisma enabled him to escape much censure from his countrymen for his free living, disdain of religion, and disrespect for tradition. When he went to Anatolia, barely escaping the clutches of the occupying powers who had already interned many other potential Turkish leaders on Malta, he was determined to restore Turkish independence and revive Turkish glory. He was truly the right man at the right place at the right time.

A nationalist core already existed in the form of local Defense of Rights societies in various parts of Turkey from Kars to Edirne. These were now combined by Kemal (who shortly resigned from the army) into a Defense of Rights Society of Rumelia and Anatolia. The society held congresses at Sivas and Erzurum in 1919 and adopted the National Pact which set out basic demands for territorial integrity and national independence. The first task, however, was military salvation. The Greeks, urged on by the other World War I allies, had launched an invasion of the Aegean area and western Anatolia. Kemal and other commanders mobilized the country into a force sufficient to repel the invaders after a struggle of over three years. At the same time, Kemal and others organized a full-blown provisional government, ostensibly to act until the Istanbul government could be liberated from occupation. The Ankara-based nationalists acted like anything but mere caretakers, however. Instead they put forth their own program and consolidated their power in most parts of the country. Virtually all Turkish leaders who had any reform sympathies and who were not interned managed to get to Ankara, where a Grand National Assembly was convened in 1920 composed of some deputies elected specifically to it, plus any members of the Ottoman parliament who could attend. The Istanbul government meanwhile was seeking to combat the nationalists by collaborating with the occupying powers, declaring the nationalists to be rebels and traitors and attempting to mobilize forces of its own. It was completely unable to achieve its aims, however, and when the Lausanne Conference was convened in November 1922 to make a settlement between the victorious Turks and the Allies, the Ankara government was Turkey's sole representative. The treaty signed on July 23, 1923 gave Turkey full sovereignty.

The Ataturk Revolution

Even before the Lausanne Treaty was concluded Ataturk began to reveal his plans for remaking Turkey. It is not clear how long he had been formulating plans for drastic changes, but it is known that his contempt for the old ways had been steadily building up over the years as he observed the dying Ottoman state, and there is little doubt that by 1922 he envisioned most of the radical breaks with tradition which followed. The first step, a vital one, was to abolish the Ottoman sultanate on November 1, 1922 and to exile all members of the Ottoman dynasty. The government of the Grand National Assembly was now the sole government of Turkey. Kemal further solidified his power by molding the Defense of Rights Society into a disciplined political organization which he soon converted into the Republican People's party. In June 1923 new elections were held which successfully routed the conservative elements (known as the Second Group of the Society) who had opposed many steps in Ataturk's rise to power.

The Republican People's party (RPP) ruled single-handedly from 1923 to 1946, with two exceptions which will be mentioned shortly. During the 1920s particularly, and frequently later, drastic reforms followed each other in rapid sequence. They were intended to achieve both complete Westernization and modernization. In pursuit of the former objective, turning Turkey's face completely away from the East, reforms included adopting the Gregorian calendar and the Western method of telling time; abolition of the fez and adoption of Western style of dress; substituting Sunday for Friday as the weekly day of rest; promulgation of civil, penal, and commercial law codes adapted from Western models; and in 1928 the most far-reaching move, the substitution of Latin for Arabic script. This last-named step not only cut newly educated Turks off from the East but had the additional effect of cutting them off from most of their past except what the new government permitted to be translated. Reforms directed at modernization included proclaiming a republic and representative government; fostering Turkish nationalism; drastic measures of secularization and the disestablishment of Islam; and large programs of education, economic development, public works, and public welfare. The modernizing reforms and the problems of contemporary Turkey connected with their implementation will be discussed in detail below. First we should complete the historical background.

During the single-party period, the RPP ruled in an authoritarian, but not totalitarian manner. Ataturk never ceased maintaining that "loyal opposition" was to be welcomed, and that democracy was his eventual goal. Twice during his presidency opposition emerged. In 1925 a group of generals and intellectuals led by Adnan Adivar, Rauf Orbay, Kazim Karabekit, Refet Bele, and Ali Fuat Cebesoy, became critical of both Ataturk's personal power and the speed and radicalism of his reforms. All were potential rivals of the president and thus had some personal motives for opposition, but they were also genuinely concerned for the traditions of Turkish culture. Unfortunately, their opposition Progressive party came at a time when Ataturk was most intent on pressing the reforms and at a time when Kurds in eastern Turkey were in rebellion, so that this, combined with Ataturk's personal resentment of their criticism, caused the government to close the Progressive down. The bitterness of feeling was such that some of the Progressive leaders did not return to Turkey until after Ataturk's death in 1938.

The second opposition incident was more interesting. In 1930 Turkey had passed through the period of the most drastic reforms and seemed to be settling down and adjusting to the new order. There was growing dissatisfaction with the economic situation, however, due to both internal underdevelopment and the world depression then at its height. Thus, several prominent Turkish political leaders expressed a desire to revitalize government economic policy just at the time that Ataturk too was of the opinion that Turkey was ready for the final jewel in its revolutionary crown, the inauguration of multiparty politics. In August of 1930 Ataturk's close, long-time friend Fethi Okyar founded the Free Republican party, with the president's strong encouragement. To everyone's surprise, it gained immediate popularity and large numbers of adherents, even though its leaders had vowed to proceed slowly and carefully on this new reform departure. It gained particular favor among many businessmen and intellectuals who were dissatisfied with certain policies, wished to have their interests better represented, or had other such "loyal" motivations. But it also gathered those who had basic opposition to the reforms, including many who hoped particularly to reverse the policies of secularism. Incidents of violence between supporters of the government and the opposition, particularly the anti-secularists, were influential in convincing Ataturk that the venture had been premature, and the Free party closed its doors after 99 days.

The RPP had been warned, however, that its popularity was on shaky foundations, and during the 1930s there were many efforts at deliberately wooing the populace and "tutoring" the country in democracy. The RPP itself was reorganized to emphasize decentralization, wider participation of party members in decision-making, and greater responsiveness to popular needs and interests. This effort (which took various forms including for several months an actual merger of the party and government to achieve better coordination and supervision) was only partially successful, as has been the case with most such self-reform attempts by single parties. Another measure was the inclusion of some "independent" deputies in the Assembly, to give the legislators experience in accepting criticism and get the public accustomed to debate by "loyal" opponents but this too was less than successful as everybody recognized its ineffectiveness in changing government policies. Still another step was the establishment of a network of "People's Houses" *(Halkevleri)* and "People's Rooms" *(Halkodalari)* throughout the country to serve as centers for adult education, community activities, and political indoctrination through things like lectures on Turkish history, culture, and public affairs. These institutions served useful purposes, but because they were run entirely by the RPP they failed in one of their main stated aims, the encouragement of free discussion and criticism of public affairs. They were closed in 1951 by the Democratic administration which had long been charging that they were nothing but RPP sinecures, which to some extent they were.

Perhaps most important for Turkey's future, however, was the intense program of economic development known as *etatism* which was inaugurated soon after the demise of the Free party in 1931. It will be discussed in detail below.

Ataturk died in 1938 and was succeeded by his long-time colleague, fellow general in the War of Independence, negotiator of the Treaty of Lausanne, and prime minister from 1923 to 1937, Ismet Inonu. Inonu carried on the reforms, and skillfully brought Turkey through World War II as a neutral. Then in 1945 pressures began to build up again for political liberalization. Internationally, Turkey had been a founding member of the United Nations which was pledged to further democracy throughout the world. Domestically, there was restiveness due to the austerity which had been necessary during the war and the martial law restraints which had been imposed. Most important of all was the legacy of promises of democracy as soon as conditions allowed, as soon as the nation was "ready." By 1945 a whole generation of Kemalist-educated youth was on hand and ready to take part in public affairs, many political leaders with over two decades of experience were available, and a variety of new interests had begun to develop and to demand a voice in running the country.

Late in 1945, therefore, the moderate wing of the RPP under Inonu's stewardship decided that the time was ripe to allow organized opposition. Conservatives in the party led by Recep Peker, a strong militant who had led much of the RPP's tutoring activity, opposed the action, particularly when the opportunity was seized by four deputies who had recently been expelled from the RPP for breaches of party discipline. The Democratic party founded by them (Adnan Menderes, a large landowner from the Aegean region, a former member of the Free party, and a deputy since 1931; Celal Bayar, a veteran nationalist from Young Turk days, minister of economics during much of the single-party period, prime minister in 1937-8; Refik Koraltan, another veteran politician; and Faud Köprülü, a highly regarded professor of history at Istanbul University) won 61 seats in the election of 1946 despite many disadvantages. In July 1947 Inonu finally managed to force Peker's resignation as prime minister and assured the opposition's survival. In the ensuing four years the Democrats vigorously pressed their criticism of the government in the Assembly and campaigned from one end of the country to another, visiting virtually every town and village. The many causes of dissatisfaction with the RPP brought the Democrats victory on May 14, 1950, whereupon Bayar became Turkey's third president, Menderes prime minister, Köprülü foreign minister. The RPP, true to its word, stepped quietly into opposition.

The Democrats' election victory had been the result of support by intellectuals, businessmen, and primarily Turkey's great peasant majority. The new government soon set about keeping many of its campaign promises. This chiefly involved changes in economic policy and lessening the pressure for drastic interpretation of the Ataturk reforms. Economically the Democrats sought to speed up development by soliciting large amounts of foreign aid, particularly from the United States under the Truman Doctrine; engaging in deficit financing; importing large amounts of both industrial and agricultural machinery; and undertaking massive public works programs. These policies did quicken economic expansion and laid foundations for a relatively rapid expansion which is still continuing, but eventually brought rampant inflation and nearly bankrupted the country. These matters will be discussed further below.

A great deal more controversial was the manner of interpreting the reforms, particularly in the area of secularism, and the speed in implementing them. The strictures against religious teaching in public schools were relaxed (the Republicans, under electoral pressure, had modified this ban just before the 1950 elections by allowing religious instruction for those pupils whose parents specifically requested it; the Democrats took it one step further by introducing such teaching for all except those specifically requesting to be excluded, something few parents were willing to do). New schools for *imams* were opened, as well as a Faculty of Divinity at Ankara University. The public works program included large numbers of mosques along with the factories. Religious sects and orders which had been outlawed were permitted or at least their reemergence was overlooked. These actions were bitterly attacked by the RPP, although it took some stretching of the imagination to consider that the Democrats were repudiating secularism as was sometimes charged. Such actions did, however, give much fuel to the RPP opposition in a sphere in which feelings were particularly bitter on all sides.

A third and more subtle area of controversy was that of the sources of political leadership. The RPP had at its core intellectuals and career civil servants, whose orientations were national rather than local and who for the most part were determined reformers in every sense of the concept. The Democrats brought in men whom Frederick Frey has described as considerably more the products of local affairs, with nonofficial backgrounds and either professional or economic occupations.[1] In part, the RPP's scorn was merely at seeing themselves replaced by other men. But this alleged anti-intellectual bias, the tendency to rely more on locally and popularly expressed interests than on elite-generated ideas as to appropriate government policies, further alienated some of the many former Republicans who had supported the Democrats in the name of furthering democracy and economic development. These former Republicans now saw how much better the new type of leader fared at the polls than did the RPP. Some joined minor parties, others returned to the RPP and sharpened the polarization more than ever.

The hostility was reciprocated by the Democrats, who further inflamed it by accusing the RPP of exploiting their political position for personal gain (some of the charges were undoubtedly true), closing the People's Houses and confiscating much of the RPP's property as well as its records on the grounds that the latter had to be examined for evidence of corruption. The Democrats also engaged in much partisan favoritism, such as giving advertising (the bulk of which in Turkey is government-generated) only to pro-DP newspapers and using the state radio for party propaganda.

The steady embitterment was further accented after the DP won a second and even greater electoral victory in 1954. The election of 1957 reduced the DP margin somewhat, but only through what is now generally agreed to have been considerable fraud. By 1959 the government had passed a repressive press law, changed the electoral and political party laws to severely curb opposition, arrested numerous journalists and opposition politicians. Serious violence began in May 1959, becoming ever more frequent. In April 1960 the government attempted to stop opposition leader Inonu from holding a rally in the city of Kayseri, and on April 28-29 there were bloody clashes at Ankara and Istanbul universities. In both incidents, and in almost daily demonstrations thereafter, the government used troops as well as police to restore order.

The armed forces now faced a dilemma. They had hesitated for a long time despite dissatisfaction with the DP by small groups of officers going back at least as far as the late 1940s. The doctrine of military abstention from politics, first advocated by Ataturk when he resigned from the army in 1919 and determinedly maintained by him, was in part responsible. So was the fact that most of the officers were themselves products of the new Turkey and strongly believed in democratic forms. When by 1960 not only was there a threat of civil war, but the army had already been dragged into politics when the government had used soldiers to put down the opposition, there could be no further delay. On May 27, 1960 the government was ousted in a military coup d'état.

From then until October 1961 the country was ruled by a National Unity

---

[1] *The Turkish Political Elite* (Cambridge: M.I.T. Press, 1965); p. 380.

Committee headed by General Cemal Gursel, a fatherly, moderate officer who had only a few months previously warned his colleagues to stay out of politics just as he himself was being passed over for appointment as army chief of staff. The 38 officers of the NUC stated that their aim was only to repair the internal rents in the national fabric, to restore democracy, and to return political power to elected leaders at the earliest possible time.

The NUC took several important steps toward these ends. First, all those who could be charged with responsibility for the recent sorry events were purged. These included all of the DP members of the Assembly and many other party officials at the national, provincial, and local levels, most of whom were put on trial on Yassiada Island in the Sea of Marmara within sight of Istanbul. The proceedings were generally considered to be fair. The charges which ranged from personal corruption to violation of the constitution resulted in many prison sentences, and the execution in September 1961 of Menderes and two of his ministers. Bayar escaped death only because of his advanced age. Others ousted included the retirement of 5,000 officers including 235 generals and admirals in August 1960; and 147 university professors in October. Many of the latter were later reinstated after considerable public pressure.

Another NUC action was to sponsor the writing of a new constitution by a constituent assembly convened for that purpose. Its main new features were many checks and balances to prevent abuses of power such as the DP had been charged with. These included addition of a senate; a constitutional court with full powers of judicial review of government actions; and writing into the constitution many specific safeguards of civil liberties and freedom of expression and assembly. Many social welfare provisions were also included. The new constitution was supplemented by a new electoral law, which among other things provided for proportional representation rather than the winner-take-all system under which the DP had been able to greatly swell their parliamentary majority. The constitution was submitted to a national referendum in July 1961, and approved by 62 percent to 38 percent, with many of the former DP strongholds voting against it as a form of protest.

On the economic front the NUC established a State Planning Organization, something long advocated by both the RPP and by foreign advisors but stubbornly resisted by Menderes. The SPO drew up a Five-Year Plan which was inaugurated in 1962. The NUC also imposed considerable austerity, curbing luxury imports and stopping work on many public works and industrial projects which were allegedly uneconomic, badly planned, or built to favor partisan interests. In addition, it sought to reform the tax structure, particularly by levying taxes on income from agricultural production which had been exempt since the beginning of the Republic and by drastic tightening of enforcement of tax collection. Neither of these efforts had more than superficial success. Altogether, the economic performance of the NUC was disappointing.

Politically, too, the soldier-rulers dismayed those who had sought radical changes and reforms. This was due largely to the fact that to a considerable extent the officers were looking over their shoulders in the manner of politicians, maintaining their aim of ruling for only a short period and to rule in cooperation with civilian politicians. This was not done though without some internal strife within both the NUC and the armed forces as a whole. The majority of the committee found it necessary in October 1960 to purge a radical minority of 14 led by Colonel Alparslan Tür Kes, who considered another period of imposed reforms necessary. This purge was much to the liking of most civilian leaders, particularly the RPP which saw itself as the coup's heir apparent. The NUC had no intention of handing the government to the RPP however, and when in January 1960 political parties were allowed to resume activity, the RPP was joined in the field by several other aspirants who were tolerated by the NUC despite the fact that some were not too far from being revivals of the DP. This was particularly true of the Justice party, which included many former second-line Democrats who had escaped the purges, and other clear sympathizers with the ousted regime and its policies. The New Turkey party, headed by economist and finance minister under the NUC Ekrem Alican, had the favor of private industrialists and businessmen, many of whom had briefly worked under the banner of the small Freedom party around 1957. The Republican Peasants Nation party was basically one of the religious conservatives, the carry-over of another minor party from pre-1960. Elections were held in October 1961, with results as indicated in the following table:

	RPP	DP-JP	NTP	RPNP	TIP
1950	40.0%	53.5%		3.3%	
1954	35.3	56.6		4.9	
1957	40.9	47.7		7.2	
1961	36.7	34.8	13.7%	14.0	
1965	28.8	52.8	2.2	3.7	3.2%

Clearly, not much had changed in Turkish electoral politics.

For a brief time the armed forces hesitated, but then they turned power back to civilian hands after exacting from the politicians several agreements to preserve many of the NUC's actions and not to work against the "principles of May 27." The officers also insisted that Gursel be elected president. The members of the NUC became ex officio members of the new senate. Also at the insistence of the armed forces, an unlikely coalition government of the RPP and the Justice party was formed, with Inonu as premier. A period of political maneuvering now set in. In February 1962 a group of dissident officers under Colonel Talat Aydemir failed in an attempted coup when the majority of the armed forces remained loyal to civilian politics. In May the coalition government collapsed, succeeded by one between the RPP and two smaller parties. The government was unable to do more than mark time, however, and as a measure to conciliate the opposition and strengthen its own popularity, began to entertain amnesty proposals for the convicted Democrats. These things led to a second attempted coup by Aydemir, again put down by the rest of the armed forces. These developments further emboldened the Justice party, which also made considerable gains in local elections in November at the expense of both the RPP and the minor parties. The latter soon resigned from the coalition, feeling that their presence there had caused much of their electoral loss. In December, again under armed forces pressure, Inonu formed a third government of his party and independents.

By 1964 the basic pattern of Turkish politics had thus been reestablished: a system of basically two major parties and a smattering of minor ones, with the more conservative (Justice party) firmly in the electoral majority. The armed forces again found themselves faced with the choice of either intervening or remaining aloof and perhaps accepting a lower pace of reform. They chose the latter course, but only after eliciting from all the parties still another pledge not to act "contrary to the spirit of May 27." This nonintervention position was bolstered when early in 1965 a moderate faction under 40-year old businessman and successful administrator Suleyman Demirel won control of the Justice party. In general elections in October 1964 the JP won an outright majority, and Demirel became premier. In January 1966 President Gürsel resigned after suffering several strokes and was succeeded by Chief of the Army General Staff Cevdet Suray.

Thus, Turkey today is in an uneasy balance between political factions (including a new and markedly leftist Turkish Labor party) with the armed forces sitting in the wings but also divided in their political ideas. How stable the balance will be depends in large measure on the handling of key political, social, and economic problems which we shall discuss after briefly summarizing a few structural aspects of the Turkish political system.

The Framework of Political Life: Institutions and Structures

Turkey is governed by a Grand National Assembly composed of the 150-member Senate of the Republic (elected for staggered six-year terms) and the 450-member National Assembly (elected every four years). The assembly elects the president of the republic for a seven-year term, and he in turn appoints the prime minister and the cabinet. The assembly has the greater legislative power. A constitutional court established in 1961 has powers of judicial review of all legislative and executive actions. In addition to the central government, there are provincial governments consisting of elected provincial councils and central-government appointed governors. Large cities have separate governments, and villages elect their own councils with more limited powers.

As has already been mentioned, Turkey has two major political parties and several minor ones. The RPP can be generally described as representing the intellectuals, civil servants, and other urban elements. It also has considerable strength among landowners in some sections, who were left relatively untouched by the RPP's failure to implement many agricultural reforms during the single-party period, and in eastern Turkey where peasants derived particular benefit from political reforms. Although the RPP is often considered the stronghold of reform, this characterization is not entirely applicable, for despite its strong commitment to continuing change the party also includes many entrenched interests which have tended to resist letting the political system open itself to include new groups. In 1965 under a new, young, and able secretary-general, Bülent Ecevit, the party adopted the slogan "Left of Center" in an effort to simultaneously uphold reform and increase its electoral popularity. Even this was too much for some other powerful party leaders, however; and in mid-1967, 48 dissident senators and deputies under the leadership of former Deputy Prime Minister Turhan Feyzioglu split away and founded the Trust party. Despite these efforts the RPP is still identified with radical reform and the authoritarian rule of the single-party period (and is still led by octogenarian Inonu, remembered personally as one of the most militant of the reformers), and its electoral prospects for the immediate future appear dim.

The Justice party which became Turkey's biggest after the election of 1965 draws largely on the business community, local leaders in areas that chafe at the central domination (such as the Aegean region centering on Izmir), and the majority of the peasantry. This base is, of course, similar to the one on which the Democratic party rested. These groups' motivations are varied, including a preference for private sector economic development rather than the RPP's etatism, a variety of degrees of opposition to radical secularism and other social change, and opposition to particular groups and individuals in the RPP (many villages, for instance, are split into rival lineages each of which belongs to a different political party). The Justice party went through considerable internal turmoil between 1961 and 1965 when the more liberal wing under Prime Minister Suleyman Demirel won control and has continued to be the dominant voice in party policy. It is generally moderate, preferring private enterprise (but not exclusively), and tending also to modern interpretations of secularism though it can by no means be really accused of betraying this aspect of the Ataturk reforms. The JP's electoral prospects appear bright, but they could be reversed by an economic downturn, or by too great dissatisfaction in the armed forces and other urban elements which made the 1960 revolution.

There are also several minor parties. The Nation party is basically a group of social and religious conservatives who have long been on the political fringe. The New Turkey party is a group of economically-oriented dissident DP and JP intellectuals who operated briefly in 1956-7 as the Freedom party. The NTP's vote declined from 14 percent in 1961 to 3.5 percent in 1965 due to organizational problems and the attraction of the moderate wing of the JP. An as yet unknown quantity is the Republican Peasants Nation party led by Colonel Türkes and others of the 14 radicals purged from the NUC in 1960. Finally, there is the Turkish Labor party, led by a group of mostly Marxist intellectuals and some labor leaders of the far left, which advocates doctrinaire socialism. It has not yet attracted large numbers of worker votes, but if economic conditions do not improve the party's potential would seem great.

Interest groups have gradually increased in number, size, and degree of organization. The business community, centered largely in Istanbul and Izmir, is still relatively small and composed of commercial and small industry elements, although it does include some large industrial empires, such as that of Vehbi Koc. Private enterprise continues to suffer from shortages of skilled management, skilled workers, and investment capital, and the competition of state-owned and subsidized factories.

Labor has had the right to organize since 1947, but won the right to strike only after 1961. Labor union weakness has been due to suspicion by all governments that union growth would open the doors to leftist infiltration; to the fact that many welfare benefits which in Western countries were fought for by unions have been provided to Turkish workers unilaterally by the government; and to the large oversupply of unskilled workers. Since 1961, labor leaders have been quite active in organizing workers, and strikes in some important industries have often succeeded both in consolidating union strength and in winning higher wages and other benefits. The unions' political role has so far been limited, both because many labor leaders feel that their most fruitful area of work is not in direct politics, and because there are many differences among unions and among Turkey's two union federations as to which parties to support.

A particularly vocal group has been the students, as is the case in so many nations both developed and "developing." Ataturk always paid special attention to Turkey's youth, glorifying and encouraging them as leaders of the revolution. The students of Turkey's six universities, many technical and vocational schools, and lycees have seldom hesitated to voice their opinions on any political subjects, and they played a notable role in the events leading up to the 1960 revolution. Not all are left wing, however, and Turkey has two national student federations which are constant and often bitter rivals as well as frequent political opponents.

Other voluntary associations are few. Agricultural groups remain largely unorganized, and cooperatives are few despite concerted efforts in the 1930s and 1940s to popularize them. A number of women's organizations exist which are concerned primarily with continuing the emancipation of women and with charitable pursuits. Professional organizations are largely profession-oriented.

The Issues of Turkish Politics

The politics of Republican Turkey since the very beginning of the Ataturk revolution has revolved around several issues which can be conveniently summarized by the question "what is the proper and most socially useful interpretation of the principles of Kemalism?"

As was mentioned earlier, the Ataturk revolution's major ideas were pulled together in the RPP program of 1931 in the form of six major principles, republicanism, nationalism, secularism, populism, etatism, and revolutionism. These include all of the important aspects of social, political, and economic change with which the Turks have been concerned. Their precise interpretation, however, has been a matter of great controversy, particularly as changing circumstances required new policies in areas such as economic development, government organization, or education. The political parties frequently accuse each other of betraying Kemalism, and such accusations were the focus of the antigovernment demonstrations of 1960. An examination of these principles is thus a useful way to proceed.

1. *Republicanism* was the most basic, the expression of the most deeply ingrained Kemalist slogan "Hakimiyet-i Milletindir" (Sovereignty Belongs to the Nation). Under its aegis the Sultanate was abolished and the Turkish Republic proclaimed on October 29, 1923. Complete political authority was vested by the 1924 constitution in the National Assembly. In 1960-61, after the Menderes experience, there was general agreement that the preservation of republican government also required checks and balances (a senate, etc.) which were inserted in the 1961 constitution without controversy.

2. *Nationalism* was intended first to restore the pride and self-respect of the Turks who had so declined from when the Ottoman Empire was at its height, and second to create the national unity on which Western nations had so successfully built their strength. Under the Ottomans, despite the fact that it was a Turkish dynasty, the mass of Turks were considered as little more than another subject group; and in fact the Turks were one of the last groups in the empire to display nationalist sentiments.

The republican government's program to develop nationalist feelings among all Turks consisted of asserting both the domestic and international power of the Turkish state and of a vast effort at glorifying all aspects of Turkish history and culture. One of the earliest steps taken in this regard had been definition of the state (embodied in the National Pact of 1920) as those territories containing an "Ottoman Muslim majority" (in effect the postwar boundaries of Turkey) and renouncing all other ambitions and irredentism. Many steps also emphasized the complete sovereignty of the Turkish state. The Lausanne treaty was its first important symbol. During the 1920s, the government ended many foreign economic concessions by buying out foreign railroad and port companies, making many activities into government monopolies, or restricting certain occupations only to Turks. National pride was also emphasized by refusal of most foreign loans which were regarded as one of the chief ways in which inroads on Turkish sovereignty had been made in the past.

Among the most dramatic efforts at instilling nationalist sentiment were historical and cultural revivals which reached their height during the early and mid-1930s. The Turkish Historical Society "rediscovered" history of the Turkish people including connections with the territory of Anatolia back at least as far as Hittite and Sumerian times. Among the cultural activities were popularization of Turkish art, poetry, and folklore. Also particularly prominent was language activity. The 1930s saw prodigious efforts to cleanse the Turkish language from the overlay of Arabic and Persian which had been incorporated by the

Ottomans, and the restoration of "pure Turkish" which was discovered by, among other things, dispatching teams to remote areas to listen to the peasants. As words were discovered they were incorporated into newspaper and journal use, the constitution and other state documents were translated from "Ottoman," and Ottoman-Turkish glossaries issued. There was also the "Sun Language Theory," which purported to show that Turkish was the original language spoken by mankind. The history and language reforms were major subjects of public attention during most of the 1930s, sometimes going to some chauvinistic excess but generally serving their purpose particularly for school children. It is difficult to say how much credit should be given directly to such deliberate indoctrination efforts, but the Turks today are extremely proud of all aspects of their culture. On the other hand, Turkish nationalism has brought difficulties in popular acceptance as full citizens of various minorities (Greeks, Armenians, Jews in Istanbul, and about two million Kurds in eastern Turkey).

3. *Secularism* was a point in which Ataturk had particularly strong personal feelings, attributing much of Turkey's backwardness to its having been held in the grip of a reactionary Islam. He maintained that although he had nothing against religion as long as it was "enlightened," religion and public affairs must be strictly separated. On these grounds he put through a series of reforms aimed at disestablishing Islam and at reforming some of its practices. In 1924 the Caliphate followed the Sultanate into history. Soon came such things as closing of mystic orders and brotherhoods such as the dervishes; abolition of the office of Sheyh-ul-Islam and creating of a Ministry of Religious Affairs and a Directorate of Pious Foundations *(Evkaf);* closing of the *medreses* (theological seminaries); promulgation of secular civil, commercial, and penal codes and the abolition of religious courts; and in 1928 removal of Islam from the constitution. Education was also, of course, completely secularized. A second set of reforms aimed at the Turkification of Islam. These included translation of the Koran into Turkish and forbidding the use of Arabic in the *ezan* (call to prayer). Public religious observance was implicitly discouraged.

Not surprisingly, secularism has been one of the most controversial of the reforms. Only a few Turks want to reverse it entirely, and few dispute the need to break the political power of the Islamic hierarchy, but many question whether or not it had to be so drastic. The Turkish people remain strongly religious, and even much of the urban middle class continue to perform such acts as observing the fast of *Ramadan.* In addition, the advent of electoral competition has tempted all the political parties to make concessions in the interpretation of secularism, examples of which were mentioned earlier.

A further problem is that despite the fact that Turkey is officially a secular state, for many Turks the concept *Turk* still implicitly means *Turkish Muslim,* and the religious minorities are not always looked on kindly or given the equal treatment to which they are legally entitled. (Official discrimination does not exist.)

There is no chance today that secularism per se will cease to be a foundation of the state in the sense, for example, that religious law might be enforced by the state. But the Turks have not yet come to a final conclusion on the proper role of religion in society, and the proper meaning of secularism is likely to remain a political football for many years to come.

4. *Populism* has also been the basis of important reforms. As was noted earlier, the dynasty was abolished and a republic took its place, governed by representatives elected by universal adult male suffrage (women getting the franchise in 1934). Other measures abolished titles, such as Bey and Pasha, though many remain in popular usage. Populism meaning such things as equality before the law regardless of social class is pretty fully practiced.

On the other hand, Turkish populism has generally meant government *for* the people more than *by* the people, and there is still a very marked elitist thread running through much of the Turkish political discussion. The persistence of considerable sentiment for returning to single-party political tutoring of the Turkish people has been noted earlier. In 1960-61 there was a good deal of talk in Ankara to the effect that the lesson of the Menderes period was that the peasants were not ready for the franchise. Much of the elitism is reflected in the educational system. Turkey has compulsory, free primary education, but shortages of teachers and facilities and other problems have resulted in a national literacy rate of only 49 percent in 1965. Secondary education is available only to relatively few. Village boys and girls very seldom indeed have the intellectual and material requirements for passing entrance examinations, enrolling in an urban lycee, and making their way into the urban, educated elite. Such a problem is not, or course, unique to Turkey.

5. *Etatism* as a basic principle was added to the RPP program in 1931 and has been one of the most controversial, becoming more so as Turkish economic development has advanced. A brief survey of the Turkish economic situation will be useful here.

Turkey emerged from her War of Independence in extremely poor economic circumstances. The country had been wracked by almost a decade of continuous war; had most of its commerce and what little industry there was either in the hands of non-Turkish minorities (the Ottomans, like other upper-class Middle East Muslims, traditionally looked down on these pursuits) or European concessionaires; had only the most rudimentary agriculture; and was hampered by various tariff restrictions under the Lausanne treaty. During the 1920s, there was relatively little advance. The government devoted its efforts to such things as buying up foreign concessions like railroads and the port of Istanbul and similar actions which had immediate political importance but only more long-range economic effects. Little attention was paid to agriculture, the most significant step being abolition of the tithe and other taxes on agricultural income, a measure which also meant a sharp reduction in government revenues.

The world depression of 1929 hit Turkey very hard, and came simultaneously with the Free party episode and its revelations of much dissatisfaction with economic affairs. These and other pressures gave rise to etatism, a doctrine under which the state undertook to deliberately and systematically promote all forms of economic development. As a doctrine it was based on practical more than ideological considerations, *i.e.*, that state action was the only way to promote development in many areas, but that where private enterprise was able and willing to operate and would do things which met criteria of national usefulness (as determined by the government) it would be not only allowed but also encouraged and helped. A large-scale development program thus began. Government promotion of industry was done through two large holding companies, the *Sümerbank* and *Etibank;* through the *Is Bankasi* (Business Bank) to assist private enterprise; through an Agricultural Bank for credit to farmers, and also numerous other miscellaneous efforts. A five-year plan was inaugurated in 1933 and a second one in 1938. Primary attention was given to industry, but, in contrast to the 1920s, agriculture also began to receive attention. During the 1920s and 1930s, most development was financed with domestic resources, as the government was extremely suspicious of foreign capitalists (whose activities had allegedly been key in eroding the sovereignty of the Ottoman government). Therefore, almost no offers of foreign loans were accepted.

The restlessness of 1946 which led to the transistion to multiparty politics was in considerable part economic. Dissatisfaction with wartime austerity and strict controls was added to the growing impatience of an increasing number of potential private entrepreneurs with etatist policies. They charged, with much justification, that officials paid only little attention to the problems of the private sector despite government denials that etatism meant favoring the public sector as a matter of principle. There were also many examples of inefficiency and poor quality goods being produced by state industries which did not need to submit to the discipline of the market and were frequently bailed out of difficulties by more and more government funds. Some piecemeal reforms were made by the RPP government before the Democratic victory in 1950 (which was in part based on a program of greatly increased emphasis on the private sector and aid to agriculture).

The DP decade saw a great quickening in economic development for several reasons. One was simply its timing: Much of the infrastructure needed for a modern economy now existed. Another was the availability of foreign aid in great quantities, particularly from the United States. American aid to Turkey during 1947-60 amounted to around $3 billion. The Menderes government also engaged in large amounts of deficit financing which in addition to new industry brought severe inflation and was one of the causes of revolt by the largely fixed-income urban educated class in 1960. Some efforts were made to increase the efficiency of state industries with moderate success. Significantly, the Menderes government did not carry out its intention of selling some state factories to private owners, possibly because the Democrats too found that keeping them under government control was politically quite lucrative.

The agricultural sector benefited from the importation of large numbers of tractors and other equipment, and from some irrigation, improved seed, fertilizer, the development of village roads, and so on provided by the government and international agencies. The effects here were only marginal, however. Mechanization benefited mainly the larger landowners; and other measures, though useful, were not massive nor basic enough to enable most of Turkey's peasants (particularly the wheat-growers and animal-raisers of Anatolia) to overcome their dependence on good weather as by far the most important factor in determining their production. In the early 1950s the Korean War and excellent weather stimulated demand for Turkish agricultural exports (particularly wheat) and rising population added domestic demand. In response, more and more marginal land was put into production, with resulting declines in productivity, less emphasis on basic improvements, and less availability of good grazing lands. The bumper crops of 1953-55 were followed by several drought years and by the end of the decade Turkey had turned from a net exporter to a net importer of wheat and peasant income remained low. No government has yet made significant progress in land reform.

Menderes' financial policies eventually brought the country to near bankruptcy, and it was only under strong pressure from the World Bank and many creditors that a stabilization program was undertaken in 1958. Further complaints of both domestic and foreign observers were the Democratic government's great aversion to planning, Menderes' penchant for large and spectacular public works projects, and the use of economic resources for partisan political purposes. On the positive side once more, however, the Menderes decade saw the growth of an impressively vigorous business community and the basis for a rapidly expanding consumer market. Thus the Democratic decade, while admittedly one of very considerable economic progress, also had serious shortcomings in creating a sound basis for further development.

On the basis of all these experiences the debate over the proper interpretation of etatism has since 1960 been more vigorous than ever. Most political groups favor a combination of public and private enterprise, lacking firm ideological views (the doctrinaire socialists, mainly in the Turkish Labor party, are few and with relatively little influence). Both sectors are handicapped by such things as lack of a significant private capital market. Large amounts of government and foreign capital recently had to be provided for a project like Turkey's second steel mill at Eregli. The government has also taken a strong hand through the State Planning Organization under whose auspices a Five-Year Development Plan was drawn up and inaugurated late in 1962. A second five-year plan was approved in April 1967. Under the NUC and subsequent governments there have been cutbacks in luxury imports and similar measures designed for increased stability. The base of foreign credits has been widened by the creation of a consortium of several European nations and recently by aid from the Soviet Union. To the surprise of many, Turkey has begun to meet many of its development targets, including that of overall rate of growth in GNP of 7 percent in 1966. Agricultural production has also been rising, but Turkey's balance of payments still shows a large annual deficit. The Justice party has generally tended to favor the private sector, but has had to take special measures to combat considerable unemployment as the rate of economic growth has not kept up with demand for industrial jobs. Large numbers of Turkish workers have recently found employment in Europe. Many workers are being pushed into the cities by Turkey's high birthrate.

In summary, Turkish economic development has advanced greatly since the beginning of the republic. The roles of the private and public sectors have tended to shift according to circumstances and shifts in political rather than ideological factors. Basic improvements, such as less weather-dependent agriculture and increased supply of skilled management and skilled workers as well as employment opportunities in industry, remain to be achieved, but conditions for further expansion seem generally favorable under pragmatic political rule. It also seems clear that economic policy is now one of the chief issues on which Turks will judge the performance of the political parties.

6. *Revolutionism,* the last of the "Six Arrows," is perhaps the most difficult to define, certainly the most difficult to achieve. It poses Turkey's greatest challenge, that of maintaining a continually revolutionary spirit, never ceasing to be open to new ideas, and willing to make new changes to approach the ideals of the Ataturk revolution. The challenge is particularly great because after having already passed into an era of multiparty politics, Turkey seems faced with the prospect of either reverting to authoritarian rule and imposing further changes, or the combination of a conservative peasant majority and a leadership intent on getting electoral support and therefore slowing down the reform pace.

Neither of these alternatives presents easy answers to Turkey's problems. Reverting to authoritarian rule is probably possible only through physical force, as became clear in 1960-61. The Turkish army could have maintained itself in power, but when faced with the tremendous pressure of many political groups which did not feel that their interests would be well served, the officers chose to give in rather than repress their own countrymen. The return to civilian, multiparty rule was reenforced by the army's tradition of noninvolvement in politics under the Republic, a tradition which weighed heavily in the thinking of many officers who were also products of Kemalist education and upbringing. If military rule is rather unlikely, rule by a single reformist party is even more so. Of course were Turkey to fall into still another crisis, such as that of 1960, or a severe economic depression, a combination of military and civilian power might well come into being to suspend democracy for a more extended period while new reforms are made.

The second possibility, a conservative electorate and opportunistic leadership, is more likely to come to pass, although it need not mean an end to reform. Turkish peasants, like their urban compatriots, have begun to see that reform and development is to their benefit even though they cling tenaciously to their religion; relatively few have as yet acquired such modern habits as realizing the value of postponing some present gains for greater future gains. On the other hand, the considerable clamor for education from villagers in almost every section of the country, the increasing physical and social mobility of large numbers of Turks, and the rapid growth of the urban middle class, all increase the prospect that the electorate will also make modernizing demands.

Thus, Turkey is truly in need of creative, imaginative political leaders. Will they be able to work out policies which can satisfy both the radical reformers and enough conservatives to provide popular backing for continued modernization? Will educational efforts, economic incentives, and other means be used so as to eventually bridge the elite-mass gap and the generation gap and to make the mass of Turks into agents of change rather than only objects of it? To do these things will require shrewd balancing of the need for rapid development and the need to go slow enough to bring the population along; but it has been said, after all, that leadership in a democracy is being ahead of the people but not too far ahead. If Turkey can continue to be revolutionary and also democratic, it will be a great achievement indeed and fully in the Ataturk tradition.

Foreign Policy

Turkish foreign policy under the Republic has been characterized by careful evaluation of the country's needs and limitations as a small power. As has been mentioned, Turkey renounced all irredentist ambitions after World War I. The single exception was the province of Hatay, whose status was left unsettled in the Lausanne Treaty and which Turkey annexed in 1938. During the 1920s and 1930s, Turkey remained relatively aloof from foreign affairs. Relations with Russia were cordial during most of the period, the Soviets wooing the Turks as natural allies in anti-imperialist revolution. Ataturk was ever wary of Soviet designs, however, and kept close watch on communist activities in Turkey. The Communist party has been outlawed since about 1925. During the War of Independence, Russia supplied the Turkish nationalists with military aid and some credits. On the west, Turkey made treaties of friendship and some collective security with most of the Balkan states. Turkey joined the League of Nations in 1932, and as relations with European powers gradually improved after the world war and War of Independence experiences, talks on an anti-axis alliance with Britain and France began in 1937, being signed soon after the outbreak of World War II.

Turkey remained neutral in the war, however, joining the allied side just in time to become a founding member of the United Nations. In 1945 relations with Russia deteriorated when the latter made unacceptable demands about the Turkish Straits, over which Turkey had gotten control in the Montreux Convention of 1936. When the United States offered aid under the Truman Doctrine in 1948 Turkey accepted, and soon thereafter Turkey became a member of NATO. In 1950 Turkey sent troops to assist the U.N. effort in Korea. During the 1950-60 decade, she maintained very close ties with the United States, receiving about $3 billion in military and economic aid. Relations with other European countries were also close economically, politically, and culturally. Turkey also joined the Baghdad Pact (now Central Treaty Organization) and entered into mutual security pacts with Greece and Yugoslavia.

The sorest point in foreign affairs has been relations with Greece, particularly over Cyprus. Under British rule the Turkish minority on Cyprus was fairly secure, but when the Greek Cypriot majority began to agitate for the end of British rule in the early 1950s Turkey became alarmed for its compatriots and about strategic problems were the island to become part of Greece. Much Turkish pressure was applied, and an agreement for Cypriot independence with guaranteed rights for the Turkish minority was reached at Geneva in 1959. It lasted only a short time, however, and in 1963 fighting broke out again, stopped by United Nations intervention.

The Cyprus dispute has had far-reaching effects. Turkish disappointment with American failure to back Turkey coincided with a general disenchantment by many Turks with the close ties to the United States and the impression of being virtually an American puppet. It was demonstrated several times in anti-American rioting; and while staying in NATO and CENTO, Turkey has also begun to seek more cordial relations with the Soviet Union. The latter is now giving Turkey economic aid, although most of Turkey's economic ties continue to be with the West. Relations with the Arab states are generally smooth. Turkish foreign policy seems headed toward more multilateral ties and a greater degree of maneuverability and independence from the great powers. It is a trend which most Turks appear to welcome.

SELECTED BIBLIOGRAPHY

The most thorough analysis of Turkish development is Bernard Lewis, *The Emergence of Modern Turkey* (New York: Oxford, 1961). Shorter treatments are Geoffrey Lewis, *Turkey* 3rd ed. (New York: Praeger, 1965) and the somewhat dated but still useful Lewis V. Thomas, *The United States and Turkey and Iran* (Cambridge: Harvard, 1951). The politics of the Tanzimat is analyzed by Roderic Davison, *Reform in the Ottoman Empire 1856-76* (Princeton: Princeton, 1963.) Kemal Karpat's *Turkey's Politics, The Transition to a Multi-Party System,* (Princeton: Princeton, 1959) is an excellent analysis of primarily the 1946-50 period. Development in 1923-60 is also discussed by Richard Robinson, *The First Turkish Republic* (Cambridge: Harvard, 1963), and Nuri Eren, *Turkey Today and Tomorrow* (New York:Praeger, 1963). The circumstances and politics of the 1960 military coup d'etat are described in Walter F. Weiker, *The Turkish Revolution, 1960-61* (Washington: Brookings, 1963). An analysis of the Turkish economy is Z. Y. Hershlag, *Turkey, An Economy in Transition* (The Hague: Van Keulen, 1958). Leadership development is analyzed in Frederick W. Frey, *The Turkish Political Elite* (Cambridge: M.I.T., 1965), and education in Andreas Kazamias, *Education and the Quest for Modernity in Turkey* (Chicago: University of Chicago, 1966). A series of excellent essays on specific aspects of Turkish modernization is found in Robert

E. Ward and Dankwart A. Rustow, eds., *Political Modernization in Japan and Turkey* (Princeton: Princeton, 1964). The best biography of Ataturk is Lord Kinross, *Ataturk: The Rebirth of a Nation* (New York: Morrow, 1965). A perceptive essay on stability and change is Dankwart A. Rustow, "Turkey: The Modernity of Tradition," in Lucian Pye and Sidney Verba, eds., *Political Culture and Political Development* (Princeton: Princeton, 1965).

chapter 8

Iran*

Introduction and Description

The Middle East has long been a key region in world affairs. Aside from its being the progenitor of three of the world's great religions and creator of a great scientific and cultural heritage, the area has taken on importance in more tangible ways. First, it serves as a key land bridge, with three countries especially crucial: Turkey, linking Europe and Asia; Egypt, linking Africa and Asia (and with the Suez Canal, Asia, and the Mediterranean Sea); Iran, linking the Middle East with the Indian subcontinent and the Far East.

A second key aspect of the region's significance lies in the energy sources which it supplies to the world. Middle Eastern oil has been crucial to fuel Western, especially European, industry and transport. Kuwait, Saudi Arabia, Iraq, Libya, and Iran pump millions of barrels of oil, most of which reach Europe but increasingly find their way to Japan, India, eastern Europe, and even the Soviet Union.

Finally, the region has become a focus for world attention as the Arab-Israeli dispute has assumed more violent forms, resulted in misery for millions of persons, and, with the introduction of major Soviet and American military forces in the area, constantly threatened world peace.

As the region is significant in world religious, intellectual, and political developments, so is Iran significant in the region. Iran is religiously distinct as the home of both the Zoroastrian religion, whose largest group of adherents are the Parsees in India, and Bahai'ism, which has become a worldwide faith. Moreover, the official state religion of Iran is the Shi'ite branch of Islam, considerably different from the Sunni branch followed by the vast majority of Muslims. A 25 centuries long cultural life with significant contributions in astronomy, medicine, mathematics, literature, and philosophy has established a

---

*Marvin Zonis, assistant director, Center of Middle Eastern Studies, University of Chicago.

permanent position for Iran in the history of the world's intellectual life. A key geographic position, a key factor among Mid-East petroleum suppliers, and the chief friend of Israel in the Middle East all additionally contribute to Iran's importance. The significance of Iran lies precisely in the fact that it has the same outstanding characteristics as the region in which it is located. The distinctiveness of the region which Iran typifies is multifaceted and vital.

Iran is a large country of some 628,000 square miles, the size of Texas, New Mexico, Arizona, and California combined or equivalent to the total area of England, France, Germany, Italy, Belgium, Holland, and Denmark. Its strategic position is mirrored in its lengthy boundaries with its neighbors. To the east, Iran shares a common border with Pakistan of 500 miles and with Afghanistan, a similar amount. Along the north, Iran and the Soviet Union meet for some 700 miles east of the Caspian Sea and 480 miles west of the Caspian, with Iran's Caspian shore approximately 400 miles long. To the west, Turkey stretches for 240 miles and Iraq for another 700 before the border reaches the Persian Gulf. Along the south, Iran has a coastline of over 1000 miles on the gulf.

In addition to its lengthy borders with diverse foreign nations, the salient geographical features of Iran are its extremes of climate and terrain. The general scarcity of water has restricted habitation to only 30 percent of the land area. Yet the southern shores of the Caspian Sea are a veritable rain forest, the Persian word for which has passed into English as *jungle*. The country is trisected by two east-west mountain ranges with peaks up to 18,000 feet, with considerable hindrance to communication and effective control by the central government. Yet the natural travel routes from Iraq in the west to the Soviet Union in the northeast have served for centuries as invasion routes and formed part of the famed "Silk Route" to China.

The people of Iran in their religions, languages, and ethnic backgrounds reflect the diversity of the geography of their land. A population of some 26 million in 1966 was counted as 98.5 percent Muslim. Yet Islam in Iran takes a variety of forms and displays a variety of interpretations. The Shi'ite and Sunni division and numerous versions of Shi'ism fragment an ostensibly united faith. In addition, there are communities of Jews, Christians, and especially Bahais who despite their limited numbers play a great role in the economic and political life of the country.

In addition to the differences of religion among urban dwellers, there are striking linguistic and ethnic differences among the people. The name Iran, which means "land of the Aryans" belies the Turkic, Mongol, and Semitic peoples who have mixed with the original Aryan invaders. Examination of a map of Iran on which has been recorded the population distribution by linguistic or ethnic groups reveals the heterogeneity of the people: to the northwest, Turkish speaking Azarbaijanis; to the north, Gilani and Mazanderani; to the northeast, Turkomans and Kurds; to the east, Arabs; to the south, Qashqais, Lurs, and Bakhtiaris; to the southwest, Arabs; to the west Kurds. The center of the country, the central plateau surrounded by the Zagros and Elburz ranges, is the home of the Iranians. The picture then is of a combination of ethnically or linguistically distinct peoples populating nearly every border area of the country. Not only are these border people cut off from the Iranians by the mountain ranges, but more threateningly are in close physical proximity with their kin across national boundaries which present no natural obstacles to movement. In the past, these groups have had closer ties with the Arabs of Iraq and Kuwait; the Kurds of Iraq, Turkey, and the USSR; the Turkomans of the USSR and Afghanistan; and the Baluchi of Pakistan than with their Iranian countrymen. The result has been mistrust of the border peoples, fear of political relations with neighboring powers, and constant concern for the dismemberment of the country.

This melange of ethnic, linguistic, and religious groups is primarily rural—some 62 percent of the population living in towns and vilages smaller than 5,000 persons. Many of these are largely uninvolved in national life and cut off from schools, medical care, the mass media. On the other hand, 10 percent of the nation's population live in its capital, Teheran, a city with the amenities and bustle of Europe. Teheran's economic, political, and cultural domination over the remainder of the country is immense. (This domination partly accounts for the importance of Iran's religious minorities who are overwhelmingly concentrated in the capital.)

The economy of Iran reflects the diversity of its peoples. In part, technically sophisticated and integrated with international economic currents, the economy remains on balance, archaic and isolated. Nonetheless, the leading sectors have succeeded in increasing the volume of goods and services available to the population. Since 1963 the economy has advanced at a near boom pace, giving Iran a rate of economic growth comparable to the world's fastest growing economies. Annual per capita income has now reached $250. While this figure is low by the standards of the more developed West, it is relatively prosperous for the Middle East, Asia, and Africa.

Iran's prosperity is based on her massive petroleum supplies. Now the largest oil exporter in the Middle East, Iran earned close to one billion dollars from her oil sales in 1968. The sum is expected to rise continually as new oil producing areas are located; as Iran locates new markets to which her oil can be sold, especially in the developing nations; and as the international consortium of oil companies responsible for the vast majority of Iran's exports agrees to expand Iran's share of international petroleum production.

Not only has the country's revenue reached a high level—in 1968 oil brought in nearly $40 for every man, woman, and child—but that revenue has grown steadily for the past 15 years. With the resumption of oil sales following the nationalization crises of 1951-53, Iran's oil revenues totalled only $22 million. Since then Iran's oil income has been mounting at an increasing rate. This annual increase in oil income has served as a tremendous impetus to economic activity, produced something of a boom mentality, and has been the key factor underlying Iran's political stability.

While oil accounts for 15 to 20 percent of Iran's gross national product, agriculture remains the basis of Iran's economic life. Some 60 percent of the population is engaged in its pursuit and together they add 40 percent of the national product. Iran's agriculture has never been of the subsistence variety but has always tied even the smallest producers into the market economy through the production of cash crops. Nearly half of all agricultural production is derived from wheat, cotton, rice, and other field crops, while livestock contributes about one-third and orchards and fruit, the remainder.

Traditionally, however, the surplus produced by the agricultural sector never found its way back to the farms. Rather than being reinvested in agriculture, these profits were shifted to the city by absentee landlords and contributed to Iran's industrial and urban growth. As a result, agriculture was the least dynamic economic sector with no increase in production during certain periods of the 1960s. Partially as a response to this and to more pressing political problems to be noted below, the government launched a vigorous land reform program in late 1962. Ultimately, thousands of landlords were displaced (although compensated for their lost lands) while hundreds of thousands of peasant cultivators became landowners (although not without having to pay the government for their new property). While the immediate results of the land reform have been to introduce a fair degree of turmoil in the countryside, it appears that substantial government intervention—in the form of agricultural credits and technical assistance to the new proprietors—will contribute to steadily mounting production even as much of the rural population is siphoned off to the cities.

Iran's industrial production is still small, although growing rapidly, and contributes some 10 percent of the total national welfare. From a state directed industrialization program in the 1930s, Iran's development lagged until the 1950s when renewed oil production began. As money again entered the economy through the government, private entrepreneurs took a more active role. Rather than sending their money to Europe, investments were made in Iran. First, office and apartment buildings were built in Teheran. Then consumer goods—soaps, cooking oils, bottled drinks, and the like—began to be produced in greater quantities. Now Iran can boast privately owned enterprises producing refrigerators, air conditioners, automobile tires, refined petroleum products, paper, shoes, textiles, as well as steel rolling mills and automobile assembly plants.

Along with these private developments and in many ways a precursor of them was massive governmental industrial investment culminating in two major complexes not yet completed. Ever since the 1920s Iran has considered the construction of a steel mill. Abortive starts were made, but in 1964 Iran disregarded the advice of the American and European governments as well as private steel producers by signing an agreement with the Soviet Union. The agreement provided for the construction of an integrated steel mill with an initial capacity of 750,000 tons, expandable in two phases to three million tons. The mill would use strictly domestic resources—Iranian coal, limestone, and iron ore. In return, Iran would pay for the $450 million plus project by constructing an 800-mile pipeline from her southern oil fields to the Soviet Union. The pipeline would supply the U.S.S.R.'s southern provinces with natural gas which to the present has been completely wasted, being burned off as it escaped from the ground. Both projects are well under way and give promise of being more economically successful than had previously been imagined.

A second major government project is a joint undertaking with a number of American corporations which will result in the construction of a major petrochemicals complex. Located on the Persian Gulf coast, natural gas and petroleum products will be used to produce chemicals and plastics for domestic consumption as well as for export. More than $100 million is being invested at this time.

Together, these two projects symbolize the economic development which it is hoped will realize higher standards of living for Iranians. But just as Iran's peoples are a melange, so is her economy a mixture of advanced and primitive elements. Economic development is poorly distributed with the major portion of wealth going to its richer, urban inhabitants. While the average per capita income is estimated nationally at $250 per year, in rural areas (for the majority of Iranians) that figure is considerably below $100. Similarly, with all the fruits of modernization—the gross rural-urban imbalances of Iran persist. Whether it be health or education, automobiles or telephones, the inhabitants of Teheran enjoy benefits to a far greater extent than do others; 69 percent of all those who have any college education live in Teheran; 77 percent of all beds in medical and mental hospitals are located in the capital; 95 percent of all daily newspapers are published and read in Teheran; 62 percent of all the nation's passenger automobiles are owned and driven by Teheranis. These and a host of similar statistics illustrate one fundamental point, viz not all Iranians participate equally in the life of their country. Gross disparities exist in life expectancy, live childbirths, education, and wealth. While current programs are ostensibly designed to reduce these disparities, critics of the present government argue that these are halfhearted attempts and, in fact, the imbalances are growing greater. Partisans dispute this and urge a historical perspective to illustrate how far Iran has progressed. Such a perspective, however, illustrates that the differences between social classes and urban and rural dwellers has hardened as new criteria for differentiation, e.g., Western education and investment capital, have been introduced by development. While statistics are lacking it does seem clear that the extreme imbalances which characterize contemporary Iran represent a considerable worsening of the previous condition and a problem which present political forces in Teheran are not significantly ameliorating.

History

The recent history of Iran manifests several themes which serve as the background to this social structure and to contemporary politics. Perhaps the dominant theme is the lengthy success of Iran in avoiding colonialism. From the introduction of European powers following the invasion of Egypt by Napoleon, Iran has been considered a prize plum. During the 18th and 19th centuries, France, Britain, and Russia competed for influence at the courts of the shahs. For the French, Iran represented a potential ally in her struggles with the British in India. When those struggles waned following the establishment of complete British hegemony French interest diminished leaving the field to the British and Russians.

It seems clear that from the late 17th century Britain's interests lay chiefly in protecting the northwestern approaches to India—the only possible invasion route unimpeded by formidable mountains. With alterations of governments and circumstances, British policy fluctuated between the aggressive pursuit of active control over the Iranian government to a passive policy seeking only to prevent Russia from doing the same. Russia seems to have been pursuing a variety of interests at different periods: from control of territory for strategic interests to capturing warm water ports on the Persian Gulf to simple economic imperialism.

Iran's success in preserving her independence was based on the art of playing off one foreign power against the other. The last half of the 19th century illustrates a series of classic manoeuvers of this type. Fearing for Iran's security, the Shah would turn to the Russians for support. When Russian influence was threatening to become too great, the Shah would turn to the British. When the British demanded a concession over Iran's railroads in return, a concession which the Shah was unwilling to give, he approached the Russians and urged them to demand a similar concession. Then he could return to the British and promise not to award the Russians rights for constructing railroads if they did not press their demands. Thus, no concessions were granted and Iran retained her independence.

Two developments altered this balance. First, foreign powers learned to make complementary rather than conflicting demands. No longer could the Shah refuse to grant demands for concessions on the grounds that the other foreign power would lose out. By the end of the 19th century, there were British and Russian banks, British and Russian trade companies, British and Russian capitulations (the right of citizens of those countries to be tried by their own rather than Iranian courts), British and Russian control over Persian customs, and so forth.

Second, Britain and Russia drawn together by the fear of a recently united and restless Germany, determined to settle their extra-European differences to concentrate on the new challenge. The treaty of 1907, among other countries, divided Iran into "spheres of influence." The Russians were given a virtually free hand in northern Iran including Teheran and Isfahan. The British received a small zone in the southeast flanking British India. In between was a large neutral zone including the city of Shiraz. Despite protestations to the contrary, Iranian nationalists viewed the treaty as a prelude to the dismemberment of their country. That fear was exacerbated by the failure of the signatories to consult or notify Iran of their agreement. Indeed, in the years preceding World War I Russia took an impressive position of supremacy in her zone.

When World War I broke Iran immediately declared itself a neutral, but this did not spare it from belligerencies. Russia and Britain on the one hand and the Ottoman Empire on the other invaded the country, established military bases, fought campaigns, and even went so far as to organize military units on Iranian territory. (These units were composed of Iranian recruits, equipped, officered, and paid by the British or Russians.)

From the direct and indirect intervention of foreign governments and the internal weakness and decay Iran's sovereignty seemed to be rapidly slipping away. Had it not been for the Bolshevik Revolution and the subsequent renunciation by Lenin of all Czarist, imperialist claims, it is likely that the 1907 agreement would have been formalized into the dismemberment of Iran and an end to its independence. But Iran was saved from that fate and as one of the few countries of Asia and Africa to have preserved her independence in the age of imperialism, strengthened a widespread sense of national pride and national identity. Moreover, Iran became an astute player in the game of international politics, a role which has been played to the present. When an outside power threatened, an appeal was made for protection to a second power, hostile to the first. Thus, the vital role of the United States in post-World War II Iran when the Soviets supported "independent" republics of Azarbaijan and Kurdestan in Iran's northwest and west. True to form, as the Shah perceived that threat diminish and his own internal political position strengthen, the value of the United States to the Shah diminished and their influence, accordingly, fell. The Iran-U.S.S.R. steel mill pact and the supplying of over $100 million worth of military supplies by the U.S.S.R. thereafter were only the outward manifestations of a return to a pattern of normal foreign relations for Iran.

Besides this theme in Iran's foreign relations (success in avoiding colonial status despite the intervention of Czarist Russia and Great Britian, more recently the Soviet Union and the United States, in its domestic affairs) two major themes run through recent Iranian history. One is the Persian Constitutional Movement of 1905-1909 which resulted in the first regulation by a formal consititution of political affairs of any Middle Eastern state. The movement had its roots in the granting of concessions to foreign companies seeking to exploit Iran in the latter part of the 19th century. Then concession hunters from Great Britain and Russia competed for the right to control Iran's foreign trade, to develop its natural resources, to build railways and bridges, to monopolize any economic undertaking which promised sizeable economic benefit.

That such benefits could accrue to foreigners was due to the total corruption of the monarch and his court, the pervasive decay of public morality, internal administrative and political anarchy, and foreign pressures. These had contributed to the near bankruptcy of the government and a pressing need for funds.

(The monarch, Nasr ed-din Shah, who ruled from 1848 to his assassination in 1896, became infatuated with travel in Europe and his three trips in 1873, 1878, and 1889 created a need for vast sums of money.) The Shah's demand for funds in combination with internal decay and external pressure made Iran a fruitful arena for concession hunters ready to bribe Iranian officials.

The incredible backwardness of Iran at the end of the 19th century meant that a virtually limitless array of projects were available and worthwhile. One perceptive British traveler, Edward G. Browne, wrote:

> When I was in Persia [in 1888], the old regime held undisputed sway, and except for the existence of the Indo-European telegraph, the conditions of life were entirely medieval. There were no railways, no banks, no paper money, no cabs, no hotels outside the capital, and of course, no telephones. The few newspapers which appeared at irregular intervals were lithographed and, being produced by courtiers and officials, contained hardly any news and no criticism, had a very restricted circulation and no sale save such as was secured by supplying them to government employees and deducting the subscription from their salaries . . . The only method of travel was on foot or horseback . . . The Government was a pure despotism, mitigated by the lack of centralization and the quasi-independence of the provincial governors, which often made it possible to escape oppression by the simple process of moving into another district under a more benign rule . . .

Into this atmosphere stepped Baron Julius de Reuter, an Austrian who had bought his title and made a fortune in England. His business acumen was revealed by a breathtaking set of concessions he obtained from the Shah. For an extremely modest annual payment to Iran, he was given a virtual monopoly on the exploitation of all Iran's natural resources (save gold, silver, and precious stones which the Shah assumed were the only true bases of real wealth), all communication facilities, all uninhabited lands and manufactories. Partly in revulsion to this sale of national wealth and partly from more narrow political considerations, a group of important officials, including the wife of the Shah, some ministers, leading *ulema* or Islamic theologians, and dissident merchants with the support of the Russian minister, combined to pressure the Shah— pressure which resulted in the cancellation of the Reuters concession.

These notables had joined in the collective political action for the first time in the history of Iran. But the Reuters concession was not to be the last time. Another startling concession—this one an 1882 concession to a British firm for a monopoly over the production, distribution, and sale of all tobacco in whatever form—generated a more immediate and more widespread reaction, for now virtually all sectors of society were affected either as consumers or producers of tobacco. And once again the coalition of government officials, clergy, and merchants coalesced. The clergy declared that tobacco which had been contaminated by the hands of the infidel concessionaires was unfit for

Muslim consumption. The merchants launched a variety of economic counter-attacks—especially the passive one of refusing to carry on trade. Government officials could bring more direct persuasion to bear at the court.

The widespread outcry against this concession in combination with opposition at the highest levels of society was sufficiently potent to cause the Shah to cancel the tobacco monopoly. Whereas the opposition to Reuters had been largely the work of a courtly cabal with little public visibility, this affair entailed the political mobilization of a widespread segment of the entire population. For the first time in contemporary Iranian history, a popular outcry was able to change the course of the government.

From these roots stemmed the constitutional movement. A revulsion against internal despotism and decay and external degradation grew. The mortgaging of the country's assets to finance foreign pleasure trips had brought Iran to the verge of colonial status. Tyranny and reaction by the Shah and his court contributed to the profound backwardness of the nation. Gradually over the last quarter of the 18th century there grew the belief that Iran could be saved from these evils by the spread of the "enlightened" culture of the more advanced societies and by formulation of a code of laws. During 1905 and 1906, these beliefs resulted in demonstrations, economic strikes, and religious protests. Finally, in the summer of 1906 thousands of Teheranis, especially the merchants and religious leaders, encamped on the grounds of the British legation and took sanctuary (*bast*) from their own government. The ultimate result of these and other pressures was the granting by the Shah of a constitution and supplemental laws which defined and limited his own powers. It also formally specified the creation of a parliament with a lower and upper house.

With the acceptance by the monarch of the constitution, Iran seemed headed for a period of internal consolidation and external strength. In fact, the next two decades marked an astounding increase in the very process which the constitution was designed to counter. Shah Mozaffar ed Din Qajar expired shortly after its ratification and his successor dedicated himself to its cancellation. Subsequent years were marked by occasionally violent struggles between the nationalists pressing for full implementation of the constitution and more conservative and reactionary elements who sought the abrogation of that instrument. A nationalist triumph seemed assured by the forced abdication of the recalcitrant monarch. But intervention by the British and the Russians on behalf of one or the other parties, the fact that the new king was not of age and was supervised by a series of more or less reactionary regents, internal dissension and rankling on the part of the nationalists kept the country divided and weak when World War I extended to Iran.

With the removal of the Russians as a major force after the revolution, British troops continued to occupy the country, and in 1919 their government offered a treaty which would have made a virtual protectorate of Iran with British officials occupying key posts throughout the state.

While Ahmed Shah, now of age and ruling with a regent, signed the agreement, the parliament refused to give its accession to a document which would, in effect, sign away its independence. Despite bribery and pressures on the Shah which resulted in new cabinet ministers, the parliament maintained its position, a position it had developed as protector of Iran's national independence, highlighting the importance of the constitution.

From its first session, whenever the regime or reactionary landlords have been unable to control its elections, the Majlis has continued to be the political seat of the most ardent nationalists. Given its constititional functions of limiting the power of the Shah, moreover, it has naturally been the subject of continual efforts by the throne to reduce its autonomy and thus its power to limit the autonomy of the monarch. With the exception of one election during World War II and another during the Mossadeq period, no Majlis since this early period has been elected free of official control. The role of the Majlis then as a check on the royal prerogative has been severely limited.

One result is that opposition to governmental policies or to the Shah has frequently taken the form of demands for liberal democracy, parliamentarianism, or more basically, constitutionalism. The widespread appeal which such slogans generate have put 20th century Iranian monarchs on the defensive. Thus even while violating its provisions they have had to act in the name of the constitution. While the document alone then cannot guarantee a constitutional regime, it does serve as a potent symbol around which Iranian political forces can find some degree of unity. It also serves as a hallmark against which to judge the performance of the regime. And it is a goal towards which the monarchs of this century have at least ostensibly directed the course of their rule.

In the face of this absolute parliamentary intransigence the British finally realized in 1921 the impossibility of attaining agreement to the treaty they had first proposed in 1919. After formally withdrawing it from consideration, Great Britain announced its intention to withdraw its troops as well. But before that event occurred, a detachment of the Iranian Cossack Brigade led by Reza Khan, in conjunction with a fiery Iranian journalist, Sayyed Ziya ed-Din Tabatabai, marched from Qazvin to Teheran, staged a coup d'état, and installed a new government with Ziya ed-Din at its head as prime minister and Reza Khan as its minister of war. The role of the British in the coup d'état remains an unsolved puzzle of recent Iranian history. Many feel that the British were responsible for the coup, believing that if they could not directly control Iran its interests would be better served by a strong centralized government in that country. It is known that the British facilitated the movement of Reza Khan from Qazvin (where a large contingent of British troops were located) to the capital. In addition, Sayyed Ziya was a notorious Anglophile. In any case, after the coup the British withdrew their troops leaving Iran for the first time in decades at its own mercies and with a need to face the realities of finding a political balance in its own government.

It shortly became clear that that balance would increasingly center on Reza Khan. Dynamic, aggressive, and in control of the only organized military force in the country—the Cossack Brigade—Reza Khan increasingly consolidated his own power. He sent Sayyed Ziya into exile and installed himself as prime minister. Then, in 1925 he did the same for Ahmed Shah, the last Qajar monarch, and crowned himself Reza Shah, the first ruler of the Pahlevi dynasty. From his coronation until his forced abdication in 1941, Reza Shah ruled with a firm hand and in an increasingly tyrannical, arbitrary, and venal fashion.

Toward the end of his rule, he boasted that his most significant achievement was to teach the Iranian people the value of labor. Whether he did this or not is questionable, but there are many other substantial achievements to his credit, achievements which illustrate the third major theme of recent history, a state initiated and state directed drive for modernization and development. Reza Shah, by imposing a rigorous tax on sugar and tea which penalized the peasants most heavily, generated funds for the construction of the Grand Iranian Railway. He introduced a fledgling industrial system, built highways between cities and new roads within the major cities of Iran. The modern state supported education system expanded at all levels with new sections of the population finding an education within their grasp for the first time. The ruler also established the first modern institution of higher learning in his country—the University of Teheran. In addition, his efforts at emancipating Iranian women, including the outlawing of the *chador,* the Iranian veil, had profound effects on the social structure. Modernizing the civil and military bureaucracies and establishing a contemporary system of government finance were also important steps in the transition from a backward monarchy to a modern nation.

In short, Reza Shah gave impetus to and laid the basis for the more radical changes which have beset Iran since his rule. Often referred to as the "Ataturk of Iran," Reza Shah operated within narrower limits than his Turkish counterpart. He himself was less worldly (his first trip outside the borders of Iran occurred toward the end of his rule with a visit to Ataturk), less well educated (it appears that at the time of his coronation he was but semiliterate), and less committed to democratic principles (with no pretense whatsoever he violated virtually every article of the constitution). Moreover, Iran at the time of his accession had much less of the foundations of modernity—a smaller cadre of technically trained persons and a poorer economic and communications infrastructure.

But working within these limitations Reza Shah began the state directed development of Iran and established a strong central government with control over the farthest reaches of his domain. These two processes—state sponsored development and the growing power of the central government—continue unabated to the present.

The power of the central government was based on a formidable military to which Reza Shah devoted more resources than any other single area.

But the invasion of Iran in August 1941 by the British and the Russians, fearful of growing German influence in Iran and desirous of using Iran as a transit route for war materials to the Soviet Union from the Persian Gulf, indicated how unsuccessful he had been. Without major resistance his army collapsed in the face of a coordinated invasion from the north and the south. One of the costs to Iran of that invasion was the forced abdication of Reza Shah. He was replaced by an inexperienced young man of 21, Muhammad Reza Pahlevi, thereafter called Shahanshah, or King of Kings. Those chaotic days, amidst foreign occupation, economic disintegration, and savage attacks on the 20-year rule of his father, highlighted the insecurity of his throne. Supported by the occupying powers who viewed him as a source of stability, by many of the elite including the military generals who had served the ex-monarch, the Shah continued to maintain a tenuous grip on the throne while devoting his efforts to eliminating his dependence on unreliable sources of support.

Following World War II, a pattern similar to the conclusion of World War I presented itself. The Soviet Union violated earlier wartime agreements with Britain and the United States by failing to withdraw its troops from Iran within six months of the ending of hostilities. With Soviet troops stationed throughout western and north-western Iran, two "Autonomous Peoples' Republics" were established. These appear to have been Soviet attempts to prepare a portion of Iran for eventual incorporation. Commonly referred to as the "beginning of the cold war," this was also the first international incident brought before the Security Council of the newly established United Nations. Intense diplomatic pressures from the United States, Great Britain, and Iran in that forum as well as extremely shrewd diplomatic maneuvering and negotiations between Iran's then Prime Minister Qavam and the U.S.S.R. resulted in the withdrawal of Soviet forces, the invasion of the region by Iranian troops, and the collapse of those "republics."

Iran was then once again independent and unoccupied, and the Shah could turn to his two principal tasks: strengthening his own bases of support and bringing his country abreast of the 20th century.

For more than a decade internal political turmoil hindered the achievement of these goals. In 1949 an abortive assassination attempt on the life of the Shah was followed by the outlawing and repression of the Iranian Communist party. Simultaneously, the National Front, a growing movement under the direction of Dr. Mohammad Mossadeq, became more vociferous about the need to nationalize the Iranian oil industry and to remove its control from the hands of the Anglo-Iranian Oil Company (a majority of whose shares were owned by the British government). And in addition, a third group, the Fedayeen-e-Islam, a fundamentalist Moslem Brotherhood organization, became increasingly militant in favor of these same objectives. The assassination of political figures by the Fedayeen culminated in the killing of the then Prime Minister Razmara, and his replacement by Dr. Mossadeq.

Meanwhile, the Majlis voted to nationalize Iran's oil. But Iran was unable to sell the petroleum for which it now claimed complete ownership for the Anglo-Iranian Oil Company had threatened to sue any other petroleum companies or governments which bought Iranian oil or carried Iranian oil in its ships on the charge that such petroleum was in fact stolen property. For months negotiations dragged on, but positions hardened. Eventually diplomatic relations were broken off and Mossadeq promised to go it alone with an "oil-less" but truly independent and nationalistic government.

Mossadeq's popularity was at a peak despite the increasingly serious financial difficulties and seemed to gather power as it flowed away from the Shah.

When the monarch attempted to reassert his power by dismissing Mossadeq and installing a more pliable prime minister, much of the population of Teheran took to the streets and rioted. With Mossadeq reappointed, a direct confrontation between the Shah and his prime minister seemed inevitable and with his attempts to gain control of the armed forces, a prerogative traditionally reserved for the King, that confrontation was manifest.

But the intense struggle for power disheartened many of the prime minister's former supporters, who either withdrew from politics or sided with the monarch. The possibility of a showdown and Mossadeq's increasingly autocratic style of rule proved too much for the bonds which had united the National Front. Then in August of 1953 the Shah once again dismissed Mossadeq who this time refused to give up his office. The Shah and his family responded by fleeing the country to Rome—according to later reminiscences—a strategic political maneuver to rouse his supporters. Then, mobs from the poorer sections of the capital poured into the streets and flowed toward the government ministries. They were joined by the military, and Mossadeq's support dissolved. The Shah returned to the country in triumph and the prime minister was arrested, jailed for three years, and subsequently placed under house arrest at his estate.

How did the monarch translate what appeared to be a self-imposed exile into a political victory within a matter of days? Many attributed his success to the machinations, both direct and indirect, of the U.S. Central Intelligence Agency. It seems conclusively clear at this stage that the CIA did have a key role in those fateful August days.

But fundamentally, Mossadeq's inability to maintain his political coalition was responsible for his collapse. While many factors underlay the collapse of his support, his direct confrontation with the king, his increasingly autocratic style of rule, and his inability to solve the oil crisis which prevented large sums of money flowing into Iran were at the root of his failure.

When the Shah returned he found himself in much the same position as he had been in 1946 and as his father had been in 1925: titled to a throne with a centuries-long tradition of charisma but whose base of support was primarily the military. To strengthen that support, the Shah conducted an extensive purge of his officer corps, arresting or dismissing hundreds of officers accused of Communist inclinations or participation in Communist activities. Undoubtedly many of these officers had been supporters of Mossadeq, but it also seems clear that a rather extensive penetration of the military had been accomplished by the Communist party. With the elimination of their supporters in the ranks of the armed forces, he then turned to eliminating their supporters throughout Iran and subduing the most ardent partisans of Mossadeq. The most threatening of his opponents being neutralized, the Shah began to experiment with new forms of control.

From 1957 to 1960 a royally chartered and directed two-party system was created. One party was to serve as the government while the other was the "loyal opposition." Both were under the direction of close personal friends of the Shah, but the "tweedledum-tweedledee" character of the parties failed to provide any meaningful channel of political expression.

Simultaneously, His Majesty convened the upper house of the parliament provided for by the constitution but never previously organized. The constitution empowered the king to appoint half of the senate's 60 members and with that power he was able to pack a second parliamentary body with established and conservative figures who could at least serve as a check on what he considered the excesses of the first.

The 1960 elections to the parliament, however, revealed that the Shah's control over the political system was still tenuous and his support unreliable. As the elections proceeded political disquiet and widely voiced complaints of electoral corruption led to the Shah's cancellation of the elections themselves. But the cancellation only fostered demands for new elections free of police control.

The second round of elections for the 20th session of the parliament began in January 1961, but were as poorly managed as the previous one. When the Shah inaugurated the new session in February of that year, students had closed the University of Teheran with widespread demonstrations, a revived National Front sponsored an ominously successful general strike, and important independent political leaders boycotted the Majlis. His Majesty responded to the mounting political chaos and the growing power of the counter-elites (and many Iranians claimed, to the inauguration of President Kennedy in January) in characteristic fashion. He made overtures to the dissident politicans by taking a number of apparently liberalizing steps without, however, allowing any fundamental diminution in his own power.

He renewed the distribution of the Crown lands to the peasants who were farming them. (These lands, which the Shah had been in the process of selling since 1961, were acquired, usually illegitimately, by his father.) He established the Pahlevi Foundation on a firm financial footing and, while he retained control over its assets, he assigned them in a perpetual endowment to charity. (This was a foundation then valued at $135 million which the Shah established with a portion of his personal wealth.) In addition, the Shah dismissed a number of unpopular military officers including the chief of the supreme commander's staff; the chief of army intelligence; and General Bakhtiar, director of the State Security and Intelligence Organization, the secret police.

But the public quietude which followed was only temporary. Shortly thereafter Teheran teachers struck for higher salaries and demonstrated in front of the Majlis. Clashes broke out with security forces, and one of the striking teachers was killed. His death galvanized the vacillators, and schools were shut down as the body of the newly created martyr was paraded through the streets. The Shah again responded, this time by dismissing the prime minister and appointing Dr. Ali Amini, popular with the demonstrators for favoring limitations on the power of the throne and reputed to be a man devoted to civil liberties and of profound personal integrity. (It was also widely claimed that he was a friend of the United States where he had served as ambassador.) By the end of the year, however, Amini had failed to satisfy any section of the politically active population. He was able to do little to alter the political or economic priorities which the Shah had established or to bring the National Front into political activities. He was unable to induce the Shah to call new parliamentary elections. What with the Shah's distrust of Amini to begin with, it was clear that his time was running out. Following a budgetary crisis Amini resigned and the Shah asked his closest boyhood friend, Assadollah Alam, to form a new government.

Alam was an ideal transition figure from the chaos of the early 1960s to the surface quiet of the late 1960s. He could be counted on to carry out His Majesty's wishes with little temporizing. And this he did. He continued to rule without a parliament while submitting a series of reform measures, collectively known as the White Revolution, to a national referendum. These reforms constituted a series of initiatives from the throne designed to alter the base of political power in Iran. Striking directly for support from traditionally excluded groups in the society, the Shah sought to cut his reliance on the military on the one hand and to the established political elites on the other hand; undercut the National Front by leap-frogging directly to the farmers, workers, and women through land reform, profit-sharing in industrial enterprises, and suffrage for women. The referendum was passed by an overwhelmingly positive vote and served as a signal for going ahead with plans to hold a parliamentary election; an election whose outcome would be more favorable to the rule of the Shah, as he determined it.

These plans were disrupted, however, with the outbreak in June 1963 of three days of nationwide urban rioting, touched off by the arrest of Ayatollah Khomeini, the leading Shi'i mullah of Iran. Khomeini had come to public attention in 1961 for his outspoken opposition to the government. Later, he was arrested for asserting that the Shah's land reform program was contrary to Islam which sanctified private property.

Khomeini's picture covered the bazaars of Iran for the religious holidays of Moharram in early June, a time of increased passions as the devout anguished over the martyrdom of Husain and Hassan the sons, and according to the Shi'ites, the rightful successors of Ali to the Caliphate. His picture seemed to symbolize the opposition to illegitimate authority which had been offered by Husain and Hassan. The authorities waited until the early morning hours of June 4, after the end of the holy days, and arrested Khomeini. Within hours crowds of protesters began to form before the bazaars of Teheran and by 10:00

a.m. the troops had opened fire. While the rioting spread to other cities it was finally put down after three days with thousands of casualties.

In previous years, such rioting would have toppled the government and shaken the roots of the regime. Coming as it did upon the heels of a month of tribal fighting in south-central Iran (fighting which resulted in the temporary capture by the tribes of the Shiraz international airport), these riots were especially threatening. But the ability and willingness of the government to employ military force to decisively put down both disturbances indicated that a new phase of Iranian politics had been entered. The government could now boast a significant monopoly of physical force and a willingness to exercise it. The opposition was disorganized, their leaders having left the country, been jailed, or withdrawn from politics; their followers being demoralized or frightened or worse. The Shah moved ahead with hardly an interruption.

New elections for the Majlis were organized far more efficiently than in the past. A "Congress of Free Men and Free Women" was held to nominate candidates who would carry on the Shah's reform plans now known as the White Revolution. A slate was produced and with few exceptions was elected to the parliament which convened in early 1964, no opposition candidates being allowed to run. These new members of the parliament were just that. Virtually none had been previously elected or even involved in politics. They were not members of politically influential families but represented those strata of Iranian society to which the Shah was now appealing: professionals, civil servants, workers, females, and even a peasant or two. On the one hand, then, the new Majlis entailed a considerable broadening of the social groups who were now participating in politics. On the other hand, the newly elected delegates had no independent political bases, having been co-opted into the parliament to serve the interest of the regime. Thus, the possibility of their challenging the regime in any way was negligible. (Moreover, the senate, still composed almost entirely of the old elites, was quiet.)

With the convening of the parliament in an atmosphere of tranquility, the Shah's confidant, and prime minister, had successfully completed his mission. He stepped down and a new government was formed by Hassan Ali Mansur, head of a grouping then being billed as the New Iran party with a majority in the parliament. By the end of his first year in office Mansur had managed to antagonize virtually all sectors of the politically aware. His arrogance and arbitrariness resulted in widespread bitterness and ultimately to a resort to a political weapon frequently used in Iran's past. Mansur was assassinated on the steps of the Majlis as he went to present a new government bill. Of significance, however, is that the Shah was able to appoint Mansur's finance minister as prime minister and to insure the continuation of his policies with little alteration in the affairs of state.

The new prime minister and many of the younger men in their 30s and 40s with Western, technical education who were brought in by Mansur have continually served to the present. Their tenure in office is nearly the longest for any such officials of this century. Nor was the continuity of the regime shaken a few months after Mansur's death by yet another assassination attempt on the life of the Shah. A machine gun wielding member of the Imperial Guards turned on the Shah in front of his office. While his two personal bodyguards were shot down, the king escaped injury. Once again he had been saved and once again his own sense of *baraka* or "divine blessing" was heightened. Whatever the truth of the latter claim, it serves to bolster support among certain segments of the population as well as the confidence of the Shah in the correctness of the course he has established for Iran and his regime. The failure of this assassination attempt to distrub the equilibrium of the regime seems to underscore this view. With virtually no exception, Iranian politics have continued to demonstrate stability since that time. The Shah has been able to push ahead with his vision of Iran, a vision of industrial development built on revenues derived from sales of Iran's greatest national assets, petroleum and natural gas; an agricultural sector which will grow smaller, to constitute but one-third of the total population by the end of the century, but an increasingly efficient sector which will make Iran nearly self-sufficient in foodstuffs; a burgeoning education system with widespread vocational and technical training at all levels, including a vastly expanded university system; a strong military to defend Iranian interests in the Middle East and especially in the Persian Gulf after the withdrawal of British military forces in the early 1970s; and a vast array of social services making medical care and other social welfare benefits available throughout the country. The realization of this vision will depend on and in turn support an urbanized, technically trained, highly literate, and economically advanced population. In short, Iran in the year 2000 will resemble Europe in the mid-20th century.

Can the Shah and Iran accomplish this vision? One element is the key factor and is also the most problematical—the political shape of Iran's future. The Shah looks forward to a widening political base with widespread consensus behind the Pahlevi dynasty. Now in his mid-forties the Shah hopes for several more decades of rule to bring this about before turning power over to his eldest son Crown Prince Ali Reza. With the solid support of the population, then, and agreement on the course of Iran's development, the king could afford to play a less interventionist role in the day-to-day affairs of state. He could reign rather than rule as he does now; he could function as a constitutional monarch as do European royalty at present.

But this vision must remain problematical specifically because it is a long-term view. In the interim, the limits of political activity acceptable to the Shah are narrow and there exists widespread if inarticulate and dormant opposition to the current political system. To the casual observer such disquiet is not evident. But when an opportunity is present it boils to the surface with force. Such is the explanation for the June 1963 urban riots. Iran's current political stability, then, seems based more on the strength and confidence of the regime and the disarray and discouragement of the opposition than on any widespread support for the Shah and his policies. Whether this will continue and allow the Shah the time he needs to build widespread support or erupt again in a more threatening fashion is the single most important unknown in contemporary Iranian politics.

The Framework of Political Life

As should be obvious from the preceding discussion, Iran possesses an array of political institutions whose functions and relations are formally delineated in its constitution and legal system. But this formal system bears only slight resemblance to the actual operations of politics. For a variety of reasons—foreign pressure, world wars and occupations of Iran, internal disunity and discord, and lack of will—the provisions of the constitution which have given Iran's political system a democratic character have not been implemented. (Nonetheless, the constitution has served as a potent hallmark against which to judge the actions of the government. It remains a remarkably strong symbol of freedom, motivating large numbers of politically active Iranians.) But in practice, except for brief periods in the 20th century, power has remained in the hands of the monarchs. And with the growth of Iran's economy and military, with increasing centralization and development, the power which the Shahanshah is able to wield has increased drastically. Rather than a detailed examination, then, of the constitution, its provisions for a bicameral legislature and limitations on the power of the sovereign, let us turn directly to an examination of the key actors in Iranian politics and their interactions.

In any study of Iranian politics, Muhammad Reza Pahlevi occupies the center of the stage; he is the keystone of the entire political system. The Shah was the third child and eldest son of a semi-illiterate Iranian officer in the Russian directed Cossack Brigade, Reza Khan. With Reza's coronation, his son was officially installed as Crown Prince. He spent six years at the Le Rosey school in Switzerland where he is reported to have learned of Western democracy. On his return to Iran he graduated first in his class from the Iranian Officers Training School and was married as a service to the dynasty to Princess Fawzia, the sister of King Farouk of Egypt.

With the forced abdication of Reza Shah in 1941, Britain and Russia established his son on the throne, a 21-year-old, ill-prepared, and self-doubting young man. To the surprise of most, the Shah faced and overcame a series of incredible obstacles, all the while strengthening his hold on the throne and the hold of the throne over the political system. His third wife the Empress Farah has now produced two male heirs to make possible the continuation of the ruling house. While countless other seemingly more powerful and popular leaders of developing countries have fallen by the wayside of political leadership, the Shah has preserved his throne, enhanced his power, and maintained the integrity of Iran.

There are other significant actors in the Iranian system, more or less powerful, but none who approaches the wide-ranging and persisting power of the monarch. Perhaps the one who comes closest is his twin sister Princess Ashraf. Rumor has it that she is a participant in every significant economic enterprise in the country. Certainly she has been able to place men on whom she can count in virtually every important area of public and private life. Her contacts, her wealth, her relationship to the Shah, all contribute to her immense influence. (Other members of the royal family are less involved in public life. A younger brother, Prince Gholem Reza, serves as His Majesty's representative in the armed forces and as head of the Iranian Olympic Committee but is generally recognized as possessing little personal power.)

Assadollah Alam, the onetime prime minister, is another individual who possesses significant personal power. The son of a major landowner whose control of eastern Iran was greater than that of the government, Alam and the Shah were boyhood playmates. He appears to be the only Iranian in whom the Shah confides and now serves the king as minister of court.

There are, of course, other individuals of importance in Iranian politics but by and large their importance derives from the institutional roles they fill in the society. A prime example would be General Hassan Pakravan, Iranian ambassador to Pakistan and formerly director of the State Security and Intelligance Organization. SAVAK, as it is known from its Persian initials, is a combination CIA-FBI, performing external and internal security functions. As such, it has pervasive power in Iran. Pakravan, as director, was one of the four most powerful individuals in Iran, along with the Shah, Ashraf, and Alam. But when the Shah was displeased with him, because of his alleged failure to prevent or contain the June 1963 riots, Pakravan was sent off to relative political exile in Pakistan. His power had come from his command of the substantial resources of his bureaucratic organization. Once he lost control over those, his personal power evaporated.

In addition to SAVAK, there are other security forces whose senior personnel are influential in political life. The Special Intelligence Office, headed by a schoolmate of the Shah's; J-2, the army intelligence unit; the Imperial Guards; the conventional military forces; the national police; and the gendarmerie command significant government resources and are key organizations. Of the nonsecurity bureaucracies, the National Iranian Oil Company is crucial. It is responsible for insuring the production, refining, export, and internal distribution of petroleum without whose revenue the present system would collapse. Its director is an ex-prime minister who wields major influence in Iran's political life. The prime minister and cabinet officials are also major political figures. The ministries of labor, agriculture, finance, economy, and foreign affairs are especially relevant to the system, and their chiefs along with the prime minister accordingly are major figures in the system. Certain members of the Majlis and senate are also powerful although those two bodies tend to rubber stamp legislation submitted by the ministries. Nor do they perform the investigative functions, through committees, as do more effective legislatures. Certain key political actors may be found outside the governmental bureaucracies, e.g., heads of important private corporations. Finally, a number of foreigners, especially ambassadors from the major powers, the United States, U.S.S.R., Britain, and France, are significant political figures from their access to the Shah, their foreign aid, and their ability to facilitate the emergence of the Shah as a figure of international stature.

These then are the significant actors in the political system of Iran. Their interactions constitute politics and it is their actual interactions rather than those specified in the constitution which must be understood. And it is on the Shah, who orchestrates, staffs, and conducts, that one must concentrate. Over the course of his 29 years of rule, the Shah has developed a variety of techniques for dealing with the political system which keep him at its center.

The style of rule which the Shah has unfolded and elaborated since coming to power centers around five techniques. First, he seeks to control the size and the composition of the politically influential segments of the population. The basis of this policy is one of recruitment by co-optation. That is, all elites and those who because of unusual popularity, charisma, wealth, skills, or knowledge are considered potential elites or counter-elites are co-opted into elite membership by being offered prestigious office or other rewards. High status positions in the civil or military bureaucracies are used as counters in the Shah's attempts to incorporate all politically relevant individuals.

This co-optative method of recruitment to the ranks of the elite fills two principal functions: to uncover talent and to hinder the formation of counterelites. In the former sense, personal representatives of the Shah are able to identify individuals with valuable skills or training, currently outside the monarch's scrutiny, but who may be induced with suitable blandishments to use their skills for the regime and Iran. In the latter sense, individuals with the qualities to lead or form counterelites rarely do so. They lack the incentive for they are rapidly assimilated. And precisely that which they value they receive as they play the game of politics in a manner acceptable to the regime; be it status, power, money, foreign travel, the rewards or recruitment by seduction are usually satisfying.

Another method for controlling the size of the politically involved is by influencing the distribution of resources which serve as the bases of political power in Iran. By regulating apportionment of these resources the Shah attempts to circumscribe entry into the political elite to those who will probably sustain his rule. Presently, membership in the elite is most facilitated by control over two resources—wealth and education. By controlling and manipulating taxation, import-export licenses, production permits, land reform, and building and supply contracts, the Shah is able to affect the wealth of his subjects. By altering examination and admission policies, tuition and other fees, and the size of different academic programs the regime is able to affect the nature of the available education and the number of pupils who are able to acquire education at the various levels.

A second component of the king's style of rule is manipulating the behavior of the politically active and influential segments of the population. We have already mentioned his liberality in offering individuals those rewards which they value; rewards attainable for "correct" political performance. There are a host of other methods available. A variety of security organizations exist to supervise, control, and, if necessary, repress activities which the regime considers a real or potential threat. Control over the mass media has been enhanced so that opportunities for the public expression of counterelite positions are negligible. The regime has also successfully demoralized wide segments of the politically dissatisfied by its internal strength, impressive longevity, and by broadening its support among foreign nations. (Since the post-1965 rapprochement with the Soviet Union the disgruntled and dismayed have lost their principal source of foreign support. Much as the 1939 Soviet-Nazi pact confused and demoralized many Americans, so the Iran-Soviet accords in recent years have strengthened the regime by confounding its critics.)

Yet a third component of the Shah's style has been to continually restrict the limits of acceptable political behavior by relying on its greater political capacity at home and more widespread support abroad. Whereas street demonstrations were common occurrences in the past, a clandestinely printed and distributed pamphlet is now a rarity. What can be legitimately done or said (in public) is narrowly circumscribed. As a result, the politically aware have few options in the face of regime policies of which they disapprove. They may resist, a course usually unacceptable to the regime, and face dismissal from their positions, exile, or imprisonment. But the latter techniques are viewed as last resorts by the Shah who seeks to manipulate the behavior of his followers through positive rewards rather than by punishment. Opponents are given every opportunity to reform and with the slightest indication of compliance are welcomed back to the fold. Some individuals, nonetheless, continue to pursue political activities but, in the face of years of failure, they do so with a deep sense of pessimism, inefficacy, disarray, and hence a lack of effectiveness.

Another central component of the Shah's style of rule is his continual personal intervention in a phenomenally wide range of affairs of state. By hard work, long hours, and intelligence refined by almost 30 years of ruling experience, the monarch is able to put his own mark on the fortunes of his people and state. His intervention takes several forms and is directed to several ends. Whenever possible, the Shah attends and directs meetings of the cabinet. He has a fixed weekly schedule of appointments with every key official in Iran. In addition, he receives daily reports from his security services and regularly sees certain individuals who, though they have no official position, are nonetheless asked by the Shah to follow the affairs of a particular organization. Through all these methods a vast array of information is acquired by the Shah—information which he translates into personal decisions.

In addition to making countless decisions in day-to-day political affairs, the Shah also frequently intervenes for the making of appointments. At all levels of the bureaucracy the Shah exercises great care in choosing his officials. His principal criterion for appointment, overriding questions of competence and honesty, is loyalty to him.

But loyalty is not assumed to be permanent and the Shah's intervention is not assumed sufficient. A final technique of his rule then is one as old as rule itself—the policy of "divide and rule." This practice, whose overriding purpose is to prevent the rise of any meaningful opposition to the power of the monarch, has several components. One basic aspect is the appointment of personally antagonistic individuals as directors of major organizations within the government. Another is to assign responsibility for the performance of any given task to a number of bureaucratic agencies. Thus, no bureaucrat can amass power because he alone can supply some wanted service. Yet another aspect is the practice of assigning individuals the task of following the affairs of an organization, mentioned above. These individuals constitute a "shadow cabinet" whose presence is known and who represent individuals to whom the king may turn if he is dissatisfied with his current officials.

This policy of divide and rule and the other techniques mentioned above constitute the king's style of rule—a style which has proved efficient as a means for manipulating the political system and assuring the loyalty of its elite or at least their ineffectiveness in challenging the autonomy of the Shah's position.

Political Issues

It would be a gross distortion of Iranian reality to conclude that the Shah is interested solely in perpetuating his own rule. As mentioned above, he is devoted to bringing his country into the 20th century. As now constituted this effort has centered about three main domestic areas—political development, economic and social modernization, and national unity. This last issue ties in directly with problems of foreign policy: the fourth of the Shah's preoccupations.

The task of political development has proven to be the most difficult of the efforts pursued by the Shah. For him, the term has come to mean the construction of a viable political system based on majority support which would prove immune to the catastrophes which frequently besieged regimes of the past. But for the issue of majority support, the Shah has been extremely successful. His regime has weathered a series of shocks which would have devastated less solid thrones. His system is viable in that it is developing, albeit after a number of false starts. The aborted, royally chartered, two party system of 1957-1961; the single political party era following the elections of 1963; and the more recent multiparty system have all been attempts to mobilize support for the regime while giving at least a semblance of participation. But fundamentally, none of these has generated widespread support, because in no period has party government entailed any significant sharing of power by the Shah.

With the failure of the political parties to generate support, the Shah has turned to other measures, most forcefully to land reform. In a program redefined and enacted with dispatch after 1961, the government has brought about the sale of land in many thousands of villages to the peasant cultivators. On the one hand, this cut the ties of the peasants to their former landlords and deprived those elites of their traditional bases of power. On the other hand, it brought the peasants under the direct control of the central government. The Shah became the principal authority figure for millions of peasant landowners.

In this way the Shah was able to generate an entirely new base of political support.

But that base is a weak one. For the peasants are the least politically aware and active segment of the society. Politics in Iran is made and enacted in the cities and, without a base in the cities, the Shah cannot rest secure. His plans for profit-sharing for industrial workers and suffrage for females can be seen as attempts to build that urban base. But the former seems to be largely a reform on paper while the latter have proven to be an unreliable but nonetheless positive source of support. His efforts at finding enthusiastic support, then, have not been as successful as his other political achievements but represent a persistent goal towards which he and his regime strive.

One of the impressive political accomplishments of which the Shah can boast is an increasingly efficient civil and military bureaucracy. Put simply the government can accomplish more than ever before, *i.e.*, the amount of power in the system as a whole has been increased. Whether it be the conduct of a literacy campaign, the construction of an irrigation dam, the operation of jet fighter planes, or the building of a road network, the presence of the government and its capabilities have become more far-reaching, pronounced, and evident.

As the power of the bureaucracies has grown, so has the power of the Shah over them. There has been no corresponding increase in the power of the people. The result has been a relative decrease in participation, a decrease in reciprocity, and a decrease in democracy. And as the importance of the government has increased, incentives for influencing its policies has also increased, and the payoff is greater. As a result, traditional practices inimical to political development have persisted and sometimes spread. Corruption, nepotism, personalism, and mistrust are the day-to-day concomitants of politics in Iran.

While political development has proceeded unevenly, at best, economic and social modernization have been more uniformly successful. Fueled by oil revenues now running over one billion dollars per year which have grown at an average rate of 17 percent since 1954, Iran's gross national product has burgeoned. New industrial plants are springing up: the steel mill; petrochemical plants; machine tool, automobile, and tractor factories; a paper mill; and new food processing industries. Nor, for the first time, is agriculture being neglected. Along with the land reform has come new agricultural cooperatives offering financial and technical assistance to the new owners. Fertilizers, irrigation, and farm machinery are more easily available and growing in use. With a continuation of the oil revenues and the absence of political turmoil, there is no reason to assume that economic growth will not continue.

But there is a less encouraging side to this picture of increasing economic prosperity. Much of the prosperity is passing into the hands of a small segment of the society. When Iranian officials boast of the 9, 10, or even 11 percent annual increase in economic product, they refer to total growth and not to distribution of that growth. It seems clear that only a relatively small stratum of the society actually benefits in any direct way. Wages are still extremely low in the industrial sphere, while the agricultural sector is very primitive. Only Teheran of Iran's cities seems to have acquired the patina of modernity. A relatively small proportion of her population appears to be absorbing the lion's share of the new wealth. Thus, old standing economic and social imbalances persist and are even exacerbated by economic development as is true of political change.

The changes now occuring in the social sphere suggest that the political and economic imbalances will be more difficult to contain in the future. A dramatically increasing percentage of Iran's youth is receiving formal education. In 1955, 800,000 boys and girls were enrolled in primary schools, the figures now approach 3,500,000. In that same year secondary schools counted 140,000 youths and now, 650,000. Universities have jumped from 15,000 to 50,000.

The percentage of women in the schools has steadily increased. We have already mentioned the extension of the vote to women. And in 1968 the first woman in Iran's history became a cabinet minister. Other significant changes have been occurring in the status of women in Iranian society, most especially reform of the divorce and family laws. Previously, divorce was not available to women, only to their husbands who merely had to utter "I divorce thee" three times for the marriage to be dissolved. Custody of the children always went to the husband. A law recently enacted by parliament has made it possible for women to initiate divorce proceedings, requires that both parties comply with rather lengthy formalities before a divorce can take effect, and leaves custody of the children negotiable. These and other changes, many spurred by the participation of Empress Farah in public life, indicate a growing role for women in Iranian society.

Along with the youth and women of Iran, we have mentioned that the peasants are being drawn into national life. It is likely that these groups will begin to make demands of the political system. Growing economic prosperity suggests that the system will be able to satisfy their material aspirations. The ability of the system to satisfy demands for true participation is more doubtful and a source of concern to the regime.

Finally, a set of political issues focus around questions of national integration. As this is one of the problems about which the regime is most sensitive, however, little information becomes public. As was mentioned above the peoples on many of Iran's borders are ethnically distinct from the Iranians proper, frequently being part of a people who live across the border, outside Iran. Over the years they have been the target of separatist propaganda movements, culminating in the establishment of the Soviet sponsored "Republics" of Kurdistan and Azarbijan following World War II. Two such groups are once again the subject of intense concern: the Kurds and Arabs.

For more than a decade the Kurds of Iraq have been challenging the central government of that country for the establishment of an autonomous Kurdish region. The possibility that their Iranian counterparts would join in that effort in hopes of winning a slice of Iran caused the Shah to devote considerable resources to winning their favor. Initially, the Iranian Kurds received extra government goods and services—large shipments of grain for the winter months, for example. Increasingly, the Iranian Kurds began to receive supplies useful to their militarily active counterparts in Iraq. Such aid culminated in the use of Iranian military forces to harass Iraqi border posts into allowing bands of Kurds to cross into Iran unmolested. While such aid has generated considerable goodwill on the part of the Kurds, the Shah realizes that such goodwill is but a temporary amelioration. More permanent methods of relating the Kurds to Iran and the regime must be developed.

Just south of Kurdistan along the western borders are found Iran's main concentration of Arabs, contiguous with Iraqi and Kuwaiti Arabs across the border. The region has long been semi-autonomous, having been called "Arabistan" or "Home of the Arabs" until subdued by Reza Shah and officially designated "Khuzestan." With a majority of its population of Semitic stock speaking Arabic, the region has become the target of clandestine radio stations charging Iranian "genocide" and demanding Arab autonomy. The regime has responded by establishing the second largest concentration of its armed forces in the province. But again, the Shah realizes that the military presence is no answer to the problems of integration.

While the Kurds and Arabs are the two most visible of peoples not yet drawn into the fabric of the national society, much of the population is in a similar position. The principal tribes have been subject to continual government pressure towards their settlement, a step which will facilitate government control. But a number of other border peoples have not yet been subject to any government intervention. The problem is compounded in Iran for some 60 percent of the total population resides in places of less than 5000 persons. These rural people are largely outside the pale of the government whose only presence is an occasional gendarmerie outpost. With the introduction of the literacy corps and the agricultural cooperatives this is beginning to change. But even the majority of Persians themselves—the peasants—have yet to be brought into the mainstream of national life.

These issues then—building a viable political system, economic and social modernization, and national integration—are the principal domestic concerns of the regime. Their accomplishment has proven more difficult than had been imagined, but in certain areas, especially the economic and social, progress is being made. The very lack of balance between changes in these areas and the political arena, however, is likely to become increasingly troublesome. An educated population, increasingly prosperous, will seek to participate meaningfully in their political life. The regime has indicated little readiness to grant such participation.

Foreign Affairs

Many of Iran's domestic issues articulate with its foreign problems. This has been a historical pattern of centuries and persists to the present. Political change, development, and integration have involved Iran with her neighbors and the great powers. From the unusually great skill of her diplomacy and the competition for supremacy by foreign countries, Iran has benefited immensely from these involvements.

The pattern of Iran's foreign relations in the 19th century was "playing off" Great Britain against Russia to receive aid and preserve her own independence. As long as two foreign powers competed for her favors, Iran was able to steer a safe course. One power unopposed, however, presented a serious threat to the state—a threat of colonial dependency. Following World War II, Great Britain withdrew from the competition leaving the Soviet Union alone in the field. Iran quickly turned to the United States. Actually from a training mission to the Iranian gendarmerie, begun during World War II, American aid grew slowly until the post-Mossadeq period. With his overthrow the United States plunged headlong into supporting the Shah, supplying military equipment, financial aid, and even direct support for the government's budget. This latter support with which the United States agreed to meet any deficit in the budget of the Iranian government was eliminated by President Kennedy. And with the realization that Iran was one of the richest of the developing countries and well on its way to economic sufficiency, President Johnson eliminated all foreign aid to Iran in 1967. From 1953 to its phasing out, the U.S. foreign aid program had supplied Iran with some one billion dollars in economic aid and another billion dollars in military assistance.

With that aid and the political support which it implied, the Shah built his regime to the impressive level of strength it has now reached. Once his own throne was secure, however, it was clear that the United States would be of much less use. On the contrary, the overwhelming presence of the United States suggested a level of influence unacceptable to Iran and opened the Shah to the considerable charge that he was a tool of the United States.

In the 1960s the Shah once again expanded relations with the Soviet Union. He visited Moscow, entertained Leonid Brezhnev in Iran, and pledged not to allow Iranian territory to be used as a base for weapons directed at the U.S.S.R. (*i.e.*, U.S. missiles and bombers). In 1965 in a little noted act, the Soviet Union symbolized by a startling act its desire for close interstate relations, forsaking indigenous Iranian communists. It extradited, for execution in Iran, a former guard who had been responsible for the escape from prison of Iran's leading communists and who fled with them to the U.S.S.R.

Subsequently, interstate relations improved impressively. The two countries signed an economic agreement of several hundred millions of dollars. Under it, the U.S.S.R. is building Iran's steel mill for which Iran will pay with natural gas to be delivered in an 800-mile new pipeline from the Persian Gulf to the Soviet border. The two projects will have an exciting array of subsidiary benefits, *e.g.*, machine tool plants, new railroad lines, and natural gas supplied to Iran's major cities.

Since the signing of that agreement the two countries have gone on to a $100,000,000 arms agreement whereby the U.S.S.R. is supplying Iran with a variety of military supplies in return for more natural gas. The introduction of Russian military equipment, however rudimentary, attests to the growing closeness of the two neighbors. It also attests to the fact that the U.S.S.R. and United States both appear to be working towards a common aim in Iran—a strong, stable, friendly regime. In this sense, the American aid effort was the great success for which its architects hoped. It contributed to the strength of the regime to the point where American help was no longer necessary.

The remaining pressing issue between Iran and the great powers is that of petroleum. The vast majority of Iran's oil revenues is derived from production by a consortium dominated by British and American oil companies. These companies, in turn, have interests in other oil exporting countries. Thus, when the Shah insists that Iran's development requires an annual oil revenue increase of 17 percent, the oil companies can oblige only by holding down production in other Middle Eastern countries, an outcome which those governments view with alarm. The result is a dilemma for the oil companies and continual pressure by Iran abetted, at least through propaganda, by the Soviet Union.

Other than its relations with the U.S.S.R., the United States, and Europe, Iran's most pressing foreign relations issues are with her Middle Eastern neighbors. A non-Semitic nation in the midst of Semites, practicing a form of Islam disdained by the Arabs, valid cultural reasons exist for poor relations between Iran and the Arab countries. But added to these are a variety of more contemporary reasons. The competition between Iran and the Arab states for increased oil production has been mentioned. Enmity and occasional hostility with Iraq have recently occurred over the Kurdish issue and concerning the exact location of the Iran-Iraq border. The province of Khuzestan is a source of potential conflict.

In addition, Iran has long maintained close, if unofficial, ties with Israel. All Israel's petroleum supplies come from Iran, and Iranian oil will be sent through Israel's new pipeline bypassing the Suez Canal. Israeli technicians contribute to Iranian agricultural development and even to the operation of its secret police.

Perhaps the most serious imminent source of conflict, however, centers about the Persian Gulf region. Great Britain has announced its intention of withdrawing all its armed forces by 1971, leaving the region to establish its own security balance. Iran has announced its intention of being the dominant power in the Gulf, having begun to bolster its navy in preparation. It is unlikely that the Arab states will allow this domination to go unchallenged. Iraq, Kuwait, and Saudi Arabia bordering on the Gulf and Egypt, who has sought to assert influence over weaker states in the region, may seek to assert their influence. (One possible commonality of interest may be between Saudi Arabia and Iran joining to prevent Egypt from spreading Arab socialism or other more radical notions to the sheikhdoms along the Gulf.) Underlying all of Iran's foreign relations appears to be a profound connection with the domestic political process. As the Shah has felt more secure on his throne, as he has built a civil and military bureaucracy to serve his regime, and as he has eliminated his domestic opposition he has become more expansive internationally. His precedent-breaking agreements with the U.S.S.R. and his growing assertion of Iranian hegemony in the Gulf attest to his sense of increasing expansiveness and of Iran's role as a major regional power. Long too weak internally to play any role outside its own borders and then a step-child of American policy in the area, Iran until recently could be safely ignored by its neighbors. No longer is this true and it will be less true in the future as Iran seeks international status as a successfully developing, truly independent nation.

Conclusion

The above description and analysis of contemporary Iran describes what appears to be a burgeoning success story. This is only partly true, however, and even its continuation is tenuous. Economic growth and social change are proceeding rapidly but in a grossly inequitable manner. The newly created wealth benefits only a small proportion of the population, those who are already relatively prosperous. Eventually, this wealth may percolate down and benefit wider segments of the people, but that is a very long-term matter and the sharpening of social class differentials may exacerbate internal politics in the interim.

Political change itself is lagging far behind, the Shah unwilling to allow wider participation in politics. Elections are still only exercises rather than means for choosing leaders. The parliament can still be counted on to carry out the wishes of the cabinet; the latter executing the decisions of the Shah. No opposition exists, for none is tolerated. How long the lid can be kept on the political life of the nation remains an open question. No serious potential for disrupting the calm seems to exist.

Yet another factor diminishing any celebration of Iran's success must be the dependence of that success on the solitary person of the Shah himself. His impressive involvement in all phases of political life seems predicated on his fears for the preservation of his dynasty were political participation to be measurably broadened. The lessons of the turbulent Mossadeq period seem to support this analysis. On the other hand, failure to broaden the base of politics in Iran is ultimately a greater threat to the regime as long pent-up demands for participation may be bitterly and violently expressed. Clearly, the timing of the transition is crucial and it may require a sensitivity of which even the Shah is incapable. In the interim, the entire political system is dependent on the good health and longevity of the monarch. While he is young enough to promise many more years of rule, the dangers of one-man rule are obvious.

But what if Iran does navigate all these potential difficulties? What if it succeeds in perserving its economic growth and learns to distribute it more equitably? What if it moderates its problems of national integration and maintains good relations with its neighbors? And what if it succeeds unlike so many developing societies and makes the transition to greater participation and greater democracy? The irony of Iran's fate and that of the developing world in general is that, even if these countries progress as well as may be expected, the end of the century will continue to find them poor, backward, and overpopulated relative to the richer nations of the present. In short, all available evidence suggests that the gap between the prosperous nations and the poor is widening rather than decreasing. The rich have gotten richer and the poor have gotten richer. But not very much and not very fast.

ANNOTATED BIBLIOGRAPHY

The literature on Iran remains weak in a number of important areas. In fact, only Iranian history has been treated with any degree of thoroughness and then primarily the earlier periods. Students of contemporary times will have to read widely in order to satisfy their interests.

Post-World War II history and politics have been treated by a few social scientists. Leonard Binder's *Iran: Political Development in a Changing Society* (Berkeley: The University of California Press, 1962) is a comprehensive and insightful study of the principal institutional and individual actors in Iranian politics and their interrelations. While the research for the book was conducted a decade ago and many of its characters are no longer as relevant to Iranian politics, the basic outlines and conclusions are as valid now as then. *Nationalism in Iran* by Richard W. Cottam (Pittsburgh: University of Pittsburgh Press, 1964) traces the idea of nationalism through 20th century Iran focusing on its manifestation during the Mossadeq period. The use of that concept as a political weapon is well documented and rather disheartening. The Shah's view of Mossadeq's role and, of course, his own, can be found in *Mission for My Country* by Muhammad Reza Shah Pahlevi (New York: McGraw-Hill Book Company, 1961). While the work is clearly meant as an apologia of his rule and that of his father, Reza Shah, it nonetheless provides valuable information and important insights to the monarch himself. Many of these have been noted and combined with other observations by Norman Jacobs in his *The Sociology of Development: Iran as an Asian Case Study* (New York: Praeger Special Studies in International Economics and Development, 1966). A description and analysis of Iran's recent economic surge is available in George G. Baldwin, *Planning and Development in Iran* (Baltimore: The Johns Hopkins University Press, 1967). Baldwin elucidates the difficulties of economic planning in developing societies and shows how much of Iran's recent economic growth is attributable to factors extraneous to all planning efforts. Finally, the author of this chapter has a book forthcoming from the Princeton University Press entitled *Political Elites and*

Political Insecurity in Iran. Based on extensive interviews with members of the contemporary political elite, the work attempts to analyze Iranian politics through a psycho-cultural perspective.

Two novels in English by Fereidoun Esfandiary, an Iranian expatriate, are brilliantly insightful portrayals of the difficulties which beset young people in Iranian society. *The Day of Sacrifice* (London: William Heinemann, 1960) concerns the political turmoil of Iran in the 1950's and the plight of a young man caught in it. *Identity Card* (New York: Grove Press, 1966) depicts the plight of a young man entangled in the gracious horror of the civil bureaucracy of Iran in the 1960's. Both give powerful and penetrating views of life in Iran. Another work of fiction, which is a literary classic, concerns an earlier period—the turn of the 18th century—but its brilliant portrayal of its hero remains an archetypal study of the Iranian character. James Morier's *The Adventures of Hajji Baba of Ispahan* has been printed in many editions, an inexpensive recent version being the Oxford University Press of 1959. Another earlier work presents a fascinating picture of Iranian society in late 19th century Iran. Edward G. Browne's account of bus travels, *A Year Amongst the Persians* (London: Adam and Charles Black, 1893) is a rich source of observations which remain pertinent for the present.

A number of important works analyze facets of the earlier 20th century but are indispensable for the student of the contemporary period. *The Modernization of Iran, 1921-1941* by Amin Banani (Stanford: Stanford University Press, 1961) traces and assays the rule of Reza Shah and his contribution to the transformation of Iranian society. Ann K. S. Lambton's profound study of rural Iran remains a classic of scholarship. *Landlord and Peasant in Iran* (London: Oxford University Press, 1953) analyzes the history of agricultural relationships in Iran while discussing agricultural production, life-ways, and political history. A work by Sehper Zabih presents another fascinating aspect of the politics of this century, that of *The Communist Movement in Iran* (Berkeley: the University of California Press, 1966).

The older history of Iran is covered in a variety of works. Edward G. Browne is the author of another impressive work in four volumes. Concentrating on the development of Iran's cultural heritage, his *A Literary History of Persia* (Cambridge: Cambridge University Press, 1953) nonetheless manages to capture the nature of the political and social background to that heritage. A second standard work covering Iran's entire history is in two volumes by Sir Percy Molesworth Sykes, *A History of Persia* (London: Macmillan and Company, Ltd., 1921).

A number of other works cover more specialized historical periods. Firuz Kazemzadeh's *Britain and Russia in Iran, 1864-1914* (New Haven: Yale University Press, 1968) is a first-rate study which offers details of the most significant events preceding the Pahlevi era. Lord George Curzon, noted British statesman, is the author of a two-volume work with a descriptive account of Iran and startlingly profound insights into the monarchy, the civil and military bureaucracies, the economy, etc. *Persia and the Persian Question* (London: Longmans, Green and Company, 1892) remains an important work.

Nikki Keddie's *Religion and Rebellion in Iran: The Tobacco Protest of 1891-1892* (London: Frank Cass and Co., Ltd., 1966) analyzes the first occasion in Iranian history when a popular outcry led to a cancellation of a monarch's policies. *The Strangling of Persia: A Record of European Diplomacy and Oriental Intrigue* (London: T. Fisher Unwin, 1912) is the story of an American, W. Morgan Shushter, who attempted to reorganize Iran's chaotic financial system and failed. Russian and British intervention based on their fear of his weakening their influence in the internal affairs of the country led to his dismissal.

Peter Avery has written *Modern Iran* (London: Ernest Benn Ltd., 1965) to recount and organize Iran's recent history into a coherent panorama. Joseph M. Upton offers a more specialized and interpretive version in *The History of Modern Iran: an Interpretation* (Cambridge: Harvard Middle Eastern Monographs, Harvard University Press, 1960).

Finally, there are a number of works on Iran which deal with Iran's culture and peoples. Herbert H. Vreeland is the editor of a comprehensive but increasingly dated survey of many facets of Iranian life: *Iran* (New Haven: Human Relations Area Files, 1957). Donald N. Wilber is the author of another general survey-introduction: *Iran Past and Present* (Princeton: Princeton University Press, 1958). An impressive and valuable survey of Iran's artistic and literary contributions can be found in *The Heritage of Persia* (London: Weidenfeld and Nicolson, 1962) by Richard N. Frye. Finally, while concentrating on the classical music of Iran, Ella Zonis succeeds in surveying many of the contemporary fine arts in *The Dastgah Music of Iran* (Cambridge: Harvard University Press, forthcoming).

While this survey introduces the reader to a number of more specialized works on Iran, there are clearly a great variety of other works available. The student interested in additional sources will want to consult these for more specific information. Most of the books reported here contain comprehensive bibliographies. With these and a search through indexes to periodical literature, many other sources can be located.

THE FERTILE CRESCENT

chapter 9

Iraq

1. The Establishment of Statehood*

Britain's military and economic interests in the Persian Gulf were factors behind its invasion of Iraq in 1914. The Turks, who had ruled the country for almost four centuries, crumbled before the British troops who achieved complete control over the country in 1918. But the British occupation was never accepted by the Iraqis, and unrest culminated in the revolution of 1920 which called for complete independence. The British government agreed to place Iraq under its mandate in accordance with Article 22 of the Covenant of the League of Nations. The British responsibility under the mandate was to render administrative advice and assistance to help the country develop its own self-government.

The Iraqis perceived the mandate as another type of occupation and demanded nothing short of independence. The British Special Report to the League aptly described that:

> (their) impatience of mandatory control and a fervent desire for independence . . . are to be ascribed, not to ingratitude nor to lack of appreciation of the efforts of the Mandatory and the League of Nations on behalf of Iraq, but to a growing national consciousness which will not be satisfied until the country is free from foreign control.[1]

With the mandate a new type of political power relation was needed in order to safeguard British interests. The indigenous national government set up on October 23, 1920, to which the direct British administration was to be transferred, was to be constructed in such a way that the British power would be

*Abdul H. Raoof, associate professor of political science, State University College at Buffalo, N.Y.

[1] Great Britain, Colonial Office, *Special Report on Iraq, 1920-31* (London, 1931), pp. 11-12.

supreme in decision-making. This was not to fragment political power among different political institutions, but to create one strong institution on which other institutions depended for advice and decisions. The republican form of government was excluded because it would encourage competition among politicians; it would impair the concentration of power. A monarchy was favored because governmental power resting with the king would provide continuity in power relation through the hereditary succession rule. The next issue the British had to decide was the selection of the king. It was felt that the nomination of an indigenous king would open an acute strife for power among the politicians which would ultimately lead to group antagonism. A non-Iraqi, but an Arab, king would not only neutralize group struggle since the king is not associated with any of them, but would also play a conciliatory role among diversified interests in the society. Furthermore, with the lack of social support to his power the king ought to be dependent on the British for support.

On July 11, 1921 the British nominated King Faisal Ibn Husayn, son of Sharif Husayn of Mecca, who had already lost his throne in Syria. His nomination was welcomed by most politicians and social groups. Since he was the "guiding spirit" of the Arab national movement, the Iraqi nationalists placed high hopes on Faisal to bring their dreams of national independence to reality.

SOCIAL BASES OF POLITICS

During the last five decades of national government, economic and social developments have been noticeable, yet the progress is slow. The per capita income has risen from $90 in 1952 to about $298 in 1965; part of this increase is attributed to the growth of the government royalty from oil which reached $354 million for the same year.

Population Structure

While the country is rich with natural resources, such as oil and water, it is still underpopulated. According to the census of 1965, the population reached 8.5 million, three times the population of 1905, with a continuing annual rate of growth of about 2.5 percent.[2] This population growth is unevenly distributed throughout the country. Because of poverty and the lack of proper medical care, the mortality rate in the countryside and small towns is much higher than in urban centers. The migration of farmers to cities accounts for the decline in the population of rural areas. The centralization of economic activities, attracting many businessmen, professionals, and skilled workers in some large urban centers, such as Baghdad, Basrah, and Mosul, accounts for the high rate of population increase in these cities.

Most of the people continue to live in rural areas and a small portion of them

---

[2] Most of the demographic statistics used in this part were drawn from Dr. Muhammad Salman Hassan's *Studies in the Iraqi Economy* (Beirut, 1966).

are still nomads. By 1947 only about 35 percent lived in towns, but this is twice the number of 1930. The central region is more urbanized than the other two regions, northern and southern, since it encompasses the largest metropolitan area of Baghdad whose population alone reached two million in 1965, or about 20 percent of the population.

TABLE 9-1
Percentage of Population Settlement
(1947)

Region	Nomads	Rural	Urban
Northern	5	59	36
Central	1	10	46
Southern	10	59	31

Almost half of the population is in the labor force, but not more than 28 percent of the population are engaged in employment. (The working age in Iraq is between 13-56 in cities and 13-51 in rural areas.) The primary sector of the economy which consists of agriculture, livestock, fishing, and hunting employed 57 percent of the economically active population according to the 1947 census. Industry (textile, oil, construction, and light industry) had 8 percent while employment in the tertiary sector (commerce, services, and administration) was 35 percent of all occupied laborers. (The U.S. corresponding figures for the three sectors are 8 percent, 30 percent, and 56 percent respectively.)

The demographic distribution of the country is an important factor in its economic and political development. The fact that the largest portion of people are economically inactive (they are consumers/nonproducers) is an explanation of why economic productivity has to be geared towards consumption of goods rather than producing a surplus to be used in future-reinvestment. Thus, capital investment cannot grow at a fast pace.

Most of these dependents are females and students. The female labor force in cities is much less utilized than in rural areas where women often help their husbands in performing their jobs. The urban family consists of a large number of dependents, and meeting the requirements of city life can be expensive. The average head of a household, feeling the financial burden but unable to increase his income because of a lack of job mobility, has to look to the government for help. Because he expects the government to change the social structure, he constantly pushes the government for direct involvement in the management of the economic system. Such development has contributed to a growing desire among citizens to identify themselves with the central government. On the other hand, it has deprived Iraqi citizens of the possibility and even the desire to come to each other's aid; the lack of trust and cooperation inhibits the political development in the country.

By the same token, with increasing political awareness among the urban settlers the government must pay special attention to urban demands and may have to pay lip service to the reform of rural areas. During the last 15 years, funds in the Economic Plans for the agrarian sector have averaged 18 percent while housing and construction of buildings alone run as high as 40 percent. The lack of an effective program for rural development contributes to the exodus of farmers to cities.

Iraq, like most developing countries, has a very young population, about half of it being under the age of twenty. This places a heavy burden on government which becomes solely responsible for directing and managing educational institutions. The government must allocate a large portion of its resources to educational development which is more often at the expense of other social and economic developments.

Unfortunately, educational development which has accelerated at a high rate resulted in a setback for political development. The growing number of graduates (from college and high school) is beyond the capacity of economic and administrative enterprises to absorb. Their unemployment, becoming wide-spread, breeds discontent and frustration and often finds expression in the radical and revolutionary movements which have promised them rapid change.

Land Tenure and Agrarian Reform

Land tenure had been a basis of social and political power in the country since the majority of the population were tied to an economic relation in which they were subjugated to the will of the landlord. The original land ownership was based on a communal system in which the cultivated land was regarded as belonging jointly to all members of the settled tribes who also shared the crops. Later in the 19th century the tribal chiefs (*sheikhs*) began to claim rights over the land, taking it away from their tribes.

The state, according to the Islamic law, claimed ownership of all land except that which had been assigned as property tenure to individuals. With the establishment of the national government, by law the bulk of the land was owned by the state (in 1950, 65 percent of surveyed land was state-owned), but in reality the land was used by powerful sheikhs, who claimed ownership and demanded settlements of their respective rights. Most of these disputes were settled on the side of the sheikhs because of their personal influence. The failure of the government to recognize the tribal communal rights served to consolidate large property in the name of a few influential sheikhs. By 1959 half of the 32 *dunums*[3] of the surveyed cultivatable land was owned by 250,000 individuals while the other half was owned by 2,480 landlords.[4] Two prominent sheikhs each owned in excess of one million dunums, and six others each owned more than half a million dunums.

The economic position of the *fallah* (peasant) was mainly determined by his

---

[3] One dunum equals 0.62 acre.

[4] Iraq, Ministry of Economics, *Report on Agriculture and Livestock Census of Iraq, 1958-59* (Baghdad, 1961), p. 7.

landlord. The fallah was a tenant-at-will whose obligation in cultivating the land was fixed in a contract lasting one season, to be renewed if the landlord thought it desirable. Under the system of crop-sharing, commonly used throughout the country, the fallah received a fixed portion of the crop; often only enough to keep him and his family on an extreme margin of subsistence. Moreover, in the areas settled by tribes or subtribes, the fallah's duties and obligations were more out of his tribal position than out of his economic function as a tiller of the soil. He had to give respect and obedience to his tribal law and fight whenever his sheikh called upon him.

The sheikh then was performing a social role in addition to his economic role. As a paramount authority in the tribe, he was regulating tribal relations and adjudicating disputes, and through him governmental laws, if they were applicable to tribes, were to be enforced. It may be said that the sheikh enjoyed an autonomous power separate from the government.

There was a marriage of convenience between the monarchical oligarchy and the sheikhs. The oligarchy, lacking wide popular support, sought support from the sheikhs who were induced by special rewards and privileges, such as seating them in parliament, giving recognition to their claimed rights over land, and consenting to their social control over their subject tribesmen. The consequence of enhancing the social stature of the sheikhs was an augmentation of their economic power. They were able to enlarge their estates by encroaching on government land since government officials feared them and yielded to their interests.

It was obvious that the revolution of 1958 would crack down on the land tenure system. The Agrarian Reform Act of 1958 was promulgated to accomplish political, economic, and social goals. The political goal is to rid the country of the sheikh class—the symbol of the old regime—by limiting their agricultural holdings. In irrigated areas the landholdings should not exceed 1,000 dunums and not more than 2,000 dunums of land irrigated by rain. The government would confiscate above the limit in return for just compensation. The expropriation of land should be completed within five years, beginning with the largest agricultural holding. The cultivatable land held in large tracts and hence subject to the law amounted to 8.5 million dunums, one third of which was held by 95 landlords.[5]

The economic goal of the law is to create a class of small owners through distribution of between 60 and 120 dunums of both the confiscated and government land. A cooperative system was established to perform management and credit service to the peasants, which was previously performed by the sheikh. The consequence of this is to raise the standard of living of the great majority of peasants. Ultimately, it leads to an increase in agricultural production which in turn will help raise the national income. The social goal is to discourage the peasants' exodus to cities and to alleviate their suffering. It provides for the abolition of all former relations and protects the peasants

---

[5] Hassan, *op. cit.,* p. 45.

against being removed from their land and from the arbitrary domination of the sheikhs over their social and economic life.

In the ten years of the revolution, progress towards economic and social goals has been slow. By 1966 only 2,334,526 dunums were distributed to 48,194 families supporting 240,970 individuals.[6] It was estimated in 1962 that 15,000 cooperatives should be instituted to carry out the reform, but only 4,000 were licensed; most of these were criticized as being controlled by the rich peasants.[7]

For the last two decades the exodus from the countryside has occurred with great rapidity. It is apparent that the revolution has expedited the exodus rather than having halted it, because 640,000 peasants moved from the interiors to cities in the period of 1958-65.[8] Most of them have migrated to the large cities, particularly to Baghdad. (In 1965 the province of Baghdad increased its population 68 percent over the statistics of 1957.) With the eradication of the sheikhs' influence in the countryside, the peasants feel free to move from the farms and seek employment with the newly generated economic activities in the cities. Breaking away from the political alienation imposed on him by the monarchy regime, the peasant in the revolutionary regime has been subject to political mobilization carried out by both the government and the political opposition groups. Accompanying such political mobilization is a social mobilization in which the peasant feels that his new political role no longer fits his social rural role. Last, the relative failure and the slow implementation of the agrarian reform has discouraged the farmer from being optimistic about his fate in farming. Conversely, he may have concluded that rural problems are far from being solved.

Industrialization and Nationalization

The industrialization of the economy did not progress until the end of World War II. Much of this growth was a result of the wartime economic conditions which were harshly imposed on the country. As the country was cut off from imports of manufactured goods, it had to rely heavily on its own products, mostly crafts, in which 4 percent of the population were employed. After the war, faced with the competition from inexpensive mass-produced foreign goods, the craft industry began to dwindle and thousands of craftsmen were thrown into unemployment. Yet the peak of the craft industry had already paved the way for the postwar industrialization. The expansion of the craft industry into many areas of production, such as textile and leather, indicated the critical needs of the country for consumer goods. The success of the industry in bringing unexpected profits not only encouraged many craftsmen to convert their shops into larger modern factories, but also encouraged the introduction of a new class of entrepreneurs to venture into this area of production.

---

[6] *The Iraqi Economy* (Baghdad), October 30, 1967.

[7] Hassan, *op. cit.,* p. 40.

[8] Mahmud al-Daurah, *The Kurdish Case* (Beirut, 1966), p. 227.

Iraqi entrepreneurs, however, remained small in number and lacked imagination because they were dependent on government for support and initiation. The government's leading role in industrialization was a response, in part, to the existence of large numbers of unemployed, particularly among craftsmen who found an outlet for their dissatisfaction with their deteriorating economic positions in communist or other radical movements.

The government industrial policy, at least until 1964, evolved around strengthening the private sector and establishing a public sector in areas where the private sector was not able to venture. To encourage the private sector to shoulder the burden of industrialization, the government used two methods. First, it exempted newly established industries from taxes and tariffs as well as provided a protective shell from foreign competition for local products. Second, it provided financial incentive by either extending credit or holding a substantial share of the capital of the supported industries.

For the purpose of creating new bases of politics, the successive revolutionary regimes have given priority to a rapid industrialization. Massive economic aid has been received from socialist states under special agreements. Under the Iraqi-Soviet Agreement of 1959, subsequently modified, the Soviet government has provided loans with a low interest of 2½ percent a year to conduct geological surveys and to supply machines and diversified industries, such as metals, plastics, and electric appliances.

Following the steps of the U.A.R., in July 1964 the government of Abd el-Salam Aref issued a series of laws under which the private as well as the industrial and commercial sectors were brought under strict government control or were nationalized; all banks and some 30 firms were nationalized. Three official reasons were given as a pretext for directing the economy towards socialism: (1) Economic growth can only be accomplished by central planning where the public sector plays a major role. (2) A state of affairs where the concentration of wealth is with a few capitalists who exploit the majority of the population is contrary to social justice. (3) The political influence and privileges of the capitalists who have stood against the national aspirations of the people for Arab unity and socialism must be eliminated.

According to these laws full compensation was given to foreign stockholders. A ceiling of ID 5,000 was established for full compensation for the Iraqi citizens, and a flat compensation of ID 500 for the exceeding shares. Seven percent of the total stockholders who owned 81 percent of the nationalized capital fell into the latter category.[9] Any company with capital exceeding ID 70,000 should be a stockholding type. Workers and staff were to share in the management of the nationalized companies and to receive 25 percent of their annual profits.

At the apex of all the nationalized companies was the Public Economic Establishment, attached directly to the office of the prime minister, with an autonomy in managing its personnel and fiscal affairs. Its purpose was to oversee, manage, and plan the whole public economic sector. The Establishment, in turn, consisted of three subestablishments along the line of economic

[9] *al-Thawrah al-Arabiyah* (Baghdad), June 14, 1965

activities: Public Establishment for Industry managed about 40 industries, Public Establishment for Commerce managed six companies with a total capital of ID 40 million, and Public Establishment for Insurance. Management experience must have overlapped and conflicted with other ministries which led the government in early 1966 to dissolve the Public Economic Establishment; the other three establishments were attached to their appropriate ministries.

Data accumulated after the first year of operation showed a jump in the profits of most of the nationalized industries. The increase was between 13 and 48 percent over their profits in 1964. This is not, however, a surprise since the government had completely eliminated foreign competition with these industries, therefore the expansion of their production was needed.

On the other hand, other companies, particularly in the commercial sectors, showed incompetence in carrying out their activities. Shortage of essential items, such as drugs and spare parts, caused complaints from the citizens which forced high government authority to directly intervene to remedy the situation. However, the experience with nationalization, which seems to have stifled the economy, may have convinced the government of its premature step and hence no further steps have been taken since 1964.

A COUNTRY OF MINORITIES

The division of the population into social, economic, and regional groups is further complicated by their division along religious, sectarian, and nationality lines. No one of these groups constitutes a majority. The religious majority are Muslims—94 percent of the population divided almost equally into two main sects: Shi'i and Sunni. They are further subdivided into a majority of Arabs and a minority of Kurds living in the northern region and comprising 15 percent of the population. In addition, there are two other nationalities, Turkish and Iranian, whose population together does not exceed 3.25 percent.

The presence of such minority groups with their conflicting values and the diversity in their orientation towards political roles has significantly inhibited national integration. The inability of a large number of individuals within each minority group to comprehend the national unity and their unwillingness to submit themselves to a national authority beyond their own immediate community has constantly placed a strain on the performance of the political system.

The problem of minorities has been further complicated by the existence of tribal organization in some groups where the chiefs had some religious authority. This has been particularly true in the case of the Kurdish minority and the Shi'i tribes of the central Euphrates. Under the Monarchy, these chiefs could effectively defy government authority—when it became a threat to their own interests—by arousing religious sentiment among their tribesmen. Because of strong social cohesion within these groups, their submergence into the national political system was improbable.

The Shi'i outnumber the Arab Sunni but have not been proportionally represented in the structure of political power. The predominant rulers, whether under the Monarchy or the Republican regime, are Arab Sunni who discriminantly used government offices against the Shi'i. Shi'i representation in the Monarchy cabinets did not exceed more than 26 percent of the total cabinet posts. Early cabinets, until 1935, did not include more than one Shi'ite for each individual cabinet, and a Shi'ite prime minister was chosen for the first time in 1947. Faced with discrimination in government employment, the educated Shi'ite tends to be radical in viewing both the government and his political role—he suspects public policy and distrusts government authority.

The Shi'i identified themselves with the revolution of 1958, and a large number of them were appointed to high government offices. Holding onto their new gains, the Shi'i remained aloof from the political movement for Arab unity because such unity would bring them back under the dominance of the Sunni. In retaliation against their opposition, the nationalists who overthrew Kassim in 1963 killed, imprisoned, and dismissed from government thousands of Shi'i. In turn, the Shi'i viewed the government's suppressive measures as acts of discrimination and since then have had a negative attitude towards the nationalist government.

The Kurdish Problem

The Kurdish problem is a different one from that of the Shi'i. The Kurds, speaking a different language, belonging to a different race, and bound by their homogeneous culture, may rightly constitute a nation which at the present time is divided among four independent states: Syria, Iran, Turkey, and Iraq. What strengthens their national feeling even more is their concentration in settled areas, whereby they not only make up the majority in these areas, but are also linked together across the national boundaries of these four states.

The spread of Western ideas after World War I for establishing nation-states and the emphasis on self-determination for all subjugated nationalities has inspired the Kurds to seek an independent state of their own. But the war settlement in the Middle East was to curve the Kurds inside the newly drawn boundaries of these four states. The Kurdish disappointment, coupled with the lack of experience and tolerance of the new governments in the Middle East on how to live and deal with another nationality, broadened rather than healed the national disintegration. Thus, the Kurds have been a source of discomfort to the states concerned, each of which has used a different method to suppress them. Iraq has been less fortunate than its neighbor states in dealing with its Kurdish problem. Since 1927, the Iraqi Kurds have been in a state of revolution, off and on demanding secession. The most serious of all is their recent revolt in which they have been engaged since 1961.

The Kurdish national revolution, at least in Iraq, was not the work of its intelligentsia like any national movement but championed by their chiefs. This is why its goal and ideology remained undefined for a long time. The growth of social transformation and the wide spread of political awareness among the populace after World War II have mobilized large numbers of previously nonparticipant Kurds around some type of indentity. Hence, Kurdish nationalism penetrated into the rank and file of the Kurdish populace, and a new generation of Kurdish intelligentsia became the dynamic force of the movement; yet its leadership is still controlled by some chiefs and particularly Mulla Mustafa al-Barazzani, chief of the Kurdish tribe, Barzzan.

As the revolution of 1958 came to reestablish new bases for social and political interactions, high expectations for a fresh look at the Arab-Kurdish relation were aroused among the members of the two nationalities. The provisional constitution of 1958 perceived for the first time both "the Kurds and the Arabs as partners of the Iraqi nation" and recognized "the national Kurdish rights" within the Iraqi unity. Mulla Mustafa al-Barazzani and hundreds of his followers, refugees for almost 13 years in the U.S.S.R., were allowed to return and were welcomed by the government. In 1960 the Communist party for Iraqi Kurdistan and the Kurdish Democratic party were licensed by the government after long operating underground.

Political forces and social groups never had so much experience in freely expressing their demands and openly carrying out their activities and recruitment. Thus, new participants were brought into the body politics of the republic. The Kurdish national movement gained new momentum, also, when Arab national groups began to press for an immediate union with other Arab sister states. Self-awareness of their future nationhood was highly reactivated and a greater autonomy for Kurdistan was stressed. But the government of Abd Al-Karim Kassim had already plunged the country into political dissention and, hence, was not able to act decisively. The Kurds were left with no other way but to carry arms against the central government in September of 1961.

The government has not been able to defeat the Kurds who at one time controlled some 250 miles of territory in the northeastern region, and only military stalemates seem to have permitted the two sides to agree on several cease-fires whereby negotiations were to start. The position of the two sides in these negotiations, however, is tempered by the country's political conditions rather than a clear understanding of the problem.

The first phase of such negotiation was in 1963 after the Baathists came to power, when the two sides agreed to recognize "the national Kurdish rights on the bases of establishing a self-government." In a short time the agreement, nebulous in its wording, was subject to different interpretations by the two sides. To the Barazzani *self-government* meant an autonomous government loosely connected with the central government, with certain exclusive powers. To the national government it meant merely decentralization of some government functions to the Kurdistan area while the central government would maintain complete authority over it.

Hostilities resumed on June 9, 1963 with no decisive results, although

Kurdish dominance in the countryside was somewhat increased. In February of 1964 another cease-fire was announced, but negotiations proved unproductive and hostilities were resumed in 1965. In June of 1966 after the failure of a spring offensive, Prime Minister Bazzaz offered the Kurds a 12-point plan which amounted to a guarantee of local autonomy. The plan provided for a decentralized administration, use of the Kurdish language in the Kurdistan area, general elections, proportional representation of Kurds in the National Assembly and in public service, Kurdish civil servants in Kurdish areas, a Kurdish political party and press, and rehabilitation of the Kurdish guerillas.[10] The leading army officers remained opposed to concessions to the Kurds, however, and an agreement about the extent of Kurdish autonomy could not be reached. When the government of Ahmed Hasan Bakr took control in June 1968 it stood behind the Bazzaz plan to the Kurds again but failed to provide the number of cabinet posts the Kurds demanded, and no reconciliation appears possible in the near future.

The stalemate in the solution of the Kurdish problem is attributed to two main factors:

First, the government's instability and the lack of popular support have impaired the development of a rational public policy. Whenever a government begins to feel the ground underneath it and is able to comprehend the issue, it is either overthrown by a military coup d'état or disrupted by dissention within the ruling group. Each government, embedded in a different political ideological group, is inclined to take a different stand on Kurdish nationalism. Though the successive regimes since 1963 have been pro-Arab unity, none of them has ever embraced a defined ideological interpretation of the role of nationalities in the future Arab union. The lack of such ideological interpretation may open the way for a pragmatic solution, but this can only be achieved when political stability prevails.

Second, the Kurdish leaders are basing their demands on the right of a certain group of people to share the political power with the ruling elite. By the same token it is to make the rulers relatively responsible to certain rules of law. But the Iraqi rulers perceived themselves as unaccountable to any political group and were not ready to share power with the people. The issue, then, is the incompatibility between democratic and authoritarian rules.

PHILOSOPHY OF THE CONSTITUTION OF 1925

The constitution of 1925, abrogated by the revolution of 1958, laid down the framework of the political organization which in accepting Western representative government marked a major departure from the Islamic institutions of government. Though these institutions were alien to the social and economic composite of the polity, they were adopted as a symbol of nationhood and as a pass for the country into the community of nations.

---

[10]*The New York Times,* June 30, 1966.

Though the constitution was ratified by a Constituent Assembly whose delegates were far from being truly elected by the populace, it was the work of a small group of British officials and Iraqi statesmen. It did not, however, reflect the thinking of these drafters for they were closely supervised and directed by the British Colonial Office and King Faisal. Those who were engaged in drafting the constitution were preoccupied with a state of affairs which was not to be changed but legitimized. Thus, the constitution was not only to regulate political institutions, but to safeguard the British interests and the monarchical institutions which had come into existence four years earlier.

After careful consideration the British arrived at the conclusion that their juridical position in Iraq should be defined in a treaty between the two governments. The Treaty of Alliance, which was proposed in 1922, envisioned that the mandatory regime would last a period of 20 years, but the Iraqis expressed gravest misgivings. When the Constituent Assembly met in 1924 the British insisted that the assembly ratify the treaty before it proceeded to discuss the draft constitution. The passing of the treaty was not in itself a guarantee to the British interests unless they were protected by the constitution. The constitution included a provision authorizing the King to issue decrees for "securing the execution of the treaty obligations." The British financial interests, regulated by the Financial Treaty of 1922 and imposing on Iraq the repayment to the British government the cost of its operations in Iraq during the periods of the occupation and the mandate, were removed from the temper of a legislative body by vesting in the cabinet the power to initiate financial bills; the parliament was not allowed to amend the treaty. All promulgations and regulations issued by the British High Commissioner in Iraq were to be abrogated or amended only by a legislative act.

The constitution provided for a dominant monarch. He was not to be paralyzed either by a legislative or by an independent executive branch; they were to be dependent on him. He had unrestricted power in appointing and dismissing his cabinet and the members of the Senate (second chamber). The power of adjournment and dissolution of parliament was granted to him. Emergency power could be declared by the king upon the advice of the prime minister.

Old social institutions were sanctioned by the constitution, particularly the sheikhs' institution and the religious communities. The sheikhs, whose power and social status were enhanced by the British, were conscious of this gain and pressed the national government to recognize their privileges. Making up half of the Constituent Assembly, they gathered before its opening to formalize their demands, which served as bargaining bases with the government for their ratification of the constitution. None of the following demands were incorporated in the constitutional document, but they were subsequently enacted in regular laws:

1. The establishment of a special court for solving disputes among tribes. The

Tribal Trials Law, promulgated originally by the British in 1917, provided special machinery for trying tribesmen by applying the tribal customs.
2. Recognition of the tribal system in which leadership within each tribe was to be hereditary.
3. Support of their rights over the cultivated land and a guarantee against the arbitrary expropriation of any movable or immovable property or goods.

Religious communities were recognized as autonomous in the newly established state. The constitution recognized the existence of two Islamic sects: Shi'i and Sunni. Each sect had the right to practice its own rites. Two separate systems of courts, one for each sect, were established to handle matters, such as marriage and inheritance, "according to the rules of their sect." The *quadi* (judge) who decided on personal status was required to be a member of the sect to which the majority of the inhabitants where he was appointed belonged. The establishment of an Islamic state promoted a fear among the other two religious groups—the Jews and the Christians. They demanded the return to the "millet" system under which each community was allowed to issue and regulate their own affairs.

POLITICAL INSTITUTIONS

The Monarchy constitution created two political institutions with unequal power. The executive—the king and his cabinet—was created as the main institution to which parliament owed its existence. The cabinet's role in the political system was enhanced by the support it received from the oligarchy, the king and his associates, which made it the focus of effective power as well as a shadow of their influence.

The Cabinet

The cabinet was a small body consisting of a prime minister and his colleagues, the ministers who were appointed upon his recommendation to the king. Because of the absence of an effective party system and the lack of a constitutional provision describing the procedure of choosing and dismissing the prime minister from office, the king enjoyed a free hand in this matter. Effective limitation was imposed on the king's power when the margin of political power in the country shifted to other social groups. Tribal uprisings during the period of 1934-35, followed by the army intervention in politics which lasted until 1941, restrained the power of the king who found himself implementing a policy dictated to him from outside.

The constitution provided that ministers must be members of parliament. It was possible for a minister to be chosen from outside the circle of the members of parliament, but he could not retain his ministerial post more than six months unless he was appointed a senator or elected a deputy before the end of that period. This arrangement was undoubtedly made in order to give expertise a place in the cabinet where it was needed. The recruitment of ministers from among bureaucrats was very common in the history of Iraqi politics. This is not, however, because bureaucratic expertise was urgently needed to advise the cabinet on technical matters; especially in the early stages of political development, bureaucracy itself had not been effectively developed. Actually the recruitment of bureaucrats was often motivated by power politics. The prime minister could easily influence his colleagues in the cabinet if they were bureaucrats because they owed him their political careers.

The cabinet, in theory, was collectively responsible to the Chamber of Deputies (lower house of the parliament). Ministers must be as one in defending the policy of the cabinet, therefore all were responsible for any decision taken by the cabinet. The cabinet had to resign if its essential policy was rejected by the majority of the Chamber of Deputies. A government was not required to ask for a vote of confidence upon entering office or thereafter; it could only be requested when support to the government was questionable. The constitutional interpretation behind this was that a government already possessed the confidence of the Chamber upon its entry into office unless the Chamber had withdrawn its confidence by express vote. However, no vote of confidence was ever passed against any cabinet, not because cabinets were formed on the assumption that they already commanded the majority support of the Chamber, but because the cabinet could dissolve the Chamber at any time before facing it or before there was any suspicion that the Chamber might not support it.

The Powers of the Cabinet

The striking features of the cabinet's strength could be seen in its possession of the following powers:

1. The power to issue ordinances: Article 26 of the constitution empowered the cabinet to legislate any matter whenever parliament was not in session if the necessity arose. The definition of a *necessity* was left completely to the discretion of the cabinet itself. The frequency with which the cabinet resorted to ordinances can easily be established by considering the number of ordinances. During the period from 1922 to 1954, parliament passed 1,685 laws while the cabinet decreed 226 ordinances, or 12 percent of the entire legislation. This, however, does not include 1,714 regulations which were issued by the cabinet.
2. The cabinet could declare martial law and a state of emergency should disturbances occur. In order to restore order, the cabinet could, in addition to the use of coercive force which was part of its function, restrict the freedom of citizens by proroguing laws and assuming special emergency power. In the period 1924-58 martial law was declared 16 times and the country had to live under emergency conditions for 10 years or almost one third of this 34 year period.

3. The cabinet could suspend and dissolve the Chamber before its legal term of four years had expired. Because the cabinet had indiscriminately dissolved the Chamber, Iraq had sixteen different Chambers instead of only eight. Only two Chambers completed their legal term while the other fourteen were dissolved before the expiration of their four-year terms. One Chamber (1954) was dissolved after its first opening meeting.

Parliament

The constitution, though it dealt with the power and the structure of the legislature in more detail than it did with the cabinet, made the legislature ineffective and powerless. The institution of a weak legislature was considered by the British government when it decided on establishing a self-government rule in the 1920s. The British Acting High Commissioner to Iraq, Sir Henry Dobbs, gave the following advice to his government on the proposed Iraqi parliament in February 1923:

> In light of experience of other Oriental Assemblies, there is to my mind real danger that irresponsible extremist majority may in early stages of self-government seek to paralyze state activities by refusing supplies for essential services. . . . It is therefore essential to have provision for enabling the Executive to carry on.[11]

Parliament was further curtailed by the elite who reduced it to a mere rubber-stamp filled with their supporters. By suppressing all political activities, banning the formation of political parties, and intervening in the election, the elite prevented parliament from reflecting the social and political interests in the society. The sheikhs and the upper class were overrepresented, and the working and farmer classes never had a single representative in the parliament.

Parliament comprised two assemblies with equal power in legislation. The Senate (upper house), whose members were not to exceed one-fourth of the number of the Chamber of Deputies (lower house), were appointed by the King for an eight-year term. Until 1952 the Chamber of Deputies was indirectly elected by the people by the use of a two-stage system. The first stage was to elect the so-called "Secondary Electors" who in turn would elect the deputies in the second stage. In 1952 the government, responding to the opposition demands, passed a new act in which the direct system was adopted.

Political Parties

Political parties, or any other form of political aggregation, were always subject to strict government regulations. A party had to receive permission from the minister of the interior before it could start operation. Vested with unlimited power, the minister might reject an application to form a party or

---

[11]Quoted in Philip W. Ireland, *Iraq: A Study in Political Development* (London, 1937), p. 373.

abrogate the license of an already established one. Party operations, finances, and records were rigidly supervised and investigated by the government.

The oligarchy of the Monarchy regime did not believe in the formulation of political parties to carry on their competition for power. Only under certain circumstances did the oligarchy form parties, but these parties died after the motive for such a move had disappeared. The few short-lived parties during the period of 1920-1935 were characterized as personal parties—centered around one or a few personalities—and lacked public support because they were born out of factions within the oligarchy.

Political awareness, penetrating deeply into social and economic groups, gave impulse at the close of World War II to the formation of five political parties by the new generation of politicians who became impatient with the old style of politics. Challenging the oligarchy, these parties were constructed along ideological or pragmatic lines and appealed directly to the people for support. These parties were: al-Ahrar, a pragmatic party; al-Istiqlal (Independence), Arab nationalist; al-Watani al-Demokrati (the Democratic National), democratic socialist; and al-Itihad al-Watani (the National Union) and al-Sh'ab (People), both Marxist socialist.

From their inception these opposition parties were subject to repressive measures by the government. In 1947 the government withdrew the license of two parties—the National Union and the People. Al-Ahrar, shattered by intra-party dissension, dissolved itself in 1948. The other two parties continued legal operations until 1954, but their activities were curtailed, and they became no more than a clique of opposition.

However, these opposition parties had put the oligarchy on the defensive. The articulation of the opposition in political parties not only made their action more effective and better unified, but discredited the oligarchy, which remained unorganized, for being against parliamentary life. The oligarchy began to realize their vulnerable position and the need for an organization to end the agitation of the opposition.

When Nuri al-Said (the master and elder stateman of the oligarchy) formed his cabinet in 1949, he began to unify his associates under his leadership. But the oligarchy had already been split into two main factions: Nuri's faction and Salih Jabr's faction (Salih Jabr was the first Shi'ite prime minister). Personal animosity between the two leaders did not allow the establishment of one party embracing the oligarchy; conversely, two parties were installed—Nuri al-Said's al-Itihad al-Dasturi (the Constitutional Union) and Salih Jabr's al-Uma al-Ishtiraki (the Socialist Nation). Both parties depended heavily upon the alignment of the sheikhs and the traditional politicians. Al-Uma's main strength, however, lay in the Shi'i and Kurdish districts.

Party life came to an end in 1954 when the government of Nuri al-Said determined to go ahead with the Western proposed collective defense for the Middle East, a course long-awaited and constantly met with protest and violence from the opposition parties. As preventive measures against any possible opposing agitation, Nuri liquidated his party and then proceeded to issue a series of ordinances in which political freedom and parties were wiped out completely. This forced both the Democratic National party and the Independence party to enter in a national front with the two revolutionary parties, the Communist and Baath both of which had already been working underground. The front successfully established contact with a group of army officers and launched a coup d'état on July 14, 1958 which brought the end of the Monarchy regime.

2.   The Republican Regime*

The Revolution of 1958

The formation of the United Arab Republic on February 1, 1958 represented a triumph for the forces of revolutionary nationalism in the Arab world and posed a serious threat to the conservative monarchy in Iraq. For Iraq's unpopular and oppressive regime had failed to meet effectively the fundamental socio-economic problems of the bulk of its subjects; as a result those subjects were extremely susceptible to the massive propaganda emanating from Cairo and Damascus calling for the overthrow of the monarchy in Iraq. In order to meet the threat posed by the U.A.R., the Iraqi government joined with the monarchy in Jordan on February 14, 1958 to form the Arab Federation, a union in which the two Hashemite Kingdoms pledged to support one another. When events in Jordan reached crisis proportions during the summer of 1958, it became necessary for Iraq to fulfill its pledge, and the government ordered army units to proceed into Jordan to support King Husein. However, Colonel Abd el- Salam Aref ordered his unit not into Jordan but into Baghdad, and on the morning of July 14th Aref conducted a coup against the Iraqi government. The Baghdad populace, overjoyed at the downfall of the monarchy, rampaged in the streets. Scores were killed in the mob violence, including King Faisal, Crown Prince Amir Abd al-Illah, and Nuri al-Said. However, order was quickly restored and by the evening of the 16th the country was under the firm control of the military. A republic was proclaimed, and a new government was formed under the leadership of Brigadier Abd al-Karim Kassim.

The first concern of Brigadier Kassim and his chief aide Colonel Aref was to consolidate their power by cementing the coalition of broad-based political support that the revolution initially enjoyed. A Council of Sovereignty representing the Sunnis, Shi'ites and Kurds was established as a symbol of unity and tripartite head of state. The first cabinet was so chosen that its members would bring a broad spectrum of political opinion into the new government. Preparations were made for a general amnesty for political crimes committed under the old regime. While a People's Court under Colonel Fadil 'Abbas al-Mahdawi tried and sentenced politicians of the old regime, exiles returned from abroad. There was little resistance to the new regime and much

*Tareq Y. Ismael.

enthusiasm for it, and it appeared that Kassim and Aref had successfully unified the nation behind their government. However, the increase in political activity and the emergence of forces previously suppressed led to conflicts before the dust had settled. Brigadier Kassim became prime minister and commander-in-chief of the Iraqi armed forces and Colonel Aref became deputy premier, minister of the interior, and deputy commander-in-chief.

On the 26th of July a constitution was proclaimed for the state. Pronouncing Iraq to be an independent Arab republic, the constitution gave all executive power to the Council of Ministers, as well as, with the approval of the Council of Sovereignty, all legislative power. All laws were declared to continue in force until amended or canceled.

The Struggle for Power

Almost immediately there arose a three-way pull for power among the pan-Arabists, the Iraqi nationalists, and the communists. This struggle was first manifested in the problem of determining the nature of U.A.R.-Iraqi relations. Colonel Aref was a supporter of the pan-Arab point of view, an immediate or an eventual union with the U.A.R. Opposed to this pan-Arab view were the National Democrats, the communists and their supporters. The communists, supported by the Kurds, opposed any union with Egypt and Syria, primarily because Nasser's opposition to communism and the larger population of the U.A.R. would allow neither the communists nor the Kurds the scope they desired. For if Iraq, a small country united with the much larger U.A.R., the percentage of communists and Kurds to the total population would then be so small that they would have almost no voice in the affairs of the country. The Iraqi nationalists, jealous of Iraq's sovereignty, took a more conservative view of Arab unity.

Kassim initially intended to seek closer relations with the U.A.R. than had the monarchy, but was determined to maintain Iraq's independent status. His refusal to submerge the state into a larger political entity was to some extent a result of his desire to maintain leadership and become the symbol of Iraq's revolution. More fundamentally, however, Kassim was cognizant of the country's heterogeneous social characteristics which are unique in comparison to her sister Arab states. The compositely large minority of Kurds, Turks, and other smaller groups would not have been sympathetic to an exclusively pan-Arabist program that might have threatened their cultural autonomy. Also, the Shi'ite majority, then, did not favorably consider the prospect of being further submerged from national political life by federation with other Arab states, most of which are predominantly Sunni.

In attempting to unify the country, then, Kassim rejected the Nasserite program. A propaganda battle with the U.A.R. resulted, as bitter as any between Nasser and the Hashemites had been, and was manifested in a power struggle between Kassim and Aref. Kassim's outlook prevailed and on September 12, 1958 Colonel Aref was removed from his position as deputy commander-in-chief of the armed forces. On September 30 he was also removed from the cabinet, along with two supporters, and appointed ambassador to Bonn. An uprising in his regiment was quelled on October 5th, and on the 12th he left the country. He never took up his post in Germany, however, and upon his return to Baghdad on November 4th was arrested and accused of plotting against the security of the state. The pan-Arabists were now out of power and were arrested at large. In February a sentence of death was pronounced upon Aref and Rashid Ali al-Gailani (the hero of the 1941 revolt), and in protest six ministers representing the right-wing nationalists left the cabinet. The Baath and the Istiqlal party were no longer represented in the government. These two groups, along with other disenchanted nationalists, subsequently formed a coalition, the National Front, as a means of gathering their forces against Kassim.

To counter the growing strength of the anti-Kassim nationalists and Nasserites, Kassim began to lean heavily upon the support of the well-organized Communist party. As a result of Kassim's complacency toward their activities, the communists were able to expand their influence considerably. They created front organizations, such as the Association for the Defense of the Rights of Iraqi Women, the Partisans of Peace, and the Democratic Youth Association. They organized labor syndicates, farmers' associations, and student unions. They infiltrated the paramilitary Popular Resistance Forces (formed in August 1958), and they were even able to gain control over the mass media through the appointments of communists as press censor and as head of radio-television.

Even more significant and fateful than the above, however, was the appointment, late in 1958, of the well-known Communist, Colonel Taha Haj Ahmad, as director of military planning in the ministry of defense. Colonel Ahmad was able to subordinate the entire ministry to his power, and through the creation of his own intelligence channels, to suppress opposition. Furthermore, communist-controlled Committees for the Defense of the Republic were set up in almost every department of the government and functioned as spy networks to rout out political renitency. Through these machinations the communists were able to bring about the removal from government and the arbitrary arrest of many nationalists and Nasserites by early 1959. Needless to say, these purges had a debilitating effect upon government administration, removing some of the most able officials and leaving the survivors timid and cautious. More fundamentally, however, Kassim, in cooperation with the communists, isolated political opposition from legitimate channels of protest and helped consolidate nationalist unrest.

The conflict with the nationalists came to a head in early March 1959 when Colonel Abd al-Wahab al-Shawaf, a pro-Nasserite who opposed the growing influence of the communists, used his Mosul based troops to stage a revolt against the government. However, the Iraqi Air Force raided Mosul, and the revolt, which was poorly organized, failed. Colonel Shawaf was killed during the raid.

As a result of Colonel Shawaf's abortive attempt at revolution, Kassim felt that communist distrust of the nationalists was justified; thus, the communists were allowed to intensify their purge. Scores of pan-Arabists, civilian as well as military, were implicated in the attempted coup and were either killed or arrested. The purge even reached into the highest echelons of government, for Muhammad Mahdi Kubbah, head of the Istiqlal and member of the Council of Sovereignty, was placed under house arrest. The communists had reached the peak of their power.

The threat of nationalist, especially Nasserite and Baathist, strength appeared to be effectively curbed. But in circumscribing nationalist power, Kassim had established a *modus vivendi* with the communists and had allowed them quite a bit of freedom of maneuver. Now they began to demand greater voice at the policy-making level of government. By the end of April 1959 a campaign by the communist press demanded full communist participation in the government. Minister of Economy Ibrahim Kubbah and Minister of Health Dr. Muhammad Abd al-Malik al-Shawaf urged the inclusion of communists in the cabinet. Although on May 23 Kassim voiced his disapproval of these demands, nevertheless on July 13 he appointed the noted Communist Dr. Naziha Dulaimi as minister of municipalities. The delicate balance of political forces that Kassim had striven for, and for which purpose he had suppressed the nationalists, appeared to be crumbling. But he was not a communist and had no intention of allowing their ascendance. His opportunity to reduce their power came on July 14, 1959, the first anniversary of the revolution, when rioting broke out in northern Iraq between Kurdish tribes and Turcoman townspeople. The communist-controlled Peoples' Resistance Forces aided the Kurdish demonstrators. Kassim, fearful of the power of the paramilitary Peoples' Resistance Forces and outraged by communist use of them in this affair, disarmed and disbanded the organization. The Communist party, in an effort to extricate itself, indulged in extensive self-criticism in July 1960. Nevertheless, further actions were taken to curtail communist influence, including the removal of Ibrahim Kubbah and later, Naziha Dulaimi from the cabinet. General Ahmad Salih al-Abdi, military governor-general of Iraq, became the nemesis of the communists through 1960 and 1961, during which time he further diminished their influence.

Kassim had at this point subdued both communists and extreme nationalists, but he had alienated both groups. His flirtation with the communists, moreover, incurred the distrust of most of the nationalist elements. Thus, within a year after he took power, he had lost the trust of most of the civilian groups who had provided his revolution with support. Evidence of this fact was provided on October 7, 1959, when members of the Baath party made an attempt upon the Premier's life that placed him in the hospital until early December. Despite the alienation of many active politicians from the Kassim regime, however, the Premier did establish an equilibrium of sorts. For in January of 1960 political parties, which had been prohibited since 1954, were again permitted the right to organize under certain restrictions.

The restrictions were primarily in regard to their membership—no military officers or government officials were allowed to join—and their organization—they were not allowed to organize in a military or paramilitary fashion. The parties were allowed to operate under licenses granted by the minister of the interior. Of the first four parties to apply, three were granted licenses. These were the National Democratic party, the Democratic party of Kurdistan, and the Iraqi Communist party (actually a minority splinter group of the Communist party paid for and supported by Kassim in an attempt to undermine and deny recognition to the majority party). Subsequently, the Iraqi Islamic party and the Progressive National party, the latter an offshoot of the National Democratic party, were also granted licenses.

Two events occurred in 1961 to significantly weaken Premier Kassim's internal and international positions. First, early in that year, the Kurdish leader Mulla Mustafa al-Barazzani launched a rebellion against Kassim's regime and by September of 1961 controlled some 250 miles of territory in northern Iraq. The government began an offensive against the Barazzani group, but the Kurds maintained their position. The war became notably sanguinary and protracted, and the apparent inability of the government forces to bring it to a successful conclusion created a dissatisfaction among many army officers. The Baathists, strengthened in Syria by the fall of the U.A.R., capitalized on this dissatisfaction and proselytized many in the army to their more militant and dogmatic ideology. As a result, Kassim's hold on the military, whose loyalty was essential to the maintenance of his regime, began to wane.

The second event occurred on June 25, 1961 when Kassim announced his intention of annexing newly independent Kuwait. Not only was this action vigorously denounced throughout the world, but it was particularly abhorred by all members of the Arab League. That same year Kuwait was accepted as a member of the League, and Iraq, in retaliation, withdrew from the meetings.

The 1963 Coup d'Etat

Internally and diplomatically isolated then, Kassim was in a most unstable position. But his opposition was also divided and fragmented, and Kassim was able, albeit somewhat precariously, to maintain his hold until early 1963. The Baathists, meanwhile, used the interim period to organize a coalition of all nationalist and independent groups in an anti-communist and anti-Kassim front.

When the Baathists were ready to strike they set up Colonel Abd al-Salam Mohammed Aref (released from prison in November 1961) as the figurehead of their National Revolutionary Command Council. On February 8, 1963 General Kassim was overthrown by a coalition of the army, the Baath, and other pan-Arab groups. He was killed the following day. The Baathists named Aref President of the Republic, but real power lay with the Premier Ahmed Hasan Bakr (one of the more recent military proselytes to the Baath party), his cabinet (primarily Baathists with a few nationalists), and the National Revolutionary Command Council (made up principally of Baathist party leadership). Trials and executions of communists, pro-Kassim elements and others, along with a purge of the army and civil bureaucracies followed the coup.

The Aref government was pro-Egyptian, and talks were begun following the Baathist coup in Syria (March 1963) in regard to a union between Iraq, Syria, and Egypt. Conflicts again arose, however, due to traditional rivalries and conflicts of interest. Although an agreement for eventual union was signed on April 17th, Nasser and the Baathists were soon at enmity. Subsequently, on May 13th the non-Baathists were forced out of the cabinet and the Iraqi government took on a strongly anti-Nasser disposition. President Nasser declared the U.A.R.'s withdrawal from the tripartite union pact in July 1963. On October 8th a Syro-Iraqi military union was announced, which was to bring the two Baathist-controlled states into closer association.

Baathist Dominance

Now in control of a major part of the Fertile Crescent, the Baathists seemed to be prepotent. However, in Iraq there were two factors which augured ill for the party. First, there was widespread dissatisfaction among the military, which in Iraq is the perennially essential element to the maintenance of power. The creation of a paramilitary National Guard shortly after the coup was the primary cause of this dissatisfaction. The Baathist apparently used the organization as a countermeasure to potential army dissidence and as a means of purging the population of political opposition. The organization became quite powerful, reportedly exceeding 50,000 members, and many officers considered its existence and activities an affront to the military and were distrustful of this curtailment of their influence.

The second factor was an ideological split within the party ranks itself. By November 1963 two factions emerged in an intra-party power struggle—the so-called moderates and extremists. The extremists, under the leadership of Deputy Premier and Minister of Guidance Ali Salih al-Saadi, had control of the Revolutionary Command Council, the highest authority in the land, and the National Guard. The extremists demanded the immediate and total application of socialism to Iraq, uncompromising continuance of the fruitless and costly campaign against the Kurds, relentless opposition to President Nasser, and suppression of all internal political opposition. On the other hand, the moderates led by Hazim Jawad, minister of the interior, and Talib Hussein Shabib, minister of foreign affairs, and supported by many among the military, were not so ideologically dogmatic and felt that accommodation and reconciliation should temper the government's policies.

On November 4, 1963 the moderates, in collaboration with President Aref, stage-managed a meeting of the Regional Command of the Baath party and elected a number of their group who were in the military to important posts of party leadership. Simultaneously, al-Saadi and some of his supporters in the council were expelled from the country. Fighting then erupted in Baghdad within the National Guard between members supporting the two factions. In an attempt to maintain party unity, Michel Aflaq and members of the International Command of the Baath party (based in Syria) came to Baghdad and proceeded to renounce the election. They proclaimed the International Command the rulers of Iraq and expelled Jawad, Shabib, and others. They were unable, however, to resolve the differences paralyzing the party. On November 18th President Aref, supported by disaffected military elements, took advantage of the consequent weakness of the Baath administration and ousted the party from the government. Aflaq and his associates returned to Damascus, but the struggle was over only when the Baathist National Guard surrendered its arms to the army.

The Aref Regime

Aref's new cabinet retained some Baathists but was primarily composed of army officers and technicians. Aref retained the presidency, appointed himself chief-of-staff, a month later giving the post to his brother General Abd al-Rahman Aref, and gave the premiership to his close friend and confidant Lt. Gen. Taher Yahya, the former chief-of-staff.

At first President Aref was strongly pro-Nasser, going so far as to establish a Joint Presidency Council (May 26, 1964). On the sixth anniversary of the creation of the Republic of Iraq, July 14, 1964, the government took some momentous steps toward implementation of the union. The first was the establishment of the Arab Socialist Union of Iraq, hailed by President Aref as the "threshhold of the building of the unity of the Arab nation under Arab Socialism."[12] The Charter or Basic Law of the A.S.U. of Iraq was identical in most respects to the charter of the Arab Socialist Union of the U.A.R. The four publicly active political groups in Iraq at the time—the Arab Nationalist movement, the Arab Socialist party, the Socialist Unionist movement, and the Democratic Social Unionists—dissolved and were absorbed by the Arab Socialist Union of Iraq.

Also on July 14, 1964 all banks and some 30 large business firms were nationalized by the government; 25.5 million Iraqi dinars were paid by the government in compensation (I.D. 1=$2.80). An Economic Establishment was formed to supervise the nationalized industries. All of these measures were designed to bring Iraq closer in aims and structures to the U.A.R. in order to make the union foreseen by the agreement of May 26th viable. The first meeting of the U.A.R.-Iraq Joint Presidency Council was held on July 15, 1964. True unity proved as elusive as ever, for although plans for union were

---

[12] *Al-Jumhuriyya* (Baghdad), July 14, 1964.

announced on December 20, 1964, the pro-Nasser ministers resigned from the Iraqi cabinet in July of 1965.

On April 13, 1966 President Abd al-Salam Mohammed Aref was killed in a helicopter crash and was succeeded by his brother Abd al-Rahman Mohammed Aref. The new president inherited the same basic socio-economic and political problems that had thwarted all of Iraq's governments since the second world war. In an attempt to solve at least one of them decisively Abd al-Rahman Aref undertook a massive spring offensive against the Kurds, involving some 65,000 troops and air bombardment of Kurdish strongholds. Aref's prime minister, the moderate Dr. Abd al-Rahman Bazzaz, the first civilian premier since the 1958 revolution, then offered the Kurds significant concessions. Outraged at this capitulation to the Kurds, the armed forces forced Dr. Bazzaz's resignation in favor of General Naji Talib. By May 1967 Aref took the office himself. Meanwhile, the Kurdish problem remained unsolved.

Return of the Baath

As the Arab-Israeli June 1967 war approached, Iraq moved closer to the other Arab states. But the loss of that war heightened already intense frustrations, and in July 1968 President Abd al-Rahman's regime also crumbled under a military coup. As a result of the coup, the moderate Baathists again returned to power under the leadership of Ahmed Hasan Bakr (the former premier, and later vice president under the first Aref).

Bakr's government seems to be following a similar pattern as the past governments. Initial attempts were made to win popular acceptance, such as lowering taxes and prices, promising merchants more financing for imports, granting amnesty to political prisoners, and restoring to their jobs civil servants discharged for political reasons by former regimes. The government also promised to implement former Premier Bazzaz's 12-point program for Kurdish autonomy and peace. Nevertheless, dissatisfaction within the country is at a high level. Testimony to this was the arrest of about one hundred military officers and some civilians in the aftermath of an attempted coup in September 1968. Conflict has also broken out with the Iraqi Communists and Kurds; but by March 1970, in an attempt to appease opposition, the government included a Communist in the cabinet and recognized Kurdish autonomy.

POLITICAL INSTITUTIONS AND PROCESSES

The Constitutions of 1958 and 1964

Although the several Iraqi constitutions have promised at least quasi-democratic institutions, authoritarian government, as a close perusal of the constitutions of 1958 and 1964 will indicate, has been the fact of political life in Iraq. For example, the constitution of July 26th, 1958 vested the prime minister with the central role in the government. It established a figurehead Presidential Council (Article 20) which Kassim dominated. The Council of Ministers (cabinet) was entrusted with the legislative function, subject to the formal approval of the Presidential Council (Article 21). The individual ministers and the Council of Ministers collectively were made responsible for administrative and executive functions (Article 22). In this system Kassim as prime minister, defense minister, and commander-in-chief of the armed forces, controlled the means of government and the primary function of the constitution was simply the legitimization of his authoritarian role.

According to the April 1964 constitution, the president is to be elected by a National Council of the Revolutionary Command which itself was made of high-ranking army officers (Articles 55 and 42). This council—theoretically supreme in making public policy—must be consulted by the president and endorse his decision before he may declare martial law or a state of emergency, or declare war or peace (Articles 48 and 49). Further, the NCRC must approve presidential assumption of emergency powers (Article 51). The Republican Council which acts for the president in case of his absence from the country or his inability to serve is composed of three members of the NCRC (Article 53). Impeachment of the president is also the province of the NCRC, a two-thirds majority of that body being required for an indictment (Article 60). The president is also enjoined by the constitution to form a National Defense Council (Article 50).

Despite these constitutional restrictions on the presidential power, however, Abd al-Salam Aref still succeeded in making the presidency the most powerful office in Iraq. For in the 1964 provisional constitution, the president was made commander-in-chief of the armed forces, appointer of the premier, deputy premier, ministers and civil servants, and holder of executive power. The cabinet was left with primarily administrative functions. Legislative power was vested in a National Assembly which has never met, nor have elections ever been held for it. In fact, the vagueness of the constitutional provisions for such a body indicate that the idea was never a serious consideration.

Political Parties

Iraqi political parties have had a notably checquered career. All parties were prohibited between 1954 and 1960 after the 1963 coup and again after the founding of the Iraqi Arab Socialist Union in 1964. Thus, the political parties have operated with varying degrees of openness and their fortunes, depending upon the political climate, have shifted frequently and sharply. For example, the chief support of the Kassim regime after it had alienated the nationalist groups, the Baath, and the Communists, was the National Democratic party *(Al-Watani al-Demokrati)* which was headed by Kamil Chadirchi and Muhammad Hadid. However, the National Democratic party split with Kassim in July of 1960, and its place as chief support of the regime was filled by a separatist group led by Hadid called the National Progressive party.

Although they were never a licensed party, the Communists were ascendant in 1958-59 under Kassim. However, they have been out of favor since that time and, after the execution of a number of their leaders in 1963 by the Baath, their activity has been mostly underground.

The Kurdish Democratic party led by Mulla Mustafa al-Barazzani is not so much a separatist party as a Kurdish interest group. This party is asking for greater autonomy within Iraq for the Kurdish people. A recent rival splinter group, the Barati (Brotherhood) party, under the leadership of Jalal Talabani, seeks much the same aim but is less hostile to the government.

The Arab Socialist Union of Iraq was the only legally recognized party in Iraq up to the July 17, 1968 coup, and it provided for organizations from the local to the national level. However, only the higher levels of the organization were ever active. In an effort to increase the effectiveness of the A.S.U., a cabinet committee to reorganize the A.S.U. was established on September 21, 1966. On February 14, 1967 *Al-Thawra Al-Arabiyya* (The Arab Revolution) of Baghdad, the Union's official newspaper, announced that "the president would personally supervise the special arrangements for convening the National Congress of 100 members from all ethnic groups for the purpose of discussing the Charter of the Arab Socialist Union of Iraq in order to approve it for this transitional stage or to amend it, using the National Charter of the U.A.R. as a guideline." However, the 1968 coup ended the organization.

Since the 1963 coup which displaced Kassim, the Baath has been the chief political party of Iraq. In collaboration with the military under Ahmad Hasan Bakr the Baath controlled Iraq from February to November of 1963 and attempted to take complete control under Aflaq in November of that year. Although Aref displaced the Baath at that time, some of his associates were Baathists. Much of the Baath's support has been within the Iraqi army, where it has competed with Nasserism for influence. On July 17, 1968 a coup sponsored by the Baath displaced Abd al-Rahman Aref, and on July 30 Bakr utilized a second coup to consolidate his power. At this writing the Baath is the dominant party in Iraq but, as always, the situation is unstable.

FOREIGN POLICY

Iraq's foreign policy has been polarized on two axes since early in the century. The first axis concerns Iraq's relations with the other Arab states, chiefly in relation to Egypt (U.A.R.) and Syria. The second is the East-West axis which is not so much a product as a tool of the Cold War competition. The move from the thoroughly British oriented policies of the monarchy to the nonalignment policies of the Republican era has been a step away from cliency toward independence, as the Iraqis see it.

The Kassim Regime

Before the revolution of July 14th, 1958 the foreign policy of Iraq was tied closely to that of Britain. Nuri al-Said, the guiding spirit of the government, was at once pro-British and anti-Communist. This led to Iraq's adherence to the Baghdad Pact. Furthermore, this orientation and Nuri's concern with the prevention of rapid social revolution in Iraq placed Iraq in opposition to Egyptian policies. The opposition of the monarchy to Nasser's revolutionary regime and its fear of liberal influences led to the formation of the Arab Federation when the establishment of the U.A.R. raised the threat of Egyptian hegemony.

After the July 14th revolution the Kassim regime changed Iraq's foreign policy orientations. Kassim was initially pro-Nasser, but conflicts in two areas of policy led to a renewal of the hostile stance previously taken. First, there was conflict within the revolutionary government as to the extent of pro-Nasser policy permissible. This conflict ultimately led to the dismissal of Aref and to increased suspicion of pro-Nasserites in Iraq. This pattern of a warming and then dramatic cooling of relations with Egypt repeated itself several times in the following ten years. Secondly, the growing friendship of Kassim for the U.S.S.R. led Nasser, who was at odds with the Soviets at the time, to suspect Russian aims in the Middle East.

The Middle East

Kassim's most notable accomplishment in foreign affairs was his singular achievement of the almost complete isolation of Iraq from its neighbors and, indeed, from the entire international community. U.A.R.-Iraqi relations, apparently greatly improved by the 1958 coup, were the first fatality. From the time of Abd al-Salam Aref's fall in September 1958 relations between the two states began to decline, and they were finally severed in March 1959. Iraq's relations with another neighbor Iran also deteriorated in 1959. In a treaty of July 5th 1937 Iraq had recognized Iranian sovereignty over certain roadsteads on the east side of the Shatt al-Arab. In December of 1959 Iraq demanded the return of these roads. Iran refused to accept the Iraqi demands, and relations between the two states became strained.

Jordan had broken relations with Iraq after the 1958 coup and had abandoned the Arab Federation in August of the same year. In October of 1960, however, relations improved. Jordan formally recognized the Kassim regime; and road, post, and telegraph contacts were resumed. In December the two states restored normal diplomatic relations.

Iraq became further isolated among the Arab states in the summer of 1961. In late June Kuwait became independent, and a few days later on June 25th

Iraq laid claim to its small neighbor. The claim was based upon Kuwait's status as part of the Ottoman *vilayet* (province) of Basra in the 19th century, but it was obviously an attempt to gain Kuwait's rich oil deposits. The Kuwaitis appealed for aid from the United Kingdom when Iraq made threatening troop movements. The British landed troops in Kuwait, and the U.N. Security Council met to consider the situation. The Kuwaiti position was supported by the United States, Saudi Arabia, Iran, Jordan, and the U.A.R., in addition to Britain. On July 12th the Arab League voted to support Kuwait with an Arab force, and on July 19th the British began to withdraw their troops. When Kuwait was admitted to the Arab League on July 20th, Iraq boycotted further meetings. The Saudi Arabian, U.A.R., Sudanese, Jordanian, and Tunisian governments sent on September 10th 3,300 troops to Kuwait, successfully deterring the threat of any military action against the state.

In retaliation to their support and recognition of Kuwait, Iraq, during 1962, severed relations with Jordan, Japan, Iran, Lebanon, the United States, and Tunisia. Finally, the Kurdish Rebellion led to Iraqi charges of Turkish complicity with the Kurds in August 1962, and the withdrawal of the Turkish ambassador on August 23rd completed Iraq's isolation in the Middle East.

The East and the West

Within a few hours after the July 14th, 1958 coup, Kassim announced that the new republic's foreign policy would be based on neutralism and nonalignment. Of course, the most immediate ramification of this policy concerned the Baghdad Pact. Although Iraq did not formally withdraw from the Pact until March 24th, 1959, it did not actually participate in the affairs of the group after July 1958.

By August of 1958 the Kassim regime had been recognized by most states, including the United States and Britain, and had, in accordance with its neutralist policy, established relations with Russia, Communist China, and other members of the Communist camp. For the first time, then, Iraq was provided with an alternative to dealing with the West, and the initial period after the revolution witnessed many commercial and cultural agreements with the East. A major technical and economic cooperation agreement was signed with the U.S.S.R. in March 1959. This agreement provided for the Soviet Union to extend a loan and for the engineering and technical staff to build factories in Iraq. Despite Britain's announcement in May of her intention to provide Iraq with arms and military planes, Iraq withdrew from the Sterling Area in June and refused further U.S. military aid.

In December of 1959 Iraq appeared to be looking both ways when a cultural agreement was signed with Britain and a technical training agreement was signed with the Soviet Union. The agreement provided for Soviet aid in several fields, including oil production, agriculture, and communications. In April of 1960 Iraq expanded her contacts with the U.S.S.R. when First

Deputy Premier Anastas I. Mikoyan visited Baghdad for the opening of a Russian industrial exhibit, and a cultural and scientific exchange convention was signed. At this time, the U.S.S.R. was given some oil exploration rights in southern Iraq. Iraq also reached an economic agreement with Czechoslovakia in October of 1960. Prague announced that the Czech government was going to build thermal, hydroelectric, and oil-refining plants in Iraq, and provide $33.6 million in credits in Czechoslovakia to the Iraqis. On the other hand, on January 23rd, 1961 the United States signed a cultural and scientific agreement with Iraq. During 1961, Iraq reached further agreements with various nations in connection with the I.D. 556,340,000 five-year plan adopted late in that year. The agreement tended to favor the East, but Western and neutral states were also represented.

The Baath Regime

After the coup d'état of February 8, 1963, the new Baathist government immediately initiated a foreign policy aimed at reestablishing Iraq in the mainstream of pan-Arab politics. A government spokesman announced that Iraq would seek friendlier relations with those Arab states antagonized by Kassim. Iraq returned to the Arab League fold and on February 16th attended a meeting of the League, the first time it had done so since July 20th, 1961. A friendlier attitude was also adopted toward Kuwait.

Nasser's government was among the first to recognize the new regime, and on March 14th President Aref spoke in favor of a U.A.R.-Syria-[13] Iraq union. A tripartite conference held in Cairo supported the idea. By April word of an agreement was released. The official announcement of a projected union was announced April 17th, and the Iraqi cabinet and National Revolutionary Council approved the agreement.[14] However, the Iraqi cabinet reshuffle in May, a reshuffling that ousted non-Baathists from that body, once again foreshadowed serious strains in U.A.R.-Iraqi relations. Although the ideal of unity continued to dominate political polemics, it appeared evident that the consolidation of Baathist rule was being placed above the formation of a union.

By late summer the two Baathist regimes of Syria and Iraq had moved closer together and away from the U.A.R. On September 2nd a joint communique announced closer Iraqi-Syrian cooperation in several areas, especially defense, and in the following month a Supreme Defense Council was formed by the two states. Meanwhile, relations with the U.A.R. grew very strained, and the Arab news media in Damascus, Baghdad, and Cairo began making the familiar charges and countercharges. It is also interesting to note that the Baathist regime's relations with the Soviet Union were also under considerable strain as a result of the Baathist witch-hunt of local communists.

[13] The Baathist government of Syria was installed in a March 8, 1963 coup.
[14] *Arab Political Documents, 1963* (Beirut, n.d.) pp. 75-213, 227-245.

The Aref Regime

When President Aref took the helm of the government as a result of the November 15-18, 1963 turbulence, he attempted to reverse the trend established by the Baath and once more set U.A.R.-Iraqi relations in harmony. By May 26th, 1964 a Joint Presidency Council with a Secretariat in Cairo had been formed between Iraq and the U.A.R. On October 16th, 1964 plans for a unified political command between the two countries were made known, and the following December the actual creation of such a command was announced. But the seemingly perpetual oscillation of U.A.R.-Iraqi affairs proved to be too pertinacious for even so ardent a Nasserite as Aref. In July of 1965 the inevitable pendulum began its swing back as the pro-Nasser ministers resigned from Aref's cabinet and relations between the two states began to deteriorate.

Some improvements in Iraq's foreign affairs were made, however, in this period. The Kuwait situation was resolved, and trade agreements with Kuwait were reached in February and again in the autumn of 1964.[15] Relations with Iran, tense because of border conflicts and the Kurdish problem, improved with the advent of lessened activity along the Iraqi-Iranian border after June of 1966. Agreement was reached on a number of issues and a cultural and trade agreement was projected.

The Arab-Israeli war of June 1967 involved Iraqi forces, although not in major proportions. In the weeks before the war, the Arab states became closer and less abrasive in their relations than previously, and some steps were taken toward the practical aim of organizing their military forces under a single command. The results of the war for Iraq, and indeed for the entire Arab world, were two-fold. First, in regard to inter-Arab relations, the war aided in the settlement of some of the outstanding differences among these states, for example, the settling of the Yemen crisis. The second effect was the enhancement of Soviet influence in the area. Previously, Soviet support for the Arab states had been rather tentative, but the sharp turn away from the Western nations undergone throughout the Arab world after the June war presented the U.S.S.R. with considerable opportunity to expand her influence. It appeared by 1968 that the only Western nation capable of challenging Soviet influence in the area was General deGaulle's France.

In the fall of 1967 Iraq was negotiating for the future of the richest oil field in the country, the as-yet undeveloped North Rumaila field which borders Kuwait. The competitors for the concession were the French-owned Compagnie Francaise des Petrole and the Soviet government. In December of 1967 it appeared as though the Soviet Union had scored a considerable success when an agreement was signed between that government and the Iraqi

---

[15] *Ibid.* (1964) pp. 433-434.

National Oil Company. However, in April of 1968 it was disclosed that the Soviets would have the position of hired technicians and that the INOC would develop the field itself.[16]

The Baathist regime that took power in July 1968 has had disaccord in inter-Arab politics, particularly with Syria and the U.A.R. The enmity among these governments has not been overt, however, because of the desire to maintain at least a facade of unity in the face of the prevailing Arab-Israeli crisis. The new government has had some success in creating better relations with Iraq's non-Arab neighbors, Iran and Turkey. Within the international sphere, the government has taken a strong anti-Western stand, in consequence of the Arab-Israeli crisis; yet Iraqi-Soviet relations have also been somewhat strained as a result of the Baathist regime's conflicts with the Kurds and the Iraqi Communist party.

It would seem that Iraqi foreign policy since the revolution has had certain points in common with that of the monarchy, and certain continuing themes do prevail: The competition for Middle Eastern leadership between Iraq and Egypt has been carried on under the revolutionary governments just as it was before; and Jordan has remained closely tied to Iraq, despite the dissolution of Iraq's monarchy. Iraq's foreign policy has been conditioned by its domestic politics. The Kassim government relied on continuing crises to bemuse the people and hold the spirit of unity to a high pitch. The Aref regimes stressed Arab unity as a theme, although they always retreated when unity began to turn from a vision into concrete reality. The new Bakr government has yet to show its colors, but the Baath has typically relied upon the party machinery and ideology to gain popular support. The one trend of pre-revolution politics which has been reversed is the East-West orientation. Iraq has moved, if slowly and irregularly, toward greater reliance upon the Soviet Union ever since the 1958 coup.

SUGGESTED READING

A good synthesis of Iraq's history from 1500 to 1900 is Stephen H. Longrigg's book, *Four Centuries of Iraq* (London, 1925). Political development under the mandate period was recorded in many books. Among them are: Philip W. Ireland, *Iraq: A Study in Political Development* (London, 1937); Henry A. Foster, *The Making of Modern Iraq* (Norman, Oklahoma, 1935). The politics of the monarchy regime is well documented in Majid Khadduri, *Independent Iraq, 1932-1958* (London, 1960); S. H. Longrigg, *Iraq, 1900 to 1950* (London, 1953); and but less scholarly, Gerald deGaury, *Three Kings in Baghdad* (London, 1961). And Waldeman J. Gallman's book *Iraq Under General Nuri* (Baltimore, 1964) is the reflections of an American Ambassador to Iraq in the period 1954 to 1958.

Few serious works have been done on the politics of the Republican

---

[16] *Christian Science Monitor* (John K. Cooley), April 15, 1968.

regime. Caractacus, *Revolution in Iraq* (London, 1959) examines the socio-economic and political causes of the revolution. Uriel Dann's study *Iraq Under Qassem* (Jerusalem, 1969) is shallow and lacks objectivity. Bernard Vernier's French volume *L'irak d'aujour d'hui* (Paris, 1963) is a useful reference work. Pierre Rossi's *L'Irak Des Revoltes* (Paris, 1962) provides an interesting eye-and-ear witness account of the first four years of republican politics. The definitive study of the post revolutionary era is Majid Khadduri's *Republican Iraq* (London, 1969).

On the Kurds' history and politics, one may consult Hasan Arfa, *The Kurds* (London, 1967); and C. J. Edmonds, *Kurds, Turks, and Arabs* (New York, 1957).

On the economy of Iraq, Doris G. Adams, *Iraq's People and Resources* (Berkeley, 1958); Kathleen M. Langley, *The Industrialization of Iraq* (Cambridge, Mass., 1961); Fahim Quabain, *The Reconstruction of Iraq: 1950-1957* (New York, 1958); Abbas Alnasrawi, *Financing Economic Development in Iraq* (New York, 1967).

chapter 10

Syria*

Disunity in Diversity

For centuries Syria has been a route for trade, conquest, migration, and settlement due to its strategic geographical position. Thus it has come to form a patchwork of divergent traditions and belief. With the Sykes-Picot Agreement of 1915 between the British and the French, the land which once was called Syria stretching from Egypt to the Turkish border, was divided after World War I and placed under foreign control. Palestine became a separate territory to be turned into a Jewish homeland. The Amirate of Jordan was established, and an expanded Lebanon was declared a state under French control. What was left of historical Syria continued to carry the name, but a Syria now under French mandate.

The new Syria, though reduced in size and exhibiting social, religious, and ethnic diversity, gave the French rulers many headaches. The mandatory authority, therefore, found it expedient to divide the country into four states on the basis of religious and ethnic distinctions: Aleppo, Damascus, Jebel Druze, and Latakia. Though eventually (1942) reunited, those divisions kindled or reinforced the separatist tendencies among the larger minorities, the Druze and the Alawites in particular. Thus, while the Syrian leaders who have been predominantly Sunni Muslim continued their strong advocacy of Arab nationalism and unity, they failed to achieve effective political and social integration within their own country.

Division and foreign domination have led Syria during the last 50 years down several connecting paths. The first was the struggle to gain complete sovereignty which lasted until 1943, at which time the country was given nominal

*Michael W. Suleiman, associate professor of political science, Kansas State University, and Kenneth E. Koehn, currently engaged in field work in Africa since completion of graduate work at Kansas State University.

213

independence. At the end of World War II, the French under Charles de Gaulle attempted to reestablish control over Syria. With help from the British, the French were denied this objective, and in 1946 the Syria of the mandate acquired complete independence.

Disunity, dismemberment, and the struggle for independence set the country back to such an extent that political development and internal stability became the exception rather than the norm—conditions that weakened the country and invited outside intervention. This stood in stark contrast to the role Syria once played among the Arab states. It had been the leading symbol of a modernizing Arab state and gained ascendancy in the nationalist struggle which began to develop around the turn of the century. After independence, however, Syria was not the most important power in the area, though it still held the key to Arab primacy. Egypt and Iraq became the leading contenders for Arab leadership, though both realized that Syria could tip the balance in favor of either. The consequence was that Syria's internal affairs came to reflect in part the contesting forces of Egypt and Iraq.

Internal social and economic forces have contributed to the country's instability. The peasant lives on an extremely low social and economic level. A wide gap also separates the rural and urban populations as well as the rich and the poor in the cities. Throughout Syria's history agriculture has been the basic livelihood. Yet until the 1958 land reform program, land ownership was dominated by a small landlord class with the peasants subsisting on a sharecropping basis. The landed class had led Syria to independence from French control but acted to maintain the status quo internally. It opposed changing the peasant-landlord relationship or helping small proprietors by distributing land owned by the state. The land reform law of 1958 was meant to give the peasant a chance at owning and farming his own land.

Because of the scarcity of natural resources to supplement agricultural growth, Syria has been slow in economic development. This is easily seen in the fact that Syria's per capita gross national product (GNP) declined in the 1950s. With so much of the country's economic force in agriculture and commerce, there has been a chronic shortage of capital for investment purposes. This is partially due to the fact that real estate and gold are the traditional forms of wealth. Also, corporate business is unpopular and family concerns are favored. Another brake on the country's social and economic growth has been the regressive system of taxation. Now drastically changed, the old system had continued the Ottoman practice of being in favor of the ruling landed interests while the general public and salaried individuals bore the heaviest burden.

Even the educational system indirectly induced instability in the country. The Syrian educational system followed much the same pattern as that of the French, but the picture has been clouded because of non-governmental schools, both sectarian and foreign-supported. The goal of many Syrian students before and after independence has been to become employed by the government. To do this, a university degree is practically a necessity. Thus, the students have looked for the degree more than for the learning associated with it. A consequence of this attitude has been the deep antagonism that is expressed by the students any time the curriculum is updated and made more difficult. With students making up the majority of the literate population and because of the respect held for learning by the Arabs, the students soon became a political force perhaps second only to the army. In fact, they began to show their interest and participation in the political realm when Syria was still under the French mandate. At that time, the students gave support to the nationalists' objectives through demonstrations and strikes. Once they realized the power they could bring to bear on governmental policies, however, students began to strike for other than political reasons. By the time of independence, political leaders in and out of government began to show a strong interest in the students especially in order to manipulate them for their own ends. Since parliament was almost completely controlled by the ruling elite, the most effective way left for the public to express its views was in demonstrations and strikes, constituting a threat to governmental stability. Though student strikes decreased in the 1960s, partially as a result of the youthful appeal of the Baathist program as well as the effective control of the military, students still must be counted as a strong force in a nation where over half of the population is presently illiterate.

One cannot close an introduction on Syria without at least mentioning the Syrian army. Until independence, the army was a small force (*Troupes Speciales du Levant*) under French control. Even after independence, the army remained small (about 5,000), but defeat in the 1948 Palestine war brought about an increase and strengthening of the country's defenses. At first the army was led largely by the upper strata of Syrian society, especially from among the minority groups. After independence, and with the increase of educational facilities for those families of modest means, more and more of the secondary school graduates of this group gained appointments at the Homs Military Academy. While at the academy, many became politicized, favoring socialist doctrines. Thus, it was at Syria's defensive training ground that the seeds of social change were cultivated.

Party Development and the Political Process

It is difficult to present a coherent, systematic analysis of the Syrian political institutions and processes of the past half century. What comes out is little more than a chronicling of events, as coups, countercoups, threatened coups, and expected coups follow one another in monotonous succession. Suspended constitutions, dissolved parliaments, unstable governments, and everchanging military tribunals have been the hallmarks of Syria's recent history. While democracy was not given a chance to flourish, the Syrians have simultaneously been denied the advantage of a stable, to say nothing about a benevolent, dictatorship. The following sections illustrate what we mean.

Under the terms of the mandate, the French were to set Syria on the road to self-government through the introduction of institutional and political reforms. But those reforms carried out by the French only worked to increase their control over Syria. Though three assemblies were elected (1928, 1932, and 1936) to draft a constitution, the French high commissioner dismissed all three before their terms were up. The high commissioner himself drafted a constitution in 1930, with its provisions subject to the approval of the French government.

In the suspension of the three constitutional assemblies elected during the mandate can be seen the emergence of Syria's first political party. Though a majority of each assembly went along with the ideas of the manadatory power, caused primarily through manipulation of the electoral process, a nationalist minority proved to be a big enough stumbling block to prevent action by the majority—hence the repeated suspension of the assemblies by the French. In 1928 the nationalists formed the National Bloc (*al-Kutla al-Wataniya*) as a means of bringing greater cohesion to those groups waging the struggle for Syrian independence. The National Bloc, though not exactly a mass party, nevertheless became the rallying point for all nationalists and dominated Syrian politics until the end of the mandate. In 1936, it adopted the National Pact which advocated: (1) complete independence for Syria with reunification of all territories lost, except Lebanon; (2) the end of Zionism in the Palestine area, and (3) a ban on all political parties except the Bloc. The Franco-Syrian Treaty of 1936 was negotiated with the Popular Front government in France and was considered an important step toward Syrian independence. But the French parliament failed to ratify it and, consequently, it was never initiated.

The National Bloc reached its pinnacle in 1936. From then on, it was a downhill journey caused by the failure of French ratification of the Franco-Syrian treaty, the claims of Turkey on that part of Syria called Alexandretta, the continuing unrest over Palestine, the administrative failures of the national government under Bloc control, and the internal opposition forming within the Bloc against the ruling faction. By 1939 there were signs that the nationalist movement embodied in the Bloc was splitting into two groups. The split was basically on personal and regional lines, and both the ruling and dissident factions were upper-class conservatives favoring the status quo for Syria internally.

Though the Bloc was in power in 1946 when the last of the French troops were removed, it soon became obvious that with the achievement of the country's independence there was little left to keep the group from disintegrating. In the spring of 1947 the ruling wing of the Bloc formed into the National party (*al-Hizb al-Watani*) under the leadership of Shukri al-Kuwatli. The party became essentially based in the Damascus area. "It produced no detailed programme, exercised little discipline over its members, and could boast of no clear hierarchical structure of command. Its electoral strength did not even depend on the personal qualities of its leaders, although some of them were very able men, but rather on the aura of their nationalist record, powerfully sustained by their family roots and affiliations in the various quarters of the city."[1] The party's failure to establish an ideology which would win younger people's support meant isolation in the late 1940s and early 1950s from this segment of society which was becoming increasingly influential in Syrian affairs.

Those of the old Bloc who were in opposition to Kuwatli joined together in 1948 to form the People's party (*Hizb al-Sha'b*). The members of this group were geographically situated in Aleppo and the surrounding northern area. The rich and powerful Atasi family lent its support to the People's party which became the chief opponent to the Damascus-based National party. Because the People's party was Aleppo-based, close to the Iraqi border, it favored the elimination of trade barriers and a breakdown of the Syrian-Iraqi frontier.

Whereas the National Bloc and the People's party concerned themselves with the politics of Syria proper, they faced competition from ideological movements that had transnational appeal and interests, namely the Syrian Social Nationalist party (SSNP), the Communist party, and the Baath. The SSNP, established in Lebanon in 1932, remained small, largely because its ideas were not popular with the masses and with advocates of other brands of nationalism. It was, however, among the first parties in Syria to have a definite program, which called for a Syrian nationalism based on the unity of "natural" or geographical Syria which eventually included Iraq, Syria, Lebanon, Jordan, Palestine, and Cyprus. It also advocated a breakdown of feudal landholding and the separation of church and state in order to end the role of religion in politics.

The Syrian Communist party started as the Communist party of Syria and Lebanon. Though it was the oldest ideological party in Syria, it was banned under the mandate and has been periodically suppressed since then. Not until the early 1950s did the Syrian Communist party become a real force or gain more than minor support in the country.

In 1943 the Arab Baath (later Socialist) party was established by a small group of men wanting to see conditions of the Arab world improved. The main force behind this group rested in Michel Aflaq and Salah al-Bitar, both of whom had received part of their education in Europe. From its very inception the Baath party was an *Arab* before it was a Syrian party, and was to become the vanguard of the Arab nationalist movement. After independence, though remaining small, the Baath took on the role of opposition to the government. Its successful opposition of legislation limiting party and individual freedom in Syria gained it much support and sympathy among members of the younger generation. In 1947 the Baath held its first national convention and adopted a constitution and internal rules. Though its numbers were small and its ranks had no experienced politicians, it went into the 1947 elections with a program that was to become increasingly popular. "In the sphere of domestic politics, the party demanded government protection of local industry, gradual termination of foreign business and investment in the country, application of progressive

---

[1] Patrick Seale, *The Struggle for Syria* (New York, 1965), p. 28.

income taxes, reform of labor laws, supervision of domestic and foreign trade, price-fixing schemes, and high excise taxes. The convention also agreed that strict limits should be placed on private property and that the party should adopt socialism as a slogan and as an ideology."[2] The Baath was equally energetic in its foreign policy proposals. It was the first party to endorse and call for nonalignment to either the East or the West; it demanded the return of the Alexandretta district from Turkey to Syria; and it called for a united Arab action against the Zionist threat in Palestine.

No single party gained a majority in the 1947 national elections. However, a large group of independents helped keep the National party in power. This large percentage of independents remained a part of Syrian parliamentary life until the union with Egypt in 1958. The independents continually held the balance between rival parties and blocs and thus tended to political opportunism within the Syrian government. They came from among the wealthiest and most illustrious and powerful families in Syria. Their success was a reminder that parties were ineffective and that personal loyalties and attachments were still strong.

Thus, in the first years following independence Syria was more divided than ever. With the Bloc splitting into two parties, the establishment of the Baath, and the clandestine activities of the SSNP and the Communist party, the political makeup of Syria only too well reinforced divisiveness. The voter had no chance of voting for a national candidate. The president was elected by the members of parliament, but these men were elected on a regional and sectarian basis. Since the National and People's parties were also sectional in their appeal, they did not help achieve a national consensus. The cabinets that were formed between 1947 and 1949 were for the most part based not on party affiliation but on personalities. They failed to pay much attention to the needs of the public. Personal aggrandizement and corruption became widespread. To this was added governmental inefficiency as well as political stalemate between the legislative and executive branches. In brief, the stage was set for a change of the regime.

Military Coups

With the partition of Palestine in 1948, Syria joined the other Arab states in opposing the Zionist elements. But the government came increasingly under attack for the poor showing of the Syrian army and for the large-scale corruption stemming from the war effort. With confidence in the government dwindling, a new coalition cabinet was set up. This cabinet, being little more than a reshuffling of the previous one, failed to restore confidence in the government. Political strikes and demonstrations began to occur throughout the country. Adding fuel to the fire was an economic slump caused by petroleum shortage. With violence increasing, the government resigned on December 1,

---

[2]Kamel S. Abu Jaber, *The Arab Ba'th Socialist Party: History, Ideology, and Organization* (Syracuse, N. Y., 1966). p. 27.

1948, leaving the country in near anarchy. "Syria, at this crucial moment in her history, was a country without either a government or the prospect of one coming from a competent civilian leadership, but possessed of a turbulent and distressed citizenry, a collapsing economy, and an army which felt itself betrayed by a coterie of scheming politicians."[3]

The politicization of the army had started earlier when some politicians began to establish contacts with members of the officer corps. Akram Hourani, who had distinguished himself as a popular leader among the peasants of northern Syria and as the leader and founder of the Arab Socialist party, was among the first to recognize the usefulness of friendships with army officers. In particular, during the first few years after independence, he made important contacts with young nationalists at the Homs Military Academy. With the Palestine setbacks, these nationalists felt betrayed by the politicians for the lack of appropriate arms and equipment at the front lines. Several members of parliament then charged corruption and inefficiency in the army. This was the breaking point. On March 30, 1949 the army marched on the capital under the orders of the Chief of Staff, Colonel Husni Zaim. The nationalist officers in the army, already under the dominant influence of Akram Hourani, were more than ready to follow Zaim, taking the view that it was up to them to be guardians of the country's welfare. Hourani threw his full support behind the new regime.

The masses greeted the death of the old regime with joy. Its leaders were not necessarily traitors, but they did display ineptness, lack of foresight concerning the real forces in the country, and practically no understanding of representative democracy. Thus, the governmental system followed in Syria was both cause and effect for the first military intervention in politics in the Middle East: cause in that it was not responsive to the Syrian situation, effect since the first political leaders were not versed in this type of government and thus were blamed for Syria's many problems.

The Baath strongly supported the early progressive measures which Zaim proposed: extension of suffrage to educated women, distribution of state lands to peasants and the placement of a limit on the amount of land owned, and end to corruption in the civil service, the revamping and enlargement of the army, a new constitution, a smaller number of deputies in parliament, and the strengthening of the League of Arab States. But Zaim was inept at handling politicians and dissolved parliament a few days after take-over. He then decided to act as his own prime minister and formed a cabinet made up of independents. Furthermore, all political parties were banned until after a plebiscite on a new constitution was held. Zaim began to rely more heavily on minority groups, such as the Kurds and Circassians; but the more deeply involved in government did these groups become; the more antagonized was the Arab population. The feudal and commercial classes feared Zaim's ideas of fiscal and land reform, and the masses became disenchanted when they saw nothing come out of his earlier promises.

---

[3] Seale, *op. cit.*, p. 31.

When Zaim took over, Syria was divided between those wanting a union with Iraq and Jordan (the Greater Syria Plan) and those who opposed such a move. The People's party, much of the population, and a top military leader Colonel Sami Hinnawi favored union with Iraq. But Egypt and Saudi Arabia were staunchly opposed to an increase in Iraqi power and prestige under Hashemite control and, consequently, gave the Zaim regime formal recognition and financial aid as a means of keeping Syria from union with Iraq. Zaim accepted the offers by Egypt and Saudi Arabia and turned his back on Iraq. This move proved to be a blunder on his part, since it alienated many of his strongest supporters. Thus, in a mere three months Zaim had lost most of the support that he once had. On August 14, 1949 Colonel Sami Hinnawi, allegedly aided by Iraq, led a coup d'état against Zaim in which Zaim and several government leaders were assassinated. A coalition government which included the Baath was formed. However, the Baath refused to go along with its partners in the government concerning unity with Iraq. It argued that Arab unity should only be contemplated with other "progressive countries," and that union with monarchist Iraq would endanger Syria's republican form of government.

Unity with Iraq was an important issue in the elections of November 1949. The People's party was among the strongest supporters of union, and it made substantial gains in the elections. As work on a new constitution proceeded and unity with Iraq became a distinct possibility, Colonel Adib Shishakli led a successful coup against Hinnawi and the unionists on December 19, 1949. After much internal dissension a new government, which was pledged to a republican regime, was confirmed by the constituent assembly which later gave its approval to a new constitution.

With Shishakli's coup, the erstwhile dominant position of the People's party became seriously undermined, although not destroyed. The party still had a commanding majority in the constituent assembly, but the army set up the general staff to counterbalance the assembly. A new phase was thus ushered into Syrian politics; the government was forced from henceforth to strike a balance between the claims of an assembly jealous of its prerogatives and an enlarged and self-confident army. It was some time before the politicians realized this and grasped the new restrictions placed upon their power.

Several governments were formed, received a little support, and fell. The problem was that Shishakli wanted to rule Syria from his army barracks while the political leaders carried out his orders. But the politicians and the People's party in particular, which because of its large membership in parliament had the key to any stable government, refused to cooperate unless the police force was freed from the grip of the army. This would be done either by placing the police force under the ministry of interior or by having a civilian preside over the ministry of defense. When no compromise was possible, Shishakli overthrew the government on November 29, 1951. Through military decrees, the legislative assembly was dissolved and Colonel Fawsi Silu was given full legislative and executive powers. Then Shishakli once more stepped into the background but, as before, he was always close by.

With his new found success, Shishakli's political ambitions increased. Instead of remaining in the background, he felt the necessity to lead publicly. He began to build a political machine with the hope of establishing his regime on a constitutional basis and elevating himself to the presidency. Having banned all political parties, he established the Arab Liberation movement in August 1952, hoping that this would become a mass party and help give his regime a broad, popular base. The party took its ideology from a variety of sources, advocating progressive social and economic measures as well as a form of militant Arab nationalism. Though several top army officers became supporters of the movement, it failed to achieve a voluntary grass roots base.

Gradually Shishakli began to lose his grip over the army and the country. He lost contact with those in the army who had supported his earlier moves and thus lost much of the earlier enthusiasm shown him. The Baath and the Arab Socialist party turned against him. In late December 1952 Hourani, Aflaq, and al-Bitar were all arrested for "deceiving" officers of the army, but escaped to Lebanon and continued their attacks on his regime. In July 1953 a new constitution was ratified and Shishakli was elected president. A new electoral law was enacted which called for a legislative assembly with only 82 deputies, split on religious and tribal lines. Elections to the assembly were set for October. All political parties that had been banned were now allowed to become active again within specified limits. Apart from the Arab Liberation movement and SSNP, the political parties were unhappy with the restrictions and showed their displeasure by boycotting the elections. Strikes and demonstrations against Shishakli's regime were organized by the Baath. However, the elections were held as scheduled, with the Arab Liberation movement winning an easy majority. This led to greater demonstrations and strikes spurred by the opposition parties. The Baath became the leading voice in denouncing Shishakli, and he responded by arresting Aflaq, al-Bitar, and Arab Socialist party leader Hourani in late January 1954. On February 25, 1954 army units in the Aleppo area rose aginst Shishakli who chose to leave for Beirut and exile to spare bloodshed.

When the Baath and Arab Socialist party leaders drew away from Shishakli, they began to cooperate in opposition against him. This cooperation ended in the merger of the two parties on March 5, 1954 to form the Arab Baath Socialist party. The reason for this union after Shishakli's downfall was that both Aflaq and Hourani were not far separated by doctrine and both felt the need for a strong opposition against the People's party—their chief opponent once Shishakli had departed the scene.

From the downfall of Shishakli until September 1954 Syria was run by a provisional government. Elections were scheduled for September and were hailed as the first truly free elections in the Arab world. The 1949 electoral law was restored, with some changes. Thus, when the elections were held all male citizens over 18 and women citizens with at least elementary school certificates had the right to vote. Also guaranteed was a completely secret ballot—a first for Syria. No less than seven parties and the usual large number of independents eventually entered the elections. When the results were in it became apparent that over the previous four years the old social and political order had weakened significantly in Syria. Both the National and People's parties lost seats. Among the major winners was the Baath, capturing about 20 seats. These were fewer than the seats won by the People's party, but they reflected the general dissatisfaction with the old line parties. Independents won close to half the seats in parliament. Of note also was the election of Khalid Bakdash as the first Communist-elected member of parliament in the Arab world.

The Baath became the leading opposition group. Because of its good organization and since the new parliament had such a diverse makeup, the Baath came to wield power in the government far beyond its numbers. Foreign policy became the focus of the Baath and the overriding issue for the party in the next several years. Egypt and the Baath were becoming more alike in their views on foreign policy, which caused the Baath to think seriously of union with Egypt as the beginning of total Arab unity. By the end of 1957 the Baath was perhaps the strongest political force in Syria, although the Communists were becoming powerful enough to endanger its position. Union with Egypt would realize a passionate dream and simultaneously blunt the Communist drive. After negotiations done mainly on Gamal Abdul Nasser's terms, the Syrian cabinet approved unity in late January 1958. The Communists in Syria had little choice but to appear to agree with unity or lose much support; yet by giving tacit approval they were digging their own grave.

Union and Secession

The new United Arab Republic (UAR) was not a federal union but one under heavy centralized control. Nasser moved fast to eradicate Communist influence in Syria and immediately began minor economic reforms. In both moves the Baath was in full support of Nasser. The Baathists believed that with the Communists gone they could hold their weight against Nasser. While Nasser had the power, the Baathists believed they alone could provide the ideology as a guiding light for the new United Arab Republic. They accepted the dissolution of all Syrian parties including their own, thinking that the new state-sponsored party, the National Union, would be organized by them and embody most of their ideas. When they failed to gain a free hand in organizing the National Union, a split started between the Baath and Nasser which was to grow rapidly.

Within seven months Nassar introduced land reform programs to Syria much like those in Egypt, whereby compensation was given to the landowners whose lands were to be redistributed by the government. Land reform was badly needed. Almost half of the irrigated land and 30 percent of the dry-land areas were held by less than 3 percent of the total landowners. These large landowners were mainly absentee landlords, whereas close to 70 percent of the people living in rural areas owned no land at all but survived as laborers or sharecroppers. To the Baath, who began to reorganize and moved their headquarters to Lebanon, the idea of compensation was viewed with horror as a compromise with the large landowners.

Elections were held in July of 1959. Baath members participated in reduced numbers as a protest against the manner in which the elections were conducted. But those Baathists who participated in the elections did not fare very well. "Particularly galling was the fact that in many places they were opposed and defeated by coalitions of conservatives, who capitalized on holding the Baath responsible for the many incidental inconveniences and irritations that the union with Egypt had unavoidably inflicted on the Syrian populace; for it was the Baath, after all, that had taken the lead in precipitating the union in the first place. It seemed ironically as if 'Abd al-Nasir, the revolutionary dictator whose causes the Baath had supported so ardently, had chosen to undermine them with the help of reactionaries by the most democratic means available, a free election."[4]

The party's poor showing in the first elections of the United Arab Republic was the beginning of a general decline. A month after the elections, a split occurred when certain party members supported the Egyptian leader at a time when he was clearly working against the Baath. With influence in Nasser's government on the wane, the Baathists in leading positions resigned en masse in December 1959. The years of Baath collaboration with the leaders in Egypt were ended. With the Baath gone, Nasser was increasingly forced to use heavy-handed methods to maintain control over Syria. Then, in the summer of 1961 new socialist laws were passed aimed at private enterprise in the United Arab Republic. These laws struck at the heart of the Syrian business community and added to the rising discontent with Nasser and union. As economic restrictions and duties on imported commodities increased, further unrest developed in many parts of Syria. This situation was aggravated by three consecutive years of drought and poor harvests. Though Nasser had no control over the weather, the poor agricultural output added to the discontent among the Syrians. Also, disaffection began to develop among the Syrian officers in the united army because of their subordinate status vis-a-vis Egyptian officers.

Differences and difficulties multiplied. On September 28, 1961 Syrian officers arrested the chief Egyptian official in Syria and put him on a plane bound for Cairo. Syria seceded from the United Arab Republic and became known as the Syrian Arab Republic. Whether or not the wealthy conservative elements in Syria were behind the breakup of the union, as Nasser and others charged, they undoubtedly benefitted most from the coup. Immediately following the split, the conservative politicians formed a government and held new elections. With the Baath and other progressive factions in disrepute, the politicians of the old school won the majority of seats. This triumph, resulting in

---

[4] Malcolm Kerr, *The Arab Cold War 1958-1967: A Study of Ideology in Politics* (New York, 1967), p. 19.

a comeback for the laissez-faire People's party, was followed by parliamentary repeal of most of the nationalization laws formulated under Nasser except for the land reform program which was however considerably weakened.

Baathist reaction to the coup was varied. While stating that several errors had been made during the union, the National (Pan-Arab) Command placed the blame for the breakup on the manner in which the unity principle was applied. It further argued that mistakes made by the Nasser regime were not reason enough for the breakup and called for a return to union—but a federal union in which political parties would be allowed and the idea of collective leadership followed. But there were those in the Syrian Baath who were completely opposed to another attempt at union with Nasser. Though both al-Bitar and Hourani had signed their names to the secession manifesto, al-Bitar later repudiated his signature. In the elections to parliament following the breakup, Hourani was successful while al-Bitar failed. Once in parliament, Hourani strongly denounced Nasser as a dictator and a puppet of the United States. Aflaq and al-Bitar chose to stay clear of the new government and to wait for new developments while simultaneously supporting reunion. These two opposing positions led Hourani to leave the Baath and form a new party in 1962.

On February 8, 1963 Iraqi Baathists in conjunction with certain military leaders, engineered a coup d'état in Iraq. This strengthened the position of the Syrian Baathists who carried out a similar coup only a month later. The Syrian coup brought an end to 17 months of political instability (four cabinets during this period) caused by schisms and quarrels among the politicians and army commanders. A National Revolutionary Command Council (NRCC) was established to govern the country. Of 20 ministers in this government, 10 were members of the Baath, while the remainder were divided among 3 lesser parties (United Arab Front, Socialist Unity Movement, and the Arab Nationalists' movement) and independents. Salah al-Bitar became premier. The council announced that these actions were taken to lead Syria back to union, but this time with both Egypt and Iraq. The new cabinet pledged itself to work for the Baathist principles of unity, socialism, and anti-imperialism. With the rise of the NRCC, Nasser for the first time since secession officially recognized an independent Syria. Again the prospects for Arab union appeared brighter.

Unity talks between the United Arab Republic, Syria, and Iraq began almost immediately after the Syrian coup, and culminated in the April Seventeenth Agreement which called for a federal union between the three progressive Arab regimes to be ruled by a president and a federal council. Full union was not to occur for a least two years. Each country during this two-year period was to be responsible for its own affairs. During this time, the lack of trust between the Baath and Nasser was apparent. This distrust became worse when 47 pro-Nasser officers of the Syrian army were dismissed or given an early retirement for allegedly plotting a coup to oust the Baathists. Then the Syrian government suppressed an attempted pro-Nasser revolution in Aleppo and closed down the two pro-Nasser newspapers. Despite or perhaps because of hostile demonstrations and lack of support, a new cabinet was formed composed solely of Baathists. The rift between the Baath and Nasser widened, and by July both sides were in full attack on each other through the mass media. It became apparent that it was futile to attempt to carry out the April Seventeenth Agreement.

The Syrian government now turned to Iraq in its hopes for unity. These hopes were soon dashed when Abd el-Salam Aref carried out a successful coup d'état against the Baath in Iraq and assumed political power. Aref now turned against Syria and began receiving aid from Egypt. With Egypt, Jordan, and Iraq drawing closer, the Baath in Syria became isolated. But instead of fortifying itself against these external forces, the government was weakened by rifts within the party. A right wing and a left wing began to form. The right wing was led by Aflaq and al-Bitar, while the left wing was led by Ali Salih al-Saadi, a leader of the Iraqi Baathists. This split was somewhat characterized by the difference in age of the two groups—the right wing being the older members of the party, while youth was a characteristic of the leftist element. The leftists called for a stronger stance toward Nasser, immediate implementation of full socialization, and a militant idealism. The Aflaq and al-Bitar faction took a softer line toward Nasser and was not ready to push socialist measures beyond the point of practicality. The al-Saadi faction was finally expelled from the party in early 1964 by the National Command in Damascus after nearly overcoming the Aflaq-Bitar segment.

The attempted coup by the pro-Nasserites, with business support, in July 1963 brought the erstwhile little-known Amin al-Hafez to the pinnacle of power. Hafez was the kind of man the Baath had been looking for. A military man, he cooperated with the civilian wing of the party, realizing that this cooperation was essential to keep himself and the Baath in power.

In late 1965 and early 1966 there developed further splits within the Baath party. Several interrelated factors were involved. To begin with, there was resentment against Nasser and the Egyptian authorities over the treatment accorded certain Syrian officials and army officers under the United Arab Republic. In particular, Mohammed Umran, Salah Jadid, and Hafez Assad constituted the nucleus of a group that became opposed to reunion almost on any terms. Their position clashed with that of many pro-Nasser or generally pro-unity enthusiasts who desired to erase the separatist mistake.

Disagreement over who was going to be the real boss, especially among the military officers, generated a competition for support and personal following. Specifically, a major conflict developed between Amin al-Hafez, a Sunni Muslim, and Salah Jadid, an Alawite. This conflict as well as others did not remain strictly personal but began to develop religious overtones. Apparently the Alawite and Druze officers, particularly the former, favored their coreligionists with the more important and sensitive appointments. Sectarianism became a serious charge that each faction hurled against the other.

Another important factor contributing to the split is the conflict over the proper place of power within the Baath. Thus, it was not quite clear as to whether the National Command or the Regional (in this instance, Syrian) Command constituted the final authority in any dispute. Especially after Jadid and his supporters controlled the Syrian Command, they acted as though the National Command had no control over their actions. Adding to the seriousness of the conflict was the fact that the National leadership was in almost complete disagreement with Jadid and his group over important issues. The main policy differences concerned socialism and unity. Aflaq, al-Bitar, and most members of the National leadership were accused of rightist leanings, especially in the application of socialist measures. They, in turn, responded by accusing their opponents of being visionary and impractical. Unity was accepted by all—in principle. However, Jadid and his supporters, dubbed regionalists by their opponents, resisted union plans that might place them under Egyptian control again—especially since the Alawites among them would thus become an even smaller minority. Al-Bitar, on the other hand, was anxious to change the image he gained as a separatist as a result of his signing the document of Syria's secession from the UAR. He, therefore, pushed the unity movement but was handicapped by the fact that many unity enthusiasts could never forgive his earlier blunder. In fact, so strong was the sentiment against him that he was at one time expelled from the party which he helped establish. Yet not only was he rehabilitated, but the National leadership had to call on him several times to become prime minister, a fact that further alienated his opponents.

Superimposed over all the previous conflicts was the most important of all, namely the civilian-military conflict. It is now quite evident that the Baath made its most serious mistake when it allowed military officers who were members of the Baath to run the show. In essence the Baath party had no control over the military, yet it needed their support in order to take over and maintain power. The consequence, especially in a pluralistic society such as Syria, was that various military officers utilized every means at their disposal to enhance their personal or sectarian power. Thus, the revolutionary Baath neglected its organization of the people and of the soldiers and petty officers. It was, therefore, fairly easy for a small group of officers to move to save the Baath from the deviationist and rightist elements. A bloody coup on February 23, 1966 toppled the Aflaq-Bitar section of the Baath party. The real force behind the coup was Major General Salah Jadid.

The new government proclaimed that the coup was necessary because socialism in Syria had been undermined by the previous government. It advocated the improvement of the lagging economy by developing and deepening the socialist experiment. Immediately after taking over, the neo-Baath announced that the first stage of the program for agrarian land reform, *i.e.*, state confiscation of surplus land, was finished and the second stage of distributing the confiscated land to the peasants would begin. While this appears to have been more talk than action, it helped the new government gain support from among the peasants. But being strongly ideological, the government became less conciliatory in its attitudes toward private business. Many businessmen, trade union leaders, and some army personnel left Syria because of the policies of the government run by the neo-Baath. Greater socialist measures took hold throughout Syria, and the country's dependence on the Communist bloc, particularly the Soviet Union, increased. In a speech marking the first anniversary of the Baathist revolution, President Nureddin Atasi extolled the accomplishments of the revolution and violently attacked Western imperialism. He called for the overthrow of the royalist government in Jordan and blamed Jordan for blocking the liberation of Palestine. In late 1967 the government declared an end to private schools and stated that these schools would from then on be under the management of the ministry of education. The swing toward a socialist state took another important step.

The neo-Baath in Syria talks as though its one and only concern is the welfare of the masses, the defense of the Arab cause, and the fulfillment of Arab unity. Its actions, however, have so far accomplished exactly the opposite aims. The masses suffer as a result of the poor economic situation and the innumerable restrictions on the freedom of movement, speech, and assembly. The heavy-handed tactics and intransigence against any form of dissent have almost depleted the supply of business, military, and professional talent the country once possessed. Those who remain are governed by fear and distrust. In the June 1967 war with Israel, the Syrian Baathists displayed greater vigor in their attempts to topple the Jordanian monarch than they did in fighting the enemies of the Arabs. Also, their constant attacks on the reactionary Arab regimes do not bring Arab unity or even solidarity any closer to realization.

In mid-1969 the Syrian Baath was attempting to widen its base of support by including in the cabinet not only Communists but Nasserite elements as well. Also, general elections were to be held for the first time in eight years. Despite reported conflicts within the neo-Baath, the party seems to have established itself as the most extremist and intransigent in the Arab world. The Syrian Baathists have refused to accept the November 22, 1967 U.N. Security Council resolution on the Arab-Israeli conflict. They train a branch of the Palestine resistance movement called *al-Saiqa* (Thunderbolt), although they refuse to allow it to operate from Syrian territory for fear of Israeli retaliation. Their disagreements with monarchist Jordan, moderate Lebanon, and the opposing Baathist faction in Iraq definitely contribute to the weakening of the eastern front in the Arabs' military strategy in confronting Israel.

Foreign Policy

When independence came to Syria, the country found itself in the midst of several conflicting forces which became reflected in the internal workings of the political system. Thus various schemes for unity of Arab, Islamic, or Syrian nations were spelled out or fought over. The Palestine issue and the Zionist-Israeli threat temporarily brought about a unity of purpose. This unity was shattered after the poor performance of the Arab, including Syrian, armies on the battlefield. The outcome was the beginning of army intervention in politics. In this respect, Syria found itself setting the pattern that was to be followed in much of the Arab world.

Inter-Arab rivalry, especially between Iraq and Egypt, combined with the competing notions of what Arab unity should be like and among which countries it should be implemented, further complicated Syria's internal problems as factions developed and championed different sides. The military coups which followed the actions of Zaim occurred partly in response to these external influences. When Shishakli made his move in December 1949, it was done in part to ward off union with non-republican Iraq. Thus, no coherent foreign policy toward neighboring Arab countries developed in Syria during the first years following independence, save the deep resentment and bitterness for the loss of much of Palestine and the establishment of an alien Israeli state.

With the second coup of Shishakli, the hopes of those wanting an Iraqi-Syrian union were completely deflated. Because of his past SSNP connections, Shishakli at first talked of a Syrian nation rather than an Arab nation. Soon, however, he turned to a policy of Arabism for Syria which was to be the vanguard for the liberation of the entire Arab world. But Shishakli was overthrown in 1954, apparently with Iraqi connivance and support. Then followed the "struggle for Syria" over the Western-sponsored Baghdad Pact. However, the sentiment in Syria began to crystallize against entanglement in foreign alliances, especially Western defense pacts. Also, progressive Egypt was favored over monarchical Iraq. Syria, as the 1954 elections had illustrated, was moving left.

When Egypt and Czechoslovakia announced the arms deal between them in late 1955, the last stronghold of Britain and the West over Egypt was broken. A month after the arms deal was made public, Syria and Egypt entered a military alliance. Though the alliance failed to achieve much militarily, it virtually gave Nasser control of Syria's foreign policy. To Iraq, the pact meant that Egypt had won, at least temporarily, the competition for Syrian friendship and support. It placed nonprogressive Iraq further from the mainstream of Arab nationalist thought than before.

As Baathist influence increased, the chances of union grew. The growing Communist influence in Syria helped speed up the formal pact of union with Egypt. The breakup of the United Arab Republic in 1961 again placed Syria between Iraq (now progressive after the 1958 coup) and Egypt. Then the Baath party gained control of Syria and Iraq. Relations between these two countries became friendly, and talk of union between them began to be heard. When the Baath government in Syria was officially recognized by Egypt, a three-way union even appeared possible. Steps were taken to implement such a union which, however, proved unsuccessful.

In the mid-1960s Syrian denouncement of the reactionary regimes of Jordan and Saudi Arabia became louder and stronger. Syria placed on Jordan much of the blame for failure to win and settle the Palestine conflict. With the left wing of the Baath gaining control in early 1966, these denouncements became a daily routine. The propaganda campaigns from Damascus against any and all reactionary regimes, the "tools of imperialism," and the "traitors" to the Arab cause displayed, perhaps better than anything else, the frustrations, futility, and weakness of the Syrian Baath. This was clearly illustrated in the June 1967 war. Although the strategic and well-fortified Golan Heights were captured by the Israelis and despite the poor performance by the Syrian army, the Syrian leaders claimed victory because the neo-Baath regime was not removed from power. The public, though apathetic, does not seem to accept this logic. Nonetheless, any move to topple the regime will most likely come from among the ruling army officers themselves. When the moderate Baath effected a bloodless two-stage coup in Iraq in July 1968, the Syrian leaders began to have the jitters.

In the East-West struggle, Syria became the first Arab nation to take a neutralist stance. Already in 1950 many Syrian leaders advocated neutrality between the two world blocs. Both the Baath and Akram Hourani's Arab Socialist party were early leaders and advocates in this direction. This strong movement toward neutralism had many roots, the most important being the lasting bitterness toward the French in their attempt to crush independence and the hatred of the West for its support of Israel. Some Syrian factions went beyond a stand of neutralism and openly advocated a move toward the Eastern bloc, though not toward establishing communism in the country. Rather, Syria found no other important power to turn to for economic and military assistance. When it rejected the Baghdad Pact in 1955, the Soviet Union came out publicly in support of Syria at a time when Turkey and Iraq were apparently ready to act against the country that had snubbed them.

The union of Syria and Egypt into the United Arab Republic placed Syria's foreign affairs in the control of Egyptian officials. Since both Syria and Egypt were on friendly terms with the Eastern bloc countries, the United Arab Republic continued this friendly relationship. The persistence of Arab-Israeli hostilities through and after the time of union, as well as the continued Western support for Israel, makes almost inevitable Syria's dependence on the Soviet Union for arms deliveries. The takeover by the military neo-Baath in early 1966 signalled even closer relations between Syria and the communist world, at the expense of conservatives or even moderate regimes—especially those in the Arab world.

FOR FURTHER READING

A general historical survey of Syria and the surrounding region may be found in Philip K. Hitti, *History of Syria, including Lebanon and Palestine* (New York: Macmillian, 1951). Three books have treated Syria and Lebanon jointly. Stephen H. Longrigg has written a very useful study of *Syria and Lebanon under French Mandate* (London: Oxford University Press, 1958). Nicola A. Ziadeh's *Syria and Lebanon* (New York: Praeger, 1957) is a historical narrative of developments in these countries since independence. A brilliant essay on the politics, history, and social thought of Syria and Lebanon is provided by Albert H. Hourani in his *Syria and Lebanon* (London: Oxford University Press, 1954).

Major social and economic changes have taken place in Syria in the past several years. Consequently, the following books are useful primarily for background reading: the International Bank for Reconstruction and Development's *The Economic Development of Syria* (Baltimore, Md.: Johns Hopkins Press, 1955), and Doreen Warriner, *Land Reform and Development in the Middle East* (London: Oxford University Press, 1962).

Patrick Seale provides an excellent analysis of Syria's internal politics and external relations in his *The Struggle for Syria* (London: Oxford University Press, 1965). It is a study of post-war Arab politics from 1945 to 1958. Malcolm Kerr's *The Arab Cold War: 1958-1967,* Sec. Ed. (London: Oxford University Press, 1967) picks up where Seale left off and carefully analyzes the various arguments and conflicts surrounding Syria's unity with Egypt, the secession and the second attempt at unity with Egypt and Iraq. Gordon H. Torrey chronicles the numerous coups d'etat Syria experienced up to the formation of the United Arab Republic in his *Syrian Politics and the Military, 1945-1958* (Columbus, Ohio: Ohio State University Press, 1964). Two qualified writers present the history and ideology of two parties which have played an important part in Syria: Labib Zuwiyya Yamak, *The Syrian Social Nationalist Party: An Ideological Analysis* (Cambridge, Mass.: Harvard University Press, 1966), and Kamel S. Abu Jaber, *The Arab Ba'th Socialist Party: History, Ideology, and Organization* (Syracuse, N. Y.: Syracuse University Press, 1966).

chapter 11

Lebanon*

Lebanon is a land of paradox and contrast. Extreme wealth and miserable poverty may be found within its borders; its mountain resorts and parts of Beirut are as modern as any European or American metropolis, yet there are areas in the south and the Bekaa Valley that are just beginning to enter the 20th century; among its leaders, and in the same administration, may be found the most idealistic revolutionaries as well as the amoral, if not immoral, corrupt politicians; personal freedom is greatly cherished and constitutionally guaranteed—yet kinship, clan, sectarian, and regional loyalties certainly limit the freedom of choice of much of the population; religious tolerance is among the highest anywhere in the Middle East, yet religious bigotry and hatred of the members of sects other than one's own are widespread; and officially banned political parties are unofficially allowed to exist, practice and seek adherents, so long as they do not endanger the security of the regime. Equality and democracy are stressed but status and personalistic leadership *(za'ama)* are major factors in the political system. Lebanon is in, but in many respects not part of, the Arab world. While it has often been attacked for its non-Arab stands, other Arab countries owe it a debt of gratitude for providing a refuge for their political exiles; in an area of the world where opposing political views are not tolerated, Lebanon places few restrictions on freedom of speech and press; group conflicts abound but a sort of balance has been attained because the various factions have been strong enough to maintain their positions but not strong enough to overcome their competitors.

Historical and Social Background

Although the Kataeb *(Phalanges Libanaises)* party argues that there is a Lebanese nation, the fact remains that most residents of Lebanon do not

*Michael W. Suleiman, associate professor of political science, Kansas State University.

231

subscribe to this idea and, furthermore, do not display strong feelings of loyalty to a Lebanese nation. In fact, historical tradition as well as present social-economic-governmental practice have contributed to the fragmentation of the Lebanese political culture, as the following brief discussion demonstrates.

In Lebanon, as in any Middle Eastern country, religion was the most important characteristic defining one's nationality under Ottoman rule. Where persecution on the basis of religious affiliation took place, the attachment to one's religious community was strengthened. This was particularly true of the Maronites and the Druzes. These two communities vied for supremacy of Mount Lebanon in the 18th and 19th centuries. The consequence was religious strife culminating in the massacres of 1860 in which the Druzes had the upper hand and which caused the death of many thousands and a great deal of destruction. The hue and cry from the European powers forced the Ottoman rulers to sign the *Règlement Organique* in 1861 guaranteeing the autonomy of Mount Lebanon. After World War I, France came into the Levant as a mandatory power, and in 1920 Greater Lebanon (which became the Republic of Lebanon in 1926) was proclaimed. The new Lebanon almost doubled the area of Mount Lebanon with the addition of the coastal regions of Beirut, Tripoli, and Sidon, and the Bekaa Valley. Also, the population increased by one half. Although the country came closer to economic viability with the expanded borders, the population became more heterogeneous since the newcomers were predominantly Muslim and were far less interested in Lebanese nationalism than they were in the Muslim or Arab variety.

But the Christian-Muslim conflict is attenuated by the splintering groups within both religious communities. Thus, officially Lebanon recognizes some 17 different sects, each with its own personal status courts. Each group works and fights for the welfare of its own members in competition with the other groups for the scarce resources which the state dispenses. For example, the Shi'ites, though a Muslim sect, have in the last several years fought for a bigger share in the various governmental agencies—a measure that displeases the Sunni Muslims (as well as the Maronites) who are overrepresented in these institutions. In general, one can say that the smaller religious and ethnic communities feel greater security from persecution under a confessional arrangement and, consequently, work hard to maintain the status quo. This group includes all the Christian sects, the Maronites not excepted, since they fear that they might be swamped by the Muslim-Arab groups both within Lebanon and in the neighboring Arab states. On the other hand, the Muslim-Arab elements, particularly the Sunnis, would like to scrap the confessional system and reduce the power and privileges of the smaller communities. It should be emphasized, however, that some members in each community disagree with the views of their own group.

Under the French mandate, the Christians, and the Maronites in particular, felt so secure and satisfied that some of them favored continued French protection. The Muslim-Arab group strongly favored independence from France and unity with Syria. In 1943 a compromise agreement, known as the National

Pact, was worked out between two leaders of the major factions: the Maronite Bishara al-Khuri and the Sunni Riyad al-Sulh. Though never explicitly expounded, the pact recognized Lebanon's "Arab face" and rejected French protection. In other words, Lebanon was to be independent, neither dominated by the French nor united with Syria or any other Arab country. Also, since neither faction was strong enough to crush or dominate the other, it was agreed to have parliamentary seats and government offices fairly distributed among the religious sects in proportion of their numbers in the population. Thus, since independence in 1943 the number of deputies in parliament has been a multiple of eleven: a ratio of six Christians to five Muslims (including the Druze in the Muslim designation). From 1960 to the present, parliament has consisted of 99 deputies distributed as follows: 30 Maronites, 11 Greek Orthodox, 6 Greek Catholics, 4 Armenian Orthodox, 1 Armenian Catholic, 1 Protestant, 1 Minorities, 20 Sunnis, 19 Shi'ites, and 6 Druze.

There is little doubt that this arrangement has strengthened the confessional character of Lebanese politics. But it is incorrect to think that without it there would have been no confessionalism or that its abolition would change Lebanon into a secular majoritarian democracy overnight. Some form of the confessional system has been applied in parts of Lebanon for over a century now, and this is about the only kind of democracy the country has known. Thus, confessionalism has deep roots in Lebanon and many factors continue to reinforce it.

Factors Reinforcing Confessionalism

One factor that contributes to confessionalism is the regional distribution of the population according to religious sect. Thus, the Sunnis are concentrated in north Lebanon and Beirut, the Maronites in Mount Lebanon and the north, the Shi'ites in the south, and so forth. Furthermore, economic development in the country has been most evident in the Maronite strongholds in Mount Lebanon and least evident in the Shi'ite areas in the Bekaa. No matter who is to blame for these conditions, the awareness of these differences is likely to create dissension and secessionist ideas or demands.

Familial and feudal ties persist. As Samir Khalaf has written: "Lebanese society is predominantly a kinship culture. Society starts with the family and is fashioned after it. . . . Filial piety is almost a sacred norm; a debt one owes one's kin, and a prerequisite for gaining approval and support."[1] Urbanization, secular education, mobility, and the desire to emulate the West have not had as much influence on loosening family ties as had been expected. Blood still runs thicker than water, and a person is expected to help his relative against the stranger, especially if the latter happens to be of a different religious persuasion. Loyalty to the family becomes a useful device for the ambitious to enhance their political power or perpetuate their leadership. Therefore, zu'ama (plural of

[1] Samir Khalaf, "Primordial Ties and Politics in Lebanon," *Middle Eastern Studies,* Vol. 4, No. 3 (April, 1968), p. 246.

za'im) or political bosses abound in Lebanon, relying not only on family ties but also on their wealth, heritage, and leadership ability.

Education is another factor which reinforces confessionalism in Lebanon. In most countries, public schools carry most of the burden of elementary and high school education—and in the process what political socialization takes place is both uniform and of a national rather than regional or sectarian character. The reverse is true of Lebanon. Private schools abound and, since a large number of them are run or financed by foreign missionaries, the graduates emerge with different and often opposing loyalties. Needless to add, these loyalties are mostly to the religious sect or to the particular nationalism with which that sect identifies.

Thus, socialization at home which tends to stress religious separatism is further reinforced by sectarian schooling. Even after graduation, in the business and professional worlds, social intercourse among the various sects is taking place only gradually—and mostly among those Westernized elites who went to similar linguistic-cultural institutions. One observes, for instance, that the French-educated and those educated in English or American schools find it difficult, if not impossible, to communicate. On the other hand, it is fair to point out that Western education is gradually producing a common set of values to replace the conflicting values of the various religious groups. Consequently, the Westernized elites are far less bigoted and more inclined to work for national rather than sectarian objectives. The grim awareness of the Israeli threat following the June 1967 war has aided this development.

Also, the press has reflected this change to some extent. By and large, however, the press in Lebanon continues to be a divisive element. To cater to the various religious and ethnic groups, many newspapers with small circulations are subsidized. Most are in Arabic, but one finds French, English, and Armenian newspapers and periodicals. Most have a specialized clientele and, consequently, a limited focus. Editorializing is more widespread than objective reporting of the news—a tendency that is made necessary by subsidies from interested parties.

This brief introduction should be sufficient to illustrate how fragmented the Lebanese political culture is. Realizing this fact, we then move on to discuss the political processes and institutions which are very much affected by this fractionalization.

The Politics of Confessional Democracy

If stability is essential for a democracy to flourish, in Lebanon democracy and freedom are indispensable ingredients for a stable political system. Indeed, the very existence of the system is founded on democracy, *i.e.,* the proportional representation of the various religious communities in the institutions of the state. This arrangement was designed to fit the Lebanese situation that developed after the creation of Greater Lebanon in 1920, when the country found itself with numerous religious communities. There were and still are some ethnic and linguistic groups but they are of minor significance and, in any case, the dominant factor is sectarian rivalry and competition.

Under the French mandate, the Sunni Muslims were alienated and out of favor. In fact, they were so opposed to the idea of a Lebanese state that they refused to take part in the consultations among the other religious communities to discuss constitutional provisions, especially concerning parliamentary representation. Nonetheless, the idea of community representation was approved and incorporated in the constitution (Article 95), albeit on a provisional basis. But even if this arrangement has come to be accepted by the communities (rather reluctantly and as a temporary measure by the Sunnis), the question of equitable representation continues to plague the Lebanese whenever interconfessional disputes arise. The argument centers around who is or ought to be a Lebanese and who is not or ought not to be. The Armenian (Christian) settlers have been given Lebanese nationality and many emigrant Lebanese, preponderantly Christian, still retain their Lebanese status. On the other hand, the Palestine refugees (mostly Muslim) and the few Kurdish Muslim tribes have been denied Lebanese citizenship. The last official census was taken in 1932, and the Muslims want another census which would exclude the emigrants and hopefully include the Palestinian refugees and the Kurds. Since this would definitely tip the balance in their favor, it has been opposed by the Christians, and the Maronites in particular.

Communal representation is possible in the Chamber of Deputies and governmental administration, but what of the executive branch? The principle of community representation and sectarian equilibrium was applied here too, but gradually and precariously. The first president, Charles Dabbas (1926-1934) was a Greek Orthodox. However, the two major communities, the Maronites and Sunnis, wanted the position for themselves. A compromise arrangement allotted the presidency to the Maronites and the premiership to the Sunnis. This has proved to be a workable system. Difficulties arise when a president uses his extensive powers to push policies viewed favorable to the Christian community and detrimental to the Muslims. At such times, demands are made to reduce the powers of the president or to have a Sunni head of state, especially since a new census would show the Muslims to constitute a majority. The Maronites, however, argue that the presidency is reserved to their community not merely because they are the largest minority in the country but rather to give them and the Christians generally a feeling of confidence and to help maintain a stable Lebanon.

The politics of Lebanon are not only interconfessional, however, but intraconfessional as well. Since all governmental positions are divided on a sectarian basis, the various leaders and clans within each sect vie among themselves for these positions. Sometimes the institutional agencies of the state are inadequate for the resolution of the confessional or clan disputes. Under such circumstances, formal or informal organizations representing sectarian or interconfessional groups confer in public and in private to work out compromises that are later formalized by the appropriate governmental officials. Examples and more detailed explanations are presented in the following sections.

Parliament and the Electoral Process

Lebanon is supposed to be a parliamentary democracy, but in practice it is very much a presidential system of government in which the Chamber of Deputies and to a great extent the cabinet are useful devices to provide representation for the various religious communities in the country. Perhaps the most important function that parliament performs is the election of the president of the republic. But once the balloting is over, the members become docile and willing tools in the hands of the president. They seek to please him in the hope of being called to serve in the cabinet. More importantly for many is the invaluable assistance they can expect to receive from him at election time.

Parliament is supposed to legislate but, as in most countries in recent years, the initiative in introducing legislation has shifted to the executive. In Lebanon parliament displays greater impotence, however, when it is denied the chance to deliberate and pass judgment on government bills. To avoid bickering and dissension, parliament often authorizes the cabinet to issue legislative decrees concerning important or controversial issues. "The most important legislation in the past decade was passed by legislative decrees issued by the Cabinets, after they had been given emergency powers."[2] The legislative power of members of parliament is further dwindled when they are presented with urgent bills. These have to be acted on within 40 days after which the president may proclaim them as law. To sum up, the Lebanese parliament does not adequately perform the functions normally associated with that institution. It does not act as a watchdog over the executive and the administration; it does not originate many especially important bills; and it is often denied the opportunity to give careful consideration to legislation proposed by the government.

But if the Chamber of Deputies is so ineffective, why do people run for parliamentary office and what kind of individuals get elected? It should be pointed out that even though the legislature as a body is not powerful, the individual members can be and often are. Election to parliament is a source of prestige not only for the individual concerned but for the whole family. Furthermore, members of parliament are the political brokers between their constituents and the impersonal governmental institutions. They can also furnish their supporters with minor jobs eithei through patronage or through influence with private businesses. Election campaigns are extremely expensive in Lebanon, and it is generally assumed by the public that the office is worth the high price paid for it.

The electoral law specifies the size of each district and the number and

---

[2] Elie Salem, "Cabinet Politics in Lebanon," *Middle East Journal,* Vol. 21, No. 4 (Autumn, 1967), p. 494.

religious affiliation of deputies to represent each constituency. For instance, in the last three elections (1960, 1964, and 1968), the 99 deputies were elected in 26 districts of different sizes. In order to reduce friction among the various religious sects, only members of the same denomination run against each other. But realizing that such a competition can turn into unchecked and harmful appeals to the extremists in each group, the single-member constituency system is discarded. Instead, the Lebanese follow the list system according to which from any one district several deputies of different religious sects are elected. Consequently, the support of voters from different religious groups is necessary to assure success. But this system, though effective in moderating interconfessional conflicts, has had some ill effects in another area. A powerful *za'im* can and often does head a list that is almost assured success, and exacts high prices from those seeking the privilege of being on his list. The price is often both material and spiritual, in the form of subservience to the will of the *za'im* in parliament—a practice not unlike that of the "pocket boroughs" in England before the Great Reform Act of 1932.

There have been many calls for electoral reform, mostly stressing the abolition of the confessional arrangement and the requirement of party membership for all parliamentray candidates. The radical measures are not likely to be implemented in the near future. Under the presidencies of Fuad Shehab (1958-1964) and his successor Charles Helou, however, many measures were taken to clean up the electoral process. The governmental administration has been reorganized to increase its efficiency and remove corrupt officials. In order to raise the standard of living, especially in the backward areas in the south, the Bekaa, and the north, scientific planning was introduced and greater funds have been allocated. The assumption is that in order to break the hold of the *zu'ama* over the populace, higher educational standards and better incomes are essential prerequisites. Furthermore, determined efforts have been made to reduce the power of the *zilm,* the henchmen of the *zu'ama,* over the average voter. Voters' lists are now photographed instead of being copied, thus eliminating much error; more polling centers are available; and the isolated election booth is finally a reality.

But are these changes enough to modernize the electoral process or is it necessary to adopt the radical reforms suggested earlier? Opinion differs. At the center of controversy is the confessional arrangement. Thus far, at least, parliamentary seats in Lebanon have continued to be the preserve of some two dozen well-known and wealthy families. The rich are favored because of the exorbitantly high costs of electioneering, especially since there is no effective limitation on campaign expenditure. Besides, the candidature fee alone is $1,000 which is forfeited unless the candidate receives 25 percent of the vote in his district—this in a country whose per capita income is less than $400 a year!

But what kind of wealthy people get elected to parliament? It is not easy to arrive at a classification system that is completely satisfactory or accurate. But it is clear that the landlords, and more generally the propertied, still constitute one of the largest if not the largest group. Lawyers, professionals, and businessmen, in that order, are making strong headway. This is encouraging, but it should not lead to excessive optimism since a strong argument can be made to the effect that these groups were elected in their capacity as wealthy people or *zu'ama* and *not* as professionals or lawyers. It is sobering to reflect that in 1964 Beirut candidates spent on the average $40,000 (not including vote buying) and that "a serious candidate's expenses could range between $6,000 and $266,000."[3] Despite this, however, there are signs of increasing competitiveness and greater voter participation in Lebanese elections. If these trends are not wholly attributable to intensified in-fighting among the various sons and relatives of the *zu'ama,* a basis for optimism is present.

Political Parties

There are 17 groups in Lebanon which call themselves political parties. Two religious organizations, *Ibad ar-Rahman* and the Muslim Group, perform about the same functions and will be discussed with parties. All 19 groups are mainly interested in gaining converts to their various causes rather than in winning elections. They are out to educate the public in their point of view, a process which futher intensifies the already existing differences among the people. This is where their impact is strongly felt.

No party or coalition of parties has succeeded in electing a majority to the legislature. In the last three elections, about one third of the members of parliament represented seven or eight parties. The rest have been either independents or members of blocs interested in pushing the candidacies of various individuals to the highest offices of the state. But if parties in Lebanon are numerous, small, and do not directly participate in policy-making, why should they be studied or mentioned? To begin with, they can at least be considered fairly stable political blocs which exercise influence on the political leadership. Secondly, their particularistic political socialization contributes to the fragmentation of the country's political culture and, consequently, affects the stability of the system. Thirdly, and most importantly, despite the fact that they do not compete for power in the Western sense, the parties constitute a basic component of the Lebanese political system. Their elimination would upset the balance of power in the country and change the nature of the system. Consider, for example, the fact that successive Lebanese governments have legally banned but unofficially tolerated six transnational groupings (the Lebanese Communist party, the Syrian Social Nationalist party (SSNP), the Arab Baath Socialist party, the Arab Nationalists' movement (ANM), *Tahreer,* and the Muslim Brotherhood) which advocate the merger of the country into a bigger entity and/or the radical transformation of the present system. Since the government is incapable or unwilling to completely prohibit the activities of

---

[3]Michael C. Hudson, "The Electoral Process and Political Development in Lebanon." *Middle East Journal,* Vol. 20, No. 2 (Spring, 1966), p. 180.

these parties, the official ban is used only when any of them endanger the security of the state.

In addition to the two religious groups and the six transnational parties, eleven parties exist which acknowledge the independence of the country within its present borders. These exclusively Lebanese parties include the three Armenian parties (Dashnak, Hunchak, and Ramgavar Azadagan), the Muslim-Arab nationalist Najjada, the Lebanese-Arab nationalist National Appeal (inactive for the past few years), the Lebanese-Muslim National Organization, the four Lebanese-Christian parties of Kataeb *(Phalanges Libanaises),* Constitutional Union, National Bloc, and National Liberals, and the Jumblatti-Druze-Leftist-Arab nationalist Progressive Socialist party (PSP).

Whether or not they admit it and whether or not they like it, all parties in Lebanon are confessional in the sense that the members in each case come mostly from one or two specific religious groups. This is not to say that some have not tried to solicit interconfessional membership. The problem is that the religious groups hold strong, definite, and often opposing views on both domestic and foreign policy issues. An appeal to one group, therefore, is likely to alienate another. A brief examination of the origins of those parties might be helpful in illustrating this point.

With the creation of Greater Lebanon in 1920, disparate religious and ethnic groups were brought together and in essence ordered to think of themselves as Lebanese. The Communist party (1925) attempted to orient the population toward an international socialist world. In 1932 the SSNP argued that the Lebanese were really part of a Syrian nation and that the religious or ethnic differences were either unimportant or superficial. The Communists appealed primarily to the minority groups, Armenians and Kurds in particular, and the SSNP attracted a large number of Greek Orthodox. In the mid-1930s, the Kataeb and the Najjada appeared on the scene to counteract the influence of the Communists and the Syrian Nationalists as well as to protect the interests of the Maronite-Christian and Sunni-Muslim elements, respectively. At the same time, two parliamentary blocs which later called themselves parties, the National Bloc and the Constitutional Bloc, emerged as contestants for the state's highest offices.

The League of National Action (1936) was a precursor of the Baath (1942) and the ANM (early 1950s) in that it expressed Arab nationalist sentiments, advocating Lebanon's unification with the Arab countries. When the Armenians arrived in large numbers during World War I and after, they imported their political parties with them. Then after Lebanon gained its independence, the various religious groups began to form parties, not only to protect their followers but also to compete for political office with their own coreligionists. Among these are the National Appeal (1944), the PSP (1949), the National Organization (1950), and the National Liberals (1959).

It is rather ironic that the presence of so many political parties, several of them interested in and at times actively seeking the downfall of the regime, has been a stabilizing factor. For one thing, no one party has been able to win out and rid the system of the others. Also, these parties have helped uphold the existing regime by acting as a check against the other political or economic groups in the country.

The Cabinet and the Presidency

There are three important political offices that are fiercely contested in Lebanon: the presidency, the premiership, and the speakership of the House. Both tradition and the 1943 National Pact have assigned these posts to the Maronites, the Sunnis, and the Shi'ites, respectively. Thus, members of each sect compete to see which clan will capture the prize. But this does not mean that each sect acts in isolation from the others. In fact, what takes place is something quite similar to the politics of list formation for parliamentary elections. Because large and effective parties are nonexistent, aspirants to each of the three major offices have to accumulate the support of numerous blocs and personalities. But a Shi'i aspirant to the speakership, for instance, realizes that his chances of winning are greatly improved if he can reach an understanding with a Sunni candidate for the premiership and with a Maronite presidential hopeful. The same reasoning motivates the Sunni and Maronite office seekers. The consequence is a never-ending process of coalition formation and re-formation in search of the correct grouping which would guarantee success—albeit a temporary one. Thus, in the summer of 1968 those favoring the return of Shehab to the presidency or the election of a pro-Shehab candidate to the post favored Rashid Karami as prime minister and Sabry Hamadeh as House speaker. On the other hand, the tripartite alliance of the Kataeb, the National Bloc, and the National Liberals was opposed to Shehab or a pro-Shehab candidate, so much so, in fact, that the parties were able to form such an alliance when each group had its own strong candidate to the presidency: Pierre Jemayel, Raymond Edde, and Camille Chamoun, respectively. This alliance to oppose the Shehabists favored Kamel el-Ass'ad for the speakership and Saeb Salam for the premiership —even though Salam was on very good terms with another presidential hopeful, Suleiman Franjieh. Since the two opposing factions were almost equal in strength following the 1968 elections, it became almost impossible to conduct any business in parliament—which provided the right excuse for the cabinet to ask for emergency powers!

The president is the most powerful figure in the Lebanese Republic. This is recognized by the Sunni community which has in recent years called for reducing these powers or the election of Sunni presidents. Miss Alya al-Sulh, daughter of Riyad al-Sulh, one of the architects of the National Pact, has recently (1966) argued that the president is the "only ruler" in Lebanon and that the premier is merely a rubber stamp. This argument appears to be well justified. The constitutional powers granted to the president are considerable. He is elected by parliament but is not accountable to it except for criminal or constitutional violations. He may propose legislation, summon parliament to special sessions, and with cabinet approval dissolve it before the end of its term. He appoints and dismisses ministers as well as many other government officials, and he has the right to negotiate and ratify international treaties.

But the president accumulates additional important powers from the peculiarities of the Lebanese political system and the psychology of the people. Whether out of fear, respect, or both, the public at election time generally supports the candidates favored by the administration in office, essentially the president. Despite commendable attempts to conduct fair and clean elections in the past few years, one cannot deny what President Bishara al-Khuri termed "the not insignificant influence the government can have if it handles the situation well."[4] This influence is translated into cooperation with the president, if not subservience to his will, after the candidates are elected. Once the president is elected, he serves for a fixed six-year term. This gives him an edge over parliament which is elected to a four-year term but which may be dismissed sooner and over the premier who serves at his (the president's) pleasure. Besides, there are half-a-dozen powerful Sunni leaders aspiring to the office. Therefore, rotation of the premiership among several of them is not only good for the stability of the system but also provides the president with added leverage to perform the job more to his liking.

It is not always easy for a prime minister to form a cabinet or to keep it in office for a long period of time. First of all, ambitious members of parliament apply pressures and ask for favors: They wish to be included in the cabinet. This is the pinnacle of power to which most of them can aspire and they are anxious to attain it. Besides, the office bestows prestige on its occupant, in addition to the power of patronage. Hence, a new cabinet or a "replastered" one—*i.e.,* dropping a few ministers, adding a few, and reshuffling the posts, the kind of practice that was popular under the Fourth French Republic—is an occasion for high hopes among many parliament members. In fact, some incumbent ministers, sensing the imminent fall of their cabinet, begin to attack it as a strategy for possible inclusion in the next one.

The second reason why it is sometimes difficult to form or maintain a stable cabinet is the necessity to have the right confessional, regional, and political balances. Malcolm Kerr discusses the example of Premier Karami's difficulties in 1962 when Osman Dana, a Sunni member of the cabinet, began to attack his colleagues: "Which Sunni Moslem could Prime Minister Karami have put in place of Osman Dana? No one from the North, as Karami himself was from Tripoli; nor from Beirut, where Salam and Mashnuq were already his opponents; Rafiq Naja was already a minister; and Adnan al-Hakim too extreme in his views to cooperate. The seven remaining Sunni deputies presented a variety of difficulties. Khalid Shihab was too bold and as a former Premier, too distinguished.

---

[4] Bishara al-Khuri, *Haqa'iq lubnaniyya* (Lebanese Truths), III (Harisa, 1961), pp. 30-31.

Kazim al-Solh would presumably have preferred to wait for a call to the premiership. Maaruf Saad would have been only slightly less uncooperative than Adnan al-Hakim. Issam Hajjar was too young and undistinguished. Qabalan Qabalan also lacked distinction, except as a friend of Camille Chamoun, which would make him unacceptable to Kemal Jumblatt."[5] It would not have been possible merely to drop a Sunni from the cabinet because then the confessional balance would have been upset. Dropping a Sunni would have necessitated eliminating one minister from each of the other five sects represented in the cabinet. This move would have undermined the cabinet by greatly reducing the amount of support it had in parliament.

But despite the extensive powers of the president compared to those of the premier, it should not be presumed that the president has a free hand to do what he pleases. It is useful to mention the various paraconstitutional forces which limit the president's authority and then to provide examples demonstrating their effectiveness or lack of it. First, there is the Maronite Church and its hierarchy, headed by the Patriarch. This is a formidable institution and only a rash president would risk its alienation. Its influence is demonstrated not only in times of crisis, as in 1958, but also in the ordinary functioning of the political process. The newspapers regularly report how the president, directly or through emissaries sent to the Patriarch's seat in Bkirki, seeks the approval or at the very least the neutrality of the Maronite Patriarch concerning important or controversial issues. Presidential candidates and potential aspirants to the presidency pay homage to the Patriarch and hope for an approving nod, although they have to be careful, both as candidates and as presidents, not to appear too close to the Church or else they would be unacceptable to the other religious groups, especially the Sunnis. The Christian communities are better organized and, therefore, wield greater power in the political system, but the Muslim communities, represented by the Higher Muslim Council and the Islamic Congress, also present demands to and exert pressures on the president which do not go unheeded.

Powerful political and feudal leaders of the president's own as well as other sects have to be satisfied. They have an independent base of power and hold a strong conviction that they deserve a share in the Lebanese political pie. If they are denied their rights, they are likely to be more than a temporary inconvenience to the president. Pressures from Arab leaders, foreign powers, the army and the *Deuxième Bureau* (military intelligence), and from business and union interests present further limitations on the president's freedom of action. Also, the various political parties are agencies representing or being used by some or all of the above-mentioned groups. Needless to say, in any confrontation, more than one group is involved and many interests have to be reconciled as the following two examples demonstrate.

---

[5]Malcolm H. Kerr, "Political Decision Making in a Confessional Democracy," in Leonard Binder (ed.), *Politics in Lebanon* (New York: John Wiley, 1966), p. 199.

Bishara al-Khuri was elected president in 1943. Article 49 of the Lebanese constitution specifies that the term of office is six years and that "he may not be re-elected until six years have elapsed since the date of expiration of his last mandate."[6] But in May 1948, long before his term was to expire, the right circumstances presented themselves for a constitutional amendment permitting Bishara al-Khuri to succeed himself for another six-year period. For one thing, Shukri al-Kuwatli of Syria had just had his term of office renewed and thus set a precedent for his Lebanese neighbor to follow. Secondly, the Palestine conflict made it necessary to avoid changing horses in the middle of the stream—ignoring the fact that the horse-switching would not have occurred for another 16 months! Al-Khuri denied that he did any untoward campaigning or pressuring to get reelected. But neither was he against renewal. In his own words: "A person has to be an angel or a prophet to refuse the renewal of his mandate under such favorable circumstances. In all humility, I declare that I am neither an angel nor a prophet!"[7]

Slowly but surely the circumstances began to become unfavorable for Bishara al-Khuri and his friends. The Palestine war ended with a defeat for the Arabs, accompanied by public frustration and bitterness against the responsible leaders. Syria began what turned out to be a never-ending series of military coups in 1949, King Abdullah of Jordan was assassinated in July 1951, and the Egyptian revolution took place in July 1952. Inside Lebanon, the al-Khuri regime succeeded in making many enemies. The 1947 elections were corrupt—very corrupt. But their worst aspect was not corruption as such, but the fact that the regime excluded powerful members of the opposition from parliamentary membership. Al-Khuri's problems increased when the Syrian Social Nationalist party intensified its campaign against the authorities. While the attempt ended in failure and the leader and founder of the SSNP, Antun Saadeh, was executed, party followers harbored ill feelings against the regime. Riyad al-Sulh, al-Khuri's favorite prime minister, was killed (1951) while visiting King Abdullah in Amman. Finally, corruption in government and the fear and suspicion generated by Salim al-Khuri, brother of the president, combined with a serious economic slump in the country to inflame passions and produce strikes and demonstrations. The opportunity was seized upon by opponents of the al-Khuri regime, especially those who had been frustrated in their bids for political power. The Socialist Front was formed comprising the following groups and individuals: Camille Chamoun, Kemal Jumblatt and his Progressive Socialist party, the Najjada, the Kataeb, the National Bloc, and the SSNP. Apart from Jumblatt and his party, no other group or individual in the Front believed in socialism. What brought this motley crowd together was political opportunism rather than ideology.

The Socialist Front denounced governmental corruption, asked for reorgani-

---

[6] *The Lebanese Constitution* (Beirut, Lebanon, 1960), Article 49, p. 20.

[7] Khuri, *op. cit.*, p. 122.

zation of the state, and demanded al-Khuri's resignation. In the midst of a cabinet crisis, the Front organized a general strike. Sensing the widespread unpopularity of the regime, the prominent Sunni leaders were not anxious to serve as premiers under al-Khuri, especially since the police as well as the army were reluctant to use force in order to end the strike. Al-Khuri then appointed General Fuad Shahab, army chief of staff, as premier and resigned from his office on September 18, 1952. Five days later, the same parliament members who had been staunchly loyal to al-Khuri found no difficulty in switching their allegiance to Camille Chamoun, whom they elected president.

Chamoun did not apparently learn much from al-Khuri's experience despite, perhaps because of, his involvement in those events. Al-Khuri was restrained to some extent by the presence of Riyad al-Sulh, a very popular and powerful Muslim leader. With his assassination, several Sunnis aspired to the premiership, none of them of Riyad's national stature. This strengthened Chamoun's hand since he could and did play them against each other. He went further and systematically alienated many powerful leaders: Druze, Sunni, Maronite, and others.

No sooner had Chamoun become president than he succeeded in infuriating Kemal Jumblatt, his Socialist Front partner, by not heeding his advice, especially concerning investigation and trial of members of the previous regime. Thus, yesterday's friends became estranged, an estrangement that shortly turned into personal and continuing enmity. In 1955 Chamoun was reported to have disapproved of the appointment of Bishop Paul Meouchi as Maronite Patriarch, a fact that did not endear him to the Patriarch. Then, in 1957 he earned the enmity of four important leaders because they failed to win in the parliamentary elections. These were the Druze Jumblatt, the Sunni Abdullah el-Yafi and Saeb Salam, and the Shi'ite Ahmed el-Ass'ad. It was also generally believed and charged by the opposition that the elections were manipulated to provide the two-thirds majority necessary for a constitutional amendment allowing presidential renewal.

Foreign policy issues added to Chamoun's internal problems. At the time of the British-French-Israeli attack on Egypt in 1956, Chamoun refused to break diplomatic relations with Britain and France and thus caused the resignation of el-Yafi and Salam who were then premier and minister of state, respectively. To add insult to injury, the new cabinet included Charles Malik as minister of foreign affairs. Since Malik was most obviously pro-Western the move was clearly intended to convey the regime's opposition to the course of action that Gamal Abdul Nasser was following at the time. Furthermore, it was generally known that Chamoun sympathized with Iraq, Egypt's rival in Arab politics, and member of the Western-sponsored Baghdad Pact. Then, on March 16, 1957 the Lebanese government gave its official acceptance of the Eisenhower Doctrine according to which the United States would militarily defend any Middle East country desiring protection against direct or indirect Communist aggression.

Reminiscent of the Socialist Front that toppled Bishara al-Khuri, a National

Front was formed in June 1957, comprising all of Chamoun's political opponents, among them Kemal Jumblatt, Rashid Karami, Saeb Salam, Abdullah el-Yafi, Ahmed el-Ass'ad, and the Constitutional Bloc. Here it should be remembered that there were three intertwined conflicts involved. First, many Lebanese politicians of *all* religious sects were determined to oust Chamoun or at the very least block his attempt to renew his term of office in retaliation for their loss in the elections or generally because their political influence had declined under his rule. The second issue centered around Lebanon's independence as opposed to its merger in the United Arab Republic (Syria and Egypt) and the Arab world generally. The third controversy concerned Lebanon's stand in the East-West cold war. The second and third issues are the same ones that divided the Muslim and Christian communities in Lebanon before independence and that found temporary resolution in the 1943 National Pact. But by 1958 many Christians, especially among the non-Maronites, began to view Nasser as their leader and Arab unity as the best policy for Lebanon. They also favored a neutralist or even pro-Eastern stand since the West was Isreal's protector whereas the Soviet Union was supplying the United Arab Republic, the pivotal Arab state, with weapons. Thus, the conflict and the civil war about to take place were not strictly confessional, even though a majority of the Muslims took one side and a Christian majority took the other.

In 1958 after the formation of the United Arab Republic, Nasser visited Damascus. Tens of thousands, mainly Muslims, crossed the Lebanese border to hear him speak. Enthusiasm was high and the prospect of a resurrected powerful Arab nation stirred the emotions of the Arab nationalists. Muslim Lebanese felt cheated and denied the privilege of sharing this potential march to victory. In contrast, they found it difficult to identify with the Lebanese nation or state, a state in which their economic status and political influence were not commensurate with their numbers. Bitterly they complained of government bias in favor of the Christian regions, which left their areas socially and economically backward. Demands were also made to have a census taken which they were certain would show a Muslim majority, in which case the ratio in government posts would be altered to favor the Muslims.

On May 8, 1958 a journalist supporting the opposition was murdered in Beirut. The National Front held the government responsible and called for a general countrywide strike in protest. Disturbances and serious clashes began to spread, culminating in a virtual civil war. The Chamoun regime accused the United Arab Republic government of instigating and aiding the rebellion, but the group of observers dispatched by the U.N. Security Council found no significant outside support or intervention.

As the country drifted into a bloody civil war, many feared a strictly Christian-Muslim confrontation that might destroy the independence and integrity of Lebanon as well as jeopardize the position of the Christian minority in the Middle East. Among the prominent Christian critics of Chamoun and his policies was the Maronite Patriarch Paul Meouchi. This displeased many

Maronites but was hailed by most Muslims and greatly helped reduce the confessional character of the conflict. Also, General Fuad Shehab, chief of staff of the army, refused to crush the rebellion. As in 1952, he was against using the army to help a particular government stay in office. But in 1958 there were the added dangers of intensifying the religious conflict and splintering the army along confessional lines. Thus, Shehab tried to use his forces to limit the conflict, and he himself became an intermediary between the government and the opposition.

On July 14th the pro-Western Hashemite regime in Iraq was toppled in a bloody coup led by Abd al-Karim Kassim. Chamoun quickly requested American troops under the Eisenhower Doctrine to land in Lebanon within 48 hours if Lebanon was not to be lost to the Nasser pro-Eastern camp. On July 15th American marines landed on the Lebanese shores. They did not engage in any fighting, neither did the civil war immediately come to an end. But their presence effectively counteracted any outside intervention. A compromise was reached within a comparatively short time. Chamoun was allowed to finish his term of office, and Fuad Shehab resigned his army command and was elected (July 31) president to succeed Chamoun on September 22nd. But when Shehab appointed as his first cabinet a group favorable to the National Front, violence erupted again until a "salvation cabinet" was formed on October 14th. It was composed of two Sunni opposition leaders, Rashid Karami and Hussein Oueini, and two pro-Chamoun Maronite leaders, Pierre Jemayel (leader of the Kataeb) and Raymond Edde (head of the National Bloc).

Foreign Policy

Lebanon is a country of minorities, all of whom are anxious to safeguard their security in the best possible way. The numerous Christian sects as well as the Christian community as a unit constitute a minority not only in Lebanon but in the Middle East generally. The Druze are a minority, and so are the Shi'ites and the Sunnis, to mention only the larger sects. So long as there is no strong Lebanese national sentiment, with religious affiliation (but not necessarily religious devotion, which is often lacking) providing the majority of the people with their most meaningful sense of identity, then the various religious sects will look for protectors from inside and outside the country. This condition more than any other has shaped the overall course of Lebanese foreign policy since the formation of Greater Lebanon in 1920.

Toward the end of the mandate, the Maronites and the Sunnis, who represented the two most important as well as most extremist factions of the Christian and Muslim communities, produced two groups willing to compromise on both domestic and foreign policy issues. The outcome was the National Pact of 1943. The pact was vaguely formulated and unwritten, which made it more acceptable to both major groups. This very vagueness, however, has contributed to misunderstandings and crises. It is a moot question, for instance, as to whether or not the pact was a convenient but *temporary* arrangement to facilitate French departure and set the country on a stable course for the initial critical years of independence. Thus, to Arab nationalists *"the Mithaq al-Watani* [National Pact] was, in retrospect, a bulwark against the disruptive potential of irrational confessionalism, and equally a roadblock that prevented the emergence of a rational and secular alternative to confessional politics."[8] The rational and secular alternative Arab nationalists suggest envisions the eventual merger of Lebanon into a unified Arab world. On the other hand, the National Bloc, which was not pleased with the pact at the beginning, strongly endorsed it after the 1958 civil war. It even called for it to be written explicitly, voted upon by parliament, and adopted by the nation.

Also, different interpretations could be given to the notion that Lebanon has an "Arab face" and that it would be "neither a station nor a pathway for imperialism." In the middle and late 1950s, Arab nationalist fervor was very high. When President Chamoun refused to cut off diplomatic relations with Britain and France following their 1956 invasion (in conjunction with Israel) of the Egyptian region, many in Lebanon, especially the Sunnis, considered this an abrogation of the National Pact. To them Lebanon's "Arab face" was not shown during that crisis. Furthermore, Lebanon was willingly turning into a "station for imperialism" when it accepted the Eisenhower Doctrine and invited American troops to land on its shores in 1958. To the Maronites, however, these acts were justified as the necessary means to maintain the independence and integrity of Lebanon, threatened as the country was by inside and outside forces.

Despite the vagueness and the differences concerning the National Pact, however, successive Lebanese governments have proclaimed several foreign policy principles to which they have attempted to adhere. Before these are discussed, it is fair to point out that although Chamoun's regime is believed to have deviated farthest from these principles, thus causing the 1958 civil war, Chamoun's presidency happened to coincide with a very volatile phase of Arab politics. It is not unlikely that a similar situation in the future will produce another crisis for Lebanon.

One cardinal principle is Lebanon's independence as a sovereign state. This right is recognized by the League of Arab States and the United Nations as well as many countries and international organizations. In order to reinforce this legal guarantee, the Shehab and Helou regimes have implemented many reforms designed to improve the living conditions of the non-Christian population. It is hoped that this will make them more attached and loyal to the Lebanese state. These groups are further appeased by another principle of the Lebanese government, namely cooperation and solidarity with the other Arab countries. However, this cooperation is subject to certain limitations, some explicit and others assumed. It is emphasized that solidarity will stop short of political unity

---

[8] Clovis Maksoud, "Lebanon and Arab Nationalism," in Binder, *op. cit.,* p. 241.

in which Lebanon ceases to be a sovereign state. Another limitation is imposed by the very nature of Arab politics. *i.e.,* disunity. Thus, Lebanon has attempted to steer a neutral course among the various factions in the Arab world, often working to minimize differences and encourage a more amicable atmosphere. One more limitation may be mentioned. Solidarity and cooperation are accepted so long as they do not run counter to the Lebanese national interest. For example, since Lebanon itself was not attacked by Israel in June 1967, the Lebanese army did not take part in the battle.

The Lebanese army is small, ill-equipped and not well-trained. It is not much of a fighting force and can hardly put down a serious internal insurrection. In other words, Lebanon is dependent on the international community and, in particular, the United Nations and the major powers for the guarantee of its territorial integrity and political independence. Thus the country places much faith in the United Nations and seeks to strengthen the role that world body plays in resolving international disputes. Also, it professes nonalignment with either camp in the East-West struggle, desiring the goodwill of both sides. The fact that it is not formally a part of the Western camp serves Lebanon's interests well. Thus, the country can avoid the unpleasant and harmful charge that it is an imperialist stooge. Furthermore, this is one small way of demonstrating its solidarity with the Arab countries, many of which have chosen to remain nonaligned. Finally, Lebanon's relations with the Afro-Asian world are better served by this policy. In this direction, Lebanon recently began a program of educational and technical assistance to several African countries.

Lebanon's dependence on the international community may suffer serious reverses if the Israeli-Zionist threat persists or is magnified. Arab nationalists have consistently warned Lebanon of Israel's expansionist designs, arguing that solidarity with the other Arab countries is the best if not the only guarantee for Lebanon's safety. Many Lebanese, especially among the Maronites, disagreed with this line of reasoning. Some argued against Lebanon's participation in the 1948 war with Israel, and others even suggested that the establishment of a Zionist state in Palestine would be to Lebanon's benefit. A reassessment of this position was becoming evident in the summer of 1968 brought about by Israeli raids on farmers and villages in south Lebanon and by statements from Zionist leaders to the effect that southern Lebanon belongs to Eretz or historical Israel and should be taken over. Thus, the more Israel displays confidence and aggressiveness, the more "Arab" Lebanon's "face" is likely to become. On December 28, 1968 Israeli forces destroyed or damaged 13 commercial aircraft worth $56 million in an attack at Beirut International Airport. The raid was allegedly in retaliation for the machine-gun attack on an El Al plane in Athens by two Palestinian commandos. Israel claimed that Lebanon was responsible for the El Al incident since the two Palestinians had gone to Athens via Beirut. This incident and the insistence of Palestinian guerrilla forces on using Lebanese territory to conduct raids against Israel were responsible for riots, demonstrations, and governmental instability in Lebanon in 1969. Thus, Lebanon's cherished neutrality was once again being challenged.

What happens to resident Lebanon is also of interest to emigrant Lebanon and vice versa. The Lebanese are known to be very enterprising and excellent traders. Many of those who sought their fortune outside the confines of the old country have kept their ties with the fatherland. The Lebanese authorities have encouraged these contacts, especially since they provide a small fortune (7 percent of the GNP) for the country every year. Despite the controversy inside Lebanon over the rights of emigrants to be citizens or to get included in the formula for electoral representation, a special ministry for emigrants was created. It is now merged with the ministry of foreign affairs under the name of ministry of the exterior and Lebanese emigrants. Also, a World Lebanese Association was formed in 1960 to facilitate contacts between emigrant and resident Lebanese and to help the country of origin. Since Lebanon favors free trade and has become the banking and trade center in the Middle East, such contacts with the outside world could attract greater foreign investment and strengthen the economy of the country.

In foreign as in domestic policy then, Lebanon operates in accordance with John Calhoun's "concurrent majority." That is to say, the government cannot make a decision stick that is unacceptable to a sizable minority, especially either the Sunnis or the Maronites. Thus far, the system has operated exceptionally well in both areas except for the 1958 crisis. Inter-Arab politics and international intervention will continue to be major factors in Lebanon's stability and prosperity for the foreseeable future.

FOR FURTHER READING

Four of the books listed at the end of the chapter on Syria are relevant for Lebanon as well. These are the volumes by Hourani, Longrigg, Ziadeh, and Yamak. A general historical survey may be found in Philip K. Hitti, *Lebanon in History* (London: Macmillan, 1957). Two books present detailed accounts of the social, economic, and political conditions in Lebanon in the 19th century: William R. Polk's *The Opening of South Lebanon, 1788-1840* (Cambridge, Mass.: Harvard University Press, 1963), and Malcolm H. Kerr, *Lebanon in the Last Years of Feudalism, 1840-1868* (Beirut: Catholic Press, 1959). The latter is a translation of an account by a contemporary observer, with a useful introduction by Kerr. *The Modern History of Lebanon* (New York: Praeger, 1965) by Kamal S. Salibi is invaluable and up-to-date.

John Gulick has written two books on the social-anthropological structure in Lebanon; namely *Social Structure and Culture Change in a Lebanese Village* (New York: Wenner-Gren Foundation for Anthropological Research, 1955), and *Tripoli, A Modern Arab City* (Cambridge, Mass.: Harvard University Press, 1967). The study of Tripoli is excellent in its delineation of the process and effects of modernization. On Lebanese economics, Yusif A. Sayigh's *Entrepreneurs of Lebanon* (Cambridge, Mass.: Harvard University Press, 1962) is indispensable.

Descriptive studies of administration in Lebanon are given by George

Grassmuck and Kamal Salibi, *Reformed Administration in Lebanon* (Ann Arbor, Mich.: Center for Near Eastern and North African Studies, University of Michigan, 1964), and Halim S. Abu-Izzeddin, ed., *Lebanon and Its Provinces* (Beirut: Khayats, 1963). Fahim I. Qubain, *Crisis in Lebanon* (Washington, D.C.: Middle East Institute, 1961) presents a balanced and well-researched analysis of the 1958 civil war. A partisan account of those events is provided by Camille Chamoun in his *Crise au Moyen-Orient* (Paris: Gallimard, 1963).

The Precarious Republic: Political Modernization in Lebanon (New York: Random House, 1968) by Michael C. Hudson is an exceptionally well-done study of the process and institutions of political development in Lebanon. The best and most comprehensive collection of articles on Lebanon is to be found in the book edited by Leonard Binder entitled *Politics in Lebanon* (New York: John Wiley, 1966). *Political Parties in Lebanon: The Challenge of a Fragmented Political Culture* (Ithaca, N.Y.: Cornell University Press, 1967) by Michael W. Suleiman deals with 19 parties and groups which operate inside Lebanon, though some of them have transnational aims.

chapter 12

Israel*

Israel has provided a common bond for the Jewish people since Biblical days. The hope and expectation that the Jews would return to the Promised Land long flourished among the Jews of the Diaspora (Jewish communities outside Israel). In the 19th century these spiritual, historical, and religious concepts of the relationship of Diaspora Jewry to Israel were influenced by the political changes sweeping across Europe—particularly nationalism—and were impacted on by the prevalence of anti-Semitism, which was an impetus for the Basle conference and the founding of the World Zionist Organization (W.Z.O.).

Concomitant with these political changes in Europe was a revival of Zionism in eastern Europe and Russia, which took the form of a practical response to anti-Semitism and which sought relief for the Jewish communities. Several groups were established in the 1880s to alleviate the problems of the Jewish communities in Europe through the establishment of Jewish settlements in Palestine. The "Return to Zion" movement, whose goal was immigration and settlement, established new Jewish settlements in Palestine. These were the forerunners of the massive waves of Jewish immigration of the 20th century.

In 1897 Theodor Herzl, a Viennese journalist who had proposed the establishment of a self-governing community for the Jewish people in his book *Der Judenstaat (The Jewish State)*, organized the Basle conference to bring together prominent leaders from the major Jewish communities and organizations. This assembly gave shape to a Zionist political movement and established the World Zionist Organization. The Basle Program, which became the cornerstone of Zionist ideology, enunciated the basic aim of Zionism: "To create for the Jewish people a home in Palestine secured by public law."

World War I provided an opportunity for the Zionist organization to attain its goal. Because of the endeavors of the W.Z.O. (which had grown into an

---

*Bernard Reich, assistant professor of political science, The George Washington University.

organized and worldwide movement) and the efforts of Dr. Chaim Weizmann (a prominent Zionist leader and chemist who contributed to the British war effort), the British government issued the Balfour Declaration (1917) that stated "His Majesty's Government view with favour the establishment in Palestine of a national home for the Jewish people. . . ."

By the end of the war British control had replaced Ottoman rule in Palestine. The Palestine mandate was allocated to Great Britain by the Allied Supreme Council on April 25, 1920 and was confirmed by the Council of the League of Nations on July 22, 1922. Between 1920 and the termination of the mandate in 1948, British control of Palestine was exercised by a high commissioner, who was responsible to the Colonial Office, and an executive council that was composed of senior British officials. Autonomous Arab and Jewish communal groups were established and each was granted powers of self-government within the framework created by British Orders-in-Council and the regulations of the mandate system.

JEWISH QUASI-GOVERNMENT DURING THE MANDATE PERIOD

During the mandate period, the Jewish community in Palestine (*Yishuv*) established institutions for self-government and procedures for implementing political decisions. All significant Jewish groups belonged to the organized Jewish community with the exception of the ultra-orthodox *Agudat Israel* which refused to participate because it opposed Zionist policies on the grounds of its belief that only by the hand of God, not man, could Israel be properly reestablished. The organized Jewish community chose by secret ballot the Assembly of the Elected *(Asefat Hanevcharim)*, which was composed of some 300 delegates, as its representative body. It met at least once a year, and between sessions its powers were exercised by the National Council *(Vaad Leumi)*, which was elected by the assembly.

The mandatory government entrusted the National Council with the responsibility for Jewish communal affairs and delegated it considerable autonomy. The executive committee of the National Council—through a number of self-created departments concerned with education, culture, health, social welfare, and religious affairs—acted as the administering power for the Jewish community. The council also controlled the clandestine recruitment and military training of Jewish youth in the defense force *(Hagana)*, which after independence formed the core of Israel's defense forces. The General Federation of Labor *(Histadrut)*, founded in 1920, coordinated labor-related matters and engaged in social welfare and economic endeavors.

Public activities and responsibilities in the *Yishuv* were not formally defined; instead, they were based on informal relations and agreement supported and reinforced by strong, common Zionist ideals and a widespread consensus on the need for self-discipline and common action. Political parties were established and they contested the elections for the several political organs. The political elite fulfilled various roles in the organs of the Zionist movement, the *Hagana*, and the *Histadrut*, and in other political institutions. However, the basic involvement of the *Yishuv's* political elite was with external political matters, especially relations with the British as the mandatory power and the promotion of Jewish immigration and settlement in Palestine.

Prototype political institutions, founded and developed by and for the Jewish community, laid the basis for many of Israel's public bodies and political processes. The party system was initiated and proportional representation was instituted. Not only were procedures established and tried but, more importantly, the masses and the elite gained experience in the functioning of political institutions. Several of the semi-governmental organizations created, most notably the Histadrut and the Jewish Agency, have continued to play important roles since Israel's independence. These have contributed to the growth of a highly developed system of Zionist political parties and the consequential prevalence of coalition executive bodies both in the Zionist movement and the local organs of Palestine Jewry.

The National Council functioned concurrently with the internationally recognized executive of the Jewish Agency for Palestine. The term *Jewish Agency* first appeared in international usage in the mandate entrusting the administration of Palestine to the British government. In Article 4 the W.Z.O. was recognized as:

> ...an appropriate Jewish Agency ... for the purpose of advising and cooperating with the administration of Palestine in such economic, social, and other matters as may affect the establishment of the Jewish National Home and the interests of the Jewish population in Palestine, and, subject always to the control of the administration, to assist and take part in the development of the country.

It was expected to:

> ... take steps in consultation with His Britannic Majesty's Government to secure the cooperation of all Jews who are willing to assist in the establishment of the Jewish National Home.

After ratification of the mandate, Weizmann, as President of the W.Z.O., negotiated with leading representatives of Jewish organizations and communities throughout the world for their participation in the work of the Jewish Agency. In August 1929 these negotiations culminated in the establishment of a new body, the Jewish Agency for Palestine, popularly referred to as "the Expanded Jewish Agency." The Expanded Agency, which included Jews and Jewish organizations sympathetic to the idea of a Jewish national home but not ideologically committed to Zionism, took over the activities—such as fundraising and maintaining liaison with foreign governments—for building a national home in which concerned Jews everywhere could participate. It conducted negotiations with the Palestine mandatory government, the United Kingdom, and the League of Nations. It also sought an accommodation with the Arabs, but was unsuccessful.

ESTABLISHMENT OF ISRAEL

Throughout much of the mandate period the Jewish and Arab communities were in conflict regarding the future of the territory included in the Palestine Mandate. By 1947 the British conceded that the mandate was unworkable. Because they were unable to work out a solution to satisfy the conflicting views of Arabs and Jews and because of the heavy cost in men and money, the British turned the problem over to the United Nations.

The Palestine issue was placed before the United Nations General Assembly in April 1947. The United Nations Special Committee on Palestine (UNSCOP) was created to examine the issues and to submit proposals for the solution of the problem. The committee recommended that the mandate be terminated and that the independence of Palestine be achieved without delay; however, it was divided over the future of the territory. The majority recommended partition into a Jewish state and an Arab state linked in an economic union, with Jerusalem and its environs established as an international enclave. The minority recommended that Palestine become a single federal state, Jews and Arabs enjoying autonomy in their respective areas, with Jerusalem the capital. On November 29, 1947 the United Nations General Assembly adopted the majority recommendation (the Partition Plan) over Arab opposition (they favored the minority report) by 33 votes to 13 with 10 abstentions. This laid the basis for the independence of the State of Israel.

The situation in Palestine deteriorated rapidly. Disorders, reminiscent of those of the 1920s and 1930s, broke out in all parts of the country, and as the end of the mandate approached, these degenerated into a virtual civil war. Israel's independence was declared on May 14, 1948, and the next morning General Sir Alan Gordon Cunningham, the last British high commissioner, departed. Armies of the Arab states entered Palestine and engaged in open warfare with the defense forces of the new state. The United Nations secured a truce and the military situation was stabilized in 1949 by a series of armistice agreements between Israel and the neighboring Arab states. The United Nations Truce Supervision Organization (UNTSO) was established to supervise the armistice. No general peace settlement was achieved.[1]

The provisional government of Israel, which was formed on independence and which was recognized by the major powers, was new in name only as it had begun to function *de facto* following adoption of the partition resolution. It drew on the experience gained by the Jewish community in Palestine during the mandatory period. Shortly after the partition vote, the United Nations sent a

---

[1] The still unresolved Arab-Israel dispute will be considered in greater detail below.

Palestine commission to effect a transfer from the mandatory power to the proposed Arab and Jewish states. That commission had to work exclusively with the Jewish community because neither the Arabs nor the British would cooperate. As early as March 1948, a temporary National Council of State chosen from the National Council and Jewish Agency Executive assumed control in many areas. On May 14th, the new provisional government proclaimed Israel's independence, repealed the British mandatory restrictions on immigration and the sale of land, and converted the Hagana into the Defense Army of Israel.

The provisional government comprised three elements—a state council of 38 members, which acted as parliament; a cabinet of 13 ministers, elected by the state council from among its members; and a president elected by the state council. David Ben Gurion, chairman of the Jewish Agency and leader of the dominant political party, *Mapai* (Israel Labor party), was chosen prime minister and minister of defense; Dr. Chaim Weizmann was elected president. The National Council of the mandate period formed the basis of the state council; the executive of the National Council became the cabinet; the presidency was entirely new. The provisional government directed the war with the Arab states, levied taxes, established administrative agencies, and conducted essential public services. It functioned from May 14, 1948 until early 1949. At its session just prior to the national elections of January 25, 1949, the state council adopted a transition ordinance transferring its authority to a Constituent Assembly and extending its own life until that body was convened. The functions of the provisional state council ceased when the Constituent Assembly convened on February 14, 1949. That assembly, which later declared itself the First *Knesset* (parliament), was a unicameral chamber composed of 120 members representing 12 of the 24 parties that contested the January 1949 elections.

BASIC ELEMENTS OF THE POLITICAL SYSTEM

Constitutional Consensus

Israel is a republic based on an unwritten constitution. The first act of the Constitutent Assembly in February 1949 was to enact a "Transition Law" ("Small Constitution") that became the basis of constitutional life in the state. Administrative and executive procedures were based on a combination of past experience in self-government, elements adapted from the former mandatory structure, and new legislation. According to the Small Constitution, Israel was established as a republic with a weak president and a strong cabinet and parliament. It was anticipated that this document would be replaced in due course by a more extensive one.

The First Knesset devoted much time to a profound discussion of the constitutional issue. The main poles of the debate were between those who favored a written constitution and those who believed that the time was not appropriate for imposing rigid constitutional limitations on the country. The latter group argued that a written constitution could not be framed because of constantly changing social conditions resulting from mass immigration and lack of experience with independent governmental institutions. There was also concern about the relationship between state and religion and the method of incorporating the precepts and ideals of Judaism into the proposed document.

The discussion of these issues continued for over a year. On June 13, 1950 the Knesset adopted a compromise that has indefinitely postponed the real issue. It was decided in principle that a written constitution would ultimately be adopted, but that for the time being there would not be a formal and comprehensive document. Instead, a number of fundamental or basic laws[2] would be passed dealing with specific subjects, which might in time form chapters in a consolidated constitution. By utilizing this technique, the basic laws could be tested in the light of experience prior to being cast in final form in the constitution. These basic laws are no different from any other legislation in the hierarchy of legal norms; they may be amended by the normal legislative process and do not constitute yardsticks by which to determine the constitutionality of other legislation. Thus, they have some psychological impact but no preemptive legal role.

Although a formal written constitution has not yet been constructed, there are several areas of general consensus, which together with the extant fundamental laws form the parameters of the Israel political system. Israel's "Jewishness" is perhaps the most significant area of agreement, although there is a divergence of views on some of its tenets and their interpretation. This general agreement centers on what are sometimes termed the goals or purposes of Israel, such as the "ingathering of the exiles"—the return of the Jewish people from all over the world to their ancient homeland (Eretz Israel—the Land of Israel)—and the establishment of a state based on "Jewish" principles. Those disavowing allegiance to these Jewish-Zionist ideals, or at least those dissociating themselves from their immediate manifestations, are regarded as outsiders in Israel's politics. Two groups—the Communists and the ultraorthodox Neturei Karta sect—are thus considered effectively beyond the pale of political life (except as protest groups). Consensus is similarly applied to the view that Israel should be a welfare state, although there are conflicting views regarding the specific scope and method of implementation of this principle. Foreign and security policy constitutes another area enjoying wide consensus because of its overriding importance in light of the continuing Israel-Arab dispute. The Israel Defense Forces (Zahal) enjoys an enviable military reputation which was enhanced by the 1967 war. It remains outside politics and under civilian control and is identified with the state rather than with any particular groups or parties. Its

---

[2]These have included Basic Law: The Knesset (1958), Basic Law: Israel Lands (1960), and Basic Law: President of the State (1964).

role in internal cohesion is increased by universal military service and the greater awareness of the security situation since the June war of 1967.

Political Institutions

The president, the government (cabinet), and the Knesset (parliament) perform the basic political functions of the state within the framework delineated by Israel's constitutional consensus.

The president is elected by the Knesset for a five-year term and may be reelected. He is head of state and his powers and functions are essentially of a representative character. In the sphere of foreign affairs these include signing instruments that relate to treaties ratified by the Knesset, appointing diplomatic and consular representatives, receiving foreign diplomatic representatives, and issuing consular *exequaturs*. In the domestic sphere, he has the power to grant pardons and reprieves and to commute sentences. Subsequent to nomination by the appropriate body, he appoints judges, *dayanim* (judges of the Jewish religious courts), *kadis* (judges of Muslim religious courts), the state comptroller, the president of the *Magen David Adom Association* (Red Shield of David—Israel's Red Cross), and the governor of the Bank of Israel, as well as other officials as determined by law. He signs all laws passed by the Knesset, with the exception of those relating to presidential powers, and documents to which the state seal is affixed. Official documents signed by the president require the countersignature of the prime minister or other duly authorized minister with the exception of those where another procedure is laid down, as in the case of the judges.

The president's powers and functions that relate to the formation of the government fall into a different category. After consultation at his discretion with representatives of the parties in parliament, the president selects a member of the Knesset to form a government. Until now this formal discretion has not been accompanied by any real choice because the political composition of the Knesset has clearly determined the selection. Nevertheless, situations are conceivable in which different party combinations might gain the support of the Knesset. Were this to occur, the president would fulfill a crucial political role in determining the person chosen to form a cabinet. The president also receives the resignation of the government. Another aspect of the presidential role that could have considerable political significance is his public position—his frequent visits to all parts of the country, his speeches, and his formal opening of the first session of each Knesset.

The member of parliament entrusted by the president with the task of forming the government establishes a cabinet, generally with himself as prime minister and a number of ministers who are usually, but not necessarily, members of the Knesset. The government is constitutionally instituted upon obtaining a vote of confidence from the parliament. The cabinet is collectively responsible to the Knesset, reports to it, and remains in office as long as it enjoys the confidence of that body. A government's tenure may also be terminated by ending the Knesset's tenure, by the resignation of the government on its own initiative, or by the resignation of the prime minister.

The Knesset is the supreme authority in the state. It is a unicameral body of 120 members elected by national, general, secret, direct, equal, and proportional suffrage for a term not to exceed 4 years. The main functions of the Knesset are similar to those of most modern parliaments. They include expressing a vote of confidence or no-confidence in the government, legislating, participating in the formation of national policy, and supervising the activities of the governmental administration. The Knesset must also approve the budget and taxation, elect the president of the state, recommend the appointment of the state comptroller, and participate in the appointment of judges. It is divided into a number of committees, each responsible for a specific area of legislation. Much of the Knesset's activities are performed in these committees. The ratio of committee memberships is generally proportional to that of the party's representation in the Knesset as a whole. There are some exceptions, such as the exclusion of the Communists from membership on the Foreign Policy and Security Affairs Committee.

Judicial authority is vested in religious as well as civil courts. The latter include municipal and magistrates' courts for civil and criminal actions, district courts for appeals from the lower tribunals and matters not triable by a magistrate, and a supreme court. The supreme court cannot review legislation passed by the Knesset, but it has the power to invalidate administrative actions and interpret statutes it regards contrary to the rule of law. Each major community has its own religious courts that deal with matters of personal status. Rabbinical courts have exclusive jurisdiction over Jews in marriage and divorce, and they may act on alimony, probate, succession, and other similar questions with the parties' consent. The Christian ecclesiastical courts have exclusive authority over marriage, divorce, alimony, and confirmation of wills, and they may judge other similar matters if the parties agree. The Muslim courts have exclusive jurisdiction in all matters of personal status. The judicial appointment procedure seeks to discourage political influence and judges enjoy tenure subject only to good behavior.

Two other institutions unique to the Israel system are significant elements of the political structure. The *Histadrut* and the Jewish Agency while technically extra-governmental perform governmental functions and their personnel often move to positions of responsibility within the government.

The Histadrut is of greater significance than the usual trade union organization. It is unique in that it combines trade unionism, economic enterprise, cultural and social activities, and social welfare. It is the largest single employer in Israel and has engaged in overseas projects in support of Israel's foreign policy. It has undertaken extensive building and development projects in Asia and Africa, has sent medical and construction experts to developing states, and has organized and administered an Afro-Asian Institute in Israel for the training of foreign students and officials in labor organization techniques. The governing body of the Histadrut, which sets broad general policy, is the General Convention. It is elected by the members usually every three to four years on the basis of proportional representation (the same method by which the Knesset is elected). Voting is generally along party lines. The General Convention elects the General Council, which serves as the "supreme tribunal" of the Histadrut between conventions. This council elects the executive committee, the operating agency of the Histadrut that reflects proportionately the party membership of the convention. It, in turn, creates an executive bureau that performs the day-to-day management functions.

The Jewish Agency for Israel, representing the World Zionist Organization, acts on behalf of Jews throughout the world who are concerned with Israel's development, Jewish immigration and settlement, and the cultural and spiritual ties and cooperation among the Jewish people. The agency is responsible for the organization of Jewish immigration to Israel; the reception, assistance, and settlement of these immigrants; care of children; and aid to cultural projects and institutions of higher learning. Also, it fosters Hebrew education and culture in the Diaspora, guides and assists Zionist youth movements, and organizes the work of the Jewish people in support of Israel. It works closely with the government to further these aims. These activities are financed through voluntary contributions from Jewish communities all over the globe.

The functions of the Jewish Agency were approved by the Zionist Congress in 1951 and were incorporated in the World Zionist Organization-Jewish Agency Status law passed by the Knesset in 1952. In 1954 a formal covenant between the Israel government and the Jewish Agency recognized the latter as the body representing world Jewry in the practical functions of immigration and the reception and settlement of immigrants in Israel. Accordingly, a division of functions and powers was instituted between the Israel government and the Zionist organization. The Jewish Agency was entrusted with the task of organizing and promoting immigration and it, in turn, delegated to its Department of Immigration the responsibility for implementing the crucial operation of ingathering the exiles. With the creation of an Israel Ministry of Absorption, the relationship established by the status law was placed under careful review and modified. However, the basic functions of the Jewish Agency remain and its status as a coordinate semipublic institution has been retained.

Political Parties and Political Diversity

Israel's political system is characterized by a wide range of political and social viewpoints that are given expression in political parties, newspapers, and a host of social, religious, cultural, and other organizations. Numerous minority and splinter factions freely criticize the government. This diversity has been most apparent in the multiple parties contesting parliamentary elections and in the various coalition governments that have been characteristic of Israel since its inception. (See Table 12-1 Political Parties and Knesset Election Results.) The

TABLE 12-1

Political Parties and Knesset Election Results

	1949 %	1949 Seats	1951 %	1951 Seats	1955 %	1955 Seats	1959 %	1959 Seats	1961 %	1961 Seats	1965 %	1965 Seats	1969 %	1969 Seats
Mapai	35.7	46	37.3	45	32.2	40	38.2	47	34.7	42	In Alignment		In Alignment	
Mapam[a]	14.7	19	12.5	15	7.3	9	7.2	9	7.5	9	6.6	8	In Alignment	
Ahdut Avodah[a]	–	–	–	–	8.2	10	6.0	7	6.6	8	In Alignment		In Alignment	
Alignment of Mapai and Ahdut Avodah	–	–	–	–	–	–	–	–	–	–	36.7	45	–	–
Rafi[b]	–	–	–	–	–	–	–	–	–	–	7.9	10	In Alignment	
Israel Labor[c]	–	–	–	–	–	–	–	–	–	–	–	–	In Alignment	
Alignment of Israel Labor and Mapam	–	–	–	–	–	–	–	–	–	–	–	–	46.2	56
State List[d]	–	–	–	–	–	–	–	–	–	–	–	–	3.1	4
Herut	11.5	14	6.6	8	12.6	15	13.6	17	13.8	17	–	–	–	–
General Zionists	5.2	7	16.2	20	10.2	13	6.2	8	–	–	–	–	–	–
Progressives	4.1	5	3.2	4	4.4	5	4.6	6	–	–	–	–	–	–
Liberal[e]	–	–	–	–	–	–	–	–	13.6	17	–	–	–	–
Gahal[f]	–	–	–	–	–	–	–	–	–	–	21.3	26	21.7	26
Independent Liberals[g]	–	–	–	–	–	–	–	–	–	–	3.8	5	3.2	4
Free Center[h]	–	–	–	–	–	–	–	–	–	–	–	–	1.2	2

[a] Included in Mapam 1949 and 1951.
[b] Formed 1965–Ben Gurion splinter group from Mapai.
[c] Formed 1968–merger of Mapai, Rafi, Ahdut Avodah.
[d] Ben Gurion splinter group from Israel Labor.
[e] Formed 1961–merger of General Zionists and Progressives.
[f] Formed 1965–merger of Herut and majority of Liberal party.
[g] Minority of Liberal party not joining in merger with Herut.
[h] Formed 1968–splinter group from Herut.

Party	%	seats	%	seats	%	seats	%	seats	%	seats	%	seats	%	seats
United Religious Front	12.2	16[i]	—	—	—	—	—	—	—	—	—	—	—	—
Mizrahi	—	—	1.5	2	—	—	—	—	—	—	—	—	—	—
Hapoel Hamizrahi	—	—	6.7	8	—	—	—	—	—	—	—	—	—	—
National Religious[j]	—	—	—	—	9.1	11	9.9	12	9.8	12	9.0	11	9.7	12
Agudat Israel[k]	—	—	—	—	—	—	—	—	3.7	4	3.3	4	3.2	4
Paolei Agudat Israel[k]	—	—	—	—	—	—	—	—	1.9	2	1.8	2	1.8	2
Torah Religious Front[l]	—	—	3.6	5	4.7	6	4.7	6	—	—	—	—	—	—
Sephardim	3.5	4	1.8	2	—	—	—	—	—	—	—	—	—	—
Fighters list	1.2	1	—	—	—	—	—	—	—	—	—	—	—	—
Women's International Zionist Organization (WIZO)	1.2	1	—	—	—	—	—	—	—	—	—	—	—	—
Yemenites	1.0	1	1.2	1	—	—	—	—	—	—	—	—	—	—
Arab Democratic list	1.7	2	2.4	3	1.8	2	1.3	2	1.6	2	2.0	2	—	—
Arab Progress and Work	—	—	1.2	1	1.5	2	1.1	1	—	—	—	—	—	—
Arab Farmers and Development	—	—	1.1	1	1.2	1	1.2	2	1.9	2	1.4	2	—	—
Arab Cooperation and Brotherhood	—	—	—	—	—	—	—	—	—	—	—	—	—	—
Alignment—affiliated Arab and Druse lists	—	—	—	—	—	—	—	—	—	—	—	—	3.5	4
Communist[m]	3.5	4	4.0	5	4.5	6	2.8	3	4.2	5	—	—	—	—
New Communists (Rakah)[m]	—	—	—	—	—	—	—	—	—	—	2.3	3	2.8	3
Israel Communists (Maki)[m]	—	—	—	—	—	—	—	—	—	—	1.1	1	1.2	1
Haolam Hazeh	—	—	—	—	—	—	—	—	—	—	1.2	1	1.2	2

[i] Elected as follows: Hapoel Hamizrahi, 6; Mizrahi, 4; Agudat Israel, 3; Poalei Agudat Israel, 3.

[j] Merger—Mizrahi and Hapoel Mizrahi.

[k] In Torah Religious Front until 1961 elections.

[l] Joint list of Agudat Israel and Poalei Agudat Israel.

[m] Split of Communist party in 1965 resulted in formation of Rakah and Maki.

Knesset is elected by a countrywide proportional representation (PR) system. Votes are cast for party lists and a minimum of 1 percent of the votes is required to secure a seat. The PR system allows political fragmentation to continue. However, the profusion of parties basically results from the strongly ideological character of most of these parties and reflects the variety and intensity of views held by various segments of the population on economic, religious, and other matters. The principle of proportional representation is a historical precedent utilized by the Tel Aviv municipality between the World Wars; by the National Council in the period of the mandate; and by the Histadrut and the Zionist congresses. Historical developments, mostly during the pre-independence period, and personal differences among the political elite are also important elements in fostering party proliferation.

Israel's parties range over the full political spectrum and express numerous combinations of political and economic views. However, the parties can be classified by their relationship to the ruling coalition. Mapai (*Mifleget Poale Eretz Yisrael*—Israel Labor party), the major member of all cabinet coalitions, is the nucleus of political life. A second group of parties is composed of those that have joined with Mapai in the government coalition at one time or another. Mapai's coalition partners have included parties both to its right and left, as well as those representing the several religious groups. A third category consists of those that have remained outside the governing coalition—the Communists and until the June 1967 conflict, the far-right *Herut* (Freedom) party. Only twice have the coalitions been truly broad-based—the pre-election provisional government and the government of National Unity formed during the 1967 crisis and maintained following the 1969 elections. Both were unusual in that they were coalitions established in times of national stress.

Mapai, organized in 1930 as a result of the merger of two smaller parties, has been the dominant party in Israel. Its role was virtually unchallenged prior to statehood. It was in control of the Assembly of the Elected and the National Council in the semiautonomous Jewish government in Palestine. In the 1931 elections it received 43.7 percent of the vote for the Assembly of the Elected and gained control of the National Council, which it maintained until 1948. It has continued its dominant role since statehood. In elections for the Knesset it has consistently obtained the largest single percentage of votes, usually about one third of the total. It has been the major member of all government coalitions and has ordinarily held the portfolios of prime minister, minister of defense, foreign minister, and finance minister. Its role in the Jewish Agency has also been significant. Although the Jewish Agency is governed by a coalition of all Israel parties, Mapai has had the largest representation on the executive board and for the most part has held the chairmanship and other major posts. Mapai has also generally won the largest bloc of representation in the Histadrut, often a majority, and has been the controlling party on the executive board. The continuing role of Mapai as the most important member of the parliament and of the cabinet, and its status in the Jewish Agency and Histadrut, are the basis for its unique position of influence and control in the Israel system. The party is one of the political institutions of the country and is identified with the state in the minds of many voters. Also, because of its long tenure of office it has permeated the governmental, administrative, economic, and other institutions of Israel.

On January 21, 1968, Mapai merged with two other labor parties, *Ahdut Ha'avoda-Poale Zion* (Unity of Labor Workers of Zion) and *Rafi* (Israel Labor List), to form *Mifleget Ha'avoda Ha-Israelit* (Israel Labor party). Together with the Mapai-affiliated Arab parties, the new party held 59 out of the 120 votes in the Knesset, only two short of a majority.[3] The turning point that precipitated the trend toward the merger of the labor parties was the June war of 1967. The Arab threat called for the establishment of a broadly based government of National Unity. When the termination of the war did not bring peace and the continuation of the conflict with an accelerated tempo was evident, prudence dictated the maintenance of the broader coalition to present a solid front in international negotiations. The need for cooperation for reasons of security and defense contributed greatly to the creation of a climate suitable to the consummation of the merger.

The establishment of the Israel Labor party might eventually bring about the parliamentary majority that Mapai has not previously succeeded in achieving and might presage the end of coalition government. Although the alignment of the Israel Labor party and Mapam did not secure a majority in the 1969 elections, Mapai will remain the single most important factor in Israel politics. Israel's political experience suggests that the merger will not eliminate the differences between the coalition's components but rather that it will shift the quarrels from the interparty to the intraparty sphere. It is within the Israel Labor party that the problems of leadership and succession will find a solution. This shift in the arena of problem-solving was clearly indicated by the maneuvering within the party from the time of the merger to the elections of 1969, a period which included the task of finding a successor to Prime Minister Levi Eshkol after his sudden death, and in Mrs. Meir's post-election efforts to form a broad-based coalition cabinet.

The multiplicity of parties has necessitated coalition cabinets, which nonetheless, have proved quite stable. Israel had only three prime ministers during its first two decades of independence. Although there have been a number of cabinet changes, most have been essentially formal: they followed the election of a new Knesset, the choice of a president, the retirement of Ben Gurion, his return to public life, his second retirement, the 1967 crisis and war, the death of Eshkol, and so forth. The stability of Israel's cabinets has been due to a number of factors. The most important are the personal stabilizing influence of Ben Gurion, Sharett, Eshkol, and Golda Meir during their tenure as prime minister and the preponderant strength of Mapai, which has had one-third or more mandates in every Knesset and has been the basis of every cabinet. The rigorous discipline of Israel's parties has curbed irresponsible action by individual

---

[3] In November 1968 this party and *Mapam* (United Workers' party) agreed to an alliance for submission of joint lists of candidates at the 1969 Knesset elections.

Knesset members. Finally, continuity of policy has been enhanced by the reappointment of many ministers in reorganized cabinets.

The coalition system has resulted in the acceptance of bargaining as a procedure for the allocation of portfolios and the distribution of power, both in the government and at high levels of administration. This has permitted the religious parties—National Religious, Agudat Israel, Poale Agudat Israel—to play strong roles in government decision-making because they were essential to secure a majority in the Knesset. The inevitable clash of interests and the persistence of partisan loyalties implicit in this procedure have limited governmental flexibility and to an extent have reduced the efficiency of the administrative machinery. Since members of the Knesset do not represent any specific constituency and since they depend on party backing for election and reelection, their attitude and actions have frequently been motivated more by party considerations than by the general will. Although there have been various suggestions for electoral reform, the basic PR system, which helps perpetuate political diversity, persists.

DOMESTIC POLICIES AND ISSUES

Jewish immigration, the status of the Oriental Jewish population, the Arab minority, the pressures of economic needs and plans, and the relationship between religion and the state are the basic domestic issues facing Israel's political system.

"Ingathering of the Exiles" and the "Oriental Problem"

A basic policy which has left its mark on every aspect of life in Israel is the encouragement of Jewish immigration. The commitment to unfettered Jewish immigration was articulated initially in Israel's Declaration of Independence,[4] was affirmed in the Law of Return of July 5, 1950,[5] and has been reinforced by the programs and actions of successive Israel governments. This concept of ingathering the exiles has had overwhelming support in parliament and from the Jewish population, and it has been implemented almost without regard to the economic costs and social dislocations caused by the rapid and massive influx of people.

Israel's commitment to immigration results from its view of its mission as the emissary of the exiled and scattered Jewish people—it is an outward expression of a bond of faith between Israel and world Jewry. It removes Jews from areas of distress and is thus envisaged as meeting the needs of world Jewry. It serves Israel's needs by providing manpower necessary for Israel's security and development.

---

[4] The Declaration of Independence proclaimed: "the State of Israel will be open to the immigration of Jews from all countries of their dispersion."

[5] The Law of Return described *Aliya* (immigration of Jews for settlement in Israel) in the following terms: "Every Jew has the right to come to this country as an *'oleh'* (Jew Immigrating to Israel)."

Myriad problems, some of them highly significant, have resulted from this policy. Unlike the period of the mandate when immigration was selective and severely limited by British-imposed restrictions, Israel has admitted whole communities, virtually without regard to their economic usefulness or the current ability of the country to deal with them. (See Table 12-2 Population and Jewish Immigration 1948-1967.) Initially the immigrants were the remnants of European Jewry, some of whom had been interned on Cyprus by the British. During the nascent years of Israel's independence, the Jewish communities of the Moslem states of the Middle East and North Africa arrived in massive numbers. The Jews of Yemen (about 45,000) and Iraq (about 123,000) were brought to Israel by air lift, popularly known as "Operation Magic Carpet" and "Operation Ali Baba." Between 1919 and 1948, about 90 percent of the Jewish immigrants came from Europe or other Western countries. Since 1948, immigration has been overwhelmingly non-Western.[6] (See Table 12-3 Jewish Immigration by Continent of Birth.)

TABLE 12-2
Population[a] and Jewish Immigration[b] 1948-1967

| Year | Immigration | Population at End of Year | | |
		Jews	Non Jews	Total
1948	101,828[c]	758,702	120,000	879,000[d]
1949	239,576	1,013,871	160,000	1,173,871
1950	170,249	1,202,992	167,101	1,370,094
1951	175,095	1,404,392	173,433	1,577,825
1952	24,369	1,450,217	179,302	1,629,519
1953	11,326	1,483,641	185,776	1,669,417
1954	18,370	1,526,009	191,805	1,717,814
1955	37,478	1,590,519	189,556	1,789,075
1956	56,234	1,667,455	204,935	1,872,390
1957	71,224	1,762,741	213,213	1,975,954
1958	27,082	1,810,148	221,524	2,031,072
1959	23,895	1,858,841	229,344	2,088,685
1960	24,510	1,911,200	239,200	2,150,400
1961	47,638	1,981,700	252,500	2,234,200
1962	61,328	2,068,900	262,900	2,331,800
1963	64,364	2,155,500	274,600	2,430,100
1964	54,716	2,239,000	286,400	2,525,600
1965	30,736	2,299,100	299,300	2,598,400
1966	15,730	2,344,900	312,500	2,657,400
1967	14,327	2,383,600	390,300	2,773,900

[a]Until 1960: present population; 1961-1966: permanent population, to nearest thousand.
[b]Including tourists who became permanent residents.
[c]May 15 to December 31.
[d]Estimated.
Source: Israel Ministry for Foreign Affairs, Information Division, *Facts About Israel 1969*, p. 59.

---

[6]In somewhat general and oversimplified terms, immigrants to Israel from non-Western countries are referred to as "Orientals" and the problem of integrating them into Israel's society is considered under the rubric of the "Oriental problem."

TABLE 12-3
Jewish Immigration by Continent of Birth

	America, Europe and Oceania	%	Asia and Africa	%	Not Stated	Total
1919-5/14/48 . . .	385,006	89.6	44,809	10.4	22,283	452,158
5/15/48-1951 . . .	334,971	50.3	330,456	49.7	18,774	684,201
1952-1954	11,187	21.9	39,978	78.1	28	51,193
1955-1957	49,630	30.0	110,714	69.1	617	160,961
1958-1960	46,460	64.8	25,926	35.8	7	72,393
1961-1964	86,748	39.4	133,561	60.6	14	*220,323
1965-1966	22,562	53.8	19,390	46.2	–	41,952
1948-1966	551,558	45.5	660,025	54.5	19,440	1,231,023

Source: Israel Ministry for Foreign Affairs, Information Division, *Facts About Israel 1969*, p. 59.

Geographically Israel is an Oriental country; culturally and socially, it is Western-oriented. The ideology and actions of the early Zionists, which were based on 19th-century European nationalism, resulted in institutions that laid the foundations for an essentially European culture in Palestine. Subsequent immigration strengthened and accelerated the trend of Westernizing Palestine. The Occidental immigrants built up the Yishuv structure of land settlement, trade unions, political parties, and education in preparation for a Jewish national state on which all their aspirations were concentrated. In this environment, the Occidental-oriented institutions of the new state were formed. Future immigrants had to adapt themselves to the society that had formed these institutions. This presented a problem when mass immigration from non-Western countries began.

Massive immigration of Jews from the neighboring Arab states, and to a lesser extent from other parts of Asia and Africa, has resulted in an influx of large numbers of people whose societal and cultural traditions are akin to the Oriental populations among whom they lived for generations, and thus different from their Western coreligionists. Arabic is often their native tongue, and their customs, practices, and attitudes are those of the East rather than the West. Family loyalty is strong; concepts of responsibility very often do not transcend the family. Suspicion of government and all its ramifications is great; resistance to taxation, rationing, and other controls is prevalent. In part because of their lack of education and experience, few members of the Oriental community have succeeded in achieving responsible government posts. Their living conditions and standards are generally lower than those of the Occidental community and only a small number attend Israel's universities.

Numerous difficulties have beset efforts to settle and absorb the masses of immigrants. Economic, social, and cultural assimilation of the immigrants in a short time-span would have been a formidable undertaking for a small country even under the most favorable conditions. In Israel, this has been attempted despite the obstacles posed by limited resources, defense needs, and the composition and character of the new immigration. Israel has been obliged to undertake the training or retraining of the immigrants for gainful employment and to provide housing, schooling, and medical facilities. While the material problems have not yet been fully solved, they are well-defined, and manifold activities are directed towards their solution. These include systematic establishment of new agricultural settlements in which newcomers are settled soon after their arrival (the "ship-to-settlement" policy) and where they are provided with training and work, medical treatment, a well-developed system of national insurance, and housing.

The non material problems, which are essentially those of cultural and social acclimation, are more complex and their resolution will require much time. Although the basic religious tradition of the Jewish population is an asset as it provides a common core of values and ideals, there are major differences in outlook, values, frames of reference, levels of aspiration, and various other social and cultural components. Army service, which emphasizes education as well as the experience of common living and working and learning the Hebrew language, helps to ameliorate the processes of acculturation and to encourage evolution in the direction of a unified, multicultural society. Despite these efforts, the integration of immigrants into Israel's society remains the state's greatest social problem.

The Arab Minority

The Arabs of Israel are confronted by problems qualitatively different from those facing Jewish immigrants.[7] Following Israel's independence and as a result of the ensuing war between Israel and the Arab states, a large number of Arabs who had lived in that part of Palestine that is now Israel participated in a mass flight and took up residence in Arab states, either as refugees or members of their permanent populations. The Arabs who chose to remain in Israel—and who now number about 300,000—form Israel's Arab community.

Immediately after the 1949 armistice agreements, activities of the Arab community were regarded primarily as functions of Israel's security system and therefore most of the areas inhabited by the Arabs were placed under military control. Military government was established in these districts and special defense and security zones were created. Israel's Arabs were granted citizenship with full legal equality but were forbidden to travel into or out of security areas without permission of the military. Military courts were established in which trials could be held in closed session. With the consent of the Minister of

---

[7]In this section, the references to the Arabs of Israel or the Arab minority are to those Arabs who have lived in Israel since its independence, or their offspring, and who are Israel citizens and not to the Arabs in those areas occupied by Israel during the June war.

Defense, the military commanders could limit individual movements, impose restrictions on employment and business, issue deportation orders, search and seize, and detain a person if it were deemed necessary for security purposes.

Those who argued in support of the military administration saw it as a means of controlling the Arab population and preventing infiltration, sabotage, and espionage. Furthermore, it was contended that the very existence of the military administration was an important deterrent measure. As evidence developed that the Israel Arabs were not disloyal, pressure for relaxation and then for total abolition of military restrictions grew in the Knesset and in public debate. The restrictions were gradually modified and on December 1, 1966 military government was abolished. Functions that had been exercised by the military government were transferred to relevant civilian authorities.

The major long-run problem for Israel's Arab minority is its social integration. Although Israel Arabs vote, sit in the Knesset, serve in government offices, have their own schools and courts, and prosper materially, they face difficulties in adjusting to Israel's modern Jewish-Western-oriented society. Most of the major factors facilitating Jewish integration are not operative with regard to the Arab minority. The Arabs tend to live in separate villages and in separate sections of the major cities. They speak Arabic, attend a separate public school system, and do not serve in the army. Centuries of foreign rule have left their impact on the basic political attitudes of the Arabs—despotic rule, violence, and extortion have engendered an attitude of suspicion and mistrust toward government. The ideological expression of these influences is a form of fatalism and determinism that relegates responsibility for faults to external forces: fate, the government, the devil, imperialism, or Zionism. There is also an emotional strain because of Israel's conflict with the Arab states and the dual identification of those who are both citizens of Israel and Arab.

Successive Israel governments have sought to bring about a more complete integration of its Arab citizens into the life of the country and to foster their economic, social, and cultural advancement. However, the problem is complex and continuing efforts are indicated.

Economic Problems

The policy of unrestricted immigration and the problems it generates, the scarcity of natural resources, and the security requirements imposed on Israel by the continuing hostility of its Arab neighbors impact Israel's economic development efforts.

Israel is poor in natural resources and thus agricultural land is a prime asset. A major obstacle is the scarcity of water, which continues to be used at an increasingly rapid pace. The Jordan River, which plays an important role in Israel's National Water Plan, is utilized to improve agricultural production for both the increasing population and for export.

Israel seeks to produce goods and generate sufficient revenues to balance its budget and achieve a stable balance of payments. In Israel's earlier years this was achieved through income from several outside sources. This included more than $5 billion in foreign capital, of which an estimated 50 percent came from private sources in the United States through the efforts of the United Jewish Appeal, Hadassah, and other agencies. German reparations payments, which ended in 1966, totalled about $900 million while foreign currency income from restitution payments to individuals totalled more than $850 million. Although U.S. grant aid to Israel ended in 1962, Public Law 480 Food for Peace programs continue and loans have been extended by the Export-Import Bank. Much of the foreign currency income is directed toward Israel's industrial program and has resulted in increased exports.

Israel's economic position has improved greatly since 1948. It has met the problems of material shortages, inflation, and much of the task of settling a million immigrants while substantially increasing its per capita gross national product and its gold and foreign exchange reserves. Having achieved relative self-sufficiency in agriculture, Israel now aims at expanding and modernizing the industrial sector, particularly those industries with export potential that can be developed to offset the country's large imbalance of commodity trade. Israel seeks the participation of foreign financial activity to supplement its own investments. To this end it has offered tax benefits, guarantees of convertibility, and repatriation of profits and capital. At the same time, Israel's objectives include a reduction in its reliance on foreign financial assistance. The combination of this and related goals of improving the competitive efficiency of Israel's production and of cultivating overseas markets will continue to provide the framework for much of its future economic planning.

Religion and the State

Israel's Jewishness is a basic element underlying its political system and provides the rationale for many of Israel's activities and policies. However, the overwhelmingly Jewish character of the state does not ensure agreement on the proper relationship between religion and the state, between the religious and secular authorities, nor on the methods and techniques to be employed by religious authorities. The poles of the debate on the role of religion in Israel are theocracy and secularism: One segment of the population seeks to turn Israel into a theocratic state; the other wishes to make it fully secular. A large uncommitted group formulates its position on each issue as it occurs. The extreme positions have had to compromise, thereby coexisting under middle-of-the-road arrangements.

Although Israel's government is secular, it takes into account the requisites of the segment of the population that observes religious tradition. The Israel Ministry of Religious Affairs is concerned with meeting Jewish religious requirements, such as the supply of ritually killed (kosher) meat, rabbinical courts, and religious schools (*Yeshivot*), as well as with meeting religious needs of the non-Jewish communities that enjoy religious autonomy. These functions are noncontroversial; few dispute the duty of the government to meet the religious requirements of the people. Nevertheless, a subject of sharp and recurrent controversy is the extent to which religious observance or restriction is directly or indirectly imposed on the entire Jewish population. Thus, the less observant Jews of Israel often argue that they do not possess religious freedom because of governmental acquiescence to demands of the observant Jewish groups to restrict public services on the Sabbath, because of the limitations placed on the role of non-Orthodox Judaism in Israel, and so forth. The observant community, through its own political parties and through its membership in government coalitions, has been able to achieve government agreement to establish separate school systems, to exempt observant girls from army service, and to curtail almost all business and public activity on the Sabbath.

The religious parties have been able to secure such concessions because the need for coalition governments has given the religious parties a larger voice in politics than is dictated by their numerical strength. In its search for coalition partners, Mapai has found that the demands of the religious parties are in areas of least concern to Mapai's leadership and thus they are attractive coalition members. Whereas the demands of other parties are in the realm of foreign policy, security, or economics—all central to Mapai's thinking—the concerns of the religious parties are generally limited to matters impinging on religion and personal status, and these are of less concern. Nevertheless, there have been several government crises over religious questions. The disagreement on incorporation of principles of religion in a constitutional document marked the Knesset debate on the preparation of a written constitution and suggested that a crisis of major proportions was imminent. There have been disagreements over the religious education of children in immigration camps, compulsory military service for women, the question of uniform national education, and even on the criteria to be applied to determine if a given individual is to be considered a Jew according to Israel's laws. After the Israel occupation of Jerusalem in 1967, a major controversy developed with regard to the status of the Western (or Wailing) Wall and the surrounding areas where the Temple of Solomon once stood. Those of different religious orientations viewed the treatment of the area in different ways although they all agreed that it was among the holiest of Jewish sites. These and numerous non-cabinet issues have been indicative of the religion-state relationship in Israel and foreshadow a continuing effort to define Judaism's precise role in everyday Israel.

FOREIGN AND SECURITY POLICY

The issues facing the Israel political system in the domestic sphere are closely linked with the more primary concerns of existence and security that are functions of Israel's foreign and security policy. Several factors impact on Israel's regional and international foreign and security policy formulation. These include the hostility of the Arab states as manifested in the continuing Israel-Arab dispute, the East-West conflict in its regional context, and concern for the Jewish communities in the Diaspora and their relationship with Israel. These factors are readily apparent in the several major foreign and security policy areas where Israel's representatives concentrate their policy efforts.

Israel-Arab Relations

The preeminent problem facing Israel and that which affects all of its policies and activities—both domestic and international—is its conflict with the Arab states. Israel's foreign relations have been influenced by this dispute in every area of concern and application since the achievement of independence. The pursuit of peace and the difficulties of existing in a region of hostility in the interim are basic conditioning factors of Israel's political life and its foreign and security policy.

The dispute between Israel and the Arab states is essentially the result of the conflict (in both theory and practical application) of two ideologies—Zionism and Arab nationalism. Zionism or Jewish nationalism strove to create a Jewish National Home and to achieve the ingathering of the exiles to protect and preserve world Jewry. This Jewish home could be established only in Palestine—its historical location. Arab nationalists seek the independence and unity of all Arab states and deem Palestine an integral part of the Arab world.

World War I provided the setting for the conflict of these opposing views. During the war, the British entered into arrangements with the French, the Arabs, and the Zionists which laid the basis for the division of the Ottoman Empire and provided the foundation for the claims of both Arab and Jewish nationalists in their dispute for control of Palestine. These included an exchange of correspondence between Sherif Husein of Mecca and Sir Henry McMahon, the British high commissioner for Egypt; the Sykes-Picot Agreement; and the Balfour Declaration. The British chose to retain control of Palestine following the war and thus the mandate period provided the context for the conflict between the Jewish and Arab communitiies of Palestine—the adherents of the opposing ideologies. The Zionists adopted a program designed to secure the establishment of a Jewish homeland in Palestine. The Arabs decided on noncooperation with the mandatory regime in an effort to achieve Arab self-government and independence. They protested Jewish immigration and land purchases in an effort to limit the number and influence of Jews in Palestine to ensure an Arab majority and Arab control when self-determination was implemented.

The submission of the Palestine problem to the United Nations in 1947 provided an opportunity for the antagonists to present their positions. The resultant Partition Plan was generally favored by the Jewish Agency while the Arab delegates strongly opposed it.

Increased hostility between the Arab and Jewish communities in Palestine followed the adoption of the partition resolution and led to conflict in late 1947. Upon Israel's declaration of independence in May 1948, the scope of the conflict was enlarged when the Arab League notified the United Nations that it was intervening in Palestine in order to restore the territory to the Palestine Arabs. In fact, the League's goal was to thwart the partition resolution and prevent the establishment of Israel. The ensuing war was halted by armistice agreements between Israel and the four contiguous Arab states (Egypt, Syria, Lebanon, and Trans-Jordan), which were signed between February and July 1949. War occurred again in 1956 and 1967, and small-scale conflict has been characteristic of the region. The fundamental issue is Israel's right to exist and the problems that characterize the Arab-Israel dispute are symptomatic of disagreement on this point. The Arab refusal to accept Israel as an independent state with defined territory and boundaries has prompted discord over the status of Jerusalem, the future of the refugees, the blockade of the Suez Canal and the Gulf of Aqaba to Israel's shipping, and the utilization of the waters of the Jordan River.

Prior to the establishment of Israel it was realized that peace and cooperation with neighboring states were vital for the survival and development of the Jewish state. Since 1948, these goals have remained cornerstones of Israel's foreign policy. The Declaration of the Establishment of the State of Israel proclaimed:

> We extend our hand to all neighbouring states and their peoples in an offer of peace and good neighbourliness, and appeal to them to establish bonds of cooperation and mutual help with the sovereign Jewish people settled in its own land. The State of Israel is prepared to do its share in common effort for the advancement of the entire Middle East.

Successive Israel governments have included these concepts in their official programs. Israel has made numerous overtures to the Arab states to terminate the dispute and has sought to negotiate a comprehensive peace settlement. Its approach rests on the belief that an end to the existing state of belligerency and tension would serve its national interest. However, there has been no progress toward that end.

One of the most controversial issues between the Arab states and Israel is the status of the Palestinian Arabs who fled Israel in 1948. Indeed, the factors precipitating the refugee flight and the actual number of refugees remain subjects of debate. Israel has dwelt on the point that the Arab League exhorted the Palestinians to temporarily flee until the invading Arab armies defeated the new state, and then return. Israel holds that the mass Palestinian Arab emigration was to facilitate the tactical military operations of the invading Arab armies and to indicate to the world that the Palestinian Arabs were being mistreated by Israel. The Arab states have charged that the flight of these Arabs was deliberately fostered by Israel in order to make room for the influx of Jewish immigrants and to facilitate confiscation of Arab lands and other possessions. Contributing factors were the confusion, violence, and anarchy that pervaded the area after the British withdrawal.

On November 19, 1948 the United Nations General Assembly created the United Nations Relief for Palestine Refugees (UNRPR) to provide immediate relief, especially food, clothing, and fuel. On December 8, 1949 UNRPR was succeeded by the United Nations Relief and Works Agency for Palestine Refugees in the Near East (UNRWA), to which the General Assembly assigned the task of relief and a considerable range of technical services for the health, welfare, education, and training of the refugees. UNRWA has established refugee camps in which it provides shelter for refugees. It also distributes basic food rations, operates health centers, and educates refugee children.[8]

There has been no progress on the refugee issue and the June war exacerbated the situation. Israel views the problem as part of the broader question of peace and security, and its policy has stressed resettlement of the refugees in Arab states with compensation for property abandoned in Israel. Limited repatriation, such as for reuniting families, would be feasible. It has based its position in part on the *de facto* exchange of population that has occurred since Israel's establishment. Israel has accepted and absorbed more than 500,000 Jewish emigrants from the Arab states. Thus, it is argued, Israel has taken Jewish refugees from Arab states and therefore the Arab states should accept Arab refugees from Israel. The Arab states demand that the Arab refugees be repatriated and given full compensation for their properties. They insist that until the refugee question is satisfactorily solved there can be no discussion regarding recognition of Israel or peace treaties.

The June 1967 war modified the content of the issues central to Israel-Arab relations. Israel occupies the Gaza Strip, the Sinai Peninsula, the west bank of the Jordan River, the city of Jerusalem, and the Syrian (Golan) heights. The resultant strategic posture is superior to any it has previously occupied. Further, Israel has indicated that it will not withdraw from those occupied territories until there are peace agreements with the Arabs that recognize Israel's sovereignty and independence. The Arab states contend that negotiations are impossible as long as Israel occupies Arab territories. The 1967 conflict thus intensified the issues between the parties.

Once it became clear to Israel that peace would not follow the signing of the armistice agreements with the Arab states after its War of Independence, Israel's major foreign and security policy efforts were directed beyond the circle of the surrounding Arab states. Israel's policy toward the Arab world has consisted of constant reiteration of its desire for peace and its willingness to meet Arab representatives at any time, with no preconditions, to discuss peace. At the same time, it has embarked on a course designed to clearly indicate to the Arab states that it intends to continue to exist as a secure state in the Middle East. It has sought to achieve a position of deterrent strength through national armed power and international support for its position.

Thus, Israel has sought to convince the Arab states to accept peaceful coexistence or, alternatively, to ensure Israel's ability to defend itself in the

---

[8]UNRWA's definition of an Arab refugee eligible for relief is a person who resided in Palestine for at least two years prior to the outbreak of hostilities on May 15, 1948 and who, as a result of this conflict, lost both his home and means of livelihood. The exact number of refugees who meet UNRWA's criteria and are thus eligible for assistance has never been explicitly determined.

event of combat. This was succinctly stated by then Prime Minister David Ben Gurion in the Knesset in May 1963:

> Israel's policy, therefore, is to prevent war, and war can be prevented—not by saying peace when there is no peace, but in two ways and two ways alone: by constantly strengthening the deterrent power of the Israel Defence Forces, and by securing the moral and political support of all those world forces that are as concerned as we are for the maintenance of peace in this area.

Israel's assessment is of a continuing Arab hostility that places it in a perilous situation. It realizes the natural Arab advantages in population, size, strategic posture, financial resources, and international bargaining power. It also realizes the risks of war and the uneven consequences of conflict. If the Arabs were defeated, the losses might encompass territory, manpower, equipment, or other political and economic consequences. If, on the other hand, Israel were defeated, it might mean the end of its existence—politicide.

Israel's response to Arab hostility has consisted of a coordinated effort in the domestic and foreign policy spheres. Internally, it has geared development planning to its defense requirements and has instituted a national service concept that assures rapid mobilization of a military force prepared to meet its defense needs. Internationally, Israel has sought to ensure a reliable supply of essential military equipment and other requisites for its defense posture. It has sought to befriend states in the international community, some of whom might provide diplomatic and political support for its integrity.

Israel and the Powers

Israel's leaders early recognized the crucial role of the great powers in ensuring the country's defense and integrity. In the Middle East the regional manifestation of the East-West contest for influence has provided the context for Israel's relations with the Soviet Union and the United States, in both their own rights and as leaders of the East and West, respectively.

In the euphoric days following independence, Israel's leaders assumed that neutrality in the cold war was possible and that Israel could establish friendly relations with both East and West. This was in accord with Israel's perception of its national interest and seemed a realistic assessment in light of the policies of both powers in support of Israel's position between 1947 and 1949. Both the United States and the Soviet Union voted for the partition resolution, supported Israel's applications for United Nations' membership, supplied arms during its War of Independence, and permitted Jewish emigration. Apparent competition between the United States and the Soviet Union for the favor of the new state was viewed by Israel's leaders as an auspicious sign presaging a policy of noncommitment in the East-West conflict. Noncommitment has remained Israel's preferred policy, but practical factors have resulted in increasing identification with the West—a posture that has become clearer since the June War.

Israel and the Soviet Union. Initially, Israel's policy toward the Soviet Union was designed to achieve the friendship and support of the Soviet Union and the Soviet bloc and, subsequently, to minimize the negative Soviet posture. At the same time, Israel has sought to secure and maintain the well-being of the Jewish communities in the Soviet Union and in the Soviet bloc and to ensure their ability to emigrate to Israel. These goals, resulting from Israel's *raison d'etre*, have not been accorded equal weight in foreign policy planning. During the initial period of Soviet support for the new state, it was held that the means to the second objective was through attainment of the first. With the subsequent shift in Soviet policy toward support of the Arab states against Israel, the second objective has received priority attention.

During the 1947-1949 honeymoon period, Israel hoped for friendship, support, and aid from the Soviet bloc as well as for immigration to Israel of Soviet Jewry. This hope was not fulfilled. Traditional Communist policies, including a ban on Zionism and Jewish emigration from the Soviet Union, were not basically modified and the political support of 1947 and 1948 was not followed by practical economic and technical assistance. Deterioration of Soviet-Israel relations between 1949 and 1953 was climaxed by the Slansky trial in Prague and the Moscow "doctors' plot" that allegedly linked Jews and Zionism with asserted treasonable cabals. Public opinion in Israel against the Soviet Union mounted and on February 12, 1953 a bomb exploded in the Soviet Legation in Tel Aviv. The Soviet Union broke diplomatic relations with Israel and they were not resumed until July of that year. The rupture of diplomatic relations prompted Israel to reconsider its hope for Soviet friendship and support. With the exception of incurable optimists who waited for a metamorphosis in Soviet policy and Israel's Communist party and fellow travelers, who were committed to a belief in the ultimate victory of the socialist system, Israel's leaders were generally convinced of the improbability of Israel-Soviet friendship and cooperation. Soviet support and expanded relations with the Arab states tended to confirm this view. Soviet use of the veto power in the Security Council on matters of little direct concern to the U.S.S.R. but of great importance to the Arab states indicated increasing support for the Arabs, at least in their anti-Israel policies. The Soviets also rendered the Security Council incapable of performing any positive role in the maintenance of international peace and security in the Middle East.

In 1955 the Czechoslovakian-Egyptian arms deal inaugurated the Soviet role as a major arms supplier to radical Arab regimes. This coincided with its diplomatic and political support for the Arab states against Israel in the United Nations and elsewhere. Since then a series of factors has been involved in Israel's increasing identification with the West and alienation from the Soviet bloc. Foremost has been the practical realization that the Soviet Union is intent on a pro-Arab course and that no Israel approach can win the Soviets over from their pro-Arab, anti-Israel policy. Nevertheless, Israel has maintained the hope that one day it will be able to receive Soviet Jewry in Israel and in the interim it is concerned for their safety. This dictated some caution in relations with the Soviet Union.

Since the June war of 1967, Soviet support for the Arab position has intensified. The Soviet Union and most of its East European allies severed diplomatic relations with Israel and increased their material support for the Arab states, particularly the supply of military equipment. This reinforced Israel's identification with the West and the Arab radical identification with the Soviet bloc. In the Four Power talks and Two Power discussions between their representatives and U.S. officials, the Soviets championed the Arab cause. Israel has increasingly come to regard the Soviet Union as an extension of Arab hostility and thus has sought to discredit the Soviets as possible arbiters in the Israel-Arab dispute.

Israel and the United States. Israel's relations with the United States began on a note of support and assistance and have proceeded along these lines. Israel has sought friendship and has generally received the diplomatic, moral, and material support of the United States. Underlying U.S. support for Israel's existence and integrity, which has been restated by successive U.S. administrations, have been several factors. In the United States there is a fund of goodwill, partially based on a similarity in outlook, which has favored the establishment and consolidation of a Jewish homeland in Palestine and which continues to favor preservation of the existence and integrity of Israel. This is a matter of some consensus and is not limited to the Jewish community. There is also the special relationship between American Jewry and Israel—the former has engaged in extensive philanthropic, cultural, social, and political activities on behalf of Israel. A third factor is the general tenor of U.S. Middle East policy which has sought an Arab-Israel peace, has supported Israel's integrity, and has provided economic and technical assistance as a part of its foreign aid programs. These factors have contributed to a basic harmony underlying the relations of the two states, though there have been differences on specific issues.

The relationship between the United States and Israel since the June war has been indicative of the long-standing positions of the two states. Since that conflict, U.S. policy has stressed the need for an effective and durable Israel-Arab peace and not merely a cease-fire or a return to the prewar armistice arrangements. It has emphasized the need for a peace arrived at by the parties and not imposed by the great powers. President Johnson's Five Principles of Peace, declared on June 19, 1967, have provided the basis for the U.S. approach during the Johnson and Nixon administrations. These include the recognized right of national life in peace and security, justice for the refugees, innocent maritime passage, limits on the wasteful and destructive arms race, and political independence and territorial integrity of all Middle Eastern states. The United States has supported the disengagement and withdrawal of Israel's forces to recognized and secure boundaries, but in a context of peace. In the interim and barring agreement on termination of the arms race, the United States has sought to prevent an arms imbalance in an effort to forestall conflict. This is compatible with Israel's position although there are areas of disagreement—such as estimates of the value of Great Power efforts to ameliorate the situation. Also, in the period following that conflict the United States became directly involved in the supply of military equipment to Israel in order to prevent an arms imbalance resulting from Soviet resupply of military equipment to several Arab states. This military supply effort became more important when President de Gaulle embargoed French military supplies to Israel. The United States became increasingly identified with the Israel position in the Four Power and Two Power efforts to achieve a settlement of the Israel-Arab problem.

Israel Between East and West

Israel's alienation from the East and increasing identification with the West, which has become particularly evident following the June War, has been a facet of Israel's foreign policy and of Middle Eastern life since the 1950s.

This identification has not been wholly voluntary on Israel's part. The intensified cold war raised several issues in the United Nations and elsewhere that required Israel to take a stand. Thus, for example, Israel supported United Nations actions in Korea and this implicit pro-Western position affected its relations with the Communist states. Israel has had an increasing need for financial assistance, in part to support the immigration and integration of Jews in Israel. The Eastern bloc has been unwilling to supply funds while the Western states have been readier sources. This has been partially due to the large sums of money provided by world Jewry, the largest portion of which comes from the United States and almost all of which comes from Western states. An important element is the status of the Jewish communities in the Communist world. Generally, the Eastern bloc has prohibited Jewish emigration and there has been an implicit conflict between Israel and communism for the bodies and minds of Eastern bloc Jewry. On the other hand, emigration from the West is unimpeded. A related factor is that the Jewish communities of the West have been able to freely maintain their cultural and spiritual ties with Israel and have shared Israel's burdens in integrating immigrants. Also, Israel has been able to exert some influence on the governments of those states to alter anti-Israel and/or anti-Jewish policies—something that could not be done to any meaningful degree in the Eastern bloc. These factors have been supplemented by specific events that seem to impel Israel toward the West. Once the cold war became a permanent factor in the Middle Eastern environment, a policy of neutrality became a practical impossibility, and following the June war, Israel's increased dependence on the United States for political support and military equipment further contributed to its policy orientation.

Israel, The European Economic Community, and the Developing World

Israel's search for international support and efforts to improve its economic situation have involved two areas of foreign policy that became important only in the mid-1950s. The establishment of the European Economic Community (Common Market or EEC), the attainment of independence by numerous states in Africa, and the increasing commitment of the Third World to modernization have become increasingly significant in Israel's foreign policy formulation. •

On March 25, 1957 the foreign ministers of Belgium, France, the Federal Republic of Germany, Italy, Luxemburg, and the Netherlands signed the Rome Treaty establishing the European Economic Community, the purpose of which is to promote greater economic cooperation among the six states. The integration of Western Europe projected in the Treaty of Rome posed both a challenge and an opportunity for Israel. It was realized that this could be beneficial to Israel's economy because of the creation of a larger and more prosperous consumer area, *i.e.*, new markets and new potential customers would be created for Israel's exports. At the same time, Israel has emphasized the dangers to its economy if it does not achieve an accommodation with the market because of its extensive trade with those states. It sees the means to a positive relationship in association or a special arrangement with the EEC.

Israel has stressed political and moral arguments in its negotiations for economic concessions. It has pointed out its natural affinity for Western Europe in general outlook as well as in geographical, cultural, and social orientation. These fundamental ties have been supplemented by European support for Israel's establishment and by continued friendship during its first two decades of statehood. Israel has argued that, in a sense, this creates a moral obligation for these states to ensure Israel's integrity and economic advance. Israel's economic arguments have stressed the importance of the European market for its products and the severe dislocations caused by the tariff of the Common Market against its goods.

Cooperation with the developing countries of the Third World remains a dominant theme in Israel's international relations. Cooperation agreements have been established with numerous countries in Africa, Asia, and Latin America. This effort has emphasized technical assistance, and Israel has provided instructors for educational institutions and technicians and specialists to aid in various Third World programs. Trainees and students from overseas come to Israel to study its achievements and to gain from its experience. Joint economic enterprises in the developing states, owned initially by Israel organizations and foreign governments or agencies, have provided a practical training ground for local personnel to assume full control of the endeavor. Israel's multifaceted program has been based on its ability to provide developing states with the benefits of its small-state approach and pragmatic experience on the problems of development. Originally an *ad hoc* effort, Israel's program of international cooperation has now reached the status of a consolidated effort based on the lessons and experiences of the past. Israel's experts have served in more than 60 countries in Africa, Asia, Latin America, and the Mediterranean area. They have emphasized agriculture and irrigation, rural planning and development, formation of pioneer and youth movements, medicine, academic and vocational education, and cooperation and community development. These subjects have also been the core of training for students who come to Israel to further their education.

The developing states have generally been willing to participate in the relationship with Israel on an ever-increasing basis because the benefits outweigh possible liabilities. The newly independent states of Africa, as well as the independent states of Asia, Latin America, and the Mediterranean basin, see few difficulties in accepting Israel's assistance. They feel that by cooperating with Israel they can achieve many of their material goals without compromising their ideals, and they believe that their goal of modernization can be significantly advanced by such ties.

Israel possesses an advanced technology consisting, in part, of a vast reservoir of skill and experience that is generally found only in larger states and therefore it is capable of extending assistance to new African and Asian states as well as to the developing countries of Latin America. The Africans and others seem to believe that this aid does not endanger the independence or impinge on the sovereignty of these states since Israel's relative economic and military weakness precludes any form of domination. Israel has skills and experience that these states need and want. Israel's combination of small size and advanced technology has enabled it to translate the latest technological achievements into a form more readily adaptable for developing states than the experiences of larger states, such as the United States or the Soviet Union. Also, the Third World desire for nonalignment can be furthered by association with Israel—a member of neither the Eastern nor the Western bloc.

Israel has been interested in maintaining and expanding this relationship because of the benefits to be derived from closer association with the developing states. Although there is a sense of mission, and friendship is the stated goal, Israel has also looked to the practical advantages to be derived from these efforts, including an expanded trade program and support in the maintenance of its security and integrity.

ISRAEL'S UNIQUENESS: A JEWISH DIMENSION

Israel's emphasis on survival and security as foreign policy objectives is not dissimilar to the stress placed on these goals by other states and the techniques designed for their achievement—national armed strength and international support—are also commonplace. There is, however, another dimension to Israel's foreign policy that affects its domestic political, economic, and social processes: It is Israel's role as the world's only Jewish state.

The impact of the Jewish factor on Israel's political system is manifold. Israel is concerned that all Jews who wish to immigrate are able to do so, and it is interested in the well-being of Jews everywhere. It seeks to ensure free and permanent contact between itself and the world's Jewish communities in order that spiritual and cultural relations may be maintained and fostered and that world Jewry may help to bear the financial burden imposed by mass Jewish immigration to Israel.

These considerations have had a practical effect on Israel's international posture. As has been seen, Israel's relations with the major powers have been partly determined by the status of Jews in those states, as well as by their ability to emigrate to Israel. Israel's *raison d'etre* provides the rationale for this factor. Israel was reestablished after more than a thousand years, partly because the Jews maintained the dream of a return to Jerusalem and the Promised Land. Israel views itself as a prime factor in the continuation of the Jewish heritage.

Israel's status as the only Jewish state is but one aspect of its uniqueness. Despite diplomatic relations with more than 90 states, Israel is isolated from the surrounding Arab world and from the general international community of which it is a part. Its borders are comprised of temporary boundary lines, established by a post-conflict armistice or cease-fire, and on these borders are hostile neighbors. Israel has no effective intercourse with the largest portion of the region—the Middle East—in which it is physically located. It is also isolated in the larger community by not having membership in any alliance or participation in the affairs of any bloc or regional grouping. It is rarely granted an important and responsible role in international organizations, such as the United Nations.

Israel is a small state. Before the June war of 1967 it occupied less than 8,000 square miles. Much of its population has emigrated from numerous other states during a short period of time, bringing with it a diverse cultural and social heritage. Because of this, Israel is both a developing and a developed state. Although many of its institutions and accomplishments may be viewed as trappings of modernization, there are large segments of the population that are committed to traditional institutions and concepts. In the political realm Israel's institutions clearly reflect those of the developed democracies of the West. In many respects, the British and American systems provide the basic models. Its political leadership consists mainly of those who emigrated to Israel from Eastern Europe and who led the struggle for independence. Israel's political leadership has not yet passed to the second generation—those "youngsters," such as Moshe Dayan and Yigal Allon, who represent the native-born (*sabra*) generation. It will be this younger generation's approach to the basic problems of security (especially the Israel-Arab dispute), economic development, and integration of the new immigrants and the Arabs of Israel that will determine the future course of the state.

Israel's future is closely tied with this concept of uniqueness, its view of its mission, and its Western-orientation. This has manifested itself not only in the emulation of the political techniques and institutions of the Western parliamentary systems and its cultures and life styles, but perhaps more significantly in the commitment to Western concepts of advanced modern education and techniques for economic and social development—for modernization. Israel's links with world Jewry offset its otherwise isolated posture and provide it with an ally in its efforts to maintain itself as an independent, sovereign, democratic, and modernizing state.

FOR FURTHER READING

A study of Israel's politics and foreign policy begins with the formation of Israel during the Mandate period, which is discussed by J. C. Hurewitz, *The Struggle for Palestine* (New York: W. W. Norton and Company, Inc., 1950) and Christopher Sykes, *Crossroads to Israel* (Cleveland and New York: The World Publishing Company, 1965). The constitutional and legal parameters of the political system are considered in several volumes. Emanuel Rackman's *Israel's Emerging Constitution, 1948-51* (New York: Columbia University Press, 1955) deals with the problems involved in the synthesis of a constitution. Henry E. Baker, *The Legal System of Israel* (Jerusalem: Israel Universities Press, 1968) and Joseph Badi (ed.), *Fundamental Laws of the State of Israel* (New York: Twayne Publishers, Inc., 1961) discuss the legal system and basic legislation. The definitive study of the parliament is Asher Zidon, *Knesset: The Parliament of Israel* (New York: Herzl Press, 1967).

The basic features and issues of the political system are described and analyzed in several volumes: Joseph Badi, *The Government of the State of Israel: A Critical Account of its Parliament, Executive, and Judiciary* (New York: Twayne Publishers, Inc., 1963); Marver H. Bernstein, *The Politics of Israel: The First Decade of Statehood* (Princeton, N.J.: Princeton University Press, 1957); Leonard J. Fein, *Israel: Politics and People* (Boston: Little, Brown and Company, 1968); Yehoshua Freudenheim, *Government in Israel* (Dobbs Ferry, N.Y.: Oceana Publications, Inc., 1967); and Oscar Kraines, *Government and Politics in Israel* (Boston: Houghton Mifflin Co., 1961).

Two members of the political science department of Hebrew University, Benjamin Akzin and Yehezkel Dror, discuss Israel's national planning process in *Israel: High-Pressure Planning* (Syracuse, N.Y.: Syracuse University Press, 1966). Yehezkel Dror and Emanuel Gutmann (eds.), *The Government of Israel* (Jerusalem: The Hebrew University, 1961) contains many of the important political documents. Political leadership is the subject of Lester G. Seligman, *Leadership in a New Nation: Political Development in Israel* (New York: Atherton Press, 1964). Jacob M. Landau, *The Arabs in Israel: A Political Study* (London: Oxford University Press, 1969) is a comprehensive survey and analysis of the role of the Arabs in Israel.

S. N. Eisenstadt, *Israeli Society* (New York: Basic Books, Inc., 1967) is a compendium containing numerous social statistics not easily available elsewhere. Immigrant absorption is the topic of Judith T. Shuval, *Immigrants on the Threshold* (New York: Atherton Press, 1963). Alex Weingrod, *Israel: Group Relations in a New Society* (New York: Frederick A. Praeger for the Institute of Race Relations, 1965) discusses problems of social integration and the attempt to create a multiethnic society. Israel's economy is discussed by David Horowitz,

Governor of the Bank of Israel, in *The Economics of Israel* (Oxford: Pergamon Press, 1967) and by Alex Rubner, *The Economy of Israel: A Critical Account of the First Ten Years* (New York: Frederick A. Praeger, 1960). The problem of religion's relationship to the state is discussed by Joseph Badi in *Religion in Israel Today: The Relationship between State and Religion* (New York: Bookman Associates, 1959). Amos Perlmutter, *Military and Politics in Israel: Nation-Building and Role Expansion* (London: Frank Cass and Co., 1969) considers the role of the military.

Israel's international relations are discussed in Theodore Draper, *Israel and World Politics: Roots of the Third Arab-Israeli War* (New York: The Viking Press, 1968) and in *Israel and the United Nations*, Report of a Study Group set up by The Hebrew University of Jerusalem (New York: Manhattan Publishing Company, 1956). Ernest Stock, *Israel on the Road to Sinai, 1949-1956* (Ithaca, N.Y.: Cornell University Press, 1967) is an incisive study of Israel's foreign policy from 1948 to the Sinai Campaign, with a sequel on the June War. Nadav Safran, *The United States and Israel* (Cambridge, Mass.: Harvard University Press, 1963) provides coverage of Israel's domestic scene as it impacts on foreign policy. Israel's Foreign Minister has presented eloquent statements of his country's policies in Abba Eban, *Voice of Israel*, Rev. Ed. (New York: Horizon Press, 1969). Walter Eytan, a ranking Israel diplomat, has written *The First Ten Years: A Diplomatic History of Israel* (New York: Simon and Schuster, 1958). Israel's international cooperation program is discussed in Leopold Laufer, *Israel and the Developing Countries: New Approaches to Cooperation* (New York: The Twentieth Century Fund, 1967).

WEST AND EAST
OF THE RED SEA

chapter 13

The Hashimite Kingdom
of Jordan*

INTRODUCTION

In the history of civilization as we know the term in the Western world,
Jordan is one of the oldest and richest sites in evidential remains, and
archaeologists are pushing ever further backward in time the dates of the
phenomena (Sanger).[1] As a nation-state, it is among the youngest, and it is with
that period we concern ourselves here.

It is now something like 50 years since Jordan emerged as a political entity
(and the very existence of that entity has never been without challenge by one
or another of an extraordinary series of internal and external opponents to the
concept). For approximately the first 35 years it was under first the legal and
then the real—if not so termed—tutelage of a great power, England; and for the
last 21 years (partly overlapping) the central fact of its existence has been an
adversary situation—twice in open warfare and the rest of the time in marred
truce—with its neighbor Israel.

During that time, its domestic rule has been dominated by two monarchs—
grandfather and grandson—one finally assassinated and the other under almost
constant threat to his throne. In addition, they were surrounded by a rather
remarkable (for both good and ill) group of advisors and helpers, both foreign
and indigenous, some well-intentioned who stayed too long and others who
betrayed or attempted to betray them. For this reason, much of what follows

---

*William Sands, executive director of the Middle East Institute and editor of the *Middle
East Journal*, Washington, D. C.

[1] Refers to bibliography at the end of this chapter. Either author's name or shortened
title is used in succeeding references.

will concern personalities rather than institutions; it has been the persons in large measure who have shaped the forms to their ends insofar as the power to do so lay in their hands. By its size and its resources and on account of its friends, its enemies, and its proximities, Jordan has necessarily been more pawn than chess master in this brief history.

Brief though this history be, we also deal with three successive entities: old Trans-Jordan, the mandate; the Hashimite Kingdom of Jordan, which in 1948-49 found itself trebled in population, some two thirds of it refugees from Palestine (mostly indigent); and Jordan, as of this writing engaged in undeclared, constant, if small scale, warfare along a line down the middle of its territory—the west bank of the Jordan River occupied by Israel after the June 1967 campaign and the east bank, or almost exactly what was old Trans-Jordan. Without the early prospect of a "real" peace, the matter must end with projections and hypotheses rather than predictions. The constants are few; the variables are myriad.

Part I: THE MANDATE AND ABDULLAH

On January 30, 1919 the Supreme Council at the Versailles peace conference decided that the liberated Arab provinces of the Ottoman Empire were not to be returned to Turkish rule; these territories included what is now the Hashimite Kingdom of Jordan. They had been part of the Syrian provinces, at least as far south as the town of Ma'an, where the governorate of the Sharif of Mecca was generally considered to begin.

This ruling of the council did not settle the complicated juggling of the settlement of promises variously made to each other by France and Britain and by Britain to the Arabs and to the Zionist movement concerning the division of the spoils of war in the area (cf. Antonious). What became Trans-Jordan (before that merely a vague geographical term Sharq al-Urdun, east of Jordan, i.e., the river) was thought of as part of the Arab National State under the rule of Sharif Faisal, third son of Sharif Husayn of Mecca, by this time King of Hijaz. Faisal had been military leader of the Arab revolt against the Ottomans (Lawrence # 18) with the encouragement and aid of the British and was proclaimed king in Damascus in 1919. He was ejected from Syria by the French General Gouraud in July 1920. By the Franco-British convention of December 23, 1920, the area of Trans-Jordan (still undefined, and the boundary with Syria not demarcated until 1932) was given up by the French to the British as coming under the latter's League Mandate for Palestine from the League. In fact, after Faisal's overthrow, the area was left in Toynbee's word "derelict" (Survey . . . Vol-I).

In August 1920 Sir Herbert (later viscount) Samuel, first British high commissioner in Jerusalem, visited Trans-Jordan and, with the aid of a few officers seconded from the British army in Palestine, helped set up some rudimentary elements of self-government.

Then, early in 1921 Sharif Abdullah, second son of King Husayn and with a field marshal's rank from him, entered the territory, marching northward with some 2,000 men toward Syria, with the avowed intention of restoring his brother Faisal to the throne of Syria. This further embarrassment to the British was solved by Winston Churchill, then minister of colonies under Lloyd George, with the help of his Middle East advisor T. E. Lawrence. Churchill, then in Cairo to regulate England's many problems in the area, went to Jerusalem where he asked Abdullah to come to see him. Both in order to avoid annoyance to the French and as some sop to the Hashimite allies of Great Britain, he recognized Abdullah as provisional ruler of Trans-Jordan on March 27, 1921—boundaries and other arrangements to be settled later. Abdullah returned to the then Circassian village of Amman, along the Hijaz railway, which he chose at his capital. The Hashimites have been there since.

Great Britain's mandate from the League of Nations for Palestine differed considerably from other "Class A" mandates in that it did not call for speedy evolution of Palestine as an independent state, but called rather for "the development of self-governing institutions." This provision was intended to allow the gradual establishment of a Zionist National Home, promised to Lord Rothschild by Great Britain in November 1917.

Article XXV of the same mandate empowered Great Britain to postpone or withhold application of the national home provisions from "the territories lying between the Jordan and the eastern boundary of Palestine as ultimately determined" and "to make such provision for the administration of the territories as he [the king of Great Britain] may consider suitable to those conditions. . . ." (Hurewitz, Document 38, pp. 106-111).

Great Britain formally assumed the Palestine mandate on July 24, 1922, and on September 16th of that year the council of the league approved Great Britain's action in setting up a separate administration for Trans-Jordan.

The *ad hoc* arrangements Churchill had made in 1921 were somewhat more formally put into effect when the high commissioner (still Sir Herbert Samuel) came to Amman and on May 25, 1923 formally proclaimed Trans-Jordan's independence under Abdullah as Amir—approximately translated prince, a title denoting in context something less than total sovereignty—and under British guidance. This guidance was given the tools for implementation by the fact that Trans-Jordan had hardly any revenue of its own and a British subsidy of some £125,000 was the mainstay of the administration.

The first chief British representative in Amman was T. E. Lawrence himself, who had suggested the arrangement with Abdullah. But administration was never his forte and he was succeeded after a few months by another *enfant terrible*, St. John Philby. Philby, as he recounts in his *Arabian Days*, really took seriously the independence of the arrangement and reduced the guidance to a minimum. There were only five British staff in Amman in 1924, the year he left after a quarrel with the ministry of colonies over the extent to which Trans-Jordan was to have self-rule.

It was not until February 20, 1928, that the agreement was formalized. The amount of guidance provided for was not inconsiderable: a British resident, under orders of the high commissioner in Jerusalem, was to be the chief adviser to the Amir. Relations with foreign powers were to be conducted through His Majesty's Government and the Amir was to be "guided by the advice" of the same in "all important matters affecting the international and financial obligations and interests of His Britannic Majesty in respect of Trans-Jordan." (Hurewitz, Document 52, Vol. II). The Amirate was "not to alter the system of control of the public finances" without consent. Similar restrictions on budgetary and fiscal policy, succession to the throne, the personal finances of the Amir (Abdullah lived simply himself, but could be extravagant in largesse) and any assumptions of territory (the British knew his desire to rule a Greater Syria very well, and his revanchist policy towards Hijaz, taken from his family in 1924-25 by the Saudi dynasty). There was to be complete free trade with Palestine. The Amir was to be guided as to the protection of foreigners and Britain reserved adjudication in disputes among religious sects. The British were to "raise, organize and control the armed forces" and retained jurisdiction over all British personnel in the Amirate. Full transit rights were to be granted to all British forces. There was to be British control over extradition and all economic concessions.

The British agreed to extend grants and loans to the Amirate during the period when its own resources were insufficient to cover the costs of government—these resources have continued to be insufficient for the 41 years since.

As is obvious, the above agreement constitutes no independence at all. Such terms, the continuation of other forms of treaty arrangements for so long, and the memory of them have continued to saddle the Jordanian government with the opprobrium of "imperialist lackey."

The Organic Law of Trans-Jordan, decreed the same year, may be briefly described: The internal functions of the Amirate not exercised by the mandatory power came under the direct rule of the Amir, with the assistance of a legislative council (alternately called an advisory council, which latter term describes its functions more precisely). The basic law remained the Ottoman *Mecelle*, as codified in the 19th century.

The first task, going back to 1921, of the new government had been to reestablish law and order after the turbulence of World War I and the uncertain years immediately after. Perhaps "create" law and order is more exact, for the Ottoman writ had hardly run beyond the settled agricultural region around Irbid and 'Ajlun in the northwest and along the Hijaz railway, whose stations were also forts. Elsewhere, the bedouin roamed at will and raided the settled places with inpunity, as had been their immemorial custom. The population may have been as much as 250,000, but this is doubtful.

Major F. G. Peake, who had been an officer with T. E. Lawrence in the desert campaign against the Turks, was called on to amalgamate the then existing soldiery left over from the war and the police into a regular armed force. This force Abdullah named *al-jaysh al-'arabi* (the Arab army), but the British thought that a little grandiose and always called it The Arab Legion, by which name it became famous. From a few hundred men the legion grew under Peake

Pasha (pasha was an Ottoman title which Abdullah continued to bestow, and generously) to a force of some 1,300 up until World War II. But create order it did. Furnished with armed transport, as it was, bedouin raiders could be and were caught and punished. Peake was a martinet of the old Imperial Indian Army, from which he must have gotten his love of magnificent regalia and accoutrements. In addition to discipline, he gave the legion its elan and Bristol-fashion smartness that have been the hallmark of Jordanian forces ever since. It is, incidentally, not true that the legion was recruited entirely from bedouins. Most personnel came from towns and villages, with a number of Circassians and Turcomans (these latter descended from soldiers settled there during the reign of Sultan Abdul Hamid II). The Royal Guard in Amman still wears the Circassian uniform, caracul cap, and crossed bandoliers on the chest.

In 1930 another unit of the legion was established, the Desert Patrol, under Major J. B. Glubb whose principal task was to control smuggling and border raids along the Saudi frontier. This force *was* recruited from the bedouin and later integrated with the legion. In 1932, as Glubb recounts it (*Story . . .*), the last of the raids across the Jordanian border took place in 1932. This marked the end of an era in bedouin history as such, and their sedentarization has proceeded steadily since. The day of the *grand nomade* is over.

Civil administration was also scanty and highly personal. The first chief ministers and other high civil servants (non-British) were largely Syrians who had fled with Faisal from Syria under the French, but most of them got along with the British mandatory power about as well as they would have with the French. They were gradually replaced to a great extent by Cis-Jordanians who, either by Hashimite sympathies or the opportunity of a civil post, moved into Trans-Jordan. Few on the east bank then had the educational background or the experience (or the desire to be desk-bound) to make satisfactory bureaucrats.

The tradition of Palestinians in the highest post of government began then long before the 1949 union and has continued to this writing. The prime minister, as of this writing, whose older brother occupied the same post in several incumbencies, is of a family originally from Safad in Galilee.

The economy remained pastoral and agricultural, and in a good year (perhaps one out of four) Trans-Jordan exported some grain, as well as hides and mutton. Trade was oriented towards Palestine, on account of the free trade agreement, and such import-export business as went on was transacted through Haifa. Trans-Jordan was a sort of desertic Graustark-Ruritania, complete to the intrigue which Abdullah still carried on with Syrian politicians, never giving up hope of ruling Greater Syria. As early as 1934 he proclaimed himself the protector of Palestine Arabs and of the Holy Places of Jerusalem. To him Palestine was still a Syrian province. The Amirate became as well that part of the Arab world where *ne plus ultra* Westerners resident became sentimentally pro-Arab, a sentiment based on the stereotype of the noble brave, austere, hospitable bedouin—as against the other Arab image of the wily, conniving townsman *effendi*.

With World War II, Abdullah again unhesitatingly chose sides and declared loyalty to the British cause. The Arab Legion, now commanded by Peake's successor Glubb Pasha, took effective part in the campaign to put down the Rashid Ali al-Gailani revolt in Iraq and the ejection of the Vichy French from Syria, both in 1941. Abdullah offered the legion for service elsewhere, but after the battle of Alamein in the western desert (1942) it was no longer needed.

After World War II, the new British Labour government formally divested itself of the mandate for Trans-Jordan and the country was on May 25, 1946 formally proclaimed independent and the name changed to The Hashimite Kingdom of Jordan, with Abdullah assuming the royal, instead of the princely, title. But the kingdom was no more able to stand on its financial feet than was the Amirate, and the subsidies continued, as did the British presence. Sir Alec Kirkbride, the British resident, became the first British minister and, as he puts it ". . . my title changed again without causing any drastic modification in my duties." On December 7, 1946 a new constitution was promulgated, with more of the parliamentary forms of government; but with Abdullah as king and Kirkbride as British minister, governmental affairs went on much the same until the death of the former and the transfer shortly thereafter of the latter.

The Anglo-Jordanian Treaty of Alliance of March 15, 1948 spelled out the relationship. Among the provisions were: the establishment of an Anglo-Jordanian Joint Defense Board; an invitation from Jordan for the Royal Air Force to maintain bases at Amman and Mafraq, and British forces at other places according to the agreement of the board; the jurisdictional and fiscal immunities of British personnel; joint training exercises and the training of Jordanian officers exclusively in British military schools; British provision of officers, arms, ammunition, supplies and aircraft, with no deviation from British types of equipment. There was also a provision for "each to come to his (the other king's) aid as a measure of collective defense in case of war," but this provision was not to be applicable if other obligations to the United Nations or other treaties were to stand in the way. It was under this latter escape clause that the British avoided aiding Jordan in the conflict with Israel that was to follow only two months later.

The Last Years of Abdullah

On November 29, 1947 the General Assembly of the United Nations partitioned Palestine into three parts: a Jewish state, an Arab state and an internationalized enclave of Jerusalem and its environs. Abdullah was as opposed to a Zionist state as much as any other Arab, but he had different ways of opposing it. He was convinced that the world community (and primarily, to him, the British) would not support the Arabs in their determination to eliminate Israel; he was advised by his military commander Glubb Pasha that the Arab Legion was not capable of doing more than to occupy central Palestine, allotted to the Arabs under partition. This he therefore decided to do, in tacit agreement with Ernest Bevin, British foreign secretary.

Both before and after the campaign (for the story of the 1948 campaign, see "The Long War" below) Abdullah had a number of secret conversations with Israeli officials as to the disposition of territories and peaceful settlement. These conversations came to no agreement on territorial dispositions (the minimum of both sides were vast distances apart) but the fact that he conducted them and that they became known made him a traitor to the Arab cause in the eyes of many. The 1948 campaign ended with Abdullah in occupation of the Old City of Jerusalem with all its major Holy Places and some 2,165 square miles of central Palestine, added to the some 34,550 square miles of old Trans-Jordan. The population of Jordan was trebled—about 400,000 old Trans-Jordanians, some 400,000 residents of Cis-Jordan, and approximately the same number of refugees from Israeli territory, who had either fled or were ejected from their homes.

The king's first steps were to regularize the occupation. On December 1, 1948 a Congress of Notables was convoked at Jericho under the leadership of Sheikh Muhammad 'Ali al-Ja'bari (then and now mayor of Hebron). The congress, in short, offered the throne of Palestine to Abdullah. On April 26, 1949 the king proclaimed in parliament the annexation of the west bank, and on April 24, 1950 a new parliament, elected by members in equal numbers from Trans- and Cis-Jordan, confirmed the fact. British recognition followed three days later, but most of the Arab countries not only refused to recognize the fact but Jordan would have been expelled from the Arab League had it not been for the veto of Iraq, then still ruled by Abdullah's Hashimite relatives.

Abdullah skillfully employed the talents of those major Palestinian families who were favorable to his rule, such as the Nashashibis and Tuqans, who had shared with him the dream of a Greater Syria. The more educated and sophisticated Palestinians, refugees and displaced persons, and those still resident on the west bank added much to the expertise of government, but many were unhappy, having no wish for a monarch and Abdullah in particular.

It was a plot by a group of the latter who ended Abdullah's 30-year reign. On July 20, 1951 as he entered the *Haram al-Sharif* in Jerusalem, third holiest place in Islam, to perform the Friday prayers, he was shot and killed. By his side was his grandson Husein, then 16. A bullet intended for him ricocheted from the Arab Legion insignia on his chest.

Abdullah ibn Husein was a paradoxical man. A *litterateur* of no mean distinction, of great charm when he wished to be, he could be ruthless and imperious as well. Even his British advisers more than once felt the rough side of his tongue. Not for nothing was he 60-odd generations in the direct line of descent from the Prophet Muhammad. He had great dreams, but above all he was a realist. He knew how to accommodate to circumstances when necessary. He correctly wagered in two world wars and never wavered in his loyalty to his alliance, whatever his private disappointments. What he perhaps did not perceive was the waning of the imperial era when kingdoms were carved out for princes in European chancelleries.

Part II: THE CONSTITUTIONAL BASIS; STRUCTURE AND ADMINISTRATION OF GOVERNMENT

The Framework

It was obvious that the almost totally personal rule of Abdullah, with its exiguous administrative personnel, would not long suit the needs of a country suddenly trebled in population—particularly a population much more sophisticated as to modern forms of government after almost 30 years of British Mandatory rule. Even before Abdullah's assassination, measures had been taken to bring the administration of government and of justice more into conformity with what is generally considered modern. During an interim period, Mandatory law applied in Cis-Jordan and many Palestinian officials remained at their posts. Under the leadership of a distinguished Palestinian jurisconsult, new criminal and civil codes were adopted during 1951-1952. The new criminal code followed largely that of Syria and is based on French legal principles; the civil code is based on the Palestine Civil Procedure Rules of 1938, in turn based largely on English common law. A new court establishment law was also passed in 1951: It provides for magistrate courts for minor offenses; courts of first instance for all major civil and criminal cases; two courts of appeal, for Trans- and Cis-Jordan; and a court of cassation, which also acts as the high court of justice. Matters of personal status are still regulated by *Sharia* (Islamic) law (*cf.* constitutional provisions below).

At the same time that the legal and judicial machinery was being overhauled, the parliament elected in 1950 from both banks began work on a new constitution. While Abdullah lived the work went slowly, for the king had little patience with any proposal to reduce or limit his authority, and so informed parliament in rather sharp language.

The brief reign of Talal, Abdullah's elder son, brought a change in constitutional as well as other matters. In his lucid periods (he was gravely mentally ill, a fact of which the general public was not aware), he actively set about to encourage the parliament to establish the constitution, as well as to attempt to better relations with the other Arab states which Abdullah had offended.

As promulgated in January 1952, the constitution, now still in effect with minor amendments, goes much further in the establishment of parliamentary and democratic institutions than its predecessors mentioned in Part I. A large number of its provisions form bills of rights of the Jordanian citizen and are the equivalent of modern systems elsewhere. They are somewhat diluted by provisions for censorship and the inclusion of a defense law article which limits these rights in time of national emergency—reaffirmation of a preexisting law largely influenced by the state of belligerency with Israel; this article, which provides for exceptional martial law measures in times of emergency, has been several times invoked. During such times, the king may rule by decree, but he has always later requested ratification by parliament and been upheld.

Parliament consists of a House of Representatives and a House of Notables (senate). The latter is appointed by the king from among persons who have distinguished themselves in various branches of endeavor; the former is elected by universal male suffrage under provisions to be made specific by an electoral law. The Electoral Law of 1960 provides for a House of 60 representatives, 30 from each bank of the Jordan, with specific representation being given to Christian and ethnic minorities and to the bedouin tribes. Minorities are actually somewhat overrepresented, according to their percentage of the population.

The legislature shares with the king the power of legislation; the House may by simple majority (according to an amendment of 1954) declare lack of confidence in the Council of Ministers, which must then resign. The House has done so, as late as 1963. The Council of Notables is appointed for life; the terms of representatives are for four years, but the king, by an amendment of 1960, may prolong the terms for as much as two years.

The powers of the king are broad. He is not responsible; he may name his heir—and Husein has done so, his brother Hasan. He is the commander in chief of the armed forces. He may dismiss the House of Representatives, and did so as recently as 1966, though he must then call for new elections. He may also dismiss the Council of Ministers, and changes of government have usually been at his behest. He has the right of pardon and commutation of sentences. By his power to dismiss as well as to appoint judges, he has important judiciary functions.

In general, the judiciary provisions incorporate the specific laws mentioned above.

The constitution was briefly suspended in 1958, when on February 14th the Arab Federation was declared between Jordan and Iraq—a response to the United Arab Republic of Egypt and Syria, but the Kassim revolt of July 14th in Iraq effectively put an end to the federation and King Husein declared it officially dissolved as of August 2, bringing back into being the 1952 instrument.

There have been two major constitutional crises since its adoption.

By the summer of 1952, it became evident that the alcoholic-psychotic episodes of King Talal were becoming more frequent and more severe. The government of the day, after much deliberation, exercised a power granted to it under the constitution with this prospect in mind. In spite of his great popularity, they requested and obtained the abdication of Talal on August 11, 1952 and proclaimed his oldest son Husein, then a minor, king under the regency of his uncle Amir Na'if. But Na'if was suspected of designs on the throne and the government prevented him from exercising the regency. The regency was actually exercised by a triumvirate of the late King Abdullah's principal confidants, Ibrahim al-Hashim, Tawfiq Abu al-Huda, and Samir al Rifa'i—all former Palestinians, as it happened. The young king then spent six months at Sandhurst in England, a period which was to greatly influence his life, as later events disclose. He formally ascended on May 2, 1953, his 18th birthday, according to the Muslim calendar.

The second of these crises, the results of which have up until the present most affected rule in Jordan, occurred in the spring of 1957. Parliamentary elections in the fall of 1956 had brought in a House with a majority of Arab nationalists sympathetic to Egyptian President Nasser's neutralism, Baathist socialists and members of the National Front, of whom several were communists. Most were republican in sympathies and favored a federal union with Syria. Their principal target, if not the king himself, was the Anglo-Jordanian Treaty of Alliance, still the symbol of subservience, though Glubb Pasha and his British officers had been dismissed from the army the year before. As early as January 1957, the king warned Premier Sulaiman Nabulsi, head of the leftist-nationalist coalition, against "the dangers of communism." On March 15, 1957 the British treaty was abrogated without objection from the king, but Nabulsi "thought Jordan would soon be liquidated" (Hussein, p. 155). Husein during this period was warned of an army plot against him also in the brewing. The king brought matters to a head by demanding the resignation of Nabulsi on April 10.

The Chief of Staff General Ali Abu-Nuwwar had been Husein's own creation, raising him to his post and rank from that of a junior lieutenant colonel—who had once been a boon companion of his bachelorhood. But Abu-Nuwwar had now joined (if not formed) the plot against the king. Warned by loyal officers, he drove himself to the main army encampment at Zarqa and there, in a dramatic confrontation, demanded the loyalty of his troops. This was given thunderously, and the matter was basically over. Abu-Nuwwar and his successor for a few days, General Hayyani, left the country for Syria—suspected of fomenting the coup. After a few days of an attempt at conciliation, the king turned again to the old guard, formed a government with Ibrahim al-Hashim and Samir al-Rifa'i,[2] disbanded political parties, and put the army on the alert in Amman, where the center of opposition to him lay. The latter measure turned out to be unnecessary.

This second crisis has been recounted at some length because it set both the image of Husein and the pattern of future rule. Everyone admires courage, perhaps especially Arabs, and Husein displayed it, to the Nth degree. "The brave young king," then only 21 years old, came into his own. He has ruled as well as reigned since, though by his own count there have been some dozen attempts on his life and more would-be plotters than he has been able to count. The other facet of his early reputation as sport car racer, water skier, jet pilot and playboy has changed with maturity. He works long and hard at the vocation of king and,

---

[2]Oddly enough, though the general assumption is that Trans-Jordanians (and principally the bedouins) form his whole basis of support and that most Palestinians would be gladly rid of him, the best known dissidents have been the former—such as Col. Abdullah al-Tall, formerly military governor of Jerusalem who revealed King Abdullah's secret negotiations with the Israelis in his memoirs published in Cairo after his defection, and both Nabulsi and Abu-Nuwwar, mentioned above. The old guard mentioned above, on the other hand, were Palestinians, as are the present prime minister and deputy prime minister, minister of foreign affairs and defense.

though still in his thirties, he gives the appearance of an older man. Seventeen years of rule put him among the elders in experience.

Structure and Administration

Along with the dislocations, the economic disaster, and the personal tragedies of the Palestine refugees, there came along with the problems not a few mitigating elements insofar as Jordan was concerned. One of these was the hundreds of Palestinians with skills in bureaucratic management to help solve the problems of a formerly tiny group who had run the elementary machine of Trans-Jordanian administration. Many mandatory officials were employed by the administration of the much larger entity. Jordan's fiscal resources for modern bureaucracy were still inadequate, but there gradually came into being more of the services which are generally expected from government, though particularly slowly in the kind of welfare state provisions included in the constitution of 1952.

The upper echelons of government, particularly the policy-making element, have undergone change and expansion as well. Upon accession, Husein was aware of his youth and inexperience. Like his father, he had as well no wish to be an autocrat, in spite of his great love and admiration for his grandfather. In 1953 he chose as his prime minister one of the more progressive of Abdullah's coterie of advisers, and Jordan entered on a two-year period of experiment in democracy, with a highly permissive attitude towards freedom of speech and of the press, of which, especially, the Palestinian majority of the population took full advantage. But the charge that the parliamentary elections of 1954 were rigged brought widespread discontent and, finally, rioting in the streets of Amman. The Arab Legion had to be called in to restore order.

A more conservative government took over, but 1955 was the year of the Egypt-Soviet arms deal, the Bandung Conference, and an increasing tendency to neutralism and socialism throughout the Arab world which affected Jordan as well. It was generally agreed that the elections of 1956 were fairly run, and they brought in a leftist-Arab nationalist majority (including Baathists and Communists and a cabinet which eventually led to the "second constitutional crisis" described above).

Since 1957 and the banning of parties,[3] all members of parliament have been elected as independents and the King has gradually built up around him his own group of counsellors and confidants. From this group have come the majority of prime ministers and incumbents of other cabinet posts. Among these are: other members of the royal family (his maternal uncle has twice been prime minister; a cousin, minister of information; and several of them are high-ranking army officers); personnel of his own secretariat (the long-time chief of the royal cabinet has also twice been prime minister); ex-army officers of whose loyalty he is certain; scions of the old Trans-Jordanian tribes and clans, such as the

---

[3] Prominently among them the Arab Nationalist Movement, the National Socialist party of Nabulsi, the Baath, and the Communists.

Fayiz' and Majalis; and, still, representatives of old, upper class Palestinian families whose Hashimite sympathies have been long established—such as the Rifa'is, Nashashibis, Tuqans, Dajanis, and Khatibs. This group revolves in office in a fairly tight circle. In the current cabinet, seven out of the fifteen are holdovers from the previous one, though some are in different posts. The previous administration held over six from the former, and so on. This proportion has held, roughly speaking, over the last several years. There is no fixed number of cabinet posts, nor indeed is any specific cabinet organization provided for in the constitution, and ministries may be combined or separated or new posts created according to the exigencies of the time. Information, tourism, and antiquities, for instance, was a logical combination particularly before June 1967 when tourist income was a major item in Jordan's economy. Ministries, such as reconstruction and development (which deals largely with refugee matters in conjunction with a Inter-Ministerial Committee for Refugee Assistance), national economy, agriculture, public works, social affairs, and health are generally held by experts who have done excellent jobs in Jordan's economic and social progress (at least before June 1967). The ministry of religious affairs, the incumbent of which is also *Qadi al-Quda'*, or head of the Islamic religious courts which still deal with matters of personal status (marriage, divorce, guardianship, inheritance, and the like) is a special feature in governments of many Islamic countries. He is also administrator of *Waqfs* (religious endowments). The ministries of defense and foreign affairs are often held jointly, along with the premiership or vice-premiership.

In practice, Husein personally conducts the foreign relations (see Part III) and the defense of the realm to a high degree. Insofar as the ministry of interior is concerned with internal security, the king also takes keen interest in its workings. This post has more than once been held by an army officer. The portfolio is as of this writing held by Akif al-Fayiz, whom the king credits chiefly with alerting him to the plot of 1957 (see above) and who, in one capacity or another, has participated in half a dozen cabinets. Other functions he leaves to experts and administrators, it being given that the broad policy lines are, as ministerial announcements always say, "under the guidance of His Majesty." He often personally presides over cabinet sessions.

In accord with modern practice elsewhere, a number of autonomous or semiautonomous boards and agencies have been created, particularly in the field of economic developemnt. Among these are the East Ghor Canal Authority, the Hijaz Railway Board, the National Phosphate and Potash Companies and the Aqabah Port Trust.

Both in theory and practice, the administration is highly centralized, with all important orders and authorizations and even some trivial ones emanating from Amman. This has been a cause of discontent in the west bank.

Foreign experts have played a considerable role in the modernization of governmental structure. An excellent research clinic and one of the best statistical bureaus in the Middle East are examples where expertise from aid-giving countries has been wisely exploited. Government publications and reports in Arabic and many in English are competently done. Close cooperation between the United Nations Relief and Works Agency in the case of the refugee population and governmental agencies has existed since the establishment of this agency in 1950. Other specialized agencies of the United Nations, such as the UN fund for economic development, have given aid and advice.

One exceptional problem is, of course, the occupation of Cis-Jordan by Israel. Many local authorities on the West Bank have remained in office, and it is known that some still receive their salaries from the respective supervisory ministries in Amman, but to what extent these officials are guided by Amman in their reaction to orders of the occupying Israeli authorities cannot be known.

Part III: FOREIGN RELATIONS—SUBSTANCE AND CONDUCT

Jordan was created as an act of foreign policy of a great power, and external concerns have been a principal occupation of its governors since. The principal determinants of Jordan's foreign policy have been: (1) its long-term dependence on foreign subvention; and (2) its position vis-à-vis its Arab neighbors, which in turn has evolved around the Palestine question and the attitude of other Arabs towards the former determinant. The two factors are closely interwoven.

The question of Jordan's viability is discussed below, but perhaps the outstanding fact of its existence since its inception is that a substantial portion of its operating budget has come from foreign sources. It has been previously pointed out how this process began under the British mandate and did not change materially with the end of that mandate. Great Britain, under the terms of the 1948 alliance, paid the expenses of the Jordanian military establishment, the Arab Legion, almost exactly half of the national budget in ensuing years. Furthermore, this subvention was paid directly into an Arab Legion account and administered by the British commander of the same. Husein and his government therefore had no ultimate control over their own army. This dependence inevitably carried over into other spheres, after long habit and under such potential sanction. In his autobiography the king related how, when a Soviet initiative for diplomatic relations was received, the prime minister of the day took the proposition first to the British embassy to discuss before the king, himself, knew anything of it.

In early 1955, with British and American backing, there came into being the Baghdad Pact, first between Iraq and Turkey. Egypt under Nasser, increasingly neutralist with an anti-Western tinge, (this was the year of Bandung) saw the pact not only as a Western cold war instrument but as one directed against Egyptian leadership in the Arab world—an influence which began with its preponderant role in setting up the Arab League and increased as many Arabs (and prominently among them the Palestinian element of the Jordanian population) blamed the West for its defeat by Israel in 1948-49 and looked for a leader to restore their rights.

In the Anglo-American effort to build up a "Northern Tier" against Soviet encroachment in the Middle East, Jordan was an obvious candidate for participance, it being given that its government had always been strongly anti-communist. Therefore, early in December 1955 Sir Gerald Templer, chief of Britain's general staff, was sent to Amman to persuade Jordan to adhere to the pact. As he recounts the story in his autobiography (Hussein), the king was dubious of the value of the Baghdad Pact and the government had announced its neutrality as to both that arrangement and the recent Egypto-Syrian and Egypto-Saudi Arabian defense pacts, organized by Nasser as countermeasures.

Nevertheless, after the Templer visit, Husein appointed Hazza al-Majali, a young Trans-Jordanian confidant of the king and a supporter of the pact, as premier. Street rioting broke out in both Trans- and Cis-Jordan and the Arab Legion had to be called in to restore order. Majali resigned and a caretaker government was appointed, but again in January 1956 even more serious street demonstrations against the pact and government erupted and once more the Legion had to take over the maintenance of order. Husein blamed the Egyptian and Saudi Arabian radios for inflaming the passions of his people in false charges. But the new prime minister, the old guard "strong man" Samir al-Rifa'i, rejected any notion of joining the pact. The neutralist nationalists, mostly Palestinian, had clearly won, and, in spite of his disclaimer, Rifa'i was almost mobbed by several hundred Jordanian university students when he visited Cairo in February in an attempt to patch up relations.

The British influence and presence underwent what was for all practical purposes the coup de grâce on March 1, 1956 when without warning Husein dismissed Glubb Pasha and his British chief of staff from command of the Arab Legion. As the king relates it, the dismissal came about over fundamental differences in strategy between Glubb and himself, but at another point in his autobiography Husein ventures the guess that Jordan would not have lasted as an independent entity another year if Glubb had stayed, so great was the hostility at home and among its neighbors to what was regarded as a subservience. With the abrupt going of the Pasha ended an epoch in the British relationship, though the Treaty of Alliance was not to be denounced until the following year (see Part II above.

The burgeoning trend towards an ecumenical Arab nationalism (particularly among Palestinians) led to one major declared goal of the new nationalist-left coalition government which came into power with the elections of 1956—a federal union with Syria. Jordan's relations with Syria had never been good, partly on account of King Abdullah's well-known desire to be ruler of a Greater Syria, a goal few Syrians shared, but the Nabulsi government was willing (so it declared) to seek what would obviously be a junior partnership in a partial fulfillment of the dream of Arab union. Husein put an end to that brief flirtation by the dismissal of Nabulsi (recounted in Part II), and relations with Syria reverted to their old bad ways.

By early 1958, a turning point in a number of ways in the Arab world, Jordan (along with its then fellow Hashimite Iraq) was almost isolated from its neighbors. Gamal Abdul Nasser was increasingly the hero of the Arabs, to them the victor of 1956-57 with the withdrawal of the Anglo-French-Israeli forces from the tripartite invasion attempt on Sinai and the Suez, and the idol of most of Jordan's own two-thirds Palestinian population. Syria joined Egypt in the three-year United Arab Republic (1958-1961) and *Sawt al-'Arab* (Voice of the Arabs) radio in Cairo referred to Husein in such terms as the "dwarf imperialist agent." Syria went so far, according to Husein's autobiography, as to attempt his assassination during an overflight of Syrian territory in late 1958. The undertaking of other Arab states to support the Jordanian army after the end of the British subsidy came to nothing, and it was the United States who came in to do the necessary—provide the means by which Jordan governed and defended itself after the long years of British support had come to a substantial end in 1957. By 1960 American aid and support was at a higher level than the British had ever been—some $40 million per annum in budgetary support and $16 million in economic assistance. Changing one imperialist relationship for another was the interpretation of the neutralist-socialist Arabs. After the short-lived Arab Federation of Jordan and Iraq (see Part II above) even this friend turned into opponent in the person of Abd al-Karim Kassim, the sole leader of the now republican and left-leaning Iraq. In July 1958 occurred the last major British effort in support of the regime; British paratroopers landed in Amman at the same time American Marines landed in Lebanon, both at the invitation of the government in power against real revolt or that felt to be incipient. The paratroopers left Amman in October and a symbolic umbrella over Jordanian sovereignty was perpetuated for a while by the United Nations in the form of the so-called "Spinelli Mission," so called after the United Nations official who was to report to the world body on any dangers to the country from without.

The year 1959 marked the low point in the confrontation—Jordan versus almost everybody else in the Arab world. Even Saudi Arabia, under the late fumbling King Saud ibn Abd al-Aziz, had gone through a seemingly ardent friendship with Nasser, accompanied by the same diatribes from Radio Mecca as from other points of the compass. Husein held command internally, however, and came through these attacks with a combination of luck, skill, and sureness of self. As an example of the first, he once narrowly escaped assassination by poisoned nose drops—he has chronic sinusitis.

It was a much more simple task to cultivate relationships with the Arab states known variously as moderate, pro-Western, or, by others, reactionary.

Saudi Arabia under the premiership of Prince Faisal (to be king in 1964) continued to draw back from his brother Saud's previous pro-Nasser, anti-Jordan policy mentioned above. Jordan joined Saudi Arabia in 1962 in a treaty of military alliance and in supporting the royalist forces in the Yemeni civil war against the new republican regime in late 1962, though Husein was later to reverse that position after it was clear that the republican government controlled almost all of Yemen. An old wound was healed in August of 1965 when an agreement was signed between the two countries as to the border between them. Until then, there had been only an undemarcated administrative boundary, set up unilaterally in 1927 by means of a communication from a British official to the Saudi regime. The new line approximately triples (to 28 miles) Jordan's formerly tiny foothold on the Gulf of Aqabah (its only outlet to the open seas); runs along more rational topographical features; and provides for transit, pasturage, and water rights of the bedouin tribes who migrate in the region according to reason and who traditionally take no heed of arbitrary lines drawn in a desert.

Upon Kuwait's independence, Jordan became one of the first recipients of the former's generosity out of its tremendous wealth. As early as 1960, Kuwait extended a loan of £1 million before the establishment of its Fund for Arab Economic Development which has since extended even further assistance. Kuwait now plays a major role, along with Saudi Arabia and Libya, in replacing the United States as principal subsidizer of Jordan's existence. Aside from major ties with the West, the two countries share as well both the benefits and some problems which arise from a large population percentage of displaced Palestinians.

Lebanon inherited, through the facilities of its ports of Beirut, the pre-1948 role of Haifa as principal outlet for Jordan's export-import trade. Despite the development of the port of Aqabah in recent years, Beirut still plays an important part in this commerce. Both countries, since they have no common border, have shared the experience of intermittent Syrian interference with transit trade.

The two shared as well, by their own request, the presence of Western soldiery in the summer of 1958, on account of the fear of the governments of communism or other subversion. The wrath of the progressive Arab states at this action was equally directed at both. They have maintained Western ties since.

Yet another moderate which has shared this disapproval is Tunisia. President Habib Bourguiba chose an official visit to Jordan in March 1965 to chide Arabs for what he considered a sterile preoccupation with revenge on Israel, and advised them to accept the fact of Israel's existence (though on the terms of the 1947 U.N. Partition, hardly an acceptable position to Israelis). The year before, in a televised press conference during an American visit, Husein had declared that peace with Israel depended upon the latter's acceptance of various U.N. resolutions and the decision when Israel "ceases to be a threat to the Arabs." The first of these conditions is not too different from that of Bourguiba, and they were widely accused of collusion in treason by some segments of Arab opinion.

Prior to the 1969 coup which overthrew the monarch and established a republic, Libya maintained friendly relations with Western powers. But this was not vital in Jordan's relationships until Libya became so as a partner in the subsidy mentioned in the paragraph on Kuwait.

The early 1960's marked first a lessening of outright hostility from and towards the progressive or socialist Arab states, then some efforts at cooperation on specific matters of common interest, though this passage was anything but uninterrupted and not infrequently marred by outbursts of the old rancors and vitriolic exchanges.

In 1960, for example, Jordan recognized the Kassim regime in Iraq, though Husein bitterly remembered that the leaders had assassinated his cousin King Faisal II. It was not until Kassim's own removal from power by death in 1963 that Iraqi relations took a really better turn.

It was also on August 29, 1960 that the prime minister of Jordan, Hazza al-Majali, was assassinated, Husein accused Syria (then still the Syrian region of the United Arab Republic) of complicity, though the two countries' representatives had met only a few days before at Shtaurah in Lebanon in an apparently successful attempt to reconcile some of their differences.

Unconfirmed reports in 1961 had it that Husein had approached Nasser personally to suggest a rapprochement in the cause of the Arab nation. During these years, Husein more than once offered to abdicate if by that act there would be created a real Arab unity. More than his person, however, lay in the way of the eventuality.

During 1962 and 1963, both Jordan and Syria—and Lebanon, to a degree—became increasingly disturbed at the progress made by Israel in its unilateral diversion of Jordan river waters by way of the National Water Carrier from Lake Tiberias as far as the Negev. Although Jordan and Egypt had, for a while, broken diplomatic relations, common enough ground was found by January 1964 for Nasser to call for the first of three Arab summit meetings, at which the Arab chiefs of state met.

The primary item on the agenda was a plan for an Arab diversion of Jordan waters above the Israeli section of the river, by dams and canals from its Syrian and Lebanese sources, and storage in Jordan. But the meeting turned largely on other matters. By Husein's account (Vance and Lauer), he was the principal adherent of an active and working Unified Arab Command to counter what Arabs considered a growing Israeli threat to them, with its recent acquisition, among other military hardware, of the "Hawk" SAMs from the United States and supersonic *Mystere* aircraft from France. Such a command was set up, at least nominally, under the Egyptian General Ali Amir.

Even more disturbing to Husein and associates was the establishment, at the summit, of the Palestine Liberation Organization (PLO) and, by that act, the implicit recognition of a Palestine identity, the intrepretation of which might include the west bank of Jordan. This impression was strengthened when a Palestine National Congress was held in Jerusalem in May 1964 and elected Ahmad Shuqayri, a Palestinian lawyer and member of the Arab League Secretariat, head of the PLO, and announced the formation of a "Palestine Liberation Army" (PLA). Jordanian Premier Wasfi al-Tall denounced Shuqayri as an instrument of Cairo and the PLA functioned only in the Gaza Strip, not in Jordan.

As Husein recounts it (Vance and Lauer), the second summit, gathered in Alexandria in September 1964, made no progress whatever in furthering the purposes of the unified command. There was announced unanimous agreement on military measures to counter Israeli diversion of Jordan waters, but the National Water Carrier had already been in operation since May of 1964, and the measures were never implemented. In fact then Foreign Minister Golda Meir stated early in 1965 that Israel would undertake preventive war on the occasion of any attempt at interference with the carrier.

Again according to Husein's recounting of the event, at the third summit held at Casablanca in September 1965, the unified command finally was set meaningfully under way. Husein, at least, envisaged a "minimum preparatory period of these years," particularly in regard to the Jordanian Air Force. The command was not to have so much time before being tested.

The year 1965 was also the year in which a new group of *fidai'yin* (commandos) took the field. This was the movement for the liberation of Palestine, which came to be known as *Fath*. Suffice it to say here that these operations led to the massive Israeli retaliatory raid against the Jordanian village of al-Samu late in 1966. The population of the west bank, infuriated at what seemed the inability of the Jordanian armed forces to protect them, rioted, demanding arms for the people and more cooperation with other Arabs.

The spring of 1967 brought Jordan ever closer to military common effort. The Israeli-Syrian air battle of April 7th, and what Ambassador Charles Yost has called "Israeli exercises in verbal escalation" increased tensions. Finally, Husein flew to Cairo on May 30, 1967 and there signed an accord with Egypt under the terms that the Egyptian General Abd al-Mun'im Riyadh was to be placed in command of Jordan's forces in event of war. War came six days later.

During the 50s and 60s (until the June 1967 campaign) Jordan's relations with the U.S.S.R. and other Communist powers were really a function of its relations with the West. To the United States it was obligated for the subsidy on which it lived; Great Britain was still the chief supplier of arms and equipment for its forces. At the height of the cold war, Husein continued Jordan's traditional anti-communism, and in ringing terms. In 1959 and in 1960, he denounced the Soviet bloc as enemies of the Arabs, in speeches at the United Nations. Although in 1963 Jordan established diplomatic relations with the U.S.S.R., as late as December 1966, in an interview with an American news magazine. Husein declared that the objective of the U.S.S.R. and China in the Middle East was to destroy every Arab. A diminution in the harshness of this attitude followed the June 1967 campaign.

BIBLIOGRAPHY

Books

'Abdullah, King of Jordan. *Memoirs of King Abdullah of Transjordan*. London: Cape, 1950. 278 pp.

Abidi, Aqil Hyder Hasan. *Jordan: A Political Study 1948-1957*. Bombay: Asia Publishing House, 1965. 251 pp.

Antonius, George. *The Arab Awakening: The Story of the Arab National Movement*. London: H. Hamilton, 1938. xi + 471 pp.

Burns, Lt. Gen. E. L. M. *Between Arab and Israeli*. London: Harrap, 1962. 336 pp.

Churchill, Randolph S. and Winston Spencer. *The Six Day War*. London: Heineman, 1967. (pap).

Dearden, Ann. *Jordan*. London: R. Hale, 1958, 224 pp.

Dodd, Peter, and Halim Barakat. *River without Bridges: A Study of the Exodus of the 1967 Palestinian Arab Refugees*. Beirut; Institute for Palestine Studies, monograph #10, 1969.

Glubb, J. B. *Story of the Arab Legion*. London: Hodder & Stoughton, 1948.

————. *Syria, Lebanon and Jordan*. New York: Walker, 1967. 236 pp.

Harkabi, Y. *Fedayeen Action and Arab Strategy*. London: Institute for Strategic Studies, Adelphi Papers no. 53. 1968.

von Horn, Maj. Gen. Carl. *Soldiering for Peace*. New York: David McKay, 1967. viii+402 pp.

Hurewitz, J. C. *Diplomacy in the Near and Middle East: A Documentary Record: 1914-1956*. Vol II. Princeton: Van Nostrand, 1956.

Hussein, King of Jordan. *Uneasy Lies the Head: The Autobiography of His Majesty King Hussein I of the Hashemite Kingdom of Jordan*. New York: B. Geis Associates; distributed by Random House, 1962. 306 pp.

International Bank for Reconstruction and Development. *The Economic Development of Jordan*. Baltimore: John Hopkins Press, 1957. xvi + 488 pp.

Jarvis, Claude Scudamore. *Arab Command: The Biography of Lieutenant-Colonel F. G. Peake Pasha, C.M.G., C.B.E.* London, New York: Hutchinson & Co., 1942. 158 pp.

Government of Jordan. *The Constitution of the Hashimite Kingdom of Jordan*. Amman: Press and Publicity Bureau, Ministry of Foreign Affairs, 1952. Trans. by Sam'an Dawud. (For amendments see Khalil.)

Khalil, Muhammad. *The Arab States and the Arab League*. Vol. I. Beirut: Khayat's, 1962.

Lawrence, Thomas Edward. *Seven Pillars of Wisdom, A Triumph*. Garden City, N.Y.: Doubleday, Doran & Co., 1935. 672 pp.

Lias, Godfrey. *Glubb's Legion*. London: Evans, 1956.

Marayati, Abid A. *Middle Eastern Constitutional and Electoral Laws*. New York: Praeger, 1968.

Morris, James. *The Hashemite Kings*. New York: Pantheon, 1959. 208 pp.

Patai, Raphael, ed. *The Hashemite Kingdom of Jordan*. New Haven: Human Relations Area Files, Inc., 1956. xiii+605 pp.

————, ed. *Jordan*. New Haven: Human Relations Area Files, 1957. xii+391 pp.

Peake, Frederick Gerard. *A History of Jordan and Its Tribes*. Coral Gables: University of Miami Press, 1958.

Perowne, Stewart. *The One Remains*. London: Hodder & Stoughton, 1954.

Phillips, Paul Grounds. *The Hashemite Kingdom of Jordan*. Chicago: 1954. xiv + 191 pp.

Qubain, Fahim I. *Education and Science in the Arab World*. Baltimore: Johns Hopkins Press, 1966.

Sanger, Richard H. *Where the Jordan Flows*. Washington: Middle East Institute, 1963.

Schumacher, Gotlieb. *Across the Jordan* (with additions by L. Ophiphant and G. LeStrange). New York: Scribner and Wilford, 1886.

Shwadran, B. *Jordan—a State of Tension*. New York: Council for Middle Eastern Affairs Press, 1959. 436 pp.

Toynbee, Arnold J. *Survey of International Affairs. 1925*. Vol. I. London, Oxford University Press, 1927.

United Nations. *Statistical Yearbook, 1968, 20th issue*. New York: U.N. Dept. Econ & Soc. Affairs, 1969.

————. General Assembly. *Report of the Commissioner General of the UNRWA for Palestinian Refugees in the Near East*. Official Records: 23rd Session. Supplement no. 13 (A/7213.) New York: United Nations, 1968.

————. Relief Works Agency for Palestine Refugees in the Near East. *Jordan Valley Agricultural Economic Survey, 1954*. 132 pp.

Vance, Vick and Pierre Lauer. *Ma Guerre avec Israel, Hussein de Jourdanie*. Paris: Albin, 1969.

Vatikiotis. P. J. *Politics and the Military in Jordan*. London: Cass, 1967.

Who's Who in the Arab World. 2d ed. 1967-68. Beirut: Les Editions Publitec, 1968.

Articles

It would outrun our space to list all the serial literature known to us on matters Jordanian within the history of the state as such. The listing below is offered for further reading on important recent landmarks on matters still of future concern.

"Is Jordan's economy dependent on the West Bank?" *Israel Economist*, 23, nos. 10-11 (O-N '67), pp. 225-6.

Campbell, D. "Jordan: The Economics of Survival," *International Journal*, 23, no. 1 (1967-68), pp. 109-23.

Dees, Joseph L. "Jordan's East Ghor Canal Project," *Middle East Journal, 13*, no. 4 (1959), pp. 357-71.

Dodd, P. and H. Barakat, "A nation in exile—Jordan's 1967 refugees: a research report," *Middle East Newsletter*, 1, no. 4 (D '67), pp. 2-5.

Furlonge, G. "Jordan Today," *Royal Central Asian Journal*, 53, pt. 3 (0 '66), pp.277-85.

Giustiniani, Gina, "Jerusalem: 1968," *Middle East Forum*, vol. XLV, nos. 1-2, pp. 101-8.

Haupert, J. S. "Recent progress of Jordan's East Ghor canal project," *Professional Geographer*, 18, no. 1 (Ja '66), pp. 9-13.

Hopkins, I. "The Hashemite Kingdom of Jordan—what is its future?" *Contemporary Review*, 212, no. 1225 (F '68), pp. 78-81.

Huizinga, J. "Can Hussein survive?" *Reporter*, 37, no. 3 (S 7, '67) pp. 34-6.

Kanovsky, E. "The economic aftermath of the Six Day War," *Middle East Journal*, 22, no. 3 (1968), pp. 278-96.

Lang, N. "Les avcaux des communistes jordaniens," *Est & Ouest*, 17, no. 371 (Nov 1-15, '66), pp. 5-10.

————. "Les communistes et les evenements de Jordanie," *Est & Ouest*, 17, no. 402 (Apr 1-15 '68), pp. 23-6.

Nassar, F. "Deepening of the political crisis in Jordan," *World Marxist Review*, 10, no. 3 (Mr '67), pp. 52-6.

————. "Jordan's road to complete liberation, democracy and social progress," *World Marxist Review*, 9, no. 1 (Jan '66), pp. 48-52.

Pepper, C. "Hussein approaches 'a point of no return,' " *New York Times Magazine*, (Apr 7, '68), 24ff.

Pharaon, H. and C. Wilson, "A year-long study of nutriture of Jordanian children," *Nutrition Review*, 25, (O '67), pp. 289-93.

Rouleau, E. "Crisis in Jordan," *World Today*, 23, no. 2 (F '67), pp. 62-70.

————. "En Jordanie," *Monde Diplomatique*, 14, no. 154, (Jan '67), p. 9.

al-Sha'ir, K. "The Jordanian economy and the seven year plan," (in Arabic) *Dirasat 'Arabiyyah*, 3, no. 6 (Apr '67), pp. 103-8.

Stroieva, L. "A trip to the Yemen, Kuwayt and Jordan," (in Russian) *Palestinskii Sbornik*, 78 (1966), pp. 228-38.

Ward, R. J. "Self help criteria in the development of Jordan," *Economia Internazionale*, 18, no. 2 (My '65), pp. 291-307.

Yaari, E. "Al-Fath's political thinking," *New Outlook*, XI, no. 9 (N-D '68).

Zabbal, S. "The Jordanian University: a new lighthouse of learning," (in Arabic) *Al-'Arabi*, no. 109 (D '67), pp. 76-90.

chapter 14

United Arab Republic

EMERGENCE OF MODERN EGYPT

In 1798 Napoleon invaded the Ottoman province of Egypt with the hope of using that territory as a base from which to threaten the British Empire by attacking India. The plan never developed, and Napoleon soon departed from Egypt, leaving behind him a French army of occupation. In 1801 this French occupation force was compelled to withdraw by the Turkish army in collaboration with British forces. When the British departed in 1803, Muhammad Ali, an Albanian junior officer, was left in control of several thousand Albanian and Bosnian troops. At that time, four forces were in competition for the control of Egypt: the Mamluks, who were the landed aristocracy; the people of Cairo; the Albanian troops; and the Ottoman pasha. Playing one faction against another, Muhammad Ali became the strongest political leader by 1806. He massacred the Mamluk leaders in 1811, and in 1815 he crushed a revolt among his own troops, thus completing the process of establishing his control over Egypt.

The effects on Egypt of Muhammad Ali's rule were profound, for it was necessary for him to completely reorganize Egyptian society to support his military aspirations. The Egyptian administration and treasury were both centralized under Ali's control. He also took ownership of all land and then redistributed it. He regularized taxation and rebuilt the agricultural base of the society in order to collect the revenues to support his military expeditions. Through the introduction of new crops and the provision of more adequate irrigation Egypt's cultivable land was increased by 140 percent and the revenues from that land were increased by 100 percent. Sanitation was also greatly improved and the annual outbreaks of cholera and bubonic plague, which in some years decimated as much as 10 percent of the population, were significantly restricted under effective quarantines and better sanitation.

Muhammad Ali's attempts to build a modern army based on Egyptian peasants necessitated higher education, particularly in technical areas, for many Egyptians. This need was met both by providing schools in Egypt and by sending Egyptians to European schools. Although the highest military posts were staffed by Turkish and Bosnian officers, the junior officers were primarily Egyptians, many of them from peasant stock. Finally, industry was needed to provide armaments for Ali's new army. Therefore he built factories and trained people to staff them.

Public reaction to all these changes kept them from complete success and permanency, but the effort toward modernization had created a small new middle class and a nucleus of forward-looking leaders.

From Muhammad Ali's death in 1849 to the accession of his grandson Ismail in 1863 Egyptian leadership lacked dynamism. Ismail, however, was as bent on Egypt's modernization as his grandfather had been. Ismail was a builder, and he spent huge sums on the construction of public works. He also attempted to Europeanize the Egyptian people by furthering education, increasing the number of schools from 185 to nearly 5,000. Finally, he bore a great part of the responsibility of opening the Suez Canal in 1869.

Unfortunately the resources of Egypt were not equal to Ismail's modernization plans and extravagances. To finance his works Ismail borrowed from European bankers. By 1874 the country was disastrously in debt and Ismail sold his 176,602 ordinary shares of Suez Canal stock to the British government in an ill-fated attempt to extricate himself from bankruptcy. However, in 1879 his creditors, England and France, forced the deposition of Ismail. Those countries placed his son Tewfik on the throne and assumed dual control over the country.

Development of Egyptian Nationalism

During the 77 years that Muhammad Ali and his successors ruled Egypt, the idea of nationalism was spreading through the country. The strongest voice in this movement was that of Jemal al-Din al-Afgani, a teacher who argued both for progressive reform through education and for popular government. Thanks to Ismail's expanded school system, Afgani's ideas filtered down through Egyptian society and touched even the peasants.

The condition of the peasantry changed very markedly between 1849 and 1880. The cessation of Muhammad Ali's expansion in 1841 lifted from the peasants the burden of supporting his military machine. At the same time, Ali's tax reforms, the increase of usable land, and Egypt's expanded trade helped many to rise above subsistence level. Then the spread of modernization and education under Ismail bound the Egyptians more tightly together. Finally, the domination of Egypt by Ismail's creditors gave Egyptians a focus for their new feelings of nationalism.

This atmosphere fostered the rapid spread of the ideas of Afgani and his followers, most notably Muhammad Abduh, an Islamic modernist who argued for a gradual reform beginning with a reform of Islam. About 1880 a number of newspapers sprang up to carry the ideas of these men. In these newspapers and in their books. Afgani, Abduh, and their followers questioned the traditional authority of Islamic leaders. They suggested that the individual had a responsibility for the condition of the world in which he lived. And by so arguing they laid the intellectual base necessary for a popular revolt.

The strongest movement against the British and French dual control of Egypt was that led by Colonel Ahmed Arabi. Many of his followers were lower ranking army officers, and Arabi himself was the son of a village peasant. His movement had a wide base of popular support.

Arabi's movement gained control of parliament as the National party and was powerful enough to force Tewfik to promise a constitution. The party then called a national assembly and in 1881 drew up a moderate reform program.

In 1882, however, Britain and France protested the formation of a constitutional government. They felt that Egypt's developing nationalism would free her from European control and jeopardize their financial interests. Britain presented two ultimatums, both of which were rejected. Thereupon Britain invaded and Arabi's forces were unable to stop her.

Arabi's revolt, although it failed, was one of the most significant events in the development of Egyptian nationalism. It was a social revolution as well as a political movement because the peasantry and the new middle class were for the first time expressing themselves as a political force through their support of Arabi. They were signifying their dislike of both foreign intervention in Egyptian affairs and of collaboration by their own leaders with foreign powers. In fact, it was because they saw their Khedive as only a puppet in foreign hands that they were able to go against the Islamic principle of obedience to any Islamic authority.

British Occupation

The British rule of occupied Egypt was very strict. The Egyptians were allowed a legislative council, but real power was held by the British administration under the British counsul general. The British began to organize Egypt's administration and to reduce her debt, but these improvements were made at the cost of any further modernization. Social and political problems and education were almost entirely ignored. Furthermore, the British administration was staffed entirely by English.

Muhammad Abduh and others worked for cooperation with the British as a means to improve Egypt. But the British refusal to allow an increase in self-government led much of the nationalist movement to develop independently. The nationalist movement during this time was markedly anti-British and oriented somewhat toward France. It derived in large part from the educated urban middle class.

In 1896 Mustafa Kamil, a French-educated lawyer, formed the *al-Watani* (Fatherland) party and rose to the leadership of the nationalist movement.

Abbas II, Tewfik's successor, allied himself with them. Then in 1906 a British officer was killed in a dispute with some peasants. British reaction was severe, and a number of Egyptians were shot and some were put to hard labor. Because popular indignation ran high, the Egyptian people were unified by the event. However, in 1908 Kamil died and the nationalist forces became disorganized. Finally, a new British administrator, Sir Eldon Gorst, brought Abbas II and his supporters back to a pro-British position.

Egyptian nationalism continued to threaten the occupation as new nationalist leaders rose to the fore. In 1913 Saad Zaghlul, a student of al-Afgani and Muhammad Abduh, became president of the newly formed legislative assembly despite British disfavor. Because by that time the British administration was incapable of dealing with Egyptian economic and social problems, resistance and noncooperation were common. Only the advent of World War I prevented a direct confrontation between the administration and the nationalists.

In 1914 Britain formally declared a protectorate over Egypt and used the country during the next four years as a military base. During this period, labor was conscripted, a large number of British forces (whose arrogance and ethnocentrism antagonized the native populations) were brought into Egypt, and rampant inflation took place because of their ability to pay higher prices for commodities. Restrictions on the production of cotton were imposed, and confiscated crops were sold at huge profits for the government. Furthermore, troops commandeered supplies, such as peasants' donkeys, and Egyptians were drafted into the army.

Thus, all levels of Egyptian society were embittered against the British as a result of these drastic war measures imposed on the country. However, nationalist leaders determined to hold their forces in check while the war lasted, but Egypt's internal pressures indicated severe Anglo-Egyptian difficulties in the near future.

Two days after the armistice, Saad Zaghlul and his followers, forming the Egyptian delegation (Wafd), presented to the British commissioner General Sir Reginald Wingate a demand for independence and the right to send an Egyptian delegation to London to present their case. Although Wingate urged his government to allow Zaghlul to proceed to London, permission was refused. The Egyptians demonstrated their protest in mass meetings, and the British retaliated by deporting Zaghlul and three of his followers to Malta. This in turn caused a popular uprising and general strike that involved all Egypt, and the British were forced to release the prisoners and allow them to attend the Paris Peace Conference. At Paris, however, Zaghlul's delegation failed to secure Egypt's independence; the British protectorate was recognized by the attending nations.

Independent Egypt

Despite Zaghlul's failure at Paris the British decided to take steps to ameliorate Anglo-Egyptian antagonisms. A commission was sent to investigate the problem and determine what form of constitution might be most suitable for

Egypt. Then in 1920 the English drew up a treaty of alliance with Egypt to replace the protectorate. Both Zaghlul and the Egyptian people turned the treaty down, fearing a disguised continuation of British occupation. The British, appreciating that Zaghlul would agitate against any treaty, deported him, and in March 1922 Britain unilaterally terminated the protectorate. Egypt became a monarchy under King Ahmed Fuad, but Britain continued to hold the reigns of power.

In 1923 Egypt wrote a new constitution. Parliment could veto the king by a two-thirds vote, but the king could dissolve parliament and rule by decree. In the first constitutional election Zaghlul's Wafd party gained an overwhelming majority in parliament and Zaghlul became prime minister. Thus, although the nationalist upheaval of the previous three years had only nominally achieved its objective, it had changed Egyptian society. Muslims and non-Muslims had broken down the barriers between themselves in their common effort. Even women had emerged in politics. Finally, the new middle class had established itself as a major social and political force.

From this upheaval there also emerged the Wafd party with Zaghlul at its head. The Wafd was Egypt's nationalist party, the one political organ representing the hopes of Egypt's people. During its 30 years of existence (1922-1952) it won every free election, but conflicts with the king invariably led to dismissal or resignation of the Wafd government and the dissolution of parliament. Thus, it actually held power for a total of only 7½ years. Even as an opposition party, however, the Wafd served Egyptian nationalism, striking out at governmental corruption and pursuing the interests of the people. Although it was oriented primarily toward the middle class and did little to recognize or ameliorate the social and economic problems of the country, its leaders—Saad Zaghlul and, after Zaghlul's death in 1927, Mustafa al-Nahas—were able to manipulate the masses. But of far more importance was the fact that the Wafd did represent the aspirations of Egyptians for freedom from foreign control and for representative government. And throughout the next three decades Egyptian politics was a three-way power struggle between the Wafd, the palace, and the British high commissioner's office.

In 1936 two events eased relations between Egypt and England: King Fuad died and was succeeded by his son Farouk; and Italy invaded Ethiopia. In the resulting climate of lessened hostility the Anglo-Egyptian Treaty of 1936 was concluded. Under the treaty the occupation was changed to a 20-year alliance, the Sudan was opened to unlimited Egyptian immigration, and the capitulations established by the protectorate were ended. In 1937 Farouk came of age and forced the Wafd from power. At the same time, the threat of war in the Mediterranean diminished, and Anglo-Egyptian relations again became strained.

At the beginning of World War II Egypt was once again turned into a British base. Although the upper echelon of Egyptian society prospered as a result of the war, the masses—farmers, rural and urban workers, and the salaried middle class—suffered severe privation analagous to their experiences in World War I.

Attempts by successive prime ministers, Ali Maher, Hasan Sabri, and Husain Siri respectively, to keep Egypt neutral resulted in drastic measures by the British. Axis sympathizers were purged from the government, the palace was barricaded, and Farouk was forced at gun-point to hand over the reins of government to Mustafa al-Nahas, leader of the Wafd party. This British-Wafdist alliance against the king caused a reaction in the military, beginning the chain of events which ended in the 1952 revolution. Nonetheless the Egyptian people stood behind the Wafd in its support for the British.

However, by the end of the war the Wafd had proven to be ineffective in administration and as corrupt as the palace. As a result of this failure and its collaboration with the British, the party lost much of its cohesiveness and popularity. When in 1944 the British withdrew their support of Nahas, Farouk dismissed him and reinstated the Saadist party, a pro-palace splinter group of the Wafd established in 1932. The Wafd did not regain power again until 1950.

By the end of the war Egypt was determined to revise the Anglo-Egyptian Treaty of 1936. The Wafd in particular agitated for this revision in the hope of regaining their lost popularity by once again focusing their campaign on Egyptian frustration with British occupation and dominance. Special grievances were the continuing presence of British troops in the Canal Zone and the status of the Sudan. Egypt demanded a complete withdrawal of British forces and insisted on the "unity of the Nile Valley."

Since Britain's establishment of the condominium over the Sudan in 1899, Egypt had sought to reunite the Nile Valley. This demand became most vocal after World War II. The unity of the Nile Valley theme was based on historical, ethnic, cultural, economic, and strategic considerations. Historically, Egypt and the Sudan had been united throughout a large part of the Pharaonic period and into the modern era. This union was primarily due to the topographic features of the Nile Valley. The great river renders the area a single geographic unit uninterrupted by physical obstacles, such as mountains or deserts. Ethnically and culturally the two countries share a common racial intermixture, and both Islam and Arabic language and culture prevail except in the southern Sudan, whose peoples are predominantly Negroid and speak various non-Arabic languages. Furthermore, both countries are dependent upon the Nile and their economies can be complementary and supplementary. But by far the foremost consideration is strategic. For the Nile River runs through the heart of the Sudan and it can therefore control the waters flowing northward. The importance of this was graphically expressed by an Egyptian army colonel in 1948:

No politician can ignore Egypt's interest in the Sudan. Its permanent and vital interest concerns Egypt's life. Egypt gets its water from the Nile, which flows through the heart of the Sudan. To Egypt the Nile is a matter of life or death. If the waters of this river were discontinued or were controlled by a hostile state, or a state that could become hostile, Egypt's life is over. Of course, whoever controls the Sudan naturally controls the northern Nile Valley. Egypt in this era of conflicting political doctrines cannot trust the neighbors of the Sudan. Today's friends may become tomorrow's enemies. For this reason, all of Egypt's efforts are to insure for herself a secure future.[1]

In 1948 Egypt joined the Palestine war. The poor performance of the Egyptian army against Jewish forces, plus the revelation that corrupt government officials had deliberately purchased faulty arms from some Western countries, deeply humiliated the Egyptian people, particularly the young junior army officers. Furthermore, Britain was considered responsible for the establishment of the state of Israel. Against this background of tension, the Wafd party came back to power in 1950. Nahas returned to the premiership, and in 1951 abrogated the 1936 Anglo-Egyptian Treaty and declared Farouk king of Egypt and Sudan. Hostilities broke out between Egyptians and British, and in December 43 Egyptian policemen were killed during a British attack on the police barracks of Ismailia. Cairo erupted in riot on the infamous "Black Saturday," January 26, 1952. Farouk used the occasion to dismiss Nahas and reinstate Ali Maher. However, he too was forced from office shortly thereafter, throwing Egypt into its most serious political crisis in a generation. It was against this background of tension, unrest, and potential anarchy that on July 23, 1952 a group of Free Officers executed a successful and almost bloodless coup d'etat.

EGYPT IN REVOLUTION

In introduction, it should be sufficient to state that the results of the July 23, 1952 coup in the (then) Kingdom of Egypt have been far different from what its opponents, outside observers, or even its participants foresaw at the time. The goals of the Free Officers' Committee were ambiguous and limited, but the coup against the corruption of the court of Farouk has become a true social and political revolution which appears to be leading to a socialist society committed to the complete modernization of Egypt and its people. It is the evolution of these revolutionary policies and the ideas which have created them that will be the subject of this section.

From Coup d'Etat to Revolution: 1952-1958

On the night of July 22-23, 1952 a group of young army officers conducted a coup against the government of Egypt. King Farouk abdicated on July 26 in favor of his son and went into exile. The Egyptian monarchy came to a formal end on June 18 of the following year, when the Republic was proclaimed. But in reality the monarchy was over the day of the coup, and from that date Egypt aspired to a new role in world affairs.

---

[1] Abdul Rahman Zaki, *al-Sharq Alawsat* (The Middle East) (Cairo, 1948), pp. 63-64.

The causes of the Free Officers' coup are numerous, and reasons for its success are not hard to find. By 1952 Egypt's socioeconomic problems had become extreme, and the existing political structure rendered them insoluble for lack of inclination or initiative in undertaking the reforms necessary to ameliorate them. Basically, Egypt's economic problem was twofold: overpopulation and poverty. At the time of Muhammad Ali's suzerainty over Egypt, the country contained a population of approximately 3,000,000. By 1952 it had grown to about 20,000,000—an increase of 566 percent in little more than a hundred years. To a large extent it was the reforms, order, and security instituted by Ali and his successors and continued by the British that made this growth possible. The improvements in sanitation and health lowered the mortality rate, while expansion of irrigation, land reclamation, improved agricultural methods, and land reform made it possible for the country to support this growth. Furthermore, the introduction and eventual predominance of cotton cultivation made the population expansion desirable, as cotton cultivation required a large and cheap labor force. However, well before 1952 the rate of population growth far outstripped the amount of cultivable land. Even the potentials for increasing cultivable land are severely limited, for Egypt is 94 percent desert and depends entirely upon river irrigation. The entire population lives on only 4 percent of the country's total area, making Egypt the most densely populated country in the world—about 1500 people per square mile.

The poverty thus augmented by overpopulation was further compounded by the concentration of land-ownership in a few hands. At the time of the revolution less than one half of 1 percent of the proprietors owned 37 percent of the arable land. Furthermore, these large landowners lived in the cities and were out of touch with conditions in the rural countryside where 80 percent of the population lived. This small group invariably controlled Egypt's political, social, and economic life, and they manipulated conditions to their own advantage.

The extreme poverty of the masses began to worsen by the 1920s as a result of the fall in money and real income. The standard of living fell from a yearly per-capita income of £12.5 in 1913 to £7.6 in 1951 at constant prices. This lower standard was further evidenced by the decline in consumption of such staple commodities as tobacco, coffee, meat, cereals, and textiles in spite of a percentage population increase. The incidence of malnutrition, undernourishment, disease, and even famine rose correspondingly in the villages.

Another result of peasant poverty was rural migration to urban areas. As Richard H. Nolte observed:

Peasant migration to the cities, where the average income level was higher, had resulted in an urban population increase at a rate twice that of the country as a whole, and had helped to create a mounting urban unemployment problem. It had also helped to create a large urban proletariat, a jam-packed, uprooted, highly mobile, easily excited, and hungry mass of people living in daily contact with the ostentatious wealth of king and pashas.[2]

The political situation in Egypt was no better. The government richly deserved the overused condemnation of political bankruptcy. Since early 1942, when the British forced the king to accept Nahas Pasha as prime minister in place of the pro-Axis Ali Maher, the king had lost the support of the nation and sank into sterile extravagances. The Wafd (delegation) party had lost dynamic leadership, and its conservative old guard were unprepared to take the radical steps necessary to improve Egypt's economic and social problems.

Despite the acquistion of large amounts of foreign exchange during World War II, by 1952 the reserves were exhausted and the foreign debt was growing rapidly. Egyptian industry had grown up behind the riff barriers and had replaced many foreign imports, but there was no sign that it would develop the efficiency to become competitive in the export trade or that it would be capable of replacing imports as a source of capital goods. Agricultural production was growing and productivity was high, although the expansion of production into marginal lands and the increasing use of expensive fertilizers cut agricultural earnings. But population growth more than matched the rise in production, and Egypt was still forced to purchase much of its food abroad. Only services were expanding rapidly in terms of numbers employed (from 1,386,050 in 1937 to 1,927,260 in 1947), and there is suspicion that this growth was caused by a migration of workers to the cities from farms on which their marginal productivity was near zero, rather than because of any great independent increase in employment opportunities. In other words, urbanization was more a product of agricultural poverty than of urban wealth.

Finally, the continued strength of foreign, especially British, influence in Egypt was distasteful to nationalist elements. The inability of the government to settle the status of the Sudan or to arrange the withdrawal of British troops from the Suez Canal Zone led to friction. The climax of these events was the Black Saturday riots in which most of the foreign quarter of Cairo was burned. The evident inability of the government to control the unstable situation left it bereft of political capital in the nation. This was the situation which led the Free Officers' Committee to take action.

The Free Officers' Committee was composed primarily of a group of young officers who had graduated together from the military college in 1938 (the first class of lower- and middle-class students permitted to enter) and who had developed a broad secret organization in the army. They became more active after the debacle of the Palestine war of 1948-49, and the government, aware of their presence, was preparing to act just prior to their coup. The acknowledged head of the group was Gamal Abdul Nasser, son of a post office clerk. Colonel

---

[2] American University Field Staff Reports, *Northeast Africa Series*, Vol. III, No. 1, "Social Change and Industrialization in Egypt," p. 29.

Nasser, a distinguished veteran of the Faluja campaign, was attached to the staff college at the time of the coup. The Free Officers were young (their ages averaged 33 years) and relatively unknown. In order to obtain wider support they chose as their nominal leader the respected officer and distinguished soldier, General Mohammed Naguib. Their youth, idealism, and patent political naivete led them to unwarranted optimism about the results of a coup. But at least one thing was evident the morning of July 23, 1952—the people of Egypt were willing to allow the young military men to make an attempt at government.

In the first months after the July coup d'etat the Free Officers under the leadership of their 13-man executive committee, the Revolutionary Command Council, attempted to reorganize the political system and restore order to Egyptian life. It had been their expectation that the older national leaders of the Wafd and such politicians as Ali Maher would take the lead in forming a viable civilian government. They had assessed the situation in Egypt as caused by a useless aristocracy and an exploitative colonial power, and had assumed that once Egypt was rid of these parasites the people would unite behind a reformed government and proceed with the modernizing of the nation. Unfortunately, there were no civilian leaders capable of overseeing a revolution, and, for the time being, the R.C.C. was forced to govern almost without assistance. As President Nasser recorded in his *Philosophy of the Revolution*, the disillusionment of the young officers, dedicated as they were to ideals of national service which had as yet affected few of Egypt's people, was great in the first years of the revolution. What Gamal Nasser and his cohorts had assumed as a condition of prerevolutionary Egyptian society—the existence of a nation in the full sense of the word—had yet to be created.

The first crisis of the revolution occured little more than a month after the overthrow of the monarchy. The Free Officers had little in the way of ideological commitments, but they were committed to certain institutional reforms, especially in the land tenure system. In early September 1952 a land reform program was proposed by the R.C.C. to Ali Maher, who had been appointed prime minister. Ali Maher and his civilian associates were not ready to attack the interests of the landowning classes. When Maher attempted to stall or dilute the reform, he was removed, and on September 9, 1952 General Mohammed Naguib assumed the post of prime minister. The land reform program proceeded immediately.

By the Land Reform Act ownership of land was limited to 200 *feddans* (1 f=1.038 acres), with an additional allowance of 100 *feddans* for families with more than two children. An estimated 7 percent of Egypt's cultivated land was confiscated and redistributed to landless peasants in two and five *feddan* plots. A rent reform was included in the land reform program, which involved rent controls on both land and dwellings. Some 150,000 families benefited from the land redistribution, but the rent controls have had greater effects upon the conditions of the lower classes in Egyptian society, especially the urban working class.

Aside from the Land Reform Act, the new regime followed traditional patterns in its economic policy. Although the R.C.C. gave more emphasis to government investment in social overhead capital than the old regime had, no new principles of economic policy or social organization were established at this time. Government interference in the economy was limited to tax and tariff policy and the control of central banking through the National Bank of Egypt, which was, however, a privately owned firm.

After the members of the R.C.C. had made a series of speaking tours in the country to establish their popularity, the regime began moves to weaken the old political parties. It was considered that the Wafd and other smaller parties were incapable of providing the type of leadership Egypt needed, and that they could only be divisive influences. On September 10, 1952 a law of political parties was promulgated which required registration of parties and declaration of financial operations. This weakened the parties enough to allow on January 23, 1953 the formation of a National Liberation Rally, and the dissolution of the old parties. On February 10 a provisional constitution was proclaimed for the period until a permanent constitution could be written. The rule by decree thus established was not to end until 1956.

Having removed the king and the old parties, the R.C.C. faced only three major obstacles to the full consolidation of their rule: the Muslim Brotherhood (al-Ikhwan al-Muslimun), General Mohammed Naguib, and the British. The Muslim Brotherhood, founded in the 1920s by Hasan al-Bana, was a right-wing extremist group, devoted to the reinstitution of an Islamic state. Its membership was reputed to number over one million, with four thousand in the secret terrorist unit. It was the only large organized group in Egypt once the political parties had been dissolved. General Naguib had been vested with the offices of president and prime minister as figurehead positions, but the younger officers began to be concerned about the extent of his power. He was more conservative than the original conspirators, and he had connections with both the old conservative classes and the Muslim Brotherhood, although the importance of the latter was probably exaggerated.

In February 1954 the dispute between Naguib and the R.C.C. became open. After some months Nasser outmaneuvered Naguib and the general was effectively stripped of power by April of 1954. He retained the largely ceremonial office of president, however, for a time. On October 26, 1954 a workman who confessed to being a member of the Muslim Brotherhood made an attempt on Nasser's life. The Brotherhood was subsequently banned and many of its leaders imprisoned. Nasser had previously purged the army, government, and police of Communists and Muslim Brotherhood members, and was easily able to disband the group. Naguib was implicated in the alleged conspiracy on Nasser's life, and in November he was removed from all posts and placed under virtual house arrest.

Anglo-Egyptian relations had been strained for many years. The two major problems were the Sudan, which was under the joint control of Britain and Egypt, and the Suez Canal, which was occupied by British troops. The R.C.C.

proved more compromising on these issues than the old regime had been. Consequently, on February 12, 1954 the two governments revoked the Anglo-Egyptian Condominium on the Sudan and agreed to a plebiscite to be held within three years in which the Sudan would decide its own fate. It was expected that the Sudanese would opt for union with Egypt, but internal divisions in the Sudan, Britain's careful cultivation of antiunion factions, and the reaction to the dismissal of Naguib who was popular among the Sudanese, contributed to the decision for complete independence.

At any rate, this cleared the way for an agreement on the terms for British evacuation of the Suez Canal Zone. In the fall of 1954 an agreement was reached by which the British were to withdraw within 20 months. The evacuation was completed ahead of schedule, by June 18, 1956.

With the British now removed as a threat to Egypt's full sovereignty, Nasser looked to the West as the logical source of friendship and support, stating, "After the Suez agreement there is nothing to stand in the way of our good relations with the West."[3] He expected Egypt's primary ties to remain with the West and arms and aid to continue to be supplied by the West. But two problems stood in the way of the full consolidation of friendly relations: U.S. Secretary of State John Foster Dulles' attempts to create Middle East defense alliances, and the West's support of Israel. Regarding the first, as early as 1953, when a defense alliance was first proposed to include Egypt, Nasser warned, "Agitation for pacts at present would be used by the Communists and ultra-nationalists to stir up hatred and violence against the West."[4] This warning was not lightly made, for Nasser could ill afford to entangle Egypt in an alliance that could be construed by the public, who had struggled so long to free themselves from Britain, as another form of subservience.

However, Secretary of State Dulles pursued a Middle East defense alliance with vigor, considering any neutralist stand in the cold war to be immoral. With Egypt unwilling to cooperate, he therefore evolved the concept of Northern Tier defense against Communist aggression. This plan was to include Iraq. Nasser, on the other hand, was pursuing his own Middle East policy, one that aimed at establishing Egypt as the leader of the Arab nations. Cairo radio and newspapers, reaching audiences throughout the Arab world, disseminated Arab nationalist ideas and excited an already impassioned public. The Baghdad Pact, as the treaty came to be called, now became the target of Cairo's frontal attacks. Nuri al-Said, Premier of Iraq and real power wielder there, in particular was villanized as a Western puppet and an obstacle to Arab progress. To Nasser the Baghdad Pact appeared an obvious attempt to isolate Egypt, with its revolutionary principles, from the Middle East and thus make the Middle East dependent upon the United States.

When in February 1955 Israel raided the Gaza Strip in force, this action convinced Nasser of the aggressive intentions of Israel and of the fact that the

---

[3] *JANA* (Colombo, Ceylon), Vol. 1, No. 5 (September 1954), p. 16.
[4] *Ibid.*

tripartite declaration of 1950—by which the United States, France, and Britain guaranteed the integrity of the territory of all the states of the Middle East—would not be effectuated against Israel. In this, too, Nasser considered that the Baghdad Pact was a method of protecting Israel. Shortly after the raid he stated, "As long as Egypt is the shield of Arabism in its fight with Zionism, complete victory for Western policies requires, first of all, the isolation of Egypt from her Arab sisters."[5] Thus, to counteract the Baghdad Pact and in response to Israel's raid, Nasser sponsored the Arab Mutual Security Pact with Syria and Saudi Arabia.

Nasser was also on a collision course with Western policies in North and sub-Saharan Africa, where he supported and aided nationalist aspirations against the colonial powers. It was at this period in April 1955, when Egyptian-Western relations were at a very low ebb, that Nasser attended the Bandung Conference of Afro-Asian Nations at which he articulated his doctrine of positive neutrality and emerged as one of the major spokesmen of anti-imperialism. There he established Egypt as a leading nation in the Third World and raised his stature to that of such leading neutralists as Nehru and Sukarno.

It was also in this period that Nasser began seeking arms to modernize his army as a result of Israel's Gaza raid. His requests from Western nations were denied. Therefore in September 1955 he announced that he had arranged for an exchange of Egyptian cotton for Czech weaponry. This was an unprecedented act on the part of a Middle Eastern state which had traditionally been within the sphere of influence of the West. The Western states correctly feared that it would set a trend for other nations, open the door to Soviet influence, and break down the traditional economic ties between the states of the area and the West. Furthermore, this act, in conjunction with Egypt's recognition of Communist China in May of 1955, convinced Secretary Dulles that Nasser was falling into the Communist camp.

It was in this background of estranged Egyptian-Western relations that the Aswan High Dam controversy arose, bringing about one of the major world crises of the century. The High Dam project was one of the cherished dreams of Egypt's revolutionary leaders. It would provide almost unlimited electric power for the delta and increase Egypt's cultivable area by about 30 percent. The High Dam project thus offered the hope of relieving the ever-increasing population pressures by providing the necessary hydroelectricity for industrialization and some 2,000,000 more acres of agricultural land. Those who cherished the dream of the High Dam considered that it would revolutionize the standard of living and bring Egypt a healthy and balanced economy. But construction of such a project was far beyond Egypt's ability to support it. Its estimated cost was $1,350,000,000. Extensive foreign assistance would be required, and Nasser began seeking methods to finance it, including the possibility of a $200,000,000 loan from the International Bank.

---

[5] *Al-Ahram* (Cairo), March 9, 1955, p. 7.

In the fall of 1955 rumors, probably unsubstantiated, began to circulate about Soviet financing of the Aswan High Dam. The United States, however, expressed interest in the project, and after financing and feasibility studies, made an offer of financing through the World Bank. The United States offered $56 million, Britain $14 million, and the World Bank $200 million. Each loan was contingent upon the others, so that the offer was an indivisible package. Nasser hesitated for some time before replying to the offer, perhaps awaiting a firm offer from the Soviet Union. At all events, he accepted the offer and the United States withdrew their portion of it at almost the same hour on July 19, 1956. Although it is uncertain why the offer was withdrawn, Nasser's hesitation probably had something to do with it and the Egyptian recognition of Communist China may have had an effect. However, the coincidence of acceptance and withdrawal created an embarrassing situation. In response to the withdrawal of the loan (both as a retort to the affront given him and as a means of obtaining financing for the Aswan High Dam), Nasser nationalized the Suez Canal.

Although it had been anticipated that the Egyptians would be unable to operate the canal, technicians were found and the level of shipping maintained. After lengthy negotiations between Egypt, Britain, and France broke down, the French and British determined upon military action. On October 29, 1956 the Israeli army attacked through the Sinai and the Gaza Strip, routing most of the Egyptian forces it met. On October 31 French and British paratroopers landed in the Suez Canal Zone. Port Said was shelled, with much destruction of property and loss of life. However, United States and Soviet diplomatic action, through the United Nations and other channels, forced the cessation of hostilities and the eventual withdrawal of the invading forces. The British and French suffered the loss of much prestige and considerable expense, especially as the Egyptian government sequestered and nationalized all French and British holdings in Egypt. Egypt also suffered from the loss of revenue by the stoppage of the canal. But what appeared to be a decisive military defeat for Egypt was transformed into a considerable diplomatic victory.

The Suez crisis established the independence of Egyptian foreign policy. It also confirmed Nasser's suspicions of Western imperialism. Its most important effect, however, was the rise in Nasser's prestige in the Middle East and the neutralist world. These three factors, with his domestic policy position, led Nasser into a more adventurous foreign policy from late 1956 until the climax of this policy in the union with Syria and the other events of 1958.

After the Suez crisis and the war of October 29 to November 6, 1956, Egypt had an established position as a sovereign state. It could no longer be regarded as a semisovereign entity, subject to the whims of the Great Powers. No longer tied to Western policies and apparently outside the legitimate sphere of Western influence, Nasser was free to find his own direction in foreign affairs.

The French and British invasion and the collusion with Israel confirmed Nasser's suspicions of Western intentions. France and Britain were regarded as the archimperialists and Israel as an outpost of imperialism in the Middle East. The actions of the United States in condemning France, Britain, and Israel gave new prestige to the Middle Eastern view of American policy, but America's connections with the colonial powers were not forgotten, and the United States was regarded as largely to blame for the situation leading up to the crisis.

Imperialism was still viewed as a primarily Western attitude, and the United States fell under this stigma. The U.S.S.R. was not so closely identified with imperialist motives, and the principles of Marxism-Leninism were certainly antimperialist. In any event, the continuation of U.S. aid to Israel was regarded as hostile to Arab interests. At this point, connections with either power bloc were unwanted, but the Eastern bloc appeared the lesser of two evils.

In early 1957 the United States unveiled its latest effort in collective security: the Eisenhower Doctrine. The United States offered to supply arms to Middle Eastern states endangered by international communism. The offer, apparently meant to reinforce the Baghdad Pact, was regarded as a further attempt to render the Middle Eastern states dependent upon American aid. United States prestige in the Middle East was significantly reduced, and Nasser began a serious campaign against the Eisenhower Doctrine and the Baghdad Pact.

Nasser's popularity in the Middle East made this campaign a serious threat to Western interests in the area, including the interests of the pro-Western rulers in the area. For his anti-Western campaign Nasser had two available strategies. He could have tried to establish close ties with all current Middle Eastern political leaders, including traditional rulers, and to organize them against the West. However, his revolutionary policies had aroused the distrust of the traditional elites in the Middle East, and his revolutionary principles prevented him from trusting them. The other course of action was to attempt to arouse popular feeling in the other states of the area in favor of his policies, and to aid revolutionary causes which might replace the traditional rulers with leaders more sympathetic with his cause. The latter course had the advantages of promising to produce leaders he could trust and deal with and of being a step toward the realization of his goals of Arab unity and revolutionary democracy. Thus, he began a series of propaganda attacks against the pro-Western governments in the Middle East, particularly Jordan and Iraq.

Meanwhile, unrest, dissatisfaction, and ineptitude brought the Syrian system to the point of political bankruptcy by early 1958. On February 1 Nasser agreed to a Syrian request for a merger of the two states into a United Arab Republic. A plebiscite in the two nations confirmed the union. This consolidation placed such great pressure upon neighboring states that the Hashemite kings of Jordan and Iraq attempted to form a union of their two states. This latter union was never effective, but it did stir up the pro-Nasser opposition to the Hashemite regimes.

Other events in the Middle East during 1958 threatened to bring to Nasser hegemony over the entire area. In March the fiscal extravagances of King Saud of Saudi Arabia brought his brother Faisal to power, although not to formal possession of the throne. Prince Faisal was notably closer in his positions to Nasser than Saud had been. This allowed Nasser to remove the threat inherent in having the power of Saudi Arabia's wealth aligned against him. In April the regime of King Husein of Jordan was threatened by Nasserite forces in the army, primarily among the junior officers. In May civil controversy in Lebanon over the attempt of President Camille Chamoun to extend his term in office by an unconstitutional four years reached the point of open disorder. By the end of June civil strife between this nation's pan-Arabists and Lebanese separatists appeared imminent.

The crisis in the Middle East reached its peak in the middle of July. In the early hours of the 14th dissident forces under General Abd al-Karim Kassim entered Baghdad. Within two hours the government was overthrown; the king, Prime Minister Nuri al-Said, and many associates of the old ruling group were assassinated; and the Republic was proclaimed. Kassim immediately expressed pro-Nasser and anti-Western sentiments and withdrew from the Baghdad Pact.

At this point, it looked as though all Western interests in the Middle East were in jeopardy and Nasserite factions would become supreme throughout the area. A federation of all Arab states in the Middle East under the leadership of Nasser appeared not only probable but imminent. The Western powers and their friends in the Middle East reestablished themselves, however, although on a weaker footing than before, and divisions in the new group of Arab leaders quickly became apparent.

The Union with Syria

From February 1958 until September 1961 Nasser's chief task was the creation of a true union with Syria. This involved the integration of the political system and, more fundamentally, the economic and social systems. The two states were very dissimilar in tradition and culture, and to integrate their societies it was obviously necessary that their institutions be brought into coincidence. Nasser attempted to export the principles and methods of the Egyptian revolution to Syria. However, they lost much in the transition.

Nasser's views of Egyptian society had been pragmatically evolved out of and were modified by the experience of the revolution. He had, as his development of the idea of positive neutralism indicates, formed from his experience in Egypt certain ideas about modernization which he felt could be generalized for all modernizing societies. Thus, he proved more dogmatic in meeting Syrian conditions. His approach to the situation in Syria was an attempt to apply these ideas. The approach proved to be unsuitable for Syrian society.

Syria in 1958 had, despite the general disorganization of its political system, a number of well-organized political parties, the Baath party being one of the largest. The wealthier classes in Syria were better organized than had been the case in pre-revolutionary Egypt. An oligarchic economic structure was a powerful factor in Syrian society. Whereas the Egyptian government had always been organized as a strong centralized state, the Syrian government had always been of a more laissez-faire order. Also, the private sector in Syria was more politically influential than the Egyptian private sector had been before the 1952 revolution.

Nasser had built his government in Egypt upon a centralized state mechanism that preexisted his revolution and was more or less accepted by the populace. In Syria he was forced to attempt to impose a powerful state upon a nation which was internally diffused, which was unaccustomed to the statist concepts, and which was far from his ideal of socialism. At the narrowest level, he had to create in Syria a governmental structure modeled after the one he had built in Egypt. He had also to modify the political system toward his ideal of equality. At the broadest level was the necessity to remake the ideals and symbols of the Syrian people so that unitary government would be possible for the United Arab Republic.

A major problem in extending the governmental system from Egypt to Syria lay in the fact that the Egyptian system was well-integrated. It proved difficult to draw Syrian personnel into the government at the higher levels and maintain the smoothly working efficiency Nasser desired. The most notable exception was the commander of the Syrian branch of the secret police, Abdal Hamid Serraj, who was a loyal personal follower of Nasser and became the United Arab Republic's minister of the interior. The prevalence of Egyptians at the higher levels of government aroused anxieties in Syria about the possible suppression of the nation's identity. Disaffection accordingly began to grow in Syrian political circles.

In the elections of 1960 the Baath party failed to gain any significant number of seats in the National Assembly, and its leaders considered that the Nasserite attitude toward parties (all parties had been brought into the National Union) would destroy the Baath as a viable movement. In the 1958-61 period Nasser was proceeding with the nationalization of Egyptian industry, and in mid-1961 laws were promulgated beginning the process of nationalization in Syria. The Syrian landowners had been largely dispossessed through land reforms in 1959 and 1960, but they retained much of their political power. After the new nationalization laws, the commercial and industrial capitalists combined with the landowning class, the disaffected persons in the government and the army, and much of the leadership of the Baath in opposition to the Nasser regime. And in September of 1961 a military coup was conducted against the Nasserite officials in Damascus, and Syrian independence was proclaimed.

Nasser decided that the use of force in an attempt to retain Syria was impractical in the face of Syrian opinion. It appears that the use of violence to enforce an Arab union was contrary to his principles of Arab unity as well. The failure of the union of Syria was a bitter blow to Nasser's hopes, and no attempt has been made to minimize the setback it was to him. However, it is probable that the difficulties of ruling the dual state had been so great that Nasser was in many respects relieved by the Syrian secession. He has continued to use the title United Arab Republic to indicate his continued hope of eventual Arab unity, but the experience of the union changed some of his ideas about the conditions necessary for a union of Arab states.

The chapter in the *Charter of Popular Forces* (May 1962) dealing with Arab unity expresses the hope of eventual unity based upon "the unity of objectives of the popular bases" in the Arab world. But the emphasis shifts from foreign imperialism to internal reactionary forces, and it seems that he calls for internal revolutionary change and the adoption of the socialist system within each state before the goal of unity may be fulfilled. Caution is evident about the efficacy of revolutionary change, however, as in the statement: "Speeding up the various stages of development towards unity would create—as experience has shown—economic and social loopholes that could be exploited by the elements opposed to unity to undermine it." In speaking of the mission of the United Arab Republic to encourage Arab unity, Nasser states in the *Charter*, "However, she cannot impose on them a precise form for revolution." Rather than attempting to achieve political unity first and then carrying out revolutionary transformations of the various states, the aim of the United Arab Republic is to encourage the revolutionary transformations that will make unity possible and, it is thought, inevitable.

NASSERISM

To the end of 1956 Nasser's approach to politics was primarily practical. The concerns of building a viable political order and maintaining the position of the Revolutionary Command Council were paramount. There was no time and little inclination to build an ideology as well. Nasser's main concern until the Suez crisis was the "domestic security of his regime of moderate revolution."[6] Even positive neutralism and the Suez crisis situation had been generated by reactions to events impinging upon Egyptian circumstances.

After 1956, as Egypt began to impinge upon the politics of other states, there developed a more deliberate construction of ideological tenets and the application of such tenets to both domestic and foreign affairs. And the term Nasserism came into general usage to explain the relationship between Nasser's ideas and Egypt's internal and external politics. It is, however, a somewhat erroneous eponym created by observers of the revolutionary movement in Egypt. Nasser continues to act with a considerable degree of pragmatism and flexibility, and Nasserism has not been much expressed as a concrete dogma. Also Nasser's thought, the basis of Nasserism, is to a large degree typical of Middle Eastern political thought and his role is simply that of the first effective articulator of policy with this general set of attitudes. Nasser himself recognized

---

[6] Leonard Binder, "Egypt's Positive Neutrality," in Morton A. Kaplan, ed., *The Revolution in World Politics* (New York and London, 1962), p. 179.

this in his 1955 pamphlet, *The Philosophy of the Revolution*, when he denies that he is in any sense a philosopher or even a historian, but merely the latest in a series of leaders of an inevitable movement.[7] Thus, the term Nasserism is misleading to some extent because the movement is neither original nor exclusive with Nasser.

Yet the force of Nasserism, the principles it embodies and the movement it designates, is real and volatile. It has spread throughout the Arab world as a new nationalism to upset the status quo and threaten the balance of power not only in the immediate area but in the world as well. In the remainder of this chapter we shall examine the major principles underlying the policies and doctrines of this force, and through this perspective bring the history of the United Arab Republic to the present and assess the Republic's prospects in its search for development, socialism, and an effective position in the world political community. As will be seen, economic, domestic, and international political and doctrinal developments are intimately interrelated. It is impossible to separate these factors from their settings without distorting reality somewhat, especially in a mobilizing socialist state in which all aspects of social life are in some degree politically relevant. However, we may separate the policies of the United Arab Republic into various aspects analytically, as long as we remember the complex interconnections and indicate where a point has significance outside the specific frame of reference. We shall first look at the doctrine of Nasserism and its development in the policy of the United Arab Republic. Then we shall look to the political structure of the United Arab Republic—the instruments of the political decision-makers and the structure of power. We shall then turn to economic policy and the development of socialism and planning. We shall consider the impact of the increasing scope of government upon the administrative and political structures. Finally, we shall look at the foreign policy of the United Arab Republic and its current position in world politics.

Principles of Nasserism

The principles by which Nasser has attempted to proceed are few and their applications have been varied as new situations have arisen, so that a firm appraisal of them is difficult. There do seem to be certain goals which Nasser has consistently attempted to apply to domestic and foreign policy. The first of these is anti-imperialism. The rejection of any form of foreign interference or influence in the Arab states is a primary tenet of the Egyptian revolution. Second, pan-Arabism is a major influence on Nasser's ideas and policies. It is Nasser's feeling that Egypt is an integral part of the Arab world, and the natural leader of the Arab states.[8] Third is social democracy. As the Nasser government has not been a notably democratic regime, this goal may seem mere propaganda.

---

[7]Washington, D.C., *Public Affairs Press* (1955), pp. 17-18.
[8]*The Philosophy of the Revolution*, p. 85.

This is not the case. Nasser regards democracy as the end goal of his regime. However, political democracy is dependent upon economic and social equality, and the achievement of such equality requires stern measures which may preclude the immediate establishment of democratic institutions. Furthermore, Nasser contends that Egypt's experience with parliamentary institutions under the monarchy demonstrates that the people of Egypt are not as yet prepared for the proper use of democracy and must be taught the necessary skills, an enterprise which requires firm leadership.

These three pervasive themes, then—anti-imperialism, social democracy, and pan-Arabism—act in various combinations in different situations, and policy is largely the setting of priorities as to the resources to be allotted to each area and the manner in which they may reinforce one another. The more specific elements of Nasserism are instruments designed to gain these ultimate goals in specific situations. Thus, a key part of Nasserism is its pragmatic approach. The doctrine of Nasserism is derived from policy decisions designed to meet specific problems. Not dogma, but the principles derived from the pursuit of distant and rather vague goals are determinant of policy. The doctrine of Nasserism is abstracted from a body of decisions and techniques never intended to form a doctrine.

In examining the doctrine of Nasserism we cannot explain it as an independent entity, as perhaps one may explain Marxism. We must rather look to the role of situational factors in the development of doctrine. Certain long-range commitments of the Egyptian regime which may be characterized by the title of Nasserism may be discerned, but it should be noted that each is related to a specific set of problems in the fairly short run.

The commitment to a participant society and political democracy will be discussed in relation to domestic politics. The commitment to socialism and a planned economy will be left to the section on economic policy. The roles of positive neutralism and pan-Arabism will be included in the discussion of foreign policy. The instruments of policy—mass media, education, political organizations, and so forth—will be discussed where appropriate. Here we will simply attempt to outline the role of doctrine and ideology in Egyptian politics.

In pursuit of the goals of the regime, ideology plays two roles: explanation and justification. Policy may be explained through an ideological view which renders apparent the necessity for a particular course of action. Rather than explain all of the complexities of the relationship between education and development, for instance, the government may make education an end in itself. Where one is dealing with unsophisticated people whose efforts are to be directed toward ends not to be realized in their lifetime, it is easier to arouse them to action if one raises instrumentalities to the level of valued ends. As well as serving the purpose of explaining instrumental actions, ideology may serve to legitimatize ends. That is, it may justify the ends to which action is directed as well as the means by which the ends are to be achieved.

The primary inspiration of Nasserist doctrine has been the modernization process. The effort to develop an independent and prosperous state has given rise to the policies and pronouncements which comprise Nasserism. Nasserism has largely arisen as post facto explanations of policy decisions previously made. The doctrine's content is primarily elaborated in the national charter of 1962, the Statute of the Arab Socialist Union (December 2, 1962), the provisional constitution of March 25, 1964, and the speeches of Nasser and other leaders of the state.

Political System of the United Arab Republic

According to the provisional constitution of the United Arab Republic, proclaimed at Cairo on March 25, 1964, the state has a well-defined governmental system with well-articulated structures and clear channels of authority. This is an oversimplification, as are most constitutions, in view of the realities of power.[9] The constitution divides power among the president, National Assembly, cabinet, judiciary, and local authorities. In addition, there is the Arab Socialist Union, the single authorized political organization of the United Arab Republic, which nominates the candidates for public office.

The President. Since 1956, Gamal Abdul Nasser has been the president of first the Republic of Egypt and then the United Arab Republic. The functions of the office of the president have been tailored to fit Mr. Nasser's style. Even with the almost unlimited powers he has in practice, President Nasser has on several occasions also assumed the duties of prime minister. Nasser's personality, energy, and leadership extend his authority far beyond any constitutional limits. He dominates the National Assembly, the cabinet, and the Arab Socialist Union. His personal charisma makes it difficult to imagine Egypt without him. He appoints a number of vice presidents as well as the cabinet, and they serve as his administrative assistants. His control of the army and security agencies is undoubted, as was evidenced when he sacrificed the popular Marshal Amer after the June 1967 war. The manner in which he was able to sustain the loss of prestige of a disastrous war, resign his position, and then be called back to it indicates that his power is not based on organization alone, but on intense public loyalty. Institutional arrangements matter little; in the United Arab Republic the center of the government and of political authority lies with Nasser and his coterie of close associates.

The National Assembly. The National Assembly is composed of 350 elected members and 10 members appointed by the president. It must pass upon all bills before they become law, must approve the budget, and must review all emergency decrees of the president. It even has the power to pass, with a two-thirds majority, a bill returned to it by the president. The provisions are

---

[9] cf. George Lenczowski, "Nasserism: Objects and Methods," in Jack H. Thompson and Robert D. Reischauer, eds., *Modernization of the Arab World* (Princeton, 1966).

similar to those for any elected national legislative body. However clear the powers may be on paper, though, in reality the assembly is the creature of President Nasser. All members must be approved by the A.S.U. before they can stand for election. The size of the filing fee restricts candidacy to those who are relatively wealthy and to those who are supported by organizations. All organizations are under the control of the A.S.U., and most of the professional men are in some manner attached to the government. The president has the power to dissolve parliament and call for new elections, and when the assembly is not sitting he may issue emergency decress which have the force of law. The National Assembly of the United Arab Republic has never provided effective political leadership or initiative.

The Cabinet. The cabinet is composed of the prime minister and such deputy premiers as he appoints, and the ministers, who are the appointed heads of the administrative divisions of the government. The cabinet is responsible to the National Assembly, which may withhold its confidence from any single minister or the entire government. But ministers are appointed by the president, in his capacity as head of state, upon the advice of the assembly, and President Nasser has not had to concern himself with the possible ill will of the legislators. The cabinet is composed of two types of individuals. There are old political allies of the president, like Zakaria Mohieddin and Ali Sabry, and there are the "technocrats," who operate the ministries in their areas of expertise. The cabinet and the executive committee of the National Congress of Popular Powers of the A.S.U., whose memberships are almost interchangeable, contain the power-holders in the United Arab Republic, but their power does not derive from their cabinet positions. The power of the cabinet derives from the leadership of President Nasser.

One major area of growing cabinet responsibility has been in economic affairs. Under a 1963 law, all publicly owned companies are organized as joint stock companies with the controlling share owned by the state, or a sufficient share owned by the state to allow effective regulation. The 400 public companies are gathered into some 40 General Organizations and 15 Authorities (most of which were inherited from the British, *e.g.*, the Railways Authority). Each G.O. is managed by a board of directors, the chairman of which is the minister under whose jurisdiction the G.O. has been placed. All decisions are subject to review by the ministry of planning and the president, who formally heads the National Planning Council.

Judiciary. Too little information exists about the operation of the judicial branch of government to make any firm evaluation of its performance. It is likely that the judges are competent in both the legal and the political sense, but it is possible that the administration of the law is determined politically, rather than by legalities.

Local Government. President Nasser of the U.A.R. takes pride in the system of local government, which extends through provinces to the village level; but its role is severely restricted. Centralized control is maintained for education, although funds (except for new buildings) are locally raised, and most other major functions are strictly regulated from Cairo. Decentralization is sought to lend the flexibility necessary for efficient government and for the attainment of democracy, but the necessities of effective planning require a great deal of firm central control. The United Arab Republic is probably overcentralized, especially as the provinces are starved of administrative talent, but no easy solution is apparent.

An effort toward decentralization was the creation of the cooperatives, which were created to enable the local farmers to better deal with their conditions. However, the ministry of agriculture has kept a close eye on the activities of the cooperatives, and it seems that more and not less centralization has been the result. The Arab Socialist Union has developed local organizations down to the neighborhood or factory level, but the flow of authority is strongly downward, and the assumption by the A.S.U. of the control of youth and women's groups has brought most social organizations under the control of the party heirarchy.

The Arab Socialist Union. In October of 1961 Nasser began to rebuild the political system of the United Arab Republic. It was his opinion that the National Union, as established in Egypt in 1956 and as taken up in Syria in 1958, had failed because reactionary elements had been able to infiltrate the organization and subvert it. As part of a completely remodeled system of government, he planned a new mass organization which would not be susceptible to this sort of subversion. There were three parts to his program. First, a National Congress of Popular Powers, embodying the principles of corporate representation, was to be established. Second, a charter was to be written, expressing the ideals of the revolution and the path of the future. Third, an Arab Socialist Union was to be created, taking the place of the old National Union. The purity of the A.S.U. would be protected by a requirement that one half of the members of any representative body of the A.S.U. must be either workers or farmers.

The National Congress of Popular Powers was launched when a 250-member Preparatory Committee was formed on November 18, 1961. From February 5 to February 19, 1962 elections were held for 1500 seats in the NCPP. These elected members joined the members of the Preparatory Committee in the 1750-man national congress. On May 21 the congress convened, and President Nasser presented to it the draft National Charter which was approved, unamended, on June 20.

On December 2, 1962 the statutes of the Arab Socialist Union were approved by the National Congress of Popular Forces.[10] This 1750-man body was established as the "supreme political authority" of the United Arab Republic. All public organizations and the press are under the control of the Arab Socialist Union. The union leadership selects the candidate for the National Assembly.

---

[10] Text in the *Egyptian Political Science Review*, No. 21 (Dec. 7, 1962).

The Arab Socialist Union provides a channel for the expression of public support for the regime and directs the popular powers into useful channels for development. In the Arab Socialist Union we see Nasser's effort to create a true political base in popular institutions. The role of the A.S.U. and its position in relation to the state is more clearly defined and its powers greater than were those of the National Union or the Liberation Rally (1953-1957). The A.S.U. provides an organization which reaches down to the grass roots of society and serves as a mobilizing medium of the masses.

The Arab Socialist Union is the embodiment of the principles of social democracy. In its effort to instill the (modern) revolutionary spirit in the people and to act as the primary force for the mobilization of the masses, the A.S.U. controls the trade unions, Student Federation, and other popular organizations. In its effort to bring revolutionary ideals to the younger generation and provide "a perpetual source of revolutionary vanguards,"[11] the Arab Socialist Union created on October 1, 1965 the Socialist Youth Organization. This organization is designed to provide loyal, active followers of the regime. Although it ostensibly intends to provide leadership cadres for the future, the training methods stifle initiative and prevent real criticism of the regime. For instance, the executive committee of the training camp will meet daily to take "note of negative elements, with a view to disposing of them."[12] Points 3 and 4 of the Objectives of the Socialist Youth Organization[13] are highly instructive as to the probable course of its operations:

3. Organizing the efforts of the youth for the realisation of the objectives of the development plan, and participating positively in the production operations so that the construction of the socialist society may be completed.

4. Participating in solving the problems of the youth, organising their creative efforts, and promoting their talents and abilities in line with the role of the youth in the new society.

Instruments of Control. Aside from governmental structures and the A.S.U., the chief instruments of the revolution in Egypt are the communications media and the control of access to them. The government has emphasized this aspect of policy since the revolution. The government maintains a monopoly of broadcasting services, and the press is controlled by the A.S.U.

Radio broadcasting for the domestic audience is a major concern of the government. While there were 15 hours of broadcasting a day in 1952, there are now 141 hours, more than in any country except the United States. There were 3.5 million radios in the country in 1965, carrying news, music, cultural and

---

[11] Arab Socialist Union, *Socialist Youth Organization* (Cairo: 1966), p. 53.

[12] *Ibid.*, p. 22.

[13] *Ibid.*, p. 53.

political programming into every corner of Egypt. Television programming began in 1961, and now totals 28 hours per day on three channels to the country's 423,000 television sets. The state also maintains traveling films, plays, and speakers, and the number of libraries is increasing steadily.

In addition, the National Publishing House publishes a book every six hours, and prints books at all levels and for all classes. The government intends to provide reading matter for every person in the nation, of any degree of literacy, in order to improve the true literacy rate. There are series for farmers, workers, students, and the like, and much is done to hasten the improvement of the general level of education in order to prepare for modernization.

The educational system is an instrument of modernization, and an instrument of economic development, as well as of political control. A program begun in 1952 to build 400 primary schools a year has been adhered to. There has been continual expansion of primary, secondary, technical, and university training. Primary education between the ages of six and twelve is compulsory and all the educational facilities are free. It is estimated that about 65 percent of school-age children are in school, and Egypt has one of the highest ratios of university students to population in the world. The improvement of the literacy rate is viewed by the government as a prerequisite for modernization and economic development, and the educational system is viewed as the best place to provide the skills and attitudes the government feels to be necessary for development. There is continuing effort to raise the standards of the provincial schools and to improve the quality of education at all levels.

There are, however, serious problems in the Egyptian educational system which may have undesirable effects upon the efforts of the government to achieve development through education. First, considerable efforts must be made and are being made to provide the newly literate with reading materials that will encourage them to maintain their literacy. Secondly, and more serious, it may be that the educational system in Egypt is inappropriately oriented.[14] There is in Egypt a need for doctors, scientists, and technically skilled personnel at all levels for industry and government. However, although there is a surfeit of college-educated people, most of them have training unsuitable for a developing nation. Most of the students in the universities in Egypt receive liberal arts degrees and expect to secure positions in the governmental bureaucracy. The bureaucracy is already overstaffed and such positions, where they exist, are grossly underpaid. Furthermore, the value placed on such an education has made entrance requirements a political issue. (In November of 1968 rioting broke out in Mansoura and Alexandria over a rumored rise in academic standards.) The government provides almost unlimited admission to universities, and many of the entrants are not well qualified. The schools of medicine, law, and the sciences are able due to lack of facilities to limit enrollment to the best qualified entrants, but the liberal arts colleges are

---

[14] Malcolm H. Kerr, "Egypt," in James S. Coleman, *Education and Political Development* (Princeton, 1965).

unable to do so, and therefore many of the graduates are ill-trained. This signifies that a large number of college graduates, many of whom are not really capable, are competing for a limited number of jobs, while in other fields there is a lack of suitably trained personnel. At the same time, the government is unable to effectively limit enrollment in the fear of alienating this potentially activist group.

All the efforts of the government of Egypt are bent to the formation of a participant society whose members have the skills and values needed for modernization. Whether the methods used are appropriate to the task is a moot point.[15] In seeking to build his participant society, President Nasser has relied upon authoritarian methods. While this accords well with Egypt's political traditions and has been successful in the economic realm, it is possible that the narrow range of meaningful political activies precludes the development of attitudes suitable for democratic politics. Nasser's reliance on authoritarian methods may make impossible the use of any other means of governing.

Economic Policy

Toward the end of 1956, after the Suez war underlined the importance of economic development, the Egyptian government began to take a more active role in the economy. Nasser began to concentrate on internal reorganization and investment. In January of 1957 a National Planning Committee was formed and given the task of preparing a comprehensive national plan. This indicated a decisive shift from the former government role of public works projects designed to meet needs on a small scale. The emphasis moved to economic planning on the aggregate level. This was made possible by a massive data project in 1954 which had collected and evaluated all data then available, and which had provided a training ground for a large number of young planners.

The first task of the National Planning Committee was the preparation of an interim plan for 1957/59. The government policy embodied in this plan was still far from radical. It undertook to provide financing for private firms in order to stimulate industrialization and devolopment. The primary areas of government activity were still to be in the areas of tax adjustments, tariff policy, investment in social overhead capital, and the like. This plan was never actuated, but its preparation provided training for the planners and much of the information processed was of use later. A major effect of these first efforts at planning was the government's nationalization of banks, insurance firms, and all credit institutions, of which it had a complete monopoly by the end of 1958.

Results of the First Five-Year Plan. The first Five-Year Plan was scheduled to begin in July 1960 and to run through June 1965. Before the plan became operative the government reorganized the banking system by dissolving the

---

[15]Leonard Binder, "Egypt: The Integrative Revolution," in Lucien W. Pye and Sydney Verba, eds., *Political Culture and Political Development* (Princeton: Princeton University Press, 1965).

National Bank of Egypt and placing all central banking functions under the newly created Central Bank of Egypt. The Five-Year Plan was within the framework of a ten-year program. The National Planning Committee advised the government that the plan should aim to double national income in 20 years, but Nasser decided that the plan should aim to double national income in 10 years. This implied a growth rate of 7.2 percent per annum, a very healthy rate indeed, considering that the growth rate for 1957/59 was 6 percent, and the latter was artificially high due to the rebuilding following the Suez war and the high investment rate occasioned by the beginning of the Aswan High Dam Project. The plan provided for a 40 percent growth for the first five years and an additional 60 percent in the second phase of the plan.

The plan was entitled the General Frame of the Five-Year Plan for Economic and Social Development, July 1960-June 1965. It was more detailed than most plans devised for underdeveloped nations, and provisions were made for annual review to generate annual supplementary plans for detailed programming. The government was still concentrating its energies upon the development of industry through investment opportunities made available by state action, and even this plan was not a socialist document.

The plan had a number of flaws. The planners had made an incorrect assessment of trends in the structure of the Egyptian economy, in that they had considered the growth of employment in services (employment rose more than one million between 1937 and 1960 in the service sector) to have peaked, whereas it continued to rise steadily. This miscalculation led to distortions in the sector growth patterns during the plan period. While the economy as a whole grew at the rate envisioned or nearly so, the industrial sector was the only one for which the predictions were accurate. While industrial growth was very close to the target level, agricultural growth fell below expectations. The goal for agriculture had been self-sufficiency in food production, but production did not rise enough to meet this objective. Egypt remained an importer of food, although, due to rising productivity in cotton growing, agriculture was a net earner of foreign exchange. Services grew well beyond the predictions of the plan. For these and other reasons, the effectiveness of the annual plans was disappointing.

The planning models do not seem to have been fully utilized and the government has proceeded in the pragmatic manner characteristic of it. The inability of changes in investment structure to stimulate growth at the desired rate and in the desired manner, and the private sectors' unreliability in meeting the demands of the Five-Year Plan led to the assumption of greater government control. By 1960 three quarters of capital investment was derived from government sources, and in July of 1961 a series of nationalizations took place which concentrated the greater part of the economy in the hands of the government, either directly or through regulatory agencies.

The tendency to socialism was thus set in 1961, despite the fact that the attempt to spread the nationalizations to Syria led to the secession of that region from the United Arab Republic. The close link between planning and fiscal policy in the United Arab Republic in this period may be seen from the fact that the ministry of planning and the treasury were in reality a single department under a single head until early 1964.

The nationalizations of 1961 were not envisioned in the Five-Year Plan, but seem to have been the product of the commitment to planning of the government. Another development not foreseen in the plan was the reduction in hours ordered by the government in 1961. The maximum work week in large firms was reduced from 48 to 42 hours. Also in 1961 social security measures were expanded considerably. The labor code of 1959 had set 14 days of paid holidays per year after one year's work, seven public holidays, and 180 days of sick pay per year at 70-80 percent of full pay. In 1961 the employer's share in payments for these benefits was set at 17 percent, while employees paid 7 percent. Furthermore, in 1961 another land reform reduced maximum land-holding to 100 *feddans* and maximum rented holding to 50 *feddans*. About 250,000 *feddans* of land changed hands, or would have had not so many landowners sold off land in their anticipation of the reform. The cotton trade was also nationalized in 1961. In addition a new set of area restrictions was established.

Thus from 1957 to 1961 the government of Egypt was well on the way to the establishment of a socialist society. Whereas the government had done little to change the policies of the monarchy prior to the end of 1956, the reforms since have been thorough enough to justify the comment the Egypt will have a fully socialist and controlled economy.

By 1962/63, 40 percent of the gross national product was generated in government-owned enterprises and public administration, and the government was receiving 23 percent of net national income. In 1963 the government extended public ownership of business and established a structure for the management of public firms. Under Law No. 60 of 1963 the 500 government-owned enterprises were divided among some 40 General Organizations. In addition, operating major public services, are some 15 firms, called Authorities (*e.g.*, the Railway Authority), most of which had been in existence since the turn of the century. Each company is organized as a joint stock company, with a board of directors responsible to the Board of the General Organization, which is headed by the minister of the appropriate department. Each minister, in turn, is provided with an advisory committee to provide expert information. The whole structure is responsible to the Supreme Council for Public Organizations, which is chaired by the president of the republic and composed of ministers and vice-presidents. This group, however, has been almost completely nonfunctional since its creation in 1961.

At present the Authorities and General Organizations control all economic life except urban real estate and farming. However, the former is tightly controlled, and the growth of supervised cooperatives has expanded government influence in the latter area. (From 1964 all cotton trade has been in the hands of the cooperatives, but this step is too recent to judge its effects.) No part of the Egyptian economy is free of government controls in some form. The government presently takes in 23 percent of gross national income and generates 18 percent of gross national product. Over 80 percent of all investments are made by the government, compared with 23 percent in 1952. This movement, which has necessitated, or at least encouraged, the replacement of the managers in the old private firms with new government-recruited personnel, has had a major effect upon the government bureaucracy. In the first place, new opportunities have been opened for many of the college-educated young men in Egypt. On the other hand, there is an increasing shortage of competent technicians. This may tend to accentuate the stress on the political system caused by the present state of the educational system, discussed above.

At the higher level of the bureaucracy, there is an increasing reliance on the planning and managerial "technocrats." There is little doubt that the government's bureaucratic managers are as competent as those formerly employed by private firms. However, they are not operating their firms under the same assumptions dominant in private industry, even though some of the government-owned firms are organized as competitive enterprises. Since it is doubtful whether the profit-and-loss statement will be as meaningful to them as to their predecessors, there may be some loss in efficiency. Government social welfare acts may also lower efficiency somewhat. For example, the reduction in maximum hours of work allowed in large firms to 42 hours per week in 1964 curtailed the rise in productivity per worker, although productivity per hour did not diminish.

The Commitment to Development. The government of the United Arab Republic has made three primary commitments in economic policy: to development, planning, and socialism. It seems apparent that the goal of economic development has been central to Egyptian policy since the revolution. Even prior to the revolution the need for change was recognized, and it was the reluctance of the government to take action which was one of the major causes of the revolution. As the junta proceeded in its efforts to encourage development, the need for comprehensive and authoritative planning became evident. The effort to accomplish effective planning has led to increasing government intervention in the economy, as discussed above. Thus, beginning from the rather vague goal of economic development, the government of Egypt has arrived at the firm and well-articulated commitment to socialism we find in the 1964 constitution.

Two problems immediately arise in developing an economy: financing and method. The first includes such problems as generating internal savings and dealing with problems of capital inflow, while the second subsumes such matters as sector emphasis and priorities. The problems are extremely complex and we can do no more than summarize the Egyptian situation.

Financing. Internal financing is derived from savings in one form or another, including forced savings, such as taxes or extreme price markups on government goods. In Egypt, as has been mentioned, the government provides most of the investment capital. This is derived from government operations in the nationalized industries and tax revenues. In part, savings are forced through a two-step process: imports are restricted so that consumers cannot spend all their earnings, then taxes may be raised by the amount of this enforced saving. One of the chief internal sources of investment capital, especially foreign exchange, has been the Suez Canal. The closure of the canal in 1967, by the Arab-Israeli war, has deprived Egypt of a valuable asset. The profits from the canal and other government enterprises are available for investment, either in the firm in which they were generated or in other areas.

External finance, in aid from other states or private investment from foreign investors, is a valuable source of development capital, especially if it is in the form of convertible currencies with which the state may buy needed imports. Egypt has received substantial aid from abroad, especially from the United States and the U.S.S.R. The United States, under its P.L. 480 program, has donated substantial quantities of surplus wheat. The United States has also provided funds and technical assistance for road and irrigation projects. The U.S.S.R. provided financing and technical aid for the Aswan High Dam project and a considerable amount of military aid. Private investment in Egypt, aside from development of some small oil fields, has not been of major significance since the nationalization of French and British property in 1956. One major problem with external finance is that much of it is in the form of loans which carry service charges and which must eventually be repaid. The amount of external finance a country can accept must be limited by its assessment of what it can eventually repay.

Sector Emphasis. The proper emphasis upon sectors in the economy is related to the problems of finance by the question of foreign exchange. Egypt is traditionally a one-crop agricultural exporter. Cotton is the only export of significance to the Egyptian economy. Emphasis on cotton-growing for export is thus one way of earning foreign exchange. However, without industrial development it will be impossible to replace the imports of manufactured goods needed for domestic consumption and capital development. A balance must be struck at some point. There was a tendency in Egypt, as in many under-developed nations, to emphasize industrial development in the first years after the revolution. However, the possibilities of import substitution in the domestic market for final goods was almost exhausted by 1952. The importation of capital goods, especially capital goods for the production of other capital goods, is extremely expensive in terms of foreign exchange, and the domestic market is too small to make it profitable. The only real possibility of making such imports worthwhile would be export expansion, and in this market the United Arab Republic has to compete with the developed nations, those of Europe, the United States, and Japan. It therefore seems that the United Arab Republic, with a growing foreign debt, a chronic balance of payment deficit made up only by external finance, and one of its chief sources of foreign exchange cut off for an indeterminate period of time, may be better advised to emphasize agricultural development and such import substitution possibilities as remain to it, rather than continue to emphasize industrial production which requires the importation of expensive capital goods, many of which seem unlikely to pay for themselves.

Aside from the financial aspect, another problem in sector emphasis is of considerable importance in the United Arab Republic. This is a matter of technical progress in skills and in techniques. It is necessary if development is to proceed for a sustained period of time that it be reinforced with continuing innovation in industry, agriculture, and services; with continuous change in methods of organization and production; with investment in social overhead capital for transportation and power; and with the training of people in new skills and in the ability to acquire new skills as they may be needed. To introduce new techniques and borrow from the more developed nations is not enough; there must be innovation in social organization if these new techniques are to be truly productive. To this end, the United Arab Republic has given considerable emphasis to education and new organizational forms in order to generate suitable skills and attitudes among the people.

The Commitment to Planning. As the original emphasis of the government upon simply providing investment for private enterprise failed to produce the results desired, the government committed itself to a program of comprehensive planning and control. This commitment, reiterated in the 1964 constitution, is one of the key concepts in the government's campaign for economic development. After the Five-Year Plan of 1960-65, the government went to a Seven-Year Plan of 1965-72. Further government intervention in the economy has followed, and it is estimated that by 1970 Egypt will have a "command economy."[16] This tendency has been accelerated by the creation of agricultural cooperatives. In 1964, according to Everett E. Hagen, the United Arab Republic had a higher ratio of government consumption to gross domestic product than any noncommunist nation.[17] The problems in planning experienced in the first Five-Year Plan may be mitigated by the increasing expertise of the personnel involved and by the increasing ability of the government to control economic activities in line with the plan.

The Commitment to Socialism. Generated by the commitment to planning, the commitment to socialism is an expression of the government's distrust of traditional forces in the society and the desire to develop the economy as rapidly as possible. By increasing government ownership of industry and services and the organization of agriculture into cooperatives under government supervision for both production and marketing purposes, the government is able to exert influence when and as it feels necessary. Also, the essential egalitarianism of the

---

[16] Patrick O'Brien, *The Revolution in Egypt's Economic System* (London, 1967), p. 311.

[17] Everett E. Hagen, *The Economics of Development* (Homewood, Ill., 1968), p. 316. (Government consumption from Economics Department I.B.R.D.)

regime has made itself felt in the idea that a fair distribution of output is a condition of successful development. Furthermore, the commitment to socialism is an outgrowth of the idea of a participant society, in which all share equally in the labor and in the rewards, and socialist organization of the economy is one means of encouraging mass support and mobilizing the masses of the people.

The Prospects for the Economy. The difficulties in dealing with problems of development outlined above and the means by which the government has chosen to deal with these problems are complex and the possibilities vary enormously. In a nation of 30 million people, with the population increasing at nearly 3 percent per year, with a per capita income of about E£75 ($180.00)[18] for a base point, the difficulty of development is great. Simply to double the per capita income requires a growth rate of 6 percent (3 percent after population growth is considered) compounded over a period of some two decades, and a 3 percent net growth rate is very respectable for an underdeveloped nation. The government is determined to succeed, and its methods appear to have a good chance of success; but, in the final analysis, the ability of the nation to develop depends upon the will of the population to deprive itself of current consumption, luxuries, and leisure time to hasten the development process.

Foreign Policy

Before considering Egypt's foreign policy it is essential to point out that it is not only an expression of Nasser's political and/or social ideology but also a result of Egypt's historic tradition, geographical location, national interest and purpose, and security requirements. In fact, these factors are inseparable, for Nasser's ideology is a product of the other components. For example, Egypt's relationship with the West is to a large degree, but not solely, tempered by historic tradition—*i.e.*, Western, particularly British, imperialism. And since freedom from foreign interference is part of Nasserism, Nasser is cautious of real or suspected Western imperial designs, such as the Baghdad Pact or the Eisenhower Doctrine. On the other hand, he is little concerned with Soviet imperialism, which has been manifested primarily in eastern Europe and the eastern provinces of the U.S.S.R. and has not been directly experienced by the Arab world. Furthermore, because of Egypt's pressing economic and human problems, foreign policy is particularly involved in domestic policy.

Nasser himself emphasized this fact in 1964 when he stated that foreign policy "is only meant to serve the U.A.R.'s home policy. Without it we would not be able to implement our development plans or raise any loans . . ."[19] To point out one example, it is only through extensive foreign assistance that the United Arab Republic can hope to ameliorate some of its economic problems and at the same time safeguard its sovereignty. Here the doctrine of positive

[18]*The Middle East and North Africa, 1967-68,* (London: Europa Publications, 1967), p. 805.

[19]*Arab Observer* (Cairo), No. 213 (November 16, 1964), p. 4.

neutrality is instrumental. The relationship between foreign policy and its above-mentioned determinants will become clearer as our discussion proceeds.

Within the context of policy determinants several foreign policy principles have evolved. According to an official government source, the foreign policy of the United Arab Republic is founded upon eight basic principles:

1. To adhere to the policy of peaceful co-existence, positive neutrality, and active participation in resolving international problems;
2. To reject membership in cold war blocs or pacts; to liquidate all foreign military bases and lessen world tension;
3. To assert the legitimate right of self-determination and liquidate all forms of colonialism;
4. To respect the sovereignty of independent states and to protect the freedom and independence of their peoples;
5. To exert all efforts for total disarmament, a total nuclear test ban, and the solution of all disputes through peaceful means;
6. To promote economic and cultural international cooperation;
7. To respect all international obligations within the framework of the U.N. Charter; and
8. To condemn the policy of racial discrimination and to respect human rights.[20]

These principles may be categorized as positive neutralism (1 and 2), anti-imperialism (3, 4, and 8), and general expressions of goodwill derived from the U.N. Charter. The items in the last category probably have little real effect upon the foreign policy of the United Arab Republic, except for a formal observance. The principles of positive neutralism and anti-imperialism are, however, major factors in determining the manner in which the United Arab Republic deals with the rest of the international community.

The principle of positive neutralism may be divided into several aspects: peaceful coexistence, nonalignment, active participation in international politics, and mutual support among the new nations. The principle of anti-imperialism also has two facets: anticolonialism and defense of the sovereign status of all states. These two principles work together to place the United Arab Republic in a secure position between the major power blocs, so that it may work for its own ends outside of and vis-a-vis Cold War politics.

Positive Neutralism. Positive neutralism, as a policy for nonaligned states, developed from the Bandung Conference in April 1955. The first condition of this policy is the prevention of nuclear war, of which the new states would be as much victims as the combatants. The second condition is that the new states must be nonaligned, that is, they must adhere to no blocs or military alliances dominated by either of the cold war opponents. Third, they must not simply allow events to pass them by; they must take an active role in world politics.

---

[20]United Arab Republic, *Statistical Handbook 1952-1965* (Cairo, April 1966), p. 265.

This is necessary if they are to advance their interests, maintain their independence, and prevent world war. Finally, they must mutually support each other, in order to make nonalignment possible and to have a real effect upon international politics.

Anti-Imperialism. The attainment of true sovereign status was an early goal of the Egyptian revolution; the long period of British influence had rendered imperialism the *bête noir* of the Free Officers, in common with many other Arab nationalists. President Nasser stated in 1954, " . . . the major concern of the revolution was the realization of state sovereignty . . ."[21] The concern with sovereignty has led to consistent opposition to colonialism. As the great imperial powers were Western powers, there has been considerable identification of imperialism with the West. This was confirmed for Egyptian policymakers by the actions of Britain and France during the Suez crisis of 1956 and reaffirmed by the Eisenhower Doctrine of 1957. The lasting concern with the sovereignty of Egypt has led the United Arab Republic to call for respect for the sovereignty of all states. As universal adherence to this principle protects the sovereignty of the United Arab Republic, and as it is a popular policy in the new states, it thus serves a twofold purpose. Opposition to imperialism and defense of sovereignty is a key to Egyptian policy and consistent with the active role called for by positive neutrality.

In the light of these general principles, we may view the foreign policy of the United Arab Republic. Egypt has adhered to no blocs or alliances and has opposed with relative success the formation of U.S. or British dominated alliances within the Middle East. Nasser's opposition to the Baghdad Pact (CENTO) has been significant in ensuring that at the present time no Arab state of the Middle East is in an effective military alliance with any state outside the area. Nasser has certainly taken an active role in world affairs. In less than 10 years, between 1955 and 1964, he participated in 13 major meetings of nonaligned nations, six of which were held in the United Arab Republic. Since Bandung he has been a leading figure in international politics. Through these conferences, extensive travel, and meetings with heads of states, President Nasser has attempted to develop the Afro-Asian nations into a group committed to the principles of positive neutrality.

The opposition of the Egyptian revolutionary regime to colonialism has included aid to independence movements in colonial possessions and diplomatic support for leaders of nationalist movements in Africa and the Middle East. The relations of the United Arab Republic with East and West will be discussed in detail later; we will note at this time only that, while dealing with both sides, the United Arab Republic has always demanded equality of status and has made no permanent commitment to either bloc. Although the United Arab Republic at times has become involved in the internal affairs of some Arab states (largely resulting from the vagaries of Nasser's pan-Arab aspirations), still it has been a

---

[21] Gamal Abdul Nasser, "The Egyptian Revolution," *Foreign Affairs,* Vol. 33 (January 1955), p. 204.

concern of the regime at least to prevent interference by imperialist or reactionary powers in the affairs of other states.

Besides the policy determinants which temper the United Arab Republic's policy and out of which certain principles have evolved, this state's foreign policy is formulated and pursued within a hierarchy of interests. That is to say, "certain interests must be defended at all costs; others should be safeguarded under particular circumstances; and certain others, although desirable, can almost never be defended."[22] For the United Arab Republic this hierarchy is determined by two somewhat concentric factors: geographic location and community of interest.

A political science textbook used by Cairo University points up the first factor, stating, "We are not exaggerating if we state that Egypt's . . . foreign policy is very much influenced by its geographic location."[23] This location puts Egypt at the crossroads of three continents, and it is the geopolitical, historical, and cultural interplay among these three continents that has shaped Egypt's community of interest. As a result of history, culture, language, and geography, the United Arab Republic has placed the highest priority upon its Arab world relations and second priority upon its African relations. In accordance with the ideas of positive neutralism, Egypt does not wish to become too deeply entangled with either cold war bloc. In consequence of its anti-imperialism, the United Arab Republic is attached to the non-Western nations. These priorities are related to the cold war; however, the primary factor is not the cold war but the interests of Egypt (which may or may not be directly affected by the world controversy).

As early as 1954, President Nasser, in his pamphlet *The Philosophy of the Revolution,* identified these priorities (although instead of the nonaligned nations he considered the Muslim world; but a specifically Islamic world policy has proven dysfunctional in view of the secularization of religion which has proceeded in most of the Muslim states. However, religion is a significant tool of the United Arab Republic's foreign policy, particularly in Africa.) The *Charter,* adopted in 1962 as an official expression of the United Arab Republic's national aspirations, identifies Arab unity, the pan-African movement, and Afro-Asian solidarity, in that order, within this country's sphere of interest. Thus, the hierarchy of interest, in a descending order, can be categorized as the Arab world, Africa, and the Third World. And influenced by the entire order are the United Arab Republic's East-West relations.

The Arab World. The Arab states are divided into two regional groupings: the *Maghreb,* or African states, and the *Mashriq,* or Asian states. Although Egypt lies

---

[22] Kenneth W. Thompson and Roy C. Macridis, "The Comparative Study of Foreign Policy," in ed. Roy A. Macrides, *World Politics,* 2d ed. (Englewood Cliffs, N.J., c. 1962), p. 3.

[23] Boutros Ghali and Mahmoud Isa, *Mabadi Al-Uloom Asiasyiah* (An Introduction to Political Science), 1st ed. (Cairo, 1962-63), p. 564.

in North Africa, its closest affinity has been with the Asian Arabs. One reason for this is historical: Egypt, like the eastern Arab states, was subject to the Ottoman Empire, while the North African states were not. Another factor is geographical. In the first place, the deserts of western Egypt and Libya effectively separate Egypt from all North Africa except Cyrenaica. Secondly, the Arab states of the east, like Egypt, border on or are in close proximity to Israel, so that the presence of that state constitutes a direct threat to them, as it does not for the *Maghreb*. The final factor is cultural: The North Africans have had a much longer and more intimate association with Europe, particularly with France, and therefore have quite different cultural values than the eastern Arabs. The result of this has been that while Nasser has dealt with all of the North African states, the only one which is somewhat subject to Egyptian influence is neighboring Libya.

The Maghreb. There are three states which together constitute the *Maghreb:* Morocco, Tunisia, and Algeria. Although Egypt's relations with the *Maghreb* have not been as intimate as her relations with the *Mashriq,* there are important areas of common concern, as in African affairs.

Nasser's relations with King Muhammad V of Morocco were cordial, due primarily to the king's foreign policy line. This culminated in 1961 in the association of Egypt and Morocco with Ghana, Mali, and Guinea in the Casablanca bloc. By 1963 conditions had greatly changed. Algerian independence in July 1962 brought a new member into the Casablanca group. Nasser's closer affinity to the revolutionary regime in Algeria led him to support Algeria against Morocco's young King Hassan II. In April of 1963 a proposed meeting of the Casablanca group was postponed (it never was held); in May Morocco was virtually isolated at the African heads of states conference in Addis Ababa; and in September the United Arab Republic supported Algeria when open warfare broke out between Morocco and that state, even to the point of reinforcing the Algerian army.

Relations with Tunisia have been consistently stormy. Although Egypt supported the independence movement, soon after Tunisia gained independence in March 1956, President Bourguiba and President Nasser disagreed. There has been a clash of personalities, but more fundamentally, Bourguiba and Nasser have different views of development policy. There was a reconciliation in 1961 after Egypt supported Tunisia in its assault on the Bizerte air station; but in 1965, after Bourguiba urged a peaceful settlement with Israel on terms no Arab leader could accept, the dispute flared up again. While Morocco is moving toward the former French possessions in Africa, Tunisia appears to be moving closer to Europe.

Algeria presents a different situation altogether. Since Nasser began support of the National Liberation Front in 1954 and supported Algeria against Morocco in 1963, as well as diplomatically throughout Africa, relations between the two states are extremely cordial. Nasser and Ben Bella were agreed on many aspects of policy, although the Algerian leader took a more militant line in sub-Saharan

Africa. The fall of Ben Bella, and his replacement by Defense Minister Boumedienne were disappointments to Nasser, as Boumedienne is less pro-Egyptian than was Ben Bella. The relations between the two countries are still cordial, however, and they lend each other diplomatic support consistently.

The Eastern Arabs. The Arab states of the Middle East are, as we have mentioned, tied to Egypt with geographic, historic, and cultural bonds much stronger than those binding Egypt to the *Maghreb*. There are two factors that pervade the United Arab Republic's relationship with the *Mashriq*. First is Nasser's conception of pan-Arabism and his view that Egypt should take the lead in the pan-Arab movement. As early as 1954, he articulated this point clearly:

> For some reason it seems to me that within the Arab circle there is a role wandering aimlessly in search of a hero. And I do not know why it seems to me that this role, exhausted by its wanderings, has at last settled down, tired and weary, near the borders of our country and is beckoning to us to move, to take up its lines, to put on its costume, since no one else is qualified to play it.[24]

Secondly, Nasser is the symbol to Middle Eastern Arabs of Arab nationalist ideals and pan-Arab aspirations. As such, he has been able to evoke considerable support among the people. This, or course, has had an incendiary effect upon many of the Middle East governments when Nasser opposes them. The governments of Jordan, Syria, Iraq, and Lebanon have all experienced mass demonstrations and even riots incited by Cairo radio. And all of them have been seriously threatened and even toppled as in the cases of Iraq, Yemen, and Syria, by Nasserite coups.

In both instances pan-Arabism is the primary element. Two forces act for pan-Arabism in the United Arab Republic's foreign policy: the desire for support from states of common interest, and the common cultural heritage and history of the states of the region, which lends strength to their perceptions of their communality. The concept of Arab socialism, or social democracy, is closely tied to pan-Arabism in the foreign policy of the United Arab Republic, especially since 1961 when the experience with unity convinced Nasser that social revolution was necessary before Arab unity could become a reality. He noted in 1962, "The development of the action for unity toward its ultimate and comprehensive objective must be accompanied by practical efforts to fill the economic and social gaps stemming from the difference in the stages of development of the various peoples of the Arab Nation." Furthermore, he added, "She [the United Arab Republic] cannot impose on them a precise form of revolution."[25]

Thus, since the union with Syria dissolved in 1961, the United Arab Republic has taken a more cautious line with its Middle Eastern neighbors. Relations with Syria, Iraq, Jordan, and Saudi Arabia have fluctuated between open hostility and

---

[24] *The Philosophy of the Revolution*, pp. 87-88.
[25] United Arab Republic, *The Charter* (Cairo, n.d.) pp. 94-95.

great cordiality over the past seven years. In the first period after the secession, the Syrian government, supported by the Iraqi government, attacked Nasser continually. The Jordanian and Saudi governments also assailed the United Arab Republic. In August 1962 the United Arab Republic withdrew from the Arab League while under Syrian criticism. The prestige of the United Arab Republic in the Arab world, despite continued popular support throughout the region, was at its lowest ebb. In September of 1962 a rebellion broke out in Yemen. Nasser immediately lent support to the republican cause, while the Saudi government supported Imam Badr. This return to the offensive in foreign policy restored much of the self-confidence of the Egyptian government and people, although the war was protracted, sanguinary, and costly.

By 1963 the pendulum had again swung in Nasser's favor. On February 8, 1963 Kassim in Iraq was overthrown and subsequently assassinated, and the pro-Egyptian Aref was installed in Baghdad. On March 8 a coup in Damascus replaced the anti-Nasser government with men more favorable to Egypt. Unity negotiations soon commenced and a Tripartite Unity Agreement was signed. However, the Baath party in both Iraq and Syria was not prepared to yield power rapidly, and the repression of Nasser's adherents in these countries led to Egypt's withdrawal from the agreement and renewed bitterness between Eygpt and the Baathists. Following the Baathist's overthrow in Iraq (November 18), friendly relations were restored with all the Arab states except Syria at an Arab summit meeting in January 1964. But the failure to settle the Yemen war led to renewed friction with Saudi Arabia, and relations with Jordan are tenuous.

Although tentative moves toward Arab unity continue, a unified political command with Iraq having been established in December of 1964, the prospects are dim for unification in the near future. Nasser firmly believes that the various states must have a unity of purpose and accomplish their internal revolutions successfully before real unity can be achieved. Even after the disastrous war of June 1967, Nasser is still the foremost leader in the Middle East. But it may be that while he overshadows all others, the area's politicians are not willing to compromise their own power nor accept Egyptian suzerainty over their affairs.

Sub-Saharan Africa. The second area of concern in the United Arab Republic's hierarchy of interest is Africa. Several factors have led to the involvement of the United Arab Republic in Black Africa. The first, in relation to the Sudan, has been the historic and strategic interest of Egypt in the security of the Nile water resources. The second factor has been the anti-imperialist policy of Egypt, which led to involvement with African independence and nationalist movements. But this support goes beyond a mere policy principle commitment. It is also motivated by strategic and geopolitical considerations. "We should watch . . . Britain in Central Africa," warned a respected Cairo publication in 1956. "She might try to create difficulties for our projects on the Nile. This puts forward our duty to support all nationalist movements anywhere. They are behind the enemy lines. Let's make them our bases there."[26] Indeed, in 1965 Mohammed Hassanien Heikal, a close confidant of Nasser and editor of

[26] *Rose El-Youssief* (Cairo), No. 1490 (Dec. 31, 1956), p. 3.

the Cairo daily *Al-Ahram,* stated, "Egypt is and should be associated with the anti-imperialist movement. In Africa itself this existing and necessary association is not only a matter of principle but is a matter of security and protection."[27]

This geo-political concern has been most clearly manifested in Egypt's relations with the Sudan. While Egypt rejected the "unity of the Nile Valley" theme following the 1952 revolution, nevertheless, the Sudan remains a paramount consideration to Egyptian policy-makers. Their primary concern is with the security of the Nile waters, which flow through the heart of the Sudan and upon which the "gift of the Nile" is totally dependent. Therefore, while the revolutionary regime respected the Sudan's right to self-determination and has not violated the Sudan's independence, it has guarded the Sudan's sovereignty from Western encroachments and has attempted to maintain close relations with this neighbor. Free from foreign pressure, the two countries have reached agreements for the equitable division of the Nile waters and for cooperation on Nile projects. The Aswan High Dam project, for example, was made possible by the November 1959 agreement regarding division of the waters and the resettlement of Sudanese displaced by the project.

As well as supporting the movements for Moroccan, Tunisian, and Algerian independence, the Egyptians have provided a refuge and a base of operations for the leaders of many of the African independence movements. Many independence movements established in Cairo bureaus from which they dispensed propaganda and organized their efforts. From 1954 to 1964 the efforts of the Egyptian government in this respect were of considerable aid to the anticolonial movements. As the first phase of anticolonialism is over, this role has diminished in importance, although the United Arab Republic continues to aid the South African nationalist movement and the Holden Roberto provisional government of Angola and it is a major contributor to the Liberation Committee of Nine of the Organization of African Unity. Egypt's efforts established her as a leader of the African nationalist struggle for independence. The policy is in accordance with the principles of positive neutralism and with Egypt's commitment to anticolonialism. More importantly, of course, Egypt is part of the African continent. In a world made so compact by modern systems of communication and transportation, on a continent seething with political and social foment, in an area coveted by the imperialist powers, Africa's fate could not but vitally affect Egypt. Thus, Nasser committed Egypt to an active role in African affairs as part of his effort to strengthen Egypt's independence and establish for her a meaningful role in world affairs.

Another reason for the United Arab Republic's involvement in Africa is economic, as Africa may provide the most promising markets for Egypt's industry and a reliable source of raw materials. Egypt's economic interests in Africa are not yet substantial, but the continent may provide the United Arab Republic with markets for its manufactured goods, so that it may play a role

---

[27]*Al-Ahram* (Cairo) (Dec. 24, 1965).

analogous to that of Japan in Asia. The difficulties with this have been the inability of the African states, embarked on their own development programs, to afford the foreign exchange necessary to increase their imports of Egyptian goods. Egypt must compete in these markets with the older manufacturing nations, such as the United States, Japan, Britain, and France; and the latter two have considerable connections with their former colonies. At present Egyptian exports to Africa are relatively small (about 2 percent of all exports in 1964) but expanding. The foreign exchange limitation may be alleviated by an increase in Egyptian imports of raw materials for industrial production. In an era of increasing concern about economic imperialism, however, too great a penetration of Egyptian industry into Africa may occasion distrust on the part of the African states; there may be, therefore, a limit to Egyptian extension into that quarter.

Egyptian interest in Africa is accentuated by the penetration of Israeli interests into the continent. The United Arab Republic has attempted at various conferences to turn the Africans against Israel, primarily by portraying Israel as an outpost of imperialism. By 1964, however, this policy appeared to be ineffective as the Black African states do not view Israel as the threat it appears to the Egyptians. Israeli economic penetration is viewed by such statesmen as Hastings Banda of Malawi as welcome aid and not a threat, unless it reaches proportions which threaten the interests or autonomy of the state involved. Thus it seems likely that the only measures the United Arab Republic can take against Israel in Africa will be in the area of offering competitive assistance and aid. However, the United Arab Republic's own economic problems and limited resources severely limit the amount of assistance it can extend.
assistance it can extend.

The United Arab Republic through educational measures and propaganda has attempted to encourage closer ties with the African states. It has been particularly successful among the Muslim Africans, who constitute a majority in some sub-Saharan countries and a significant minority in many others. By promoting and expanding religious ties, the United Arab Republic has succeeded in creating much goodwill for its policies and leadership. However, since the majority of African states are now independent and involved with their internal problems and since the first generation of African leaders, such as Nkrumah, with whom Nasser dealt in earlier years, seems to be yielding to younger men, the extension of Egyptian influence will no longer be possible through propaganda and diplomatic support alone; if Egypt cannot offer to the African states concrete services and advantages, the future of the United Arab Republic in Africa will be limited.

The Nonaligned Nations

The Third World is viewed as a countervailing force to the major power blocs. Although it constitutes neither a bloc nor an alliance in the strictest sense, it has proved to be a cogent alignment of the smaller nations in their pursuit of an effective voice in the international community vis-à-vis the cold war powers. It emerged as a force in world affairs from the Bandung Conference of 1955, and the participants' common goals and community of interests have been further affirmed through other conferences such as the Brioni Conference of 1956, the Belgrade Conference of 1961, and the Cairo Conference of 1964. Nasser, as we have seen, is one of the outspoken advocates of nonalignment. He has taken a leading role in all these conferences and in the attempt to implement this group's goals through the United Nations. Of the nonaligned nations' mission he stated in 1961:

> There is no power able to serve peace like the community of states following the policy of nonalignment. These states which live with the problems of their world, and do not isolate themselves therefrom and which do not submit in their stand vis-à-vis these problems to the pressure of one of the blocs dictating a certain attitude or a line of action, these states, inspired by the urge of peace based on justice, irrespective of any other consideration, are particularly capable of placing at the service of peace—justly and without bias—all their material and moral potentialities.
>
> In this way we are in a better position to act freely, with integrity, and without bias, between the two blocs to narrow the gap separating them and consolidate the possibilities of understanding, particularly since the policy of nonalignment has earned the respect of all world powers, including the states within the sphere of the great blocs.
>
> As a result of all this we, nonaligned states, bear a special responsibility towards peace which is the cherished hope of our peoples and that of the peoples of the whole universe.
>
> In the atmosphere of peace alone we can develop life in our countries and augment its creative genius.
>
> In the atmosphere of peace we are able to help many other peoples still not free, and who ask us to lend them a helping hand so they can start anew shaping their destiny.
>
> In short, we should be the power of conscience in this world of ours.[28]

The assumption by the United Arab Republic of a position of leadership of the neutralist nations has meant that Nasser, like the other participants, has a platform from which to expound his ideas and a base of support at the international level. His concern with the neutralist nations is on both ideological and practical levels. He supports anti-imperialist and independence movements, both from a commitment to the principles involved and because it is in the interests of Egypt.

---

[28]*President Gamal Abdel Nasser on Consolidation of the Cause of World Peace: Speeches pronounced in International Conference Abroad and Joint Communiques with Heads of State,* comp. and trans. Ministry of National Guidance, State Information Service (Cairo, 1968), p. 142.

According to a Cairo publication:

We believe that our freedom is in danger as long as there are any colonized nations. Our prosperity is in danger as long as there are exploited nations . . . We should secure our frontiers and we should consider that they are located wherever imperialism exists. Whenever a battle against imperialism occurs, Egypt will support it and bless it, and if it can, Egypt will participate in it because of our interests, idealism, and history.[29]

Furthermore, Nasser has pointed out that the unity of all freedom-fighters is an important factor for the success of any revolutionary movement.[30] Thus, in the existence of a strong and fairly united group of neutralist states Nasser finds support for his policies and a means of advancing his country's international interests, an influence that the United Arab Republic as a small, weak, and underdeveloped nation could not possess of itself. At the same time, leadership in such a bloc provides him with strength at home, as such leadership gives the people of the United Arab Republic a sense of national pride and pride in the regime.

East-West Relations

Nasser's relations with the West have been influenced by his anti-imperialist policies and the West's support of Israel. He is suspicious of the West, which fostered colonization, and feels that they will circumscribe the United Arab Republic's sovereignty and his revolution if they are allowed to maintain substantial influence in the Middle East and Africa. His long-standing opposition to Western dominated Middle East defense alliances stems from this suspicion. His accusation that the dissolution of the Syrian union was caused by reactionary forces in Syria stems in part from his conviction that the West is primarily a force for reaction in the Middle East. Furthermore, Israel is viewed as an outpost of Western imperialism. Inasmuch as Israel is a Western creation and a thorn to Arab nationalism, the West's continued support of her and their maintenance of Israeli military superiority create a constant strain in Egyptian-Western relations, climaxed in the complete severance of Egypt's diplomatic relations with the United States following the June 1967 war.

To some extent a result of the relative decline in Egyptian-Western relations, the United Arab Republic and Russia have developed friendly relations, and they support each other diplomatically in many areas, particularly in Africa. However, Soviet-Egyptian relations are on a state-to-state level. Nasser has little use for communists in Egypt or elsewhere in the Middle East and has consistently opposed them. It appears to be Nasser's view that while Western imperialism works directly, Soviet imperialism could only work indirectly

[29]Editorial, "Misr Fikrah Wa Laysat Dawla" (Egypt is an Idea, Not a State), *Rose El-Youssief* (Cairo), No. 1451 (April 2, 1956), p. 3.

[30]*Al-Ahram*, (Cairo) (April 3, 1961), p. 17.

through domestic Communist parties. Thus, by denying local Communists any power, he is well defended against any threat from the U.S.S.R.

Nasser has maintained his position well in the narrow zone between East and West; he has not yet overcommitted himself to one side or the other. Since Suez he has placed more reliance on the Soviet Union, but he has also sought to exploit the Sino-Soviet split to maintain a balance. Relations with the West are strained, but there has been little evidence that Nasser would cut himself completely off from the Western nations. The chief Egyptian concerns in foreign policy matters concerning the cold war are the maintenance of sovereignty, domestic development, and enhancement of Egyptian prestige. The United Arab Republic is willing to accept aid from either side, and has done so. The tenets of positive neutralism, however, which are followed consistently, proscribe permanent attachments to either one of the blocs. The freedom of maneuver gained by the United Arab Republic through these methods has allowed Nasser to pursue a number of prestige building programs, such as the Aswan High Dam which the Soviet Union financed subsequent to the U.S. withdrawal from the project in 1956. The ability to shift his ground allows him to choose the party he wishes to support and to defy the other. He is totally dependent upon neither side and thus can take risks not possible under conditions of dependency. In essence, tied to neither bloc, but capable of supporting either, Nasser has carved a niche of independent action which is greater than his power alone could create.

A key to Nasser's success at treading so precariously between East and West is in part a function of the United Arab Republic's geographic location, Nasser's ability to manipulate the Arab masses, and his leading role among the nonaligned nations. The interests of the West in the Middle East center around the economic and strategic importance of this area; no guarantees are possible of its continued security without Egyptian cooperation. The interests of the Soviets are far more political than economic and relate to Africa almost as much as to the Middle East; Nasser provides them with a link to both areas.

The primary key to Nasser's foreign policy in regard to East-West relations is flexibility. Although he has moved closer to the East over the years, and the June 1967 war with Israel has caused closer Soviet supervision of their military aid program, he is still keeping the lines open to the West.

The U.A.R. vis-a-vis Israel

Egypt's confrontation with Israel is the most central problem of her foreign relations. As we have seen, the Arab-Israeli conflict somehow influences almost every aspect of Egypt's external relations: It is the fulcrum of her Middle East policy, the arbiter of her East-West relations, and the propellent of her African policy. Why? It has escalated to this magnitude over some two decades.

Nasser's initial opposition to the state of Israel—indeed, the opposition of Arab nationalists throughout the Middle East—stemmed from the irreconcilable aims of Arab nationalism and Zionism over the land of Palestine. The world's denial of the Palestinians' right to self-determination, even while recognizing these rights of all peoples under the United Nations Charter, violated a fundamental tenet of Arab nationalism—of nationalism per se. And the resulting degradation of the Palestinian population, a once energetic and creative people interred in refugee camps and turned into hapless dependents of world philanthropy, served as a constant reminder and ultimately a symbol of the struggle of Arab nationalism.

These are the considerations that motivated Egypt vis-à-vis Israel in the period immediately following Nasser's revolution. But they certainly were not central to Nasser's policies or problems at this time. Nasser's opposition to Israel was primarily rhetorical. Egypt, or the entire Arab world for that matter, could pose no real threat to Israel, as Nasser well enough knew and the world perceived. The 1948 war had effectively demonstrated for all that the Arab East was no match for Israel. Small in terms of population, but thoroughly modern relative to organization and technology, Israel was able to defeat the Arab states and would likely outstrip them for a long time to come. Involved as Nasser was in an internal revolution to entirely reshape Egyptian society, he could little afford to take on Israel, although he did take on the responsibility of spokesman for Arab nationalism. After 1948 Israel was a *bête noire* to the Arab states and they battled her, but the attacks were mainly verbal, not physical. Their only really effective weapons were economic boycott, denial of passage through the Suez Canal, and diplomatic isolation from the Arab world.

How, then, has Israel emerged as the fundamental issue of Egypt's foreign policy? Through her attacks on Egypt in 1955, 1956, and 1967. As for any state, the maintenance of the nation's security and territorial integrity are the *sine qua non* of the Egyptian government. The perception of Zionist policies as expansionist, the revelation of February 1955 that Israel could indeed easily encroach upon Egyptian territory, and the confirmation of October 1956 that Israel would do so, raised in Egypt the specter of gravely endangered national security. Israel was no longer merely the *bête noire* of Arab nationalism. The problem of Israel was no longer the displacement and deprivation of the Palestinians. Israel now appeared as a formidable foe, supported by powerful allies, bent on territorial conquest. Viewed through this perspective, as the Egyptians do indeed view it, the paramount role Israel plays in Egypt's foreign policy is easily understood. Of course, Israel's June 1967 blitzkrieg against the Arab states deepened Egyptian fears and polarized Arab and Israeli positions.

The 1967 war had two major consequences. The first was Israel's occupation of large parts of Arab territory—Jordan's west bank, Syria's Golan Heights, and Egypt's Sinai Peninsula and the Egyptian administered Gaza Strip. The second was the emergence of several Palestinian liberation movements and the mobilization of the Palestinian people into armed struggle. Affected by these developments, the foreign policy of the U.A.R. now distinguishes between the

Palestine problem proper and the Arab-Israeli dispute.[31] The official position is that the solution of the former problem could only be reached if the Palestinians themselves are a party to any settlement. As to the latter, the U.A.R. has accepted the November 1967 United Nations resolution as a basis for the peaceful settlement of the conflict. Its position has been repeatedly reiterated by top-ranking government officials and by President Nasser himself. A settlement, it is felt, would allow the U.A.R. to concentrate once more on internal reforms and economic development; a movement whose progress the war has severely arrested. In an interview with a senior editor of *Newsweek* and published in its issue of February 10, 1969, Nasser asserted that if Israel evacuated its troops from the captive areas, the Arab states would favor: (1) a declaration of non-belligerence; (2) the recognition of the rights of each country to live in peace; (3) the territorial integrity of all countries in the Middle East, including Israel, in recognized and secure borders; (4) freedom of navigation on international waterways; and (5) a just solution to the Palestinian refugee problem. However, on February 26, 1969, Nasser warned in a *New York Times* interview that if Israeli forces did not withdraw from Arab territory there was the possibility of another full-scale war. But, he cautioned, Israeli withdrawal alone would not bring a settlement. Israel, he insisted, must permit the return of the "more than one million Arabs" who had been expelled from Palestine since 1948 if there was to be "lasting peace." Thus, while Egypt has left the door open for a peaceful settlement,[32] its foreign policy, nevertheless, is being formulated on the supposition that a renewed large scale military confrontation is likely.

Nasserism in Perspective and Prospective

In 1954 Gamal Abdul Nasser wrote regarding the role of his revolution, "It is a role such as to spark this tremendous power latent in the area surrounding us; a role tantamount to an experiment . . ."[33] Indeed, the revolution did spark a tremendous power that has completely remodeled Egyptian society with its concepts of social democracy and national dignity. In overflowing Egyptian borders the revolution has created a movement among the Arab masses paralleled only by the Islamic tide centuries before it. Nasserism has brought the Arab peoples into a full light of the modern world with all its potentialities, promises, and problems—an overwhelming tide of rising expectations; it has brought in its wake a rejuvenation of the Arab creativity which so enlightened the Medieval world. But it has also been the portender of upheaval and instability. In failing to take full responsibility for the Nasserite tide that has risen throughout the Arab world—i.e., in failing to establish an Egyptian based pan-Arab Nasserite movement with himself as head—Nasser has been unable to

---

[31] *Christian Science Monitor* (February 14, 1970).
[32] *Christian Science Monitor* (February 6, 1970).
[33] *Philosophy of Revolution*, p. 88.

control the means and manifestations of Nasserism outside Egypt. All breeds of politicians and opportunists have been able to utilize Nasserism, merely to gain popular support and power. But even more importantly, the truly dedicated proponents of Nasserism have often been frustrated or alienated because they have little or no real influence in the policy-making processes that have created Nasserism. Without proper communication channels between Nasserite forces throughout the Arab world and Nasser—channels that would exist in a party structure to carry information both to and from Nasser—Nasser has sometimes pursued policies detrimental to his advocates. Within a party structure Nasserite forces would have been able to effectively articulate, aggregate, and coordinate their interests and Egypt's. Instead, various Nasserite proponents have had to seek their own ways, willy-nilly, sometimes finding themselves in disagreement with Egypt's policies, often finding themselves in opposition to other Nasserites within their own countries and/or within neighboring Arab states. Thus, while Nasserism has remained by far the most popular force throughout the Arab world, without a well articulated program to rally around or an integrated structure to work within, Nasserite proponents have been unable to transform it into a constructive program.

In foreign policy Nasserism is manifested in the resolution of the state to retain its sovereign status in the world community against outside pressures, real or perceived, with those instruments available to it. Due to the relative weakness of the state these instruments are largely persuasive rather than coercive. The principles underlying the use of such instruments are expressed by the doctrine of positive neutralism which calls for the resistance of the neutral states to the great power centers by taking an active part in the world. As in other countries, foreign policy is largely determined by domestic needs, and the United Arab Republic's development needs demand that it take some positive action in the international community. If it is both to maintain its independence and sovereign status and obtain aid for development, it must maintain a balance between the two great power blocs. In order to succeed at this, it must maintain its prestige at a level high enough to retain the recognition of the international community.

Within the Arab world, Nasser's relations with the other Arab leaders have at times been strained; at other times he has had considerable support throughout the area. His attempts to export his revolution have brought him the enmity of a number of the leaders in the area, but he is still the leading Arab statesman and the head of the most powerful state in the area. The success of Nasser's foreign and domestic policies cannot be denied, despite his failure to deal successfully with the problem of Israel. His influence among the Arab masses is due in part to the role of his regime as a model for development and in part to his personal charisma. Nasserism has been accepted throughout the Middle East as an expression of the desires of many of the Arab people and as the only indigenous policy-ideology complex to have any great success in practice.

The June war of 1967 confronted Nasser, and Nasserism, with their severest test. Nasser's prestige was badly damaged abroad by the disastrous war, and there have been serious domestic repercussions. First, the United Arab Republic government went through a cabinet reshuffle, in which such long-standing officials as Zakaria Mohieddin and Ali Sabry were removed and the civilian proportion of cabinet posts was increased. Then, in March of 1968 Nasser announced the establishment of a more democratic system of government. Seven points were to govern the drafting of a new constitution:[34]

1. Egypt must remain "part of the Arab nation;"
2. The "Socialist gains" of the revolutionary governments since 1952 would be maintained;
3. There must be new guarantees of individual liberties including freedom of thought and expression;
4. Egyptians must accept the fundamental importance of work as a basis of their society;
5. Constitutional court must be set up to rule on the constitutionality of all laws. (This, like the previous point, reflects in part concern in Egypt about curbing the past power of the military police and intelligence services, qualified observers believe.);
6. Egyptians must be guaranteed legal immunity;
7. State executive posts must be limited in time and "reconsidered every five years." Greater competition and selectivity must be introduced in choosing candidates for them.

The scandal of a military plot against the government in the summer of 1967, added to the disastrous war, has produced substantial limitations upon the power of the military. This is likely to mean that even if Soviet influence in the military increases, its impact upon the government will be minimized.

In foreign affairs, the United Arab Republic and Britain resumed diplomatic relations in March of 1968, and United Arab Republic-American relations became friendlier. Nasser appears to be attempting to offset increasing Soviet commitments with Western counterbalance. The negotiations on the Israeli-occupied territories have been utterly unsuccessful, but another long-standing dispute, the Yemen War, has been settled. In return for Saudi payments to offset their war losses, the Egyptians are withdrawing from the Yemeni conflict.

The economic and political difficulties created by the June war present President Nasser with grave problems. In the main, however, two things appear evident. One is that his position at home and in the Arab world is only slightly less secure than before. The crisis has shaken but not toppled him. According to the *New York Times*, "Even after the demoralizing defeat they [the Egyptian people] face a future by no means hopeless. They are still confident that Mr. Nasser can hold them together."[35] Indeed, according to the same paper, "If free elections were held in the U.A.R. tomorrow, Mr. Nasser would win hands down

[34]*Christian Science Monitor* (April 3, 1968).
[35]*New York Times* (Sept. 17, 1967).

against any comer. Similarly, he has retained his paramountcy among Mideast leaders despite a severe buffeting of the U.A.R.'s prestige abroad."[36]

The principles and policies of Nasserism, as applied to the United Arab Republic's domestic and foreign policy, will remain substantially the same, and so will the problems. The prospects for the United Arab Republic are still in doubt, but the June war may have changed them less than is often asserted. Nonetheless, the ideology will long outlive the man, and Nasserism will continue to influence events in the Middle East well into the future.

SELECTED BIBLIOGRAPHY

Two excellent surveys of modern Egyptian history are John Marlowe's book, *A History of Modern Egypt and Anglo-Egyptian Relations, 1800-1956*, (2d ed., Hamden, Conn., 1965) and Mahmoud Y. Zayid's book, *Egypt's Struggle for Independence* (Beirut, 1965). Jamal M. Ahmed, in *Intellectual Origins of Egyptian Nationalism* (London, 1960), examines the philosophic origins of the nationalist movement. For an examination of the role of the Muslim Brotherhood, see *Nationalism and Revolution in Egypt* (Stanford, 1964) by Christina Phelps Harris. An excellent examination of the forces shaping the internal and external policies of the United Arab Republic is *Modern Egypt* (New York, 1967) by Tom Little. For an account of the early days of the revolution, the following three books provide the insight of the men who were the key figures shaping Egypt's policies: Mohammed Neguib, *Egypt's Destiny* (New York, 1955); Gamal Abdul Nasser, *Egypt's Liberation: The Philosophy of the Revolution* (Washington, D.C., 1955); Anwar Sadat, *Revolt on the Nile* (New York, 1957). Nadav Safran's book, *Egypt in Search of Political Community, an Analysis of the Intellectual and Political Evolution of Egypt 1804-1952* (Cambridge, 1961), is an excellent survey of prerevolutionary Egypt. *Egypt in Transition* (New York, 1958) by Jean and Simone Lacouture is a very useful account of revolutionary Egypt. For the role of the military in Egyptian politics, see P. J. Vatikiotis, *The Egyptian Army in Politics, Pattern for New Nations?* (Bloomington, Ind., 1961). Morroe Berger's book, *Bureaucracy and Society in Modern Egypt: A Study of the Higher Civil Service* (Princeton, 1957) is a sociological study of civil service attitudes based on field research in Egypt. The following books provide a survey of the United Arab Republic's economic system: Bent Hansen and Girgis A. Marzouk, *Development and Economic Policy in the U.A.R. (Egypt)* (Amsterdam, 1965); Charles Issawi, *Egypt in Revolution: An Economic Analysis* (New York, 1963); Donald C. Mead, *Growth and Structural Change in the Egyptian Economy* (Homewood, Ill., 1967); and Patrick O'Brien, *The Revolution in Egypt's Economic System: From Private Enterprise to Socialism, 1952-1965* (New York, 1966). For an evaluation of agrarian reform in the United Arab Republic, see *The Egyptian Agrarian Reform 1952-1962* (New York, 1967) by Gabriel S. Saab, and Peter Mansfield's *Nasser's*

[36] *Ibid.* (Nov. 19, 1967).

Egypt (Baltimore, 1965) is a short and sympathetic study. A recent reader giving excellent coverage of the issues of Egyptian politics is P. J. Vatikiotis' (ed.) *Egypt Since the Revolution* (New York, 1968). A comprehensive view of Egypt's role in Africa is Tareq Y. Ismael's book, *The U.A.R. in Africa: Egypt's Policy under Nasser* (Evanston, Ill., 1970).

chapter 15

The Kingdom of
Saudi Arabia *

If Saudi Arabia is known to the West, it is known for the wealth provided by the oil industry, for the leisure life of its rulers, and for its societal backwardness. The sudden wealth of the country in the post-war period has begun to slowly reshape the society; particularly in the last decade the government has started to channel some oil revenues into social and economic development. Yet Saudi Arabia is still considered one of the least developed countries in the Middle East because its traditional society remained isolated from the modern world until the last two decades.

THE DEVELOPMENT OF THE KINGDOM

The Kingdom of Saudi Arabia, as it became known officially in 1932, was created by King Abdul Aziz Ibn Saud (1881-1953). For almost 24 years (1901-1925), Ibn Saud led successive campaigns against the tribes of the Arabian desert and united them under his rule. Before the creation of the kingdom, the tribes of Arabia lived in a constant state of insecurity, and tribal rivalry was the main principle conditioning the life of the desert. The two main rivals were the Saudi dynasty, the present ruling family, and the Rashidi dynasty of the Shammar tribe. In 1891 the latter overthrew the Saudi ruler in Najd, the central land in the country, and imposed its rule over the other tribes. The defeated Saudi family went into exile in Kuwait. But Ibn Saud never accepted the defeat; he nurtured the dream of returning to Najd and reinstalling the rule of his own family.

*Abdul H. Raoof, associate professor of political science, State University College at Buffalo, N.Y.

The beginning of this long campaign against the tribes took place in 1901 when Ibn Saud with 50 of his men marched from exile to capture al-Riyadh, the capital city of Najd, from Muhammad Ibn Rashid. Al-Riyadh surrendered to him after he had ambushed and killed the Rashidi governor in Najd on January 15, 1902. Relief from the ruthless and tyrannical rule of Ibn Rashid and admiration of Ibn Saud's courage motivated the bedouin tribes to welcome him and swear allegiance to his rule. Ibn Saud was declared governor of Najd, though he did not have complete control of the region until 1906. The following years were not easy for him since many tribes and rulers were aware of the danger of the expansion of his reign and were very hostile to him.

Tribal relations in Arabia were influenced by the Ottoman Empire whose domain included most of the Middle East; even those territories not in the empire were under its influence. Najd was independent, but Ibn Rashid was a paid ally of the Turks. Thus, the defeat of Ibn Rashid and claim by Ibn Saud for independence from the Turkish Sultan's authority constituted a real threat to the interests of the empire. In 1904 Ibn Rashid wanted to restore his rule in Najd and asked the Turks for military help. Eight Turkish battalions were sent to fight Ibn Saud and temporary victory over him was achieved. But the Turkish army, struck down by cholera in the summer of that year and unable to withstand the attack of Ibn Saud's army, retreated and abandoned its supplies. The bedouins with Ibn Rashid, seeing the Turkish army's defeat, ended their fighting and fled. The ramifications of this battle were obvious. The Turkish influence and the Rashidi rule in Najd were terminated for good. Other tribes which doubted the ability of Ibn Saud to stand against the Turks now realized his military strength and accepted his leadership.

The period between 1906 and 1912 was marked by a halt in the skirmishes. Ibn Saud had to assess his rule in Najd and to strengthen his control over the fragmented tribes; much effort was spent in converting these tribes to Wahabism, which will be discussed later. Once he was assured of his military strength, Ibn Saud began a new series of conquests running from 1912 to 1925.

His domain was extended to the Persian Gulf when he captured al-Hasa region on the eastern border of the country from the Turks in 1913. The capture of al-Hasa brought Ibn Saud into close contact with the British Empire, acting through its regional office—the Persian Gulf administration in Kuwait. The British Empire, which had been watching the development in Arabia for the last decade, was not interested in engaging itself in tribal quarrels because Arabia was too poor to interest the British as a colony; the only interest they had was the protection of their route to India. At the outbreak of World War I, the British decided to rally Ibn Saud to their side against the Turks. But this marriage of convenience did not last long when Allied war activities in the Arabian peninsula were turned over to the Arab bureau in Cairo, the British colonial office for Middle Eastern affairs, which had already backed Sharif Husayn of al-Hijaz, Ibn Saud's main rival.

Both Ibn Saud and his reign were different from Sharif Husayn and his. Sharif

Husayn was a descendent of Prophet Muhammad and an urban Arab, but Ibn Saud was a bedouin who never abandoned his culture. Najd and al-Hijaz also represented a contrast. Al-Hijaz was an urban region with a continuous wealth derived from pilgrimages, and its government was modeled to some extent after the Turkish government. Najd was a stretch of desert inhabited mainly by impoverished bedouin tribes whose economy was based on raising camels and goats. Ibn Saud's kingdom was a desert and a primitive land. Moreover, as a Wahabi who regarded urban Muslims as revisionists, Ibn Saud regarded Sharif Husayn as the prime example of the moral decadence which Wahabis were sworn to fight.

The active support of the British government to Sharif Husayn in part encouraged him in 1916 to declare himself king of all the Arabs—a move which led to intensified efforts by the two rivals to win other chiefs of tribes over to their sides. In 1917 Ibn Saud successfully won the chief of the Oasis of Khurma, on the northeastern tip of al-Asir, to his side. In 1919 Husayn started a direct assault on Khurma by sending in a force of nearly 6,000 men. It was ambushed by Ibn Saud's force in the dark, and heavy losses were inflicted—about 5,000 were killed. This battle undermined the morale of Husayn and discouraged him from initiating any other direct assault. Yet, he did turn to stir up the chiefs of his neighboring region, al-Asir, against Ibn Saud. This maneuver was doomed to failure when Ibn Saud sent a force of tribesmen under the command of his son Faisal, the present king, to capture al-Asir. By 1920 all Arabia but al-Hijaz was brought under the control of Ibn Saud. Hence, he emerged as the sole leader in Arabia, recognized by the British government as Sultan of Najd and its dependencies.

The direct confrontation with King Husayn came to a showdown in August 1924. King Husayn had already proclaimed himself as caliph in a move intended to rally the Muslims to his side. Contrary to what he expected, his claim for the caliphat met with the contempt of many Muslim leaders. Ibn Saud and his Wahabi followers were particularly annoyed by this claimed leadership. Promptly they marched to Mecca, the seat of Husayn's power. With the capture of Mecca and the abdication of Husayn, the leaders of al-Hijaz proclaimed Ibn Saud the king of al-Hijaz and sultan of Najd.

In the subsequent years Ibn Saud devoted his efforts to consolidating his rule and to maintaining security, order, and unity where raiding, assassination, and intrigue had prevailed for so long. One may wonder how these conflicting interests of tribes, towns, and villages were neutralized and finally subdued to a higher authority. The answer to this question lies in the effective leadership that Ibn Saud provided and in the use of religion as a system of values unifying people.

Ibn Saud's Leadership

Ibn Saud was barely 18 when he began his expeditions to regain his homeland from the Rashidi family. Youth and hatred of the Rashidis made him a forceful man, and self-confident in realizing his dreams. Personal ambition and religious motives, upholding the teachings of the Wahabi sect, were the two good reasons for fighting vigorously against his rivals who had neither. His deep understanding of the social organization in the desert and the bedouin personality guided him in overruning his opponents. Intrigues and assassinations were the customary modes in the intertribal relations which Ibn Saud utilized during his first years of conquests. The bedouin idolizes courage and bravery, as well as mercy and forgiveness, all of which Ibn Saud demonstrated. An example of this is his handling of al-Rashidi rulers in al-Hail, the northern part of Arabia, whom he defeated in 1920. The Rashidi family expected an annihilation by the Saudi force after the defeat. Instead, Ibn Saud won their gratitude by giving them his personal guarantee of security and brought them to al-Riyadh where they lived on royal subsidies. To assure their security, he and his eldest son Saud married two of their daughters.

Wahabism and the Ikhwan Movement

The second factor in the success of Ibn Saud's control over the desert was religious. Tribal organization, values, and norms remained intact in the new political order, but they were required to operate under religious order. The new social and political relations were to be based on the tie of Islam rather than kinship.

The teaching of Muhammad Ibn Abd al-Wahab, which had found support within the Saudi house since 1744, was a fanatical Islamic revivalist movement. It was directed against the laxity of manner and the sins of towns and tribes. In his zeal to restore the purity of Islam, Ibn Saud organized the Wahabi Ikhwan (Brotherhood) movement.

In order to spread Wahabism among tribesmen, Ibn Saud set up Ikhwan colonies by converting the vicinity of each oasis and spring into an agricultural settlement. Supervised by a Wahabi missionary, each settlement served as a military cantonment, farm, and center for the Islamic faith. Within a decade more than a hundred Ikhwan colonies spread through central Arabia. Encouraged by the success of these colonies, and in order to strengthen the faith of the tribesmen, Ibn Saud ordered tribal chiefs to attend religious schools, and be sent *Ulama* (religious teachers) to preach to the tribes.

The result of this movement of conversion was to produce a zealous group of warriors ready to sacrifice for propagating Wahabism and to rally behind its leader, Ibn Saud.

SOCIAL STRUCTURE

The Saudi society, though it is undergoing some change, still mainly manifests traditional character. The bulk of its estimated population of 7 million are nomads who live in tribal organization. About 15 percent of the people live in villages, and somewhat less than 20 percent live in growing cities.[1] The mode of livelihood and organization provide the basis of the political system.

The tribe is the main social organization in Saudi Arabia. There are about 100 major tribes with a membership of 100 and more. Kinship is the main principle on which tribes are organized—members of the same tribe are related to each other. They are unsettled pastoral tribes which migrate with their camels, sheep, and goats where they can find water. Before Ibn Saud imposed his control on Arabia, raiding villages and cities and attacking caravans provided them with another source of subsistence.

Bedouins are arrogant and proud of their way of life. They are contemptous of any kind of manual work. Hence, they look down on the farmers and townsmen, whom they call *al-Hadhar* (civilized). Individualism and equality among members of the same tribe are the other features of tribal values. Bedouins are very independent and unwilling to accept another's superiority. More than 500 years ago the Arab philosopher Ibn Khaldun described them as "the least capable, among all people, of governing or being governed." In the absence of diversity of specialization within the tribe, social status, class, or privilege do not exist on which the members may be stratified. The desert life, however, necessitates the subordination of individual to his tribe, which can provide him with protection against any attack.

The tribe is an autonomous political entity which demands loyalty from its members. Governmental laws and regulations applicable to cities and villages are not necessarily applicable to the tribe. Intertribal and intratribal relations are governed by the tribal law—the accepted customs and precedents of the tribes.

Authority is hierarchically arranged in the tribe. It extends from the family head the oldest male in the extended family up to the sheikh (chief) of the tribe and the paramount sheikh of the mother tribe. Political power and prerogatives in the tribe tend to be concentrated in the hands of a particular family from whom the sheikh is selected. The sheikh is not necessarily an autocrat; rather, there exist some institutionalized countervailing forces which act as checks on the arbitrary exercise of his power. The first force is the tribal council (*majlis*). Composed of a certain number of the senior males in the tribe, the tribal council hears grievances from any member in the tribe and endeavors to solve disputes. Decisions must be reached by a consensus among the members. The second force is the subordination of the sheikh to a paramount sheikh. The grievance which is not solved in a way satisfactory to the petitioner can be

---

[1] The exact population in Saudi Arabia is still undetermined because there has been no official census. All the statistics which are cited in this article have been drawn from the two official documents: Ministry of Finance and National Economy, Central Department of Statistics, *Statistical Yearbook, 1385 A.H. 1965 A.D.;* and Saudi Arabian Monetary Agency, *Annual Report 1385-86 A.H.* A point of clarity should be made here. Saudi official documents should be consulted with caution because they do contain inaccurate and even contradictory statistics. I have tried to mention only those figures which seem close to correctness.

appealed to the chief of the main tribe who may overrule the decision of the lower sheikh.

Due to the lack of sufficient water, agriculture has never played a preponderant role in the Saudi economy. Villages, dispersed throughout the country, exist around wells or springs. There are 1,915 agricultural villages occupying an area of 2,575,000 acres. The two main types of land ownership are communal and individual. The communal land tenure is common in villages which are settled by tribes. The land is considered the property of the tribes whose members work the land and share the produce together. The individual land tenure is linked to the extended family whose members jointly own the land from which they derive their livelihood. Of the 105,000 agriculture workers the ratio of family workers to nonfamily workers is 6 to 1. Large ownership, generally speaking, is not as common as in many countries of the Middle East. Of the total 45,000 landholdings, less than 3,400 landholdings exceed 40 acres.

Villages are two types, tribal and nontribal. The tribal villages are settled by nomadic tribes who became either completely or partially sedentary, with the tribe continuing to be pastoral, moving away from the village and returning for planting and harvesting. Though tribal organization in this type of village is perpetuated, tribal values and norms tend to be modified. First, by accepting the cultivation of land the bedouin no longer has contempt for the villagers or townsmen who are engaged in manual work. Consequently, the traditional animosity between bedouin and non-bedouin is decreased, and the bedouin becomes more able to move into the new sectors of the modern economy in the country. Second, the political power and prerogatives of the sheikh are reinforced by the fact that he becomes the head of an economic unit—the tribe as a producing group. Tribesmen are aware of their needs for governmental loans and machines which can be supplied to farmers. They become increasingly dependent on the sheikh's will as he has to act as their liason with the central government. Lastly, tribal loyalty has been replaced by territorial loyalty because the settled subtribe tends to terminate its relationship with the main tribe.

The second type of village is nontribal. Kinship is no longer the collective tie of all the villagers; they are an amalgamation of various ancestories. Social cohesion is not as high as in tribal villages. The unpaid head of the village is not the chief of a tribe, but he is a local administrator managing the affairs of the village.

Cities and towns, few in number, have existed in Saudi Arabia for a long time. Mecca and Madinah, dating back to the pre-Islamic period, are two holy cities of the Islamic world. Other cities have been created to serve as either centers of political power, such as the capital al-Riyadh, or as centers for trade with the surrounding villages and tribes, such as Houfouf. Cities such as Jidda, the port city on the Red Sea, and al-Dharan, the center of the oil company (ARAMCO), are extended villages which owe their expansion to the new economic activities.

Up to recent times Saudi cities, like most of the old cities in the Middle East, were amalgamations of groups constituted on the basis of occupation, ethnic, or social status. Often these groups lived in separate quarters of the city, and each quarter developed its special characteristics. The insufficient intergroup contact produced the feeling on the part of the dwellers that they were only a part of their group rather than of the larger urban area. Yet the mode of life forced some contacts to exist among groups, the effect of which was to produce a city personality which differed from that of the villages.

The two-class system is predominant in the city; upper class and lower class. The upper class is composed of families with political or social power, such as the royal family and its relatives, sheikhs, and merchants. The lower class is made up of small merchants, artisans, and members of the lower echelon of government organization. A middle class has begun to emerge in cities as a result of increasing economic activities and educational attainment.

CHANGING THE TRADITIONAL ORDER

The disruption of the traditional society of Saudi Arabia began with the exploration for oil in 1934. Yet the effect of the oil industry on the society was contained until the end of World War II. In the following years oil production steadily increased, and the government royalties from oil production followed suit. The new wealth and the recent government developmental program set the society in motion; the result of which has been the growth of the urban centers, widespread education, and detribalization of the society.

The Developmental Policy

By 1964 Saudi Arabia was the fifth largest oil-producing country with 694 million barrels. The oil revenue—based on a 50-50 share in profits between the government and ARAMCO (Arabian-American Co.)—constituted the largest share in the government revenue, about eight times all other sources (see Table 15-1). This amounted to a steady growth of about 10 percent in the gross national product. The per capita income rose from a mere subsistence level in the late forties to about $280 in 1967. (However, these figures may not be accurate since the exact population is not known.)

Government interest in modernizing the country was aroused mainly as a result of the political and social change which has been sweeping the other Middle Eastern countries. Political unrest and government instability in these countries were the result of the social injustice and the inability of these regimes to produce an effective developmental program which would bring rapid economic change. The political revolutions in the Middle East—in particular, the Yemen revolution in 1962—served as a warning to the Saudi royal family. The direct involvement of both Saudi Arabia and the United Arab Republic in the war in Yemen led to personal recriminations against each other's leadership. The Saudi monarch was in a vulnerable position when he became a target of United

TABLE 15-1
Budget Estimates
(Million Saudi riyals) [a]

	1963-64	1964-65	1965-66	1966-67
Revenues				
Oil revenues	2,268	2,592	3,166	3,974
Other revenues	358	370	448	476
Allocations for general reserve & economic development fund	60	150	347	575
Total	2,686	3,112	3,961	5,025
Expenditures				
Development budget	550	762	1,402	1,717
Operating development departments [b]	654	740	863	910
Defence & national security	496	534	731	1,137
Royal treasury	183	173	173	173
Other administrative expenditures and subsidies	803	903	792	1,088
Total	2,686	3,112	3,961	5,025

[a]$1.00 equals 4.5 Saudi riyals.
[b]Includes the departments of Communications, Agriculture, Education, Health, Labor and Social Affairs, and Civil Aviation.
Source: Kingdom of Saudi Arabia, Saudi Arabian Monetary Agency, *Annual Report, 1385-86 A.H.*, p. 4.

Arab Republic propaganda which accused him of being an authoritarian ruler, spending the oil revenue on his own lavish life but not for his people. Such an image could only have been changed by accelerating the government involvement in economic and social development.

The propaganda warfare pushed the already existing rift within the royal family to a climax. Pressure for incorporating certain modern elements into the country, without the intention of evolving them very far beyond the traditional organization, has always been associated with Crown Prince Faisal in the 1950s. Out of his association with his country's foreign ministry and his frequent visits to western countries since he was 11 years old as a representative of his father on very important diplomatic missions and conferences, Faisal became intrigued with the possibilities of improving his country.

The breakthrough in the government developmental policy took place in January 1961 by a royal decree which established The High Council of Planning, with the function of formulating an overall plan for economic development. The implementation of the plan would be entrusted to the various operating ministries and departments, *e.g.* ministries of communication and health. Financing the developmental program was defined two years later on November 6, 1962 by allocating to it half of the oil revenue.

The objectives of economic development, as officially stated, are to "diversify the economy, to ensure gainful employment, and to secure a more equitable participation of all sections in the economic life of the country." Yet the developmental policy is neither guided by a political ideology nor by comprehensive planning for all sectors of the economy. The government's anti-communism and anti-socialism policy indicates a rebuff to accepting a plan which will lead directly to radical change in the main social and economic institutions. It is apparent that allocations are mainly made to projects of communication, transportation, construction, health, education, bedouin settlement, and water development. Less emphasis has been placed on the industrialization of the country. Continuing its policy of free enterprise, the government industrial policy has not gone beyond the encouragement of private enterprise. The government neither owns nor operates any industrial project except a few public companies which are set up to supply electricity to towns and some rural areas.

As much as this developmental policy is disturbing the traditional institutions, modern media (mainly owned and controlled by the government) are expediting this process. Radio, newspapers, and television, bringing news and views of the world to the remote areas, have expanded the vision of the masses beyond their immediate environments. Television, in particular, has become the vehicle of change in the country. It was recently estimated by a Saudi newspaper that there are over 100,000 television sets in the kingdom. The government plan is to link all the country with a television network. Huge amounts of broadcast time—up to 30 percent—are devoted to education and the promotion of national interests. The overall effect is penetration by modernization into all levels of the social system.

Urbanization

The cities in Saudi Arabia have been the main target of social and economic change. There has been marked growth in city population. The rate of urban growth for the last 15 years is about 100 percent—the largest metropolitan areas are Mecca with a half million and al-Riyadh with approximately 300,000 inhabitants. Since 1963, the rate of urbanization has entered a period of even more rapid growth.

The growth of cities has been due less to a natural increase in population than to a large migration from rural areas, as well as from neighboring Arab countries and from the Islamic world. The result of introducing new economic activities to the cities was an increase in job opportunities. Most of those who migrate are being attracted by those jobs which promise them a better way of life and a higher standard of living than what their villages can offer. Tribesmen are pushed to the ghettoes of the cities because of the bankruptcy of the tribal economy, under the pressure of using motor vehicles rather than camels as a main means of transportation.

Few of these immigrants become part of the productive labor force because the number of immigrants is much larger than the number of jobs available in the cities. It is also true that these immigrants lack the skill and the required training for handling the new jobs. The result has been low wages and persisting social and economic insecurity. Many of them are congested in poor housing which lacks proper sanitary facilities. Worst of all are the immigrants from West Africa who settle in Jidda and Mecca and live in shacks made of tin and wood. All this, of course, breeds restlessness and violence.

The growth of cities has been the strongest factor in breaking the traditional ties—kinship ties have begun to lose their significance in job and occupation where achievement and merit are now the criteria. Yet many of these immigrants settle in separate quarters where they continue to practice their customs and traditions.

On the other hand, the process of urbanization has had a negative effect on national development. The Westernization of a few cities is the main factor attracting the new Western-educated to jobs with the government, but only in a big city. The result is an overstaffed central bureaucracy with centralization of programs and plans. This has often led to overlooking vital programs for rural areas. Knowing most of the incoming wealth is spent in the cities, villagers and tribesmen continue to have hostile attitudes towards city dwellers and tend to view the government unfavorably.

Cities are centers for diffusion of new ideas and culture. Foreign experts, businessmen, and visitors have brought with them new ways of life which represent progress to many Saudis. The puritanic society which veiled women has accepted their emancipation in the last few years—though few women can even now be seen unveiled in al-Riyadh and Jidda.

Education

With the emphasis on economic and social development, the government came to realize the vital role of modern education in producing the professionals needed to carry out the national development programs. In recent years education has always received priority over most other development projects. During the last five years, budgetary allocations for education have increased threefold. By 1966 the number of students enrolled at all levels of education (primary, secondary, and higher) reached close to a quarter of a million students. Compared to 1961 there was an increase of 39 percent in the number of teaching institutions, 64 percent in the number of students, and more than 38 percent in the number of teachers.

The character of public education is also changing. Religious subjects continue to be taught in almost every academic year, but they tend to be squeezed out by the introduction of new subjects in the physical and social sciences. There has been extensive development of technical and trade schools aimed at producing skilled artisans, craftsmen, and clerks. At the higher level of learning, there are the two universities in al-Riyadh and Jidda offering various specialities.

A notable development in this field is the education of women. Early in 1960, a royal decree was issued announcing the creation of formal government-sponsored education for girls. By 1966 the number of girls enrolled in school increased to 60,000 students, and the number of girls' schools have increased from 15 schools in 1961 to 266 schools in 1966.

Government interest in furthering religious education is more than paramount. Aimed at challenging the leading role of the United Arab Republic in educating religious leaders for the Islamic world, the government of Saudi Arabia established the Islamic University of Madinah in 1962. Parallel to the University of al-Azhar in Cairo, the new university offers the degree of Bachelor of Arts in Islamic theology.

Widespread education in Saudi Arabia is a dynamic factor in social and political change:

1. To the extent that it is not geared toward a privileged class, the free education and, in many cases, monthly allowances paid to the student through his years of learning offer the son of the poor family an opportunity to change his social and economic status. Thus, education is the most important factor in broadening the social base from which future elite are to be recruited.

2. The integrative role of education in nation-building is self-evident. The unified and centralized system of education is exposing the Saudi students to certain ideas and educational themes, the effect of which is the creation of a national conscience. Parochialism, tribalism, and provincialism have been pushed aside by the national identification. To a great extent many of these new intelligentsia have looked to an even larger identification with the Arab nation. On the other hand, education is broadening the gap between the new generation and the old political elite which is dominated by the royal family. Lacking formal modern education, the political elite are vulnerable and they will continue to show their incompetence in managing the affairs of a society which becomes increasingly complex. Thus, the intelligentsia comes to challenge the legitimacy of the existing political relation.

3. The number of graduates from high schools and colleges is much larger than the number of jobs available in public and private enterprises. This will ultimately lead to restlessness and dissatisfaction with the present system.

Detribalization

One of the most fundamental changes now in progress is the rapid decline of the tribal patterns of organization. The very subordination of the tribal sheikhs to a central figure—King Ibn Saud—marked the beginning of their declining power. The sheikh must act in a way which does not upset his relation with his superior. On the other hand, the king, being aware of the deep-rooted tribal principles among his subjects, has to confine the exercise of his authority to the minimum required for the perpetuation of his role over the tribe. Thus, this new political relation is based less on the exercise of force than on compromise and accommodation.

In order to gain the loyalty of the sheikhs, King Ibn Saud and his successors had to distribute subsidies to them. In the early years when the Privy Purse was almost empty, the royal bounties to the sheikhs were in small amounts. With the increasing wealth of the king these bounties were generously distributed—tribal subsidies in the 1957 budget reached 14 percent of the total budget expenditures. As a result of both the decline of the tribal economy (based on camel transportation and the raiding of cities) and the sheikhs' adoption of the leisure life of the cities, they became more and more dependent on these royal subsidies. Furthermore, the king, wanting to reduce the power of the sheikhs, encouraged them to settle on the outskirts of al-Riyadh, where wells are dug and they are provided with free food by the government.

The growing power of the central government has also drawn many of the sheikhs to the major cities and particularly to al-Riyadh where they can be close to the seat of power. Thus, the sheikh has become an absentee leader of his tribe. Being unable to manage the daily affairs of his tribe, the sheikh has lost influence over his fellow tribesmen. As a frequent visitor to the cities, the sheikh comes in very close contact with the social change which is sweeping the country. He may even foresee the future when there will no longer be a paramount place for the sheikh. To render his place secure, the sheikh now sends his son to school and hopes that through his son he will continue to derive advantages from the political system.

POLITICAL INSTITUTIONS

The exercise of political power in Saudi Arabia is a reflection of its social structure. The central political figure is the king who in theory rules his country according to the Islamic law—the Koran and the Traditions of Sayings and Deeds of the Prophet Muhammad. Sharing political power with the king are the many social autonomous units, such as the tribal and village communities. Long-honored tradition has endowed these units with the legitimacy of deciding matters within their own territorial jurisdiction. The sheikh, aided by his *majlis*, makes rules for his subjects and decides on disputes as long as the members of the tribe remain subject to the tribal authority structure. The social change and the expansion of government power has been affecting the degree of control exerted by these units.

Less influenced by the West, the formal governmental structure is neither modeled after Western political institutions nor operates under concepts innovated in the West. Concepts, such as the rule of law, the citizens' duties and rights, and public accountability, are irrelevant to the operation of government. The basic framework of modern governmental agencies, legislative and judicial, is generally unknown. Even when modern institutions were introduced to the country, they were modified to suit the existing social norm and order.

Constitutionalism and the Constitutional Law

The concept of constitutionalism which refers to the confinement of the exercise of political authority to a higher law, the constitution, has been relatively accepted by the king and the people. The higher law from which the king actually seeks guidance is the *Sharia* law and the customary law. Both laws, deeply imbedded in the mind and conscience of the people, bring condemnation on those who violate them. The customary law, though it ranks second to the *Sharia* law, is in essence more effective than the *Sharia* law in restraining the king from abusing his power. The simplicity and explicitness of the customary law preclude the possibility of disagreement about the meaning of the rules and the ways of enforcing them—an inherent element in any complicated written law. In this way the king has no justification for his action if he violates the law. Furthermore, since customary law recognized the legitimate authority of the autonomous groups to regulate the relations of their members, these groups act in defense of their prerogatives when they are about to be breached.

The *Sharia* law lacks these advantages of the customary law. Its rules are general and implicit, and they must be interpreted by the *Ulama* (religious leaders). The very existence of this privileged group is not unrealistic in that the king may influence if not control the decision-making process within this group. The king as Imam is also endowed with the right to interpret the law—this gives him a great deal of discretion in dealing with his subjects. The generality of the *Sharia* rules provides further disagreement about its applicability to the present conditions. Whenever the king is interested in introducing some modern elements to the country, and if he is challenged about the vitality of this modernization, he simply answers, "There is nothing in the Koran or the words of the Prophet Muhammad against this. Show me a Koranic phrase to prohibit me from doing so." Last the *Sharia* law does not have the backing of militant social groups to defy the acts of the king.

The gradual expansion in the power of the king, while other centers of power began to lose their vitality, demanded the institutionalization of his prerogatives. Much of this process of institutionalization had to be defined and described in written documents, the purpose of which were far from limiting the king's power. The only document describing the organization of government which may be considered the constitution of the kingdom is the Organic Instructions for the Kingdom of al-Hijaz of 1926 and their subsequent amendments. With the issuance of these instructions, Najd and al-Hijaz were separated and ruled by two forms of government. Najd continued to be ruled by a patriarchal system of government based on personal authority without specialized governmental machinery. Al-Hijaz, influenced by the Turks and having already experienced an administrative system introduced by Sharif Husayn and modeled after the Ottoman Empire's administration, was to be ruled by a more advanced system of government. A viceroy, appointed by the king, was aided in ruling al-Hijaz by both a consultative assembly carrying out legislative functions and a council of deputies. The viceroy was president of both.

With the consolidation of both Najd and al-Hijaz in 1932, the integration of their separate administrations slowly proceeded. The absorption of al-Hijaz government by the central government was completed by the 1940s. During this process of integration, the Organic Instructions were amended from time to time so that they were applicable to the whole country. To the effect that they merely describe the organization and the main functions of government institutions, they are far from being a constitution in the modern sense. Individual rights and obligations, the government's scope of power and responsibilities, methods of amending the constitution, and protection of the constitution against the abuse of governmental power are all missing. While a constitution should regulate only the main principles of government and leave the other details to other forms of public law to regulate, these Instructions regulated many matters, including personnel, which could have been left to other public laws.

A new constitution for the whole kingdom has been promised by the three successive kings. A royal decree, issued in September 1932, requested the Council of Ministers to prepare a constitution, but the decree was never carried out. Again King Faisal, then crown prince and prime minister, in stating the policy of his government in November 1962, expressed the desire to prepare a new constitution which was to evolve around the establishment of a "progressive limited monarchy." To this writing no serious step has been taken in this direction.

The Monarch

The pluralistic nature of a traditional society requires a political leader who, in order to legitimize his power among the autonomous social groups, must combine in his person various roles appropriate to their value system. The king in Saudi Arabia fills three traditional roles: that of religious leader (Imam), tribal leader, and head of state and government (king).

Leader of the Believers (Imam al Mu'mimien). The identity of state with the religious community in Saudi Arabia presupposes the amalgamation of political and civic order with religious and moral order. The Saudi king has been endowed, at least in theory, with the mission of spreading Wahabism among the Muslims. Under the influence of the modern world—the division of the Islamic community into independent nation-states with each claiming immediate loyalty to the nation rather than to the religious community—this role of the king has been reduced to no more than a ceremonial one which symbolizes the trust of the holy cities of Mecca and Madinah. The religious role of the king within his country, nevertheless, remains unshaken. The increasing dependency of the religious institution on government financial support led to an enduring consequence: the control of the king over the religious institution.

Head of All Sheikhs (Shaikh al-Mashayikh). The process of unifying the country evolved less around replacing the traditional bonds and allegiance than with adding new bonds and allegiance to the state. All that mattered was to transfer the loyalty of the sheikhs to the person of King Ibn Saud and his successors. Commanding such loyalty, the king has to work with rather than against the prevailing tribal value and system of authority. Maintaining sheikhly character, the king must show generosity, courageous leadership, and honesty. As *Shaikh al-Mashayikh*, the king should oversee the welfare of all his tribes and should attempt to solve disputes which involve more than one tribe according to tribal custom and tradition.

Adhering to the tribal values, the role of *Shaikh al-Mashayikh* was emphasized more by Ibn Saud than by his two successors. Once Ibn Saud insulted a sheikh as being a "son" of a craftsman. When the sheikh's wife heard the accusation, she went to Ibn Saud requesting permission to divorce her husband because it would be demeaning for a bedouin woman to be married to a townsman. The recent eclipse in the power of the sheikhs reduced the king's dependence on the tribes.

King. The most important of the three roles is the role of king. As a king the monarch is the head of both the state the the government. As the head of state he presumably symbolizes the unity of the nation. To the extent that a nation can only exist whenever various social groups are willing to transfer their parochial loyalty to a larger political unit, the Saudi nation does not yet exist. The king represents the fragile unity which exists among the social groups. In perpetuating the unity for the sake of legitimizing his political power, the king must perform the role of mediating among social groups rather than arbitrating their claims in the union. The role of the king as head of state, therefore, is not distinguishable from his role as chief policy-maker. Each supplements the other. In this sense, in attempting to bring a consensus among the groups, the king may have to influence them by emphasizing his supreme role in making executive, legislative, and judicial decisions.

In the absence of a definition and institutionalization of the king's power, the exercise of this role is much dependent upon the incumbent king. Any failure in carrying out his role is attributed as a failure on him personally rather than of his office. In order to avoid possible failure, the king must concentrate much of this power in his own hand rather than delegating it to independent institutions. Much of the political power of the king was concentrated in his Royal Court or in the Council of Ministers, both shadows of his influence. Up to 1958 King Ibn Saud and his successor and eldest son King Saud (d. 1969) had strengthened their Royal Court. The court assisted them in managing their private affairs, and it was their instrument of control over government agencies. King Saud had five councilors serving on the Council of Ministers.

The Council of Ministers

A Council of Ministers to manage the affairs of the whole country was instituted by a royal decree in 1953, a month before the death of King Ibn Saud. The reason for establishing the council was in part "the increase in the number of obligations and the responsibilities which were placed upon the state," which the king could no longer discharge. Its prototype was the Council of Deputies which was set up in al-Hijaz region in 1931 and disappeared in the 1940s as a result of the complete integration between Najd and al-Hijaz.

The Council of Minsters, as an executive branch, assists the king in deciding the public policy. But its jurisdiction over the public policy is not precisely defined. According to Article 7 of the council regulations, "State policy within the country and abroad shall be under the surveillance of the Council of Ministers." Such functions may include the approval of the annual budget, planning, administration, international agreements and treaties, and preparing and amending regulations. Moreover, the jurisdiction of the council extends to matters presented by its president and to those which the council itself decides to examine. This should not suggest that the council has been endowed with extensive power. On the contrary, the council was not even intended to be the main organ for carrying out executive policy. It was the president of the council, but not the council itself, who was invested with the power of coordinating the policy of the ministries, and the supervision and control over all their work. The president "may also ask any minister (to refer) any matter whatsoever to him, in order to examine it and to issue instructions in connection with it."

Like the American cabinet, the Saudi council is dependent on the king's whim and is left with no power to bargain. The council's decisions are merely recommendations and can be carried out only after approval by its president and sanction by the king. The president and vice-president are directly responsible to the king while the rest of the ministers are responsible to the Council of Ministers and to the king. The king has wide discretion in selecting, dismissing, and even in accepting the resignation of his ministers. The council's power and organization can be redefined by the king. For this reason the council would rather side with the king in case of a dispute on the direction of public policy than to lose its power. On the other hand, the Saudi cabinet resembles the British cabinet. By virtue of its wide jurisdiction over the executive function, it discusses any matter pertinent to public policy and attempts to coordinate, as its president may wish, the activities of the ministries and administrative agencies. Because of both its lack of precision of functions and authority and the absence of a legislative institution sharing the formulation of public policy, the Saudi cabinet has a wider scope of function than the British cabinet.

The Saudi cabinet performs a function which neither the American cabinet nor the British cabinet may perform: the function of aggregating interests. This function can be seen by the membership composition of the cabinet. Membership in the Council is in three categories:

1. All heads of the various ministries, ministers of state, or heads of independent agencies may become members of the council by a royal decree.
2. Those advisors of the king whom he designates may serve on the council. (This category of membership was abandoned in 1958).
3. Individuals who are not holding government positions may be appointed to the council "as long as their service is valuable to the council."

It is particularly interesting to note that the third category of membership may include representatives from some selected social and economic groups. These represented groups bring their demands and claims to the council and seek to influence its policy. Whatever accommodations the council may provide for these influential interests, it provides a forum for deliberation on public policy through which the king may become aware of these divergent interests.

Ministries and Bureaucracy

As the central government expands its function, more ministries and agencies are created. There are 13 ministries—nine of which have been instituted since 1954. Many ministers of state have been increasingly appointed either to supervise an administrative agency below a ministry or to perform a particular function which has not been assigned to a ministry or to an administrative agency. By 1967 there were 24 departmental ministers and ministers of state.

Ministries and agencies are set up on the basis of function and specialization and organized along modern principles of organization. At the top of each ministry is a minister with an overall responsibility for the work of administration and implementation of the council decisions and the king's instructions. The ministry is subdivided into bureaus; each bureau is in charge of performing a segment of the function of the ministry.

Ministers and senior officials have always been recruited from a very narrow social base; the royal family and the upper class. Since the government is still based on the personal rule of the king, he must have trust in his public servants. Most of the ministers are members of the royal family and some are notable sheikhs. Senior officials have also achieved their positions through family influence. They were sent abroad to study on government scholarships which were mainly awarded on the basis of patronage and family relations. Therefore, it is accurate to say that the top echelon of the Saudi bureaucracy have a stake in the present system and their loyalty to the king is not doubtful.

The homogeneity of the ministers and their immediate subordinates is bound to be altered in the future. As the government activities begin to increase and become more specialized, the number of individuals entering the government service must also be increased, and they must be hired on the basis of their competence to perform these specialized roles. The number of civilian employees in 1959 was 41,912, and it jumped to 92,170 in 1965. The government, in order to fill these new jobs in its organization and because the upper class families may have already utilized their manpower, must recruit individuals from low economic and and social strata. Broadening the social basis of recruitment becomes possible with the new widespread education in the country. Moreover, as these new entrants push their way up, by means of promotion, through the hierarchy of the government organization, the corps of the senior officials becomes more heterogeneous.

As the bureaucracy is undergoing change, conflict among its members is intensified. Syrians, Lebanese, Egyptians, and Iraqis have continuously supplied the Saudi bureaucracy with experts and specialists in the fields of science, education, and law. Saudi officials, lacking the proper expertise, are jealous of many of these Arab employees who, because of their training, occupy high positions in the government. On the other hand, these Arab employees are frustrated when they find themselves placed under the supervision of Saudi officials who may not be as competent as they are themselves in performing their official duties. Such a situation is aggravated in the crisis of intra-Arab relations where the Arab employees take different sides in supporting the policy of Arab unity and socialism which is not popular among the Saudi senior officials. Conflict among Saudi officials is also obvious. Sources of such conflict are, for example, kinship, family ties, and the discrepancy in the education of those who went to traditional schools and those who received western education.

Court and Law

The main law regulating legal relations such as marriage, civil contracts, and criminal offenses is the *Sharia* law. In dealing with new situations arising from social and economic change for which the *Sharia* law does not provide rules, there is a growing number of secular codes for governing such matters as banking, industrial safety, and traffic offenses. While there is no movement in the country for replacing the *Sharia* law with a modern legal system, there is a liberalization in applying some if its unsuited rules to the modern world, in particular some of the criminal rules. The *Sharia*, for instance, requires the punishment of a thief by severing his hand from his arm and of the adulterer by stoning him to death. According to an American reporter, since 1962 no adulterer has been stoned to death, and no thief has lost his hand since 1966. Yet, in 1964 there were 747 thefts and 285 adultery cases officially registered with the court.

Judiciary organization consists of religious courts which at the lowest level are headed by a judge appointed by the chief judges in al-Riyadh. In some areas local governors and tribal sheikhs may act as judge. Courts of appeal exist only in a few major cities to review the decisions of the lower courts. The High Council of Justice, set up in 1963, is the highest court of appeal. Tradition in Saudi Arabia, however, still considers the king, who should dispense justice to all his people, as the final source of petitioning grievances. To relieve the king from such ever increasing duties, the Grievance Board was established in 1954 as a division within the Council of Ministers with the purpose of providing equity for anyone who has a complaint against any government organization or against any individual. Complaints submitted to the board which fall within the scope of the *Sharia* law are submitted to the religious court for trial. Other grievances are investigated first by the board, then settlements for the grievances are recommended to the king who has the final decision.

Local Government

The country is administratively divided into five main regions called provinces, and each province is subdivided into smaller administrative units called districts (there are 31 districts). At the head of each province is the *amir* (governor) who is appointed by the king and to whom he is responsible. The amir's function, as it is defined by the Royal Decree of 1932, is to maintain order, to conciliate disputes between tribes, and to execute the laws in accordance with the *Sharia* within his own province. A council headed by the amir with members varying from four to eight is set up in each province. The head of the district is a local chief; he may be a tribal sheikh appointed by the amir. The local chief rules the district in consultation with a local council which is composed of some local officials and important persons in the district.

The municipality system, constituted in major urban areas, tends to be unified and controlled from the center. Each municipality has a chief administrator appointed by the minister of the interior and two councils; the Administrative Council and the Municipal Council. The first council, presided over by the amir or the judge of the municipality, assists the chief administrator in carrying out his official duties. The Municipal Council, elected for a three-year term, is empowered to make regulations pertinent to housing, water supply, health, and construction and maintenance of roads.

POLITICAL STRIFE AND THE EVOLUTION OF POLITICAL INSTITUTIONS

The disappearance of the charismatic leadership of King Ibn Saud from the political scene in 1953 brought discontinuity to the old patterns of political relations. The transfer of power to his eldest son Saud seemed, at first, peaceful and acceptable to all the members of his family, the *Ulama*, and the tribal sheikhs. But from the beginning, the new king, lacking the leadership of his father, found himself unable to exercise his power alone without giving some consideration to the political interests and the personal ambitions of his brothers, uncles, and the early comrades of his father. Of these individuals, his youngest brother Faisal, the present king, was the most powerful. Dissension within the royal family replaced the unity which had prevailed under Ibn Saud. Among the many consequences of the long-lasting struggle between Saud and Faisal was its impact on the evolution of the political institutions in the country.

The first impact was on the settlement of the problem of political succession, though it might not be firmly settled, and the institutionalization of the crown prince role. In hereditary monarchies the principle of succession is to appoint the king's eldest son as crown prince. This pattern of succession was followed only by King Ibn Saud when he nominated his eldest son Saud as the crown prince. Due to the disposition of King Ibn Saud himself, the nomination of his crown prince was accepted by all the members of his family, who took oath before the death of their father to support the rule of their oldest brother. The two subsequent nominations of Crown Prince Faisal and Khalid in 1954 and 1964, respectively, marked a shift in the political succession. By nominating the king's brother as a successor to the king, the succession has been solved with the intention of accommodating the rival interests within the royal family. Thus, a new element of continuity has been introduced to the political rule of the royal family.

The emergence of the crown prince as a rival or a potential rival to the king endows him with political significance. Essentially the king must share his political power with him to some extent. By the same token, the crown prince, in order to keep his grip on political power, must make his power felt by the king, by the members of the royal family, and by other influential leaders in the country. When all is said, the crown prince has to play a second-man role in the kingdom—even though he may sometimes overshadow the king himself—and hence to be appointed to important political offices such as the presidency of the Council of Ministers or vice-president when the king acts as president of the council. Moreover, the crown prince's cabinet emerged as an independent political institution, separated from both the Royal Court and the Council of Ministers, and charged with some important functions, such as supervising bedouin affairs. This institutionalization of the crown prince's role can be readily seen in the increasing financial appropriations to his cabinet—these were doubled within four years after it was established in 1962.

The second change was the decreasing personal power of the king and the decline of his court as an instrument of control over other government institutions. The first step in this direction was taken in 1958 when King Saud issued a royal decree giving the then crown prince and Prime Minister Faisal full power in managing public affairs. Upon his assumption of power, Faisal reshuffled his cabinet, as a result of which the five king's councilors were dropped from the membership of the Council of Ministers. Four non-Saudi ministers—two Syrian and two Palestinian citizens—lost their ministerial posts because of their close association with King Saud.

The crisis of 1964 resulted in a major reform in the monarchial institution. In both the Royal Court and the Royal Private Affairs Office, there was an overhaul of personnel and a reduction in their annual appropriations to one third in 1965 over the 1963 appropriation. The private purse of the king was also substantially cut from 17 percent of the state budget in 1959 to 5.5 percent in 1964. A further development was the removal of the immediate control of the king over some military forces. The Royal Guard was transferred to the ministry of defense and the white army, composed of tribal soldiers and organized by King Ibn Saud, was renamed the National Guard and attached to the ministry of the interior.

The third political institution, the one most affected by the disunity of the royal family, was the Council of Ministers. There is no doubt that the evolution of the Council of Ministers was essentially the result of the new economic and social changes in the country. Yet the internal strife has left a far greater impact on this development.

From the beginning, the Council of Ministers owed much of the expansion of its functions and of its scope of power to Prince Faisal, who served most of the time as its president or vice president. Due to his long experience and administrative competence (he had served as a viceroy and as president of the Council of Deputies of al-Hijaz, in addition to his duties as foreign minister since 1932) Faisal came to dominate the council. In the early years of the life of the council, as its vice president, Faisal presided over its meetings, rather than his brother King Saud who was still president of the council.

The rift between the two brothers was widened in 1957 and forced Faisal to leave the kingdom—leaving his brother Saud alone to manage the kingdom's affairs. Subsequent developments in the Middle East and at home discredited King Saud in handling the public policy of his government. The accusation of the Syrian Security Chief Abdul Hamid Serraj on March 5, 1958 against King Saud who had attempted to bribe him to assassinate President Nasser was an embarrassment to both the king himself and the government of Saudi Arabia. The king's overspending and mismanaging of the oil revenues led to a substantial debt and depreciation in the Saudi economy.

Thus, some princes and other influential Saudis began pressing the king to reconcile his differences with his brother Faisal. Responding to this pressure in August 1958, the king appointed Prince Faisal to the presidency of the Council of Ministers with unlimited power to govern the country.

The significance of this development was far more than separating the head of state from the head of government; this separation did not last longer than December of 1960 when Faisal tendered his resignation and King Saud resumed the position of premier. The very limitation on the king's powers had shaken the concept of absolute monarchy in the country and made it possible to foresee a limited monarchy in the future. The loss in the king's power was a gain for the Council of Ministers. For the purpose of bringing order into the disturbing financial and political crisis in the country, the ministry of finance, for a long time controlled by the king, was brought under the direct control of the Council of Ministers, and new ministries were formed to deal with the government's problems. With the return of Faisal to the presidency of the Council of Ministers in late 1961, his power was increased to include the right to select and appoint the members of the council.

As a chief executive, Faisal was now in a better position to obtain overwhelming support from tribal and religious leaders and even from some nationalist groups. The culmination of this support brought the reign of King Saud to an end in 1964. Both the religious leaders and the royal family members met during the period of December 17, 1963 through January 14, 1964, in order to convince King Saud to leave the throne to his brother Faisal. Saud gave a deaf ear to this decision. On March 29, 1964, 12 religious leaders, under the chairmanship of the Grand Mufti, issued a *fatwa* in which they resolved that Prince Faisal would carry out "all the internal and external affairs of the Kingdom without referring back to the king in this regard." The *Ulama* gave the reason for their decision as the poor health of King Saud and the enlargement of difference between Faisal and Saud beyond restoration of unity. The *fatwa* was approved by the royal family council which was composed of 68 princes. A complete transfer of power was carried out on October 31, 1964, when both the council of the royal family and about 80 religious leaders met again to dethrone King Saud and to proclaim Faisal as king. The Council of Ministers was requested by the royal family "to take necessary measures" to put both decisions—the decision to limit the king's power and the decision to depose king Saud—into effect. By allowing the council to act in this matter, extensive executive power which went beyond the mere administration of public policy was confirmed upon it. In this sense the Council of Minsters has shown a *potential* political significance.

With the elimination of his main rival, Faisal had to consolidate the two roles of king and head of government in his person. This was far from being a return to the old practice. First, the council now has two vice presidents; the first vice president is the crown prince who presides over most of the meetings. Second, proliferation of the ministerial activities is forcing the king not to be involved with the day-to-day decisions of the council. Third, as decisions are being made to solve many technical problems which are facing the government, the experts and specialists rather than the king or the minister concerned begin to exert some influence on the work of the council.

THE FOREIGN POLICY

The foreign policy of Saudi Arabia represents primarily the interest of the royal family and the traditional elite. To the extent that this interest revolves around the perpetuation of both royal family rule and traditional institutions and the sustentation of oil production at a high rate, the foreign policy has been characterized as conservative and pro-Western. Nevertheless, Arab nationalism and unity are also input factors in the Saudi foreign policy. For this very reason the government found itself supporting a course of action in its foreign policy which may be too radical for its own political system.

Relations with the Arab Countries

Due to the lack of historical definition of the boundaries of the newly created states in the Middle East after World War I, Saudi Arabia was engrossed for a long time in border disputes with its neighboring countries. The hostility between the Saudi dynasty and the dynasties which were in control of these countries added another difficulty to the solution of these disputes. In 1922 with British support, border agreements establishing Neutral Zones on the borders with Iraq and Kuwait were signed. Settlement with Jordan over their boundaries was temporarily reached in 1927, and a nonaggression agreement was concluded. The ambition of the Imam of Yemen in the bordering region al-Asir led to a direct conflict between the two countries in 1934. The Saudi forces carried the war inside Yemen and forced the Imam to sue for peace. A treaty between the two countries was signed confirming al-Asir as part of Saudi Arabia. The border treaties accomplished all but establishing cordial relations with these countries. In contrast to this, Saudi Arabia began to improve her relations with Egypt after 1936. There were sufficient grounds to draw the two countries into a close relation; the two kings of Saudi Arabia and Egypt shared their hostility to the Hashimite rule in Iraq and Jordan. Also, Saudi Arabia was much in need of Egyptians to staff its educational institutions and government administration.

Polarization in Arab politics in the 1950s drew Saudi Arabia into closer relations with Egypt because both, for a different reason, opposed the proposed military alliances in the Middle East. For the Saudi Arabian government these proposed alliances would ultimately strengthen the Hashimite kings in Iraq and Jordan.

The climax in this marriage of convenience was reached in 1956 after the Suez war. The Saudi king, who hated the British, denounced the aggression and hoped to increase his influence among the Arab nations by adopting a national Arab policy. But, on the other hand, the Suez war was a turning point in Egypt-Saudi Arabia relations. In the aftermath of the war Nasser emerged an Arab hero and enjoyed great popularity among the Arab nations. Hence, he championed Arab unity and the elimination of reactionary regimes in the Arab countries. (The Egyptian military attaches in Iraq, Lebanon, and Jordan were accused of plotting against the governments in these countries.) Drawing closely to U.S.S.R. and other socialist countries, Nasser's political regime was reoriented towards socialism at home.

These developments in the Egyptian policy encouraged the doubts of the Saudi rulers about the merit of their close association with Egypt. A rapprochement with Iraq and Jordan came into being. But the Saudi King felt uneasy about going along with them when the two countries formed the Arab Federation in 1958.

The Iraqi revolution of 1958 tipped the balance of power in favor of the progressive Arab rulers. In self-defense, the Saudi government in the subsequent years has had to adopt an active foreign policy supporting the traditional rulers in other Arab countries. Jordan and Saudi Arabia joined together in a unified foreign policy aimed at halting the spread of Arab socialism and unity.

When the British government decided in 1961 to terminate her treaty with Kuwait and grant her independence, the Saudi government, defying the Iraqi claim over Kuwait, supported the independence and provided military assistance. King Saud cabled Premier Kassim of Iraq on June 30, 1961 to avoid any action which would be likely to "break Arab solidarity and lead to foreign interference in the affairs of the Arab states." In the meantime, he put pressure on the Arab League to commit itself to the defense of the independent Kuwait. The Arab force, formed by the decision of the League on July 20 to replace the British troops in Kuwait, was placed under a Saudi commander, and the Saudi government's contribution to it was 1,200 soldiers. The Saudi force stayed in Kuwait until it was called for duty in the Yemenite war.

Aiming at containing the Arabian peninsula from social revolution, the Saudi government heavily committed itself to the support of the Royalists in Yemen after the deposal of Imam Muhammad al-Badr. Shortly after the revolution on October 21, 1962, Prince Faisal recognized the Imam as a legal ruler and promised him military support. The military intervention of United Arab Republic and Saudi Arabia did not achieve more than a stalemate in the civil war in Yemen. This direct intervention, however, ended after the June war of 1967 because of the United Arab Republic's willingness to withdraw its troops from Yemen.

Undoubtedly the war in Yemen, combined with many other factors, has left a great impact on the foreign policy of Saudi Arabia. A conciliatory policy rather than direct involvement has been sought in Southern Yemen. The collapse of the South Arabian Federation and the transfer of the political power to the nationalist group, National Liberation Front on November 30, 1967 were intolerable to the Saudi rulers. Nevertheless, King Faisal refused to offer the former traditional rulers of the Federation any assistance more than refuge. It has been reported that the king even encouraged these former rulers to come into agreement with other nationalist groups in the Republic.

Saudi Arabia and the Islamic World

The Saudi rulers are consciously and deliberately seeking closer relations with the Muslim world. The religious basis of the Saudi rule is a partial explanation of this policy. Second, the pilgrimage traffic was the major source of income to the government before the discovery of oil, and now it has dropped to second place providing about one twentieth of the total government revenue. Thus, the continuation of this income depends upon good relations with the Islamic countries.

A sense of identity with Islamic ethos and culture permits the Saudi rulers to improve their image to the ouside world and to arouse political support to its policy in attacking social reform in the Middle East. To this end a revival of Islamic unity came into being in 1961. In May of that year King Saud addressed the pilgrims in Mecca and urged all Muslims to unite in an Islamic union "to defend Islamic interests and world peace." This call for Muslim unity may have been less serious than Faisal's call three years later. Aimed at attacking the Arab socialists' notion that Islam has been a force retarding Arab society from achieving progress, Faisal deplored the decline in "Muslim piety" as the very cause of the backwardness of the Muslims. He suggested that representatives from all the Muslim countries meet in Mecca to consider the ways to revive Islam and unite the Muslims. Nasser, assailing the proposal, stated that the purpose of King Faisal in calling for such a conference was mainly to attack Arab socialism and the revolutionary regimes in the Arab countries.

Anxious to take the plan off the ground, on January 31, 1966 Faisal announced the establishment of a preparatory committee for the Islamic summit conference. Seeking support to the conference, Faisal flew to Pakistan on April 19, 1966 to induce the endorsement of Ayoub Khan. Ayoub Khan, sensing the real intention of the proposed conference, may have discouraged the idea. The official five-day visit was concluded with the issuance of a communique in which the two heads of state pledged cooperation between their respective countries in the fields of economics and education, but with no reference to the summit conference.

To promote the relations with other Muslim countries in Asia and Africa, extensive official visits have been exchanged between King Faisal and the heads of these states. Particular interest was paid to the improvement of Saudi relations with African Muslim countries. The Islamic University of Madinah, opening its door to African students, sent a mission on August 4, 1964 to East and Central Africa to study their Islamic needs and to inform them of the services the university is providing. A few months later the government announced that it had allocated about half a million Saudi riyals for the propogation of Islam in Africa.

Saudi Arabia and the West

The British support of the Hashimite dynasty in al-Hijaz, Iraq, and Jordan was the main cause of the cool relations between Britain and Saudi Arabia. This relationship deteriorated further in the 1950s as a result of Buraimi dispute. (The Buraimi Oasis borders Saudi Arabia, Muscat-Oman, and the Trucial coast.)

Saudi Arabia claimed sovereignty over the Oasis while the British refused to accord this claim. Peaceful settlement through international arbitration and mediation, which had been sought from 1954 to 1961, did not produce more than a stalemate. Saudi Arabia was inclined to abandon its claim when the Buraimi was included in the newly formed Confederation of the Gulf Emirets in April, 1968.

The American oil investment in Saudi Arabia since 1933 has been the backbone of the cordial relations between Saudi Arabia and the United States. Aiming at protecting these investments and at securing a place for the United States in the Middle East in the post-war period, American strategists in 1943 constructed an air base in al-Dahran, where ARAMCO had its wells and installations. (The two governments agreed to allow the lease on this base to lapse in April 1962.)

The United States-Saudi Arabia relations have been strained from time to time because of American support to Israel. In the aftermath of the June war of 1967, Saudi Arabia did not follow the lead of other Arab countries who severed their diplomatic relations with the United States and stopped oil shipment to the West. Nevertheless, the Saudi King continued to criticize American policy for supporting Israel—a policy which he attributed to the low prestige of America and to the Soviet penetration in the Arab world.

American recognition of the republican government in Yemen left unhappy memories with the Saudi rulers. In a special letter to Prince Fasial on October 25, 1962, President Kennedy stated: "You may be assured of full United States support for the maintenance of Saudi Arabia's integrity."[2] Later military and political developments in the Middle East brought the United States closer to the Saudi government. The poorly trained and equipped Saudi army was not able to defend the southern region of the country which became a victim of continuous attack by Egyptian airplanes. The control of the Baath party in Iraq and Syria in 1963 and the immediate discussion for union among the United Arab Republic, Iraq, and Syria marked the triumph of the Arab progressive bloc. The government of the United States expressed its concern over these developments. In a press conference on May 8, 1963, President Kennedy announced that in case of direct or indirect aggression in the Middle East the United States would support United Nations effort to bring settlement, as well as taking appropriate measures on its own. A few months later the United States announced "the USAF units would conduct joint training exercises with Saudi Arabia" in July.[3]

Though Saudi Arabia has close relations with the United States, it has joined the neutral camp. It participated in the Bandung Conference (1955) and was invited to the Belgrade Conference (1961); King Saud was not able to participate in the Belgrade Conference because of illness. The Saudi claim of neutrality,

---

[2]*New York Times* (January 9, 1963).
[3]*New York Times* (June 30, 1963).

however, was not pushed, as with most neutral Arab countries, to close relations with the Communist bloc.

The objectives and goals of the foreign policy of Saudi Arabia have been defined with more precision during the last decade. The rising tide of Arab nationalism and socialism has forced the Saudi rulers to ally themselves with the traditional regimes in other parts of the Middle East. The development of the June war of 1967 provided a new lease on life for the Saudi rulers. Their rivals, the revolutionary leaders, have been degraded by the Arab nation and have become financially dependent on their subsidies. Thus, the freeze in inter-Arab quarrels provides suitable conditions for national development. This, of course, depends on the willingness of the Saudi rulers to accept the rationalization of their political, social, and economic systems.

ANNOTATED BIBLIOGRAPHY

Little attention has been paid to the study of Saudi Arabia, and the few published works, most written by Western diplomats, have been a record of the Saudi rulers. Gerald deGaury, *Faisal: King of Saudi Arabia* (New York: 1967) is a biography of the present king. David Howard, *The Desert King: Ibn Saud and His Arabia* (New York: 1964) is a biography of King Abdul Aziz Ibn Saud. Richard H. Sanger, *The Arabian Peninsula* (Ithaca: 1954) contains a large section surveying both the history of the rise of Ibn Saud's power and the tribal customs of Arabia. The late H. St. J. B. Philby, a scholar and an experienced British officer on the Middle East, did much serious research on Arabia, all of which is indispensible. Among them is *Saudi Arabia* (New York: 1955), which is a historical survey of the Saudi House from the 18th century until 1953; *Arabian Oil Ventures* (Washington, D.C.: 1964) is an account of the oil discovery. B. Bayly Winder, *Saudi Arabia in the Nineteenth Century* (New York: 1965) is a systematic history of Arabia.

The Human Relation Area File's volume *Saudi Arabia: Its People, Its Society, Its Culture* (New Haven: 1959) is the only available book in English describing the Saudi's social organization and political structure. The socio economic development in Saudi Arabia was assessed by Karl S. Twitchell, *Saudi Arabia: With an Account of the Development of Its Natural Resources* (Princeton: 1958).

chapter 16

Yemen*

CONTEXT OF THE POLITICAL SYSTEM

Geographical Background

The southwestern corner of the Arabian peninsula, characterized as Arabia Felix ("happy Arabia") by the ancient world because of its well-known prosperity, is today divided between the two states of Yemen and the People's Republic of South Yemen (PROSY).

Physically, Yemen is markedly different from the remainder of the peninsula, and an appreciation of the country's geographical characteristics is important for an understanding of the economic, religious, and political development which has taken place within the last two millenia. Within its frontiers there are two distinct regions: (1) a relatively narrow (c. 25-40 kms.) coastal strip along the Red Sea, known as the Tihama; and (2) the mountainous interior, which has individual peaks of nearly 4,000 meters interspersed with numerous plateaus.

The Tihama is an almost waterless stretch of soil-sand desert extending the entire 450-kilometer length of Yemen's seacoast, from Maydi on the northern frontier with Saudi Arabia, to Bab al-Mandab in the south. Characterized by extremely high temperatures and humidity, the Tihama has undergone only a minimum of agricultural and industrial development. Sparsely populated and lacking in good natural harbors, it is climatically, economically, and demographically very different from the highlands of the interior. The most important city, both in terms of population and economic activity, is al-Hudayda (Hodeida), populated by a cosmopolitan mixture of mountain Yemenis, Somalis, Danakils, Negroes, Indians, Malaysians, Persians, and Europeans.

---

*Manfred W. Wenner, associate professor of political science, Northern Illinois University.

East of this coastal strip begin the foothills of the central mountain range. Divided by innumerable narrow valleys (Arabic: *wadi*), these hills increase in height, ridge after ridge, until the central massif where the majority of Yeminis live is reached. It is within these hills and mountains that the major cities and towns are located, including the capital of San'a', at about 7,500 feet above sea-level. On the other side of the highest chain, the mountains slowly decrease in height again in another series of ridges until the great central desert of the Arabian peninsula, the Rub' al-Khali (the Empty Quarter), is reached.

The highlands are unusually fertile; unlike the remainder of the peninsula, they receive a regular annual rainfall of substantial proportions (between 20 and 40 inches per year), thus permitting extensive cultivation. The combination of fertile soil and sufficient water supports a far larger population than other regions of Arabia; in addition, the overwhelming majority of the population is settled and does not need to engage in nomadism and animal husbandry for its livelihood. For approximately 3,000 years, Yemen has had relatively large and populous cities, the residents of which are engaged in agriculture, commerce, and industry.

Demographic Background

Although no census has ever been taken, most authorities agree that the total population numbers approximately 3.5 to 4.0 million. In order to appreciate the political system of modern Yemen, it is necessary to understand the factors which divide this population into a variety of distinct groupings.

The Arabs of the peninsula have been separated into two distinct groups since the beginning of recorded history. Although racially and linguistically related, the differences in physical characteristics and way of life were sufficient to require an explanation. The "northern"Arabs of the Hijaz and Najd were primarily nomads; the "southern"Arabs were settled cultivators or town dwellers. While the northern Arabs were engaged in animal husbandry, the southern Arabs established a series of highly civilized kingdoms and empires. The most well-known among them—the Sabaean, the Minaean, and the Himyarite— were quite powerful, both politically and economically. Their trade routes extended from southest Asia to the Mediterranean, and their commercial activity was a significant element in the life of the Mediterranean empires of the ancient world, especially during the Persian and early Roman empires.

In order to explain the differences in language, culture, and physique, Muslim historians and genealogists adopted the Hebrew traditions and genealogies. According to this explanation, all Arabs were descended from a common ancestor, Shem, the son of Noah (*Sam ibn Nuh*); the pure or southern Arab (*Qahtani*) is descended from Joktan ben Eber (*Qahtan ibn Abir*, or *Hud*, as he is often called in southern Arabia). The derived or northern Arab (*'Adnani*) is descended from Ishmael (*Ismail*) through 'Adnan. This distinction is still of some importance within Yemen. The Rassi Dynasty, to which the 20th century Imams belong, claimed to be the inheritors of the Himyarite empire which ruled Yemen before its conquest by the Muslims, thus claiming Qahtani ancestry. In fact, they were all Adnanis, as their other and more probable claim to descent from the Prophet Muhammad through Hasan indicates. During the 1960s, when the opposition to the continued rule of Imam Ahmad became most obvious and widespread, the population of the northern highlands demanded that someone of Qahtani descent be made the new Imam to replace Ahmad, thus providing some indication of the depth of feeling which this very ancient division can engender. In fact, many of the northern tribes of Yemen consider the Imams as foreigners, despite their presence in Yemen for over 1,000 years.

It was, however, the conquest of Yemen by Islam that is of greater relevance today. The two major sects within Islam, Sunni and Shi'a, are both represented in Yemen. Due to the lack of precise statistical data, it is not possible to establish with any accuracy which is in the majority; both, however, claim numerical superiority.

Perhaps as a result of Yemen's pre-Islamic preeminence in Arab affairs and the need for an Islamic justification for similar rank within the new Muslim empire or perhaps simply because the mountains of Yemen provided an obvious refuge for those who adopted a minority viewpoint within the Islamic world, Yemen soon became associated with those who supported the claim of 'Ali. Two of these Shi'a groups are still found in Yemen today: the Zaidis and the Ismailis.

Zaidis. The rise of the Zaidi Imamate in the 9th century A.D. was undoubtedly the most important event in Yemen since its conquest by Islam, for the religious and later political domination of the Zaidi sect deeply influenced and changed the social structure, the attitudes, and the political life of Yemen.

The Zaidis derive their name from Zaid, one of the two grandsons of Husain. As is the case with other Shi'as, the Zaidis recognize as their spiritual leaders (Imams) only descendants of the Prophet Muhammad through his daughter Fatima and his son-in-law and cousin 'Ali and their two sons, Hasan and Husain. The Zaidis differ from other Shi'as, however, in their recognition of Zaid as the fifth Imam rather than his brother Muhammad al-Baqir; they have as a result been often called the "Fivers."

The Zaidis differ from other Shi'as in numerous respects: They actively discourage saint worship, mysticism, temporary marriage, and the extensive celebrations associated with the death of Husain (the 10th of Muharram). By far the most important difference, however, is the Zaidi view of succession to the Imamate. According to Zaidi theory, 'Ali's succession to the Imamate was due to his particular merits; therefore, in Zaidi Islam inherited familial rule is not a major criterion for accession. Far more important is whether the candidate meets the 14 commonly accepted prerequisites for the office required by Zaidi law and tradition. Within Yemen, only one of these effectively eliminates the majority of the population, i.e., descent from Fatima and 'Ali. An important corollary of this reasoning, which has a profound influence on Yemeni political development, is that a candidate for the Imamate must publicly declare himself and seek general recognition of his claim.[1]

The position and powers of the Imam in Zaidi religious theory are unlike those of any other ruler in either Shi'a or Sunni Islam. After accession, an Imam is considered to be imbued with the "guiding light of God;" his decisions on matters of faith, morals, law, and even the personal lives of the community of believers, of which he is both the spiritual and temporal head, are infallible. In fact, of course, the Imam's power is limited by the Quran, the Sunna (tradition), and Islamic law according to the Zaidi theoreticians.

Upon assuming office, the Zaid Imams have always adopted other names, usually descriptive phrases indicative of their piety and/or learning. Imam Yahya (1904-1948), for example, styled himself *al-Mutawakkil ala Allah* (the relier on God); Imam Ahmad (1948-1962) adopted the title *al-Nasr li-Din Allah* (he who aids the religion of God). Among their other titles are *Amir al-Mu'minin* (commander of the faithful) and *Khalifa* (successor to the Prophet); both of these emphasize the Zaidi Imams' claim to be the head of the only true Islamic community. As a result of the thesis that other Muslims have deviated from the true path, there has been a tendency among the Zaidis toward fanaticism in their view of other Muslims.

The Zaidi state of Yemen, if one remembers the conditions for accession to the Imamate, was clearly based on the right to rule of the descendents of Muhammad; the total of all those with a claim to descent from Muhammad (the Sayyids) was estimated to number between 5,000 and 50,000 prior to the revolution of 1962. Under the Zaidi Imams, Yemen was administered largely in the interest of this minority. Theoretically elected by his fellow Sayyids, the Imam was forced to take their interests and desires into consideration. In order to satisfy this interest group, the Imams dispensed patronage in the form of

---

[1]There are fourteen commonly recognized prerequisites for the Imamate. The candidate must be: (1) male; (2) free born; (3) a taxpayer; (4) sound in mind; (5) sound in all the senses; (6) sound in the ends, that is, perfect hands and feet (this is designed to eliminate criminals who have suffered the Quranic punishment required by the *Sharia*); (7) just; (8) pious; (9) generous; (10) endowed with administrative ability; (11) 'Alawi, that is, a descendent of 'Ali; (12) Fatimi (this is designed to eliminate members of Ismaili sects from candidacy); (13) brave (more specifically, this means the ability to resort to the sword if necessary for offense or defense and is designed to eliminate children and "concealed" Mahdis from candidacy; it is a specific statement to the effect that the Zaidis must have a living Imam); (14) a Mujtahid, that is, one learned in Muslim law and theology and able to interpret the Qur'an and therefore make new laws when required.

A number of religious authorities, however, have claimed additional conditions which must be fulfilled. Among the most commonly listed is excellent horsemanship. The frequent listing of this attribute and the stress on bravery have, perhaps, placed an unfortunate amount of emphasis on unrestrained might or power as the major determinative. It is to this factor that many trace the frequency of civil wars which have plagued Yemen for centuries.

Zaidi theory permits the existence of multiple Imams if one Imam is unable to fulfill all the conditions. Consequently, there have been Imams for war and Imams for theology and law at the same time. There have also been frequent "anti-Imams"; if an anti-Imam is able to oust his predecessor or rival, he is recognized as the legal Imam.

government positions. As a result, many of the affairs of state were in the hands of the Sayyids; they administered justice, assessed taxes, and supervised tax collections as well as all the other myriad functions of even a relatively unsophisticated and primitive government. The Sayyids, who were not an independently wealthy landed or commercial aristocracy, were forced to obtain their income from other sources. Their control of the administration of justice and taxation naturally provided them with many opportunities for the extortion of funds from both the farmers and the commercial classes of the cities.

The Imams were largely separated from the population by this intervening oligarchy of Sayyids, against whom there was much popular resentment. In his encounters with the government, the average Yemeni never dealt with the Imam or even his personal aides, who were usually commoners (non-Sayyids) raised to important positions as advisers and assistants to the Imam (primarily because the Imams felt they could not trust other Sayyids). They dealt with this Sayyid oligarchy, and consequently the generally tyrannical nature of the Imam's regime was associated in the popular mind with the Sayyids. It was the Sayyids that the average Yemeni had to bribe and mollify if he wanted decisions made or affairs settled. The Imams, therefore, were able to command a good deal of public respect, loyalty, and even love from a large portion of the population.

Ismailis. The other group of Shi'as historically associated with Yemen are the Ismailis. Unlike the Zaidis, and like other Shi'as, the Ismailis believe in the Mahdi (hidden Imam) who will one day return to save the world. In Ismaili theology, the last recognized Imam was the seventh, Isma'il ibn Ja'far al-Sadiq; this has resulted in their other name, the "Seveners." Within Yemen, the Ismailis are called al-Makarima, because during the 17th century the leadership of the community devolved to the al-Makrami family, from which all Ismaili leaders (termed *da'i*, the caller) since that time have come.

In earlier centuries, the number and extent of Ismaili settlements in Yemen appears to have been larger than at present, for Ismaili governments during the Middle Ages are known. At present, their number probably does not exceed 25,000, all found primarily in the mountains around Manakha (Jabal Haraz). Nevertheless, it is interesting to note that all of the republican governments between 1962 and 1968 had at least one Ismaili cabinet member.

Shafi'ites. Orthodox, or Sunni, Islam is represented in Yemen by the Shafi'i school of law, whose adherents outnumber other Sunni schools in southwestern Arabia. Shafi'ites predominate in the Tihama, the foothills, and the southern regions of the country, whereas the Zaidis live almost exclusively in the highlands of the center and north as well as the eastern desert regions. Like the Ismailis, the Shafi'ites have in the past exercised a greater amount of political power than in the 20th century and have at various times suffered some mistreatment at the hands of the Zaidi government.

The Shafi'ites, as adherents of Sunni Islam, recognize no legal or religious right of the Zaidi Imam to interpret or create law. They have acknowledged, with varying degrees of sincerity or passivity, the Imam's position as temporal ruler of Yemen (prior to 1962), but they do not accept him as their religious overlord. As may be imagined, there was considerable disagreement within Yemen over the Imam's powers, and the conflict between Sunni and Shi'a Muslims was and remains a frequent accompaniment to the various civil disturbances which have affected Yemen.

Nevertheless, the average Yemeni understands very little, if anything, of the doctrinal differences between Shafi'ites and Zaidis, which deal largely with relatively obscure points of law. Indeed, the Sunnis of south Arabia even refer to the Zaidis as the "fifth school" of Islamic law because of their doctrinal similarities with Sunni Islam. The greatest distinctions between them are found in their oral traditions, epics, and tales concerning themselves and others, which each sect has as a part of its culture. In addition, there are few outward signs of the differences between the Shafi'ites and Zaidis. There has in fact often been interfaith cooperation on many political issues and problems, for Shafi'ites have often acted in the interest of the Imam and the Zaidi state in times of revolution and public disorder. It is not uncommon for Shafi'ites and Zaidis to intermarry and use each other's mosques.

Jews. For centuries the Jews were the largest non-Muslim minority in Yemen, numbering approximately 60 to 75 thousand. Resident in Yemen since prior to the Jewish state established by Dhu Nuwas, they were governed as a *millet* (nation) according to traditional Muslim legal theory concerning *dhimmis* (protected peoples). Apparently the Zaidis have been especially tolerant of the Jews, for few lived within the Shafi'i districts. Subjected to a number of special laws, and not assigned any special position within Zaidi theory with respect to the governing of Yemen, they were an important economic group but not relevant to the politics of Yemen. Shortly after the establishment of the state of Israel, the overwhelming percentage of Yemeni Jews were transported there (in Operation Flying Carpet). The many Jewish villages and the large Jewish quarter in San'a' are almost totally deserted; recent estimates of the total number remaining in Yemen are between 1,500 and 2,000.

Tribal-Urban Divisions. More important, perhaps, for an understanding of the modern history of Yemen is the division in the population between those who are tribally oriented and the commercially inclined independent town dwellers. As has already been pointed out, the vast majority of the population of Yemen are settled either as cultivators or as merchants or artisans within the towns and cities. The traditional tribesman, the nomad who ekes out a meager existence in his lifelong trek from water hole to water hole in search of grazing lands for his flocks, represents only a small minority of the population and is confined to the arid, relatively barren eastern areas and some regions of the north.

Nearly all the tribes of Yemen long ago settled themselves into the innumerable valleys which cleave the great Yemeni plateau. They have established small villages and, following the traditions of their ancestors, they keep large flocks of animals which necessitate some seasonal migration. At the same time, they are involved in at least a minimum of agricultural activity on land which they usually own. They produce most of their own food and fodder for their animals as well as some products which they exchange at weekly markets.

Although the majority of the tribes are semisettled cultivators, their traditions of independence and fierce dislike of the permanent town dweller engaged in commerce or manufacture have diminished little over the years. They cherish an attitude of contempt for the comfort and effeminacy of city life and the inability of city people to settle their arguments and feuds themselves. In other words, they denigrate urban residents' dependence on a government which has undertaken to protect their lives and property and to apply certain standards of justice. They also criticize the townsman's inability or unwillingness to carry arms—the certain sign of a tribesman in Yemen.

Shafi'i tribes constitute about one fifth of the total number of tribes in Yemen. They are located primarily in the Tihama foothills, while the remaining four fifths, the Zaidi tribes, are located in the central and northern mountains. The fact that the population is almost evenly divided along religious lines means that more Shafi'ites than Zaidis are engaged in commerce, manufacturing, and trade and thus more reside in cities and towns. This means that the religious differences among the population are, in many cases, strengthened by this tribal-urban division.

Tribal people consider themselves to be the elite of Yemen because of their ancestry. They are nearly all Qahtani, and most can trace their genealogies to the great pre-Islamic civilizations and confederations.[2] In many ways they do form a privileged class, primarily because they constitute over half the population and hold the preponderance of power in the state. All Yemeni tribes are very conservative; any attempt to introduce administrative, religious, or other innovations is extremely difficult. They have their own unwritten laws and usages, called 'urf which are passed down from generation to generation, and their own courts for settling water, boundary, and other kinds of disputes which arise between them, including, in many instances, criminal cases.

Each tribe is in reality a small nation with its own territory, grazing ground, wells, market towns, allegiances, friends, enemies, history, and the like. All its members give fealty to their own leader or sheikh, who, in the case of a Zaidi tribe, in turn owes allegiance to his spiritual leader, the Imam. Most tribes have their own system of shifting alliances, which they utilize when they believe that a wrong has been done them. Unless the central government is capable of prohibiting it, intertribal warfare is used to settle even the most petty grievances.

---

[2]Traces of the ancient pre-Islamic kingdoms persist in the names of many tribes, although these tribes may be of much diminished stature today. Most are no longer located in the areas from which they first derived their names: the Banu Ma'an (Ma'in), Banu Himyar, Banu Ma'afir (Maphar), Qutaybi (Qataba), for example, all are now located east and southwest of the areas covered by the great pre-Islamic kingdoms. T. E. Lawrence is undoubtedly correct in attributing this movement to population pressure in the interior, with stronger clans pushing weaker ones into the desert, where they became nomads in order to keep alive. See T. E. Lawrence, The Seven Pillars of Wisdom (New York: Doubleday, 1935), pp. 35-37.

Until the 20th century most of the tribal districts, because of their geographical isolation, had never come under any type of foreign rule.

DOMESTIC POLITICS

Historical Background

With the defeat of the Ottoman Empire in World War I, its possessions in the Arabian Peninsula faced an uncertain future. Very few had an obvious alternative government to which the Turkish administrators could legally transfer authority and sovereignty. Yemen was one of those with a clear successor available.

Throughout the last period of Ottoman rule in Yemen, which had begun shortly after the opening of the Suez Canal in 1869, the Zaidi population of the highlands was in an almost continual state of revolt. These rebellions were led by the Imams as secular as well as religious heads of the Zaidi community. Because of the difficult terrain, the endemic instability, and the apparent impossibility of ever effectively administering the Zaidi districts, the Turkish authorities granted the Zaidi community autonomy prior to World War I. Consequently, when the war ended the Imam appeared to be the logical inheritor of Ottoman rule. Indeed, in November 1918 the Ottomans recognized the Imam as their legal successor in Yemen.

The Imam at this critical point was Yahya ibn Muhammad, of the prominent Hamid al-Din family, who had become Imam upon the death of his father in 1904. Recognized by the Ottomans as responsible for the autonomous Zaidi districts, he had already gained some administrative experience. Centuries of Muslim and Zaidi tradition, as well as the peculiar set of circumstances surrounding Yemen's reemergence as an independent state combined to create not the conciliatory government which might have resolved domestic cleavages but rather a thoroughly autocratic government determined to restore ancient prerogatives and recreate an unalloyed Islamic state. The factors which brought about this particular development merit some elaboration.

First and foremost was the Zaidi view of the authority of the Imam in both religious and temporal affairs. Islam, it must be remembered, makes no clear distinction between religious and secular affairs; specific Zaidi interpretations of the prerequisites and conditions for assuming the Imamate, added to centuries of Zaidi precedent wherein Imams not only were considered capable of but necessarily required to personally handle both affairs of religion and the state, helped create Imam Yahya's conception of his own role.

Second, the territory of the new state of Yemen consisted solely of the predominantly Zaidi mountain districts. Under Ottoman rule the predominately Shafi'i Tihama had been governed separately, and after the war, the Turks handed over the Tihama to one of the Imam's wartime opponents, the ruler of the principality of Asir, immediately to the north of Yemen on the Red Sea coast. Consequently, Imam Yahya considered the restoration of the "historic and natural" frontiers of Yemen as one of his major tasks. Because territories which in fact had formerly been considered part of Yemen had been incorporated into the surrounding states in the interval and now were administered by other governments, this irredentist policy inevitably led to foreign wars. In addition, the Ottoman government, although it had granted the Zaidi community a measure of autonomy in religious and civil affairs, had not extended the privilege to military and police matters. The result was that, in the view of the Imam, his most immediate task was the creation of an effective army, or military establishment, which could maintain internal security, collect taxes, prevent rebellious tribes from interfering with either commerce or the government, protect the frontiers of the new state, and perhaps even assist in expanding them.

During the inter-war period, Imam Yahya devoted his resources on the domestic level to the consolidation of his rule. To accomplish this end he employed his military establishment, under the leadership of his son Ahmad, to bring the many tribes of the north and east under his suzerainty. Almost simultaneously, he brought the Shafi'i districts of the southwest and the Tihama under his administrative control. Throughout, the Imam was determined to eliminate any alternative sources or centers of power; it was made abundantly clear to the tribes, the townsmen, the commercial class, as well as his own Sayyid aristocracy, that Imam Yahya was not only Imam of the Zaidis, he was also king of Yemen—a title he arrogated to himself in the mid-1920s.

A significant by-product of the Imam's campaigns was the creation of the first extended period of domestic peace which the country had known in more than a century. Any equitable assessment of Yahya's reign must take cognizance of this achievement; on the other hand, it may be equally as persuasively argued that the cost—in creating and perpetuating domestic political cleavages and in lost opportunities for even a minimum of economic and social reform—was too great. For the means by which the Imam consolidated his personal rule, created this domestic peace, and laid the cornerstone for continued Hamid al-Din control of the instruments of power were unquestionably a major cause of the revolutions of 1948 and 1962.

Beginning in the 1930s, political opposition to the despotic rule of the Imam began to grow. By the post-World War II period it was largely concentrated in the largest metropolitan area of the southwestern Arabian region: Aden. The number of Yemeni political exiles, at first relatively small, began to increase rapidly; they soon managed to create a variety of political organizations, publishing houses, and business enterprises designed to provide the movement with its necessary capital.

By 1948 the political exiles in Aden and other cities in the Red Sea area had established links with elements of the Sayyid elite who were displeased with the Imam's rule. While most of the latter were opposed to Yahya because he sought to perpetuate his family's ascendancy, there were also groups who sought to modernize Zaidi Islam and those who objected to Yahya's near total monopoly of trade and commerce. These rather disparate opposition elements cooperated to effect the first attempt at revolutionary change of the traditional pattern of government, an effort which resulted in the assassination of the Imam in February of that year.

In the succeeding weeks of civil war, the inability of these opposition elements to submerge their policy differences made it possible for Yahya's son Ahmad and some of the latter's brothers to lead a successful counterrevolution. By mid-March, Ahmad was officially recognized by the Zaidi Ulama as the new Imam.

Ahmad, like his father, was imbued with the Zaidi traditions concerning the powers of the Imam, the frontiers of natural Yemen, and the techniques of government. Although certain symbolic concessions to opposition forces were made, the new Imam Ahmad soon was administering and governing the state in the age-old Zaidi manner. It was not long, consequently, before opposition elements were re-forming and organizing their next attempt at some modification or reform of Yemen's government. By 1955 the demand for reforms again resulted in violence; this time, Ahmad's brother Abdullah sided with the revolutionaries. Unfortunately for Yemen, this unsuccessful attempt at reform brought about increased repression, rather than a stepped-up pace of reforms, whether real or symbolic. Until his death in September 1962, Ahmad depended upon a combination of domestic supports to retain full and complete control of the state apparatus: a shifting alliance of Zaidi tribes, an increasingly modernized army (largely trained and equipped by a combination of Egyptian officers and Soviet materiel), and finally (as the army became less dependable during the early 1960s), the Sayyid elite which increasingly feared that a major revolution would deprive all of them of their position and prerogatives.

Although Ahmad died of natural causes on September 18, 1962, his son and successor Muhammad al-Badr was not able to withstand the pressures and effectively allay the already well-advanced plan for the overthrow of the Imamate. On September 26 the Imam's palace was shelled, and a new group of revolutionaries declared the Republic of Yemen.

Patterns of Government under the Imams

Under the rule of the Zaidi Imams, Yemen was governed according to Zaidi politico-religious theory insofar as possible, creating probably the closest modern approximation of a theocracy. In theory, God rules the Zaidi state; in political terms, God is represented by the Quran, the Hadith, and the Zaidi interpretations of the significance and contents of these two basic sources. The Imam, as such, is merely God's temporal representative. Again in theory, all judicial, executive, and legislative powers are vested in the Imam. In practice, of course, strict adherence to the theory was impossible and there inevitably grew up a complex set of arrangements designed to deal with the immediate problems of administering the political entity known as Yemen.

Undoubtedly the two most important elements which brought a modicum of secular administration into being were: (1) The fact that the overwhelming number of nominally Zaidi tribes of the Yemeni highlands settled disputes and regulated their internal and external affairs for centuries according to tribal law (*'urf*), and (2) the fact that a substantial minority of non-Zaidis (Shafi'ites as well as Ismailis and Jews) were brought under the temporal rule of the Imams by Yemen's emergence as an independent political unit. Neither the powerful tribes nor the large number of non-Zaidis could be expected to accept the authority of the Imam as unquestioningly as the Zaidis, nor did they.

Judicial Powers. Much of the inter-war period is the story of Imam Yahya's campaigns to consolidate his position within the new state. While the Imam no doubt wanted to establish the preeminence of his own family, the Hamid al-Din, and indeed perpetuate it, he was also evidently motivated by (Zaidi) Islamic fervor. This is most clearly demonstrated by the tremendous effort—in time, money, and manpower—to introduce and then enforce Islamic law in the many tribal districts of the north, northeast, and east which had little or no knowledge of Islamic legal principles.

In this attempt he was not wholly successful. By the outbreak of World War II, the Imam was forced to give official recognition to the continued existence, vitality, and validity of customary tribal law (*'urf*). He was, however, successful in arrogating to himself the power to appoint the judges for the customary law. This meant that the Imam now appointed two judges for each administrative district within the country, one for Islamic law cases, and one for *'urf* cases. In other words, Yemen in effect had two legal systems: (1) a civil and secular law, which was administered by the governor of each district, and (2) the canonical Islamic law, administered by trained judges also appointed by the Imam.

The highest court of appeal for cases from both systems was the Imam, although he could also be the court of first instance. In practice, however, the Imam rarely became the final appeal from cases carried through the Islamic system, for these usually were decided by a special high court of appeal. The Imam, however, made certain that the cases within the customary law system were always passed to him for final appeal, thus making certain that the authority of the Imam as secular ruler was made clear and that basic principles of Islamic law were increasingly applied to such decisions.

Executive Powers. Executive power was vested solely in the Imam. For centuries the Imams had been more or less able to fulfill both the spirit and the letter of Zaidi expectations: They personally handled an incredible number of responsibilities, from essential foreign policy decisions to written approval of such trivial matters as the number of bottles of ink to be assigned to any schoolteacher or lower echelon administrator for his office. However, as the size of the areas effectively under the Imam's control as well as the numbers of people being administered increased, personal control over all matters of state became increasingly difficult.

Despite this, Imam Yahya, until his failing health during World War II made his task almost impossible, conscientiously attempted to carry out the monumental task of personally administering the whole country. As had apparently been the case in the past, the Imams resorted to the services of trusted aides and assistants. In nearly all cases for which records are available, these aides can be grouped into two categories: (1) relatives, usually brothers or sons, upon whose loyalty the Imams seemingly could most frequently depend because of their obvious interest in maintaining the preeminence of their own family; and (2) commoners, that is, non-Sayyids, of sufficient education and training who, because they owed their positions of power to the Imam and his family, could also be trusted with administrative duties. Under the Hamid al-Din, certain families of commoners became closely associated with the Imamate. Often they provided numerous advisors for a great variety of functions and duties. For example, the al-'Amri family (sometimes incorrectly given as Umari, or Umri) served both Imams Yahya and Ahmad in a number of sensitive capacities. In no case were Zaidi Sayyids from other families who contended for the Imamate selected for such positions.

It was, however, not possible for all the administrative levels below governorates, of which there were at first only four and later seven, to be fully staffed with such relatives and trusted commoners. Therefore, provincial and lower administrative positions were filled with local officials, nearly always Sayyids, who it was hoped and assumed would be loyal because of the fact they had received their position through the Imam. In most instances, this policy was reasonably effective in the sense that provincial or district rebellions were infrequent.

It is necessary to add that, until the last years of Imam Ahmad's reign, no ministries or similar executive agencies were even established. Under a combination of domestic political pressures, failing health, and the suggestions of foreign advisors—both Arab and non-Arab—decrees establishing such ministries were issued during the 1950s. However, none of them were ever provided with any independent authority, competitively recruited staff, or the means for effective action. They were a facade of modernization and in fact represented only an enlargement of the differentiated spheres of responsibility meted out to the Imam's trusted retainers and advisors. While certain complex technical affairs were turned over to recognized experts by the Imam—for example, the operations of Yemen Air Lines—the Imam retained full and complete ultimate authority to decide on flights, their frequency, destination, and similar related matters.

Legislative Powers. As already indicated, only the Imam had legislative powers in the modern meaning of the term. There was, of course, no regularly constituted body which proposed laws or enacted bills or suggestions submitted to it. One reason is the fact that, at least in theory, there was little or no need for new laws since previous documents, the Quran and the Hadith, provided all the legislation which would ever be needed; their origin was divine and therefore unimpeachable. While the Zaidi community no doubt usually accepted the

Imam's interpretations of the body of Zaidi law with whatever modifications or alterations approved by the Ulama, this was not the case with the non-Zaidi population.

The Jews were governed as a *millet*, a separate nation, subject to their own laws and procedures and only required to give obedience to the restrictions which had been placed upon their activities as well as to pay the stated taxes directly to the government. The Ismailis, although no specific provision within Islamic or Zaidi law requires it, were usually similarly treated by the Zaidi Imams.

The most important problem arose with the Shafi'i population, which of course had no religious reason for recognizing the legislative powers of the Imam. While most recognized the Imam as king of Yemen and with greater or lesser degrees of acquiescence or apathy accepted him in that role, his religious authority was nil. As a result, in a limited sense the Shafi'ites also retained some autonomy, and the Shafi'i theological centers in the Tihama continued to operate, although clearly under great restrictions. In fact, Shafi'ites from outside Yemen (primarily from among the population of the present-day People's Republic of South Yemen) frequently traveled to these centers, notably Zabid, in order to have their disputes settled there.

Nevertheless, the Zaidi Imams could not and did not allow Shafi'i autonomy in nonreligious affairs. This, of course, necessitated a certain amount of secular administrative rulings which affected Shafi'i commercial activities. Although there is no precise data, the evidence which is available indicates that whatever regulations and decisions were issued had been arrived at on a purely *ad hoc* basis. This is to say, the Imam decided all such matters on a day-to-day basis, the major criterion being whether or not the resultant decision was likely to benefit the Imam and the Hamid al-Din and their political allies. No attempt at codification nor consistency nor appeal to precedents ever appears to have been undertaken. It is for this reason that the Shafi'i portion of the Yemeni population was so prominent in anti-Imam political movements and organizations and why it probably remains the most alienated portion of the general population.

It is only fair to note that upon his accession to power, Imam Muhammad al-Badr undertook to implement a series of reforms, the effect of which would have been to introduce some very substantial changes into the political structure of the Imamate. Among those affecting domestic policy were a general amnesty for political prisoners, cancellation of debts, abolishment of the feudal mortgage laws, as well as decrees establishing municipal councils, and a consultative council of 40 members of which 20 were to have been elected.

It is well to remember that not all of the many political opponents of Ahmad's reign as Imam sided with the Republican government upon the latter's establishment. Indeed, a substantial number of Yemeni reformers and political opponents of the *ancien regime* who were released as a result of the amnesty thereafter joined the staff of the new Imam.

During the lengthy civil war, the Royalists placed some limitations upon the powers of the Imam, while the military tactics employed required a considerable decentralization of authority. By early 1964 a variety of proposals were under consideration for reforming the Imamate, all including the creation of a Council of Ministers, a consultative assembly, and political and administrative decentralization. In January 1965 a new national charter was promulgated incorporating these reforms, as well as a number of articles more precisely defining the powers of the Imam, the numerous councils, the assembly, and the judiciary. It was, however, clear that the principles of Zaidi Islam would continue to play a substantial role in the system of government which the Royalists would establish upon their presumed return to unquestioned supremacy.

Patterns of Government under the Republic

The Yemen Arab Republic was declared on September 27, 1962 by the newly formed Council of the Revolutionary Command. Composed of representatives and participants in all the varied conspiracies which were developing during the early 1960s, it was headed by Colonel Abdullah al-Sallal, former commander-in-chief under Imam Muhammad al-Badr's brief unopposed reign as Imam.

Although it was briefly believed that the Imam and his major advisors had died in the artillery attack on the palace in San'a, evidence was soon available that the Imam in fact had survived and escaped from San'a in order to recruit support for a counterrevolution in the northern mountains. Indeed, the counterrevolution was soon a credible threat to the continued existence of the Republic, whereupon the latter appealed to the government of the United Arab Republic and President Nasser for assistance. The request for assistance and support was immediately honored: By October 1 Egyptian paratroopers and materiel began to arrive in Yemen, and the first ships carrying additional support, less than one week later. By mid-October of 1962 it was clear to most observers that a civil war was in progress.

The presence of Egyptian troops and equipment in support of the Republic occasioned the intervention in the conflict of Saudi Arabia, which soon was providing financial and military assistance to the supporters of the Imam, dubbed the Royalist side. Yemen had become, in effect, not only a battleground between opposing views of which form of government was best for Yemen but also between two opposing ideologies and their relevance to the political future of the Arab world as a whole.

In other words, the Yemenis who originally organized and effected the revolution had only a brief opportunity to determine the outlines and structure of the government which they sought to create in place of the Imamate. The circumstances surrounding the revolution's development—the continued and determined resistance by the Royalists and the presence of tens of thousands of Egyptian troops and advisors—provided little or no opportunity to implement the vast array of reforms originally promised. In addition, the very serious disagreements and conflicts which arose within Republican ranks shortly after the outbreak of the revolution and continued to plague them throughout the entire civil war, also made any consistency in the patterns of government difficult. In fact, constitutions, cabinets and councils, and similar documents and bodies came and went with distressing frequency. In the majority of instances, expediency or necessity dictated specific changes in either structure or personnel. In the view of many observers, in both the Republican and Royalist areas of the country inertia, the experience of decades of authoritarian and arbitrary rule, and the relatively unsophisticated and uncomplex way of life of the majority of the inhabitants made possible some semblance of order when, in fact, no effective government existed in either area.

Nevertheless, the Republican government undertook to introduce a complete reorganization of both the government and the society upon its accession. Precisely what these were and some description and analysis of the Republican government's organization follows.

Executive Powers. From the outset, it was clear that the Council of the Revolutionary Command (CRC), the author of the revolution, was primarily an organization of Yemeni army officers. The first governmental decrees were all issued by the "Supreme Command of the Yemeni Army," and it was this organization which established the CRC, the Presidency Council of the Republic, as well as the first Council of Ministers announced on September 28, 1962. From the very beginning, in other words, army officers of the new Republic of Yemen exercised fundamental powers in the new government, and the army has continued to remain the basic source of the Republic's authority to the present day.

On October 31, 1962, the CRC issued its first constitutional proclamation. In a total of 11 brief articles, the objectives of the revolution were outlined as well as the framework of the system of government. In Article 7, the CRC assumed "the duties of supreme sovereignty," including the right to dismiss and appoint ministers in the cabinet, which was assigned the purpose of carrying out the duties of the executive authority. Article 10 established a higher defense council, all members of which held the rank of minister, responsible for state security. Under Article 11, the CRC elected (Brigadier General) Abdullah al-Sallal president of the Republic, premier, and supreme commander of the armed forces and promised to establish a permanent constitution and a parliament to approve the permanent constitution as well as hold elections for the parliament, which was to be responsible for selecting future presidents. Clearly, all authority within the new government was in the hands of the army, under the leadership of Abdullah al-Sallal.

On April 13, 1963, a provisional constitution of the Yemeni Arab Republic was announced. In 60 articles, it elaborated some of the same points as the original document with respect to objectives, rights and duties of citizens, and similar issues. Of the total, 21 articles were devoted to explaining in greater detail the responsibilities and powers of the executive. The powers of the president, still Abdullah al-Sallal, remained essentially the same; however, his legal authority to issue laws and decrees was broadened, subject only to approval by the presidential council, which in its powers resembled the former CRC and which absorbed its membership.

One new body was created, the executive council; according to Article 46, it was "the highest executive and administrative body of the state." It was made responsible to the presidential council, and assigned the duty of implementing "general state policy in accordance with the law and the decisions of the presidential council" (Article 48), as well as the drafting of laws, budgets, economic development plans and supervision of the work of all government ministries, departments, and other organizations. As many observers were quick to point out, there was nothing in this provisional constitution which could be described as democratic, especially in view of the fact that Article 2 stated, in part, "the source of authority is the state," and there was no provision for a parliament. The dissolution of the CRC, the omission of any mention of an elected assembly, the establishment of the presidential and executive councils showed the increasing influence of the United Arab Republic and its advisors on the Yemeni government; indeed, the new organizational structure conformed very closely with that of President Nasser's government.

Although President al-Sallal in February 1963 issued orders for: (1) the formation of a presidential council which would include tribal leaders (sheikhs), army officers, and professional economists; and (2) elections for a tribal house of representatives which was to include between 160 and 180 sheikhs, no implementation of these directives was ever undertaken. It is more than likely, however that the president's decree in late May which prohibited the formation of political parties and organizations (except those with a social, cultural, or religious purpose) was in part due to the discussions among tribal groups as to how they could most effectively organize to make their demands known to the government.

The Republican government faced increasing domestic difficulties after it became clear that the Royalists would not be as easily defeated on the battlefield as first expected. The latter's unabated resistance, and the increasing role of Egyptian advisors and officials within the Republic as a result of the latter's dependence upon them for its existence, seemed to bring about increasing frictions between the various members and leaders of the Republic. The next few years are characterized by rapid cabinet changes and a bewildering series of *ad hoc* alterations in the organization and structure of the Republican government.

On June 2, 1963 President al-Sallal suspended the provisional constitution and declared a state of emergency prior to his departure for Egypt and other Arab nations in connection with the proposed plan, current at the time, for a loose federation or association between Egypt, Syria, and Iraq. General Hasan al-Amri, the vice president, was declared interim president and, during his tenure, presided over joint sessions of the presidential and executive councils, thereby officially signalling the end of any division of responsibility between the two bodies.

During September 1963 at a rally in Amran, a list of 27 resolutions were approved which included demands for a parliamentary rather than presidential system of government and the placing of limitations upon the authority of the president. It was, in effect, a direct challenge to President al-Sallah's authority and, while it did not effect specific changes, it was obvious that the discontent expressed at Amran had to be mollified. On January 7, 1964 al-Sallal issued two reorganization decrees; One established a political bureau as the highest authority for political and legislative affairs, while the second created a national defense council, responsible for military and defense affairs, with himself as presiding officer on both. But, the executive council, which was organized on February 10, apparently continued to be the supreme executive body, again with al-Sallal as its head.

No doubt at least in part due to increasing discontent with the government and due perhaps to the confusion caused by the previous *ad hoc* reorganizations, a new constitution was promulgated. Unlike the first two, it lacked the adjective "provisional," although there were immediate indications that it too was considered temporary.

The new document consisted of 155 articles in seven general "chapters" devoted to general principles, economic and social goals, public rights and duties, legislative powers, executive powers, judicial powers, and "general rules." Of most immediate relevance were some 15 articles scattered throughout the document which, in effect, clearly placed nearly all powers in the hands of the president. The new charter, however, did foresee the creation of a consultative assembly, very much like the Egyptian National Assembly, (Articles 46-91) which was designated as "exercising legislative powers" and overseeing the work of the executive bodies. No article, though, specifically defined the number of members, their method of selection, or when such selection would be made—all this was left to later implementing legislation (Article 48).

By December 1964 the opposition to President al-Sallal's governmental methods had become so intense that within a two-week period nearly the whole cabinet and literally hundreds of other officials resigned. At that time, the head of the consultative council, Ahmad Muhammad Nu'man, and some others among the resigning officials proposed an unofficial new interim constitution. By early January 1965 the situation necessitated the president's declaring a state of emergency, an almost completely new cabinet, as well as new reorganizations. Among these were the creation of a new consultative council, a national security council to replace the previous national defense council, as well as the formation of a series of committees to investigate, and special courts to try, previous governmental members for charges brought against them.

On April 21, 1965, a new presidential council was formed, which in effect limited the president's powers, and which was led by Ahmad Muhammad

Nu'man—a well-known and respected Shafi'i who favored heightened efforts at some sort of negotiations with the Royalists. In late April and early May, a national peace conference was held in Khamir (north of San'a); on May 8, largely as a result of these efforts, another interim constitution of 78 articles was announced. Although it drew freely on the 1964 constitution, it was clear that one of its major purposes was a further curtailment of the president's powers. The presidential council was increased in size, and perhaps most important, it foresaw the president subject to a 90 member consultative assembly which, as supreme legislative authority, was to prepare a permanent constitution which was to be approved by a national referendum to be held at the end of an unspecified interim period. Significantly, the assembly was given the power to remove members of the Republican council, a separate body to which the president was also made subject. This Republican council was assigned the function of head of state; headed by the president, it was also to include the commander-in-chief of the armed forces of the Republic, with the rest of its members to be designated by the consultative assembly. The Council of Ministers, i.e., the cabinet, was made the executive and administrative authority within the new order. Shortly thereafter, a supreme national defense council was created, with responsibility for the creation of a People's army. The 16 members of this council and the new army were supposed to give the Republican government an increased voice in the direction of the war with the Royalists and to limit the influence and control of the Egyptian advisors and officers.

President al-Sallal, obviously displeased with the turn of events, established a supreme council for the armed forces, an indication of his increased dependence upon the army for his support. Prime Minister Nu'man and his predominantly civilian cabinet resigned, giving as one of their major reasons the establishment of this clearly unconstitutional body. By early July 1965 President al-Sallal had taken over the government and eliminated the civilian leaders of the Republic from nearly every position of responsibility. Both sides in this domestic dispute, as well as representatives of the National Peace Conference, sent representatives to Cairo in order to persuade President Nasser to support their view of the best path for Yemen's Republican government; the incident provided an indication of how dependent upon Egypt the Republican government had become.

The Egyptian President, who had already begun to make arrangements for some sort of settlement with King Faisal, of Saudi Arabia, could not afford to have a conciliatory Republican government in control of Yemen at the time; in order to obtain the best possible terms as far as Egypt's and President Nasser's own prestige were concerned, a militant and hard-line government was necessary. Consequently, the United Arab Republic supported President al-Sallal and his overwhelmingly military and uncompromising Cabinet. This led to an exodus of nearly 300 Republican leaders from Yemen.

Shortly after the Jidda Agreement of August 1965, which laid down the compromise conditions for a settlement and provided for the withdrawal of

Egyptian troops, a new government under al-Sallal was formed which included some civilian members of the earlier cabinets as well as former Premier Nu'man himself. The Haradh Conference in late 1965, which was to work out the details of the Jidda Agreement, failed. In early 1966 the intransigent Republican cabinet was forced to resign under Egyptian pressure, but no further progress on a settlement was reached.

In April 1966 leaders of the Republic returned from Cairo with new plans for the government, including national elections, and a consultative assembly. Discussions for implementing these proposals continued into the summer when, once again, a wave of anti-Egyptian sentiment swept the Republican government and many of its prominent leaders. President al-Sallal returned to Yemen after a lengthy absence, once again supported by Egyptian units and troops. By September a near open break with the United Arab Republic had been reached; General Hasan al-Amri, previously considered one of the major supporters of al-Sallal appeared to become the major leader of the anti-Egyptian Republican forces in the country. On September 18 President al-Sallal once again took over the government; his cabinet, exceedingly small by previous standards, with some individuals holding more than two ministerial portfolios, was dominated once again by pro-Egyptian military leaders.

A purge took place; prominent political figures in the Republic during the four previous years of its existence were arrested, and at least seven (including former ministers) were executed; by late October most sources reported that more than 2,000 had been detained and additional deaths.

Administratively, President al-Sallal's new government undertook some changes; a new defense council was organized, for the first time publicly including senior Egyptian officers. A constituent committee was formed to create a popular organization which would support the revolution and be modeled after the United Arab Republic's.

Unlike previous similar decrees, including the proposed Yemeni Arab Union of January 1965, the latter decree was implemented. On December 14, 1966 the Popular Revolutionary Union was publicly formed and on January 18, 1967 held its first session. Very similar in design and organization to the Arab Socialist Union in the United Arab Republic, the PRU was to become "a major stronghold for whose principles all of us would die." It was, in other words, an attempt by President al-Sallal and the current government to create a basis of popular support for the government at a time when continued arrest and executions of former members of the Republic's political leadership were taking place.

For the next six months, President al-Sallal appeared to be in firm control and administered the affairs of the country in accordance with his personal predilections with regard to ministerial positions as well as the exercise of all legislative, judicial, and executive functions. It was not until the aftermath of the Arab-Israeli war of June 1967 that the situation again underwent substantial change.

Obviously as a direct result of the Egyptian defeat, President Nasser began the phased withdrawal from the central highlands of the estimated 35,000 United Arab Republic troops operating in the Republic. Although some reinforcement of air units took place and there was a step-up in air attacks against the Royalists, these actions seem largely to have been calculated to convince the latter that the withdrawal was not in fact as total as indicated.

President al-Sallal thereupon repudiated the Jidda Agreement of August 1965, whereas during the Khartum Conference President Nasser and King Faisal decided to fully implement this earlier peace proposal. Once again, it was agreed that Egypt would withdraw all of its forces and Saudi Arabia would completely cease all aid to the Royalists. Withdrawal was to be completed within three months, at which time a transitional government would be established; this government would be headed by President al-Sallal who would, however, be lacking in all executive powers.

By early September the Yemeni leader capitulated and accepted the new agreement. He appointed a new all-Yemeni four-man supreme council for the armed forces, (headed by himself), to replace the former national defense council to which Egyptians had belonged. Leading officers in the army continued to demand reforms, including the creation of a more representative government for the country, the repatriation of political exiles, release of political detainees, professionalization of the administration; all were included in the national document submitted to him during the consultations on the formation of a new government. On October 12 a slightly broadened cabinet was formed; President al-Sallal however, retained the positions of prime minister and foreign minister, and deliberately chose to exclude any official who favored some sort of negotiations with the Royalists.

At this point the United Arab Republic released a substantial number of Yemeni leaders who had been in Cairo in exile; all were known to favor conciliatory talks with the Royalists. On the night of November 4, 1967 al-Sallal was overthrown in a bloodless coup; it was reliably reported that the remaining Egyptian troops in Yemen had been asked by Cairo not to intervene. Although the former president, who was in Baghdad at the time, was reported as vowing he would return to eliminate the new regime, all indications were that he had received prior warning. Indeed, he was also reported as saying that he considered the coup a "constitutional act" since his term as president had technically expired in May of 1967.

Certain changes were soon evident: A new three-man Republican council was formed; all of its members were said to favor a compromise settlement with the Royalists. One of these was former Premier Ahmad Muhammad Nu'man, who had achieved reknown for his conciliation efforts more than two years earlier. The new government also created a Permanent National Reconciliation Committee to win over former Royalist supporters and implement some program for just such a reconciliation.

Within three weeks, however, new frictions appeard. Nu'man resigned, charging that other government members had no intention of seeking a settlement, reconciliation, or any sort of compromise. General Hasan al-Amri took his place on the council, and rapidly became the dominant figure in the new government; in December 1967 he formed the Popular Resistance Force, a paramilitary organization to support the Republic, and the government immediately fell. Shortly thereafter, al-Amri formed a new cabinet, "the cabinet of defense and mobilization," and it was clear that the government was once again committed to a hard line.

After the defeat of the strongest Royalist threat upon the Republic in many months in early 1968, and perhaps as a result of new criticism of the government's intransigence, a new two-man committee was created in mid-April 1968 to draw up a national charter. Its purpose was to more clearly outline the responsibilities of governmental officials, provide appropriate limitations upon the powers of public officials, as well as lay down guidelines for the state and its leaders. Somewhat later, in late May a higher planning council under the chairmanship of General Hasan al-Amri was created, to which all appropriate ministers belonged, for the purpose of studying the financial, economic, and social development of the country.

Once again, during July and Early August a number of reorganizations took place; the new eight-member national defense council, under al-Amri's leadership, also set up a committee to prepare for a permanent constitution, as well as a constituent assembly. Then, in August the divisions within the Republic again came into the open—many of them, as had been the case in previous disputes, centered on the number of representatives within the cabinet from each of the two major Islamic sects.

In an effort to cope with political and religious extremist elements, an 11-man committee of ministers and military and tribal leaders was created on August 24th and asked to make recommendations. In an unusual display of speed, the committee submitted its decisions within three days, and the following set of new decrees were issued on August 28th:

First, unauthorized political activity and sectarianism were banned. Second, in a new attempt at broadening the base of the government, it was decided to set up an interim national assembly to assist the government in dealing with the many political, military, and social issues facing it until a new consultative council could be established. Third, a state security tribunal was established to deal with suspected or real efforts at weakening the Republic.

Apparently neither the committee nor its recommendations were sufficient to calm the situation: Al-Amri at first resigned in order to form a new government, one in which the balance between Shafi'ites and Zaidis was approximately equal and which represented some more moderate elements. Shortly thereafter, however, al-Amri became the military governor of Yemen, and was "given all powers for reorganizing the armed forces." In effect, al-Amri had become former President al-Sallal's successor as the leading political figure, or "strong man," in the Yemeni Republic.

In brief then: The Republic of Yemen from the outset had a highly centralized presidential system of government. As the above summary shows, the direction of state policy, the actual policy outputs, and their implementation were and still are all concentrated in the hands of the president of the Republic.

Over the years, a large number of executive bodies were established, either officially or unofficially, to assist the president in the carrying out of his duties. With the exception of the military and defense councils created for the purpose of providing better coordination of the Republic's efforts in these arenas, none of these had any real power to direct state policy in any direction other than that desired by the president. In fact, only the army and its higher officers had any independent powers and were capable of influencing governmental policy.

Legislative Powers. As the above summary shows, no independent legislative authority or body has existed in the Republic since its inception. All legislative powers have, since September 1962, been in the hands of the president of the Republic: in the actual determination of state policy, however, he has frequently had the advice and counsel of either specially created advisory bodies, or executive councils of one sort or another.

During the six years since the birth of the Republic, various documents have made provision for some sort of independent legislative authority; indeed, many of the Republic's internal difficulties stemmed from the demand for such bodies or their equivalent on the part of leading civilian political figures. No implementing directives or action appear to have been taken with respect to the creation of the tribal house of representatives originally proposed in early 1963, which constituted the earliest concrete suggestion for a parliament to fulfill the provisions of Article 11 of the first constitutional proclamation of October 1962.

In late September 1968 the government of General Hasan al-Amri was reported to have said that a new national council would be created prior to mid-March 1969. This new body would represent all the provinces of the country and would replace the consultative council provided for in the provisional constitution. In addition, it would be granted full powers to question national policies, act as a legislative body, and hold public meetings. On the other hand, it was implied in the original statement that its members would be nominated and not elected.

It seems unlikely that the Republican government will be able or will wish to implement this most recent decision in the direction of creating an independent legislative authority for the Republic any more than it was in the case of earlier decrees to the same end. While it may be argued that the Republic and its governmental forms are closely modeled after those of the United Arab Republic and therefore there is little determined interest in creating a truly independent legislative authority, this is clearly not the whole story.

There are numerous points of similarity with the United Arab Republic within the basic documents of the Yemeni Republic, especially with regard to the legislative authority. It should, for example, be noted that President al-Sallal and many of his aides put forth the same arguments and decrees designed to limit if not prohibit the formation of any independent sources of power within the state, primarily for fear that these would become either divisive elements or the instruments of outside powers. Also, the formation of the Yemeni Arab Union in 1965 and the Popular Revolutionary Union in 1,966 were evident efforts to create within Yemen the same base of popular support, as well as a committed but relatively independent and representative mass organization which could play a vital role in the formation if not approval of legislation, as does the Arab Socialist Union in the United Arab Republic.

On the other hand, it must also be remembered that the Republic during its first six years of existence was in a constant state of war with the Royalists and therefore not as free to create such legislative bodies as some of its leaders may have wished. There was and still remains the fear that any such broadly based body could become an instrument of the Royalist faction and their sympathizers within the new government.

It appears then that it will take a lengthy period of domestic peace and governmental consolidation before *any* government in Yemen will be able to establish a freely elected legislative body with independent powers.

Judicial Powers. Although all of the constitutions issued by the Republic provided for an independent judiciary, and a major reorganization of the rudimentary Ministry of Justice which existed under the Imamate was undertaken, some indication of the relative unimportance attached to this particular aspect of government may be obtained from the very small number of articles in these basic documents devoted to elaboration of the structure and procedures of the courts and the appointment and tenure of personnel.

Islam remained the major source of all law; for the complex new activities in which the Republic found itself engaged, however, there was substantial drawing upon the secular codes of the United Arab Republic and European nations in more technical matters.

In the tribal areas which were under the administrative jurisdiction of the Republic, there was little if any attempt to modify the existing tribal law, primarily for fear of losing the allegiance of tribesmen in the continuing civil war. Within the major cities, however, there was a far more conscientious effort to alter both the law itself as well as the administrators of the law.

Draft laws were prepared for a new penal code, as well as new civil and criminal statutes. In most instances, however, implementation was severely impeded by the generally unstable conditions in the country and the inability of the Republic to adequately recruit and train personnel to staff the new court systems.

Although this conscious effort to completely overhaul the old system was an important objective of the Republican government, the continuing civil war and the exigencies of the situation resulted rather in a confusing array of *ad hoc* courts which were established for specific purposes. Many were created to hear cases regarding the implementation of decrees related to the new ministries and national organizations of the Republic. Others were set up at various times to hear cases involving the security and defense of the Republic, as for example, the state security tribunal (or its various predecessors) which heard cases of treason.

It appears that the majority of cases were heard in one of two separate systems; the overwhelming number of disputes, claims, and personal injury suits of various types were probably heard by a slightly modified version of the traditional Islamic courts. These were administered by an Islamic judge (called a *hakim* in Yemen) who was unquestionably aware of the purposes, regulations, and procedures of the Republican government and consequently tried to administer justice in a manner which would take into consideration both Islamic principles and the new government's requirements.

The second coexisting system consisted of the military courts, operated both by Yemenis and in some instances Egyptians and deriving their authority for the most part from the fact that the Republic found it necessary to operate under the equivalent of martial law during the first six years of its existence. Disputes and claims which involved the state or military apparatus and their requirements were assigned or arrogated to this particular system.

Again, it will probably not be possible for the Republic to elaborate a complete set of modernized codes or undertake a total revision of the judicial structure in Yemen for many years to come. Many writers and observers of Yemen have indicated that the pattern of life which has prevailed in large areas of the country subject to periodic anarchy or instability and other side-effects of war has tended automatically to fall back to previous, well-established and often Imam-oriented habits and traditions. It will unquestionably require considerable time, perhaps measured in decades, before the older judicial patterns can be replaced with a more secular and stable court system.

FOREIGN POLICY

Since the revolution of September 1962, both the Royalists and Republican factions in the civil war have been primarily concerned with the international aspects of their dispute, which may for the sake of brevity be categorized as essentially ideological and political. This has involved, above all, the search for military support and assistance as well as commitments from other nations throughout the world with approximately the same ideological outlook.

In fact, however, these foreign policy issues were not preeminent in the past. And, it may be argued that Yemenis, regardless of their present allegiances in the current internal war, are in substantial agreement on what has been the major foreign policy issue of the past, namely, what are the legitimate boundaries of Yemen. Alternatively stated, in the past and probably in the future as well, irredentism has probably been the dominant determinative of Yemeni foreign policy. Although the Zaidi Imams have, more often than not, ruled in a severely restricted area of southwestern Arabia, usually no more than the central highlands of Yemen, they have at the same time entertained substantially more grandiose ideas of what constituted their domains. This was due to: (1) their conviction that they were the successors of the ancient pre-Islamic empires which ruled in this area; (2) the Zaidi claim to be the one true Islamic faith and therefore the only legitimate government; and (3) the fact that at various times the Zaidi Imams had in truth administered and governed much larger areas of the southwestern portions of the peninsula.

The boundaries of Yemen as it appears on maps today were delineated in the 20th century; in only one instance did Yemenis have any voice in the creation of these frontiers. The eastern border, which merges with the Rub' al-Khali (the Empty Quarter) has always been and remains undemarcated. The northern frontier was marked by a binational commission established at the close of the war with Saudi Arabia in 1934. The southern frontier was set down by an Anglo-Turkish Boundary Commission in 1902-1904 and remains today as the frontier between Yemen and the People's Republic of South Yemen.

The Imams considered the latter border completely devoid of any legal validity; their argument was that it had been established by two foreign powers (the Ottomans and the British) during their temporary military occupation of Yemeni territories. Neither had any sovereign rights in Yemen, and Yemen itself had been neither a member of the commission which drew the frontier, nor a party to the convention which legalized it.

During the inter-war period, Imam Yahya undertook a series of political maneuvres designed to regain those territories which he considered to be part of historical and natural Yemen, as well as to obtain some form of international recognition of his position as sovereign. His first objective was to regain the Tihama, which had been taken over by Great Britain at the end of World War I and then ceded to their wartime ally, the ruler of Asir. The Imam was able to occupy and incorporate the Tihama with little or no difficulty; and, more important, his actions precipitated no protest from Great Britain.

Thoroughly convinced of the effectiveness and superiority of his armed forces, the Imam thereupon embarked upon a military occupation of some of the small sheikhdoms and principalities on his frontier but part of the British Aden protectorates, while simultaneously undertaking an active policy to gain for his country the province of Asir and the Oasis of Najran from Saudi Arabia in the north.

These irredentist policies soon involved Imam Yahya in wars. In 1934 he lost the war with Saudi Arabia and was forced to recognize the presently existing frontier with that country. In the same year, the Anglo-Yemeni Treaty was signed—six years after the Imam's troops had finally been expelled from nearly all of the protectorate areas and after countless negotiations concerning a permanent frontier. In effect, the treaty formalized the stalemate which existed, since both sides promised only that they would respect the status quo. Since no precise agreement could be reached on what constituted the status quo, the southern frontier of Yemen remained, as it had been since its demarcation, the primary source of Yemeni grievances against Great Britain and the latter's position in south Arabia. The question of this frontier and its future status remained a major element in Yemeni foreign policy until the departure of the British from the former South Arabia Federation in November 1967.

During Yemen's long dispute with Great Britain over this frontier, it sought to obtain allies and assistance in the international arena. In as many instances as possible, Imam Yahya sought to sign treaties or other types of international acts with non-Arab states while he was in actual possession of portions of the protectorate, for such agreements signed while he occupied these territories implied the other signatory's recognition of this occupation. No doubt Italy, the first European power to sign an agreement with Imam Yahya's government (in 1926), was sympathetic to Yemeni overtures because it saw the treaty with Yemen as a means whereby it could expand its influence in the Red Sea region where it already had colonial ambitions (e.g., Ethiopia, Eritrea, Somaliland). The Imam was cognizant of the Italo-British friction and sought to use it for his own ends.

Two years after the Italian agreement was signed, in 1928, Yemen signed a Treaty of Friendship and Commerce with the Soviet Union. The latter nation was quite clearly an opponent of Britain in the international arena and, as such, both Yemen and the U.S.S.R. expected that their association would lessen British influence in the peninsula. No doubt the British decision, in the same year, to finally act decisively with respect to the Yemeni occupation of portions of the protectorate was closely linked to the Yemeni decision to enter into an agreement with the U.S.S.R.

In 1927 also, Yemen sought an agreement with the United States; while it may be argued that the timing was fortuitous, there is reason to suspect Yemen's request for such an agreement at that particular time. It seems equally clear that the U.S. government was perfectly aware of the anti-British implications of any decision on its part to associate itself in any way with the Imam's government, for its explanation that it had not yet decided on the status of former Ottoman territories in the peninsula as the reason for not entering into an agreement seems weak, at best.

Shortly after the 1934 treaty with Great Britain, but primarily during World War II, Britain increased the number of, and simultaneously strengthened the political ties implied by, the treaties which it negotiated with the member states of the Aden protectorates. Precisely which states, and the exact wording of these treaties is no longer of particular relevance; what is important is that the Yemenis saw these treaties, and the closer links with Great Britain which they contained or implied, as a violation of the status-quo which had been agreed upon by the 1934 treaty. As a result, there began two decades of frontier agitation, skirmishes, propaganda, and subversion between the various Proectorate states in order to counter British influence. Despite a brief interlude in 1950-1951 when a *modus vivendi* of passing import was worked out, these differences over the frontier and the extent of British influence in the protectorates remained the most important foreign policy issue of the Yemeni government. Great Britain, in an attempt to strengthen its position, embarked upon a variety of programs to link the protectorate states in some sort of federal or confederal scheme. By 1954 Britain had succeeded in obtaining, through advisory and protectorate treaties, a sufficiently large number of tribal allies to sponsor a formal scheme for a federation in the Protectorates.

The Yemenis under Imam Ahmad were outraged and intensified their campaigns of bribery, infiltration, propaganda, and subversion. Aware of the relative weakness of his own forces when compared to the political and military might of Great Britain, the Imam decided that Yemen needed powerful non-Arab allies who could assist in weakening Britain's position while simultaneously strengthening Yemen's hand. Like his father, Imam Ahmad felt that the most obvious place to seek such allies was from among Britain's opponents in the international arena. As in the inter-war period, this would include the Soviet Union; equally clearly, this included the U.S.S.R.'s allies.

The electric reaction among the European and Western states to the Soviet Union's offer and Egypt's decision to accept Soviet arms in 1955 was fully appreciated by Imam Ahmad. And, he expected that Great Britain's reaction to his own acceptance of Soviet assistance would be equally panicky: At best, Britain would weaken in her resolve to remain in Aden and continue with her announced plans for the protectorates; at worst, Britain would become more willing to discuss the issue with Yemen and reach an acceptable compromise with the Yemenis. Consequently, Imam Ahmad in November of 1955 signed a friendship pact with the U.S.S.R. and shortly thereafter had his son Muhammad al-Badr make an extensive tour of the Soviet Union's allies in eastern Europe as well as the People's Republic of China, with which diplomatic relations were established in 1956. In early 1957 an arms agreement with the Czechoslovakian government was revealed.

Yet the Imam was at least as aware as his father before him of the dangers to Yemen's traditional government, domestic policy, as well as maneuverability in foreign affairs if there developed a too great dependence upon any one outside ally. Consequently, Ahmad sought to associate Yemen, even if only on a relatively trivial basis, with a number of additional powers—including the United States—in an effort to retain the flexibility which he deemed necessary to the success of his purposes.

Despite these relatively sophisticated plans, Great Britain chose not to abandon the protectorates; instead, it diligently went ahead with its various proposals to create at least a semiautonomous political entity in the protectorates. Although the Imam expanded his links with the Soviet Union and its allies and even undertook some negotiations with the British, it was clear by the early 1960s that there was little reason to expect any concession from either side. By the end of September 1962, when the revolution broke out, no significant change had taken place with respect to Yemen's determination to limit British influence in the protectorates and eventually to incorporate these areas into a greater Yemen.

Great Britain, on the other hand, had succeeded in making some significant alterations in the status of the many principalities found in the protectorates. Throughout most of the 1950s, there had been little if any interest in the plans of the British; the creation, in 1958, of the United Arab Republic (UAR) between Syria and Egypt, however, brought about a dramatic change. The subsequent creation of the United Arab States, which was nothing more than the adherence of Yemen to the United Arab Republic agreement as an associate member, changed the image of Imam Ahmad's Yemen which had prevailed until that date in southwestern Arabia. Until the United Arab States, the Imam's government had been considered hopelessly reactionary among the more than 80,000 Yemeni exiles employed in Aden as well as the Arab nationalist political parties. After the United Arab States, these exiles and the political parties and organizations moved to support a much closer relationship with Yemen; as a result, the rulers of the protectorate states saw their position in an entirely different light.

In the past, these rulers interpreted any British-sponsored federal proposal as a means by which Britain could perpetuate its position indefinitely in Aden and southwestern Arabia. They now saw the same proposal as the most effective means for retaining their prerogatives in a collective organization which would protect them against the political ideas of Egypt, Syria—and now also of Yemen. Great Britain was able, therefore, to make significant progress toward political unification in the protectorates, and by 1959 began the establishment of the Federation of the Amirates of the South, later termed the South Arabian Federation after a number of additional principalities decided to adhere to the original agreements.

The Yemeni government, of course, totally disapproved; it once again escalated its commitment to intrigues, subversive activities, bribery, and the like in order to nullify as much as possible these developments. Until 1961, at which time Imam Ahmad withdrew from the United Arab States agreement, however, these campaigns were seen as emanating from increased pressure for such activities from Egypt, and therefore they only succeeded in hastening the process of federation in the protectorates.

Post-Revolution Policies

The revolution of 1962 brought about a significant change in the international position of Yemen. It becomes necessary, however, to distinguish between the Republican and the Royalist factions in the conflict which followed upon the revolution of September.

The assistance which the Egyptian government began to provide—troops as well as materiel—shortly after the outbreak of the revolution to the new Republican government meant that the Royalists would also be forced to seek outside support if their counterrevolution were not to fail. In view of some of the public statements made by leaders of the Republican government—including both overt and covert threats to existing monarchical regimes on the Arabian peninsula—it was inevitable that the Royalists would seek assistance from Saudi Arabia. The latter was basically a conservative Islamic monarchy, as Yemen had been under the Imams, and deeply concerned about the possibility of Egyptian support for domestic movements and organizations which sought to effect a revolution within its own frontiers.

The other Middle Eastern monarchies—Jordan, Morocco, and even Iran—saw the Yemeni situation as a possible precedent for the overthrow of their own governments by Republican regimes. Consequently, they were at least sympathetic to the Royalist faction and, in some cases, provided military assistance in the form of equipment and personnel.

Conversely, the Republican government appealed to the Republican regimes in the area: Besides Egypt, these included Iraq, Syria, and Algeria—all of which at one time or another provided at least token support to the new government. Aware of the strength of the basically conservative Zaidi tribesmen, as well as of the financial and other assistance being provided primarily by Saudi Arabia, the new government sought to consolidate its position in the international arena as the first step toward permanence. In this connection, it sought diplomatic recognition from the major Western powers and the United Nations as soon as possible. Most of the Soviet Union's allies and associates, as well as the U.S.S.R. itself, granted diplomatic recognition within the first few weeks.

The international affiliations and alliances which the two Yemeni sides made during the first six years of the civil war were by and large completely predictable just as soon as the ideological policy lines had been clearly drawn.

[In general, this may be summarized as follows: the Royalists were recognized by the more conservative states in the Middle East and elsewhere, while the Republicans were recognized by the republican, progressive, Arab nationalist states of the Middle East, as well as most of the Western European democracies, and the newly independent states of Africa and Asia. Great Britain, with its extensive interests in the Arabian peninsula region, as well as its concern with the precedent which such revolutionary action and substantial Egyptian military intervention implied, was one of the few Western states which continued to recognize the Royalists.]

The policy with respect to the South Arabia Federation was not as forcefully stated, nor indeed were there any overt indications of immediate Republican interest in these areas. Friction between the British and the new government, however, appeared as soon as it became clear that Britain would not recognize the new Republican government. By 1963, the first of a series of organizations to direct and organize resistance against the British position in South Arabia was created in San'a: the National Front for the Liberation of South Yemen (NLF); later, its arch-rival Front for the Liberation of South Yemen (FLOSY) also established its headquarters within Yemen, in Ta'iz. The complex story of the conflict within South Arabia for hegemony after the projected British withdrawal from Aden is covered in detail in the chapter on the People's Republic of South Yemen; suffice here to indicate that the Republican government, as well as its major ally the Egyptian government, provided some assistance to these liberation forces (although to different ones at different times) and they are generally acknowledged to have supported—financially as well as militarily—the Radfan revolt against Britain in the spring of 1964.

In general then, the Republican government adopted one of the basic foreign policy tenets of the Imams: reintegrate into Yemen those territories which a variety of foreign powers had illegally usurped in past centuries. In the northern frontier regions—the former principality of Asir and the Najran Oasis—the Republican government had no influence, for it was precisely this region which the Royalists controlled, largely as a result of the generous assistance provided by their Saudi allies.

In the south, although some measure of ideological agreement was clearly evident (at least among the nationalist groups opposed to the continued political domination of the sheikhs and sultans of the federation), it was also evident that a separate interest had developed within the old protectorates. Perhaps the clearest indication of this is provided by the fact that no concrete steps for union between PROSY and the Republic had been initiated despite more than two years of independence on the part of the former by the end of 1969. Nevertheless, the choice of name at the same time provides some idea of the vague affinity which does exist and which may possibly be of immense significance in the future. In this connection, it is wise to remember that the overwhelming portion of the population of PROSY is Shafi'i, and those areas of Yemen held by the Republic are also predominantly Shafi'i in persuasion. Should the seemingly endless civil war continue and some form of *de facto* partition take place, it is not impossible to foresee an amalgamation of the Shafi'i Yemeni Republic with PROSY, leaving a truncated Zaidi state of Yemen in the northern highlands of the present state.

With the June 1967 Arab-Israeli war and subsequent developments in that region of the Middle East, the southwestern portion of the peninsula and its problems have tended to recede from the headlines. The conflict, however, is not yet concluded; in the meantime, there is no basis for assuming that the present frontiers and political arrangements in this area will prevail for long. With the departure of most Western diplomatic representatives—including those of the United States—from Yemen in 1967, international interest in the area waned noticeably. In the meantime, both the Yemeni Republic and PROSY have substantially increased their political, military, and economic ties with the Soviet Union and its allies; the consequences of these recent developments await the future.

CONCLUSIONS

As the previous pages have made clear, it is very difficult to describe adequately, much less with precision, the political structure and behavior of a nation in the middle of a protracted and extremely divisive internal war.

The simple fact of mobilization, the actual battles, and the flexibility needed to cope with the constantly changing exigencies of the conflict make it inevitable that both the political structure and behavior patterns will remain in a state of flux. One may assume, of course, that once a semblance of stability is brought into being (whether this involves a semipermanent stalemate or the eventual victory of one side or the other), some of the older patterns of government and behavior will make their reappearance, modified to the extent necessary or consistent with intervening events and developments. For that reason alone, it has been necessary to describe at some length the patterns of government under the older Imamate.

Despite the withdrawal of the Egyptian forces, the Republican government has been able to maintain its control of the major cities, indicating more clearly than ever before the very deep division of interests and outlook between the urban centers and the tribal rural population. It would seem that some sort of compromise between the two sides is possible, with the creation of a government of sufficient flexibility to enable it to apply varying standards and techniques to the divisions which exist—with perhaps in the very long run, an eventual coming together of both through the adoption of increasingly convergent patterns of administration.

It remains in 1969, as in previous years, as difficult as ever to predict the eventual outcome of the conflict. Perhaps, however, the simple fact that neither side is operating within the glare of worldwide publicity, as was so frequently the case in the past, will permit a softening of previous stands and viewpoints for the eventual compromise which will be necessary. When that point is reached, it will be easier for political scientists to effectively describe, analyze, and study the politics of this relatively isolated Middle Eastern nation.

BIBLIOGRAPHICAL NOTES

Readers interested in further information on all aspects of Yemen can consult, for extensive bibliographical material, the following:

Macro, Eric, *Bibliography on Yemen.* (Coral Gables, Fla.: University of Miami Press, 1960).

Macro, Eric, "The Yemen, Some Recent Literature", *Royal Central Asian Society Journal*, Volume XV (January, 1958), pp. 43-51.

Wenner, Manfred W., *Modern Yemen, 1918-1966.* (Baltimore: Johns Hopkins Press, 1967), pp. 234-247.

Wenner, Manfred W., *Yemen: A Selected and Annotated Bibliography since 1960.* (Washington, D.C.: The Library of Congress, 1965).

The following works are especially recommended for additional information:

Fayein, Claudie, *A French Doctor in the Yemen.* (London: Robert Hale, 1957). Especially valuable for its detail on life in Yemen under Imam Ahmad.

Gerlach, Richard, *Pictures from Yemen*. (Leipzig: 1960). Brief text; finest collection of pictures of life in Yemen under the Imams.

Holden, David, *Farewell to Arabia*. (London: Faber and Faber, 1966). Written by a British correspondent with many years of experience in the Middle East; valuable personal knowledge of events at some crucial points in time during the last two decades.

Ingrams, Harold, *The Yemen: Imams, Rulers and Revolutions*. (London: John Murray, 1963). By one of the most famous British experts on southern Arabia; personal experiences and knowledge add immensely to the value of this treatment of Yemen since independence.

Macro, Eric, *Yemen and the Western World*. (New York: F. A. Praeger, Inc. 1968). Although weighted toward the earlier history, it is valuable for an alternative summary and view of the significant events of the post-World War II period.

Pawelke, Günter, *Der Jemen–Das verbotene Land*. (Düsseldorf: Econ Verlag, 1959). Informative alternative view of Yemen under the Imams by former German ambassador, especially on the political climate in the latter years of Imam Ahmad.

Reilly, Sir Bernard, *Aden and the Yemen*. (London: H.M. Stationery Office, 1960). By the former High Commissioner in Aden; although presenting the British viewpoint, valuable for material on relations between Yemen and the Aden Protectorates and Aden Colony.

Schmidt, Dana Adams, *Yemen: The Unknown War*. (London: The Bodley Head, 1968). By the Middle East correspondent of the *New York Times*; extensive experience on both the Royalist and Republican sides throughout the civil war. Extremely valuable for developments since 1962.

Scott, Hugh, *In the High Yemen*. 2d ed. (London: John Murray, 1947). Although somewhat dated in its political coverage, this remains an essential work on Yemen for the modern era; extensive detail on the country, its people, and the government under Imam Yahya.

Wenner, Manfred W., *Modern Yemen 1918-1966*. (Baltimore: Johns Hopkins Press, 1967). Provides extensive background information on the reigns of Imams Yahya and Ahmad; divided into three parts, covering domestic policy, foreign policy, and the civil war up to 1966.

chapter 17

The People's Republic of
South Yemen *

BACKGROUND

The modern state known as the People's Republic of South Yemen (PROSY) occupies the area generally characterized as "south Arabia," that is, the southern fringes of the Arabian peninsula. During the great pre-Islamic empires, this region was an integral part of the domains of the Sabaean, Minaean, and Himyarite kingdoms; in more recent times, it can best be characterized as the collection of principalities and sheikhdoms which managed to retain their autonomy into the 20th century through the direct intervention of Great Britain into this region early in the 19th century. Formerly, the immense wealth of south Arabia was due primarily to its near-monopoly over the production of frankincense and myrrh; in modern times, agriculture provides an insignificant percentage of the national income, and the economic prospects for the future do not appear heartening.

The People's Republic of South Yemen consists of four distinctly different geographical regions. The most inhospitable of these is the great Arabian desert known as al-Ruba' al-Khali (the Empty Quarter), whose southern fringes are the northern boundaries of PROSY. Probably most economically important is the great Wadi Hadramawt (Valley of the Presence of Death), probably so named by the pre-Islamic rulers to discourage foreign discovery of the major production area of frankincense. The Hadramawt Valley completely dominates the eastern regions of PROSY, and was divided into two separate states until the creation of the South Yemeni Republic in November 1967: the Qu'ayti State of Shihr and Mukalla on the seacoast, and the Kathiri State of Sayun in its upper reaches.

In the western areas of PROSY, the mountainous highlands which rise in

---

*Manfred W. Wenner, associate professor of political science, Northern Illinois University.

412

Yemen and fall off to the west dominate the area. Their height, often over 8,000 feet, results in more regular rainfall; extensive terracing and water preservation methods make cultivation feasible in much of this area. The coastal plain, extending from the Red Sea coast along the fringe of the peninsula and containing most of the population, makes up the last of the four regions.

Despite the easy categorization of geographical regions within PROSY, its boundaries are everywhere either nonexistent or in dispute—with Yemen, with Saudi Arabia, and Muscat and Oman. The fact that no precise cadastral survey has ever been undertaken means that an exact figure for the land area of PROSY is impossible. Perhaps the best estimates are those made by the British government during its 128 years of sovereignty in this area: roughly 115,000 square miles. Within this relatively limited space more than 25 independent or autonomous states, principalities, sheikhdoms, naqibdoms, and other political entities were to be found, although again no clear frontiers were ever demarcated between them.

Similarly, no census has ever been taken. Estimates by the British, by long-time residents and administrators, and by the present government range between about 800,000 and 1,500,000 persons. By far the majority of these are engaged in the traditional pursuits of farming and animal husbandry, although some are engaged in fishing, pearl-diving, and other sea-oriented livelihoods. The major industry, developed since the 1950s, has been the petroleum refinery located in the city of Aden, which processes in the neighborhood of about 6 million tons of crude oil per year. Most of this is imported from the Persian Gulf states, and was used to refuel the large number of ships which used Aden as a way-station. In addition, because of its strategic location, protected deepwater, and outstanding berthing facilities, Aden also became the prime outlet for the exports of the southwestern region of the peninsula in general, including those of Yemen and even some parts of Saudi Arabia.

During most of the British administration of this area, the constituent states retained their autonomy in nearly all arenas. The many treaties which were negotiated between the states and Great Britain specifically reserved jurisdiction over foreign affairs to the latter, of course, but left internal policy and procedures the prerogative of each ruler. Consequently, it was not until the very recent past that Britain undertook to begin or to implement any specific projects related to economic development or industrialization. The largest of the projects was the Abyan project, which as a result of scientific irrigation and modern agricultural methods contributed significantly to an increase in domestic production of foodstuffs.

Political Background

Population. The origins and history of the Arabs inhabiting south Arabia is obscure; in certain regions of the interior a number of non-Arabic languages, all apparently related to ancient south Semitic, are still spoken. It has been suggested by some authorities that one or more of these languages may be the remnants of the languages spoken in the ancient pre-Islamic empires. Certainly some of the peoples speaking these languages, all of whom it might be added live in what was formerly known as the eastern Aden protectorate, give evidence of having resided in other areas in the past and having been pushed aside by more recent population migrations and tribal wars.

In the western Aden protectorate there appears to be a greater degree of population homogeneity, with no major groups of persons speaking non-Arabic languages. Nevertheless, certain characteristics of the Arabic language even in this region show the influence of the ancient south Semitic tongues [e.g., the frequent use of Am- or An- for the definite article in place of the classical Arabic al-].

The greatest difference which exists in the area is that between the racially, linguistically, and religiously mixed population of Aden and some of the coastal cities and the purer Arab of the interior regions. Aden, as a long time entrepot and commercial shipping center, has a cosmopolitan population of Arabs (many of whom are of Yemeni origin), Somalis, Danakils, Ethiopians, Indians, Pakistanis, as well as a variety of Europeans; Muslims of course predominate, but there are also colonies of Christians, Parsees (Zoroastrians), and until very recently, a substantial community of Jews. In the larger coastal cities, such as Mukalla, one finds Pakistanis, Indians, Indonesians, Malaysians, Baluchis, as well as Negroes and mixtures of all with Arabs. Because the eastern Aden protectorate is the location of a tomb of great religious significance, that of the Prophet Hud (the Biblical Ebir), this particular region has never had any Jewish colonies. Among the relatively isolated population of the remoter valleys in south Arabia, there is also abundant evidence of shamanism, animism, and other varieties of paganism.

Islam, of course, is the religion of probably at least 90 percent of the population of southwestern Arabia. But Islam is represented by both Shi'a and Sunni sects, and an appreciation of their distribution and relations between them is an important part of the explanation for the complex relationship between Yemen and the states of the former Aden protectorates.

Shi'a Islam is represented in southwestern Arabia primarily by the Zaidi sect, though Ismailis are also present. The rise of the Zaidi Imamate in the mountains of Yemen in the 9th century A.D. has been attributed to a combination of Yemen's particular pre-Islamic background as well as its inaccessability, thus providing a safe refuge for dissident sects. The Zaidi Imams have continued, with numerous interruptions, to provide whatever political leadership has existed in that country until the middle of the 20th century.

Sunni Islam, on the other hand, is represented primarily by the Shafi'i school of law, though in certain isolated areas both the Hanbali and Maliki schools have their adherents. More important, however, is the fact that the Shafi'ites of southwestern Arabia predominate in the coastal and lowland regions throughout this area, including those within Yemen. Consequently, while there is considerable debate as to the actual percentage distribution of these sects within Yemen (both claim a majority), it is quite clear that Shafi'i Islam is overwhelmingly predominent in PROSY.

Despite the fact that even the Sunnis of south Arabia refer to the Zaidis as *al-madhhab al-khamis* (the fifth school) of Islamic law and to the far greater number of doctrinal similarities between Zaidi and Sunni Islam than between Zaidi Islam and other Shi'a sects, Zaidi Islam has always been associated with the political overlordship of the Imams of Yemen—not all whom were magnanimous or tolerant in their treatment of Shafi'ites, thus creating considerable suspicion and mistrust of Zaidi rule in Shafi'i areas and districts.

History. The origins of European interest in the Red Sea region and the Gulf of Aden are found in the voyages of the Portuguese in the early 16th century. Later, other European powers entered the scene—to participate in the lucrative Indian trade and compete for prestige and commercial interests: the Dutch, the Danes, the French, the Swedes, and of course, the British.

It was the latter who were to become of greatest importance to the future development of the political situation in south Arabia. Interested, as were all the other powers, in controlling the Red Sea trade, the British in the early 19th century had been denied substantial participation in the coffee trade centered in Mocha (Yemen). As a result, Britain began to demonstrate a greater interest in the port of Aden, which at that time was a part of the domains of the Sultan of Lahij—the largest of the former western Aden protectorate states now a part of PROSY. The Sultan of Lahij had declared himself independent of Yemeni suzerainty in 1728, and was clearly the strongest of the south Arabian rulers. After reconaissance voyages in the 1820s and 1830s to determine which port would be best suited for an entrepot for the India route and a series of incidents associated with the Indian trade, the British decided on Aden. In January 1839 Aden was stormed and taken by Britain, beginning the more than 128 years of British administration which finally ended in November 1967.

To the British, their spoils logically included a portion of the Adeni hinterland, not only because this area was claimed by the sultan whom they had defeated but also because the security of Aden was necessarily related to this hinterland. No doubt the expansion of Egyptian influence in the Arabian peninsula, especially in the Hijaz and Yemen, also played a role in the decision, for it seems likely that the British government was sufficiently concerned with the possibility of long-term Egyptian control that it felt it prudent to establish a prior claim to at least a portion of the peninsula.

For most of the 19th century, there seemed to be little cause for any border disagreement between Yemen and Great Britain with respect to their claims in the southwestern corner of the peninsula. The major event which changed this relatively peaceful coexistence was the opening of the Suez Canal; almost immediately the strategic value of Aden and the surrounding areas, including Yemen, increased significantly. Indeed, the Ottoman Empire returned to Yemen, and the British set about more systematically to obtain sovereignty over certain islands and territories felt to be of potential maritime or military value: Perim, the Kuria Muria Islands, Kamaran, Socotra, and the like.

As friction on the border with Ottoman-administered and controlled Yemen increased, the interest of Britain in the status of the many principalities also increased. This and the difficulties which arose with a number of the tribal states soon led to a lengthy series of agreements which in most instances provided for a monthly stipend to the ruler, a promise not to alienate territory except to the British government or with its approval, and assignation of foreign policy and foreign defense to the British government. Generally these agreements provided for a British protectorate, hence the adoption of the collective names, western Aden protectorate and eastern Aden protectorate. Through purchase, the size of the Aden settlement grew, attaining an area of approximately 75 square miles.

Primarily because of the importance of India and the fact that the original conquest of Aden had been undertaken through the Bombay government (the governor-general of India), it was attached for administrative purposes to that government. By the post-World War I era, however, the lines of communication and administration had become so confused and contradictory that adjustments were needed. In 1928, for example, the defense of Aden was transferred to the Royal Air Force; when partial autonomy was granted to India in 1931 by the Statute of Westminister, the Arab population of Aden feared that Indian officials would replace British ones—a prospect with little to recommend it in the view of the Arabs, whose opinion of and relations with the Indian community in Aden were not the best. Consequently, in 1932 Aden became a chief commissioner's province, directly under the control of the central government of India. This did not satisfy the Adenis, who asked that the city and surrounding areas be placed under the control of the colonial office in London (which had been responsible for relations between the settlement and the protectorates since 1928). The result, in 1937, was that Aden became a crown colony, directly administered by the London colonial office.

At the close of World War I and with the demise of the Ottoman Empire, the status of the many former Turkish territories in the Arabian penninsula was in doubt. In at least one instance, however, a legal transfer of sovereignty was effected: the former vilayet of Yemen.

Yemen under the leadership of the Imam of the Zaidi sect had been engaged in an almost unceasing revolt against the Ottoman authorities since shortly after the turn of the century. It was this Imam, Yahya, that the Turkish authorities considered their legal successor and to whom the reins of government were given. The Ottoman administrators however did not cede the coastal plain, the Tihama, to the Imam; this had been a separate governmental administrative jurisdiction, and was ceded to the neighboring principality of Asir, which was allied with Great Britain.

Imam Yahya, although concerned with the many domestic and foreign policy problems any ruler faces, soon opted for a major effort devoted to restoring Yemen's historic and natural frontiers. No doubt the knowledge of the great pre-Islamic empires and the extent of their domains, as well as the relatively more recent, though oft-interrupted, Yemeni suzerainty over nearly all of southwestern Arabia contributed to the Imam's grandiose conception of what was included in "historic and natural" Yemen. The decision of the Yemeni government to vigorously pursue a policy of irredentism naturally conflicted with the territorial claims of neighboring authorities. In this case: with the Saudi rulers of Najd, with the rulers of Asir (soon to fall under a Saudi protectorate), and most importantly, the British in Aden. The latter based their claims to territories formerly [in the 18th century] under Yemeni suzerainty and now at least nominally included in the protectorates upon: (1) the collection of protection agreements signed with some of these states as a result of the occupation of Aden in 1839, and (2) the Anglo-Turkish Boundary Agreement negotiated prior to World War I between the Ottoman Empire administrators of Yemen and the British government.

In the inter-war period, the Yemeni government made numerous attempts to annex the areas it claimed. On its northern frontier, these attempts finally led to a Saudi-Yemeni war by 1934, with the result that all of Asir was incorporated into the new Saudi Arabian state. In the south, Yemeni troops occupied the Tihama and many of the smaller states in the protectorate. It was primarily to assist in the elimination of these Yemeni forces that the Royal Air Force was, as mentioned above, assigned responsibility for the defense of Aden and the Protectorates.

By 1934 Britain's increased determination to retain her control in the Protectorates, and the attempt by Yemen to simultaneously wrest irredentist territories in the north, necessitated at least a temporary agreement with Great Britain: the Ango-Yemeni Treaty. The treaty, however, did not succeed in creating a permanent settlement to these frontier issues; its vague terminology led to conflicting interpretations and the result was that, with the exception of a brief period during World War II, the border continued to be a major source of friction between Yemen and Great Britain.

The latter, in order to make its legal and administrative jurisdiction in the protectorate areas more effective and generalized, signed a further round of protection, advisory, and similar agreements with those states which had not previously entered into any binding relationship with Britain.

The death of Imam Yahya in 1948 and the accession later that same year of his son Ahmad led to a new round of border conflicts and difficulties between Yemen and the protectorates. In 1950-1951, a so-called *modus vivendi* agreement between the two nations was negotiated in London. Its effect was, however, minimal. In 1952 the British extended their influence by obtaining advisory treaties with additional protectorate states.

By January 1954 a sufficient number of these treaties had been signed for the British high commissioner in Aden to announce that the government was going to sponsor a scheme for a formal federation of the various states in both the eastern and western Aden protectorates. According to a former commissioner, most of the tribal chiefs "agreed in principle though the details of any scheme which would be generally acceptable would have to be worked out."[1] The decision to embark upon the creation of a federal association of the many principalities in the protectorates was, in effect, an attempt to resuscitate a similar earlier proposal. In the early 1930s, at a time when the British position in the protectorates was weakened by the continued attempts by the Yemenis to reassert their suzerainty over these states, almost exactly the same suggestion was proposed by certain British officials to strengthen the several states against either the blandishments and/or the military incursions of the Yemenis. At that time, it was argued by certain officials that such a proposal was impractical and instead of creating a more modernized political structure would only perpetuate the kind of fractious tribalism which prevailed. When a political settlement, the Anglo-Yemeni Treaty of 1934, appeared in the offing, the proposal was abandoned.

The Yemeni government took violent exception to what it considered to be a violation of the 1934 treaty and the clause which read:

> . . . the high contracting parties agree to maintain the situation existing in regard to the frontier on the date of the signature of this treaty . . .

This was interpreted by Yemen to mean that the political status quo would be maintained. Consequently, the Yemenis undertook an intensive campaign of bribery, infiltration, propaganda, and exploitation of inter-tribal disputes to void the British decision to bring a greater amount of political unification to the area.

While it seems clear that many of the tribes and the population of some of the state governments displayed varying degrees of sympathy toward Yemen, there were clearly limits to this sympathy. Some of the reasons for a sympathetic relationship were: (1) Yemen was governed by an Arab ruler; and (2) Yemen has within its frontiers certain cities of religious significance to Shafi'ites. On the other hand: (1) The ruler was of the Zaidi persuasion, (2) the Yemeni government would enforce taxation, and (3) Yemen would not tolerate the existence of autonomous units and clearly would establish a unitary state. The efforts of Yemen, supported by the Arab League and other Arab nations who saw the plan as a means whereby Britain could perpetuate itself indefinitely in south Arabia, had the result of lessening the interest of most of the rulers.

In 1956 the governor of Aden reported that he had had conversations with certain rulers of the protectorates with regard to their future status. In a public statement he suggested that the protectorate states "should seek some form of closer association with each other for mutual assistance and support and in order to strengthen their internal economy and social organization."[2]

Eventually, it was events in an entirely different area of the Arab World which brought about greatly increased interest among the protectorate states for the proposed Federation. In early 1958 Egypt and Syria created the United Arab Republic—the first union of independent Arab states. The subsequent affiliation

---

[1] Sir Bernard Reilly, *Aden and the Yemen* (London, H.M.S.O., 1960), pp. 37-38.
[2] *Ibid.*, p. 43.

of Yemen with the United Arab Republic (UAR) in the even larger association known as the United Arab States (UAS) completely altered the status of the Imam's government among the Arab nationalist elements in Aden colony.

Previously, the ultra-conservative nature of the Imam's government had made it abhorent to the Adenis, as well as to the thousands of Yemenis employed in Aden's industries. While most of the latter had originally emigrated to Aden in the search for employment, their association with the politically sophisticated Adenis—in clubs, trade unions, and on the job—made the majority *political* self-exiles within a relatively brief period. Now, on the other hand, Yemen's association with Egypt, clearly the most progressive and nationalistic of all the Arab states, indicated that a major reassessment was necessary. The nationalistic groups, some of the political parties, and the dissident sheikhs in the protectorate who disapproved of British policy changed their view. The prospect of closer association with the UAR/UAS held out the hope of substantial progress toward the type of goals and policies advocated by President Abdel Nasser. And, as a consequence, these groups and the nationalistic leaders began to agitate for some far closer relationship with Yemen, perhaps even union.

The reaction of the majority of the rulers in the protectorate states was entirely different. The prospect of Aden and the protectorates joining with Yemen implied two related and thoroughly disagreeable prospects: (1) their demise as even minimally automonous rulers under what would presumably be a centralized republican government, and (2) the complete elimination of their special status, prerogatives, subsidies, and separate territorial existences. By mid-1958 five of the protectorate states were sufficiently interested in the proposals for federation to visit London and discuss the project. Britain's support was not long in forthcoming, and this precipitated the addition of another state. After discussions over the draft constitution, events moved more rapidly, and on February 11, 1959 the rulers of six (of 20) states in the western protectorate signed a document creating the Federation of the Amirates of the South. In the following months and years, other protectorate states acceded to the federation, whose relationship with Great Britain was essentially that of the former "protection and advisory" treaties signed by the individual rulers in previous decades. Britain retained responsibility for foreign affairs and defense, with the federation agreeing to accept Britain's advice on governmental matters except those dealing with religious affairs and not to enter into any agreement, treaty, correspondence, and the like with any other power without the previous knowledge and consent of Great Britain.

By far the most significant hurdle which all the parties concerned had to face in the process of creating a viable political entity in south Arabia was the future status of the crown colony of Aden with respect to the federation. By the end of the 1950s, Aden colony was the world's third busiest port; it had one of the Middle East's most important oil refineries and the heterogeneous industries and commercial operations which both the port and the refinery had spawned; it had a large and diverse population, especially when compared to the protectorates; and, perhaps most important, it had developed under British tutelage and protection a remarkably sophisticated complex of specialized social, economic, and political institutions, most of which bore far greater similarity to those in developed nations than the essentially tribal, patriarchal, and traditional institutions found in the protectorate states.

INDEPENDENCE

In retrospect, it is clear that the issue of the future status of Aden colony set the stage for the eventual independence of PROSY. On the other hand, the sizeable discrepancies between the colony and the protectorates, as well as the traditional conflicts within the latter provided the new rulers with monumental nation-building problems.

Aden's economic importance has already been mentioned. While still under British administration and while the Suez Canal remained open, Aden's primary significance lay in its bunkering trade. Even in 1964, after preindependence violence had already begun to disrupt port operations, Aden annually handled about 7,500 ships of nearly 32 million tons net registered tonnage—surpassed only by London, Liverpool, and New York. Able to provide ships with fuel and water, Aden also appealed to the passengers of all transit vessels because of its free port status. No doubt of greatest significance to this bunkering and transit trade was the construction, between 1952 and 1954, of the British Petroleum Refinery at Little Aden, expanded a number of times until by independence it had an annual throughput of 6.5 million tons of crude oil—more than half reserved for bunker fuel for transit shipping.

It was, however, not only the bunkering and transit facilities which made Aden so valuable. Indeed, its military and strategic importance in Great Britain's defense posture "east of Suez"—rarely if ever questioned until the mid-1960s—cannot be ignored. After the independence of Cyprus and the transfer of Britain's east African facilities to Aden following the independence of Kenya and Tanganyika, the military value of the bases located at Aden appeared to be essential to the whole British position. In addition, the R.A.F. base at Khormaksar and related army facilities were Aden's biggest employer, and provided more than $30 million in income annually to Aden.

In order to retain these facilities, Great Britain was slow to permit full political freedom to the Adeni population. At the same time, the many communal frictions which existed among the population and the inability of the indigenous political parties and groups to agree upon any compromise with respect to the franchise contributed to the seemingly perpetual postponement of revised electoral machinery and extension of the limited franchise which existed.[3]

[3] The legislative council in office at the time of the Aden merger with the federation had been elected in 1959. Out of an estimated total population of 180,000, only 21,554 were eligible voters. The 1959 elections had been boycotted by most of the parties due to these differences, and only about 27 percent of the eligible voters actually cast ballots.

On the other hand, Britain had permitted and even encouraged the formation of trade unions, of which there were more than 30 joined in the Aden Trades Union Congress (TUC), and had assisted in the establishment of a Legislative Council with some popularly elected Arab members as well as a ministerial form of government. When the crucial question of Aden's incorporation into the new Federation was raised, a series of difficult political, economic, social, and even military issues were raised. As far as the politically articulate Adenis were concerned, these concerned primarily such issues as Aden's future status within the federation, economic arrangements which would not prejudice Aden's position, and the expansion of representative and more democratic forms of government and administration, again in order to avoid prejudicing Aden's advanced position.

After long and often acrimonious debate, Aden colony was merged with the protectorates in January, 1963; the new association was renamed the Federation of South Arabia. As far as the Adenis were concerned, none of the major issues had been settled, and plans for a conference to be held in London to discuss the outstanding problems were made. By mid-1964, after a year of increasing tension and unrest marred on occasion by violence, the main purposes and objectives of the conference were more clearly defined: (1) setting an approximate date for the eventual independence of the federation; (2) widening of the franchise in both the federation and Aden; (3) reorganization of federal institutions and procedures for the purpose of democratizing them—in both form and content; and (4) the issue of British financial assistance, and the schedule of payments (rent) for the continued use of the military facilities in Aden. Eventually, on July 4, 1964 the participants at the conference signed an agreement which recognized 1968 as the year of independence for the Federation, with appropriate arrangements for the base, constitutional revisions, and related matters to be more precisely defined at another conference proposed for 1965.

As differences of opinion grew between the British, federation leaders, and Adenis as to the outstanding issues, so did the divergence of opinion among the Adeni political parties. The issue of the franchise and governmental forms and procedures continued to be the major catalyst for these differences. For example, the Adenis on the whole began to lean in the direction of independence outside the federation, while federation leaders began to insist upon the incorporation of the former eastern Aden protectorate states into the planned independent state in order to counterbalance the economic and political power of Aden as well as its greater population.

Beginning in December 1963 with the assassination attempt upon the life of the British High Commissioner Sir Kennedy Trevaskis, nearly all the political groupings in Aden moved in the direction of employing varying forms of political violence in order to emphasize their opposition to Britain's proposals and plans for the future of Aden. While assassination attempts as well as bombings of various sorts remained rather isolated at first, boycotts, general strikes, and smaller scale disruptions became an ever more frequent characteristic of the Adeni political and commercial scene.

As a result of increasing violence and the wide differences of opinion among the parties, the London conference was postponed. Special commissions were established both by Great Britain as well as the special committee of 24 of the general assembly of the United Nations to investigate the Adeni situation. At the same time, other Arab nations, especially Egypt and Republican Yemen, began to demonstrate an increasing interest and concern over developments in south Arabia. Many of the political groups in Aden began to agitate for some form of association with Republican Yemen, with at least one grouping, the Front for the Liberation of Occupied South Yemen (FLOSY) headquartered in Ta'iz in Yemen and actively supported by the Egyptian government. The Saudi government, concerned about the whole future of the southern area of the peninsula, also entered the scene more actively and supported different factions.

In August 1965 the second London conference, with most political factions in attendance, met to outline future arrangements more specifically; it failed to create any consensus, and immediately thereafter terrorism and violence increased sharply as the various groups began to fight openly for control of both Aden and the federation. A complex and confusing array of blocs, organizations, parties, and *ad hoc* alliances characterize the Adeni political scene during the two years prior to independence. It will not be possible here to detail these developments; the accompanying chart provides a brief summary of these shifting relationships.

Of immense importance to an understanding of the increasing militancy and reluctance to compromise on the part of the various political factions was the release in February 1966 of the British White Paper on defense. Its importance for Aden's future lay in the decision to evacuate all British troops from Aden by December 31, 1968 and the related decision *not* to have any defence treaty with the independent state of South Arabia. The effect of the White Paper upon the strategy of the various parties and groupings was devastating: Up to this point the federal leaders had counted upon the continued presence and support of the British; on the other hand, the Adeni political groupings had assumed that Britain would retain some interest in the base, and their activities were designed to extract the greatest number of concessions and the highest annual payment possible. In the aftermath of the White Paper, the Federalis, as they were known, began to seek allies among the leading anti-British parties in Aden; similarly, the Adeni political parties who had attempted to act within the British-dominated framework of Adeni politics sought accommodations and compromises with the original parties who had been far less reluctant to resort to violence and terrorism to extract concessions. Without question, the two most important of these groups were the National Liberation Front (NLF) and the Front for the Liberation of South Yemen (FLOSY).

Political Parties in South Arabia

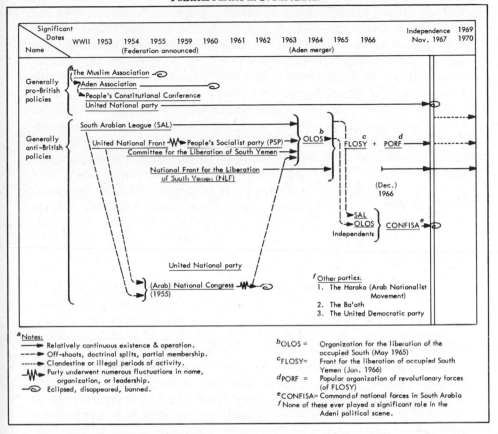

Throughout the remainder of 1966, the federation struggled to retain its separate existence; it finally approved the 1963 U.N. resolution favoring a plebiscite in South Arabia, thus bringing about a second U.N. Committee on Colonialism attempt at conciliation, which unfortunately was no more successful in 1966 than it had been three years earlier. Indeed, all attempts during that year to create a consensus, or a compromise arrangement embracing all the parties, were a failure. By mid-1967 a condition of near anarchy prevailed, at least in part precipitated by Britain's newly set departure date—January 9, 1968—and the fact that the federation leaders now refused to hold public office. In fact, the federation was completely dead; even its army had largely joined the forces of the Adeni parties struggling for control over the whole of its former territories.

In early September 1967 the British high commissioner finally saw the necessity of meeting with the nationalists, *i.e.*, the various revolutionary groups which were clearly in the ascendant—specifically the NLF, which Britain had formerly refused to acknowledge as anything more than an Egyptian-led and controlled terrorist organization. In fact, the NLF at this time controlled more than one half of the 20 odd states in the old federation, and had managed to gain the support of many disparate elements in the federation precisely because it had retained its independence from Cairo—definitely not the case with the Yemeni-based and Egyptian-controlled FLOSY.

A brief attempt at a coalition government and·cease-fire between the two rival organizations failed to last more than intermittently between mid-September and mid-November; by the latter time, it was clear that the NLF was in control of considerably more than half of the federation, and so it was with the NLF leaders that British Foreign Minister George Brown held talks concerning the transfer of authority. By November 30, 1967 the last British troops left Aden, and the NLF proclaimed the new People's Republic of South Yemen.

NATION-BUILDING

The new government immediately faced the kinds of problems which are characteristic of most new nations. No doubt the two most important of these were (and are): (1) the building of a national consensus, and (2) economic development.

Although it seems relatively clear why the NLF achieved supremacy over the forces of FLOSY, the traditional allegiances, rivalries, and political associations are not so far in the past as to be irrelevant to any analysis of the future development of PROSY. Among the reasons advanced for the apparent victory of the NLF would be: (1) its recruitment patterns—the NLF had recruited solely among the indigenous population of south Arabia, and perhaps more important, it had members from among many of the tribal associations and states which had existed within the federation; as a result, it avoided being associated either with the British, or the Egyptians; (2) its cohesiveness—the NLF had succeeded in avoiding the divisive and destructive intramural fighting which had characterized many of the other political alliances as well as refusing to associate itself (except very briefly and only tentatively) with other organizations; (3) the political neutrality of the federal army prior to the summer of 1967, at which time it finally opted to support the NLF; (4) the withdrawal of the United Arab Republic from Yemen following the Arab-Israeli War, which also resulted in a cut off of the primary sources of revenue and support of FLOSY.

This, of course, is not to argue that a domestic consensus had or has been established. Indeed, PROSY during its first two years of independence was plagued by an intermittent series of revolts and rebellions. At least in part, many of these internal upheavals were the direct result of the NLF's accession to power; while the NLF was threatened by political opponents, and seeking to attain uncontested control over south Arabia, the disparate elements contained within the Front found it easy to cooperate. On the other hand, as the experience of a multitude of other newly independent single-party states in the Third World shows, disputes over both means and goals between the constituent elements of such pre-independence political alignments appears almost immediately. So it was with the NLF: What soon became characterized as the moderate faction of the NLF (under the first Prime Minister, Qahtan al-Sha'abi) found itself attacked from the Right as well as from the Left. During PROSY's first two years, it was the Left which appeared to be gaining the upper hand. By the latter half of 1969, it seemed that the disputes within the NLF were also directly related to its foreign policy alignments: A pro-Soviet Union faction (the more moderate wing, concerned primarily with support for Arab causes in general, economic development, and more interest in specifically PROSY and Yemeni affairs), and a pro-People's Republic of China faction (in the ascendant after the deposition of al-Sha'abi) which actively supported revolutionary liberation movements directed against the "Occupied Gulf," Ethiopia, and Dhofar, Musqat, and Oman, while in domestic policy favoring a policy of "scientific socialism" and the establishment of "popular councils" to spread "popular democracy."

Despite surface appearances, however, it would be a serious over-simplification if analysis of PROSY since independence were restricted to an investigation of doctrinal disputes within the NLF combined with a survey of the activities of the former contestants for political power, the South Arabian League (SAL) and the Front for the Liberation of Occupied South Yemen (FLOSY). Clearly, the latter two had not fully reconciled themselves to the continued one-party rule of the NLF in PROSY. During PROSY's first two years, it was clear that either singly, together, or in combination with other governments (notably elements of the Republican government of Yemen and Saudi Arabia), they continued to attempt a comeback by supporting deposed and unreconciled tribal leaders, tribesmen within the territory of PROSY, and/or allying themselves with elements within the NLF.

It was inevitably as a result of the continued existence of tribal rivalries, jealousies, and conflicts that the former contestants had their greatest successes in the post-independence period. For, despite some appearances to the contrary, a substantial number of the doctrinal disputes and internal political frictions within and among the competing groups had their bases in long-established and continuing tribal frictions. Indeed, these tribal rivalries tended to take on modern political overtones simply in order to find opportunities within the limited political framework of the one-party state that PROSY had become for expression of their continued disputes.

Illustrative of this problem, which is by no means restricted to the Arabian peninsula states, is the role of the army in PROSY. As is the case with many other single-party states where army support frequently plays a crucial role, the demographic makeup of the armed forces is of paramount significance. Under the British, despite a program to broaden the population mix represented in army ranks, it was tribesmen from the upper Aulaqi sheikhdom who predominated—because of their willingness to serve, reliability, and effectiveness, as well as the fact that the Aulaqi sheikhdom lay across the major overland access routes toward the northeast and east from Aden. Almost inevitably, the special role of the Aulaqis aroused resentment among the other states, especially among the traditional rivals of the Aulaqis, the Dathina. After independence, the NLF favored the Dathina and began a purge of Aulaqi elements; consequently, the Aulaqis became a natural focus of opposition and resentment to the continued dominance of the NLF. The result was that in the post-independence period the defeated parties in the battle for control of PROSY (FLOSY and the SAL) and their foreign supporters (elements of Republican Yemen and the Saudi government) sought influence among the Aulaqis; at the same time, the complex array of traditional tribal alliances and antagonisms which characterized inter-tribal/state relationships became part of the conflict. In brief, there is considerable evidence that the ideological elements involved in recent domestic unrest—whether in the Bayhan, Aulaqi, Haushabi, Subayhi, Hadrami areas or elsewhere—are often a modern overlay on far older antagonisms and rivalries.

Here then, as in so many other Middle Eastern states, the problems of nation-building, and the creation of a viable national consensus present the current political elite with substantial problems. While the leaders of the NLF as well as the leaders of FLOSY and the SAL are unquestionably motivated by ideological considerations that transcend the borders of PROSY, as well as possessed of an awareness that the issues and problems they face are not unique, the overwhelming percentage of the population of PROSY is only slowly becoming aware of political alternatives and is reluctant to part with old ways. It seems that the pattern of other nations is likely to be repeated in PROSY: extensive domestic unrest while a large variety and number of groups contest the reins of power, until it becomes possible for one group—often the army simply because of its access to and control of the means of violence—to control the machinery of government effectively enough to control or eliminate overt opposition while consolidating itself and its ideology.

As indicated above, the issue of economic development is an important part of the whole process of national independence and political development. PROSY presents a set of characteristics all too common among newly independent, former colonial states: a primitive infrastructure, limited natural resources, a shortage of managerial and technical skills, little or no investment and development capital, with little or no possibility of mobilizing such capital from among its own population, and a limited number of commodities or services available for foreign trade.

The juncture of independence with the semipermanent closing of the Suez Canal had devastating effects upon the economy of Aden Port and derivately therefore on all of PROSY. Although the British Petroleum refinery continues to operate at capacity and is able to find a ready market in the Red Sea region for its output, petroleum refining is not a labor intensive industry. Prior to independence and the closing of the Suez Canal, Aden Port and the British base provided employment for roughly 65,000 to 70,000 unskilled and semiskilled laborers—many of whom were Yemenis. While the departure of many of the ethnic communities which dominated Adeni commerce and trade (Indians, Pakistanis, Jews, and Somalis) was not regretted, and the drifting back to Yemen of most of the occasional laborers of Yemeni origin (probably more than 40,000) helped to alleviate the unemployment problem, the government admitted in late 1969 to unemployment of more than 25,000 persons in a total estimated population (in Aden) of 190-200 thousand. Much of this is due to the catastrophic decline in shipping through Aden—rarely more than 110-125 ships per month, compared to the pre-independence struggle total of roughly 570-610 ships per month. At the same time, the largely subsistence agricultural methods which characterized the long-neglected Protectorate state economies has not been amenable to rapid improvement (despite a land reform and distribution program) due to the lack of the necessary capital and skills.

The immense disparity in levels of income, expenditure, and development between the various former states of the federation (e.g., between the relatively sophisticated, export-conscious and trade-oriented eastern states, and the barely subsistence level economies of the far more backward former western states) and Aden has not been bridged. Discussions between PROSY and Great Britain over the amount and kind of economic assistance which the latter is "supposed to provide" continue to take place sporadically, despite considerable disagreement between the parties. Assistance in the form of grants, development aid, and the like comes today largely from a variety of eastern European and Asian states under Communist governments, as well as through a variety of United Nations agencies. In view of the limited resources at the disposal of the government, the continued closure of the canal, the endemic political instability, as well as the problematical future significance—economic or political—of the southern regions of the peninsula (especially in light of the fact that extensive searches for petroleum resources have so far proved fruitless), the economic outlook for PROSY appears bleak. It is to be expected that these difficulties will have their domestic repercussions, as well as a long-term effect upon PROSY's foreign policy.

PROSPECTS FOR THE FUTURE

Among the most cherished of all Arab political goals is, of course, that of unity—that is, the unification of the many distinct Arab political entities into a single Arab nation. Southern Arabia is unique in that it contains two states with basically the same name: Yemen and South Yemen. And the conscious adoption of the name of South Yemen by many of the pre-independence parties as well as the subsequent independent state was an indicator of the depth of the common heritage, culture, and political concerns which the two states felt they shared. It was indeed expected that some form of unification between the two entities would not be long in forthcoming, and indicative of the mutual interests was the creation in each country of a ministry of all-Yemeni affairs.

To the outside observer, however, it appears that the gulf between the two states is widening, as each struggles to create a national consensus and attempts to deal with the idiosyncratic domestic problems it must face. The insistence upon ideological purity which characterizes the political elite of PROSY also contrasts markedly with the greater emphasis upon pragmatic solutions which Republican Yemen proposes after more than seven years of civil war. Despite extensive efforts at secularization and modernization, both nations are discovering that traditional rivalries within their diverse populations tend to reappear in the guise of ideological conflicts within the context of the prevailing orthodoxy.

In sum, the chances of unification between the two Yemens in the near future is problematical at best. In southern Arabia, as in much of the rest of the Middle East and other developing areas, the primary problem appears to be whether the new elites are willing and able to help create a political culture which can peacefully accomodate both traditional and modern conflicts of interest. Until this is accomplished, we are likely to continue to see endemic unrest and violent changes in and among the political elites.

SELECTED BIBLIOGRAPHY

Brinton, J. Y. *Aden and the Federation of South Arabia.* (Washington, D.C.: American Society of International Law, 1964). Primarily a compilation of the relevant documents and legal materials related to the establishment of the Federation; a short introduction provides a summary of the origins and development of the idea of Federation in South Arabia.

Great Britain Central Office of Information. *Aden and South Arabia.* (London: British Information Services Booklet R.5671, 1965). A summary of the political, economic, and social characteristics of South Arabia, as well as a chronology of developments to the date of publication. Presents in concise format basic data as well as the British government view of the significance of South Arabia.

Hickinbotham, Tom. *Aden.* (London: Constable, 1958). Although dated, the volume provides important background information on developments in the Protectorates and Aden through the mid-1950s. The author was British High Commissioner in Aden.

Holden, David. *Farewell to Arabia.* (London: Faber & Faber, 1966). A very interesting, though impressionistic, survey of the Arabian Peninsula during the early and mid-1960s by a highly competent British journalist; covers political developments and their significance in all the states of the Peninsula, especially with respect to British foreign policy.

Ingrams, Harold. *Arabia and the Isles*. (London: John Murray, 1966). The third edition contains the reflections of one of the most famous British administrators in southern Arabia after the political scene in South Arabia had been radically altered during the late 1950s and early 1960s. The remainder is a fascinating account of his service during the 1930s and 1940s.

Johnston, Sir Charles H. *The View from Steamer Point*. (London: Collins, 1964). The highly impressionistic account of developments in Aden by a British High Commissioner during the early 1960s. Though lacking an accurate index, highly instructive reading for the viewpoint of a traditional British Colonial official during a turbulent period in Adeni development.

King, Gillian. *Imperial Outpost—Aden*: (London: Oxford University Press, 1964). A publication of the Royal Institute of International Affairs; an excellent summary of the significance of south Arabia to British Strategy; the causes and development of Adeni political activism; and the relationship between events in the Protectorates and Aden and other areas in the Middle East.

Little, Tom. *South Arabia*. (New York: Federick A. Praeger, Inc., 1968). A fine study of the development of the issue of the Protectorates, the idea of Federation, and the establishment of the People's Republic. The presentation is clear, and unlike most other studies, includes criticisms and commentary on British actions and policies.

Reilly, Sir Bernard. *Aden and the Yemen*. (London: H.M.S.O., 1960). An important, though highly colored account of the situation in southern Arabia up to the beginning of the decade. More concerned with the relationship between Aden and the Protectorates and independent Yemen. The author, also a former High Commissioner, presents the best summary of British official opinion.

Trevaskis, Sir Kennedy. *Shades of Amber*. (London: Hutchinson, 1967). A sober and thoughtful account of the end of British rule, by the next-to-last High Commissioner. The author was one of the very few British officials who grasped the complex relationship between the parties and the political situation both in Aden and the former Protectorates and who recognized the consequences of the many policies which Britain either proposed or adopted.

chapter 18

Kuwait and the Eastern
Arabian Protectorates*

The present chapter deals with two types of political units: the independent state and the Emirates (or Sheikhdoms) protected by the British government as the result of special treaty relations. For the sake of convenience the independent state of Kuwait (until 1961 also to some degree a British protectorate) will be considered first, and the other protectorates, the Sheikhdoms of Bahrain, Qatar and the seven Trucial States (the Sheikhdoms of Abu Dhabi, Dubai, Sharjah, 'Ajman, Umm al-Qaiwain, Ras al-Khaimah and Fujairah) will follow.

The territory covered by Kuwait and the protected sheikhdoms runs on the western shore of the Persian Gulf from its northernmost edge to its southernmost end with only one intermission—that of al-Hasa, a territory lying between Kuwait in the north and Qatar in the south and forming a part of Saudi Arabia. In spite of the fact that the area we are considering contains the varying political units, it should be noted that there is a common factor uniting those same units, *i.e.,* that they are all Arabian territories inhabited in the main by Arabian tribes designated today as belonging to the 'Adnani, the northern division of Arabs, or the southern Qahtani.

KUWAIT FROM SHEIKHDOM TO STATE

A brief recollection of its early history is needed to fully appreciate the political development of Kuwait. The state was named after its capital city, orginally a very small fishing center on the northwestern corner of the gulf. The

*A. M. Abu-Hakima, visiting professor of history, Middle Eastern Institute, Columbia University (on leave from the University of Jordan).

name Kuwait is a diminutive of *kut,* meaning a small fortress. This town was also known to the 18th-century European travelers by the name of Grane (sometimes spelled Grain or Graen), a diminutive of the Arabic, *qarn,* meaning a small hill. The town's earliest history might date back to the mid-17th century and is not to be seen as ancient. Kazima, in the same neighborhood, was famous in the seventh century A.D. and is alluded to in various Arabic verses.

The 'Utub

The earliest settlers of Kuwait, of whom we have historical record from the 17th century, were the Bani Khalid tribes, rulers of eastern Arabia in the 16th, 17th, and 18th centuries. It was their Amir Barrak who is said to have established Kuwait. Later in the 17th century, a number of Arabian tribes, united under the name of 'Utub, travelled from the southern part of central Arabia to the coasts of the gulf near Qatar. These dispersed along the shores of the gulf and finally met again at Kuwait where they gradually established their independence from the Bani Khalids in the middle of the 18th century. From the start, Kuwait was a tribal society.

Famous among the 'Utub confederacy were the al-Sabah, al-Khalifa, and al-Jalahima clans. It might be useful to note here that these 'Utub (singular 'Utbi) were the cousins of al-Saud and that they all claimed descendency from Jamila, a branch of the Great 'Anaza tribe now inhabiting northern Arabia.

Rise and Development of Kuwait in the 18th Century

The al-Sabah became rulers of Kuwait about 1750. By the end of the 18th century it had become an established sheikhdom, politically and economically. Its fleet, together with that of Muscat, was said to have monopolised the conveyance of trade in the Persian Gulf, and its Arab ruler was independent of all foreign control, including the Ottoman. Sheikh 'Abd Allah ibn Sabah, the second and most efficient ruler to whom Kuwait owes not only its independence but also its prosperity, rose to power about 1762 after the death of his father Sheikh Sabah ibn Jabir (who gave the present ruling family its name). Sheikh 'Abd Allah ruled unchallenged until his death in February 1815. This long reign was destined to go through certain political and economic difficulties, but of interest to us now is the actual structure of the early Kuwaiti society, for this structure remained unchanged until the 1950s when oil began to change the face of it.

The rule of Sheikh 'Abd Allah set the pattern for government and statesmanship in Kuwait for a long time to follow. European sources speak of an early paternal system of government and point out that al-Sabah became rulers of the town by local choice. There are two aspects of Kuwait's internal political structure noteworthy here: (1) that Sheikh 'Abd Allah received the right to rule from his people and did not simply inherit his power (actually he was the youngest of several brothers), and (2) the choice of the ruler was made mainly by merchants. Of the latter we note that Kuwait was from the start a society in which merchants, because of accumulated wealth, played a great role in the running of current affairs. Not only was their own political influence on their ruler important, but members of the ruling family themselves maintained their own businesses. Though the rulers, relying upon the advice of merchants, settled disputes among the townspeople, local tradition speaks also of a *qadi,* or a judge, who settled matters relating to Islamic law. This internal political structure remained intact until Kuwait became an independent state in 1961.

We might also note that much of this internal policy was dictated by the external situation, *i.e.,* the state of affairs in the neighboring countries. Two factors have always had their influence on Kuwait and the eastern Arabian protectorates: the waters of the gulf and the policies of the countries surrounding those waters. Considering Sheikh 'Abd Allan ibn Sabah's rule in the 18th and early 19th centuries, one can detect the work of each of these two factors and see them affecting the politics of Kuwait. These concerned Britain's growing interests in the gulf waters and their elimination of the other maritime powers of Europe (the Portuguese, Dutch, and French) and land forces, such as the Wahabis on the eastern Arabian shores, the Ottomans in Iraq, and the Persians on the eastern shores of the gulf. Though it is beyond the scope of this chapter to go into the details of how each of the above mentioned factors worked in moulding the policies of Kuwait, it could be briefly stated that Sheikh 'Abd Allah built a fleet to defy the local fleets in the gulf and that he maintained friendly policy toward the British.

Sheikh Mubarak the Great and the "Exclusive" Agreement of 1899

No major change took place in the sheikhdom's foreign policy until the first few years of the rule of Sheikh Mubarak al-Sabah (1896-1915). Then, "in 1898 Sheikh Mubarak of Kuwait, anxious to avoid any extension of this control (Ottoman in Iraq), turned to Great Britain and in 1899 signed a comprehensive treaty which contained most of the provisions included in the various agreements with Bahrain and the Trucial states." Under this agreement Kuwait agreed to have no direct relations with any other foreign power and not to sell, lease, or cede land to any such power. These agreements are usually referred to as the "exclusive" agreements, and by them Great Britain became responsible both for conducting the foreign relations of Kuwait and for protecting it against foreign aggression. Sheikh Mubarak entered readily into this agreement. At the time, Kuwait's continued independence could be insured only by British protection.

After the signature of this treaty of 1899 and until 1946 when the golden oil tap was turned by Sheikh Ahmad al-Jabir al-Sabah, no radical changes in the policies of Kuwait took place. The Berlin-Baghdad railway project at the opening of the 20th century and World War I, however, were major factors in promoting the Anglo-Kuwaiti relations which continued until the days of independence. And World War II had, of course, its effects on Kuwait's internal as well as external political development. The huge jump in human communications through the various media of air transport and radio broadcasting stations and receivers accelerated social, political, and economic change. However, the role of oil was paramount.

It is not possible to include in this brief section on Kuwait the history of oil discovery, but it might be useful to note that because of the cordial Anglo-Kuwaiti relations, and following the lines of the 1899 exclusive agreement, Sheikh Mubarak the Great offered the British another exclusive agreement regarding the search for oil in Kuwait in 1913.

Effects of Oil in Kuwait

The discovery of oil in Kuwait was bound to have effects on its society. The changes which were to come could be measured by the amount of oil and money earned per capita and what use was made of this fabulous wealth.

Until the reign of Sheikh Ahmad al-Jabir al-Sabah (1921-1950), Kuwait consisted of about 15,000 square kilometers with only one large town— Kuwait, the capital. Its boundaries were fixed at 'Uqair in Saudi Arabia in 1921. Sheikh Ahmad al-Jabir continued to administer the sheikhdom in the traditional manner though he tried to form a consultative assembly in the 1920s to help him in his administration. That assembly, however, was doomed to die soon after its birth. Of greatest importance here is to note the traditional role of Kuwaiti merchants who continued to help the sheikh run the administration of their country until time became ripe for the birth of real Kuwaiti democracy.

Oil was struck during the year 1938, but oil production started in 1946. With this came a great human influx into Kuwait. Together with the original Arab people of Kuwait, the newcomers who flooded there from the Arab countries of the Middle East began to transform the Kuwaiti traditional society. Their right arm was the newly discovered wealth drilled from the earth. Oil was to develop the society.

Sheikh Ahmad al-Jabir did not live long enough to witness the great changes that were to come. This lot fell to his successor Sheikh 'Abd Allah al-Salim al-Sabah (1950-1965). Thanks to the latter's internal and external policies, Kuwait was transformed into a modern democratic state and reached its present position and prestige, not only among the gulf states, but also among other Arab countries. The transformation can be seen in population and economic statistics.

The census of 1958 placed the population of the Shaikhdom at about 300,000 with the majority living in the town of Kuwait. The census of 1965 read 467,789. More than half of this increase came from both neighboring and distant Arab countries. Among the foreign population, a few thousand Persians from the opposite littoral of the gulf, Arabs by descent, are numbered as well.

Economic increase was more drastic. Kuwait earns most of its income, if not all of it, from oil. During the last five years of Sheikh Ahmad al-Jabir's life (1946-1950), oil revenue rose from £280,000 in 1946 to more than £4,000,000 per annum. *The London Times* on May 18, 1961 estimated Kuwait's annual oil revenue at about £150,000,000. The £200,000,000 mark was reached by 1963. The official *Year Book* published by the Ministry of Information and Guidance gives the figure of 248,127,432 Kuwaiti dinars for revenue (K.D.—$2.80). These figures put Kuwait at the top among the nations of the world when computing income per capita ($3,410 in 1969) and reflect Kuwait's share of the oil wealth. Kuwait Oil Company, which is half-owned by British Petroleum and half-owned by Gulf Oil, is said to have enjoyed an overall income of $1,700 million each during the 12 years, 1946-58. The *New Statesman* has estimated that Britain benefits to the tune of $600 million a year from Kuwait, including British Petroleum profits, the sterling income from the sale of oil and the Sheikh's investments. There are also considerable private Kuwaiti investments in England.

Although Kuwait had not been cut off from modern influences before the oil age (the wealth of certain Kuwaiti merchants was estimated by millions of Indian rupees before the 1940s), Sheikh 'Abd Allah al-Salim laid the solid foundations of modernization in Kuwait. His role in the transformation of his society cannot be underestimated.

This period of change extending from 1950 to 1968 can be divided into two periods: 1950-1961 and 1961-1968. During the first 11 years, the main lines of democratic progress of Kuwait were demarcated. A few examples demonstrate this, such as in the fields of education and health. Money was alloted which made education at all levels free to those living in Kuwait. The British system of national health service was embraced by the Department of Health, and free medical treatment, hospitalization, and medicine have since been extended to all who live in Kuwait—foreigners as well as natives.

Private enterprise was also given ample chance to help develop the country and was generously compensated by the government. Schools whose costs exceeded $10 million each were built in large numbers. Roads were paved first in the town of Kuwait, and before 1961 dual-carriage roads were connecting almost all parts of the country. The social pattern kept pace with this rapid development in building and road construction. Free education was extended to include studies abroad, and Kuwaiti youth were sent on scholarships to obtain university degrees elsewhere. Such young people returned to run the various government departments and brought with them Western patterns of thinking and behavior which were modified by local traditions to suit the Kuwait Arab environment. These changes in society and urbanization effected in the 1950s readied Kuwait for the new phase in its history—the transformation into an independent state.

THE STATE OF KUWAIT 1961-TO PRESENT

The treaty of 1899 with Great Britain could not continue to serve the relations of Kuwait and Britain in the 1960s. The replacement of that treaty by the treaty of 1961 therefore was welcome. Kuwait became, on June 19, 1961, completely independent of Great Britain. By July 16th of the same year Kuwait joined the League of the Arab States and was accepted two years later on May 14, 1963 as a member of the United Nations.

As soon as the 1961 treaty was made, Sheikh 'Abd Allah announced a provisional system of government, and a constituent assembly was established to carry out two duties. The first was to draft a constitution for the country within a year, or not later than January 1963. The other was to fulfill the duties of a chamber of deputies, or House of Commons. The assembly finished its work in January 1963, but the draft of the constitution was prepared a few months before that and was approved by Sheikh 'Abd Allah on November 11, 1962.

The National Assembly

The first elections to fill the 50 seats of the assembly were held on January 23, 1963. Though the amir (sheikh) of Kuwait appoints the ministers, they are responsible to the assembly which can force them to resign by a vote of no-confidence. The assembly also has power with respect to the prime minister. If the deputies find that they cannot cooperate with him, their house will notify the amir who either dismisses him or dissolves the assembly. If the then newly elected assembly finds that it cannot cooperate with the prime minister, he must resign. The National Assembly meets for eight months of the year. The amir delivers a speech at the opening session in which he reviews the conditions in the country and the important public events of the previous year. He also outlines the projects and the governmental plans for the coming 12 months.

The Constitution

The constitution, drafted by an elected committee of five assembly members, has 183 articles and is divided into five sections. The first of these deals with the system of government and its articles represent many of the political attitudes of the state. These read as follows:

Article One: Kuwait is an Arab, independent, fully sovereign state. Neither its sovereignty nor any part of its territory may be relinquished. The people of Kuwait form a part of the Arab nation.

Article Two: The religion of the state is Islam, and Islamic law shall be a main source of legislation.

Article Three: Arabic is the official language of the state.

Article Four: Kuwait is an hereditary Emirate, the succession of which is confined to the descendants of the late Mabarak al-Sabah.

A special law issued within one year of the date on which the constitution comes into effect, shall lay down the other rules concerning the succession of the Emirate.

Article Six: The system of government in Kuwait shall be demo-
                      cratic, under which sovereignty is vested in the nation,
                      the source of all powers.

Other articles deal with guarantees for personal liberty, public rights, and duties. The Kuwaiti constitution, in brief, reflects modern trends in a country where preparations were being effected during its early tribal years to meet those trends. And while such internal structure grew, at the same time, Kuwait was preparing to meet its external commitments to both the Arab countries and the rest of the world.

Foreign Policy

In one degree or another, a sense of Arabism—from the extension of generous brotherly help on one hand to the expression of Arab nationalist feelings on the other—dominates Kuwait's foreign policy. Other factors also play their part in molding the relationships which Kuwait now enjoys with neighboring Arab and other states. Although Kuwait's enormous wealth from oil revenues has enabled her to boost her importance in the Arab world, even before the discovery of oil, Kuwait followed a policy which enabled her to get along very well with her neighbors. After creating in 1961 the Kuwait Fund for Arab Economic Develop-ment (with an initial capital of 50,000,000 K.D.s to be covered from the Kuwait government reserves), Kuwait extended financial aid to her Arab sister countries. By 1966-67 the capital reached the 200,000,000 K.D. mark, and by 1967 ten Arab countries were given long-term credits from this fund. The total amount of loans to those countries reached 56,550,000 dinars.

The case differed with the aid extended to the poor sheikhdoms of the Trucial coast—Sharjah, Dubai, 'Ajman, Fujairah, 'Umm al-Qaiwain, and Ras al-Khaimah. Kuwait supplied those sheikhdoms freely with teachers and medical aid as early as 1953. By 1958 schools and clinics were built by Kuwait in those sheikhdoms. The minister of external affairs has likened this aid to the seven Trucial states to "brothers sharing a loaf."

On the international scene Kuwait follows the nonalignment line. This policy has been stressed more than once by its minister for external affairs.

THE SHEIKHDOMS OF BAHRAIN AND QATAR

Again for the sake of convenience and geographical order in looking at the eastern Arabian coast, the Sheikhdom of Bahrain comes to focus first in this chapter, followed by the Sheikhdom of Qatar.

Geographically, Bahrain lies between al-Hasa (a province of Saudi Arabia) and the Sheikhdom of Qatar on one side, and the waters of the gulf on the other. In examining the governmental and political systems we find this location has made Bahrain the contested bone among the powers that exert influence in the whole Persian Gulf area. Before discussing such claims and anti-claims to Bahrain, a short historical background to the Bahrain Islands is in order.

One does not need to relate the ancient and medieval history of Bahrain here but notation should be made that the earliest recorded medieval history of the area tells us that Bahrain was ruled by 'Abd al-Qays, Arabian tribes, centuries before the advent of Islam to eastern Arabia early in the seventh century A.D. And another fact relevant at this point is that Bahrain, during the Middle Ages and until about the early 16th century, was a geographical name given not only to the present archipelago but to the entire eastern Arabian coast—from near Basra in the north to the Trucial coast in the south. Under the 'Abbasid Caliphate of Baghdad, and even earlier under the Umayyad Caliphate, Bahrain formed one of the caliphate's several provinces. With the coming of the Portuguese to the gulf early in the 16th century, Bahrain became one of their strong outposts in the gulf. This might mark the first contact between Bahrain and the European nations who were to follow the Portuguese not only to the East Indies but also to the gulf. The Dutch, the French, and the English were the most important European nations who left their mark on the history of the area. It was during the ascendancy of British influence in the gulf in the late 18th century that the incessant rule of al-Khalifa, rulers of Bahrain, began.

Al-Khalifa, Rulers of Bahrain, 1782

As noted earlier in the chapter, al-Khalifa, cousins of al-Sabah, were living in Kuwait together with al-Sabah and other 'Utbi families early in the 18th century. These cousins are related to al-Saud, rulers of Saudi Arabia, as off-springs of the Great 'Anaza tribe. Al-Khalifa remained in Kuwait until 1766, and then migrated to Qatar in the south where they established the town of Zubara on the peninsula's coast opposite Bahrain Island. Bahrain was at that time under the rule of an 'Umani Arab tribe whose headquarters were at Bushire on the Persian coast of the gulf. Sheikh Nasr al-Madhkur was the chief of that tribe with his residence at Bushire. Hostilities between the 'Utub, of both Kuwait and Zubara, and Bushire made Sheikh Nasr attack Zubara in 1778 and 1782. As a result of the unsuccessful 1782 attack, the 'Utub of both Kuwait and Zubara attacked and occupied Bahrain in November 1782. For the first few years after the capture of Bahrain, al-Khalifa ran its affairs from Zubara in Qatar. But later in the century al-Khalifa moved to Bahrain, and Zubara in Qatar became a deserted town, especially following the Wahabi attacks of 1796-98.

Bahrain, the 'Utbi Sheikhdom

Since 1782 and until the present day, Bahrain has been under continuous

'Utbi administration—that of al-Khalifa. The present ruler of Bahrain, Sheikh 'Isa bin Salman al-Khalifa, is the 10th Sheikh of the Khalifa family to rule in Bahrain since it was conquered by his ancestor Sheikh Ahmad ibn Muhammad al-Khalifa. The conquest of Bahrain seems to have been such an important event in the history of the Khalifas that Sheikh Ahmad is usually nicknamed Ahmad the Conqueror.

Early Government and Involvements

The 19th century in eastern Arabia was perhaps one of the most politically disturbed periods of its history. Bahrain was involved in that turmoil, but much of her involvement in the wars of the time was forced upon her because of previous claims to Bahrain by Muscat. The first half of the century was also a time when piracy in the gulf became paramount, and Bahrain, under the Khalifa rule, was involved in piratical incidents. It was under the pretext of subduing such piracy in the gulf that Britain's political relations with Bahrain and other sheikhdoms of eastern Arabia began. It should be remembered too at this junction that in Bahrain and the remaining other sheikhdoms of eastern Arabia, political sway was in the hands of one man, the sheikh, or ruler. Thus, from a political and administrative point of view, Bahrain was run by its al-Khalifa sheikh through almost all of the 19th century.

Britain and Bahrain

After the third British expedition of 1819 (the first took place in 1806, the second in 1809) against Ras al-Khaimah, Bahrain signed the 1820 Treaty of Peace with the British government. This treaty contained agreement by the sheikhs to abstain from plunder and piracy by land and sea except by way of acknowledged war. This treaty with Britain was followed by others in a manner that was unique in the history of eastern Arabia. Not only Bahrain signed such treaties, but also the other sheikhdoms of what (after one of those treaties) came to be called the Trucial coast. Among other treaties signed by Bahrain with Britain was the 1861 Perpetual Treaty of Peace and Friendship concerning such matters as slavery, maritime aggression, and trade.

Although Ottoman presence in eastern Arabia was nominal in the 18th century, the situation was reversed in the 19th century when the Ottoman sultan in Constantinople sent first his viceroy, Muhammad Ali Pasha of Egypt, against the Wahabis in the first half of the century and then Midhat Pasha in the latter half. The revival of Ottoman influence in eastern Arabia, from the British point of view, would have endangered their position in the gulf.

From time to time during the remaining years of the 19th century, the British government rejected Ottoman claims to sovereignty over Bahrain (as in the years 1870 and 1874), while at the same time the British took the opportunity to consolidate their power in Bahrain by means of two treaties signed between sheikh 'Isa al-Khalifa and the British government in December 1880 and March

1892. By these treaties the sheikh bound himself not to enter into any relationship with a foreign government, other than the British, without the latter's consent, and there were also stipulations about the disposal of Bahrain territories.

In 1902 a British political agent was posted in Bahrain, and in July 1913 a convention was signed by the British and Ottoman governments which included the recognition of Bahrain's independence and control of a number of islands near her. Three years later Ibn Saud signed a treaty with the British government in which he also agreed to refrain from aggression against Bahrain.

Modern Bahrain, 1935-to Present

In April and May of 1923 there were internal troubles in Bahrain which led to the abdication of the Sheikh 'Isa after a reign of 54 years and to the succession of his son Hamad, first as deputy ruler for 12 years and, on the death of Sheikh 'Isa in 1935, as sheikh of Bahrain.

With the accession of Sheikh Hamad the story of modern Bahrain begins, and during the 19 years of his rule, Bahrain moved toward modernization. Bahrain was traditionally a great pearl fishing center; and conditions in the pearl industry were reformed, the position of the divers was bettered, and municipalities, education, and other public services were developed. In 1930 Sheikh Hamad signed a concession agreement with the Bahrain Petroleum Company, and three years later the first tanker load of oil left Bahrain. On February 20, 1942 Sheikh Hamad died and was succeeded in turn by his son Sheikh Salman al-Khalifa. Under the new ruler the march of progress continued in all areas already mentioned and in the field of external affairs as well. Sheikh Salman visited Saudi Arabia in 1958 for a meeting with King Saud ibn 'Abd al-Aziz and, as a result of this visit, an agreement was signed between the two rulers providing for the sharing of profits derived from any oil found in an area that had hitherto been the subject of dispute. The importance of this political step lies in the fact that Sheikh Salman, by negotiating with King Saud, not only solved that problem, but also took Bahrain forward in the field of international politics. It was also during the later part of Sheikh Salman's reign that the British government transferred to Bahrain a number of responsibilities previously held by Britain, including such matters as the legal jurisdiction over Muslim foreigners.

In 1961 and on Sheikh Hamad's death, his eldest son Sheikh 'Isa ibn Salman succeeded him at the age of 28 years. The new ruler had acquired experience in administration during his father's life, and despite his youth competent administrative progress continued in the various councils and committees by which Bahraini government is run.

Councils and Committees in Bahrain

In Bahrain, as in Kuwait, the sheikh held the upper hand in administration. However, while Kuwait (after obtaining complete independence in 1961) is now run by the assembly and various ministries, in Bahrain (which has not yet gained full independence) the sheikh is helped by departments which are run by councils and committees. Usually one finds a member of the ruling family on the top of the administration in each department. This same structure is found in the municipal councils of the six big towns of Bahrain. The president of each municipal council is a member of the Khalifa family. Within the departments, one finds a president from the Khalifa family on top, assisted by a director who could be either a native of Bahrain or a Britisher. Of the 170,000 people living in Bahrain, according to the last census carried out in 1959, 143,213 people live in the six towns with the municipal councils. Those who live in towns have the right to vote and select the members of the municipal council. Women are not excluded from voting; as a matter of fact they were given this right long before some of their sisters in larger Arab countries.

It should be remembered that the story of the administrative system in Bahrain does not go much beyond 30 years. The first committee to be established was that of education in 1931. Since then a stable and efficient administration has been built up with numerous departments to deal with public health, public works, education, labor affairs, and minors' estates. In addition to these departments, a number of committees have been established to deal with matters affecting the public interest. These committees include among others the Committee of Trade Disputes and Diving Matters and the Religious Endowment Committee (Awqaf). The members of some of these committees were nominated, while the members of others were partly elected and partly nominated.

The creation of these committees and departments came about no doubt as a result of local pressure on the ruler by the people of Bahrain. By participating in these committees the people of Bahrain began to take an increasing part in the administration of their country and were, in fact, the first people of the gulf to do so. Bahrain is no exception to the rule concerning this political aspect of government in the sheikhdoms of the gulf. The same symptom can be seen spreading in every particular sheikhdom. But this has not, of course, minimized the abilities of members of the ruling families in the field of administration. By examining the various political establishments in Bahrain, one can easily observe that the ruling family is very well represented in the various councils and committees.

External Relations

It has been indicated that Bahrain has been in treaty relations with the British government since 1820. Under such conditions, foreign relations of Bahrain have been left to Britain to deal with and, as a matter of fact, Bahrain's relations with Britain and other foreign countries are conducted through a British political agent. It might be stated here as well that Bahrain is the place where the British political resident for the gulf sheikhdoms has been accommodated since 1946. In Kuwait, after independence, the British political agency became the British embassy.

Bahrain and Persian Gulf Politics

It has already been pointed out that Bahrain used to be the most contested bone in the Persian (Arabian) Gulf area before the discovery of oil in other parts of the gulf. But after the 1930s Bahrain was not contested for its rich pearl fisheries. The Persian (Iranian) claim still stood, together with claims from Bahrain herself to territories in the neighboring Qatar peninsula. In addition Saudi Arabia, during the zenith of Wahabi power in the 19th century, had practiced some sort of control for short intervals on Bahrain. The Sultan of Muscat did not, in the 19th century, drop his ancestor's claim to Bahrain.

The details of any of the four mentioned claims would take lengthy study, but to ignore them completely will not do Bahrain justice. Many studies of the Persian claim to Bahrain were published in learned journals and books in this century. The majority of those scholars tend to approve of Bahrain's independence under the Khalifa family and to turn down the Persian claim on a legal basis. However, the last Persian claim to Bahrain was made in January 1968, on the eve of a state visit to Teheran by the Sheikh of Kuwait. Although the statement of claim was most inopportune, the Sheikh of Kuwait nonetheless left for Teheran and paid his state visit to Persia. The situation will no doubt become different if the newly proclaimed Union of the Arabian Gulf Sheikhdoms materializes. Reference to this union will be made later in the chapter.

Bahrain's claim to Zubara in Qatar is based on the fact that Zubara was owned by al-Khalifa for a considerable period after they established themselves there in 1766. Zubara was more or less an al-Khalifa property until the 1870s when the Ottomans occupied al-Hasa and Qatar and appointed al-Thani, the present rulers of Qatar, as rulers over the area in which Zubara lies. Zubara, where many of the Khalifa family are buried, will always remain a site which al-Khalifa desires to regain.

Neither Muscat nor Saudi Arabia seem to be keen on their previous claims to Bahrain. Yet it was understood that both the Shah of Persia and King Faisal of Saudi Arabia, during the six-day state visit by the Shah to al-Riyadh (starting on the eighth of November 1968), would be looking into the various political problems of the gulf including the proposed Union of the Arabian Gulf Sheikhdoms. Bahrain is one of the very active members of this union.

The Sheikhdom of Qatar

The peninsula of Qatar, which is now the Sheikhdom of Qatar, only recently attained its importance in the area with the discovery of oil. Al-Thani rule of the peninsula is not as old as the rule of al-Sabah or al-Khalifa in eastern Arabia. Until oil was found in Qatar in the 1940s the country was inhabited mainly by nomadic tribes.

The Population

After the discovery of oil in Qatar the population of the peninsula almost doubled; *i.e.,* from 20 thousand or so people to more than 40 thousand. The early inhabitants of Qatar belonged to various Arabian tribes mainly descended from Najdi or central Arabian origin. Al-Thani themselves came from Najd early in the 18th century.

Al-Khalifa in Qatar

As has already been stated, in 1766 al-Khalifa departed from Kuwait and settled at Zubara in Qatar. Until the occupation of Bahrain by al-Khalifa in 1782, Zubara was the center of their trade which was mainly fishing and the marketing of pearls. With the occupation of Bahrain, al-Khalifa's trade multiplied because of their trade with India. Zubara shared in that successful trade, but the Wahabi attacks on Zubara toward the end of the 18th century forced al-Khalifa to withdraw for some time to new settlements in Bahrain. Al-Khalifa returned partially to Zubara early in the 19th century and showed great interest in keeping the place as one of their domains on the main land, but Qatar was slowly drifting from them as other tribes moved into the political scene.

Perhaps the most important event in the history of Qatar in the 19th century was the return in the 1870s of Ottoman rule to eastern Arabia into which Qatar was incorporated, and its sheikh of al-Thani was made a Qa'im-Maqam, or an Ottoman province ruler of the peninsula.

Al-Thani, Rulers of Qatar

Al-Thani claim their descent from Thani ibn Muhammad ibn Thamir ibn 'Ali of the Bani Tamim, one of the largest subdivisions of Mudar, or Nizar—the northern Arabs or 'Adnan. According to al-Thani's local tradition, their ancestors left al-Washm in Najd and settled at Jibrin oasis in eastern Qatar late in the 17th century. They soon travelled to the north and inhabited Zubara, where they stayed for some time, but later they departed to live at al-Doha, the present capital of Qatar, which was then a very small town. Local tradition also states that al-Thani ruled al-Doha as vassals to al-Khalifa, rulers of Zubara. This point is interesting for those who will go into the details of claims and counterclaims to Zubara by both al-Khalifa and al-Thani. It was Muhammad ibn Thani, ruler of al-Doha, who was the first among al-Thani sheikhs to seek independence for his tribe from al-Khalifa's dominance. Yet Muhammad does not seem to have been successful in achieving independence on his own. It was not until 1872, and by

Ottoman help, that he became independent of al-Khalifa. At that point in the history of Qatar the peninsula became a part of the Ottoman (Turkish) province of al-Hasa.

It should be recalled in this connection that during the Ottoman rule of eastern Arabia, the Ottoman Pasha asked the various sheikhs for only nominal allegiance. Thus, under Ottoman rule the sheikhs of Qatar were virtually independent. This case becomes very clear under Muhammad's successor, Sheikh Kassim, son of Muhammad (1878-1913), who was a great fighter and who managed to spread his influence all over the peninsula. He fought the British, the Ottomans, and many of the local sheikhs who threatened his individual rule over the peninsula, including al-Khalifa of Bahrain.

'Abd Allah ibn Kassim al-Thani

However, this zeal for a free hand in the running of Qatar affairs did not outlive Sheikh Kassim, for during the reign of his son 'Abd Allah (1915-1949), Qatar became a British protected sheikhdom. The Ottomans continued to recognize the Sheikh of Qatar as their local deputy ruler until 1914, *i.e.*, until the beginning of World War I, but on the eclipse of Ottoman rule in Arabia, the Sheikh of Qatar signed a treaty in 1916 with Britain embodying the provisions contained in what was called the "exclusive" treaties already signed by Bahrain and Kuwait. It should also be remembered that it was under 'Abd Allah that Zubara was annexed to Qatar in 1937. Zubara has always been the heel of Achilles in Bahrain-Qatar relations.

Oil and State

Sheikh Ahmad al-Thani and his predecessors ruled Qatar after the same traditional local tribal government to be seen predominating as a form of state in other eastern Arabian sheikhdoms. No major changes took place in Qatar in the field of government even after the exploitation of oil. The sheikhdom is headed by the sheikh who, since the treaty of 1916 with the British, is chosen from among the al-Thani family with the formal blessings of the British political agent who usually resides at al-Doha, the capital. In accordance with the provisions of the treaty, the political agent runs the external affairs of the sheikhdom, and, though not officially, he is consulted on important decisions affecting the internal affairs as well.

The enormous wealth which oil brought into Qatar has had its effects on the internal administration of the sheikhdom. As a result of the spread of education and the rapid growth of towns, roads, and the like, a great deal of the administration of the various departments passed to the hands of the civil servants, both Qataris and foreigners. However, this should not indicate that a radical change in the tribal system of government is taking place. The Sheikh of Qatar is still the sole ruler. There is no assembly as in Kuwait.

Qatar, Bahrain, and the Trucial States

In the field of politics in the area, Qatar has always been on bad terms with Bahrain. This resulted from the Zubara affair. Bahrain did not accept Qatar's annexation of Zubara in 1937. But Bahrain seems helpless, for the time being, in doing anything to reassert its rights there. Another political problem is the demarcation of the southern boundaries with Abu Dhabi. A similar problem arises with Saudi Arabia too. Will Qatar through the newly proposed Union of the Arabian Gulf Sheikhdoms find a solution to those border disputes? And if so, what will Qatar offer Bahrain to compensate her for Zubara?

Qatar and the Persian Gulf States

Since the British government has indicated its willingness to withdraw from the Gulf area in 1971, it becomes quite apparent that Qatar's 1916 treaty with Britain will have to be replaced by another, and not necessarily with Great Britain. Here again there is the possibility of the Union of the Arabian Gulf Sheikhdoms taking over certain responsibilities from Great Britain. But the Union might be unable to work on its own, when other powers in the area are taken into consideration, since Persia, Saudi Arabia, and Iraq each have by far a larger population than all those sheikhdoms put together.

Qatar, however, can still play an important role in shaping new policies in the remaining years of this 20th century in the Persian Gulf area working jointly with the other sheikhdoms bordering on the gulf and lying to the south of Qatar.

The Trucial States (Sheikhdoms)

As has already been pointed out, there stretch on the western shores of the gulf between Qatar and Oman the territories of the Trucial states on what is called Trucial Oman or the Trucial Coast. The denomination (Trucial) came from the Perpetual Treaty of Peace which was signed by the various Arab sheikhs of that coast in 1853. The names of these sheikhdoms running from west to east, are Abu Dhabi, Dubai, Sharjah, 'Ajman, Umm al-Qaiwain, Ras al-Khaimah, and Fujairah. Perhaps the best introduction to the study of the governments and politics of these sheikhdoms will be found in a brief narrative describing their rise as states on the eastern Arabian shores.

Historical Background. As early as 1498, Shihab al-Din Ahmad ibn Majid, the famous sea pilot from Ras al-Khaimah, met Vasco da Gama in Malindi on the East African coast and directed him to the sea route leading from there to India. So it was a native of Ras al-Khaimah who directed the Portuguese to India, a fact significant enough to prove that the Trucial coast was a center of seafaring as early as the 15th century. But with the coming of the Portuguese to the Indian

Ocean and the Persian Gulf, Ras al-Khaimah and other centers of trade on the western littoral of the gulf were occupied by the Portuguese, and their trade and even their political life came to a standstill. After the expulsion of the Portuguese from Oman and the gulf early in the 17th century, Ras al-Khaimah and other ports came to life again, and by the 18th century Ras al-Khaimah was famous as a residence of the Qawasim (sometimes called Jawasim, plural of Qasim or Jasim) who were a great seafaring people and who, towards the end of that century, became notorious pirates—hence the name the Pirate Coast.

The Qawasim were masters of the Trucial coast for the second half of the 18th century and the early years of the 19th as well. Said to have emigrated to eastern Arabia from Samarra in Iraq in the 17th century, the al-Qawasim belong to the northern branch of Arabs, *i.e.,* Mudar or 'Adnan. There were other Arab tribes living in this littoral of the gulf before the arrival of the Qawasim. Famous among these tribes, mention must be made of the Bani Yas, perhaps the largest confederation of all. The Bani Yas gave their name to the same coast as it was called "Sir Bani Yas" or Oman al-Sir. This denomination was kept until the early years of the 18th century where we can trace it in Arab authors from Iraq and the Arabian peninsula.

Worthwhile noting in this context is that among the population of the Trucial sheikhdoms, which totals about 120,000, the great majority are settled Arabs. The following table illustrates the population break down among the Trucial area:

TABLE 18-1
Estimates of Area and Population

Trucial State	Area Square Miles	Population		Persons per Sq. Mile
		Capital Town	*Whole Country*	
Abu Dhabi	26,000	8,000	25,000	1.0
Dubai	1,500	40,000	60,000	40.0
Sharjah	1,000	9,000	15,000	15.0
Ras al-Khaimah ...	650	5,000	12,000	18.0
Fujairah	450	2,000	3,500	7.8
Umm al-Qaiwain ...	300	2,500	3,000	10.0
Ajman	100	2,000	2,500	25.0
Total	30,000	68,500	121,000	4.0

From a glance at this table one can see that Abu Dhabi is the largest in area, Dubai is the most densely populated, while Ajman is the smallest. Among the population are a few Persians, Balauchis, Pakistanis, and Indians, as well as many expatriates from other parts of the Arab world—especially Palestinians and Iraqis. Following is a similar table concerning neighboring countries, for the sake of comparison with the Trucial states:

TABLE 18-2
Countries Bordering the Persian Gulf

Country	Area Sq. Miles	Population in Thousands	Persons per Sq. Mile
Saudi Arabia	927,000	6,000	6
Persia (Iran)	628,000	21,000	33
Iraq	172,000	6,539	38
Muscat Oman	82,000	550	7
Trucial Coast	30,000	121	4
Kuwait	6,200	468	75
Qatar	4,000	45	11
Bahrain	213	143	761

Britain and the Trucial Sheikhdoms

Early in the 18th century, Britain, represented by the English East India Company, began its monopoly of the trade and politics of the gulf area. Ras al-Khaimah, together with other Qasimi ports, was attacked in 1819 by the Indian navy. A series of treaties were signed by the various sheikhs of the Trucial coast during the 19th century, and the once united coast under the Qawasim divided into separate small sheikhdoms or political entities, the last of which to come into existence as a sheikhdom was Fujairah in 1952. It should also be stated that out of seven Trucial sheikhdoms, five were orginally under Qasimi control or belonged to the Qasimi tribe. These are Sharjah, Ajman, Umm al-Qaiwain, Ras al-Khaimah, and Fujairah.

Administration of the Trucial Sheikhdoms

Change that swept over the old administration in Kuwait, Bahrain, and Qatar as a result of the discovery of oil will soon reach the Trucial sheikhdoms. Indeed, it has reached Abu Dhabi which has recently become a rich oil-producing sheikhdom. However, until a noticeable change in administration becomes clear, a study of the present system which is run by the British government is in order.

The seven sheikhdoms have been dealt with collectively by the British government ever since treaty relations were established. For many years relations with them were conducted through an Arab residency agent with his head-quarters at Sharjah. Then at the beginning of World War II, a British political officer was appointed to Sharjah. In 1953 his status was raised to that of political agent, and in 1954 his headquarters were transferred to Budai, where a new agency was built for him. In 1951 a Council of Trucial States Rulers was formed with the object of inducing them to adopt a common policy in administrative matters, such as regulations for motor traffic, the issue of nationality and passport laws, and so on. This council meets two or three times a year, and education and health committees have been established. It is hoped that as a result of the discovery of oil in Abu Dhabi and the prospects of its discovery in the other sheikhdoms, a central administrative office will be set up.

In 1951 the British government, with the cooperation of the rulers, raised a force called the Trucial Oman Levies for the maintenance of law and order and the protection of the sheikhdoms against external aggression. Its strength was originally 500 men, but soon it was raised to 1,000. These forces, who came to be called the Trucial Oman Scouts, are recruited locally but are officered and trained by British personnel who volunteer for the service. Recently, police forces coming under the authority of the states themselves have been established in Abu Dhabi and Dubai. The headquarters of the Trucial Scouts, however, is Sharjah—and they played a major role in driving the Saudi forces away from the Buraimi Oasis during the crisis of 1955.

The rulers mostly administer "palm tree justice" personally in cases which are not referred to a *Qadi* for settlement according to *Sharia* (Muslim) law and exercise jurisdiction only over their own or each other's subjects. All foreigners, whether Muslims or non-Muslims, are subject to the jurisdiction of the political agent. Some cases of mixed nature are settled by a joint court presided over by the political agent and the ruler concerned. In the British House of Commons on May 15, 1963 the Lord Privy Seal stated that the British government would relinquish jurisdiction when the development of satisfactory legal and judicial systems justify such action. Already steps are being taken in this direction in Abu Dhabi.

To recapitulate the British relations with the Trucial sheikhdoms, one might say that though Britain was ultimately responsible in administration, the actual handling of affairs was delegated. Until 1858, all contacts of a diplomatic or administrative nature were conducted through the East India Company: from 1858, by the government of Bombay acting for the British crown; and from 1873 to 1947, by the government of British India. Since 1947, when India attained independence, negotiations and contacts have been effected through the foreign office in London.

By virtue of the 1892 excluse treaty, the British government became responsible for the external affairs of the sheikhdoms. These affairs were entrusted to the political resident for the gulf at first, but later became the responsibility of the political officers on the Trucial coast in Sharjah who later became political agents in Dubai and Abu Dhabi.

Internal Affairs

Having discussed the British role in the external affairs of the sheikhdoms, it might be useful to underline some unseen acts of British interference in the domestic affairs of the sheikhdoms. "The close personal contact maintained between the political agents and the rulers," says a political resident, "is an outstanding feature of the British position in the Persian Gulf. They meet each other frequently, and more often socially than for official talks. Possibly the social meetings are more important than the official ones, as a hint dropped here and there in the course of casual conversation is often more effective than formal advice, and the rulers, being Arabs, are quick to resent any attempt to teach them their business." Another Britisher writes, "The British government does not interfere in the internal affairs of the various states except that jurisdiction over certain classes of foreigners is in the hands of the political agents." This neutrality of the agents could be questioned in such events as when two rulers were deposed: Sheikh Saqr ibn Sultan al-Qasimi of Sharjah who was deposed in 1965, and Sheikh Shakhbut ibn Sultan of Abu Dhabi, deposed in August 1966 and replaced by his younger brother Sheikh Zaid.

The Frontiers Problems

Since no agreement has yet been reached on the frontiers of the seven Trucial sheikhdoms, there will always arise points of dispute among those rulers. The same thing applies to the boundaries with other neighboring sheikhdoms, sultanates, and kingdoms, such as the boundaries of Abu Dhabi with Qatar, and the boundaries with Saudi Arabia and Muscat. Perhaps the sharpest dispute has been that of al-Buraimi among Abu Dhabi, Muscat, and Saudi Arabia.

The Union of the Arabian Gulf Sheikhdoms

The Union of the Arabian Gulf Sheikhdoms was proposed in February 1968, as a response from the sheikhdoms of Bahrain, Qatar, and the Trucial coast to the British decision to withdraw from the Gulf by 1971. To appreciate the idea behind establishing a union of this nature, the student of Persian Gulf politics must keep in mind the Persian claims to Bahrain, the Saudi interests in the lands of the sheikhdoms forming the Union, Iraq's presence in the area, and last but not least, the position of Kuwait towards the union.

It is difficult for most experts on the gulf to visualize the idea of a union of this nature among the concerned sheikhdoms. Yet, if the British do withdraw, it is only natural for these sheikhdoms to look to their right and left in search of someone to protect their interests, especially their wealth of petroleum. Each of the sheikhdoms has a problem with one or more of its neighbors, but the surrounding big powers will think twice before attacking any one sheikhdom which is a member of a union of sheikhdoms.

It should not be assumed that the union has been successfully formed by this date. Certain questions, such as those relating to border disputes, are facing the rulers who will meet to facilitate the establishment of the proposed union. The question is, will the union be born in the near future or not? There are certain factors which indicate the chances of success. The danger of being swallowed by more powerful neighbors will certainly tell the rulers that "in unity there is strength." Also, the tribes of the sheikhdoms, as we have continuously pointed out, are related in the main. Together, such factors have already promoted a natural unity. Some of the rulers in whose territories oil was found first, began helping the poorer sheikhdoms in a manner which did not make the latter feel that they were given alms. Indeed, Sheikh Zaid of Abu Dhabi made it clear that Abu Dhabi's oil was not her own but to be shared by the neighboring sheikhdoms, in whose territories oil is still being sought. And Kuwait, though not yet a member of the suggested union, has been giving aid in the fields of health and education since 1955. Whether it will be possible for Kuwait, if the union materializes, to keep from joining the union or not associating herself with it remains to be seen.

SELECTED BIBLIOGRAPHY

There are several monographs and official government publications written in Arabic which deal with eastern Arabia in modern and contemporary times. These should be consulted by any one who wants to comprehensively understand developments in government and politics of the area. The following list of authorities will help shed light upon the early modern period and the contemporary period too.

Abu-Hakima, Ahmad Mustafa, *History of Eastern Arabia (1750-1800)* (Beirut, 1965); Belgrave, Charles, *The Pirate Coast* (London, 1966); Belgrave, James H. D., *Welcome to Bahrain* (London, 1965); Fenelon, K. G., *The Trucial States, a Brief Economic Survey* (Beirut, 1967); Hay, Rupert, *The Persian Gulf States* (Washington, 1959); Hewins, Ralph, *A Golden Dream, the Miracle of Kuwait* (London, 1963); Kelly, J. B., *Britain and the Persian Gulf, 1795-1880* (Oxford, 1968) and *Eastern Arabian Frontiers* (London, 1964); Landen, Robert Geran, *Oman Since 1856* (Princeton, 1967); Lorimer, J. G., *Gazetteer of the Persian Gulf, 'Oman and Central Arabia*, two vols. (Calcutta, 1915); Low, Charles Rathbon, *History of the Indian Navy (1613-1863)*, vols. 1 & 2 (London, 1877); Marlow, John, *The Persian Gulf in the Twentieth Century* (London, 1962); Moyse-Bartlett, H., *The Pirates of Trucial Oman* (London, 1966); Wilson, A. T., *The Persian Gulf* (Oxford, 1954); Winder, R. Bayly, *Saudi Arabia in the Nineteenth Century* (New York, 1965).

part IV

INTERNATIONAL RELATIONS OF THE MIDDLE EAST

chapter 19

The Middle East in
World Affairs*

The Middle East is an important factor in the politics of the world primarily because of its geographical location as an international crossroads between the Eurasian and African continents and of its vast resources of petroleum. As Stephen H. Longrigg has maintained, the primary task of providing the world with next century's demand for energy and fuel seems "ineluctably to belong to the Middle Eastern oilfields." Even with the advances in nuclear technology, the "wells of power" strewn along the crossroads may still be of significance, and the West will overlook the strategic and economic significance of the Middle East only at its peril. By 1967 daily production was estimated at some 10.3 million barrels, as compared with 8.6 million for the United States, and crude reserves were estimated at 250 billion barrels, perhaps three fourths of the world total. In 1967 Middle Eastern fields supplied some 90 percent of Japanese requirements for crude oil and about one half of European requirements. By 1977 it was calculated that the Middle East would be supplying more than 20 million of the 58 million barrel daily requirement in the world market. These are very material considerations. But it may also be observed that the Middle East was of interest and concern to peoples over the world because it was the birthplace of three of the great world religions: Judaism, Christianity, and Islam. The Middle East had been a center for the propagation of principles, institutions, and cultures through which much of the Western world had become civilized.

I

Granted its strategic position along the shores of the Mediterranean—the inland sea—and its position at the international crossroads, it is perfectly natural

---

*Harry N. Howard, professor, School of International Service, The American University, Washington, D.C.

that the Middle East should have been involved in world affairs, as it were, from the dawn of written history, as indeed it has been. One need not recount the ancient story here, but he may observe that the Turkish Straits have been a bone of contention and conflict since the period of the Trojan Wars (1194-1184 B.C.) and that the Suez problem may be said to date from the era of Cambyses (531-521 B.C.) in the sixth century before the birth of Christ. The Athenian Empire, the Roman Empire, and the Byzantine Empire built up much of their power in the East around the position of Constantinople (Istanbul) and the Straits, and control of the Middle Eastern land routes, in an earlier period, was important to the wealth, power, and prestige of the more ancient empires. Similarly, the Arab empires, during the medieval era of western Europe, found the center of much of their power and position and wealth in what is now the Arab East. Here the Ottoman Empire grew and expanded over the centuries (ca. 1453-1699) and entered into its era of decline, with its center at Constantinople, astride Europe and Asia, at the Turkish Straits. Today the nexus of air routes through the Middle East must be added to those of the land and the sea to complete the strategic picture of world interest and concern.

II

The modern phase of the Middle East in world politics came with the advent of Napoleon into the area, in his attempt to strike a mortal blow at the British Empire (1798-1799) along British routes to India, and with the introduction of the new French revolutionary doctrines of "Liberty, Equality, and Fraternity" and the new technologies and science which were to bring about basic transformations in the Middle East. Already the Ottoman Empire had long been in contact with the Kingdom of France (1535), and in the 17th and 18th centuries it had fought numerous wars with the Hapsburg and Russian Empires. These struggles culminated in the treaties of Karlowitz (1699), which marked the decline of the Ottoman Empire, and Kuçuk Kaynarca (1774), which signaled the weakening of Ottoman dominance in the Black Sea and the Straits and the more definite beginnings of Russian ambition and influence in the region of Constantinople (Tsargrad). Russian influence reached a kind of zenith with the signature of the treaty of Hünkar Iskelese (1833), with the achievement of an Ottoman-Russian alliance, under which the Straits were to continue barred to non-riverain warships, when the empire was under severe attack by the forces of Muhammad Ali and his son Ibrahim of Egypt. Although that treaty lasted a bare six years, its influence remained, and the principles embodied in it became one of the cornerstones of Imperial Russian and later Soviet policy in the Middle East.

The primary influences in the Ottoman Empire and the Middle East during the 19th century, however, undoubtedly were those of France and Great Britain. France had had long association with the Middle East dating, in a certain mythical sense, from the period of the Christian Crusades in the 11th to the

13th centuries. Francis I had made a landmark treaty with Suleiman Kanuni (the Magnificent) in 1535, which, among other things, embodied the capitulatory regime, giving foreign traders and residents in the Ottoman Empire very special rights as distinct from subjects. The impact of the Napoleonic invasion in 1798, whether in Egypt or later in the Balkan peninsula, had been profound and helped to initiate the modernizing tendencies both in Cairo and Constantinople, as well as along the Mediterranean seaboard of Syria and Palestine. Moreover, France annexed Algeria in 1830 and later turned it into a part of metropolitan France. In 1881 it made a protectorate out of Tunisia, and in 1904, in the Entente Cordiale with Great Britain, France similarly converted the independent Kingdom of Morocco into a French protectorate. Syria and Lebanon also came under strong French influence (1860-1861), with large French commercial penetration and profound French cultural institutions (St. Joseph University, 1875), while French influence at Constantinople was also very significant during the mid-19th century.

Great Britain, it has been well remarked, really had no Middle Eastern policy as such, but was interested in protecting British routes to India, the crown jewel of the empire. She also wanted to prevent the Ottoman Empire from falling under the control of any other states, especially of Imperial Russia as the Crimean War (1853-1856) well demonstrated, to say nothing of British policy during the troubled era of 1875-1878 and the Russo-Ottoman war of that period, when Russian armies seemed on the point of taking Constantinople. British policy held to the maintenance of the independence and the territorial integrity of the Ottoman Empire until the advent of Imperial Germany on the Middle Eastern scene, after the creation of the German Empire in 1871. With increasing German economic and political pressure toward the southeast, especially after the advent of William II to the throne of his fathers, British policy changed signally if subtly, whether as to the integrity of the Ottoman Empire or as to relations with Imperial Russia. Already, in 1875 it secured 44 percent of the shares of the newly constructed Suez Canal (1869), and in 1882 it occupied Egypt and took over the administration of that unhappy land, as it had begun administration of the island of Cyprus in 1878. Now the British government came to the conclusion that the Ottoman Empire might not, indeed, be maintained in its territorial integrity, that bargains might have to be struck with its rivals in the area, and that, in newer arrangements in the Turkish Straits (1902), the Russian fleet might be allowed in the Mediterranean, under suitable conditions, to redress the naval balance in the inland sea. Bargains were struck with Germany around the great project of the Baghdad Railway (1903, 1914) on the very eve of the outbreak of World War I, in projects for the partition of the Ottoman Empire into spheres of interest and influence, from which, however, Imperial Russia, which was not yet interested in partition, was excluded.

Meanwhile, although it is seldom noted in the standard histories of the "Eastern Question," there was another power which was developing an interest and concern with the Middle East, especially in the 19th century, even if it had no politico-strategic interest in the area. This was the United States of America. Already, as early as the 18th century, American merchant vessels were plying their uncertain trade in the Middle East. The Continental Congress had sought the recognition of the Sublime Porte in the Ottoman Empire, and a treaty was signed with the sultan of Morocco during the Washington administration which recognized Moroccan independence (1792). Early in the 19th century, under President Jefferson, the United States fought a naval war with the Barbary states along the North African coast of the Mediterranean Sea (1801-1805). American missionary educators began going out to the Middle East to inaugurate the great work which culminated, in many ways, in the foundation of such institutions as Robert College (1863), the American University of Beirut (1866), the Istanbul Women's College (1871), and the American University of Cairo (1919), along with many other institutions of lesser status, out from which radiated a profound influence in the area. The first American businessmen also went out to the Middle East during this period, and on May 7, 1830 the United States signed its first treaty with the Ottoman Empire—a commercial treaty which stressed freedom for American commerce with most favored nation treatment, the maintenance of capitulatory rights (which the United States gave up with great reluctance after 1923), and freedom of commercial transit and navigation in the Turkish Straits. Indeed, in 1871 the United States enunciated the principle that the Sublime Porte had no legal right to close the Straits while the empire was at peace, even to American warships, and refused to recognize the right *de jure*, although it made no special issue in the matter. While the commercial-economic interest remained largely aspirational rather than actual down to the period of 1939, and there were no politico-strategic interests, it may be observed that two Americans, Henry Eckford and his assistant Foster Rhodes, practically rebuilt the Ottoman fleet after the Battle of Navarino (1827) in the 1830s, while a group of former Union and Confederate officers supervised the modernization of the Egyptian armed forces, carried out extensive surveys, and projected a dam at Aswan during 1870-1883. But the missionary-educational-philanthropic enter-prise remained the most enduring of American interests and concerns in the Middle East.

III

World War I brought about dramatic and far-reaching changes in the Middle East, which proved to be one of the important theaters in that great conflict. During the war, plans were drawn up among the Allies for partition of the Ottoman Empire, under which, generally, Russia was to have Constantinople and the Straits, France was to have Syria, and Great Britain was to have Mesopotamia and Palestine in addition to areas which it already held, to say nothing of territory assigned to Italy. Agreements were reached with some of the Arab leaders, among them kings Husayn and Ibn Saud, and declarations and statements of policy were issued in the interest of assuring victory in the war. On the one hand, the British government issued the Balfour Declaration on November 2, 1917, with its promise that a national home for the Jews would be established in Palestine, subject to the two conditions that the action would not prejudice the civil and religious rights of the "indigenous inhabitants" (the Arabs, about 92 percent of the population) or the rights and status of citizens of other countries who happened to be of Jewish faith or heritage. On the other, France and Great Britain, in a declaration of November 7, 1918 advised the Arabs that their aim in fighting the war in the Middle East was "the complete and definite emancipation of the peoples so long oppressed by the Turks and the establishment of national governments and administrations deriving their authority from the initiative and free choice of the indigenous populations." Herein lay some of the basic issues underlying the conflict, a conflict between two secular and genuine nationalisms over Palestine which the Arabs wanted to keep and the Zionists to take. From that time on, it would appear, the conflict was inevitable and irrepressible, granted the Arab determination to resist what they deemed to be the Zionist intrusion into an Arab land.

But, as Arthur James Balfour, the British foreign secretary, explained at the Paris Peace Conference on August 11, 1919, the promises were often conflicting in substance. The documents were "not consistent with each other"[1] and represented no clear-cut policy. The policy which they adumbrated was "not really the policy of the Allied and Associated Powers," although none had entirely lost its validity or could be treated as of merely historic interest. As to Palestine, the British foreign secretary observed that the powers had "made no statement of fact" which was "not admittedly wrong, and no declaration of policy which, at least in the letter," they had "not always intended to violate." Nevertheless, with the end of World War I, it was clear that the Ottoman Empire was passing into history, and there was the basic issue as to what was to be done with the remnants.

While President Wilson had sought a settlement of Middle Eastern problems on the basis of reasonable consideration and the principle of self-determination, and sent a commission to that area to study the problems of peacemaking on the ground, little attention was paid at the time to its findings. In the end, settlement was made on the basis of the secret interallied agreements negotiated during World War I. Syria and Lebanon were placed under French, Palestine with its Jewish national home and Transjordan under British mandate, while Iraq became an independent state in 1932. Egypt remained a British protectorate until 1936, while King Ibn Saud achieved independence in 1927 in Saudi Arabia. North Africa—the Maghrib—remained under French rule, while Italy remained seemingly in firm control of Tripolitania and Cyrenaica (Libya). Under the guidance of Mustafa Kemal Ataturk, the Turkish nation emerged from the matrix of the Ottoman Empire and moved through a great series of

---

[1]E. L. Woodward and Rohan Butler, eds., *Documents on British Foreign Policy, 1919-1939*. First Series, IV, pp. 340-349.

revolutionary reforms toward modernization, after having fought a war with Greece during 1919-1922. Peace did not come to the Middle East until a signature of the Treaty of Lausanne on July 24, 1923.

During the interwar era, as Hans Kohn pointed out almost 40 years ago, the Middle East entered an epoch in which nationalism was "the highest and most vitally symbolic social and intellectual form" and set "its stamp upon the whole era," in contrast to religion which hitherto had been the determining factor in the area.[2] While the force of nationalism did not oust religion, it took its place beside it, sometimes fortified it, and sometimes transformed and impaired it. National symbols acquired religious authority, and the truth which men would "defend with their lives" was "no longer exclusively religious . . . but in increasing measure national." While France, with the exception of North Africa, gradually receded from the Arab East during the interwar period, that period was, in reality, Britain's moment in the Middle East, when it seemed supreme as arbiter of Middle Eastern destinies. But the winds of change were blowing. World War II was to alter the picture fundamentally. Almost immediately thereafter the nationalist storm signals went up throughout the Middle East.

IV

The Middle East again was a significant center of military and diplomatic activity during World War II, as Germany moved down through the Balkan peninsula toward Turkey (especially after 1940) and the heart of the area, and Italy and Germany struck through North Africa, only to be ultimately stopped by the British Eighth Army. At the very outset of the war, Turkey entered into alliance with Great Britain and France (October 19, 1939), while the Soviet Union moved in seeming consonance with the Axis. In November 1940 during and following the Hitler-Ribbentrop-Molotov discussions in Berlin, the Soviet Union demanded a change in the Montreux Convention of the Straits (1936) which would enable it to control passage into the Black Sea, through what it considered to be a Soviet security zone; and it appears she also wanted territorial cessions in eastern Turkey (the Kars-Ardahan area). These demands, coupled with others, as a price for possible Soviet adherence to the Axis, alarmed the German government, however and, in any event, on June 22, 1941 German forces attacked the Soviet Union. The German campaign to take Alexandria in the drive across North Africa following conquest of the Balkan peninsula and Greece, with control of the Middle East as the objective, did not succeed, thanks to the British Eighth Army under General Montgomery.

The end of World War II introduced a new era into the international politics of the Middle East, which remained a center of rivalry and contest. On the one hand, the states of that area moved even more clearly and often with much violence toward independence and sovereignty. On the other, the United States

---

[2] Hans Kohn, *Nationalism and Imperialism in the Hither East* (1932), pp. 19-22, 120-121.

and the Soviet Union became the primary rivals among the Greater Powers in the area, with Great Britain, however important its interests at the outset of the period, and France in the secondary roles. Following the war, it was clear that the Soviet Union under the Stalin dictatorship had set out on a course of domination throughout the Middle East, as it had in eastern and southeastern Europe. This was clear in the Berlin discussions of November 1940, and there was little or nothing in the record to indicate any basic change immediately following the war.

During the Yalta Conference (February 4-11, 1945), before the formal conclusion of the conflict, the Soviet Union made known its position relative to the Straits, and on March 19, 1945 it denounced the Turco-Soviet nonaggression agreement of December 17, 1925. As the price of a new agreement with Turkey the Soviet Union demanded a new regime of the Straits, with military bases in the area, to be elaborated by Turkey and "the Black Sea powers" and cessions of territory in eastern Anatolia before making a new treaty, which would have converted Turkey into a Soviet satellite on the model of those being established throughout eastern and southeastern Europe. In June 1945 these demands were reiterated with emphasis and, as the war came to an end in Europe, renewed pressures were brought against Turkey on the part of the Soviet Union. At the same time, the United Kingdom and the United States entered the diplomatic lists against the Soviet position in behalf of Turkey and supported the Turkish government in its opposition to the Soviet demands to make the Straits a Soviet-Turkish preserve, both at the Potsdam Conference (July-August 1945) and in the diplomatic exchanges and consultations which followed in 1945 and 1946. Indeed, as the pressures on Turkey continued, on August 15, 1946 the United States advised the Turkish government of its very firm position although, like the United Kingdom and even Turkey, it was willing to make legitimate concessions in the regime of the Straits, even if unwilling to have the entire area fall under Soviet control. Insofar as the United States was concerned, President Truman had already characterized the seriousness and importance of the problem throughout the Middle East in an Army Day address of April 6, 1946, when he stated:

> This area contains vast natural resources. It lies across the most convenient routes of land, air, and water communications. It is consequently an area of great economic and strategic importance, the nations of which are not strong enough individually or collectively to withstand powerful aggression.
>
> It is easy to see, therefore, how the Near and Middle East might become an arena of intense rivalry between outside powers, and how such rivalry might suddenly erupt into conflict.
>
> No country, great or small, has legitimate interests in the Near and Middle East which cannot be reconciled with the interests of other nations through the United Nations. The United Nations have a right to insist that

the sovereignty and integrity of the countries of the Near and Middle East must not be threatened by coercion or penetration.[3]

President Truman had well described the situation in the Middle East, although it was only part of the story at the time. The Soviet Union, which had refused to withdraw its armed forces from Iran within six months after the end of the conflict, brought pressures against that country, not merely through the maintenance of the Red army in Azerbaijan and the establishment of the socalled Kurdish Republic in Iran, but through the subversive activities of the Tudeh party in Iran. Similarly, during this early period of 1945-1946, the Soviet Union demanded a trusteeship in Libya, and held up the Italian peace treaty with Greece until it could secure a commercial (naval) base in the Dodecanese Islands, a demand which, however, was given up in 1946. In Greece, the Soviet Union encouraged guerrilla action against the Greek government through its Balkan satellites, Albania, Bulgaria, and Yugoslavia, and sought to dominate the country through the EAM and the Communist party (KKE). Had it achieved its aims, Greece too would have become a satellite, and the Soviet Union would have arrived on the European side of the Turkish Straits in the eastern Mediterranean Sea. But not merely that. If one adds to the Soviet ambitions in Greece, Turkey and Iran those relative to the Arab world, it is easy to see that the entire Middle East would have fallen under Soviet influence, and the threat to western Europe would have been grave, indeed.

This was the grand Soviet design which brought the United States into the Middle East after the end of World War II in an enduring sense of the term. As early as December 3, 1941, in extending lend-lease assistance to Turkey, President Roosevelt had declared the defense of Turkey essential to that of the United States and ultimately, during World War II, the defense of the Middle East had been declared vital to that of the United States. Now the challenge, it seemed, had come in the period immediately following the war from the Soviet Union. The United States Sixth Fleet, the most powerful which the inland sea had ever seen in all its long history of peace and war, came into being in 1946, and it had come evidently, after more than two decades, to stay.

The test in Turkey was met. Now that Greece was under threat not merely from domestic troubles and problems after World War II, but from guerrilla activity aided and abetted from across the frontiers in Albania, Bulgaria, and Yugoslavia, the United States moved through the United Nations to find out what was going on along the northern frontiers of Greece. With the United Kingdom no longer able to bear the burdens in Greece and Turkey, on March 12, 1947 in one of the most far-reaching of the great pronouncements of American foreign policy, President Truman announced that the United States was prepared to assist both Greece and Turkey in defending their independence.[4] He not only

---

[3] Raymond Dennett and Robert K. Turner, eds., *Documents on American Foreign Relations, 1945-1946,* VIII, p. 29.

[4] *A Decade of American Foreign Policy: Basic Documents, 1941-9.* 81st Congress, 1st Session. Senate Document No. 123 (Washington, D.C., 1950), pp. 1253-1257.

indicated that if Greece fell under the control of an armed minority, the effect upon Turkey "would be immediate and serious," but "confusion and disorder might well spread throughout the entire Middle East." Moreover, if the United States, the only country at the time capable of rendering assistance, failed to aid Greece and Turkey "in this fateful hour," the effect would "be far-reaching to the West as to the East." President Truman believed that "it must be the policy of the United States to support free peoples who are resisting attempted subjugation by armed minorities or by outside pressure," that they must be assisted to "work out their own destinies in their own way," and that the assistance should be primarily through economic and financial aid. Congress was asked to provide authority for assistance to Greece and Turkey in the amount of $400,000 for the period ending June 10, 1948.

V

Like the United Kingdom and France, the United States was interested in the containment of the explosive situation surrounding the Arab-Israel conflict, following the establishment of the State of Israel and the ensuing conflict during 1948. The Western powers, along with the Soviet Union, had supported the partition of Palestine (November 29, 1947), and armistice agreements were achieved in 1949, even if peace were not to be attained. A Conciliation Commission for Palestine, on which France, Turkey, and the United States were represented, failed to move the contending parties to the conference table, although a United Nations Truce Supervision Organization (UNTSO) policed the armistice lines and served to limit the incidence of conflict. On May 25, 1950 France, Great Britain, and the United States issued a Tripartite Declaration which recognized that both the Arab states and Israel needed to maintain a certain level of armed forces to assure "their internal security and their legitimate self-defense and to permit them to play their part in the defense of the area as a whole," and recalled "their opposition to the development of an arms race between the Arab states and Israel."[5] Moreover, the three governments declared: their deep interest in and their desire to promote the establishment and maintenance of peace and stability in the area and their unalterable opposition to the use of force or threat of force between any of the states in that area. The three governments, should they find that any of these states was preparing to violate frontiers or armistice lines, would consistently with their obligations as members of the United Nations, immediately take action both within and outside the United Nations to prevent such violation.

The statement was received as a declaration of policy on the part of the three powers relative to the Arab-Isreal conflict, which embodied no direct commitments to either side, much less an alliance with any state. On May 25 President Truman emphasized the desire of the United States "to promote the maintenance of peace in the Near East," and the belief the the declaration

---

[5]*American Foreign Policy: Basic Documents, 1950-1955,* II, p. 2237.

would stimulate increased confidence in future security and contribute toward the well-being of the peoples of that area. While it may be questioned that it did so, and its spirit was soon violated (1954) in secret Franco-Israeli arms arrangements, the declaration remained as the only public position of the United States relative to the Arab-Israeli conflict, as a policy of containment, in which the major interest and involvement of the United States was officially expressed.

By 1952 the particular threat to Greece had come to an end, and the Soviet pressures on both Turkey and Iran had eased. Indeed, after the death of Stalin on March 5, 1953, Soviet tactics in the Middle East shifted considerably, even if the basic aims of policy had not necessarily changed. During the latter part of the Truman administration, partly in order to solve certain problems in Anglo-Egyptian relations centering around the presence of British troops in the Suez Canal Zone, the United States, the United Kingdom, France, and Turkey proposed the establishment of a Middle East Command (October 13, 1951), inviting Egypt to become a founding member of an Allied Middle East Command as an equal partner in the defense of the area against external aggression. Among other things, it was pointed out that Egypt belonged to the "free world" and that consequently its defense "and that of the Middle East in general" was "equally vital to other democratic nations." If Egypt were prepared to cooperate, the United Kingdom would be prepared to agree to the suppression of the Anglo-Egyptian Treaty of 1936 and to withdraw from Egypt such forces as were not allocated to the Middle East Command. The Egyptian government, however, rejected the proposal on October 15, and the four inviting powers, on November 1, among other things reiterated their view that peace was "indivisible," that defense of the Middle East was "vital to the free world," and that it could be secured "only by the cooperation of all interested states." Within that context, the Middle East Command was "intended to be the center of cooperative efforts for the defense of the area as a whole; the achievement of peace and security in the area through the Middle East Command" would bring it "social and economic advancement." Its function was to assist and support cooperating states in defense of the Middle East against external aggression. It would not interfere in problems and disputes arising within the area, such as the Arab-Israel conflict (although Israel and the other Arab states were invited to cooperate with it), and would not affect existing arrangements relating to such matters, notably the armistice agreements of 1949 and the Tripartite Declaration of May 25, 1950.[6]

Nothing came of this ill-conceived project. As early as November 24, 1951, the Soviet Union charged that it represented an attempt to draw the Middle East into "the aggressive Atlantic bloc," which would deprive the Middle Eastern states of their national independence. Nevertheless, when Prime Minister Churchill visited Washington in January 1952, the United Kingdom and the United States reaffirmed their resolution "to promote the stability, peaceful

---

[6]*Ibid.*, II, pp. 2180-2187.

development, and prosperity of the countries of the Middle East" and considered it essential "for the furtherance of our common purposes that an Allied Middle East Command should be set up as soon as possible." As regards Egypt, they were confident that the proposal offered "the best prospect of relieving the present tension." By 1952 the proposal took a somewhat different form in the Middle East Defense Organization (MEDO), but it was realized now that it could not be worked out overnight. By this time, however, it seemed a dead proposition, and it was no longer pushed. It had failed partly because the Arab states by this time had what they considered to be their own security arrangements under the Arab League (1945), partly because Israel was included in the project, and partly because of Arab recollections of past Western imperialism in the Middle East and fears of restoring it under another guise before the remnants had been completely cleared away. In any event, as Mr. Dulles discovered when he visited the Middle East during May 1953, shortly after becoming secretary of state, to most of the Arab governments and peoples Israel and Zionism appeared a greater danger than the Soviet Union or international communism.

Mr. Dulles, therefore, broached the idea of the Northern Tier defense system. Greece and Turkey had already become members of the North Atlantic Treaty Organization (NATO) on their own initiative on February 15, 1952, and Mr. Dulles felt that the states which bordered on or were, in any event, in the more immediate neighborhood of the Soviet Union, would be more amenable to the kind of regional defense arrangement relative to the possible danger of Soviet domination of or aggression against the Middle East. Initial steps in this direction were taken in the signature of a Turco-Pakistani agreement on April 2, 1954 and of American mutual defense arrangements with Iraq and Pakistan. Moreover, on February 24, 1955 Iraq and Turkey signed a Treaty of Mutual Cooperation at Baghdad, despite the misgivings of certain other Arab states (notably Egypt, Syria, and Saudi Arabia) and Soviet strictures concerning the pact which became the foundation of the so-called Baghdad Pact (CENTO after 1958) to which the United Kingdom, Pakistan, and Iran soon adhered although France and the United States did not. Ultimately, the United States became a member in all but name; it sent representatives to all meetings of the ministerial council; and on March 5, 1959 it signed bilateral agreements with Turkey, Iran, and Pakistan. While the pact appeared to have little military significance, there can be little doubt that the pact (which served further to split the Arab world) proved useful in the sphere of economics and communications, but the Soviet Union, as it were, was soon able to hurdle the barrier and make its own arrangements in the Middle East.

Indeed, there was much reluctance on the part of the Arab states especially, to play any role in what was deemed to be a Western contrivance which would suck the Middle East into the vortex of the "cold war." While Iraq had become an original member of the Baghdad Pact, the spirit of neutralism, so much condemned by Mr. Dulles, prevailed among the Arab states. The Chamoun government was somewhat attracted to the idea, but dared not move in that direction thanks to the delicate politico-confessional balance in Lebanon, unless all other Arab states did so. Jordan was almost torn asunder under British pressure to adhere to the Baghdad Pact during 1955-January 1956. Egyptian adherence was altogether improbable, particularly after the Bandung Conference of April 1955, when President Nasser became one of the leaders of the neutralist states, and then moved to a position of positive neutralism. Nasser's Egypt not only eschewed any association with the Western powers under a security arrangement, but went in the direction of the Soviet Union to the point where it was thought in the West that Egypt was falling under Soviet domination, not merely seeking and obtaining Soviet assistance.

Secretary of State Dulles expressed American concern with the threatening situation in the Middle East in an address of August 26, 1955 which dealt particularly with the Arab-Israel conflict, in which he noted three basic problems left unresolved by the armistice agreements of 1949: (1) the tragic plight of 900,000 refugees who had formerly lived on territory occupied by Israel,[7] (2) the pall of fear hanging alike over Arabs and Israelis, and (3) the lack of fixed boundaries between Israel and its neighbors. He offered American assistance in solving these problems and, among other things, declared that given a solution of other related problems, the president would "recommend that the United States join in formal treaty engagements to prevent or thwart any effort by either side to alter by force the boundaries between Israel and its Arab neighbors." While the U.N. secretary-general welcomed the American overture, and the United Kingdom endorsed it, along with some other states, it was received with caution and reserve throughout the Middle East.

In this situation, the Soviet Union did not miss the opportunities which now became available to it, especially in 1955 when the Baghdad Pact developed into something of a reality, and particularly after the Israeli attack in the Gaza Strip on February 28, 1955. When President Nasser failed to obtain arms from the West (the United Kingdom and the United States) on terms which he considered consonant with Egyptian independence, he turned toward an arms arrangement with the Soviet Union through agreement with Czechoslovakia on September 27. The United States sent Assistant Secretary of State George V. Allen to confer with President Nasser about the matter on September 28, although the right of a sovereign state to purchase arms wherever it might do so was freely granted. The Egyptian government, in its turn, indicated that it had sought unsuccessfully to purchase arms from France, the United Kingdom, and the United States, a position which was fully supported by the council of the League of Arab States; and Saudi Arabia and Syria indicated their willingness to make similar arrangements. The situation was further complicated by Soviet promises of extended economic and technical assistance in the Middle East and, of course, there was always the prospect of an unbridled arms race in the Middle East, with Israeli insistence on the "prime necessity" of defensive armaments, and pressures for special "security arrangements" with the United States.

---

[7]*Ibid.*, II, pp. 2176-2180.

By this time another element entered into the picture. Together with the United Kingdom and the International Bank for Reconstruction and Development (IBRD), the United States was interested in the project for the construction of the High Dam at Aswan on the Nile River, both for hydroelectric power and irrigation purposes, the total cost of which, over a 20-year period, was then estimated at some $1 billion. The project was to become a symbol of the new Egypt under the guidance of President Nasser, not merely another grandiose economic project. On December 17, 1955 it was announced that the United Kingdom and the United States had assured Egypt of their support of the project, "which would be of inestimable importance in the development of the Egyptian economy and in the improvement of the welfare of the Egyptian people."[8] Financial assistance was to be given in the initial stages, and the two countries were prepared "to consider sympathetically in the light of then existing circumstances further support toward financing the later stages of supplement World Bank financing." But events did not follow that course, as the Egyptian government itself procrastinated in accepting the Anglo-American-IBRD offer and as relations between the United States and Egypt deteriorated, especially after the Egyptian-Czechoslovak arms arrangement of September 1955. On July 19, 1956 the United States decided not to participate in the initial financial stages of the Aswan project, and the Soviet Union stepped in to finance, supervise, and assist in the construction of the great dam.

Now another episode came in the Arab-Israel conflict, ostensibly over the Suez Canal. Seven days after the Anglo-American announcement relative to the Aswan High Dam on July 26, 1956, President Nasser announced the nationalization of the Suez Canal Company (1856), which had built and managed the Suez Canal. While there were many elements which entered into the subsequent picture of the Suez conflict, in which Israel joined with France and the United Kingdom in attacking Egypt, and much yet remains to be written and said, a number of elements seem clear. One is that nationalization of the Suez Canal Company served as a pretext for later military action. A second is that the problem of the Suez Canal appeared on the road to solution by October 13, 1956, when the U.N. Security Council, which was seized of the problem, adopted principles set forth by the British government especially for the governance of transit and navigation of the Canal, and that implementation was to have been worked out among France, the United Kingdom, and Egypt on October 29—the very day on which the Israeli army was to attack in the Gaza Strip and the Sinai peninsula. A third is that neither France nor the United Kingdom was interested in a settlement of the Suez problem, and that their reference to the U.N. Security Council was a deceptive charade to provide suitable U.N. cover for military operations already planned by France and Israel, in which the United Kingdom was soon to join, as the United States suspected. A fourth is that the United Kingdom, France, and Israel were determined to get rid of President Nasser: The United Kingdom, because of the prime minister's obsession with the alleged threat of Nasser (who was compared with Hitler or

---

[8]*Ibid.*, II, p. 2230.

Mussolini) to British prestige and interests in the Suez region and the Middle East generally; France, because of its problems in Algeria, for which Nasser was held largely responsible; and Israel, because of the *fedayeen* raids from Gaza into Israel and the problem of passage through the Strait of Tiran into the Gulf of Aqaba.

As a military operation, the *blitzkrieg* soon succeeded. In accordance with Anglo-Franco-Israeli plans and schedules worked out during October 22-23, Israeli forces attacked on October 29, Anglo-French ground forces went into action on November 5, and by November 10 the basic action had been completed. The Gaza Strip and the Sinai peninsula were occupied, the Strait of Tiran opened, and the Suez Canal blocked to traffic. But in the face of this crisis the United States, under the leadership of President Eisenhower, had denounced the Israeli-Anglo-French action, as did the Soviet Union, and ultimately pressures forced the end of the conflict, and a new UN force, the United Nations Emergency Force (UNEF), was established in November 1956 to police the Egyptian-Israel lines from the Gaza Strip to Sharm El Sheikh, although it was never permitted to operate on Israeli soil. While Egypt was defeated in a military sense, ultimately it won a diplomatic and political victory. In a very real sense, the Suez conflict became a turning point in the Middle East, for Egypt emerged under President Nasser as the unrivaled leader among the Arab states, perhaps primarily because the Egyptian leader had shown that an Arab could successfully defy the Western powers. Now Egyptian neutralism would become more positive than ever. Other Middle Eastern states, like Syria and Iraq, to say nothing of Algeria and the Sudan, moved in a similar direction, while the great oil-producing states, with their markets largely in the West, maintained a more cautious position and were, in any event, somewhat more inclined politically toward the West, without being formally associated with it.

In the period of the Suez conflict the United States had been much concerned with the promotion of equitable solutions. In that which followed President Eisenhower, concerned with a possible Soviet domination of the area, reiterated that the United States supported "without reservation the full sovereignty and independence of each and every nation of the Middle East," and proposed that it step into the "power vacuum" in the area. On March 9, 1957, in the so-called Eisenhower or American Doctrine, the Congress authorized the President: (1) to cooperate with and assist any nation or group of nations in the Middle East desiring such assistance in the development of economic strength "dedicated to the maintenance of national independence;" and (2) to undertake military assistance programs with any nation or group of nations desiring such assistance. Since the United States regarded "as vital to the national interest and world peace the preservation of the independence and integrity of the nations of the Middle East," she was prepared, if the president considered it necessary, "to use the armed forces to assist any such nation or group of such nations requesting assistance against armed aggression from any country controlled by international communism." But aside from allies of the United States, such as

Greece, Turkey, and Iran, there was little or no enthusiasm for the new American Doctrine which had its antecedents in the Truman Doctrine, and much outright criticism and opposition. In fact, it was much more the framework of a policy at the time than a genuine policy for action.[9]

VI

Like other states in the period following World War II, those of the Arab East developed their own groupings and regional arrangements. Projects for Arab unity, like that of the Fertile Crescent, were as common as olives at an Arab table. Following an original protocol signed at Alexandria on October 7, 1944, Egypt, Iraq, Jordan, Lebanon, Saudi Arabia, and Yemen agreed to a charter of the League of Arab States on March 22, 1945, and in later years as they became independent, Algeria, Morocco, Tunisia, Libya, the Sudan and Kuwait became members. Moreover, provision was made in the charter for the representation of Palestine and for its membership, if and when it became independent. The charter established a council, composed of representatives of all members, each with a single vote, and a secretary-general as its directing head.

The purposes of the league were to: (1) strengthen the ties among the Arab states and coordinate their activities in order to effect genuine collaboration, maintain their integrity and independence, and in general examine Arab problems and interests; and (2) insure closer cooperation and collaboration in the political, cultural, health, economic, legal, and social fields. Over the years the League of Arab States moved in a number of directions. Members participated in the United Nations Conference on International Organization at San Francisco during April-June 1945 and, among other things, sought both a definition of regional arrangements (which would have confined the concept to regional groupings of states within a geographical neighborhood sharing a common culture, civilization, and destiny) and recognition of its status as a regional arrangement under the United Nations Charter. It achieved neither of these objectives but, like the North Atlantic Treaty Organization and the Organization of American States, the League of Arab States received a kind of observer status, when the General Assembly on November 1, 1950 approved a resolution inviting its secretary-general to attend sessions as an observer. As early as 1945, a Cultural Treaty was signed by members of the league, and in 1950 a Treaty of Joint Defense and Economic Cooperation. In 1953 an Arab Telecommunications and Radio Communications Union was formed, followed by an Arab Postal Union in 1954. In 1959 an Arab Development Bank was established, followed in 1962 by an agreement to establish economic unity, and in 1965 by an Arab Common Market. Many of these projects, of course, remained in the paper stage, whatever the more concrete objectives of the members.

There were, however, grave problems among the members of the League of

[9]*American Foreign Policy: Current Documents 1957,* pp. 771-872.

Arab States relative to Egyptian domination of the league which at times seemed practically a branch of the Egyptian foreign ministry; the secretary-general, from the beginning, has been an Egyptian. Moreover, there was a general lack of unity in matters both of general policy and with respect to intra-Arab problems. While it was often said that there was unity only as to the Palestine problem, even on that question there was disunity in moments of crisis, as when Jordan in 1950 annexed the Old City of Jerusalem and the west bank of the Jordan River and was threatened with expulsion from the league because of its action. There was the further question of whether the Arab League (or other regional arrangements), unless associated with a Great Power or Powers, could serve effectively as a regional security arrangement, whatever else it might be able to do.

Over the years, there was much dissatisfaction with the performance of the Arab League on the part of Arab politicians, statesmen, and thinkers, both because of Egyptian dominance and because of its weaknesses as a security instrument in the Middle East; and there were many proposals for reform in the direction of strengthening it and encouraging unity among its members. These too failed to materialize. In 1958 it will be recalled, Syria and Egypt established the United Arab Republic (February 1, 1958), with Yemen added (March 8, 1958) to form the United Arab States, while the Hashemite Kingdoms of Iraq and Jordan constituted the Arab Federation (February 14, 1958). But these forms of unity soon broke up. The Arab Federation was, perhaps, not a viable structure in the first instance, and it appeared largely as a Hashemite creation. The Iraqi revolt of July 14, 1958, which ended the monarchy, delivered a mortal blow to the federation. The unitary United Arab Republic, dominated by Egypt, came to an end on September 30, 1960, when Syria revolted. While it remained formally on the books, the United Arab States was of little evident significance from the beginning. On the other hand, the programs for Arab unity cannot merely be dismissed with a sneer. However vague and inchoate, there is a subsuming sentiment among many Arabs for unity despite the obvious national and cultural differences, leaving aside the vast expanse of territory which separates Kuwait, for example, from Algeria and Morocco; the significant differences in the regimes which govern the countries of the Arab world; and the obvious differences in national and regional interest. It would seem that the League of Arab States would, perhaps, remain as the only institutionalized form of Arab unity. Despite the reservations concerning the League on the part of states like Lebanon and Tunisia, for example, and the rivalries between the United Arab Republic and Saudi Arabia, it seemed likely to endure.

VII

The relationships between the states of the Middle East and the United Nations also require brief exploration. As already observed, the League of Arab States may certainly be viewed as a regional arrangement under the United Nations Charter and especially Articles 52-54, which deal particularly with the problem of regional arrangements and actions taken thereunder. One may also make the same point as to Greece and Turkey under NATO and Turkey, Iran, and Pakistan under CENTO, whatever the specific differences embodied in these latter regional groupings. Secondly, the Middle East has been a theater of United Nations operations, whether in the form of such peace-keeping activities as the UNTSO, UNEF, or the activities in Yemen and Cyprus (on the one hand) or the work of the United Nations Relief and Works Agency for Palestine Refugees in the Near East (UNRWA), UNICEF, the U.N. Special Fund, the WHO and FAO, to say nothing of other U.N. agencies.

But the area also brought to the United Nations more persistent and seemingly insoluble problems than any other area of the world. In the very beginning of the world organization, came the problems of the withdrawal of Soviet troops from Iran and those of France from Syria and Lebanon, followed in 1951 by the problem of the nationalization of the Anglo-Iranian Oil Company, in 1957 by that in Syria, and in 1958 by the difficulties in Lebanon, which had occasioned the dispatch of some 15,000 American troops to that country and of British troops to Jordan. U.N. observation groups or peace-keeping forces were sent into Lebanon (1958), Yemen (1963), and Cyprus (1964).

The fact that some of the persistent problems with which the Middle East confronted the United Nations fell within the context of the East-West conflict, in part even during a seeming detente between the United States and the Soviet Union, highly complicated solutions. This was particularly true of the problems of Palestine, Cyprus, and Yemen; and there were no easy or simple answers. The problem of Palestine, the origins of which go back to the turn of the century, found no solution. To the contrary, it burst into flames once more in the *blitzkrieg* of June 5-11, 1967, and it was difficult to see how the problem could be solved without basic adjustments in the attitudes and policies involved and solutions of the political, social, and economic problems which surround the question. By the fall of 1968 there was little indication of progress toward settlement, with Israel holding essentially to direct negotiations and the Arab states rejecting that procedure, although willing evidently to discuss substantive issues under the auspices of the United Nations. While the U.N. Security Council had unanimously approved a resolution on November 22, 1967—with proposals for possible settlement involving Israeli withdrawal from occupied areas, the end of belligerency, freedom of navigation through international waterways, a just settlement of the refugee problem, and guarantees of the territorial integrity and political independence of all states in the area—few moves were made in that direction. The special representative of the secretary-general, Ambassador Gunnar V. Jarring, had worked for almost a year on the problem, but the secretary-general reported on September 24, 1968 that "the basic situation in the Middle East remains much the same as it was eight months ago."[10] It seemed doubtful, in any event, that any solution of the problem would prove

---

[10] U.N. Doc, A/7201, Add. 1, paras. 42-60.

possible without agreement among the Great Powers, and more particularly between the United States and the Soviet Union, although it was equally doubtful that the giants could impose a solution on the contending parties. As the secretary-general indicated, the primary responsibility for peaceful settlement of conflicts inevitably rested with the parties themselves. Without their cooperation, no U.N. peace mission, however skillfully conducted or strongly supported, could prove successful. Given that cooperation, the United Nations could be of inestimable assistance, and it was fortunate that Ambassador Jarring returned to the area for further delicate work in the fall of 1968. Grave issues of war and peace in the Middle East, with possibilities of direct Soviet-American confrontation, were at stake.

Similarly, there was no solution of the long-standing conflict involving (after 1959) Greece, Turkey, and the island of Cyprus. Like the Palestine conflict, the Cyprus issue involved the struggle of seemingly irreconcilable nationalisms, not merely of the Greek and Turkish Cypriots who inhabited the island and constituted the Republic of Cyprus under the presidency of Archbishop Makarios, but Greece and Turkey as well, in view of the ethnic character of the population and the strategic location of the island some 40 miles off the Turkish Mediterranean coast of Asia Minor. Moreover, both Greece and Turkey were on the southern flank of the NATO alliance and, as such, were important to the great alliance as the chief makeweight in the containment of the Soviet Union. Curiously enough, there appeared more opportunity for possible adjustment in the problem with the emergence of an authoritarian government in Greece (April 21, 1967) than there had been in years past, after a near blow up in the fall of 1967. As the U.N. secretary-general reported in September 1968, after four years of tension and conflict during which the situation in Cyprus was kept to no small degree within limits by the U.N. peace-keeping force, a number of significant developments had occurred. The armed clashes in November 1967 had brought the intercommunal confrontation to "an explosive state", and for a time international peace and security in the eastern Mediterranean were gravely threatened. The United States, NATO, and the United Nations, however, took dramatic action and the danger of war receded. An adjustment was reached under which Greek and Turkish military personnel in excess of the respective national contingents were withdrawn. Since the beginning of 1968, there was a steady relaxation of tension marked by increasing contacts among Greek and Turkish Cypriots, a reduction in incidents, a significant effort by the government to return to normality by eliminating economic restrictions, and the granting of freedom of movement to Turkish Cypriots. Although there was no settlement, there now seemed some prospect of progress in that direction.

VIII

There is much evidence that the Middle East will remain an area of interest, concern, contention, and strife in world politics, despite the halting and sometimes faltering efforts toward orderly adjustment of its manifold and complex problems both within and outside the United Nations. While the great political, social, economic, technological, and cultural changes had done much to revolutionize the world at an accelerated pace, they have not yet shifted the Middle East from its strategic position at the intercontinental crossroads of Eurasia and Africa or significantly reduced the importance of access to the Middle Eastern "wells of power." The force of Middle Eastern nationalism had brought new states and nations into existence, and the outside Great Powers were now dealing, not with subordinate peoples in a colonial area, but with sovereign states which though weak and fragmented were determined to maintain their independence. This was a new element in the picture of the Middle East, especially after World War II.

The major contending powers in the area no longer were the old powers, such as France, Great Britain, Imperial Russia, Austria-Hungary, or Germany, seeking imperial answers to the Eastern Question, but the United States and the Soviet Union. France, as a major element, had been receding in the Middle East since the end of World War I. After World War II France's power diminished even in North Africa when Algeria, after a long costly and bloody struggle, as well as Morocco and Tunisia achieved their independence. France sought to regain something of its prestige, if not its former power and influence, after the tragic events of June 1967. Great Britain—whose moment of dominant influence occurred during the interwar era with significant politico-economic interests in the Middle East, especially in oil and in freedom of transit and navigation through the Suez Canal—was also drawing back. British withdrawal from the Red Sea, the Indian Ocean (Aden), and the Persian (Arabian) Gulf threatened to leave a power vacuum in these parts of the Middle East and, in the immediate future, perhaps to give some occasion for increased disorder.

The Soviet Union, however, maintained the Imperial Russian strategic interest and supported it with a new totalitarian dynamic in an area touching its Black Sea shores and its frontiers in the Caucasus and Soviet Central Asia. Following the *blitzkrieg* of June 1967, the Soviet Union enhanced its position, especially in the Arab world, to the disadvantage of the United States. It not only exploited its support of the Arab states in their contest with Israel, but increased its influence through both military and economic assistance. By the end of 1968, it was estimated that the Soviet Union had given the United Arab Republic at least $1 billion in military and $2,500 million in economic assistance, while Syria and Iraq had received some $1,500 million, Algeria $500 million, and Iran sought a $900 million credit. The Republic of Turkey received a $250 million credit in 1968 in technical and economic assistance. During 1967 no less than 6,192 Soviet merchant ships transited the Turkish Straits, or some 26,631,409 tons, out of a total of 17,398 ships, of 59,512,793 (44 percent), along with 240 warships. A Soviet fleet of some 50 to 60 warships shared the Mediterranean Sea with the United States Sixth Fleet. Although the Soviet Union sought no direct confrontation with the United States in the Mediterranean or the Middle East, there was every indication that the Red Fleet was there to stay, to exercise its psycho-political influence along the shores of southern Europe, North Africa, and the Arab East. As a Black Sea naval power, it was clear that the Soviet Union was interested in the Mediterranean and the passageway through the Straits.

Similarly, the United States maintained its basic strategic interest in Middle Eastern communications and in access to Middle Eastern oil, in which American concerns had invested some $3 billion. The United States had also invested an estimated $20 billion in public funds and $8 billion in economic and technical assistance. Although it had no direct commitments, and their national interests were by no means identical, the United States had supported Israel over the years, and it continued to do so in military and economic assistance during 1967 and thereafter. Professedly interested in the peace, security, and orderly progress of all states in the Middle East, it remains to be seen whether American policies will prove constructive, whether within or outside the United Nations in these directions; and there is much ground for question and skepticism, as well as calls for more balanced policies and less favoritism as to particular states.

As the Arab-Israel conflict continued to develop in the Middle East by the end of 1968, there was an evident reluctance on the part of the United States and the Soviet Union, to say nothing of other interested powers, to become involved in direct confrontation (for very obvious reasons) and to seek some kind of political settlement. Nevertheless, the prospects for conflict in the Middle East seem so great that intervention is conceivable if adjustment does not prove feasible, and the stakes, indeed, are very high. All one can foresee for the immediate future is the prospect of further basic change in a troubled Middle East, with problems of fundamental interest and concern to the world community.

SOME SUGGESTED READINGS

Anderson, M. S. *The Eastern Question.* (New York: St. Martin's, 1966), 475 pp. Following the model of Sir George A. R. Marriott's classic, Professor Anderson covers the period of 1774-1923. Much use of Russian materials. Bibliographical essay.

Badeau, John S. *The American Approach to the Arab World.* (New York: Harper and Row [for the Council on Foreign Relations], 1968), 208 pp. Perceptive treatment by the Director of The Middle East Institute, Columbia University, and former American Ambassador to the United Arab Republic.

Campbell, John C. *Defense of the Middle East: Problems of American Policy.* (New York: Praeger, 1961), 400 pp. Background and development of U.S. policy, with consideration of political, economic, and military problems facing the United States in the Middle East. By the Director of Political Studies, Council on Foreign Relations.

Davis, John H. *The Evasive Peace: A Study of the Zionist-Arab Problem.* (London: John Murray, 1968), 124 pp. Brief treatise, with discussion of conflict between political Zionism and Arab nationalism and the illusive peace between Israel and the Arab states.

De Novo, John A. *American Interests and Policies in the Middle East, 1900-1939.* (Minneapolis: University of Minnesota, 1963), 447 pp. Detailed and balanced work, dealing with American policy and interest, which is being carried down to date.

Evans, Laurence. *United States Policy and the Partition of Turkey, 1914-1924.* (Baltimore: Johns Hopkins University, 1965), 424 pp. Discussion of American policy substantially from beginning of World War I to and immediately after the Lausanne Conference (1923).

Finnie, David H. *Pioneers East: The Early American Experience in the Middle East.* (Cambridge: Harvard, 1967), 333 pp. A fascinating and scholarly account, which deals with diplomatists, traders, missionaries, and educators and concentrates on both the early American experience and the heritage.

Fisher, Sydney N. *The Middle East: A History.* (New York: Knopf, 1968), rev. ed. A standard general text on the subject which brings the story up to date.

Gallagher, Charles F. *The United States and North Africa.* (Cambridge: Harvard, 1963), 275 pp. Brief discussion of American policy and interest, with concentration on development and problems of North Africa.

Gordon, Leland J. *The United States and Turkey, 1830-1930: An Economic Interpretation.* (Philadelphia: University of Pennsylvania, 1932), 402 pp. A standard account, based on archival research.

Hoskins, Halford L. *The Middle East: Problem Area in World Politics.* New York: Macmillan, 1954), 311 pp. Well-balanced account, centering on major problems.

Howard, Harry N. *The King-Crane Commission: An American Inquiry in the Middle East.* (Beirut: Khayats, 1963), 369 pp. American policy during 1919-1923, based on Commission papers.

Kerr, Malcolm H. *The Middle East Conflict.* (New York: Foreign Policy Association, 1968), 63 pp. Headline Series 191. Well-written, forthright account of the problems and issues.

Khouri, Fred J. *The Arab-Israeli Dilemma.* (Syracuse: N. Y., Syracuse University, 1968), 436 pp. Well-written, balanced consideration of the Arab-Israel conflict and the prospects and problems of peace in the Middle East.

Kirk, George E. *The Middle East in the War, 1939-1946; The Middle East, 1945-1950.* (London: Oxford [RIIA], 1953, 1954), 511, 338 pp. Excellent discussion of international politics and developments and problems in the Middle East during the period covered.

Laqueur, Walter Z. *The Soviet Union and the Middle East.* (New York: Praeger, 1959), 366 pp. Now out of date, but useful, although the author makes too sharp a break between imperial Russian and Soviet policy in the Middle East.

Lall, Arthur. *The U.N. and the Middle East Crisis, 1967.* (New York: Columbia,

1968), 322 pp. Based largely on U.N. documentation and particularly useful for that reason, but somewhat overoptimistic as to the U.N. role.

Lenczowski, George. *The Middle East in World Affairs.* (Ithaca, N. Y.: Cornell, 1962), 723 pp. A standard text which concentrates on international relations relative to the Middle East.

Love, Kennett. *Suez: The Twice Fought War: A History.* (New York: McGraw-Hill, 1969), 767 pp. An excellent study of the Suez crisis and its international context.

————, Project Director. *United States Interests in the Middle East.* (Washington, D. C.: American Enterprise Institute, 1968), 132 pp. Well-balanced presentation, both of American policy and of American interest.

MacDonald, Robert W. *The League of Arab States: A Study in the Dynamics of Regional Organization.* (Princeton, N. J.: Princeton University, 1965), 290 pp. A well-rounded, dispassionate account.

Monroe, Elizabeth. *Britain's Moment in the Middle East, 1914-1956.* (London and New York: Oxford, 1966), 310 pp. A study of the period of British dominance in the Middle East and the subsequent decline.

Nutting, Anthony. *No End of a Lesson: The Story of Suez.* (New York: Potter, 1967), 205 pp. A brilliant study of the Suez Conflict, which corrects a number of myths, by a former British Minister of State in the Foreign Office.

Polk, William R. *The United States and the Arab World.* (Cambridge: Harvard, 1965), 320 pp. A discussion of American policy and interest, which concentrates on the development and problems of the Arab world.

Safran, Nadav. *The United States and Israel.* (Cambridge: Harvard, 1963), 341 pp. Especially good on the Israeli economic and defense systems.

Sayegh, Fayez A. *The Dynamics of Neutralism in the Arab World: A Symposium.* (San Francisco: Chandler, 1964), 275 pp. A discussion of Arab neutralism by a number of authors, primarily Dr. Sayegh.

Spector, Ivar. *The Soviet Union and the Muslim World, 1917-1958.* (Seattle, Washington: University of Washington, 1959), 328 pp. Excellent work, which develops the historical continuity between Imperial Russian and Soviet policy.

Stevens, Georgiana E., ed. *The United States and the Middle East.* (Englewood Cliffs, N. J.: Prentice-Hall, 1964), 182 pp. An excellent symposium on American policy and interest and the problems which the United States faces in the Middle East.

Thomas, Hugh. *Suez.* (New York, Harper and Row, 1967), 261 pp. A scholarly study of the Suez conflict (1956), which should be read in connection with the Nutting volume.

Thomas, Lewis V. and Frye, Richard N. *The United States and Turkey and Iran.* (Cambridge: Harvard, 1951), 391 pp. Out-of-date, but still a useful summary presentation of the subject.

Tibawi, A. L. *British Interests in Palestine, 1800-1901.* (London: Oxford, 1961),

280 pp. An excellent account of the development of British interests, with special attention to the missionary-educational enterprise.

——————. *American Interests in Syria, 1800-1901: A Study of Educational, Literary and Religious Work.* (London and New York: Oxford, 1966), 333 pp. A study especially of the religio-educational enterprise which well supplements the Finnie volume.

Xydis, Stephen G. *Greece and the Great Powers, 1944-1947: Prelude to the "Truman Doctrine".* (Thessaloniki, Greece: Institute for Balkan Studies, 1963), 758 pp. A detailed and comprehensive study, based in part on Greek archival material, which also covers Turkey in this period.

Wainhouse, David, et al. *International Peace Observation: A History and Forecast.* (Baltimore, Johns Hopkins University, 1966), 663 pp. A well-balanced work, which gives ample coverage to U.N. peace-keeping operations in the Middle East.

Documentary Collections

Department of State, Historical Office. *American Foreign Policy: Basic Documents, 1950-1955.* 2 vols. Annual after 1956 as *Current Documents.* Indispensable for American interest and policy.

Hurewitz, J. C., ed. *Diplomacy in the Near and Middle East, 1535-1914, 1914-1956.* 2 vols. (Princeton, N. J.: D. Van Nostrand, 1956). Indispensable and convenient. Excellent editorial notes and annotations.

World Peace Foundation and Council on Foreign Relations. *Documents on American Foreign Relations.* (1938 to date). Published by the Council on Foreign Relations since 1952 (New York: Harper and Row, 1953-1967; Simon and Schuster, 1968-). Convenient documentary source.

INDEX

Index

479

This book has been set in 10 point Press Roman, leaded 1 point. Part and chapter numbers are in 24 point and 18 point Univers Medium; part and chapter titles are in 24 point and 18 point Bodoni Bold. The size of the type page is 27 by 45½ picas.